On the Road to Total War is a collection of essays, originally presented at a conference of the same title, which attempts to trace the roots and development of total industrialized warfare (which terrorizes citizens and soldiers alike). Scholars from the United States, Germany, France, Canada, Switzerland, New Zealand, and Britain focus on both the social, political, economic, and cultural aspects and the impact on local society of the American Civil War and the German Wars of Unification. Certain social forces, such as mass mobilization of people and resources and growing nationalism, led to this totalization of war in industrialized nations in the nineteenth century.

PUBLICATIONS OF THE
GERMAN HISTORICAL INSTITUTE,
WASHINGTON, D.C.

Edited by Detlef Junker
with the assistance of Daniel S. Mattern

On the Road to Total War

THE GERMAN HISTORICAL INSTITUTE, WASHINGTON, D.C.

The German Historical Institute is a center for advanced study and research whose purpose is to provide a permanent basis for scholarly cooperation between historians from the Federal Republic of Germany and the United States. The Institute conducts, promotes, and supports research into both American and German political, social, economic, and cultural history, into transatlantic migration, especially in the nineteenth and twentieth centuries, and into the history of international relations, with special emphasis on the roles played by the United States and Germany

Other books in the series

Hartmut Lehmann and James J. Sheehan, editors, *An Interrupted Past: German-Speaking Refugee Historians in the United States after 1933*

Carol Fink, Axel Frohn, and Jürgen Heideking, editors, *Genoa, Rapallo, and European Reconstruction in 1992*

David Clay Large, editor, *Contending with Hitler: Varieties of German Resistance in the Third Reich*

Larry Eugene Jones and James Retallack, editors, *Elections, Mass Politics, and Social Change in Modern Germany*

Hartmut Lehmann and Guenther Roth, editors, *Weber's Protestant Ethic: Origins, Evidence, Contexts*

Catherine Epstein, *A Past Renewed: A Catalog of German-Speaking Refugee Historians in the United States after 1933*

Hartmut Lehmann and James Van Horn Melton, editors, *Paths of Continuity: Central European Historiography from the 1930s to the 1950s*

Jeffry M. Diefendorf, Axel Frohn, and Hermann-Josef Rupieper, editors, *American Policy and the Reconstruction of West Germany, 1945–1955*

Henry Geitz, Jürgen Heideking, and Jurgen Herbst, editors, *German Influences on Education in the United States to 1917*

Peter Graf Kielmansegg, Horst Mewes, and Elisabeth Glaser-Schmidt, editors, *Hannah Arendt and Leo Strauss: German Emigrés and American Political Thought after World War II*

Dirk Hoerder and Jörg Nagler, editors, *People in Transit: German Migrations in Comparative Perspective, 1820–1930*

R. Po-chia Hsia and Hartmut Lehmann, editors, *In and Out of the Ghetto: Jewish-Gentile Relations in Late Medieval and Early Modern Germany*

Sibylle Quack, editor, *Between Sorrow and Strength: Women Refugees of the Nazi Period*

Mitchell G. Ash and Alfons Söllner, editors, *Forced Migration and Scientific Change: Emigré German-Speaking Scientists and Scholars after 1933*

On the Road
to Total War

THE AMERICAN CIVIL WAR AND THE
GERMAN WARS OF UNIFICATION, 1861–1871

Edited by

STIG FÖRSTER

and

JÖRG NAGLER

GERMAN HISTORICAL INSTITUTE
Washington, D.C.
and

CAMBRIDGE
UNIVERSITY PRESS

PUBLISHED BY THE PRESS SYNDICATE OF THE UNIVERSITY OF CAMBRIDGE
The Pitt Building, Trumpington Street, Cambridge, United Kingdom

CAMBRIDGE UNIVERSITY PRESS
The Edinburgh Building, Cambridge CB2 2RU, UK   http://www.cup.cam.ac.uk
40 West 20th Street, New York, NY 10011-4211, USA   http://www.cup.org
10 Stamford Road, Oakleigh, Melbourne 3166, Australia

First published 1997
Reprinted 1999

Printed in the United States of America

Typeset in Bembo

A catalogue record for this book is available from the British Library

On the road to total war: the American Civil War and the German Wars
of Unification, 1861–1871 / Edited by Stig Förster and Jörg Nagler.
p. cm. – (Publications of the German Historical Institute)
Includes index.
1. United States – History – Civial War, 1861–1865. 2. Franco-
Prussian War, 1870–1871. I. Förster, Stig. II. Nagler, Jörg.
III. Series..
E468.9.05   1996   95–50625
973.7 – dc20   CIP

ISBN 0 521 56071 3 hardback

Contents

v

PART FOUR: THE HOME FRONT

PART FIVE: THE REALITY OF WAR

Acknowledgments

It remains the obligation and pleasure of the editors to thank all those who made this book possible. First, we are grateful to the former director of the German Historical Institute in Washington, D.C., Hartmut Lehmann, who helped to bring about the original conference and gave the editors leeway to follow through on their ideas. We also thank all those colleagues who participated in the conference as chairpersons and as contributors to the debates whose remarks and ideas could not be published here, although they certainly influenced the results. We are just as grateful to these colleagues as we are to those who wrote for this book. We finally thank the staff of the German Historical Institute, whose work was indispensable for the success of the project: Daniel S. Mattern, who did the editorial work; Kenneth F. Ledford, whose advice kept us going; Dieter H. Schneider, who helped us iron out all logistical problems; Christa Brown and Bärbel Bernhardt, who did a tremendous secretarial job; Pamela Abraham, Birgit Beck, and Dierk Walter, who aided in the production of the manuscript; and Gaby Müller-Oelrichs, who helped to get us all the books we needed and whose peaceful library rooms we cruelly disrupted for the duration of the conference.

We would also like to thank the social sciences editor at Cambridge University Press, Frank Smith, for supporting the publication of this large book. Last, but certainly not least, we are grateful to the two outside reviewers who undertook the tremendous job of reading the manuscript and who gave us valuable advice for its improvement. Finally, we hope that the readers will find as much food for thought in this book as did the participants at the conference in Washington.

Contributors

Stéphane Audoin-Rouzeau is a professor of history at the Université de Picardie–Jules Verne, Paris.

Annette Becker is a professor of history at the Université Charles de Gaulle, Lille.

Richard E. Beringer is a professor of history at the University of North Dakota, Grand Forks.

Manfred Botzenhart is a professor of history at Westfälische Wilhelms-Universität, Münster.

Roger Chickering is a professor of history at Georgetown University, Washington, D.C.

Richard N. Current is a historian living in South Natick, Massachusetts.

Carl N. Degler is a professor of history at Stanford University.

Wilhelm Deist is a former director of the Militärgeschichtliches Forschungsamt and currently an honorary professor of history at the Albert-Ludwigs-Universität, Freiburg/Breisgau.

Stanley L. Engerman is a professor of history at the University of Rochester.

Michael Fellman is a professor of history at Simon Fraser University, Vancouver, British Columbia.

Stig Förster is a professor of history at the Universität Bern.

J. Matthew Gallman is a professor of history at Loyola College, Baltimore.

Joseph T. Glatthaar is a professor of history at the U.S. Army Military History Institute, Carlisle Barracks, Pennsylvania.

Edward Hagerman is a professor of history at Atkinson College, York University, Toronto, Ontario.

Herman M. Hattaway is a professor of history at the University of Missouri, Kansas City.

Earl J. Hess is a professor of history at Lincoln Memorial University, Harrogate, Tennessee.

Donna Rebecca D. Krug is a historian living in Orange County, California.

Gerd Krumeich is a professor of history at the Albert-Ludwigs-Universität, Freiburg/Breisgau.

Alf Lüdtke is a research fellow at the Max-Planck-Institute für Geschichte, Göttingen.

Jay Luvaas teaches at the U.S. Army War College, Carlisle Barracks, Pennsylvania.

James M. McPherson is a professor of history at Princeton University.

Manfred Messerchmidt is a former director of the Militärgeschichtliches Forschungsamt, Freiburg (now Potsdam).

Reid Mitchell is a professor of history at Princeton University.

Jörg Nagler is director of the Kennedy Haus in Kiel and a guest lecturer at the Universität Kiel.

Mark E. Neely Jr. is a historian at the Lincoln Museum, Fort Wayne, Indiana.

Phillip S. Paludan is a professor of history at the University of Kansas, Lawrence.

Jean H. Quataert is a professor of history at the State University of New York, Binghamton.

Thomas Rohkrämer is a lecturer in history at Lancaster University.

William Serman is a professor of history at the Université de Paris I.

Robert Tombs is a university lecturer in history at St. John's College, Cambridge.

Hans L. Trefousse is a professor of history at Brooklyn College, City University of New York.

Ulrich Wengenroth is a professor of history at the Technische Universität München.

1

Introduction

STIG FÖRSTER and JÖRG NAGLER

WARFARE IN NORTH AMERICA AND EUROPE, 1861–71

The age of cabinet's war is behind us, – now we only have people's war. ...[1]

Such a people's war, on both sides, has never happened before since the existence of large states. ...[2]

With these words, the conservative Prussian Field Marshal Helmuth von Moltke and the left-wing military analyst Friedrich Engels, clearly two very different characters, summed up their impressions of the German Wars of Unification and of the American Civil War, respectively. They were both talking of wars that had taken place in the same decade (1861 to 1871) but on two different continents, for very different reasons, and apparently under very different circumstances. Yet, both men used the same term – people's war – to characterize these military conflicts. We may therefore ask to what extent were there structural similarities between the German Wars of Unification and the American Civil War. Never mind the large differences between these wars; there should have been similarities if such otherwise opposing personalities such as Moltke and Engels looked at them in the same way.

It is certainly true that the war in North America was a civil war caused by the break-up of a nation, whereas the Franco-Prussian War was fought between two more or less clearly distinct nations. To compare these two conflicts is therefore a problematic task. Yet, as some of the chapters on the Civil War indicate, an increasing number of people on both sides of the Mason-

---

1 Speech by General Field Marshal Helmuth von Moltke in the Reichstag, May 14, 1890, quoted after *Stenographische Berichte über die Verhandlungen des Reichstages*, 1890-91, 1:76. All translations were made by the editors.
2 Friedrich Engels to Col. Joseph Weydemeyer (a German immigrant serving in the Union army), Nov. 24, 1864, Karl Marx and Friedrich Engels, *Marx-Engels-Werke*, ed. Institut für Marxismus-Leninismus beim Zentralkomitee der SED, 39 vols. (Berlin, 1958-68), 31:424.

Dixon Line looked upon themselves as members of a community different from the one of their enemies. Sectional, social, economic, and even political history separated the North and the South. The war itself definitely enlarged this gap. Defining nationhood in North America was therefore at least as questionable as indeed it was in Germany in 1866, when Prussians, Austrians, Hanoverians, Saxons, and other Germans fought against each other. It should also not be forgotten that the Germans in 1870 did not enter the war against France as citizens of a united nation state. Carl N. Degler makes an important point in this context by emphasizing that the wars in North America and Central Europe between 1861 and 1871 were largely fought to complete the unfinished project of nation building.[3] What on the surface appear to be rather different, on a deeper level and under the circumstances of that fateful decade, were two phenomena (civil war and war between nation states) based on structural similarities that make a comparison not only possible but also fruitful.

Indeed, even a brief investigation of the Franco-Prussian War of 1870–71 in particular and the Civil War demonstrates that they had a lot in common.[4] They both began as rather limited conflicts, fought for limited war aims: the prevention or fulfillment of German unification and the break-up or preservation of the United States. But as the wars lingered on and grew ever more bitter, the war aims, at least those of the stronger sides, became more and more radical: annexations, if not the total subjugation, of France and destruction as well as revolutionizing of the Old South. Both wars started with regular armies: semiprofessionals versus conscript armies in Europe and large-scale militias in North America. But the harder the wars got, conscription became the primary basis for recruiting ever-more troops. In addition, while the regular armies fought it out, civilians turned into guerrillas and took part too. In Germany, France, and North America, public opinion did not only play an important role in getting these wars started in the first place but also had great impact on its conduct. Nationalism, racism, and particularism were among widespread public sentiments that helped to bring the wars about and contributed to keep them going. The populace on the whole participated as citizens in these wars, not only as subjects of authoritarian states. More than perhaps in any previous war, the "home front," particularly in France and in the Confederacy, became the backbone of warfare, as civilians including women worked to supply the armies and as morale depended

---

3   See Carl N. Degler's essay in this book (Chapter 3).
4   Probably the best overviews over these two wars still are Michael Howard, *The Franco-Prussian War: The German Invasion of France, 1870–71* (London, 1961) and James M. McPherson, *Battle Cry of Freedom: The Civil War Era* (New York, 1988).

on public support.[5] The civilian populations in the nations under attack were not only indispensable in keeping the war effort going but became themselves the targets of enemy action, from Sherman's march through Georgia and South Carolina to the shelling of Strasbourg and Paris. A strategy directed against civilians thus began to form an important part of modern warfare.[6]

Technologically and economically, both wars stood at the beginning of industrialized warfare. More than ever before, technological change and industrial production of weapons, ammunition, and equipment influenced the course of war. Rifled handguns and artillery, the first forms of machine guns, ironclads and armored gun boats, breech-loaders and heavy artillery, and above all the systematic use of railroads, all created a new kind of warfare: the beginning of industrialized mass warfare. Due to the enormous increase in firepower, the character of combat developed new dimensions, as the defense gained tactical advantage over the offensive. Some generals, such as Moltke, realized the import of these changes and found new ways to remain successfully on the offensive.[7] Others, like Ambrose E. Burnside (at Fredericksburg) and Robert E. Lee (at Gettysburg) demonstrated to the detriment of their troops that they had not yet fully grasped the terrible power of modern firearms. Nevertheless, in the end, both wars produced the suitable answer to improved firepower: trench warfare (at Petersburg and at the fortress in France, for example).

Transported by railroads, mass armies with modern weapons had to be supplied by industrial production. More than ever before, therefore, a somewhat industrialized economy became the basis of warfare, especially the longer the war lasted. Cooperation between the state and private industry was indispensable for the war effort. In countries that were relatively underdeveloped such as the Confederacy, or partially under foreign occupation like post-imperial France, the governments had to organize the use of the limited resources themselves. The results were immediate state intervention into the economy, a new phenomenon in the age of developed capitalism.

---

5   On the American home front, see Jörg Nagler's contribution to this book (Chapter 16).

6   John Charles Frémont, one of the foremost radical political generals during the war exclaimed in Nov. 1862, "For no matter how begun, this is the People's war." *Missouri Democrat*, Nov. 3, 1862, 2, cited in Jörg Nagler, *Frémont contra Lincoln: Die deutsch-amerikanische Opposition in der Republikanischen Partei während des amerikanischen Bürgerkrieges* (Frankfurt/Main, 1984), 102.

7   As early as 1865, Moltke investigated the tactical influence of the new firearms and came to the conclusion that attacks across open field on a well-covered body of infantry had become suicidal. The only way to remain on the strategic offensive therefore was to force the enemy by outmaneuvering him to attack himself. The catastrophic losses he was bound to suffer would allow a successful counterattack and thereby keep the overall offensive going. This was Moltke's famous blend of strategic offensive and tactical defense. See Helmuth von Moltke, "Bemerkungen über den Einfluss der verbesserten Feuerwaffen auf die Taktik" [1865], in Stig Förster, ed., *Moltke: Vom Kabinettskrieg zum Volkskrieg* (Bonn, 1992), 147–64.

The introduction of conscription, the need to influence public opinion by keeping the antiwar opposition under control, and in general the necessity to coerce the more and more disillusioned population into participating in an evermore strenuous war effort in order to rally the human resources of the nation, all led to first steps toward transforming the state into the modern "leviathan."[8]

These similarities – and more could have been mentioned – seem to indicate that in spite of all the differences, in the decade between 1861 and 1871, the problem of war and society had reached a comparable level on both sides of the Atlantic. In France, Germany, and North America, mass societies, in which public opinion and the general participation of the citizens had gained political importance,[9] stood at the threshold of a new phase of industrialization. Under these circumstances, large-scale warfare in the western world took on a new quality: industrialized people's war.

PEOPLE'S WAR AND TOTAL WAR

This raises of course the question: What is the term *people's war* all about? After all, as has been seen, contemporaries already used this term when explaining what had happened in North America and Continental Europe. However, it would probably not be too useful to analyze in detail here Moltke's and Engels's understanding of people's war. It certainly makes more sense to look at this phenomenon on the basis of the latest research, for it is in this context that we will have to raise the questions about warfare in the 1860s and early 1870s.

The age of people's war began with the American and French Revolutions of the late eighteenth century. The "Atlantic Revolution"[10] not only brought about the more or less successful quest for participation of the citizens in

---

8 For the Union, see, e.g., Richard F. Bensel, *Yankee Leviathan: The Origins of Central State Authority in America, 1859–1877* (Cambridge, 1990) and Mark E. Neely Jr., *The Fate of Liberty: Abraham Lincoln and Civil Liberties* (New York, 1991).

9 In order to avoid misunderstandings, it is important to note here that the participation of citizens in politics and indeed in warfare is not necessarily equivalent to democracy. The introduction of people's armies, whether as militias or via some form of conscription, for example, has been practiced by such undemocratic regimes as those of the two Napoléons, nineteenth-century Prussia, Wilhelmine Germany, the National Socialists, and the Stalinist Soviet Union. In addition, all these régimes had their parliaments and, in the twentieth century, tended to form state-run mass movements. In other words, whether democratic or not, since the French Revolution of 1789, all modern régimes are in a competitive world dependent for survival on the participation of their citizens. This is of course particularly true under the strains of mass warfare. For a deeper analysis of this problem, see Roland G. Foerster, ed., *Die Wehrpflicht: Entstehung, Erscheinungsformen und politisch-militärische Wirkung* (Munich, 1994), 55–70.

10 Robert R. Palmer, "La 'révolution atlantique' – vingt ans après," in Eberhard Schmitt and Rolf Reichardt, eds., *Die Französische Revolution – zufälliges oder notwendiges Ereignis? Akten des internationalen Symposiums an der Universität Bamberg vom 4.–7. Juni 1979*, 3 vols. (Munich, 1983), 1: 89–104.

the political process within their state. It also led to tremendous wars in which those citizens took immediate part in order to defend their political aspirations. Citizens became soldiers in people's armies or participated on the home front to support the war effort. For the first time in modern history, public opinion asserted an important role in fighting wars. Thus in the War of American Independence and even more so in the French Revolutionary wars, warfare assumed a new quality: Mass armies composed of citizens fought for national war aims to which the people could relate.[11] The age of eighteenth-century-style cabinet's war, fought by relatively small professional armies for the limited war aims of their monarchs, was over. As Carl von Clausewitz put it when referring to France: "Suddenly war again became the business of the people – a people of thirty millions, all of whom considered themselves to be citizens."[12]

People's war, however, composed a threat to the state's monopoly of using force, which had been established in Europe during the eighteenth century. The tendency of people to take up arms on their own account weakened the central government's control over the military effort. Moreover, barely trained mass militia armies lacked of efficiency and were in constant danger of dissolving after a few months of service. On the other hand, tapping the human resources of the nation for large-scale warfare became an irresistible temptation for political and military leaders especially in Europe. People's war therefore had to be channeled and organized by the state in order to make it more efficient and to use it as an extremely powerful tool to force through wide-ranging war aims. Carnot and later on Napoléon I were the first to experiment with conscription as a means of regaining control over the new quality of warfare. During the Wars of Liberation, however, it was Prussia that brought this development to its logical and most radical conclusion: universal conscription.[13] But channeling the forces of people's war into a state-run affair was only one direction in which the new kind of warfare developed. The less tight system of militia armies continued to exist, particularly in the United States. Perhaps even more striking was the most radical form of people's war: guerrilla warfare. Where control by the state in form of a central government collapsed altogether under the weight of an invading enemy, people sometimes took matters entirely in their own hands and

---

11 See, e.g., Christopher Ward, *The War of the Revolution*, 2 vols. (New York, 1952); Russel F. Weighley, *History of the United States Army*, 2d ed. (Bloomington, Ind., 1984), 29–95; Don Higgingbotham, *War and Society in Revolutionary America: The Wider Dimensions of Conflict* (Columbia, S.C., 1988); and Albert Soboul, *Précis de l'histoire de la révolution française* (Paris, 1962).

12 Carl von Clausewitz, *On War*, ed. Michael Howard and Peter Paret (Princeton, N.J., 1976), 592.

13 For an overview of this epoch, see Geoffrey Best, *War and Society in Revolutionary Europe, 1770–1870* (London, 1982), 63–190.

began a campaign of irregular warfare, carried out by armed civilians. No-where did the whole meaning of *guerrilla* warfare become more apparent than in the country that invented the word: Spain (after 1808).[14]

The wars following the Atlantic Revolution therefore brought about three military types of people's war:

1. *Guerrilla war.* This was the most radical form of people's war, in which loose bands of armed civilians, virtually under no government control whatsoever, fought an irregular campaign against an invading regular army. The examples were Spain, Calabria, the Tyrol, and to a certain degree Russia in 1812.
2. *War with militia armies.* Here citizens volunteered in more or less large numbers to fight for the interests of "their" state, which they regarded as their own interests. Such armies were under the general control of the state authorities but retained a certain spirit of independence, which hampered their efficiency and made them not always reliable. The examples were the Continental Army in North America and the first French revolutionary armies.
3. *War with conscript armies.* In this system, the central government assumed the role not only of the leader but of the organizer of people's war via measures to coerce citizens into fighting for the state. Under such circumstances, people's war reached its most destructive level of power, and the state tended to gain more control over society on the whole than ever before. It was the birth of the modern military state that was to penetrate domestic civilian life and to wage well-organized people's war abroad. The early examples were France under the Jacobeans and Napoléons, as well as Prussia since 1814.

Until 1815, however, the military revolution of people's war took place under largely preindustrial circumstances. This limited the scope of the changes in modern warfare. The third type of people's war, conscription warfare, in particular, remained on a rather low level, as armies equipped with eighteenth-century-style weapons had little need of industrially pro-duced supplies and as poor communications hampered the state's effort to gain control over society. But the foundations of momentous change had been laid.

Yet for decades after Waterloo, the implications of the military revolution stayed somewhat dormant. The United States, which stuck to the second type of people's war, fought only one major war during that period: the war against Mexico. In Europe, the conservative regimes even attempted to turn the clock back by reintroducing professional armies (with the notable excep-tion of Prussia) and by avoiding war altogether. The wars that finally took place in the 1850s, on the Crimea and in Northern Italy, were therefore in many respects reminiscent of cabinet's wars. Peoples were not directly

---

14 See David Gates, *The Spanish Ulcer: A History of the Peninsular War* (London, 1986) and Rainer Wohlfeil, "Der Volkskrieg im Zeitalter Napoléons," in Heinz-Otto Sieburg, ed., *Napoléon und Europa* (Cologne, 1971), 318–32.

involved. On the other hand, these wars demonstrated the first impacts of industrialization.[15]

The big turning point came in the 1860s. The American Civil War and the German Wars of Unification, as has been shown, carried all the elements of people's war in them. This time, however, in contrast to the wars before 1815, people's war was conducted in an age of beginning industrialization. The parameters of modern warfare had been widened to such an extent that the conflict between state and society, inherent in all three types of people's war, assumed a new quality. Large-scale mass warfare required better organization, and modern means of communication provided new opportunities for tighter government control. As militias and semiprofessional armies proved insufficient, conscription became the order of the day: in North America in 1862–63, in Prussia from the outset, and in France toward the end of 1870. Along with this kind of warfare, which carried the third type of people's war to a new high, went coercive measures by the governments in domestic politics, economy, and society in order to rally the nation's resources.

To alert contemporaries, such as Moltke and Engels, it was obvious that in the decade between 1861 and 1871, warfare had reached a new quality. They were able to describe the changes that had taken place, but they refrained from categorizing the new developments in an academic fashion. Instead they used the label of *people's war* in a vague fashion. It remained to historians of later generations to come to terms with the exact meaning of what had happened in that fateful decade. This task was complicated and also made more interesting by the fact that many developments in the 1860s and early 1870s were reminiscent of large-scale warfare in the first half of the twentieth century. Was there a structural connection between *people's war* and *total war*? Did the year 1861 mark the beginning of *modern warfare* or perhaps even the *age of total war*, which was to last until 1945? It was certainly no accident that some American historians shortly after the end of World War II began to regard the Civil War as the first in a series of total wars. In 1948, John B. Walters published an influential article, "General William T. Sherman and Total War."[16] Four years later, T. Harry Williams wrote: "The Civil War was the first of the modern total wars, and the American democracy was almost totally unready to fight it."[17]

The validity of such notions are of course to a large extent a question of definition. It is at this point that the greatest difficulties and misunderstandings

---

15 See Best, *War and Society*, 191–308.
16 John B. Walters, "General William T. Sherman and Total War," *Journal of Southern History* 14 (1948): 447–80.
17 T. Harry Williams, *Lincoln and His Generals* (New York, 1952), 3.

have arisen. Historians, who tried to come to terms with the modern aspects of the Civil War and the German Wars of Unification, used labels like *people's war, industrialized people's war, citizen's war, total war,* or simply *modern war.* The chapters of this book are full of such contradictory, sometimes overlapping, but in any case confusing terminology. It proved impossible to find common ground amongst the contributors, to agree on definitions, or even to determine conclusively the degree of modernity that these wars reached. For the most part, the reader will have to fend for him- or herself when trying to find answers. In fact, in the absence of agreement amongst historians, the only aim that could be achieved here was to demonstrate the current state of the debate by inviting the most prominent specialists in the field to state their opinions. The outcome of this controversy, it is to be hoped, may form a basis for future research that will aid our understanding of the changing nature of warfare since the second half of the nineteenth century.

This introduction is not meant to go beyond the essays in the book. It would be unwise and unfair to judge the merits of each individual approach and thereby try to find a solution to the controversial issues. This task must be left to reviewers and readers. However, it might help if we clarified some of the labels that have been used to analyze the nature of warfare in North America and Europe between 1861 and 1871. Thus, the concept of this book will become easier to understand. As has been shown, the phenomenon of people's war reaches way back to the revolutionary wars of the eighteenth century. At its core, it meant simply that the phenomenon of increasing participation of ever-larger parts of the population in the political process found its equivalent in warfare. The people took up arms and, whether mobilizing themselves or being organized from above, waged war – with all the consequences involved. This form of warfare contrasted sharply with the cabinet's wars of the eighteenth century, which were largely fought by mercenary armies. There is no doubt that the American Civil War and the German Wars of Unification were people's wars in that sense. All three different forms of people's war, guerrilla warfare, warfare with militias, and warfare with conscript armies were present in these military conflicts. Indeed, the wars under consideration firmly established the concept of people's war against all attempts of the first half of the nineteenth century to turn the clock of history back. From now on it was certain that any major war in the Western world would be a people's war. Influenced by Moltke, the German officer and military writer Colmar von der Goltz emphasized well after 1871 that in the "age of people's war" no alternative was possible.[18] In 1905, Moltke's

---

18   Colmar Freiherr von der Goltz, *Das Volk in Waffen,* 2d ed. (Berlin, 1883), 138–47.

nephew, Helmuth von Moltke the Younger, who was to become chief of the General Staff until after the start of World War I, told Kaiser Wilhelm II that another war against France could be nothing but a huge people's war.[19] Indeed, it may be said that both world wars in the twentieth century were people's wars in the aforementioned sense. If people's war meant the mobilization of the population in and for war, total war was nothing but an extreme form of that phenomenon, driving its principles to the most radical end.

The term *people's war*, which seems to be more or less equivalent to the occasionally used term *citizen's war*,[20] appears to be rather useful when analyzing the development of warfare since the late eighteenth century, especially when it is contrasted to cabinet's war. Still, this concept has its limitations. It is far too broad to help us grasp all the changes that took place in warfare until 1945. In particular, the new quality of warfare that was introduced between 1861 and 1871 cannot be entirely explained by relying on that term. After all, the American Civil War and the Franco-Prussian War were not fought on the same level as the wars of revolutionary France around 1800. As people's wars, they were all alike, but Grant, Moltke, and Gambetta had different and more powerful means at their disposal than Napoléon. Technological change played a surprisingly little role in the "*French Wars*" between 1792 and 1815. But after 1861, the acceleration in industrialization made itself felt on the battlefield as well as in transport and supply. This made war more complicated, swifter, and even more destructive. Improved communication meant that the home front became more implicated. It makes sense therefore to use the term *industrialized people's war* when talking about warfare in the Western world between 1861 and 1871.[21] Again, however, this term is not fully satisfying. Its main purpose is to distinguish warfare in the 1850s from people's war around 1800. It does little to help us determine whether the decade between 1861 and 1871 marked a turning point that stared off the development toward the murderous wars of the twentieth century.

Some historians tried to find a way out by reverting to the term *modern war*.[22] This seems to provide a compellingly simple solution, as it indicates that there was a connection between warfare in the 1860s and the twentieth century without going into too many details and without offering a too narrow framework. But it may be asked: Is *modern war* too imprecise a term? After all,

19 Moltke the Younger reporting about a meeting with Wilhelm II in a letter to his wife on Jan. 29, 1905. See Eliza von Moltke, ed., *Generaloberst Helmuth von Moltke: Erinnerungen, Briefe, Dokumente, 1877–1916* (Stuttgart, 1922), 308.
20 See the essay by Robert Tombs in this book (Chapter 25).
21 See Stig Förster's essay in this book (Chapter 6).
22 See, e.g., Edward Hagerman, *The American Civil War and the Origins of Modern Warfare* (Bloomington, Ind., 1988). Several contributors to this book also used this term.

where does modernity begin, and what does it mean? Perhaps it would make sense to equate modernity in our context with the age of industrialized mass societies. If so, the decade between 1861 and 1871 would stand at the very beginning of modernity. Clearly, the problems addressed in this book are closely interconnected with the issue of modernization. But does the concept of modernization applied to warfare help us to understand the catastrophe of the late nineteenth century and the first half of the twentieth century? Did modernity in warfare necessarily imply mass slaughter?

Still, the use of the label _modern war_ has its uses, if only as to hint that the 1860s did indeed mark a watershed. But what were the consequences? As has already been indicated, several historians have used the more definite term _total war_ when talking about the interconnections between the American Civil War and the world wars of the twentieth century. Indeed, World War I and certainly World War II have often been described as total wars. But there is no such thing as a widely accepted definition of the term _total war_. Since the term first appeared in France during World War I, it has been used by politicians, soldiers, journalists, and of course by historians. But the term was given many different meanings.

General Erich Ludendorff was perhaps among the first to attempt something like a systematic definition. To him, total war meant total mobilization of all human and material resources for the purpose of fighting a war for life or death of a nation. But it also included complete control by a (military) government over every aspect of social, political, and economical life. Such a radical system was to prepare the nation single-mindedly for the ultimate war well before its outbreak.[23] Ludendorff's militaristic dream (or nightmare) became the core of all further attempts to define total war. Complete mobilization, organized by a gigantic military and bureaucratic machine, which was firmly in the hands of the national leadership, was the key. But the experience of World War II added further dimensions. Unlimited war aims such as unconditional surrender, the total destruction of the enemy state, and the idea of _Lebensraum_ gave the total means of complete mobilization a total objective. The physical annihilation of the enemy's soldiers and civilians alike added a gruesome dimension to the field of the conduct of war itself. Above all, the state, which in the dawning of the age of people's war was meant to become a tool to foster the general interests of its citizens, now turned into a murderous fighting machine that used its citizens as "human material" (_Menschenmaterial_).

It may be said that the phenomenon of total warfare in this sense existed in earlier epochs of history as well. The Roman wars against Carthage,

23 Erich Ludendorff, _Der Totale Krieg_ (Munich, 1935).

Genghis Kahn's war against China, and certainly Tamerlan's style of warfare carried many elements of total warfare in them. It could even be claimed that the societies then involved were rather highly organized and controlled by relatively powerful states. But they were certainly not industrialized mass societies. Warfare approaching total mobilization for total ends was only possible under such modern conditions. The term *total war* should therefore be limited to modernity. Any definition of total war has to take all of these elements into account.[24]

A formal and satisfactory definition of *total war* is still missing. It will therefore come as no surprise that the contributors to this book use conflicting ideas about the meaning of total war. Many of the controversies between the authors have to been seen in that light.

And yet it appears to the editors that the arguments by Walters and Williams, according to which the American Civil War marked the beginning of the fateful road to total warfare in the twentieth century, deserve further investigation. If total war, at least theoretically, consists of total mobilization of all the nation's resources by a highly organized and centralized state for a military conflict with unlimited war aims (such as complete conquest and subjugation of the enemy) and unrestricted use of force (against the enemy's armies and civil population alike, going as far as complete destruction of the home front, extermination, and genocide), then at least some of these elements can be found, albeit on a much lower level, in the third type of people's war. As the American Civil War and later on the Franco-Prussian War clearly drifted toward conscription warfare, and at the same time were the first industrialized people's wars, it may well be asked: Did they form something like a link in the otherwise certainly not teleological development from nineteenth-century people's war to twentieth-century total war? Asking such a question is not the same as claiming that the wars under consideration have already been fully developed total wars. We intend to pursue a more cautious line by looking for the seeds of total warfare way back in the decade between 1861 and 1871. To try to find some answers to these questions is the raison d'etre of this book.

THE UNITED STATES AND GERMANY IN THE AGE OF TOTAL WAR

The best way of coming to something like a watertight definition involves empirical historical research into the development of total warfare until 1945.

---

24 For further details on the discussion surrounding the term *total war*, see Mark E. Neely Jr.'s essay in this book (Chapter 2).

As this would be a very tall order indeed for just one scholar to achieve, the German Historical Institute in Washington, D.C., has decided to undertake a series of conferences solely devoted to this topic. International scholars are invited to contribute to these conferences in order to define the meaning of total war and to investigate its relationship to state and society. The history of modern warfare from 1861 to 1945, as well as its impact on and roots within society, will be looked at from many different angles. Certainly the revolutionary wars at the end of the eighteenth century constituted the all-important prelude to warfare after 1861, as they truly marked the beginning of the age of people's war. Yet they were somewhat separated from developments almost a hundred years later by a kind of lull after 1815. Moreover, industrialized warfare only began in the second half of the nineteenth century, and it was only after 1861 that the beginning of industrialization and the phenomenon of people's war formed a powerful and gruesome combination, which bore the seeds of twentieth-century's warfare. We therefore believe that it makes sense to start our conference series with the year 1861. Even at this point, it is debatable whether the wars of the subsequent decade were truly modern. After all, some of the contributions to the book cast doubts as to the very modernity of the American Civil War and the German Wars of Unification. In any case, we consider it a useful undertaking to trace the origins of total war as far back as possible.

The conference series focuses on the examples of the United States and Germany. After all, these two nations were not only among the highest developed and most powerful in the period under consideration and participated in both total wars of the twentieth century; in their political structures, they both formed striking opposites within the Western world. A structural comparison therefore allows us to take into account many different factors in the development of total warfare. Nevertheless, other nations will have to come into the picture as well, since they played major roles in this development, too (for example, France in 1870–71).

The first conference of the series took place in Washington, D.C., in April 1992. It was devoted to a comparison between the American Civil War and the German Wars of Unification. A comparative approach promises to deliver more results than a thorough investigation of just one example. It gives us more data and more information and provides us with an opportunity to distinguish between specific and general developments. Total warfare moreover was a structural phenomenon that hit not just one or two nations but eventually engulfed more or less the whole modern world. Only comparison could help us to lay some of these structures bare. In addition, a comparison between the American Civil War and the German Wars of Unification is an interesting undertaking in itself. Some historians have talked about similarities, but so far no serious attempt has been made to start a comparative investigation. Specialists on both sides of the Atlantic Ocean have for the most part concentrated on their own field, without looking over the fence. The same is true for those colleagues whose careers led them to specialize on the history of distant shores. They were usually too busy learning about the country of their academic choice to follow the research into the history of their own land. Consequently, historians of the respective wars seldom met to exchange ideas. It was a purpose of this conference to provide an arena for such a meeting to take place. The results of the exchanges were interesting and at times even fascinating. Much of this has been incorporated in the revised essays published here. As there are desperately few historians, however, whose expertise enables them to undertake a comparison of these wars, the vast majority of the contributions analyze only aspects of one side. With the exception of Carl Degler and Annette Becker, we could not find anyone who embarked on the risky adventure of writing a comparative paper. Thus, it remains mostly to the reader to draw comparisons from the specialized contributions. This approach, however, allowed for more detailed investigations into each individual case, which benefits the depth of analysis.

This book contains revised versions of most of the papers presented at the conference. Not all of them could be published, however, since some contributors did not "deliver." The editors decided moreover to include Mark E. Neely Jr.'s important article on the question of how total the Civil War really was. Neely's essay puts a fundamental question mark behind the main idea of the book. Indeed, the almost inflationary use of the term *total war* has led some historians to apply it freely to the American Civil War. In his masterpiece, *Battle Cry of Freedom*, James McPherson emphatically claims that the second half of that war was total in a rather modern sense.[25] Neely's criticism of this thesis has made it even more interesting to look into the question of how total the Civil War was. Still, it appears to the editors that elements of total warfare, at least as far as they are included in the third type of people's war, were indeed found in the Civil War.

Apparently, nobody ever claimed the German Wars of Unification to have been something like total wars. Even the most violent of these conflicts, the Franco-Prussian War, has traditionally been regarded as a rather limited affair. Helmuth von Moltke and his Prussian General Staff did their best in the official histories to portray the war of 1870–71 as an almost traditional

---

25 McPherson, *Battle Cry of Freedom*. See also his contribution in this book (Chapter 14). For criticism of this and other assertions in the same direction, see Neely's article (Chapter 2).

military campaign between regular armies, which was decided in big battles and could have been an almost classical cabinet's war had it not been for those nasty French republicans.[26] But research in the last couple of decades has demonstrated that the Franco-Prussian War in its intensity and quality was indeed a rather modern war that carried elements of World War I in it.[27] A most recent analysis of atrocities perpetrated by Bavarian troops against French civilians has made the point perhaps clearer: A relatively backward and undisciplined conscript army with the consent of its commanders waged people's war against suspicious civilians with increasing brutality. Old-fashioned and modern elements thus came together to create warfare in a transitional state between people's war and total war.[28]

The Franco-Prussian War is curiously much less researched than the Civil War. More has to be done. Some of the best specialists in the field have contributed essays to this collection, however, to make a comparison possible. One of the major characteristics of comparative history is that it will always reveal similarities as well as divergence. By comparing, we are able to highlight certain structural patterns of a social or military phenomenon that we would most certainly have overlooked without this approach.[29]

Since comparison is one of the purposes of this book, we have refrained from including articles on the direct involvement of third powers on both sides of the Atlantic Ocean in the wars under consideration. It would certainly have been interesting to look into the diplomatic activities of these neutrals while those wars raged. Moreover, it cannot be denied that Europe's great powers exerted considerable direct and indirect political, economic, and even military influence on the course of the Civil War.[30] American involvement in the German Wars of Unification, even in the Franco-Prussian War, was certainly of lesser importance. Some indirect influence might have been there, particularly in supplying France for the continuation of war after

---

26 Helmuth von Moltke, "Geschichte des Krieges, 1870–71," in Förster, *Moltke*, 236–594, and Kriegsgeschichtliche Abteilung des Grossen Generalstabes, eds., *Der deutsch-französische Krieg, 1870–71,* 8 vols. (Berlin, 1874–81).

27 See, e.g., Howard, *Franco-Prussian War,* and Stéphane Audoin-Rouzeau, *1870: La France dans la guerre* (Paris, 1989).

28 Mark R. Stoneman, "The Bavarian Army and French Civilians in the War of 1870–71," M.A. thesis, Universität Augsburg, 1994.

29 For comparative historical analysis, see, e.g., Gabor S. Boritt, ed., *Civil War–World War II: Comparative Vistas* (New York, 1995); Erich Angermann, *Challenges of Ambiguity: Doing Comparative History* (New York, 1991); C. Vann Woodward, ed., *The Comparative Approach to American History* (New York, 1968).

30 See, e.g., Eugene H. Berwanger, *The British Foreign Service and the American Civil War* (Lexington, Ky., 1994); D. P. Crook, *The North, the South, and the Powers* (New York, 1974); Baldur Eduard Pfeiffer, *Deutschland und der amerikanische Bürgerkrieg* (Mainz, 1971); Harold Hyman, ed., *Heard around the World: The Impact of the Civil War* (New York, 1969); Serge Gavronsky, *The French Liberal Opposition and the American Civil War* (New York, 1968).

Sedan. But we felt that these topics had perhaps not that much to contribute within the context of our agenda. After all, this book is already sizable enough.

Still, in order to find some answers to the main questions of this project, the authors set out to investigate many different fields, which appeared important to us if we wanted to come to a deeper understanding of the wars under consideration. One thing was clear right from the beginning: it would not suffice to stick to the traditional ways of military historiography. A "battle history of war," although certainly not without its merits,[31] is merely an analysis of military operations, and is certainly not enough to grasp war in its totality. It may still be popular unfortunately to indulge in the exploits of commanders and soldiers, but such a popular approach, if done in isolation, can only distort our view of reality. It was the great military historian Basil Liddell Hart who quite some time ago condemned a too narrow-minded approach to military history with harsh words: "To place the position and trace the action of battalions and batteries is only of value to the collector of antiques, and still more to the dealer of faked antiques."[32]

Since the purpose of this collection goes far beyond battlefield history, we had to make use of virtually every methodological approach that modern historiography has to offer. Political history, history of diplomacy, social history, economic history, cultural history, gender history of daily life, all come together to enrich military history to a point where the relationship between war and society can be investigated in its broadest sense. This seemed the only way to us to foster a general interpretation of our theme. Indeed, if modern warfare tends to implicate all aspects of social life, then all historiographical methods have to be applied to understand its real meaning. This is even more the case when we are looking for the development of total warfare. As Roger Chickering put it so neatly during the second conference of our series: "Total war requires total history."[33]

CONTRIBUTION AND CONTRIBUTORS

The theoretical model – or to use Max Weber's term, the *ideal type – total war* offers an intriguing new look into the most traumatic social activities of which human beings are capable: wars.

---

31 See, e.g., the wonderful book by John Keegan, *The Face of Battle. A Study of Agincourt, Waterloo, and the Somme* (London, 1976), which has helped to enlarge considerably our knowledge about what actually happens on battlefields.

32 Basil H. Liddell Hart, *Sherman: Soldier, Realist, American*, 2d ed. (New York, 1958), viii.

33 The papers of the conference, "Anticipating Total War: The United States and Germany, 1871–1914," held in Augsburg in 1994, will be published in due course.

The two introductory essays in Part I provide a general theoretical and conceptual framework and a guiding line and point of reference when reading the subsequent contributions. The two essential conceptual elements and core questions of this book – total war and comparability – are examined in these essays from different angles and points of view and impressively demonstrate the complexity involved.

By taking the concept of nationalism or nationhood as a point of reference, Carl N. Degler in "The American Civil War and the German Wars of Unification: The Problem of Comparison" (Chapter 3) reflects on the theoretical dimension of the problem of the comparability between the American Civil War and the German Wars of Unification. Although the comparison between the two "secessionist" states Prussia and the Confederacy is tempting, Degler rightly states that in contrast to Prussia, the South was struggling against the forces of modernization. It was determined to defend its central institution – slavery – against the free industrialized Northern states. Compared to Austria, Prussia under Bismarck was significantly more modernized in economic and military terms. Here it resembled more the Northern development of accelerated industrialization. Within the comparative paradigms of nationhood, Degler analyzed then the nature of American nationalism and its Southern variation before 1860 and its overall meaning to the process of the American national unification. He argues that the existence of a Confederate proto-nationalism demonstrated the relative weakness of American nationalism before 1860, also detected by contemporary Europeans. In other words, was the United States in 1861 an unfinished nation in much the same way that Germany was? The Civil War then was not a war for preserving the Union but rather for creating a new nation with all the forces of economic, technical, and organizational modernity. This might explain the totality of warfare on both sides of the Mason-Dixon Line and the will to sustain devastation and destruction.

Everyone can imagine how excited we were about the appearance of Mark Neely's essay "Was the Civil War a Total War?" (Chapter 2, this volume) in the March issue of 1991 in *Civil War History* when we were just in the middle of the conceptualization and planning of our conference. Evidently, something in the zeitgeist was ripe for the question we asked – and obviously for some other colleagues. Neely concentrated on elementary theoretical considerations of the way(s) in which the American Civil War could – or could not – be called *total*. Although his conclusions negate the applicability of the total war concept to the American Civil War, it nevertheless brings the core questions of the ideal type of *total war* sharply into focus.

These two basic essays render a provocative stimulus and frame of reference for the subsequent contributions to this book. We consider these essays stimulating and suggestive enough for the reader that he or she will remember certain hypotheses even when reading the last essay.

Six major interconnected components structured the conference; hence, this publication reflects our basic concerns. No hierarchical structure for the outline in terms of importance was intended, and consequently the parts of this publication reflect this intention: Basic Questions (Part One); Nationalism, Leadership, and War (Part Two); Mobilization and Warfare (Part Three); The Home Front (Part Four); The Reality of War (Part Five); and The Legacy (Part Six). Needless to say, these six components are all interrelated. Interwoven—and often reoccurring—motives produce a fabric with certain patterns and structures that yield a new look at the wars discussed.

Richard E. Beringer and Hans L. Trefousse address the first component, "Nationalism, Leadership, and War" in Part Two, and thus join Degler's reflections on this important issue. In his contribution "Confederate Identity and the Will to Fight" (Chapter 4), Beringer examines the questions of Southern distinctiveness, identity, nationalism, and ideology. He also discusses major driving forces behind the Confederate will to sustain such a horrendous war for four years. It was not primarily an identification with a "Confederate Nation," except in a geographic sense, as Beringer states, but rather regional and individual loyalties that motivated soldier-citizens to continue to fight.

The victorious side of the war is dealt with in Trefousse's essay on "Unionism and Abolition: Political Mobilization in the North" (Chapter 5). The author focuses on the Union and examines central ideological and political motives behind the successful mobilization of the North. He also investigates the ways in which Northern leaders appealed to the maintenance of the Union and the perpetuity of popular government. The main ideological carrier of popular government, who called the Civil War a "people's contest," was Abraham Lincoln; consequently, Trefousse delineates Lincoln's achievements and developments during the war, which also reflect the changing character and quality of this conflict.

In the age of people's war, the relationship between military command and political leadership was perhaps more complicated than ever. Stig Förster in "The Prussian Triangle of Leadership in the Face of a People's War: A Reassessment of the Conflict between Bismarck and Moltke, 1870-71" (Chapter 6) explores the gray area between the logic of policy and the grammar of war. He analyzes the impact of people's war on the dualism between civilian government and military high command personified through

Bismarck and Moltke and the conflict's culmination during the Franco-Prussian War. Edward Hagermann in "Union Generalship, Political Leadership, and Total War Strategy" (Chapter 7) also addresses the subject of a civilian–military coexistence and its logic in the decision-making process under the impact of war. He looks at the relationship between political and military leadership during the Civil War and its influence on the nature of warfare in the context of an increasingly industrialized democracy.

Closely connected to the subject of political decisions and military planning is the aspect of mobilization and warfare, the subject of Part Three. Civilians become soldiers in wars, and their attitude toward war might be decisive for the outcome of a war. This component addresses issues such as the transition from limited war to total war in America, France, and Germany, and the creation and structures of armies in these countries. The major subjects discussed are the political preconditions for mobilization and the will to fight in each respective society. The creation of two large and complex separate armies within a relatively short time span in the United States was a unique and new phenomenon in the Western world. How was this achieved, and by what means?

In his contribution, "The Civil War Armies: Creation, Mobilization, and Development" (Chapter 8), Herman M. Hattaway first investigates the creation of both armies and then concentrates on the pertinent evolutionary changes that took place both in the Confederate and the Union armies during the war. Hattaway argues that development rather than creation or mobilization was the key factor for explaining the potency of the Civil War armies. He also investigates the question: How did the organizational structures of the opposing armies differ, and what might have been the reasons for these differences?

Arthur Marwick rightly emphasizes that total war requires the "involvement, whether in the army or on the domestic front, of hitherto underprivileged groups."[34] With the shifting goals and hence character of the Civil War – from preservation of the Union to the emancipation of the slaves – the destruction of the institution of slavery became a major driving force behind the Northern political and military mobilization efforts to win the war. With black enlistment in the North – in Marwick's words, the "involvement ... of hitherto underprivileged groups" – Lincoln aimed directly at the very social and economic foundations of the South.

Joseph T. Glatthaar in "African-Americans and the Mobilization for Civil War" (Chapter 9) examines the developments that led to the decision to arm Afro-Americans and the significance of the enlistment of 179,000 blacks for

---

34 Arthur Marwick, ed., *Total War and Social Change* (New York, 1988), xvi.

the Northern military expansion. The impressive performance of black troops for the Union and the desolate Confederate military situation doubtlessly affected Southern attitudes regarding Afro-Americans, as demonstrated by Southern politicians opting for black enlistment–a proposal unthinkable before the outbreak of war in 1861. This is clearly an indication that the war transformed social and cultural actualities under the stresses of warfare into a new reality.

Stanley L. Engerman and J. Matthew Gallman in "The Civil War Economy: A Modern View" (Chapter 10) analyze the economic dimension and the various assumptions concerning the relationship between industrialization and the Civil War. They wisely examine the industry's role in the fighting of the Civil War and the importance of the war in the United States' subsequent industrial development, because only by comparing wartime developments with the conditions of peacetime can a sensible analysis be possible. Engerman and Gallman conclude their essay with an important finding concerning mobilization of resources during the war, a finding that sheds light on our attempt to understand the mechanism of total war. The more modern and industrialized Union with its evident quantitative advantages over the Confederacy did not choose the path toward total war. Because of this superiority, the Union did not have to develop the full spectrum of total war. The Confederacy, however, much less modernized than the Union and traditionally resistant to change, was more or less forced into revolutionary changes and thus to commit itself to total war in order to sustain the conflict.

In "Industry and Warfare in Prussia" (Chapter 11), Ulrich Wengenroth looks at the involvement of private industry in Prussia and the degree to which its potential was used. He also analyzes industry-based warfare and modern armament industry, the scale and scope of civilian production, and the shift from army factories to civilian mass-producing industry.

In the next chapter, "The Prussian Army from Reform to War" (Chapter 12), Manfred Messerschmidt looks at the nexus between army reform, military successes and German unification, and the role of the prince regent behind the reform project. Again this addresses the issue of the relationship of policy makers and military leaders.

In his contribution, "French Mobilization in 1870" (Chapter 13), William Serman examines the way in which French mobilization took place and discusses the reasons for the French shortcomings in the enterprise. He explores the transformation of the Imperial army into a mass people's army under the guiding influence of Gambetta and Freycinet. Their combined effort boosted the defensive national spirit and also raised the morale of the soldiers. Serman documents that with this spirit, industrial production increased and the collection of capital was improved. Still, the National Defense Government failed to utilize effectively the economic resources of the country and to convince especially the rural population to wage guerrilla warfare against the Germans. Serman argues against the interpretation that the French were committed to total war in this conflict.

As the title of his essay indicates – "From Limited War to Total War in America" (Chapter 14) – James M. McPherson argues with Neely's position that the American Civil War was still a limited war. McPherson examines the developments and events that demonstrated an accelerated drive toward violence and devastation on both sides and the waging of unlimited hostilities that transformed this war into a total war. In "Remarks on the Preconditions to Waging War in Prussia-Germany, 1866–71" (Chapter 15), Wilhelm Deist analyzes the military consequences of a general conscription that was based on the Prussian military reform. He also focuses on the new technical aids and developments – especially the rapid transport of troops by railroads on the Prussian side – and their consequences for the conduct of war and discusses whether the German conduct of war evolved from a cabinet war to industrialized people's war, or whether it evolved instead more in the direction of total war. Deist argues that in the war of 1870–71 mobilization of manpower resources remained limited, and one cannot speak of a mobilization of material resources. On the Prussian-German side, the forms of an industrialized people's war cannot be recognized according to Deist. Although the appearance of the franc-tireurs and the *guerre à outrance* posed great problems to German military leaders, they scarcely changed their essential elements of warfare.

In every modern war, the inclusion of the civilian population is essential for the war effort. Without the home front, loyal and committed to a cause, politicians in a democratic state hesitate to support a war, because ultimately the battle front collapses. Indeed, the domestic front is pivotal in sustaining a war. We believe that to understand the complexities of the home front and its relationship with the battlefields is also to understand the mechanism of total warfare. Hence, Part Four focuses on the political, cultural, and economic forces at the domestic front and its relation to the battle front, including issues such as women and war, propaganda, and dissent. Total war requires the concentration, mobilization, and utilization of all available economic resources of a nation for sustaining a war. Hence, looking at the political economy during war is pivotal in understanding the mechanism of total war.

In "Loyalty and Dissent: The Home Front in the American Civil War" (Chapter 16), Jörg Nagler focuses on the underlying ramifications behind the significance of loyalty and dissent in the context of the American Civil

War and how this subject relates to the overall methodological and thematic framework of the concept of total war. Loyalty becomes the psychological touchstone on which to base national cohesiveness and the ability to motivate civilians to become soldiers, to leave their families, homes, friends, and communities, and to risk the ultimate sacrifice–death–for a cause, a nation, or both combined. Propaganda, hence, becomes essential to keep the "home fires burning." Propaganda in modern warfare is closely connected to the evocation of atavistic emotions to dehumanize the enemy and thus further to attempt mentally to mobilize and strengthen the morale of the populace for sustaining the will to fight.

In " 'The Better Angels of Our Nature': Lincoln, Propaganda, and Public Opinion in the North during the Civil War" (Chapter 17), Phillip S. Paludan places the definition of the term *propaganda* within the context of American society and then examines how Northern opinion makers propagandized during the war, concentrating on the "Great Communicator" Abraham Lincoln.

War accelerates the repression of dissenters on the home front. The surveillance, control, and policing of civilians becomes pivotal for the state's successful continuation of the war effort. In his contribution, "The Permanence of Internal War: The Prussian State and Its Opponents, 1870–71" (Chapter 18), Alf Lüdtke emphasizes the continuity of the repression by Prussian agencies and state officials of opponents of the dominant classes and elites since the revolution of 1848–49. During the Franco-Prussian War, large parts of the North German Confederation were declared to be under a state of siege, and seemingly unpatriotic civilians were detained. In the aftermath of the Paris Commune, the Prussian police intensified its surveillance and repression of political dissenters such as the socialists. According to Lüdtke, the perpetual internal "small war" of the authorities against "others" was thereby enhanced by the forces of the real war of 1870–71.

As with Paludan, Stéphane Audoin-Rouzeau in "French Public Opinion in 1870–71 and the Emergence of Total War" (Chapter 19) focuses on the psychological mobilization of the populace during wartime and asks if the seeds of total warfare were already present in public opinion in 1870–71. He also analyzes the spirit of the army and the civilians and looks at the different patterns of public opinion that emerged in the city and the countryside.

Total war with the inclusion of civilians into the war effort automatically addresses gender relations and roles and their change under the impact of war. This subject is deeply embedded in the overall cultural and social dimension of war and the ideological framework necessary for the war effort. When citizen-soldiers go to war, their wives and mothers play their appropriate roles for the war effort and maintain the social order at the domestic front.

In "Women and War in the Confederacy" (Chapter 20), Donna Rebecca D. Krug looks at the war's effect on Confederate women's lives and at the changing patterns of gender roles in view of the absence and deaths of husbands. How were male gender roles changed with the collapse of their nation? In "German Patriotic Women's Work in War and Peace Time, 1864–90" (Chapter 21), Jean H. Quataert explores through a women's history perspective how the representations of war and particularly their gender symbolism shaped collective memory and solidified state power long after conclusion of the peace. She focuses on the short- and long-term implications of the mobilization of a group of patriotic German women for war work.

Although we have thus far investigated the various dimensions of war, we have not looked at the battlefields, the soldiers involved, their lives in the trenches, and their everyday experience. Accordingly, Part Five, "The Reality of War," concentrates on the questions of the front experience, guerrilla warfare, and the treatment of prisoners of war. Again, we are not so much interested in the course of battles but rather in the character of warfare under the paradigm of total war. Civil War soldiers were tested by the reality of combat more terribly than in any other previous American war. Earl J. Hess examines the changes that took place on and off the battlefields in "Tactics, Trenches, and Men in the Civil War" (Chapter 22). He investigates the new tactics which modern war making demanded and which significantly changed the combat experience of Northern and Southern soldiers.

In "Daily Life at the Front and the Concept of Total War" (Chapter 23), Thomas Rohkrämer examines the long-neglected daily life of common soldiers during the Franco-Prussian War. He analyzes the attitudes, behavior, and beliefs of soldiers of all ranks within the changes from limited war to *guerre à outrance*. In "At the Nihilist Edge: Reflections on Guerrilla Warfare during the American Civil War" (Chapter 24), Michael Fellman draws a wide historical circle between the pre-modern Thirty Years War and the wars of the 1860s and analyzes the cultural factors that determined the level of violence in the American Civil War. He takes a close look at the conditions of the hill country of the border states and the up-country South, where guerrilla war broke out spontaneously after the beginning of war.

Robert Tombs examines the two wars waged against Paris between September 1870 and May 1871, the first by the German army, the second by the French, in "The Wars against Paris" (Chapter 25). Tombs looks in detail at the German motives and beliefs that animated the attack on Paris and at the key political and ideological developments that were to contribute to the twentieth-century concept of total war.

People's war and total war also changed the fate and treatment of prisoners of war – the forgotten victims of history. Traditional forms of enemy prisoner treatment might collapse under the stress of a highly emotionalized war hysteria. Prisoners of war are now one of the least studied subjects relating to the Civil War and also to the Franco-Prussian War. By looking at the prison system, we might detect new forms and a new quality of warfare. In " 'Our Prison System, Supposing We had Any': The Confederate and Union Prison Systems" (Chapter 26), Reid Mitchell sheds new light on the approximately 195,000 Union soldiers and 215,000 Confederates who spent some time in enemy hands. Mitchell scrutinizes the motives and policies behind the treatment of prisoners of war on both sides of the Mason-Dixon Line. In "French Prisoners of War in Germany, 1870–71" (Chapter 27), Manfred Botzenhart also covers new terrain in examining the treatment of French prisoners of war in Germany and how the Germans coped with the utterly new situation in European history – namely, how to supply housing and provisions for the masses of French prisoners that poured into Germany after the capitulation of Sedan, Metz, and other fortresses.

Each war leaves an imprint in the collective national memory. One can assume that depending upon the character of a war – and the outcome – the profundity of the creation of myths and legends will vary. The legacy of a war, the subject of Part Six, can be long-lasting and enshrined in the national memory for generations and can have various ramifications in the political, social, and economic realm of a nation.

In "The Influence of the German Wars of Unification on the United States" (Chapter 28), Jay Luvaas deviates from the approaches taken thus far by interconnecting the two separate national (military) histories of the United States and Germany. He examines the direct influence of the German Wars of Unification upon the United States in the post – Civil War era up to 1914 and scrutinizes the nature and extent to which German military thinking and models shaped U.S. Army and military institutions and organizations.

In "From Civil War to World Power: Perceptions and Realities, 1865–1914" (Chapter 29), Richard N. Current examines the questions: to what extent did the Civil War and its legacy spur the growth of the United States to a world power, and how do contemporary Americans perceive and interpret the legacy of the war concerning the American extension of global power?

In "The Myth of Gambetta and the 'People's War' in Germany and France, 1871–1914" (Chapter 30), Gerd Krumeich explores the question of whether and in what way French warfare after the defeat at Sedan was regarded as a step on the way to total war. Krumeich does not intend to determine whether the "people's war" (*Volkskrieg*) organized by Gambetta between September 1870 and January 1871 objectively represents a new type of war but, rather, asks the question of whether and in what way the people's war represented a milestone in German and French memory and military theory between 1871 and 1914.

In the American Civil War, 618,000 soldiers died, and in the Franco-Prussian War, probably 320,000 German and French soldiers lost their lives. Does the character of a war also influence the way people commemorate their dead? This was an important question for us to ask. A modern people's war with soldier-citizen armies excludes the idea of commemorating only the generals and officers. The common soldier, the American "Billy Yank" and "Johnny Reb" or the French *moblot*, now also appear on war memorials by individual names.

It seems appropriate to end this part of the collection with a study of war memorials erected to commemorate the victims and supposed heroes of very bloody wars. In the aftermath of wars, the collective memory must reconstruct itself. Both the victors and the vanquished have to come to terms with commemorating the dead. The cause of the sacrifices made and the memories of the past war – its myths and legends – can be instrumentalized for the next war by governments, as Annette Becker demonstrates in "War Memorials: A Legacy of Total War?" (Chapter 31). In a comparative approach Becker concentrates on the memorials that were built in France and Germany after the Franco-Prussian War and in the United States after the Civil War both on and off the battlefields.

Roger Chickering's conclusion, "The American Civil War and the German Wars of Unification: Some Parting Shots" (Chapter 32), offers us a cautionary note to this story of total war and attempts to draw together the various strands that comprise this collection of essays.

As has been indicated previously, the outcome of our endeavor is ambivalent and even contradictory. We cannot present clear-cut results, general answers, or even common agreements. Instead, we ended up with a rather mixed bag. The full range of individual findings and opinions reaches from a denial of even the very modernity of the Civil War and the Wars of Unification to the ready, albeit cautious application of the term *total war* at least to the Civil War. This may come as no surprise, as the congregation of so many excellent scholars was bound to lead to differences in opinion. The exchange of such differences was after all one of the purposes of the conference, and, as in most academic meetings, it was unlikely that one position would carry the day. This book therefore represents the current state of the debate. Moreover, many of the disagreements stem from the different angles from which we looked at the problem. If the seeds of total warfare might become visible in the plight of Southern women, in General Sherman's operations, or in Moltke's plans for the total subjugation of France, this might not be the case for Bismarck's policy, the mobilization of the Union's economy, or the operations of General Lee. To some extent, therefore, every scholar was shackled by his or her own subject.

There might also be a deeper reason for the disagreements amongst our contributors. These wars themselves presented contradictory pictures. They were modern and old-fashioned at the same time. They tended in some ways to become unlimited, while in others they clearly remained wars in the traditional style of the Victorian age. They were people's wars and yet retained elements of romantic chivalry. They stood at the beginning of industrialized warfare but were fought by still overwhelmingly agricultural societies. In short: They were wholly ambivalent.

Perhaps the aforementioned example of the Bavarians may indicate what these wars really were. They seem to have been wars of transition that stood at the dawning of the industrial age of mass societies. They already carried some of the seeds of total war in them, but, in spite of all their horrors, they never reached that terrible point of utter destruction that future generations were to suffer.

PART ONE

Basic Questions

2

Was the Civil War a Total War?

MARK E. NEELY JR.

In a recent article, Charles Strozier, a Lincoln biographer and co-director of the Center on Violence and Human Survival, argues that the United States' demand for unconditional surrender in World War II, and ultimately the use of two atomic bombs on Japan, found antecedents in President Lincoln's surrender terms in the Civil War.

Precedent, it might be said, is everything in human affairs. [Franklin D.] Roosevelt's inventive reading of the surrender at Appomattox draws us back into that most curious of American events, the Civil War, as the crucible in which the doctrine of unconditional surrender was forged. In this first of modern wars, a new technological capacity to kill and destroy emerged, along with a strikingly new set of ideas about military strategy, the relationship between a fighting army and noncombatant civilians, and the criteria that determine when war is over. The latter are of enormous significance and relate directly to the brutality, length, and totality of twentieth-century warfare.[1]

The crucial term here is not *unconditional surrender*, a phrase perhaps coined by Gen. Ulysses S. Grant at Fort Donelson early in 1862, but the ideal of *totality* in war, a concept that comes from our own century. "It was Lincoln, Grant, and the Civil War that incorporated total war into modern experience," Strozier maintains. "There is a clear connection here between the emerging nation-state, a new type of deadly warfare, and an ending in which an enemy capitulates completely. To put it epigrammatically, the totality of the modern state seems to require unconditional surrender as a necessary correlative of its total wars. The American Civil War brought that into focus."[2]

---

1 This chapter was originally published in *Civil War History* 37, no. 1 (1991), and is reprinted here with the permission of Kent State University Press. A few minor revisions were made for this book. John Y. Simon, editor of *The Papers of Ulysses S. Grant*, and William E. Gienapp, Harvard University, carefully read this essay in draft, criticized it, and offered useful suggestions for improvement. They helped me a great deal, but they do not necessarily agree with my arguments.

2 Charles Strozier, "The Tragedy of Unconditonal Surrender," *Military History Quarterly* 2 (Spring 1990): 12, 14; Charles Strozier, *Unconditional Surrender and the Rhetoric of Total War: From Truman to Lincoln*, Center on Violence and Human Survival Occasional Paper no. 2 (New York, 1987); see also James M. McPherson, *Lincoln and the Strategy of Unconditional Surrender* (Gettysburg, Pa., 1984), 11–13, 23–4.

The assertion that President Lincoln insisted on unconditional surrender in the Civil War can be quickly proven wrong. Grant's terms at Fort Donelson were not those of Abraham Lincoln in Washington. As the war approached its conclusion, Lincoln on four occasions wrote his peace terms down on paper. In the first instance, instead of demanding unconditional surrender, he insisted on two conditions for surrender. On July 9, 1864, he told Horace Greeley, who was about to meet Confederate agents in Canada, "If you can find, any person anywhere professing to have any proposition of Jefferson Davis in writing, for peace, embracing the restoration of the Union and abandonment of slavery, *whatever else it embraces*, say to him he may come to me with you...." Lincoln would negotiate any other terms the Confederate agents might have in mind. As the summer wore on, the Northern military cause, and with it Republican political fortunes, sank dangerously low. On August 24, Lincoln drafted a letter about peace for *New York Times* editor Henry J. Raymond, saying, "you will propose, on behalf this government, that upon the restoration of the Union and the national authority, the war shall cease at once, *all remaining questions to be left for adjustment by peaceful modes.*" The president chose not to use this letter and later insisted on the two conditions previously stipulated to Greeley, but he remained willing to negotiate other things.[3]

True, Congress might have some say as well, and the 1864 Republican platform called for unconditional surrender. *Union* and *emancipation*, Lincoln's terms, amounted to a great deal when one considers that the Confederate states seceded in order to become an independent nation and a slave republic. Yet there were many other things that a less lenient president might reasonably have demanded: the exclusion of Confederate political leaders from future public office, disfranchisement of Confederate soldiers, enfranchisement of freed blacks, legal protection for the Republican party in former Confederate states, recognition of West Virginia's statehood, the partition of other Southern states, no reprisals against ex-slaves who served in Union armies, and so on. More important, agreement to the abandonment of slavery did not consider how slavery would be abandoned, and this would matter a great deal five months later at the Hampton Roads peace conference, discussed later. For the purposes of this article, however, what Lincoln might have insisted upon is not the point. The point is that he had, for much of the Civil War at least, only two conditions for surrender. Abraham Lincoln was *not* committed to unconditional surrender.

In his annual message to Congress of December 6, 1864, even after his reelection, the president still did not call for unconditional surrender. Instead,

---

3 Roy P. Basler et al., eds., *The Collected Works of Abraham Lincoln*, 9 vols. (New Brunswick, N.J., 1953–55), 7: 435, 517 (italics added).

he stated "a single condition of peace," by which he meant "that the war will cease on the part of the government, whenever it shall have ceased on the part of those who began it." He explained that "if questions should remain, we would adjust them by the peaceful means of legislation, conference, courts, and votes, operating only in constitutional and lawful channels." He still retracted "nothing heretofore said as to slavery." That meant that he would not modify the Emancipation Proclamation or return to slavery anyone freed under it. By January 31, 1865, as Confederate resistance appeared increasingly senseless, Lincoln added a third condition (in his instructions to Secretary of State William H. Seward for the Hampton Roads peace conference): "no cessation of hostilities short of an end of the war, and the disbanding of all forces hostile to the government." Such conditions more nearly approached unconditional surrender, but Lincoln also instructed Seward to tell the Confederate peace commissioners "that all propositions of theirs not inconsistent with the above, will be considered and passed upon in a spirit of sincere liberality." Thus, Lincoln was still willing to negotiate on other matters if the Confederates agreed to Union, emancipation, and peace.[4]

For their part, the Confederates considered Lincoln's peace terms tantamount to unconditional surrender. This was especially true of President Davis, who never shared the optimism of the Confederate negotiators at Hampton Roads. When the Southern commissioners returned, Davis saw to it that the report on the conference given to the Confederate Congress embodied his own view that Lincoln had refused to offer any terms except "those which the conqueror may grant, or to permit us to have peace on any other basis than our unconditional submission in their rule...." Although Davis described the terms as "unconditional submission," Lincoln, after returning to Washington, immediately drafted a bill offering $400 million as compensation for slaves if the rebellion ended before April. He had discussed compensated emancipation at Hampton Roads. In other words, to say that Lincoln's terms amounted to unconditional surrender is to adopt the views of his worst political enemy, Jefferson Davis himself.[5]

The attribution of the concept of unconditional surrender to Lincoln has gained prominence only recently in serious historical writing, but the idea in which it is rooted, that of the Civil War as a total war, has been around a long while. In fact, it might be said to constitute the prevalent interpretation of the nature of the great American conflict. Its appeal transcends the

4 Ibid., 8: 1551–2, 250–1.
5 Edward Chase Kirkland, *The Peacemakers of 1864* (New York, 1927), 253, 258; Basler et al., eds. *Collected works of Abraham Lincoln*, 8: 260–1.

sections in Civil War debates, and the idea lies at the heart of most modern interpretations of the war by the most respected and artful writers.

The term *total war* was first applied to the Civil War in John B. Walter's article, "General William Tecumseh Sherman and Total War," published in the *Journal of Southern History* in 1948.[6] After this initial use of the term, it was quickly adopted by T. Harry Williams, whose influential book *Lincoln and His Generals*, published in 1952, began with this memorable sentence: "The Civil War was the first of the modern total wars, and the American democracy was almost totally unready to fight it." Among the more popular Civil War writers, the idea also fared well. Bruce Catton, for example, wrote in a 1964 essay on "The Generalship of Ulysses S. Grant" that "He was fighting... a total war, and in a total war the enemy's economy is to be undermined in any way possible." Scholarly writers continued to use the term as well. In his masterful *Battle Cry of Freedom: The Civil War Era*, Princeton University's James M. McPherson writes, "By 1863, Lincoln's remarkable abilities gave him a wide edge over Davis as a war leader, while in Grant and Sherman the North acquired commanders with a concept of total war and the necessary determination to make it succeed." Professor McPherson's book forms part of the prestigious Oxford History of the United States. In another landmark volume, "*A People's Contest*": *The Union and the Civil War* (Harper and Row's New American Nation series), historian Phillip S. Paludan writes, "Grant's war making has come to stand for the American way of war. For one thing, that image is one of total war demanding unconditional surrender."[7]

Surely any idea about the military conduct of the Civil War that has been championed by Williams, Catton, McPherson, and Paludan, which is embodied in the Oxford History of the United States and in the New American Nation series, can fairly be called accepted wisdom on the subject. Most writers on the military history of the war, if forced to articulate a brief general description of the nature of that conflict, would now say, as McPherson has, that the Civil War began in 1861 with a purpose in the

---

6 John B. Walters, "General William Tecumseh Sherman and Total War," *Journal of Southern History* 14 (Nov. 1948): 447–80; see also John B. Walters, *Merchant of Terror: General Sherman and Total War* (Indianapolis, Ind., 1973). Paludan mistakes the origins of Walters's ideas as being a product of the Vietnam War era, ignoring the anti-Yankee roots of the idea apparent in the earlier article. See Phillip S. Paludan, "*A People's Contest*": *The Union and the Civil War* (New York, 1988), 456. Other books on Sherman embracing the total war thesis include John G. Barrett, *Sherman's March through the Carolinas* (Chapel Hill, N.C., 1956); Burke Davis, *Sherman's March* (New York, 1980); and James M. Reston Jr., *Sherman's March and Viet Nam* (New York, 1984).

7 T. Harry Williams, *Lincoln and His Generals* (New York, 1952), 3; Bruce Catton, "The Generalship of Ulysses S. Grant," in Grandy McWhiney, ed., *Grant, Lee, Lincoln and the Radicals: Essays on Civil War Leadership* (New York, 1966), 8; James M. McPherson, *Battle Cry of Freedom: The Civil War Era* (New York, 1988), 857; Paludan, "*A People's Contest*," 296.

North "to suppress this insurrection and restore loyal Unionists to control of the southern states. The conflict was therefore a limited war...with the limited goal of restoring the status quo antebellum, not an unlimited war to destroy an enemy nation and reshape its society." Gradually, or as McPherson puts it, "willy-nilly," the war became "a total war rather than a limited one." Eventually, "Union generals William Tecumseh Sherman and Philip [H.] Sheridan saw more clearly than anyone else the nature of modern, total war, a war between peoples rather than simply between armies, a war in which the fighting left nothing untouched or unchanged." President Lincoln came to realize the nature of the military contest and "sanctioned this policy of 'being terrible' on the enemy." Finally, "when the Civil War became a total war, the invading army intentionally destroyed the economic capacity of the South to wage war." Northern victory resulted from this gradual realization and the subsequent application of new and harsh doctrines in the war's later phase.[8]

The idea of total war embodies a rare quality among interpretations of the American Civil War: It is without sectional bias. Walters, after all, was a Southerner; he saw in Sherman's doctrines the breeding ground of a counterproductive hatred at odds with the North's mission to heal the nation after the war. Williams and Catton were both Northerners, and McPherson and Paludan might fairly be termed neo-abolitionist in their interpretations of the war. Yet all agree that it was a total war. Modern writers on the Confederacy also remain ready to regard the war as a total war. Indeed, the idea provides the key to historian Emory M. Thomas's book, *The Confederacy as a Revolutionary Experience*, which argued that "by 1865, under the pressure of total war, the Confederate South had surrendered most of its cherished way of life."[9]

Northerner and Southerner alike have come to agree on the use of this term, *total war*, but what does it mean exactly? It was never used in the Civil War itself. Where does it come from?

The roots of the term are instructive. It was coined in 1921 by Giulio Douhet, the pioneering Italian advocate of air power, when he wrote: "The prevailing forms of social organization have given war a character of national totality—that is, the entire population and all the resources of a nation are sucked into the maw of war. And, since society is now definitely evolving along this line, it is within the power of human foresight to see now that future wars will be total in character and scope." Such ideas were rife in the

---

8 James M. McPherson, "Lincoln and the Second American Revolution," in John L. Thomas, ed. *Abraham Lincoln and the American Political Tradition* (Amherst, Mass., 1986), 148–9, 151.

9 Walters, "General Sherman and Total War," 480; Emory M. Thomas, *The Confederacy as a Revolutionary Experience* (Englewood Cliffs, N.J., 1971), 135.

1920s among military thinkers who had witnessed the appalling slaughter on the Western Front in the Great War, and who fancied how much better it would be to vault over the stalemated trenches and attack the enemy's industries and centers of population remote from their armies.[10]

Although the idea began mainly as an apology for air power, and is therefore virtually unthinkable outside a technological environment that includes airplanes and strategic bombing, it was related to another term that originated in the 1920s and shared the same root word, *totalitarianism*. In fact, the first book to use *total war* in its title was *Der totale Krieg*, written by the German Great War general Erich Ludendorff and published in Munich in 1935. Ludendorff used the term to suggest that modern wars fought by the totality of society needed totalitarian political control by a general at the top, a military dictator (presumably Ludendorff himself).[11]

These seem like strangely unattractive origins for an idea that would take American historians by storm. Douhet briefly served the Fascists in Rome, and his works were republished by them, while Ludendorff's ideas were conservative competitors of Adolf Hitler's. Nevertheless, *total war* took on new meaning and respectability during World War II, when it invoked, along with its old associations, the idea of planning and mobilization of the domestic economy for the war effort. In the 1940s, titles began appearing such as these: *Total War: The Economic Theory of a War Economy* (1943) by Burnham P. Beckwith; *Fiscal Planning for Total War* (1942) by William Leonard Crum; and *Financing Total War* (1942) by Robert M. Haig.[12] World War II became synonymous with *total war* and greatly accelerated interest in the idea and use of the term. In 1946, for example, constitutional scholar Edward Corwin delivered a series of lectures at the University of Michigan called "Total War and the Constitution." By 1948, Walters began his landmark article on Sherman by saying, "Within recent years the term 'total war' has become … definitely accepted as a part of the everyday vocabulary."[13]

Unfortunately, like many parts of everyday vocabulary, *total war* is a loose

---

10 Giulio Douhet, *Command of the Air* (New York, 1942), 5–6; Klaus Knorr, "Military Power Potential," in David L. Shills, ed., *International Encyclopedia of the Social Sciences* (New York, 1968), 10:327; Michael Sherry, *The Rise of American Air Power: The Creation of Armageddon* (New Haven, Conn., 1987), 24; Edward Warner, "Douhet, Mitchell, Seversky: Theories of Air Warfare," in Edward Mead Earle, ed., *Makers of Modern Strategy: Military Thought From Machiavelli to Hitler* (New York, 1966), 488.

11 Hans Speier, "Ludendorff: The German Concept of Total War," in Earle, 307–8, 315–17.

12 Published respectively by Meador in Boston, the National Bureau of Economic Research in New York, and Columbia University Press.

13 Walters, "General Sherman and Total War," 447; Edward S. Corwin, *Total War and the Constitution: Five Lectures Delivered on the William W. Cook Foundation at the University of Michigan, March 1946* (New York, 1947). Note also the title of one of the standard histories of World War II: Peter Calvorcoresis et al., *Total War: Causes and Courses of the Second World War* (New York, 1989).

term with several meanings. Since World War II, it has come to mean, in part, a war requiring the full economic mobilization of a society. From the start, it meant the obverse of that idea as well: making war on the economic resources of the enemy rather than on its armed forces alone. Yet there was nothing really new about attacking an enemy's economy; that was the very essence of naval blockades, which long predated the Civil War. The crucial and terrible new aspect of the notion of total war was embodied in the following idea, part of a definition of the term cited in the *Oxford English Dictionary*: "Every citizen is in a sense a combatant and also the object of attack." Every systematic definition of the term embodies the concept of destroying the ages-old distinction between civilians and soldiers, whatever other ideas may be present. Another citation in the OED, for example, terms it "a war to which all resources and the whole population are committed; loosely, a war conducted without any scruple or limitations." *Webster's ... Unabridged* dictionary describes total war as "warfare that uses all possible means of attack, military, scientific, and psychological, against both enemy troops and civilians." And James Turner Johnson, in his study of *Just War Tradition and the Restraint of War*, asserts that in total war "there must be disregard of restraints imposed by customs, law, and morality on the prosecution of the war. Especially ... total war bears hardest on noncombatants, whose traditional protection from harm according to the traditions of just and limited warfare appears to evaporate here."[14]

Applying to the Civil War this twentieth-century term, the product of the age of strategic bombing and blitzkrieg and powerful totalitarian governments capable of mobilizing science and psychology, seems fraught with difficulty. Surely no one believes, for example, that the Civil War was fought "without any scruple or limitations." From the ten thousand plus pages of documents in the eight full volumes of the *Official Records* dealing with prisoners of war, to the many copies of General Orders no. 100, a brief code of the laws of war distributed throughout the Union army in 1863, evidence abounds that this war knew careful limitation and conscientious scruple. Even World War II followed the rules bearing on prisoners of war. Any assessment of the Civil War's nearness to being a total war can be no more than that: an assertion that it approached total war in some ways. By no definition of the term can it be said to *be* a total war.

14 *Oxford English Dictionary*, 2d ed. (Oxford and New York, 1989), 18:286–7; James Turner Johnson, *Just War Tradition and the Restraint of War: A Moral and Historical Inquiry* (Princeton, N.J., 1981), 229. The U.S. Department of Defense, incidentally, says that the term is "not to be used." See Joint Chiefs of Staff, *Department of Defense Dictionary of Military Terms* (New York, 1988), 362. Edward Luttwak and Stuart L. Koehl in *The Dictionary of Modern War* (New York, 1991), 625, call the idea "propagandistic and literary" and say it could not be accurately applied even to Hitler's Germany.

Occasionally, the term total war approximates the meaning of *modernity.* Williams used the terms interchangeably, as in his passage from a later work in which he hedged a bit on calling the Civil War a total war: "Trite it may be to say that the Civil War was the first of the modern wars, but this is a truth that needs to be repeated. If the Civil War was not quite total, it missed totality by only a narrow margin."[15]

Modernity is not a very useful concept in military history. Surely every war is thought to be modern by its participants – save possibly those fought by Japan in the strange era when firearms were consciously rejected. "As a historian's term, *modern* when applied to warfare has a widely accepted meaning different from *total.* Modern warfare generally connotes wars fought after the French Revolution by large citizen armies equipped with the products of the Industrial Revolution and motivated more by ideology than the lash or strictly mercenary considerations.[17] The Civil War certainly was a modern war in that sense, but it was not a total war in the sense that civilians were commonly thought of as legitimate military targets.

Perhaps no one who maintains that the Civil War was a total war means it so literally. Historian Brian Bond provides a useful idea when he writes, "strictly speaking, total war is just as much a myth as total victory or total peace. What is true, however, is that the fragile barriers separating war from peace and soldiers from civilians – already eroded in World War I – virtually disappeared between 1939 and 1945."[18] Seeing how often that fragile barrier broke in the Civil War will tell how nearly it approached being a total war. All such matters of degree contain dangers for the historian trying to answer the question; the risk of sinking under a mass of piecemeal objections raised afterward by critics is very high. Even the most conservative of Civil War generals occasionally stepped over the boundaries of customarily accepted behavior in nineteenth-century warfare. Gen. George B. McClellan, for example, did so in the Peninsula campaign, after only about a year's fighting. On May 4, 1862, he informed Secretary of War Edwin M. Stanton: "The rebels have been guilty of the most murderous & barbarous conduct in placing torpedoes [land mines] *within* the abandoned works, near wells & springs, near flag staffs, magazines, telegraph offices, in carpet bags, barrels of

15   T. Harry Williams, *Americans at War: The Development of the American Military System* (Baton Rouge, La., 1960), 47. Williams was also more guarded in his *History of American Wars from 1745 to 1918* (New York, 1981), 202–3.

16   Noel Perrin, *Giving Up the Gun: Japan's Reversion to the Sword, 1543–1879* (Boston, 1979) .

17   "With Napoleon, if not with the wars of the French Revolution, modern war begins." So says Robert B. Holtman in *The Napoleonic Revolution* (Philadelphia, 1967), 52. See also similar views in John Gooch, *Armies in Europe* (London, 1980), 1; and Gunther E. Rothenberg, *The Art of Warfare in the Age of Napoleon* (Bloomington, Ind., 1978), 11, 95.

18   Brian Bond, *War and Society in Europe, 1870–1970* (New York, 1983), 168 .

flour etc. Fortunately we have not lost many men in this manner – some 4 or 5 killed & perhaps a dozen wounded. I shall make the prisoners remove them at their own peril."[19]

Confederate Gen. James Longstreet essentially agreed with McClellan and did not "recognize it as a proper or effective method of warfare" to use torpedoes. Eventually, the secretary of war in Richmond, George Randolph, was forced to render an opinion on the practice:

Whether shells planted in roads or parapets are contrary to the usages of war depends upon the purpose with which they are used.

It is not admissible in civilized warfare to take life with no other object than the destruction of life. Hence it is inadmissible to shoot sentinels and pickets, because nothing is attained but the destruction of life. It would be admissible, however, to shoot a general, because you not only take life but deprive an army of its head.

It is admissible to plant shells in a parapet to repel an assault or in a road to check pursuit because the object is to save work in one case and the army in the other.

It is not admissible to plant shells to destroy life and without other design than that of depriving your enemy of a few men, without materially injuring him.

Walters cited General Sherman's use of prisoners to clear mines as an example of his total war practices, but Sherman's reaction was in fact exactly like McClellan's. When Sherman saw a "handsome young officer" with all the flesh blown off one of his legs by a Confederate mine in Georgia in December 1864, he grew "very angry," because "this was not war, but murder." Sherman then retaliated by using Confederate prisoners to clear the mines. What at first may seem an incident suggesting the degeneration of warfare, in fact proves the belief of the protagonists in rules and codes of civilized behavior which have in the twentieth century long since vanished from the world's battlefields. The real point is that Union and Confederate authorities were in substantial agreement about the laws of war, and they usually tried to stay within them.[20]

Leaving aside similar isolated instances caused by temporary rage, can a historian seeking to describe the war's direction toward or away from total war examine larger aspects of the war where the "fragile barriers" between soldiers and civilians may have broken down? Since the conscious application of a new doctrine in warfare forms part of the total war inter-

---

19 Stephen W. Sears, ed., *The Civil War Papers of George B. McClellan: Selected Correspondence, 1860–1865* (New York, 1989), 254.

20 *The War of the Rebellion: A Compilation of the Official Records of the Union and Confederate Armies,* 128 vols. (Washington, D.C., 1880–1901), ser. 1, vol. 4, pt. 3, 509–10, 608 (hereafter cited as, *OR;* all references are to series 1 unless otherwise noted). North and South agreed, too, on the senseless killing of pickets. See Richard Shelly Hartigan, *Lieber's Code & the Laws of War* (Chicago, 1983), 58; Walters, "General Sherman and Total War," 467; William Tecumseh Sherman, *Memoirs of General W. T. Sherman,* 3d rev. ed., 2 vols. (New York, 1892), 2:194.

pretation, can a historian focus on certain figures in high command who consciously held such doctrines and systematically applied them to the enemy in the Civil War? Throughout, can the historian keep an eye on the dictionary definition of total war to measure the proximity of the Civil War to it? Surely this can be done, and short of a study of the Civil War day by day, there can hardly be any other test.

Sherman, Grant, and Sheridan are the obvious figures for study, with particular emphasis on the March to the Sea and the campaign in the Carolinas from 1864 to 1865, and actions in northern Virginia in 1864. Likewise, some attention to President Lincoln's views would also fit the traditions of the literature on this subject.

Sherman is the Civil War soldier most often quoted on the subject of total war. An article about him gave rise to this interpretation of the Civil War, and indeed it is now widely held that, as historian John F. Marszalek has expressed it, Sherman was the "inventor of Total Warfare."[21] "We are not only fighting hostile armies, but a hostile people, and must make old and young, rich and poor, feel the hard hand of war, as well as their organized armies," Sherman told Gen. Henry W. Halleck on Christmas Eve, 1864. As early as October 1862 he said, "We cannot change the hearts of these people of the South, but we can make war so terrible ... [and] make them so sick of war that generations would pass away before they would again appeal to it."[22]

The gift of sounding like a twentieth-century man was peculiarly Sherman's. Nearly every other Civil War general sounds ancient by comparison, but many historians may have allowed themselves to be fooled by his style while ignoring the substance of his campaigns.

Historians, moreover, quote Sherman selectively. In fact, he said many things and when gathered together they do not add up to any coherent "total-war philosophy," as one historian describes it. Sherman was not a philosopher; he was a general and a garrulous one at that. "He talked incessantly and more rapidly than any man I ever saw," Maj. John Chipman Gray reported. "It would be easier to say what he did not talk about than what he did." Chauncey Depew said Sherman was "the readiest and most original talker in the United States." And what Sherman said during the war was often provoked by exasperating, momentary circumstances. Therefore, he occasionally uttered frightening statements. "To secure the safety of the navigation of the Mississippi River I would slay millions," Sherman told Gen. John A. Logan on December 21, 1863. "On that point I am not only insane, but

21   John F. Marszalek, "The Inventor of Total Warfare," *Notre Dame Magazine* 18 (Summer 1989): 28–31.
22   OR 44: 798, OR 17, pt. 2: 261.

mad... for every bullet shot at a steam-boat, I would shoot a thousand thirty-pounder Parrotts into even helpless towns on Red, Oachita, Yazoo, or wherever a boat can float or soldier march." This statement was all the more striking, coming from a man widely reputed by newspaper critics to be insane. On another occasion, Sherman said, "To the petulant and persistent secessionists, why, death is mercy, and the quicker he or *she* is disposed of the better [italics added]."[23]

In other moods and in different circumstances, Sherman could sound as mild as Robert E. Lee. "War," the alleged inventor of total war wrote on April 19, 1863, "at best is barbarism, but to involve all—children, women, old and helpless—is more than can be justified." And he went on to caution against seizing so many stores that family necessities were endangered. Later, in the summer of 1863, when General Sherman sent a cavalry expedition toward Memphis from Mississippi, General Grant instructed him to "impress upon the men the importance of going through the State in an orderly manner, abstaining from taking anything not absolutely necessary for their subsistence while traveling. They should try to create as favorable an impression as possible upon the people." These may seem hopeless orders to give General Sherman, but his enthusiastic reply was this: "It will give me excessive pleasure to instruct the Cavalry as you direct, for the Policy you point out meets every wish of my heart."[24]

Scholars who pay less heed to the seductively modern sound of Sherman's harsher statements, and look closely instead at what he actually did on his celebrated campaigns in Georgia and the Carolinas, find a nineteenth-century soldier at work—certainly not a man who made war on noncombatants. Joseph T. Glatthaar's study of Sherman's campaigns confirmed that, for the most part, Sherman's men did not physically abuse civilians who kept to themselves: atrocities were suffered mostly by soldiers on *both* sides; in Georgia and the Carolinas, Sherman's army recovered the bodies of at least 172 Union soldiers hanged, shot in the head at close range, with their throats slit, or "actually butchered." And only in South Carolina, the state blamed for starting the war, did Sherman fail to restrain his men in their destruction of private property. Before the idea of total war came to Civil War studies, shrewd students of the conflict had noted the essentially nineteenth-century nature of Sherman's campaigns. Gamaliel Bradford's *Union Portraits*, for example,

23 McPherson, *Battle Cry of Freedom*, 809, John Chipman Gray and John Codman Ropes, *War Letters, 1862–1865* (Boston, 1927), 425, 427; Edmund Wilson, *Patriotic Gore: Studies in the Literature of the American Civil War* (New York, 1962), 205; OR 31, pt. 3: 459; OR 32, pt. 2: 281.

24 OR 24, pt. 3: 209; John Y. Simon, ed., *The Papers of Ulysses S. Grant*, 16 vols. (Carbondale, Ill., 1967–c1995), 9: 155, 156n.

written during World War I, observed: "Events…have made the vandalism of Sherman seem like discipline and order. The injury done by him seldom directly affected anything but property. There was no systematic cruelty in the treatment of noncombatants; and to the eternal glory of American soldiers be it recorded that insult and abuse toward women were practically unknown during the Civil War."[25]

Although not a systematic military thinker, General Sherman did compose a letter addressing the problem of noncombatants in the Civil War, and it described his actual policies better than his frequently quoted statements of a more sensational nature. He sent the letter to Maj. R. M. Sawyer, whom Sherman left behind to manage Huntsville, Alabama, when he departed for Meridian, Mississippi, early in 1864. Sherman also sent a copy to his brother, Republican Senator John Sherman, with an eye to possible publication:

In my former letters I have answered all your questions save one, and that relates to the treatment of inhabitants known or suspected to be hostile or "Secesh." This is in truth the most difficult business of our army as it advances and occupies the Southern country. It is almost impossible to lay down rules, and I invariably leave the whole subject to the local commanders, but am willing to give them the benefit of my acquired knowledge and experience. In Europe, whence we derive our principles of war, wars are between kings or rulers through hired armies, and not between peoples. These remain, as it were, neutral, and sell their produce to whatever army is in possession.

Napoleon when at war with Prussia, Austria, and Russia bought forage and provisions of the inhabitants and consequently had an interest to protect the farms and factories which ministered to his wants. In like manner the allied Armies in France could buy of the French inhabitants whatever they needed, the produce of the soil or manufactures of the country. Therefore, the general rule was and is that war is confined to the armies engaged, and should not visit the houses of families or private interests. But in other examples a different rule obtained the sanction of historical authority. I will only instance one, where in the siege of William and Mary the English army occupied Ireland, then in a state of revolt. The inhabitants were actually driven into foreign lands, and were dispossessed of their property and a new population introduced. … The question then arises, Should we treat as absolute enemies all in the South who differ from us in opinion or prejudice, kill or banish them, or should we give them time to think and gradually change their conduct so as to conform to the new order of things which is slowly and gradually creeping into their country?

When men take up arms to resist a rightful authority, we are compelled to use like force. … When the provisions, forage, horses, mules, wagons, etc., are used by

25   Joseph T. Glatthaar, *The March to the Sea and Beyond: Sherman's Troops in the Savannah and Carolinas Campaigns* (New York, 1985), 72–3, 127–8; Gamaliel Bradford, *Union Portraits* (Boston, 1916), 154n–5n. Paludan, although he says Sherman "helped announce the coming of total war," also states that "Sherman's idea of war was more description than doctrine." Paludan, "*A People's Contest*," 291, 302.

our enemy, it is clearly our duty and right to take them also, because otherwise they might be used against us. In like manner all houses left vacant by an inimical people are clearly our right, and as such are needed as storehouses, hospitals, and quarters. But the question arises as to dwellings used by women, children and non-combatants. So long as non-combatants remain in their houses and keep to their accustomed peaceful business, their opinions and prejudices can in no wise influence the war, and therefore should not be noticed; but if any one comes out into the public streets and creates disorder, he or she should be punished, restrained, or banished.... If the people, or any of them, keep up a correspondence with parties in hostility, they are spies, and can be punished according to law with death or minor punishment. These are well-established principles of war, and the people of the South having appealed to war, are barred from appealing for protection to our constitution, which they have practically and publicly defied. They have appealed to war, and must abide its rules and laws... .

Excepting incidents of retaliation, Sherman by and large lived by these "principles of war."[26]

Leaving the "whole subject" to local commanders nevertheless permitted considerable latitude for pillage or destruction and was in itself an important principle. Moreover, Sherman, who was a critic of universal suffrage and loathed the free press, thought a volunteer army, the product of America's ultra-individualistic society, would inevitably loot and burn private property. His conservative social views thus led to a career-long fatalism about pillage.[27]

Sherman's strategic purposes in the Georgia and Carolinas campaigns, usually pointed to as the epitome of total war in the Civil War, are obscured by two months of the general's letters to other generals describing his desire to cut loose from Atlanta and his long, thin line of supply to march to the sea. From mid-September to mid-November 1864, Sherman worried the idea, and his superiors, explaining it in several ways. At first, he argued from his knowledge of the political disputes between Davis and Georgia Governor Joseph E. Brown that the march would sever the state from the Confederacy. "They may stand the fall of Richmond," Sherman told Grant on September 20, "but not of all Georgia." At the same time, he belittled the effects of mere destruction:"... the more I study the game the more I am convinced that it would be wrong for me to penetrate much farther into Georgia without an objective beyond. It would not be productive of much good. I can start east and make a circuit south and back, *doing vast damage to the State* [italics added], but resulting in no permanent good. ... "[28]

26   Rachel Sherman Thorndike, ed., *The Sherman Letters: Correspondence between General and Senator Sherman from 1837 to 1891* (New York, 1894), 228–30.
27   Ibid., 175–6, 181–2, 185; M. A. DeWolfe Howe, ed., *Home Letters of General Sherman* (New York, 1909), 209.
28   *OR* 39, pt. 2: 412.

Less than three weeks later, Sherman gave a rather different explanation to Grant: "Until we can repopulate Georgia, it is useless to occupy it, but the utter destruction of its roads, houses, and people will cripple their military resources. By attempting to hold the roads we will lose 1,000 men monthly, and will gain no result. I can make the march, and make Georgia howl."

Ten days after that, he more or less combined his different arguments in a letter to General Halleck. "This movement is not purely military or strategic," he now said, "but it will illustrate the vulnerability of the South." Only when Sherman's armies arrived and "fences and corn and hogs and sheep" vanished would "the rich planters of the Oconee and Savannah" know "what war means." He spoke more tersely to his subordinates. "I want to prepare for my big raid," he explained on October 19 to a colonel in charge of supply, and with that Sherman arranged to send his impedimenta to the rear.[29]

With plans set, more or less, Sherman explained to Gen. George Thomas, who would be left to deal with Confederate Gen. John Bell Hood's army, "I propose to demonstrate the vulnerability of the South, and make its inhabitants feel that war and individual ruin are synonymous terms." Delays ensued and Sherman decided to remain in place until after election day. On the twelfth, he cut his telegraph lines, and the confusing explanations of the campaign ceased pouring out of Georgia.[30]

Sherman did not attempt the "utter destruction" of Georgia's "people." He did not really attack noncombatants directly or make any serious attempt to destroy "the economic capacity of the south to wage war," as one historian has described his purpose. After capturing Atlanta, for example, Sherman moved to capture Savannah and then attacked the symbolic capital of secession, South Carolina. He did not attack Augusta, Georgia, which he knew to contain "the only powder mills and factories remaining in the South."[31] Although he did systematically destroy railroad lines, Sherman otherwise had little conception of eliminating essential industries. Indeed, there were few to eliminate, for the South, in comparison with the North, was a premodern, underdeveloped, agrarian region where determined men with rifles were the real problem – not the ability of the area's industries to manufacture high-technology weapons. Despite scorching a sixty-mile-wide swath through the Confederacy, Sherman was never going to starve this agrarian economy into submission either. He had remarked in the past on how well fed and even shod the Confederate armies were despite their backward economy.[32]

What Sherman was doing embodied traditional geopolitical objectives in a civil war: convincing the world and the enemy's people that the Confederate

29   Ibid., pt. 3: 162, 358.   30   Ibid., 378.   31   Ibid., pt. 2: 412.
32   Thorndike, ed., *The Sherman Letters*, 185.

government and upper classes were too weak to maintain nationhood. He was "illustrating" or "demonstrating" the "vulnerability" of the Confederacy. He did this with a "big raid." "If we can march a well-appointed army right through his [Davis's] territory," Sherman told Grant on November 6, 1864, "it is a demonstration to the world, foreign and domestic, that we have a power which Davis cannot resist." In *Battle Cry of Freedom*, this statement is followed by ellipsis marks and the statement, "I can make the march, and make Georgia howl!" But that appears to be a misquotation. In fact, Sherman went on to say something less vivid and scorching:

This may not be war, but rather statesmanship, nevertheless it is overwhelming to my mind that there are thousands of people abroad and in the South who will reason thus: If the North can march an army right through the South, it is proof positive that the North can prevail in this contest, leaving only open the question of its willingness to use that power.

Now, Mr. Lincoln's election, which is assured, coupled with the conclusion just reached, makes a complete, logical whole.

And Mr. Lincoln himself endorsed the view. In his letter congratulating Sherman on his Christmas capture of Savannah, the president counted the campaign "a great success" not only in affording "the obvious and immediate military advantages" but also "in showing to the world that your army could be divided, putting the stronger part to an important new service, and yet leaving enough to vanquish the old opposing force of the whole – Hood's army." This, Lincoln said, "brings those who sat in darkness, to see a great light." Neither Sherman nor Lincoln put the emphasis on the role of sheer destructiveness or economic deprivation.[33]

If Sherman had his politic moments, there was hardly a more politically astute general in the Northern armies than his military superior and friend, General Grant. To depict Grant as an advocate of total war is to take him at his word when he spoke in temporary anger and frustration, and, more important, to make him appear a clumsy and brutal slugger, whereas he was really a deftly political puncher.

Of course, the doctrine of total war has its political side, but the point here is that no general as politic as Grant was going to embark on a single-minded strategy for the war that was certain to offend Victorian sensibilities throughout the world and make permanent enemies of all persons in the South. Grant, therefore, did not make as many "mad" remarks as Sherman did about killing "millions." He was a more reticent man. Nevertheless, the logic

---

33 OR 39, pt. 3: 660; Basler et al., eds., *Collected Works of Abraham Lincoln*, 8: 181–2; McPherson, *Battle Cry of Freedom*, 808.

of military conscription and the frustrations of guerrilla or partisan warfare could drive even Grant to make statements well beyond the accepted bounds of warfare in the middle of the nineteenth century.

The ultimate limits of Southern manpower figured ever larger in Grant's strategic thinking by 1864. Manpower shortages in the underpopulated Confederate states had led their Congress to embrace conscription even before the North did. On April 16, 1862, Southern males eighteen to thirty-five were made liable to draft, and two years later the age limits had been expanded to seventeen and fifty. In defense of Confederate conscription, even Robert E. Lee could sound like a total warrior. According to one of his staff officers, Lee "thought that every other consideration should be regarded as subordinate to the great end of the public safety, and that since the whole duty of the nation would be war until independence should be secured, the whole nation should for the time be converted into an army, the producers to feed and the soldiers to fight." Grant realized as early as the summer of 1863 that the Confederates were conscripting everyone they could lay their hands on. Every mobilizable male had become a proto-combatant. The categories of noncombatant shrunk accordingly. When guerrilla or partisan warfare further exasperated him, Grant proposed radical measures. In August 1864, to stop the pesky Confederate cavalry leader John Singleton Mosby, Grant suggested a blistering raid by General Sheridan:

> If you can possibly spare a Division of Cavalry send them through Loudo[u]n County to destroy and carry off the crops, animals, negroes, and all men under fifty years of age capable of bearing arms. In this way you will get many of Mosby's men. All Male Citizens under fifty can farely be held as prisoners of war and not as citizen prisoners. If not already soldiers they will be made so the moment the rebel army gets hold of them.

Mosby provoked another savage order from Grant to Sheridan at the same time:

> The families of most of Mosby's men are know[n] and can be collected. I think they should be taken and kept at Fort McHenry or some secure place as hostages for good conduct of Mosby and his men. When any of them are caught with nothing to designate what they are hang them without trial.

Grant seemed to be acquiring an unwholesome taste for summary execution, a policy he had rejected in his early days of command in Missouri at the beginning of the war.[34]

34   J. F. C. Fuller, *Grant and Lee: A Study in Personality and Generalship* (Bloomington, Ind., 1957), 252; Simon, ed., *The Papers of Ulysses S. Grant*, 12:13, 15.

The partisan cavalry under Mosby had troubled Union authorities for months. Sheridan willingly testified in his *Memoirs* to their effectiveness in depleting his "line-of-battle" strength by forcing him to provide large escorts for his supply train. Nevertheless, Sheridan was at first too busy campaigning in the Shenandoah Valley to order the special operation against Mosby that Grant desired. When the Confederate partisans subsequently killed Sheridan's chief quartermaster and his medical inspector, he decided to turn his attention to them after the campaign slowed in the later autumn. His orders of November 27 to cavalry commander Wesley Merritt embodied the scorched-earth aspects of Grant's suggestions, but the wholesale rounding up of civilian population seems not to have been attempted.

This section has been the hot-bed of lawless bands, who have, from time to time, depredated upon small parties on the line of army communications, on safe guards left at houses, and on all small parties of our troops. Their real object is plunder and highway robbery. To clear the country of these parties that are bringing destruction upon the innocent as well as their guilty supporters by their cowardly acts, you will consume and destroy all forage and subsistence, burn all barns and mills and their contents, and drive off all stock in the region.... This order must be literally executed, bearing in mind, however, that no dwellings are to be burned and that no personal violence be offered to the citizens. The ultimate result of the guerrilla system of warfare is the total destruction of private rights in the country occupied by such parties.

In this instance, the ordinarily fierce Sheridan retained more sense of distinction between guilty and innocent civilian populations than Grant, but the logic of military events was driving him to similarly ruthless-*sounding* conclusions. More than likely, Sheridan spared the civilians less out of considerations of conscience than practical military necessity. Thousands of civilian prisoners in tow would hardly have made the Union cavalry's task of rounding up Mosby's men easier. After all, the partisans were, as Merritt ruefully reported, "mounted on fleet horses and thoroughly conversant with the country."[35]

In the end, both Grant and Sheridan stopped well short of obliterating the distinction between noncombatants and soldiers even while fighting the aggravating Mosby, and few arrests were made.[36] Union authorities talked tough about Mosby, even to each other, but their actions fit the traditional standards of civilized warfare.

It required the extreme provocation of the frustrating campaigns of the summer of 1864, knowledge of the relentlessness of Confederate

---

35 Philip H. Sheridan, *Personal Memoirs of P. H. Sheridan*, 2 vols. (New York, 1888), 2:99–100; *OR* 43, pt. 2:679; *OR* 32, pt. 1:671.
36 Mark E. Neely Jr., *The Fate of Liberty: Abraham Lincoln and Civil Liberties* (New York, 1991), 80–1.

conscription, and the embarrassing irritations of partisan cavalry to drive Grant to declare that essentially all white Southern males between the ages of seventeen and fifty be treated as combatants. And afterward, no one really acted on the new declaration. The Union armies never gathered all white males, ages seventeen to fifty, from any area, let alone the whole South, as military prisoners. Sheridan, who was specifically told to do so in his area, did not.

Wholesale military arrests of citizens never came about, in fact, for the war was fought mostly by practical men like Ulysses S. Grant who tailored their actions to accommodate day-to-day realities. Even in its most extreme formulation, in his letters to Sheridan, for example, Grant included only draft-age males and the known relatives of guerrillas in his new broad definition of belligerent population, not women, children, or the aged. Within days, as new information came to him, he was forced to modify his own drastic orders to suit the political realities in the field. "I am informed by the Asst. Sec. of War," Grant told Sheridan, "that Loudo[u]n County has a large population of Quakers who are all favorably disposed to the Union. These people may be exempted from arrest." He qualified the order again two weeks later, instructing Sheridan to exercise his own judgment "as to who should be exempt from arrest and ... who should receive pay for their stock grain &c. It is our interest that that County should not be capable of subsisting a hostile Army and at the same time we want to inflict as little hardship upon Union men as possible."[37]

Ulysses S. Grant never applied a unitary military philosophy to the South, not total war or any other doctrine. Rounding up civilians and destroying the crops and livestock by which a local army could live – these were strategies that Grant ordered only in bitterly disloyal areas infested with guerrillas. Where the political complexion of the local populace appeared different, Grant's orders took a different tone. After Vicksburg's fall in 1863, for example, he issued a general order counseling restraint on the part of U.S. forces, which now controlled the western third of Mississippi. He called upon the people of the state "to pursue their peaceful avocations in obedience to the laws of the United States" and assured them that if they did so, the occupying forces would be "prohibited from molesting in any way the citizens of the country." "In all cases," he added, "where it becomes necessary to take private property for public use a detail will be made, under a Commissioned officer, to take specified property, and none other. A staff officer of the Quartermaster or Subsistence Dept. will ... give receipts for all property taken, to be paid at the end of the war, on proof of loyalty or on proper adjust-

37   Simon, ed., *The Papers of Ulysses S. Grant*, 12: 63, 127.

ment of claim under any regulation hereafter established." Even proof of loyalty was not always necessary to receive humane treatment from Grant's armies. For Warren County, which had been "laid waste by the long presence of contending Armies," he made provision to "issue articles of prime necessity to all destitute families" who called on the Union armies for them. The local generals could make "such restrictions for the protection of Government as they may deem expedient," but for his part, Grant did not stipulate proof of loyalty as a requisite for receiving U.S. aid.[38]

Political judgment, more than humanitarian sentiment, dictated Grant's differing policies. Where the potential for reconstructing civilian loyalty appeared high, he treated the local populace gently. Grant told Halleck that Mississippi and Louisiana "would be more easily governed now than Kentucky or Missouri if armed rebels from other states could be kept out." Later, Loudoun County, Virginia, the logistical base for Mosby, seemed to merit different treatment, but Grant did not grow steadily harsher as the war wore on. In 1864, for example, after he was given overall command of the Union armies, he learned from an old general, Henry Price, that Gen. Eleazer A. Paine, whom Grant had known in Missouri, was oppressing the people of Kentucky. Price protested "in the name of God and of all my countrymen who respect the rights of mankind." Grant ordered Paine removed from command in Paducah:

He is not fit to have a command where there is a solitary family within his reach favorable to the Government. His administration will result in large and just claims against the Government for destruction of private property taken from our friends. He will do to put in an intensely disloyal district to scourge the people but even then it is doubtful whether it comes within the bounds of civilized warfare to use him.

Paine was later court-martialed and reprimanded.[39]

Grant was not growing soft; he always believed that commanders ought to be tailored for the districts commanded. Thus, he thought Benjamin F. Butler worthless as a soldier, but in "taking charge of a Dept.mt where there are no great battles to be fought, but a dissatisfied element to control no one could manage it better than he." As late as the summer of 1864, Grant contemplated a restructuring of military districts that would put Butler in command of Kentucky or Missouri. These areas Grant had seen himself, and he regarded them as more difficult to control than Mississippi. Butler, whose notorious treatment of civilians in occupied New Orleans earned him the nickname "beast" and made him an outlaw in the Confederacy,

---

38 Ibid., 9 : 133–4.
39 Ibid., 9 : 173–4; 12 : 124–5n; E. Merton Coulter, *The Civil War and Readjustment in Kentucky* (Chapel Hill, N.C., 1926), 221–2

seemed to Grant ideal for the intractable western border states. General Grant adapted his policies to the situation at hand, but he remained always "within the bounds of civilized warfare."[40]

For his part, Sheridan consciously grasped the economic part of the modern idea of total war. In his *Memoirs*, he stated clearly:

I do not hold war to mean simply that lines of men shall engage each other in battle, and material interests be ignored. This is but a duel, in which one combatant seeks the other's life; war means much more, and is far worse than this. Those who rest at home in peace and plenty see but little of the horrors attending such a duel, and even grow indifferent to them as the struggle goes on, contenting themselves with encouraging all who are able-bodied to enlist in the cause. ... It is another matter, however, when deprivation and suffering are brought to their own doors. Then the case appears much graver, for the loss of property weighs heavy with the most of mankind; heavier often, than the sacrifices made on the field of battle. Death is popularly considered the maximum of punishment in war, but it is not; reduction to poverty brings prayers for peace more surely and more quickly than does the destruction of human life, as the selfishness of man has demonstrated in more than one great conflict.[41]

Of course, he did not embrace the doctrine of making war on noncombatants.

Ultimately, what is most interesting about Sheridan's statement is its contrast with the memoirs of Sherman and Grant, neither of whom proclaimed discovery of a new form of warfare approaching the modern idea of total war. Sherman's memoirs are, in fact, terribly disappointing in that regard. Not only does he repeatedly express his belief in "the rules and laws of war," but he also fails to lay claim to any broad originality as a commander. His Chapter 25, for example, is entitled "Conclusions – Military Lessons of the War." There he enumerates some nineteen lessons, mostly logistical, but covering such details as mail service to the troops, the use of judge advocates, and the necessity not to neglect the dead. There is nothing about noncombatants, the enemy's economy, science, psychology, or any of the other ideas usually associated with total war. And he definitely chose in his *Memoirs* to downplay any originality in the conception of the most famous campaign of his career.

I only regarded the march from Atlanta to Savannah as a "shift of base," as the transfer of a strong army, which had no opponent, and had finished its then work, from the interior to a point on the sea-coast, from which it could achieve other important results. I considered this march as a means to an end, and not as an essential act of war. Still, then, as now, the march to the sea was generally regarded as something extraordinary, something anomalous, something out of the usual order of events; whereas, in fact, I simply moved from Atlanta to Savannah, as one step in

40 Simon, ed., *The Papers of Ulysses S. Grant*, 11:155.
41 Sheridan, *Personal Memoirs of P. H. Sheridan*, 1:487–8.

the direction of Richmond, a movement that had to be met and defeated, or the war was necessarily at an end.[42]

No Northerner at any time in the nineteenth century embraced as his own the cold-blooded ideas now associated with total war. If one seeks the earliest application of the idea (rather than the actual term) to the Civil War, it lies perhaps in the following document, written in the midst of the Civil War itself:

> They [the U.S.] have repudiated the foolish conceit that the inhabitants of this confederacy are still citizens of the United States, for they are waging an indiscriminate war upon them all, with a savage ferocity unknown to modern civilization. In this war, rapine is the rule: private residences, in peaceful rural retreats, are bombarded and burnt: Grain crops in the field are consumed by the torch: and when the torch is not convenient, careful labor is bestowed to render complete the destruction of every article of use or ornament remaining in private dwellings, after their inhabitants have fled from the outrages of a brutal soldiery.
>
> Mankind will shudder to hear of the tales of outrages committed on defenseless females by soldiers of the United States now invading our homes: yet these outrages are prompted by inflamed passions and madness of intoxication.

The source of the idea was, of course, Confederate, and it was a high Confederate source indeed: Jefferson Davis.

It may sound as though Davis was describing Sherman's March through Georgia or perhaps Sheridan in the Shenandoah Valley – most probably in a late speech, in 1864 or 1865. In fact, President Davis made the statement in 1861, in his Message to Congress of July 20. Davis not only described total war three years before Sherman entered Georgia; he described total war before the First Battle of Bull Run had been fought! It was fought the day *after* Davis delivered his message to Congress.[43]

The first application of the *idea* to the Civil War came, then, in Confederate propaganda. Although it may not be a sectional interpretation now, it was an entirely sectional idea in the beginning.

Its origins give perhaps the best clue to the usefulness of the idea in describing the Civil War. *Total war* may describe certain isolated and uncharacteristic aspects of the Civil War, but it is at most a partial view.

The point is not merely semantic. The use of the idea of total war prevents historians from understanding the era properly. Taking the notion, for example, that total war hitches science to the military cause, one can see the inappropriateness of applying this idea to the Civil War. As Robert V. Bruce notes in *The Launching of Modern American Science, 1846–1876*,

---

42 Sherman, *Memoirs of General W. T. Sherman*, 2 : 220–1.
43 Jefferson Davis, *Message of the President* (Richmond, Va. [1861]), 3–4.

there was no Civil War Manhattan Project. The war, in fact, mainly hampered science by killing young men who might have become scientists later. Neither Yankee ingenuity nor Confederate desperation, as Bruce shrewdly reveals, caused technological breakthroughs of significance for the battlefield. And the great symbol of American science in the era, the Smithsonian Institution, flew no national flag during the Civil War. Science remained neutral, although individual scientists enlisted as their sectional preferences dictated.[44]

Likewise, the economic aspect of total war is misleading when used to describe characteristics of the Civil War reputedly more forward-looking than naval blockades. The ideas of economic planning and control from World War II cannot be applied to the Civil War. Hardly anyone then thought in such macro-economic terms. Abraham Lincoln did calculate the total cost of the war, but he did not do so to aid long-range economic planning for the Union war effort. Instead, he used the figure to show how relatively inexpensive it would be for the U.S. government to purchase the freedom of all the slaves in the border states through compensated emancipation. At $400 a head, the $2 million daily war expenditure would buy every slave in Delaware at "less than one half-day's cost," and "less than eighty seven days cost of this war would, at the same price, pay for all in Delaware, Maryland, District of Columbia, Kentucky, and Missouri."[45]

From the Confederate perspective, the economic insight seems ironically somewhat more appropriate. The blockade induced scarcities on which almost all Confederate civilian diarists commented — coffee, shoe leather, and needles were sorely missed. The Confederate government's attempts to supply scarce war necessities led some historians to call the resulting system "state socialism" or a "revolutionary experience." Yet these were the outcome less of deliberate Northern military strategy (the blockade aside) than of the circumstances that the South was agrarian and the North more industrialized.[46]

For its part, the North did little to mobilize its resources — little, that is, that would resemble the centralized planning and state intervention typical of twentieth-century economies in war. There was no rationing, North or South, and the Yankees' society knew only the sacrifice of men, not of materials. As Paludan has shown, agriculture thrived, and other parts of

44   Robert V. Bruce, *The Launching of Modern American Science, 1846–1876* (New York, 1987), 279–80, 299–300, 306.

45   Basler et al., eds., *Collected Works of Abraham Lincoln*, 5 : 160.

46   Louise B. Hill, *State Socialism in the Confederate States of America* (Charlottesville, Va., 1936); Emory M. Thomas, *The Confederacy as a Revolutionary Experience* (Columbia, S.C., 1991). Hill deals mainly with foreign trade and finance. See also Charles W. Ramsdell, *Behind the Lines in the Southern Confederacy* (Baton Rouge, La., 1944), 42–82.

Northern society suffered only modestly; college enrollments fell, except at the University of Michigan, but young men still continued to go to college in substantial numbers. Inflation and a graduated income tax did little to trouble the claims made by most Republicans of surprising prosperity in the midst of war. The Republican president stated in his annual message to the United States Congress in December 1864:

It is of noteworthy interest that the steady expansion of population, improvement and governmental institutions over the new and unoccupied portions of our country have scarcely been checked, much less impeded or destroyed, by our great civil war, which at first glance would seem to have absorbed almost the entire energies of the nation.

... It is not material to inquire *how* the increase has been produced, or to show that it would have been *greater* but for the war. ... The important fact remains demonstrated, that we have *more* men *now* than we had when the war *began.* ... This as to men. Material resources are now more complete and abundant than ever.

The national resources, then, are unexhausted, and, as we believe, inexhaustible.

Democrats generally conceded prosperity by their silence and focused instead on race and civil liberties as campaign issues.[47]

The *essential* aspect of any definition of total war asserts that it breaks down the distinction between soldiers and civilians, combatants and noncombatants, and this no one in the Civil War did systematically, including Sherman. He and his fellow generals waged war the same way most Victorian gentlemen did, and other Victorian gentlemen in the world knew it. That is one reason why British, French, and Prussian observers failed to comment on any startling developments seen in the American war: There was little new to report.[48] The conservative monarchies of the old world surely would have seized with delight on any evidence that warfare in the New World was degenerating to the level of starving and killing civilians. Their observers encountered no such spectacle. It required airplanes and tanks and heartless twentieth-century ideas born in the hopeless trenches of World War I to break down distinctions adhered to in practice by almost all Civil War generals. Their war did little to usher in the shock of the new in the twentieth century.

47 Basler et al., eds., *Collected Works of Abraham Lincoln*, 8:151; Paludan, "*A People's Contest*", esp. 133, 151–69.
48 Jay Luvaas, *The Military Legacy of the Civil War* (Chicago, 1959); Viscount Wolseley, *The American Civil War: An English View*, ed. James A. Rawley (Charlottesville, Va., 1964), xix, xxxiii–xxxiv.

3

The American Civil War and the German Wars of Unification: The Problem of Comparison

CARL N. DEGLER

Except for Annette Becker's essay (Chapter 31), my obligation seems to be the only one that is unabashedly comparative in conception. By that very fact, my anxiety level along with my responsibility are considerably raised since it seems I am expected to provide the fundamental justification for this Conference! (It is only fair to the organizers of the conference for me to admit that their suggestion was only that I would keep the conferees from making "premature comparisons.") Yet, behind the project stands the implication that there is a sound reason for bringing these two military activities into historical comparison. It is true that they happen to occur in a narrow time frame. Yet a common time frame is hardly a sufficient basis for comparison. For, if it were, why not include the Taiping Rebellion in China, which was both contemporaneous, occurring between 1850 and 1864, and much more costly in loss of life – always a good historical measure for significance, after all – than the American Civil War and all three of the German Wars of Unification taken together. It has been reliably estimated that more than 30 million people perished before the Taipings were put down.[1]

Moreover, the Chinese struggle, like the American Civil War, was a rebellion, whereas the German wars were said to be conflicts to create a new Empire rather than to disrupt or change an established one. Furthermore, the official name of the American conflict is the War of the Rebellion, a title which, on the face of it, seems to make it have more in common with the Chinese struggle than with the three German wars, especially when this conference places the latter under the rubric of Wars of Unification. Don't be alarmed; I am not going to make a case for including the Taiping Rebellion in this Conference. I do intend the reference to serve, however, as a way of suggesting at least one of the problems inherent in historical comparison. The Chinese war, aside from its being a rebellion, actually had little in common

---

1   S. Y. Teng, *The Taiping Rebellion and the Western Powers* (London, 1971), 411.

with the American rebellion of roughly the same time, for the American struggle, despite its official name, was more than a revolt or rebellion. It was at the very least a remarkable attempt to give birth to a new country – the Confederate States of America – out of an established one.

Does a comparison between the Southern strike for independence and the temporally overlapping German Wars of Unification of 1864, 1866, and 1870–71 provide a better basis of comparison? Curiously enough, there is a rather striking similarity that might yield some comparative insights if one does not become too beguiled by the idea of linking those three wars into a single drive for the creation of a united Germany. Helmuth von Moltke, it is true, in his memoirs spoke of *die drei deutschen Einigungskriege* (the three wars of German unification), as many essays in this volume do. And as recently as 1990, a British historian of Germany, William Carr, published a book entitled *The Origins of the Wars of German Unification*, by which he meant precisely these three wars.[2] Yet, when one reads Carr's book, it becomes clear that along with a number of other German historians, Carr has real doubts that unification was a central concern behind any of the wars. Indeed, of the three wars, the one about which Carr knows the most – namely, the war of 1864 waged by Prussia and Austria to detach Schleswig-Holstein from Denmark – is only peripherally a war of unification. Indeed, it can be seen as a war of unification only if one has in mind the idea that there was such a thing as Germany instead of the myriad of states that constituted "Germany" in the minds of most Europeans. For as James Sheehan and others have pointed out, it was not foreordained and certainly not established out of which elements a united Germany was to be forged, either under Bismarck or under the liberals who had sought to bring a united Germany into being in 1848.[3]

The very vagueness of the concept of Germany geographically makes a comparison with the American Civil War problematic. (After all, the geographical boundaries of the United States were quite definite in 1860.) Today, of course, we have a pretty good idea of what Germany consists, but before the creation of the German Empire at Versailles in 1871, that idea was not only debatable but a source of military conflicts. There was a Germany, of course. It had been created at the Congress of Vienna out of the truly ancient Holy Roman Empire of the German Nation. It was called the German Confederation, consisting of most of the German-speaking states, with Austria

---

2   William Carr, *The Origins of the Wars of German Unification* (London and New York, 1990).
3   James J. Sheehan, "What Is German History? Reflections on the Role of the *Nation* in German History and Historiography." *Journal of Modern History* 53 (March 1981): 1–15, and his "The Problem of the Nation in German History," Otto Busch and James J. Sheehan, eds., *Die Rolle der Nation in der Deutschen Geschichte und Gegenwart* (Berlin, 1985), 20.

and Prussia as the recognized leaders. The Confederation was a loose aggregation of thirty-nine German states, most of which were quite small, and in which the division of power between Austria and Prussia was sufficiently uncertain as to be a potent source of hidden – and not so hidden – rivalry between them.

In this context, the joint war by Prussia and Austria against Denmark was a war of unification only because it sought to bring into the Confederation a stretch of territory on which Germans resided. The effort was joint simply because that was the only way Bismarck at that time could settle the issue of Schleswig-Holstein. For similar reasons, the war of 1866 between Prussia and Austria was hardly a war of unification; indeed, on the face of it, just the opposite was the case. Its immediate and Bismarck's intended result was to destroy the German Confederation and thereby remove Austria from the Germany he envisioned. Instead, at least for the moment, Bismarck brought into being the North German Confederation, with Prussia as the dominant member.

In sum, if one is seeking analogies or comparisons between German unification and the American Civil War, the most obvious analogy with the war of 1866 is between Prussia and the Confederate States of America! For in making war on Austria and decisively defeating her at Königgrätz, Prussia in effect had entered upon a civil war in order to secede from the German Confederation. Bismarck emerges in that context, as a German Jefferson Davis, creating a new state – the North German Confederation – out of the older and larger unit of which it had been a part for the preceding half century.

Men and women at the time frequently perceived the war as a *Bruderkrieg* (fratricidal war), just as Americans were prone to call their civil conflict a war between brothers. "The war of 1866," wrote Carr, "was not just a clash of arms between two sovereign states but a civil war in which Germans fought Germans. And the outcome of the war was the exclusion of German Austria from the rest of Germany."[4] Nor did it appear to be a war of German unification when observers recognized that Italy was allied with Prussia. Pertinent for our purposes was the comment of an American historian interested in comparisons between the German wars and the Civil War. Of the Prussian victory at Königgrätz in 1866, Robert Binkley dryly remarked, "This Gettysburg was won by the secessionists."[5] And the comparison between Prussia and the Confederacy was even neater than simply sharing a common secession: Both "secessionists" fought their decisive battles outside their own territories.

4 Carr, *Wars of German Unification*, 134.
5 Robert C. Binley, *Realism and Nationalism, 1852–1871* (New York, 1935), 269.

Should we then narrow our focus to a comparison between Prussia and the Confederacy? Insofar as secession was an issue in both cases, that might suggest a comparison. Closer inspection of the larger circumstances and aims, however, rightly warns us away from an analogy. After all, a South determined to preserve its historic institution of slavery, and to escape its perception of domination by the free states, hardly fits Bismarck's modern economic policies and aggressive use of force. To defeat Austria and secede from the Confederation, Prussia invaded its neighbors Saxony, Hanover, and Electoral Hesse. Prussia, in short, was no slave South with its back against the wall of modern thought, facing down a threatening North that was rapidly growing in population, industry, and wealth. Prussia, rather, was the strongest German state both militarily and economically, easily outrunning Austria, its erstwhile competitor.

If, in subsequent German historiography, 1866 was transformed into a major step toward the unification of Germany, few saw it that way at the time. Bismarck, it is true, in his memoirs so defined his motives, but that memory suffered not only from the usual inadequacy of retrospective assertions of motives but also from Bismarck's well-known dislike for either nationalism or popularly directed policies. The fact was that throughout the German-speaking states and principalities, the war was worrisome simply because it was engineered by Bismarck, who was not popular even in Prussia. Indeed, only the army stood firmly behind his policies.[6] Even his king harbored grave doubts about breaking up the Confederation and allying Prussia with Italy in a war against another German state. The North German Confederation, which Bismarck created out of the victory at Königgrätz, was not intended to be an independent state as Davis hoped to make the Confederate States of America. In Bismarck's mind at the time, whatever he may have said later, the North German Confederation was only a way station on the road to uniting the north and the south under Prussian domination. Unfortunately, from the standpoint of Bismarck's program, the southern states of Baden, Württemberg, and Bavaria had scant interest in joining a union in which Prussia would be the dominant power, an attitude of which Bismarck was well aware. Indeed, as recently as 1869, he thought he would probably not live to see a united Germany, so problematic did the achievement of unity appear to him.[7]

---

6   Carr, *Wars of German Unification*, 134.
7   In a letter to Georg Freiherr von Werthen in February 1869 Bismarck still perceived German unity as "unripe fruit." He continued, "If the time that lies ahead works in the interest of unity as much as the period since the accession of Frederick the Great has done, and particularly the period since 1840, the year in which a national movement was perceptible for the first time since the war of liberation, then we can look to the future calmly and leave the rest to our successors." Quoted in Gordon A. Craig, *Germany, 1866–1945* (New York, 1978), 20.

Why was Bismarck so dubious about the creation of a united Germany? Partly, of course, because he was determined to have a *Kleindeutschland*, in which Prussia would be the dominant state and Austria would be excluded. Many Germans did not view that arrangement as a united Germany. The *Grossdeutschland* and *Kleindeutschland* division was only the beginning of the problem of how to create a united Germany. Beyond that stood historical and social divisions, which offered little support for unification. As Mack Walker remarked years ago, the difference between the politics of Germany, on the one hand, and that of the United States, Britain, and France, on the other hand, has been a quite different political experience. German politics had long been rooted in the towns, which lacked the connectedness to a state that political parties supplied in the United States, that parliament offered in England, and that the monarchs and their courts provided in France. Or put more broadly, Germany was divided historically not only by regions and states but even more significantly by "social and occupational groupings, mutually exclusive and often hostile, and without the need of submerging or compromising their special variants to a common interest or a common master."[8]

Beyond politics, Germans were also divided by religion, ethnicity, and class. At the time of the Frankfurt Parliament in 1848, for example, religious concerns far outran secular. Of the signatures on the 2,000 petitions sent to the conclave, 163,000 were appended to requests concerned with church-state relations, 54,000 with economics, and only 20,000 with politics.[9] Nor were aristocrats enamored of national identity. Leopold von Gerlach, a confidante of Frederick William of Prussia made no secret of his condemnation of what he called "the vice of patriotism." "Why do I detest patriotism, 'the dearly beloved fatherland,' and things of that sort?" he asked. Partly because they are empty and hypocritical, but largely because they are wrong. "Loyalty to the king and love of our fellow man, which can just as well be extended to Russians, Englishmen, and Frenchmen, are quite enough."[10] Agreement on a drive for nationality was no more obvious among those who had little or no claim to aristocracy. The major organization during the 1860s pushing for national unity, the Nationalverein (National association) counted no more than 25,000 members.[11] Ordinary citizens, Theodore Hamerow concluded in his history of German unification, were simply uninterested in national unity; they lacked a real conception of nationalism. Rather,

---

8 Mack Walker, *German Home Towns: Community, State, and General Estate, 1648–1871* (Ithaca, N.Y., 1971), 108–10.

9 James J. Sheehan, *German History, 1770–1866* (Oxford, 1989), 695n.

10 Quoted in Theodore S. Hamerow, *The Social Foundations of German Unification, 1858–1871: Ideas and Institutions* (Princeton, N.J., 1969), 191.

11 Sheehan, *German History*, 868–9.

unification "appealed... to men of means, most of them bourgeois, whose ideals and interests stimulated their support for political unification"—nationalism would advance their businesses and wealth.[12] Or as Bismarck himself put the matter in his memoirs, Germans needed dynasties in order to focus their loyalties. A German, he continued, is "much more ready to demonstrate his patriotism as a Prussian, a Hanoverian, a Württemberger, a Bavarian or a Hessian than as a German. And in the lower classes and in parliamentary parties it will be a long time before it is any different."[13]

The point of sketching the obstacles to creating the kind of Germany that Bismarck later brought into being is to relate them to the historical divisions that also characterized the United States. Just as Bismarckian policy before and after the Franco-Prussian War sought to reduce the traditional barriers to unity among Germans, so the American Civil War was intended to end the divisions that had disrupted the Union. But more on that matter a little later.

The similarities are surely there, but a comparison between the German Wars of Unification and the American Civil War is threatened from the outset with illegitimacy by a rather inconvenient historical fact. Unlike Germany at the time of its wars of unification, the United States at the opening of the Civil War had been a united country for more than three-quarters of a century! Under such circumstances, is it proper or legitimate for us to compare the German wars and the American struggle? I think it is.

If we are to make that comparison, however, then we have to introduce the concept of nationalism or nationhood. There can be no doubt that in 1860 the United States was in truth a political entity. It was recognized abroad and at home as a government or state; it exerted judicial and political authority over its citizens; it collected taxes, maintained an army, and even fought foreign wars in 1812 and again in 1846 in behalf of its citizen's interests. Yet at the same time, many of its own citizens and leaders doubted that the United States comprised a nation or a people. Paul Nagel in his study of the concept of Union among Americans points out that in the first twenty-five years of the country's existence, the Union was frequently spoken of by statesmen and citizens alike as an "experiment" rather than as an enduring polity. It was, Nagel observed, more a means to achieve nationhood than a nation itself.[14]

Certainly the early history of the country reflects a loose conception of the Union. Within ten years of the founding of the new government, Thomas Jefferson in his Kentucky Resolutions boldly asserted a state's right to nullify an oppressive act of Congress. Five years later, citizens who objected to the

12   Hamerow, *Social Foundations*, 396–7.
13   Quoted in Carr, *Wars of German Unification*, 136.
14   Paul C. Nagel, *One Nation Indivisible: The Union in American Thought* (New York, 1964), chap. 1.

acquisition of Louisiana openly talked of secession from the Union as a remedy for their discontent; within fifteen years, even louder and more widely disseminated suggestions for getting out of the Union came from New England in the course of the War of 1812. None of these suggestions, of course, disrupted the Union, but they surely measure the essentially political, as opposed to the national or organic, nature of the United States. States may seek to secede or withdraw from a political connection, but people do not secede from their national identity.

The most striking challenge to the permanence of the Union, of course, came not from New England, but from the South, from South Carolina in particular during the nullification crisis of 1828–33. And although no Southern state at that time supported South Carolina, increasing numbers of Southerners over the next two decades began to follow South Carolina's conception of the nature of the Union. At the root of the change, of course, stood the peculiarly Southern institution of slavery, on which, Southerners increasingly recognized, their prosperity, their racial security, and in time, their identity rested.

American historians have disagreed in their conclusions about the growth of Southern distinctiveness or what some have called *Southern nationalism* in the course of the thirty years before 1860. And we do not need to enter that debate here. But the very assertion of a Southern nationalism is pertinent to the question before us. For the existence of a Southern nationalism, even if only weakly rooted, as its deriders contend, supports the argument being made here that the United States even as late as 1860 was still not a nation.

It is easy in retrospect to deny the existence of a true sense of national identity among Southerners before 1860, or by 1865, as many historians have done. For we know that once the war was over, that sense of difference among Southerners diminished precipitously – only a handful of Confederates found it necessary to leave the country after Appomattox. Yet, for our purposes here, that sense of difference or of proto-nationalism does not have to be fervent or deeply rooted. It needs only to have begun to be felt in order to demonstrate the weakness of *American* nationalism. And that sense of difference is what developed among white Southerners in the course of the thirty years before 1860.

To bring a Southern confederacy into being, its proponents needed materials to work with, events, and personages around which to build, and through which to sustain their incipient national feeling. For white Southerners, the underlying source of that sense of difference from other Americans was slavery, the wealth-producing capacity of which fixed the South as a region of agriculture and rurality at the very time that the North and West were increasingly diversifying their agriculture with trade, industry, and cities. Slavery, however, was more than a labor system; by the middle years of the nineteenth century, it had become a source of deep political and moral division in the country. It could even be frowned upon by many white Southerners from Jefferson to Henry Clay as contrary to the values of a republic, but its eradication was difficult to accomplish. Increasingly, it was seen by both Southerners and Northerners as peculiarly Southern.

Once there had been a time when slavery was established in all the states that had fought and won the Revolution. And at one time, Americans in both sections had worshipped in Baptist, Methodist, and Presbyterian churches that were national in organization. By 1861, however, thanks to differences over slavery, all of these most popular of Protestant denominations had split into Northern and Southern branches. It did not require nullifiers like John C. Calhoun or secessionists like Robert Barnwell Rhett or William Lowndes Yancey to point out the differences to white Southerners, but those Southern peculiarities certainly provided ingredients from which the Rhetts and Yanceys could begin to fashion an ideology of Southern nationalism.

Along with slavery as a source of Southern difference from the rest of the United States went social and economic differences, which, together with the election of an antislavery president, helped to convince many white Southerners by 1860 that the Union, which their ancestors had played such a large part in forming in 1787, was not the Union in which they then found themselves. Not only had all the states at the time of the Revolution accepted slavery, but they had all been agricultural in economy and rural in society, as well as proud of their republican ideology that had been fashioned in the fires of their common revolt against Britain's central authority. It did not escape Southerners' attention that the American nationalism being fostered by the expanding urban and industrial economy of the North did not include them or their region. As a Texas politician told the correspondent of the *London Times* in early 1861, "We are an agricultural people.... We have no cities – we don't want them.... We want no manufactures; we desire no trading, no mechanical or manufacturing classes. ... As long as we have our rice, our sugar, our tobacco, and our cotton, we can command wealth to purchase all we want."[15] The South's prosperity, which slavery and the plantation had generated, only deepened the divisions between the regions and sharpened the recognition that Northerners were not like Southerners, that the South was a different place, that Southerners were strangers in the house of their

---

15 Quoted in James M. McPherson, "Antebellum Southern Exceptionalism: A New Look at an Old Question," *Civil War History* 29 (June, 1983):233. This article splendidly develops the argument that it was the North, not the South, which changed over the course of the first half of the nineteenth century.

fathers. At the time Northerners, too, acknowledged that the Union had not become a nation. "Let us not … too anxiously grieve over the Union of 1787," abolitionist Wendell Phillips told a New York audience in 1861. "Real unions are not made, they grow." The old Union had been made "like an artificial waterfall or a Connecticut nutmeg. … It was a wall hastily built, in hard times, of round boulders; the cement has crumbled and the smooth stones, obeying the law of gravity, tumble here and there."[16] As the historian Allan Nevins later wrote, "South and North by 1857 were rapidly becoming separate peoples. With every passing year, the fundamental assumptions, tastes, and cultural aims of the sections became more divergent."[17] This recognition of the Union's transformation since its founding is nicely reflected in Confederates' frequent insistence that their cause was nothing less than a rerun of the Revolution against England.

The existence of Southern nationalism, even the attenuated variety that I am asserting here, is admittedly not a settled issue among American historians. Indeed, I suspect that most of them agree with Kenneth M. Stampp and think of its assertion in the late 1850s as a subterfuge, almost a trick played upon the mass of Southerners by a relatively few so-called Southern "fire-eaters" like Yancey and Rhett.[18] That certainly seems to be the view that shapes historian William Freehling's recent study of the *Road to Disunion*.[19] And there were, indeed, many men and women in the South in 1860 who spoke of themselves as Unionists. Lincoln, too, along with many other Republicans, thought Southern alienation from the North was but a ploy to gain concessions. Yet, despite such widely held doubts, by April 1861 eleven Southern states had withdrawn from the Union and then proceeded to defend that decision by sustaining for four long years the bloodiest conflict of the nineteenth century (after the Taiping Rebellion, of course). The proportion of Southerners who died in that struggle far exceeded that experienced by Americans in any other war and in a European context was exceeded only by the losses sustained by Germans and Russians during World War II. That straightforward quantitative fact, I think, provides the most compelling response to Stampp's doubts that Southerners were truly alienated from the United States.[20]

European observers at the time well recognized the incomplete nature of American nationalism, even if Lincoln did not. William Gladstone, the

16 Quoted in Nagel, *One Nation Indivisible*, 31.
17 Allan Nevins, *Ordeal of the Union*, 4 vols. (New York, 1947-50), 2:533–4.
18 Kenneth M. Stampp, *The Imperiled Union: Essays on the Background of the Civil War* (New York, 1980), 255–6.
19 William W. Freehling, *The Road to Disunion Secessionists at Bay* (New York, 1990).
20 See his provocative essay "The Southern Road to Appomattox," in his *Imperiled Union*.

English chancellor of the exchequer in 1862, could not conceal his conviction, as he phrased it, that "Jefferson Davis and other leaders of the South have made an army; they are making, it appears, a navy; and they have made what is more than either, they have made a nation."[21] In short, when the Southern states seceded in 1860–61, that fact measured not only the failure of the Union but, more important, the incomplete character of American nationhood. Or as Erich Angermann has reminded us, the United States in 1861, despite the Union of 1787, was still an "unfinished nation" in much the same way that Germany was.[22]

When we recognize that in 1860 only a truncated nationalism existed among Americans despite the eighty-year history of the Union, then the American Civil War suddenly fits well into a comparison with Bismarck's nation-building efforts of those years. The Civil War, in short, was a struggle not to save a failed union but to create a nation that had not yet been born.

The father of that nation was Abraham Lincoln. Is there any basis for seeing him as comparable to Bismarck, the acknowledged creator of the German Reich? Few American historians like to make that equation. As David Potter once wrote, "the Gettysburg Address would have been as foreign to Bismarck as a policy of 'blood and iron' would have been to Lincoln."[23] And certainly Bismarck would never have defined his new Germany as a "government of the people, by the people, and for the people" even if he did surprise many by introducing universal manhood suffrage and the secret ballot into his new Reich.[24] Yet the two leaders have things in common that help us to see the two struggles for nationhood as comparable, aside from their sharing the same height – six feet four inches – and an avidity for Shakespeare.

For one thing, both men are the most written about of any other political figure in the modern history of the two countries.[25] That they are so

---

21 Quoted in Belle Becker Sideman and Lillian Friedman, eds., *Europe Looks at the Civil War* (New York, 1969), 186.

22 Erich Angermann, *Challenges of Ambiguity: Doing Comparative History* (New York, 1991), 8. True, a deep sense of nationhood existed among Americans, but it was confined largely to the North. Indeed, to acknowledge that nationalism is probably the soundest way to account for the remarkable explosion of popular support that greeted Lincoln's call for volunteers to enforce the laws in the South after the fall of Fort Sumter.

23 David M. Potter, "Civil War," in C. Vann Woodward, ed., *The Comparative Approach to American History* (New York, 1968), 143.

24 And, of course, Bismarck freed no slaves! But, then, the American Civil War turned out to have *two* quite distinctive purposes and results: creating a nation, and ending slavery. Obviously, the American Civil War can be compared with the German Wars of Unification only in connection with the first result, which was also Lincoln's sole purpose when the war began.

25 Even before Bismarck's death, some 650 books on his life had already appeared; by 1908, the number of titles reached 3,500. Louis L. Snyder, *The Blood and Iron Chancellor: A Documentary-Biography of Otto von Bismarck* (Princeton, N.J., 1967), ix. Professor Don Fehrenbacher has informed me that Frank J. Williams's annotated bibliography of writings about Lincoln will contain between 5,000 and 6,000 items.

endlessly analyzed and commented upon is only tangentially accounted for by their personalities yet much accounted for by the role each played in establishing his own people's sense of nationhood. In the case of Bismarck, the intention may not have been as clear as nationalists immediately after 1870 and Bismarck and historians subsequently liked to make out. As Michael Howard pointed out thirty years ago, "the explanation that the conflict [with France] was planned by Bismarck as the necessary climax to a long-matured scheme for the unification of Germany – an explanation to which Bismarck's own boasting in old age was to give wide currency – is one which does not today command general assent."[26] And even thirty years after Howard's conclusion, few historians subscribe to the idea that Bismarck was a true nationalist seeking identity for Germans. Yet Bismarck's Germany has become the heart of German nationalism; history rightly or wrongly has made him the father of that nationhood whatever his intentions may have been. Our own recent experience of living through the reunification of Germany, after its forty-five-year dismemberment following the fall of the Third Reich, testifies to the endurance of Bismarck's vision of Germany.

Lincoln's vision of the American Union, to be sure, differed from Bismarck's. Lincoln was a nationalist from the outset, believing that the Union was created by the Revolution; it was not dependent even upon the formation of the Constitution. That is the meaning of the postwar remark by Lincoln's erstwhile congressional colleague, and Confederate vice-president, Alexander Stephens – that for Lincoln "the Union... in sentiment rose to the sublimity of a religious mysticism."[27] That mystic nationalism, however, was far in advance, as we have seen, of the state of the actual Union, which the alienated Southern states disrupted in 1860–61. To most Americans, the conflict that ensued was intended to save the Union, but at its end they recognized that the Union had become "a new nation, under God" as Lincoln phrased it in his Gettysburg Address.

That Address, as Potter has remarked, may not have been a Bismarckian document, but Lincoln's unrelenting prosecution of the war came closer to Bismarck's "blood and iron" than Americans like to remember. It was certainly a most bloody war, killing off some 600,000 Americans in the name of national unity. And Lincoln's willingness to risk war and to sustain a lengthy and bloody conflict reflect the iron in his determination. "The tug has to come, & better now than anytime hereafter," he advised his fellow Republicans

---

26 Michael Howard, *The Franco-Prussian War: The German Invasion of France, 1870–171* (London, 1981), 40.
27 Quoted in Mark E. Neely Jr., *The Fate of Liberty: Abraham Lincoln and Civil Liberties* (New York, 1991), xi.

when the Crittenden compromise was before Congress.[28] Like Horace Greeley, Lincoln was determined to call what he considered the South's bluff, that is, its frequent threat over the years to secede in an effort to extract one more concession to ensure the survival of slavery. He himself was so convinced of the power of American nationality that at first he counted on the mass of Southerners to rally around the national standard, only to find that loyalty to the Union was largely absent in the region of his birth. Only military force kept even his native state of Kentucky within the confines of the Union that he cherished.

Bismarck's application of comparable power really came in 1866, when, in support of Prussia's war against Austria, he ordered the invasion of the independent states of Hanover, Saxony, and Electoral Hesse, because they would not accept his vision of a *Kleindeutschland* dominated by Prussia. The war with France was Bismarck's device to bring the south German states into his new Reich. Even though the southern states quickly joined in the war against France, their adhesion to Bismarck's Reich was so problematic that Bismarck felt he must deny King William the coveted title Emperor of Germany out of fear that the title would alienate the southerners.[29]

The growing economic power of Prussia, which certainly impressed when it did not simply intimidate the southern German states, suggests another parallel with the Lincoln administration in the course of the American Civil War. Hamerow has identified the years of the North German Confederation as the foundation of German industrialization. Bismarck pushed through the legislature significant measures to free economic movement and enterprise, among which were the ending of guild and artisan controls over work, the repealing of laws against usury, the adoption of the metric system, and the relieving of corporations of state controls over their formation. Helmut Böhme, in turn, has identified the economic superiority of Prussia as the controlling factor in the establishment of a *Kleindeutschland* by simply keeping an economically weaker Austria out of Bismarck's contemplated Germany.[30]

The Lincoln administration also instituted modernizing and economic development measures in the course of its war for unification. It enacted, for example, a new banking and monetary system, a protective tariff for industry, and a homestead law to speed up the settling of the west; it authorized the building of a transcontinental railroad and gave federal financial aid to higher education for the first time. Doubts have been expressed that the war itself

---

28   Quoted in James M. McPherson, *Battle Cry of Freedom: The Civil War Era* (New York, 1988), 253.

29   Helmut Böhme, ed. *The Foundation of the German Empire: Select Documents* (Oxford, 1971), 1–2.

30   Theodore S. Hamerow, *The Social Foundations of German Unification: Struggles and Accomplishments* (Princeton, N.J., 1972), 338–45; Helmut Böhme, *Foundation*, 43.

was not as stimulating to economic development as Charles Beard and others once thought.[31] Yet there can be no doubt that in the post–Civil War United States, as in post-1870 Germany, industrialization, urbanization, and wealth production in general soared.

German historians have not been in agreement on the forces that brought about the final creation of the Bismarckian Reich in 1871. Some argue for an upswelling of national sentiment from the *Volk* (the people), while, more recently, others have been emphasizing the political contrivance at the top. Historian Geoff Eley, for example, has referred to the *Reichsgründung* (founding of the German Empire) as a "radical, even revolutionary departure. ... Indeed, it is doubtful whether Germany ever corresponded to the nationalist desideratum of the nation-state."[32] The very presence of disagreement brings us closer to the American situation, where the moment of the nation's creation is not settled either. In both the German and American examples, there is no question that Lincoln and Bismarck were at the center of their respective creations. And war was the means used by both.[33]

In Lincoln's case, force was brought in directly to hold the dissidents within the confines of his nation. Self-determination was neither Lincoln's principle nor Bismarck's. The Iron Chancellor deliberately excluded German Austria from his unified Germany while including Lorraine, which was hardly German. (Prussia had long since, of course, included more than a million Poles within its "German" boundaries.) In Bismarck's mind, the decisive element was the strategic importance of Alsace and Lorraine for the security of the new German state.

Lincoln, in his actions as well as in his ideas, came closer to Bismarck than is usually admitted. There is nothing in Lincoln's record that is comparable to Bismarck's clever editing of the so-called "Ems dispatch," which set the stage for France's declaration of war in 1870. Over the years, the dispute among United States historians about whether Lincoln maneuvered the South into firing the first shot of the Civil War has not reached the negative interpretation that clings to Bismarck's Ems dispatch. Yet Lincoln's weeks

31 See Thomas C. Cochran, "Did the Civil War Retard Industrialization? " *Mississippi Valley Historical Review* 48 (Sept. 1961): 197–210.

32 Geoff Eley, *From Unification to Nazism: Reinterpreting the German Past* (Boston, 1986), 64. See also James J. Sheehan, "What Is German History? Reflections on the Role of the *Nation* in German History and Historiography," *Journal of Modern History* 53 (March 1981): 1–23.

33 Otto Pflanze in his recent biography of Bismarck broadens the comparison into a kind of principle: "It is worth noting," he writes, "that the quest for national self determination whether by a divided or a subject people, has seldom been achieved without war. Britain fought hers in the seventeenth century, the Netherlands in 1568–1648, the United States in 1775–83 and 1861–65, France in 1792–1815, Italy in 1859–66." Otto Pflanze, *Bismarck and the Development of Germany*, vol. 3: *The Period of Fortification, 1880–1898* (Princeton, N. J., 1990), 436.

of delay in settling the knotty issue of Fort Sumter exerted great pressure upon the Confederates to fire first, just as the Ems dispatch maneuvered France into declaring war. To that extent, Lincoln's actions display some of the earmarks of Bismarck's actions in 1870. For at the same time that Lincoln was holding off from supplying Sumter, he was firmly rejecting the advice of his chief military advisor Winfield Scott – that surrendering the fort was better than provoking the Confederates into beginning a war. Lincoln's nationalism needed a war, but one that the other side would begin, just as Bismarck's unification of his Germany needed a war that would rally the southern German states to join his Reich.[34]

The way in which Lincoln fought the war also reminds us at times of Bismarck's willingness to use iron, as well as shed blood, in order to build a nation. Throughout the war, Lincoln denied that secession was a legal remedy for the South, yet his own adherence to constitutional limits was hardly flawless. If Bismarck in 1862 in behalf of his king's prerogative interpreted constitutional government out of existence in Prussia for four years, Lincoln's interpretation of the American constitution followed a similar if somewhat less drastic path. As James G. Randall remarked years ago, Lincoln employed "more arbitrary power than perhaps any other President.... Probably no President has carried the power of proclamation and executive order (independently of Congress) as far as did Lincoln." Randall then proceeded to list those uses of power: freeing slaves, accepting the dismemberment of Virginia by dubious constitutional means, providing for the reconstruction of states lately in rebellion, suspending the writ of habeas corpus, proclaiming martial law, and enlarging the army and the navy and spending public money without the necessary Congressional approval. "Some of his important measures," Randall points out, "were taken under the consciousness that they belonged within the domain of Congress. The national legislature was merely permitted," Randall continues, "to ratify his measures, or else to adopt the futile alternative of refusing consent to accomplished fact."[35] Lincoln himself justified his Emancipation Proclamation on the quite questionable ground

---

34 See John Shipley Tilley, *Lincoln Takes Command* (Chapel Hill, N.C., 1941), chap. 15, in which Tilley quotes Lincoln as taking "no small consolation" from the failure to resupply Sumter because the effort was "justified by the result," that is, the supportive response of the North. For other evidence along the same line, see Ludwell H. Johnson, *Division and Reunion: America, 1848–1877* (New York, 1978), 78–9.

35 James G. Randall, *Constitutional Problems Under Lincoln*, rev. ed. (Gloucester, Mass., 1963), 513–14. At one point in his book, in discussing the constitutionality of the blockade, which Lincoln initiated, Randall came close to identifying Bismarck's and Lincoln's repudiation of constitutional limitations. If the Supreme Court in the *Prize Cases* had found that Lincoln exceeded his powers in proclaiming the blockade and expanding the army and navy, Randall wrote, then the Court "would have seemed to legitimize a dictatorship analogous to that of Bismarck from 1862–1866." Ibid., 57.

"that measures otherwise unconstitutional might become lawful by becoming indispensable to the preservation of the Constitution through the preservation of the nation."[36]

The wars that Lincoln and Bismarck waged in behalf of national unity shared more than a common purpose. In both instances, economic modernity helped to reshape the weapons and the organizations that were employed. Moltke's reorganization of the Prussian General Staff and army is generally credited with the surprisingly quick and decisive victory at Königgrätz and the later French surrender at Sedan.[37] Beyond the organization was technology. Among the Prussian innovations in arms was the breech-loaded "needle-gun," which was first used significantly and with devastating effect by the Prussians at Königgrätz. A breech-loaded gun was also introduced in the early years of the Civil War, but too slowly to be equally decisive despite Lincoln's pressing it upon the Ordnance department. For as one Confederate general later admitted, had it been widely used by the Union armies, the war might have ended before Gettysburg.[38] The importance of the breech-loading rifle was that it permitted a soldier to load and fire without standing up and presenting an inviting target for the enemy. Even Gen. Philip H. Sheridan's cavalrymen could use it effectively as they demonstrated with their carbines at Winchester during the Shenandoah campaign.

Undoubtedly, though, the railroad was the transforming innovation of the two wars. Railroads made feasible the mobilization of the enormous armies that distinguished the great battles of the Civil War and those of Königgrätz and Sedan. At Königgrätz, thanks to the railroad, the forces mobilized on the two sides reached almost a million men. In 1870, the North German Confederation alone, thanks to Moltke's General Staff's mastering of the logistics of the railroad, brought together twice the force – that is, about 1.2 million men – that Napoléon had led into Russia.[39] (Moltke's insight into the value of railroads began early. In 1843, when only a major on the General Staff, he published a technical essay on the value of railroads for the military, for national unity, and for moving goods rather than only passengers.)[40]

Finally, the German and American wars are comparable in their revival of the idea of total war, that is, a war against populations as well as armies, such as had not been seen since the horrors of the Thirty Years' War. The military

36 Quoted in Randall, *Constitutional Problems*, 378.
37 Geoff Eley, *From Unification to Nazism*, 96.
38 See Robert V. Bruce, *Lincoln and the Tools of War* (Indianapolis, Ind., and New York, 1956), chap. 7; the Confederate general's remark is on page 102.
39 Michael Howard, *War in European History* (New York, 1976), 99.
40 Helmut von Moltke, *Essays, Speeches, and Memoirs of Field-Marshall Count Helmut von Moltke*, 2 vols. (New York, 1893), 1: 227–63.

aim, of course, was to destroy civilian morale and thus induce the military forces to give up. That this tactic was introduced deliberately and effectively in the American Civil War is well known and particularly associated with Gen. William Tecumseh Sherman and his march through Georgia and the Carolinas, and with General Sheridan's destruction of the supplies and communications in the Shenandoah Valley of Virginia. More recently, however, Charles Royster has argued that the idea of destruction and killing as the proper way to deal with enemies in the Civil War began with the civilian population. It was people outside the military who called for attacks on populations rather than simply other armies. Only later did the military respond to the cry for devastation of the civilian order.[41]

Appropriately enough, the idea of total war brought the American and German wars together in 1870 in the person of General Sheridan himself. He had gone to France to observe the conflict on the German side. Once there, he took it upon himself to advise Bismarck how to proceed against the French guerrillas during the siege of Paris. On several occasions, Sheridan personally urged Bismarck to learn the lesson of his Shenandoah Valley campaign of 1864. He told Bismarck that so far in their war against the French, the Germans had been too humane. They ought to inflict as much damage on the enemy as possible and cause "the inhabitants so much suffering that they must long for peace, and for their government to demand it. The people must be left nothing but their eyes to weep with over the war." At the time, Bismarck responded favorably to the suggestion. Soon thereafter, a companion, who was present, reported that Bismarck issued orders to burn any French village to the ground, hanging all male inhabitants, where guerrilla acts were committed. To show mercy, Bismarck was reported to have said, was "culpable laziness in killing."[42]

Count Alfred von Waldersee, who later succeeded Moltke as Chief of the General Staff of the army, also witnessed Sheridan's advising Bismarck. Waldersee himself was worried about the effect of the French franc-tireurs, contending that "we must have recourse to terrorizing in order to nip this evil in the bud." Many people find terror too harsh in these civilized times, he noted, but anything that will bring a war to an end more quickly certainly has much to recommend it. Better to burn down houses than shoot innocent soldiers. "General Sheridan, who was with us until Sedan," Waldersee remarked, "said to Bismarck: 'You know how to hit an enemy as no other army does, but you have not yet learned how to annihilate him. One must see

41 Charles Royster, *The Destructive War: William Tecumseh Sherman, Stonewall Jackson, and the Americans* (New York, 1991), 39.
42 Quoted in Paul Andrew Hutton, *Phil Sheridan and His Army* (Lincoln, Neb., 1985), 202, 204–5.

more smoke of burning villages, otherwise you will not finish with the French.' And I am convinced that man is right. If we allowed our cavalry to carry out campaigns of destruction throughout the country à la Sheridan," Waldersee concluded, "many Frenchmen would lose their taste for playing at being franctireurs."[43] And that was the course that the Germans followed in the months after Sedan.

In both the German and the American cases, it is evident that the movement of the military against the civilian population grew out of the persistent resistance of the enemy. We know that Bismarck planned and hoped for a quick, decisive war against France analogous to his earlier wars against Denmark and Austria. Napoléon III surrendered at the time of Sedan, to be sure, but the continued resistance by Paris and by the new Republic caused the Germans to rephrase the old Clausewitzian cliché: Continue war by new means. Similarly, it was the persistent resistance of the Confederacy that convinced Grant to authorize Sherman's famous march through Georgia and across South Carolina and to order Sheridan to pursue "to the death" the Confederate forces of Gen. Jubel Early in the Shenandoah Valley.[44]

As Royster has recently pointed out, Sherman came late to making war against civilians. When he did arrive at that point, Royster remarks, he defended his actions as a part "of the process by which Americans attached themselves to their nation. This crucial union; of citizens, not just of states," Royster emphasizes, made possible as far as Sherman was concerned, "the prosperous powerful country Sherman endlessly extolled." Indeed, Royster reminds us, "Americans did not invent new methods of drastic war during the Civil War so much as they made real a version of conflict many of them had talked about from the start. Despite their differing fates in this kind of war," Royster concludes, "people in both sections understood it to be their means to vindicate a nation."[45]

Sheridan and Bismarck were not the only contemporaries to see connections between the two struggles for national unification. Senator Charles Sumner, in a lecture on American nationalism on the fourth anniversary of Lincoln's Gettysburg Address in 1867, pointedly regretted Germany's failure to achieve nationhood. "God grant that the day may soon dawn when all Germany shall be one."[46] President Ulysses S. Grant was sufficiently impressed

43 Alfred Count von Waldersee, *A Field-Marshal's Memoirs: From the Diary, Correspondence, and Reminiscences*, cond. and trans. Frederic White (London, 1924), 74–5. Translation slightly revised on the basis of Alfred H. K. L. Waldersee, *Denkwürdigkeiten des General-Feldmarschall Alfred Grafen von Waldersee auf Veranlassung des Generalleutnants Georg Grafen von Waldersee*, ed. Heinrich Otto Meisner, 3 vols. (Stuttgart and Berlin, 1922), 1:100–1.
44 Quoted in McPherson, *Battle Cry of Freedom*, 777.
45 Royster, *Destructive War*, 39, 89, 322.
46 Charles Sumner, *Works*, 15 vols. (Boston, 1877), 11:204.

by the unification of Germany that he called upon Congress, in a special message, to celebrate the new Germany by raising the financial status of the U.S. minister to Berlin to that of the ministers to France and Great Britain. In Grant's view, German unification signified the attainment of "the cherished aspiration for national unity, which for ages has inspired the many millions of people speaking the same language, inhabiting a contiguous and compact territory, but unnaturally separated and divided by dynastic jealousies and the ambition of short-sighted rulers." The American people, Grant told Congress, see in the new federal government of Germany "an attempt to reproduce in Europe some of the best features of our own Constitution, with such modifications as the history and conditions of Germany seem to require."[47]

The similarities extended beyond forms of government. Since both wars were fought on behalf of nation building, it is not surprising that in both societies the process would go on after the fighting ended. In the United States, it meant ending the source of the disunity – slavery – and purging the Southern states of those social and economic traits that slavery was believed to have fostered. The South's political system must be broadened and democratized, its industry stimulated, its economy diversified, and its loyalty to the nation deepened. In Germany it meant among other things the reduction of regional differences, the incorporation of smaller states, and the compelling of the Polish population to abandon its different ways, including its language, although at one time that had been permitted.[48] In time it would also mean mounting a Kulturkampf against the Roman Catholic Church.

National unification in the two countries through total war stimulated comparable reactions from neighbors. In each case, the recently displayed power of the new national states aroused concern about the future. Soon after the war, Lord Acton, in a letter to former Confederate Gen. Robert E. Lee explained why he had welcomed the Confederacy. "I saw in State Rights," Acton wrote, "the only availing check upon the absolutism of the sovereign will, and secession filled me with hope, not as the destruction but as the redemption of Democracy. ... I deemed that you were fighting the battles of our liberty, our progress, and our civilization; and I mourn the stake which was lost at Richmond more deeply than I rejoice over that which was saved at Waterloo."[49] The striking triumph of American arms made clear to France

---

47   James D. Richardson, ed., *Messages and Papers of the Presidents* (Washington, D.C., 1897), 9 : 4074–5.
48   Hans-Ulrich Wehler, *The German Empire, 1871–1918* (Leamington Spa and Dover, N.H ., 1985), 110–11; see also Pflanze, *Bismarck*, 3 : 198–209.
49   John Emerich Edward Dalberg-Acton, *Essays in the History of Liberty*, ed. J. Rufus Fears (Indianapolis, Ind., n.d.), 363.

that its imperialistic adventure in Mexico was doomed, and it stimulated the British in 1867 to grant a new autonomy and union to Canadians in order to thwart any expansionist tendencies within the recently emboldened nation to the south.

As far as Germany was concerned, Disraeli's well-known remark in February 1871 on "the German revolution" captured some of Europe's apprehensive reaction to the newly unified Germany. That revolution, Disraeli dramatically asserted, is "a greater political event than the French Revolution of the last century." He admitted that it was not as great a social event as the French upheaval, but "there is not a diplomatic tradition which has not been swept away. You have a new world. … The balance of power has been entirely destroyed, and the country which suffers most, and feels the effects of this great change most, is England."[50]

This essay began with a dubious comparison of the Taiping Rebellion with the American Civil War. Let me close with another unconventional comparison: the as yet unresolved nature of Canadian national unity. As I write, a question of the special status for Quebec threatens to disrupt the Canadian Union. It is, of course, a Union forged during that climactic era of national unification in Europe and the Americas. Unlike contemporary instances of nation building, Canada's was accomplished without the violence of war. Yet the troubled history of that Union, even more than a century after its consummation, suggests that without the cement of blood, a Union may fall short of nationhood. After all, in the making of nations, as Sherman advised, one must be prepared to use violence, even to the extreme of total war, if necessary. Abraham Lincoln, the lowly born democrat, and Otto von Bismarck, the aristocratic autocrat, could have agreed on that.

---

50 Quoted in Walther Hofer, ed., *Europa und die Einheit Deutschlands: Eine Bilanz nach 100 Jahren* (Cologne, 1970), 16.

PART TWO

Nationalism, Leadership, and War

4

Confederate Identity and the Will to Fight

RICHARD E. BERINGER

INTRODUCTION

Comparative history is extraordinarily difficult. Any two cases that might have enough similarities to encourage comparative study will also have enough differences to cast doubt on the effort. Thus, we should note one of the fundamental differences between the German Wars of Unification and the American Civil War that makes comparison difficult. In Germany, independent political bodies moved toward agreement. It was a voluntary unification. The wars of unification were fought against the foreigner (*Ausländer*). In the United States, on the other hand, consensus broke down; the war was waged against one's own to secure an involuntary unification. Looking at the world today, it would seem that it is much easier to destroy unions than to create them. Presumably the Southern task in 1861–65, being divisive rather than unifying, was easier than the Northern task. How, then, do we account for the result?

This chapter will attempt to answer that question. My remarks will be more suggestive than conclusive. I would like to buttress a hypothesis for further consideration at other times and places, for one cannot present an entirely convincing argument even within the generous limits allowed here.

In brief, my hypothesis is that during the American Civil War large numbers of Southerners, a significant minority if not a majority, did not identify themselves primarily as Confederates, except in a geographic sense. Southerners in general lacked the nationalistic identification to be expected in an emotional, in-group sense of distinctive, shared history, culture, and nationality. The few true Confederate nationalists did not comprise a positive reference group for many Southerners. Instead, they served as a negative reference group for those who looked to their personal safety, their localities, their families, and the old Union for guides to appropriate behavior and loyalty. Many Confederates (and these are overlapping categories): (1) identified

75

themselves instead as besieged and embattled inhabitants of threatened land and therefore sought individual and collective safety; (2) identified themselves as citizens of their own back yards and went to great lengths to maintain local stability; (3) identified themselves as husbands, fathers, and brothers and therefore attempted to provide for the welfare of their families; and (4) often continued to identify themselves as Unionists, dreamed of restoring the past, and were unable to give whole-hearted commitment to the new Confederacy. In the course of discussion, this essay may seem to stray from the underlying theme of the road to total war. The reader must keep in mind the commentary on that issue by Mark Neely, who points to the ambiguous meaning of the term *total war* and cogently argues that the American Civil War was not *total*; it did not erase the distinction between civilians and soldiers, it did not commit the full resources of either side – especially of the North – to the war, it did not attack both troops and civilians by any available means, and it did not deny protection to noncombatants.[1]

The American Civil War was therefore not a total war, although it was total enough if you were the civilian who was shot or whose home was destroyed. Nevertheless, it approached total war in its effect on the civilian population. Several of the other essays in this collection mention the role of the enemy civilian population and its relation to the concept of total war. War approaches totality as that population becomes a military objective in an effort to undermine the enemy's will to fight. What is absent in these discussions is the recognition that total war also involves what you are willing to let the enemy do to your own civilian population. To win is everything; victory becomes so important that one is not only willing to inflict devastation upon enemy civilians, but, as the Confederate States of America illustrate, the leadership also becomes willing to accept tremendous sacrifice, including suffering and death, by its own civilians. Confederates on the home front did suffer, for a variety of reasons, as we shall see. So, too, did the French, the other defeated people in this comparative study. Indeed, in some respects it is not the wars that should be compared but the experiences of the defeated – the Confederacy with France – and the victorious – the Union with Germany. Both of the defeated powers suffered an application of force upon the civilian community that played an important role in determining the outcome of the war, while both of the victorious powers experienced much less disruption of their civilian populations.

---

1 Mark E. Neely Jr., "Was the Civil War a Total War?" *Civil War History* 37 (March 1991) : 10–11. See also Daniel E. Sutherland, "Abraham Lincoln, John Pope, and the Origins of Total War," *Journal of Military History* 56 (Oct. 1992): 567–86, who believes Neely's definition of total war is too narrow (568, n.l).

In an effort to emphasize the negative forces acting upon the American South, this essay may appear to overemphasize the weakness of Confederate identity; some readers will no doubt wonder that any Southerners showed up to fight at the First Battle of Manassas. On the other hand, there should be little doubt as to why so few were left to surrender at Appomattox Court House and Durham Station.

IDENTITY AND NATIONALISM

"People do not fight and die for dollars and cents, as individuals sometime do," Raimondo Luraghi reminded us twenty years ago; "but they are ready to fight it out to the last ditch for what is (or seems to them) a scale of moral values."[2] This reminds us that as Americans squared away against each other in 1861, both sides had to mobilize not only military forces but also economic, political, social, and psychological forces. That is to say, ultimately the war would be won or lost in the hearts and minds of the citizens. And thus the question of identity becomes so important. In both Union and Confederacy by 1861, there were "political classes which had reached so high an ideological self-awareness that an uncompromising war became an immediate danger."[3] Indeed, "Modernization released a volatile combination of private and public loyalties and ideals that made war an acceptable solution to the crisis of national political authority and identity."[4] Americans of both sections were willing to trade bullets for ballots. But Southern values were not so distinctive that a Confederate nationalism was created that was strong enough for Southern citizens to identify with and sustain a prolonged war effort.

Confederates spent four years trying to hammer Southern sectionalism into Confederate nationalism. Did they succeed? Perhaps by 1865, or later, but they surely did not begin secession with much sense of Confederate nationalism. Certainly there were exceptions. Perhaps Judah P. Benjamin, Edmund Ruffin, and Robert Barnwell Rhett, father and son, fit the description of the Confederate nationalist. But just what is Confederate nationalism – or any sort of nationalism, for that matter? In an essay derived from his recent book *The Fire-Eaters*, Eric Walther has maintained that Southern nationalists were really localists and thus not nationalists at all. He did not define nationalism, but in discussion he claimed that "Nationalism is like a

---

2 Raimondo Luraghi, "The Civil War and the Modernization of American Society: Social Structure and Industrial Revolution in the Old South before and during the War," *Civil War History* 18 (Sept. 1972): 242.
3 Luraghi, "Civil War and the Modernization of American Society," 242. See also Richard D. Brown, *Modernization: The Transformation of American Life, 1600–1865* (New York, 1976), 159.
4 Brown, *Modernization*, 163.

duck. I know it when I see it."[5] There is much to be said for this pragmatic approach, but I shall also retreat to some observations on the point by Hans Kohn.

"Nationalism," suggested Kohn, "is a state of mind, in which the supreme loyalty of the individual is felt to be due the nation-state." It involves "a deep attachment to one's native soil, to local traditions, and to established territorial authority." It is usually marked by "certain objective factors ... like common descent, language, territory, political entity, customs and traditions, or religion."[6] However, the most important "element is a living and active corporate will. It is this which we will call nationalism, a state of mind inspiring the large majority of a people and claiming to inspire all its members."[7] By Kohn's criteria, Southern nationalism was not much different from United States nationalism in 1861. The "objective factors" characterizing Southerners were similar to those characterizing Northerners; descent, language, territory, political system, customs, and religion were much the same. Ideas of ethnicity were also much the same; Northern racism was only expressed differently from Southern racism. Many Northerners were antislavery because they wanted to avoid blacks.[8] As for a "living and active corporate will," Southerners were again much like their Northern counterparts.

Perhaps we can also define nationalism by present-day examples. As we look over this confused world, we may see distinct nationalism in Croatia and Serbia but not in Yugoslavia, in Quebec but not in Canada, in some of the republics of the former Soviet Union but not in the new commonwealth that replaced it. And what of the United States? Does not the current emphasis on multiculturalism have a denationalizing effect?

Some Southerners attempted to create an ideology that would lead to a distinctive nationalism which would have claims to moral superiority. Among the several moral aspects – " trust, benevolence, generosity, fidelity" – was the system of slave labor. But these ideals, including slave labor, "embraced only some people, not necessarily a majority of the region." Nevertheless, some sense of community was created, a dichotomy of "we" versus "they." But "they" was not only "the negative reference group on the other side of the Mason-Dixon line,"[9] as Richard D. Brown indicates; owing to internal divisions, "they" were also to be found in the South itself. Northerners too

5   Eric H. Walther, "Fire-Eaters and the Riddle of Confederate Nationalism," 16, paper presented at the annual meeting of the Southern Historical Association, 1991, Fort Worth, Texas; Walther, *The Fire-Eaters* (Baton Rouge, La., 1992).
6   Hans Kohn, *Nationalism: Its Meaning and History* (Princeton, N.J., 1955), 9.
7   Ibid.
8   Charles P. Roland, *An American Iliad: The Story of the Civil War* (Lexington, Ky., 1991), 3.
9   Brown, *Modernization*, 171–2.

had created an ideology, based on free labor, and Northerners also looked to a "negative reference group on the other side of the Mason-Dixon line." But differing reference groups do not establish distinct nationality or identity, only differing behavior and aspirations. Confederates knew they were Southerners, but that label provided merely a geographic identity; it gave most of them precious little sense of national identity, especially Confederate identity. That four slave states remained in the Union, and North Carolina and Tennessee were more or less dragooned into the Confederacy, reminds us of that fact.

Michael Barton has made an interesting effort to examine this identity question. Pointing out that men may "find their identities in the act of committing themselves to something larger than themselves," he sees the Civil War as a test of whether Southern soldiers did in fact identify themselves with the larger cause, that is, the Confederacy. The conclusion, derived from the study of the diaries of both officers and enlisted men, is that most Confederate soldiers identified with themselves or their units; few identified with the Confederacy.[10]

There is a growing literature on the question of Southern distinctiveness and nationalism, which is probably more useful and precise in this context to call *Confederate* distinctiveness and nationalism. The most noted supporter of the idea is Emory Thomas, who emphasized nationalism in two books: *The Confederacy as a Revolutionary Experience* and *The Confederate Nation*. In the former work, Thomas claimed that the Confederacy "embraced centralized nationalism."[11] To Thomas, this nationalism developed as organizational features of the war effort – conscription, industrialization, urbanization, and the like. The revolution came with the abandonment of state rights, and the identity came only toward the end of the war. Southern nationalism, to say nothing of Confederate nationalism, does not appear to have existed in 1861, except perhaps for an incipient cultural nationalism. In *The Confederate Nation*, Thomas contends that "the Confederate era was an extended moment during which Southerners attempted simultaneously to define themselves as a people and to act out a national identity." Nevertheless, Thomas concludes, "the South began as a section instead of a nation." It was the experience of war – not antebellum sectionalism – that made the South a nation, if anything did.[12] Perhaps Thomas's views may be summed up conveniently

---

10 Michael Barton, "Did the Confederacy Change Southern Soldiers? Some Obvious and Some Unobtrusive Measures," in Harry P. Owens and James J. Cooke, eds., *The Old South in the Crucible of War* (Jackson, Miss., 1983), 75, 166.

11 Emory M. Thomas, *The Confederacy as a Revolutionary Experience* (Englewood Cliffs, N.J., 1971), 134.

12 Emory M. Thomas, The Confederate Nation, 1861–1865 (New York, 1979), xv, 297. See also Emory M. Thomas, "Reckoning with Rebels," in Owens and Cooke, eds., *Old South*, 9–10.

in his essay, "Reckoning with Rebels." The most salient part of that essay was the simple statement that "The Richmond government was characterized by centralization and nationalism. The conscription of troops and labor, suspension of the writ of habeas corpus, governmental control of manufacturing, railroads, and vital raw materials, impressment of goods, fixing of consumer prices, and ultimately state socialism were but some of the manifestations of Confederate nationalism."[13] But is this truly nationalism? Thomas speaks more to the organization of the Confederate war effort than he does to the hearts and minds – the identity – of the Southern people.

David Potter observed that Southern nationalism developed primarily in antagonism to the North, and he concluded that "the South did not want a separate destiny so much as it wanted recognition of the merits of Southern society and security for the slave system." Southern nationalism did evolve, thought Potter, but only "from the shared sacrifices, the shared efforts, *and the shared defeat* ... of the Civil War." Potter concluded that the cause and effect relationship was that the war produced Southern nationalism, illustrated by the cult of the Lost Cause, not vice versa. Southern nationalism did not cause the war.[14] "In fact," believed Potter, "the readiness with which the South returned to the Union will defy explanation unless it is recognized that Southern loyalties to the Union were never really obliterated but rather eclipsed by other loyalties with which, for a time, they conflicted."[15]

One of the strongest affirmations of nationalism has been made by Drew Gilpin Faust, who wisely aimed her argument at Confederate nationalism, not Southern nationalism. She too finds that Confederate nationalism was not a preexisting characteristic of the South but rather an "effort to build a consensus at home, to secure a foundation of popular support for a new nation and what quickly became an enormously costly war." The creation of Confederate nationalist identity was therefore a conscious wartime event.[16] A skeptic might remark, however, that if you have to create it, you don't have it. No wonder so many common folk – excluded from decision making but not from suffering – opted out.

13 Thomas, "Reckoning with Rebels," in Owens and Cooke, eds., *Old South*, 9–10.
14 David M. Potter, *The Impending Crisis, 1848–1861*, completed and edited by Don E. Fehrenbacher (New York, 1976), 469 (emphasis mine).
15 David M. Potter, "The Historian's Use of Nationalism and Vice Versa," in *The South and the Sectional Conflict* (Baton Rouge, La., 1968), 78. See also John M. McCardell, *The Idea of a Southern Nation: Southern Nationalists and Southern Nationalism, 1830–1860* (New York, 1979), 9; and Steven A. Channing, "Slavery and Confederate Nationalism," in Walter J. Fraser Jr. and Winfred B. Moore Jr., eds., *From the Old South to the New: Essays on the Transitional South* (Westport, Conn., 1981), 221–4.
16 Drew Gilpin Faust, *The Creation of Confederate Nationalism: Ideology and Identity in the Civil War South* (Baton Rouge, La., 1988), 7, 14, 16.

In a similar vein, Don E. Fehrenbacher argues that by 1861 there was a "genuine Southern nationalism" but only "*in the sense of wanting independence from the North.*" In fact, he concluded that whatever Southern nationalism existed before the war was "*converted readily into Confederate antinationalism* [in the sense of opposing a strong central government]."[17] The weight of evidence appears to be on the side of those who deny the existence of a nationalism that provided Southerners unique Confederate identity, at least until after the war or perhaps at the very end. Kenneth M. Stampp refers to Southern nationalism as "that most flimsy and ephemeral of dreams,"[18] and in my own work, done in collaboration with three other authors, we expressed the opinion "that the people of the South had no widely accepted mystical sense of distinct nationality," for "the Confederacy functioned as a nation only in a technical, organizational sense, and not in a mystical or spiritual sense."[19] Paul D. Escott seems to agree. Although Jefferson Davis was able to keep Confederates fighting, "an inspiring sense of nationalism did not emerge to give purpose to the effort. The Old South could not transform itself as the crisis required.... The creation of the Confederacy," believes Escott, "was ... a declaration of a sense of nationalism that was not yet present." It was defeat, Reconstruction, and the bloody shirt that set the South apart and gave it its distinctiveness.[20] Charles P. Roland, author of the most recent civil war history, believes that Southern nationalism was "inchoate and not pervasive" and that one of Jefferson Davis's tasks was to build an identifiable nationalism, but he failed.[21]

Confederates opted for war, but most of them hardly realized it when they promoted secession, or went along with their states because that seemed the safest or most appropriate thing to do at the time. Jefferson Davis, on the other hand, understood that Northerners would fight, and after the war he remembered that he had never expected peaceable secession to be possible.[22] It was

---

17 Don E. Fehrenbacher, *Constitutions and Constitutionalism in the Slaveholding South* (Athens, Ga., 1989), x, 62, 70 (emphasis mine).

18 Kenneth M. Stampp, "The Southern Road to Appomattox," in Stampp, ed., *The Imperiled Union: Essays on the Background of the Civil War* (New York, 1980), 257.

19 Richard E. Beringer et al., eds., *Why the South Lost the Civil War* (Athens, Ga., 1986), 66, 77.

20 Paul D. Escott, "The Failure of Confederate Nationalism: The Old South's Class System in the Crucible of War," in Owens and Cooke, eds., *The Old South in the Crucible of War*, 16, 18, 27.

21 Roland, *American Iliad*, 46, 260.

22 Jefferson Davis, *The Rise and Fall of the Confederate Government*, 2 vols. (New York, 1881), 227, 230–1. See also Varina Davis, *Jefferson Davis, Ex-President of the Confederate States of America: A Memoir*, 2 vols . (New York, 1890; reprinted New York, 1971), 2:4–5, 9–10. In Jan. 1861, Davis feared "that fiercest of human strife, a civil war. The temper of the Black Republicans is not to give us our rights in the Union or allow us to go peaceably out of it." Dunbar Rowland, ed., *Jefferson Davis, Constitutionalist: His Letters, Papers, and Speeches*, 10 vols. (Jackson, Miss., 1923), 5:37. Davis also recalled that most Confederates thought secession would be peaceful, or at least would involve only brief conflict. Davis, *Rise and Fall*, 1:227, 304 .

a confusing question at the time. Shortly after the war, William Alexander Graham, a North Carolina Unionist of 1861 who had gone into the Confederacy with his state, wrote to a Northern acquaintance that he and others like him "had ever been sincere and zealous adherents" of the Union, but they had gone along with secession when "the only alternative left us, was the choice of the side we should espouse, when a favorable result to either, was to be little short of ruin to us."[23] Similarly, Thomas J. Foster of Alabama claimed that in the secession crisis "upon all occasions and in every circle both public and private I denounced the plans and purposes of the secession faction...[and] denied their wild and impracticable dogma of *peaceable secession*." Why had he gone along with secession? Foster believed that one owed primary allegiance to one's state.[24] Foster had many companions among Confederate politicians. James G. Ramsay of North Carolina claimed to be a "consistent and active Union man, until after the war began" who "would rather be ruled by Black Republicans of the North than the Red Republicans of the South."[25] David P. Lewis of Alabama was an opposition member of that state's secession convention, a minority on the committee that reported the ordinance, who only signed it "under special instructions from his constituents." He did raise a volunteer company, but it was never mustered in; when it was called upon to serve for three years, he disbanded it instead. He declined another commission, became a judge and then a miller to avoid conscription, and finally fled to Union lines.[26] Burgess S. Gaither of North Carolina opposed even the exercise of the right of revolution in 1861.[27] In Tennessee, a newspaper editor in April 1861 mourned "the destruction by its own people of the greatest, the freest, the most beneficent and powerful government ever known to man."[28] Such individuals, and these are only a few examples, were desolated by the turn of events. Most of them would make very unenthusiastic Confederates and would never identify themselves as Confederate nationalists.

---

23 William Alexander Graham to Robert C. Winthrop, Feb. 1, 1867, Winthrop Family papers, Massachusetts Historical Society, Boston.
24 Thomas J. Foster to Andrew Johnson, May 30, 1865, Foster petition, Amnesty papers, Alabama, Adjutant General's Office, record group 94, National Archives.
25 James G. Ramsay petition, Amnesty papers, North Carolina; *South Carolinian*, March 25, 1861, copied in Ramsay amnesty petition.
26 David P. Lewis petition, Amnesty papers, Alabama.
27 Burgess S. Gaither petition, Amnesty papers, North Carolina.
28 *Nashville Republican Banner*, April 17, 1861. Jefferson Davis remarked on the decidedly cool reception he received in Tennessee, which had not yet seceded, when he passed through that state on his way to Montgomery for his inauguration as provisional president of the Confederacy. Davis to Varina Davis, Feb. 20, 1861, in Hudson Strode, ed., *Jefferson Davis: Private Letters, 1823–1829* (New York, 1966), 123.

Clearly, there were widespread misgivings in the South about the course Southerners had decided to pursue that makes the notion of wartime Confederate nationalism somewhat fanciful. Although many Northerners, Abraham Lincoln included, overestimated the strength of Southern Unionism, nevertheless it was strong enough in many localities to influence the course of Confederate history. The existence of Union slave states is proof enough of that, but there was also notable opposition to secession in most of the other Confederate states. In many areas, secession was anything but a popular movement, at least before the fall of Fort Sumter. Of the states in the first wave of secession, only Texas held a popular referendum. Even then, intimidation of Unionists helped to ensure the outcome. In the upper South, only Tennessee held a referendum.[29] In the three border states of Virginia, North Carolina, and Tennessee, only Lincoln's call for troops after the fall of Fort Sumter caused thousands of would-be Unionists to join the Confederacy, and many of them did so with reluctance, feeling betrayed by Lincoln.[30]

The hesitancy of so many Confederates underlines a key weakness in the Confederate war effort – a lack of widely shared feelings of distinct nationality. It would be difficult under these circumstances – especially after the war began to go badly and the passage of the conscription law put men into the ranks against their will – to convince the average Southern soldier that this was truly his fight, and not just a conflict to protect the special property of a special class. To the extent that this was a revolution, it was imposed from the top, not inspired from below.

Indeed, there was significant opposition in every state except South Carolina; in Alabama, Unionism was strong enough in certain areas that the Union army managed to raise six regiments of white troops, approximately 2,600 men – which is not many but is more than Confederates recruited in, for example, Illinois or Pennsylvania. Arkansas, too, contributed not just individual soldiers but fourteen white regiments for 8,300 troops. Two regiments were raised in Florida, one in Mississippi, and four in North Carolina – all these without counting black units or those white units raised in western Virginia, eastern Tennessee, or the New Orleans area.[31]

29 Ralph A. Wooster, *The Secession Conventions of the South* (Princeton, N.J., 1962); Walter L. Buenger, *Secession and the Union in Texas* (Austin, Tex., 1984), 155, 161, 173, 181.

30 Daniel W. Crofts, *Reluctant Confederates: Upper South Unionists in the Secession Crisis* (Chapel Hill, N.C., 1989), xviii, 360.

31 Frederick H. Dyer, *A Compendium of the War of the Rebellion*, vol. 1 (New York, 1959), 11, 113–253. See also the recent work by Richard Nelson Current, *Lincoln's Loyalists: Union Soldiers from the Confederacy* (Boston, 1992), 218. Current believes that "at the very least, 100,000 white Southerners served in the Union army."

Planters and extremists convinced multitudes of other Southerners that slavery was worth a war, or at least the risk of one, and that was no little accomplishment. Although "ultras outmaneuvered them," however, John Niven claims that there were so many conservatives that "it is probable that a majority of the white Southern population opposed secession."[32] Escott comes close to agreement "that – for Southerners – the Confederacy was an unwelcome experience, a change that the majority of Southerners came to oppose."[33] Under the circumstances, it would be unreasonable to expect anything approaching Southern unanimity on the question of disunion. After all, what was so distinctive about the Confederacy that it caused a war? Slavery only, not state rights.[34] And once formed, and the war begun, what held the Confederacy together? Only one thing, says recent Jefferson Davis biographer William C. Davis, "their regional hostility to the old Union. Once out of the old compact and the enemy – politically at least – lay beyond their borders, their commonality as Southerners was not enough to bind them."[35] Thus, Grady McWhiney's complaint that too many historians have magnified "the differences between Northerners and Southerners out of all proportion"[36] seems appropriate. Edward Pessen agrees: "For all their distinctiveness, the Old South and North were complementary elements in an American society that was everywhere primarily rural, capitalistic, materialistic, and socially stratified, racially, ethnically and religiously heterogeneous, and stridently chauvinistic and expansionist."[37]

True Confederate nationalism would have had some degree of permanence about it. However, some Confederates were worried that victory might undo them. Before the Confederacy was a year old, Attorney General Thomas Bragg feared it might disintegrate into a middle and a Southern component.[38] During the later years of the war, there were strained relations between Interior members of the Confederate Congress, who represented districts that were not occupied or threatened by the Federal army, and Exterior members of the border South, whose constituents suffered under

---

32 John Niven, *The Coming of the Civil War, 1837–1861* (Arlington Heights, Ill., 1990), 131.
33 Escott, "Failure of Confederate Nationalism," 18.
34 See, e.g., Kenneth M. Stampp, *The United States and National Self-Determination: Two Traditions*, Fortenbaugh Memorial Lecture Series (Gettysburg, Pa., 1991), 12.
35 William C. Davis, *Jefferson Davis: The Man and His Hour* (New York, 1991), 444, 598, 704.
36 Grady McWhiney, *Southerners and Other Americans* (New York, 1973), 3–4.
37 Edward Pessen, "How Different from Each Other were the Antebellum North and South?" *American Historical Review* 85 (Dec. 1980): 1122, 1149, 1247. See also McCardell, Ideal of a Southern Nation, 2–3, 9, who disagrees with McWhiney and Pessen to the extent that he sees a growth of Southern nationalism but agrees that "it is incorrect to think of Northerners and Southerners in 1860 as two distinct peoples."
38 Thomas Bragg diary, 1861–1862, no. 3304, microfilm copy of original, Southern Historical Collection, Library of the University of North Carolina at Chapel Hill.

enemy occupation. Exterior congressmen frequently supported harsher war measures than Interior congressmen would agree to. The resulting tensions were never far beneath the surface and even led to suggestions of break-up within the Confederacy.[39] A clerk in the War Department remarked in his diary that "I hope we may soon conquer a peace with the North; [but] then I fear we shall have trouble among ourselves. Certainly there is danger, after the war, that Virginia, and, perhaps a sufficient number of the States to form a new constitution, will meet in convention and form a new government."[40]

And just why had Southerners gone to war in the first place? Not for independence, although that would necessarily be the consequence of a successful war effort. Very few Southerners were nationalistic enough to desire independence for its own sake; it was, rather, a means to an end – the perpetuation of slavery and the safety of their communities. Toward the end of the war, Georgia's Governor Joseph E. Brown felt it necessary to remind his fellow Georgians that "Some persons in authority seem to have forgotten that we are fighting for anything but independence."[41] Few Confederates claimed in 1861 that independence was a goal in itself. "We seek no conquest, no aggrandizement, no concession of any kind," Jefferson Davis reminded his people in May 1861. "All we ask is to be let alone."[42] But wishing to be left alone is not Confederate identity or Confederate nationalism, nor is it a very sophisticated reason for fighting one's own.

The answer to the question of identification varied from individual to individual, but this much is certain: Many inhabitants of the Confederacy – enough to make a difference – did not identify themselves as Confederates. If they had, they would have acted like Confederates. Instead, they thought of themselves as threatened and embattled inhabitants of an invaded land and feared for their safety; they understood their roles as husbands, fathers, or brothers who had obligations to loved ones back home; and they thought of themselves as citizens of their own back yards; many others never took

39 Thomas B. Alexander and Richard E. Beringer, *The Anatomy of the Confederate Congress: A Study of the Influences of Member Characteristics on Legislative Voting Behavior, 1861–1865* (Nashville, Tenn., 1972). See U.S. Congress, Senate, *Journal of the Congress of the Confederate States of America, 1861–1865*, 7 vols. Senate doc. no. 234, 58th Congress, 2d session (Washington, D.C., 1904–5), 7:524, and the debate that followed in the "Proceedings of the … Confederate Congress," *Southern Historical Society Papers* 52 (1959): 266–9.

40 John Beauchamp Jones, *A Rebel War Clerk's Diary at the Confederate States Capital*, 2 vols. (Philadelphia, 1866), 1:156, entry for Sept. 26, 1862.

41 Joseph E. Brown to the [Georgia] Senate and House of Representatives, February 18, 1865, in Allen D. Candler, ed., *The Confederate Records of the State of Georgia*, 6 vols. (Atlanta, 1909–11), 2:853–4.

42 Message to the 2d session of the Provisional Congress, April 29, 1861, James D. Richardson, ed., *Compilation of the Messages and Papers of the Confederacy, Including the Diplomatic Correspondence, 1861–1865*, 2 vols. (Nashville, Tenn., 1906; reprint: New York, 1966), 1:82; Rowland, ed., *Jefferson Davis, Constitutionalist*, 5:84.

off the mantle of Unionist, or put it on again after Federal troops came to their neighborhoods and it seemed safe to express their thoughts. It was these identifications that motivated behavior and, in the end, persuaded thousands to quit.[43]

SAFETY

Two things seem to have separated North and South in 1861. Neither of them were sufficient to create a distinctive nationality, but both were closely involved with the decision to secede in order to maintain individual and group safety. The most obvious was the presence in the South of a large black population, mostly enslaved, and concern about how that population might behave if set free.[44] Equally important was a "defensive group consciousness" in which Southerners felt that national and world environments threatened Southern culture and ideals. A conviction that Northerners considered Southerners to be inferior and felt that the South was "the victim of malevolent forces" put Southerners on the defensive and prompted them to use violence for redress. Often this sort of defensiveness "leads to an aggressiveness that seems almost paranoid" – as indeed it did – and encourages "a quickness to take offense and a readiness to strike back."[45] Speaking of the present, but clearly referring to the past as well, historian Sheldon Hackney discerned "a sense of grievance ... at the heart of the Southern identity." Southern consciousness was strongest in the face of attack from outside forces such as abolition and the Union army.[46] If true, had there been no hostile outsiders, there would have been no Confederacy.

This is not the material out of which successful revolutions are made, which may explain why most leading Confederates seemed to deny the revolutionary implications of what they were doing, even as they claimed a parallel to the stirring events of 1776. Howell Cobb seemed to deny the whole notion of revolution when he claimed that the movement was most notable for its conservatism.[47] Jefferson Davis claimed that "ours is not a revolution." Rather, the Confederate States of America was merely a "new government on the basis of ... [inherited] rights." Davis went on to the ringing declaration that "We are not engaged in a Quixotic fight for the rights of man."[48]

43 According to Confederate army returns of Dec. 31, 1864, 53 percent of the Confederate soldiers were absent from their units, many wounded, many prisoners, but mostly deserters. The figures got even worse in the last months. Beringer et al., eds., *Why the South Lost*, 480.
44 Roland, *American Iliad*, 2.
45 Lewis M. Killian, *White Southerners* (New York, 1970), 5.
46 Sheldon Hackney, "Southern Violence," *American Historical Review* 74 (Feb. 1969): 922, 924–5.
47 *Journal of the Confederate Congress*, 1: 845.
48 Speech at Augusta, Georgia, Oct. 5, 1864, Rowland, ed., *Jefferson Davis: Constitutionalist*, 6:357.

J. D. B. Debow claimed that "we are not revolutionists – we are resisting revolution."[49] The point takes on added significance in the secession movement in North Carolina. When Unionists there realized that they would lose the question, they sought to base secession on the right of revolution, only to be outvoted by secessionists, who denied that revolution was involved at all.[50] As Frank E. Vandiver, one of the leading authorities on the Confederacy, so accurately noted about the Montgomery convention, "They did not believe there was any revolution in what they did," for "revolution was anathema to them all."[51]

Instead of revolutionaries, Confederates believed themselves the embattled inhabitants of an invaded and threatened land. And the homes of many Confederate soldiers were in dangerous proximity to the field of action at one time or another. Governor Joseph E. Brown of Georgia tried to play on local-ist fears as he attempted to persuade fellow Georgians to join the colors. In 1862, he warned his people that the Yankees were going to confiscate all Southern lands and incite rebellion among the slaves.[52] Such dire predictions did not always encourage sufficient enlistments, but other tactics could be used. In 1863, for example, Governor John Gill Shorter of Alabama author-ized one of his state colonels to raise troops for thirty days' service in the southeastern portion of his state. These were men who had escaped con-scription and wished to protect their families. They would volunteer for short state service now, however, because the area had recently suffered from Federal raids. Once in state service, moreover, Shorter planned to transfer these localists into Confederate service – a piece of bait-and-switch sales-manship necessary to sustain Confederate manpower.[53] The problem was that state militias were often a safe haven for those whose horizons extended no farther than their own back yards and therefore, by definition, might not even be loyal to the Confederacy if called upon to fight outside of their own states.

Of course, there was real revolution in the Civil War, but it emerged with the Emancipation Proclamation in 1863, not with the secession ordinances

49   J. D. B . Debow, "Our Danger and Our Duty," *DeBow's Review*, 1st ser. 33 (1862): 44.
50   Wooster, *Secession Conventions of the South*, 195, 198–9. "I do believe the people of a State have a revolutionary right to do so, but I do not believe the States had *sufficient* cause to secede at the time they did." James G. Ramsay to Andrew Johnson, July 8, 1865, Amnesty papers, North Carolina.
51   Frank E. Vandiver, *Their Tattered Flags* (New York, 1970), 19.
52   Steven Hahn, *The Roots of Southern Populism: Yeoman Farmers and the Transformation of the Georgia Upcountry, 1850–1890* (New York, 1983), 121.
53   Gov. John Gill Shorter to Jefferson Davis, Jan. 10, 1863, Governor Shorter administrative files, Alabama Department of Archives and History, Montgomery, Jefferson Davis Association. Materials from other depositories that were examined at the Jefferson Davis Association, Rice University, Houston, Texas, will hereafter be designated JDA. For additional detail on the especially interest-ing situation in Alabama, see Georgia Lee Tatum, *Disloyalty in the Confederacy* (Chapel Hill, N.C., 1934; reprint: New York, 1970), 62–9.

in 1861. That is why some Southerners had always sought safety in the Union. They feared what would happen to slavery—and to themselves—without it. Some Mississippians believed that the Union was the great protector of slavery, and without it bondage would disappear.[54] In North Carolina, many of the Unionists agreed; secession would bring war, and war would bring abolition.[55] "Slavery is doomed if the South sets up a Southern Confederacy," complained Jonathan Worth of North Carolina. "With Canada in effect for her Northern border . . . all hating us, it is madness to think of anything else only to cut the throats of the negroes or have our own throats cut." He had no desire to launch, "probably through civil war, upon the dark sea of experiment."[56] In July 1862, Edward Stanly, the Lincoln-appointed military governor of North Carolina, warned his old planter friends in eastern North Carolina that if rebels persisted, "the end would be to incite the negroes [to rebellion]."[57] Stanly exaggerated, as it turned out, but the implication that without the Union the protector of slavery would be gone was proven by events.

Even some South Carolinians were among those who paused at the brink of secession because they feared it would render their slave property insecure and disturb the social order. To these men, "the arms and laws of the national government offered a sanctuary for the peculiar institution in a hostile world."[58] "That was one reason why I was a Union man," groused James Chesnut Sr. "I wanted all the power the United States gave me—to hold my own."[59] Likewise, one delegate to the Virginia secession convention was convinced that "it is nothing but the prestige and power of the General Government that now guarantees to the slaveholder his right."[60] Sometimes fears took on a special concreteness that made them especially vivid. Lawrence M. Keitt, one of the leading fire-eaters, took himself and his fears much more seriously after his brother was murdered by one of his slaves. Keitt had thought the relation of master and slave was one of kindness, and the dissonance between what Keitt believed about slavery and what he learned about

---

54 Lillian A. Pereyra, *James Lusk Alcorn: Persistent Whig* (Baton Rouge, La., 1966), 38, 40.
55 Marc W. Kruman, *Parties and Politics in North Carolina, 1836–1865* (Baton Rouge, La., 1983), 207–8.
56 Worth to J. J. Jackson, Dec. 17, 1860, Jonathan Worth, *The Correspondence of Jonathan Worth*, ed. J. G. deRoulhac Hamilton (Raleigh, N.C., 1909), 1:127; "Mr. Worth's Address to the People of Randolph and Alamance," no date but c. Jan. 1861, ibid., 133.
57 Wayne K. Durrill, *War of Another Kind: A Southern Community in the Great Rebellion* (New York, 1990), 107.
58 Steven A. Channing, *Crisis of Fear: Secession in South Carolina* (New York, 1974), 145–7.
59 Mary Boykin Chesnut, *Mary Chesnut's Civil War*, ed. C. Vann Woodward (New Haven, Conn., 1981), 241, entry for Nov. 20, 1861.
60 George H. Reese, ed., *Proceedings of the Virginia State Convention of 1861* (Richmond, Va., 1965), 3:169–70.

his brother forced him to believe that somehow abolitionists must have been involved. Life and death were now at stake, for in Keitt's mind, "the threat that a Republican regime would turn slave against master had become horrifyingly real."[61]

However, many Southerners had foreseen that war to save slavery would destroy it, and Unionist planters feared inevitable "anarchy and revolution."[62] Alexander H. Stephens summed up the Unionist position: "I consider slavery much more secure in the Union than out of it," he wrote in July 1860. "We have nothing to fear from anything so much as unnecessary changes and revolutions in government."[63] The institution was threatened; to the shrewdest of Southern thinkers, safety was all, and it lay in the Union.

Others disagreed; for them, safety lay outside the Union. The pressures of the differential pace of modernization resulted in dissonant views of slavery. Despite the reams of proslavery apologies, it is clear that one of the key motivating factors behind the secession movement was simply fear. Few historians have made this so vividly clear as Steven A. Channing. In South Carolina, and in other states as well, fear of a black population uncontrolled by slavery drove people to disunion. Abolition was horror, its consequences apocalyptic because emancipation would surely lead to black rebellion.[64] By most accounts, there were few voices of caution left in South Carolina on the eve of secession, although the most noted Unionist, James L. Petigru, is supposed to have warned secessionists that "South Carolina is too small for a republic, but too large for an insane asylum."[65] Throughout the South, uncompromising secessionists were angry, threatened, fearful people, and they reacted in accordance with their fears. Like anyone else, they sought safety from danger.[66]

The fear that a black population was to be set free to "violate his home and family" was motivation for many a planter, and yeoman too, to look to secession for safety.[67] A threatened people had turned increasingly to the politics of slavery to ensure their safety over the previous fifteen or twenty years. Even

61 Walther, *The Fire-Eaters*, 184–5.
62 James L. Roark, *Masters without Slaves: Southern Planters in the Civil War and Reconstruction* (New York, 1977), 4.
63 Alexander H. Stephens to J. Henly Smith, July 10, 1860, in Ulrich B. Phillips, ed., *The Correspondence of Robert Toombs, Alexander H. Stephens, and Howell Cobb*, Annual Report of the American Historical Association for the Year 1911 (Washington, D.C., 1913), 2: 487.
64 Channing, *Crisis of Fear*, 6, 20–1, 58–9; see also Lacy K. Ford Jr., *Origins of Southern Radicalism: The South Carolina Upcountry, 1800–1860* (New York, 1988), chap. 10.
65 Sally Edwards, *The Man Who Said No* (New York, 1970), 65, quoted in Ford, *Origins of Southern Radicalism*, 371.
66 Frank L. Owsley, "The Fundamental Cause of the Civil War: Egocentric Sectionalism," *Journal of Southern History* 7 (Feb. 1941): 6 (emphasis mine).
67 Ford, *Origins of Southern Radicalism*, 372.

so, in the aftermath of the election of 1860, Southerners still believed that "their liberty had never been so insecure."[68] "Whether ultimate or imminent, the extinction of slavery was precisely what the South feared," concludes James M. McPherson.[69] In the bitter days of January 1865, the *Raleigh Daily Conservative* reminded its readers that Unionists had warned at the very beginning that breaking up the old Union "jeopardized the institution of slavery a thousand-fold more by secession, than by carrying on the contest under the old government."[70] Secession came not as an expression of a separate Southern nationality but as a defensive reaction to a fear of apocalypse.

LOCALISM AND ONE'S OWN BACK YARD

Some Southerners found themselves at odds with the Confederate movement simply because they had rather narrow horizons. Some were state rights men, but others were simple folk who just wanted to be left alone. Any government that bothered them would have been thought hostile. These localists were most concerned with "their own back yards," to repeat Walther's phrase.[71] A number of students of the Confederate experience have noted that Southerners tended to stiffen their resistance when hostile troops were in their own areas. The inevitable destruction and the seizure of crops, livestock, and other goods naturally got citizens upset. For some prospective soldiers, such threats were enough to persuade them to put on a uniform after all. Thus, much of "the primary bonding element at first was a common hostility to the alleged oppressor," not Confederate nationalism, and part of the sense of national identity that did develop was based merely on the "ordeal of the conflict."[72] John Shelton Reed remarks of Southerners that "exposure to non-Southerners can heighten Southerners' regional consciousness through a reactive process."[73] His observations of our own time apply as well to the nineteenth century, for this is precisely what happened as Union soldiers penetrated the South ever more deeply. Many peoples feel their greatest sense of identity and cohesiveness under threat of war or natural catastrophe. Thus, one Federal soldier is said to have asked a captured Confederate why

68 William J. Cooper Jr., *Liberty and Slavery: Southern Politics to 1860* (New York, 1983), 200, 255–8, 267. See also Richard H. Sewell, *A House Divided: Sectionalism and the Civil War, 1848–1865* (Baltimore, Md., 1988), 71, 76-9; and Robert F. Durden, *The Self-Inflicted Wound: Southern Politics in the Nineteenth Century* (Lexington, Ky., 1985), 38–9, 47.

69 James M. McPherson, *Ordeal by Fire: The Civil War and Reconstruction*, 2d ed. (New York, 1992), 135–6.

70 *Raleigh Daily Conservative*, Jan. 2, 1865.

71 Walther, "Fire-Eaters and the Riddle of Confederate Nationalism," 16.

72 Fehrenbacher, *Constitutions and Constitutionalism*, 59.

73 John Shelton Reed, *Southerners: The Social Psychology of Sectionalism* (Chapel Hill, N.C., 1983), 38.

he fought. The answer had nothing to do with state rights, slavery, or Confederate identity. It was simply because "you're down here."[74]

However, many Southerners did not even have enough sense of nationality to be sure what their land was, outside of their own back yards. Others, such as the Jones County, Mississippi, men deserted because they "did not propose to fight for the rich who were at home having a good time." Such deserters thought of themselves as men who "were fighting in defense of their homes and their rights."[75] Trans-Mississippi troops, for example, thought of their homes in the west and became reluctant to fight east of the river. The governor of Arkansas feared that Missouri troops would simply desert if moved east.[76] There were fears about the Arkansas troops as well. Arkansas Senator Robert W. Johnson informed Davis that if Arkansas were not well defended, the legislature might order Arkansas troops home.[77] And after Confederate Gen. John C. Pemberton surrendered at Vicksburg and was promptly paroled, he warned Davis that his paroled troops might as well be furloughed, because if and when they were exchanged they would not be available for duty; Pemberton expected them to desert and go home, and many of them did.[78] They returned to their own back yards. For such men, Confederate nationalism – or Confederate identity – was simply too weak to sustain the will to resist. "I tell you, sir," wrote one Confederate soldier, "we have trampled our own Liberties under our feet in attempting to establish a Nationality which was not intended for us."[79] Localism thrived, for his own back yard was as much of the Confederacy as many a provincial could identify with. An anonymous soldier from South Carolina announced with refreshing directness that "I go first for Greenville, then for Greenville District, then the up-country, then for South Carolina, then for the South, then for the United States, and after that I don't go for anything."[80] For the most part, the up-country people only wanted to be left alone – by both governments.[81]

74 Unfortunately, the source of this incident has been lost.
75 Tatum, *Disloyalty in the Confederacy*, 97–8.
76 H. Flanagin to Jefferson Davis, Autograph file, Dearborn Collection, Harvard University, microfilm copy, JDA. By permission of the Houghton Library, Harvard University.
77 R. W. Johnson to Jefferson Davis, June 18, 1863, Clements Library, University of Michigan at Ann Arbor, microfilm copy, JDA.
78 Jefferson Davis to John C. Pemberton, July 16, 1863, United States, War Department, *The War of the Rebellion: A Compilation of the Official Records of the Union and Confederate Armies*, 70 vols. in 128 (Washington, D.C., 1880–1901), ser. 1, vol. 24, pt. 3: 1006–7; Pemberton to Joseph E. Johnston, July 16, 1863, ibid., 1007; Pemberton to Davis, July 17, 1863, ibid., 1010; and Pemberton to S. Cooper, July 23, 1863, ibid., 1025.
79 Alfred Blevins to James Blevins, Dec. 31, 1864, Ashe County Civil War Letters collection (copy), Ashe County Public Library, West Jefferson, North Carolina.
80 Walther, "Fire-Eaters and the Riddle of Southern Nationalism," 17.
81 Frank L. Owsley, "Defeatism in the Confederacy," *North Carolina Historical Review* 3 (July 1926): 450.

In a study of contemporary Southerners based upon public opinion sur-
veys in North Carolina, Reed claims that "the starting point for many
Southerners, it appears, is 'localism'"–defined in the words of Robert
Merton as "an orientation to local social structures."[82] Put into the Civil War
context, Reed's contemporary observation helps to explain the numerous
references to men who deserted or evaded conscription but were perfectly
willing to enlist in local companies and make themselves available in case of
invasion of their own localities.[83] In March 1863, reported Charles W.
Ramsdell, the governor of Virginia complained that "five sixths of the 'state
Line' had deserted...because they were about to be transferred to the
Confederate service." Similar events occurred in other states.[84] One Georgia
private objected to fighting with soldiers from other states or being sent outside his state to fight. "I expected to fight through this war as a Georgian not
as a Mississippian, Louisianan, Tennessean nor any other state, and if I cannot
fight in the name of my own state I don't want to fight at all [sic]."[85] Such
men identified with their states, not the Confederacy; it is not surprising
that they lacked the will to fight as Confederates.

HUSBANDS, FATHERS, AND BROTHERS

Thus, some Southerners sought safety first, and others concerned themselves
only with their own back yards. Many of these, and others besides, lacked
commitment to Confederate success because they identified themselves primarily as husbands, fathers, and brothers. They had obligations on the battle
front, but in case of conflict with obligations to their families, their families
took precedence. By the thousands, they left the army to take care of the folks
at home, as economic difficulties pressed heavily on their loved ones before
the war was a year old. Skyrocketing prices for essentials such as food, cloth,
and tools caused widespread suffering among soldiers' families. When the
Southern poor entered the service, it was understood that their families
would be cared for, but whatever assistance they received was inadequate.[86]

Throughout the Confederacy, farm folk were ravaged by troops and
deserters from both armies. "The whole country is full of men on horseback,"

82 Reed, Southerners, 53.
83 See, e.g., James N. Arrington to J. M. Withers, Jan. 30, 1865, Official Records, ser. IV, 3: 1042–3;
    M. A. Baldwin to Jones M. Withers, Jan. 30, 1865, ibid., 1043–4; and G. T. Yelverton to M. A.
    Baldwin, Jan. 15, 1865, ibid., 1044.
84 Charles W. Ramsdell, Behind the Lines in the Southern Confederacy (Baton Rouge, La., 1944; reprint:
    New York, 1969), 54.
85 Hahn, The Roots of Southern Populism, 119, quoted in Walther, "Fire-Eaters and the Riddle of
    Confederate Nationalism," 16.
86 Ramsdell, Behind the Lines in the Southern Confederacy, 20, 23–5.

complained one anonymous letter writer to Davis, "claiming to belong to the Cavalry, going through the land destroying what is left by the Soldiers for their wives & little ones & often without remuneration. ... Can't you protect the families?"[87] Governor Milton of Florida feared that the exactions of the impressment officers would force some men fighting in Georgia and Virginia to come home to protect their families from the ravages of impressment.[88]

If the government could not, surely soldiers would attempt it themselves, even if it meant desertion. "It has been a Rich man's war and a poor man's fight throughout the war. ... But it will not be so long," threatened another anonymous letter writer, for "our poor tender-hearted men will not stand it to read there letters that come from home saying that me and your poor little children are nearly staard [starved] and I have knowed it many cases."[89] Such protests were made as early as 1861. One discontented soldier warned Davis that "many such men proclaimed that they would '*fight for no rich man's slaves*' and would not enlist at all."[90] Naturally, many soldiers for whom the slaveholding aristocracy was a negative reference group expressed their feelings by deserting from the Confederate army or avoiding conscription in the first place.[91]

Such letters filled the files of the Confederate secretary of war. "Now we are tired of fighting for this negro aristocracy," wrote "Many Soldiers" to Davis. "Now we are tired of this favoritism we call loudly for a change and a change we will have ... or we are determined it [the war] shall cease as far as we are concerned."[92] It can be no surprise that when learning of the situation back home, thousands of Confederate soldiers, identifying more with their families than with a new country created to protect slavery, decided their families had the first call upon their loyalties. In December 1862, one poor soldier reminded Governor Pettus of Mississippi, "*our families first and then our count[r]y* ... we are forced to this or starve.[93] "Fundamentally," concluded Ramsdell, "the men with Lee and Joseph E. Johnston and the people back home were one" so that disaster at home meant disaster for the troops as well.[94] Obviously, such men had lost the will to fight, and who can blame them?

87   Anonymous to Jefferson Davis, May 5, 1864, Letters Received by the Confederate Secretary of War, M-437, roll 118, frames 443-45, JDA.
88   Tatum, *Disloyalty in the Confederacy* 87–8.
89   Anonymous to [unknown], July 25, 1864, Letters Received by the Confederate Secretary of War, roll 118, frames 519–22, JDA.
90   [first name unknown] Brooks to Jefferson Davis, May 13, 1861, RG 109, National Archives, quoted in William C. Davis, *Jefferson Davis*, 333.
91   Tatum, *Disloyalty in the Confederacy*, 97.
92   "Many Soldiers to Jefferson Davis, Sept. 7, 1864, Letters Received by the Confederacy Secretary of War, roll 118, frames 702–4, JDA.
93   Ramsdell, *Behind the Lines*, 28.
94   Ibid., 83.

Similar letters from other soldiers frequently underlined the problem. "Soldiers do not enter the service to maintain the Southern Confederacy alone," wrote one state governor, "but also to protect their property and defend their homes and families."[95] In Mississippi, many soldiers heard of threats to their families by Federal soldiers and by "tories and Southern thieves" as well. Such men deserted their units to protect their families; once home, many "remained and gone to bushwacking."[96] One officer in western Virginia reported a remarkable deterioration in morale by August 1863. Citizens felt defeated. Deserters passed through the area in large numbers, and when "asked for their furloughs or their authority to be absent from their commands, they just pat their rifles and defiantly say, 'This is my furlough'."[97]

Such desertion was inevitable, and as Ramsdell pointed out, "the evidence shows that thousands of them had become resentful at the unrelieved privations of their families at home."[98] Davis was well aware of the problem and hoped that state legislatures would have "relieved the sufferings of the poor and have quieted the anxiety of the soldiers in regard to the condition of their families," but not enough was done.[99]

The pathos of this situation, and the pressure it placed upon the soldier is illustrated in the semi-autobiographical work of Joel Chandler Harris. In the story of his boyhood adventures in the South during the war, he wrote the following:

"What do you call those here fellers . . . what jines inter the army an' then comes home arter awhile without lief or license?"

"Deserters," replied Joe, simply.

"So fur, so good," said Mr. Pruitt. "Now, then, what do you call the fellers what jines inter the army arter they'er been told that their families'll be took keer of an' provided fer by the rich folks at home; an' then, arter they'er been in a right smart whet, they gits word that their wives an' children is a lookin' starvation in the face, an' stedder gittin better it gets wuss, an'bimeby they breaks loose an' comes home ... They hain't got nothin' but a little piece er lan'. They goes off expectin' their wives'll be took keer of, an' they comes home an' fines 'em in the last stages. What sorter fellers do you call them?"[100]

95 H. Flanagin to Jefferson Davis, Jan. 5, 1863, Autograph file, Dearborn Collection, Harvard University, microfilm copy, JDA. By permission of the Houghton Library, Harvard University.

96 A. E. Reynolds to Jefferson Davis, Jan. 20, 1863, Autograph file, Dearborn Collection, Harvard University, microfilm copy, JDA. By permission of the Houghton Library, Harvard University.

97 *Official Records*, ser. 4, vol. 2:721.

98 Ramsdell, *Behind the Lines*, 51.

99 Jefferson Davis to Theophilus Holmes, Jan. 28, 1863, letterbook (55-D vol. 1). Courtesy of the Louisiana Historical Association Collection, Jefferson Davis papers: Letterbook I, Manuscripts Department, Tulane University Library.

100 Joel Chandler Harris, *On the Plantation: A Story of Georgia Boy's Adventures during the War* (New York, 1892; reprint: Athens, Ga., 1980), 138–9.

In April 1863, the issue of hunger was brought home to the Confederate government in a particularly vivid manner. A husky woman, armed with a knife and gun, persuaded a women's meeting in Richmond that it was time to "demand goods at government prices or forcibly take them."[101] Her argument was successful, and soon three hundred women, most of them wives of workers at the vital Tredegar Iron Works, marched on the capitol to demand bread, adding men, boys, and more women as they went.[102] "We celebrate our right to live," said one of them. "We are starving." From there they marched with weapons in sight to some stores, where they looted bread but also jewelry and clothing.[103] The governor of Virginia called out the city militia and threatened to fire on the crowd. Davis arrived also, made the same threat, gave the crowd time to disperse, and checked his watch to count down the minutes. The crowd dispersed, and some of the rioters served jail time for their behavior. In the meantime, the government took no chances. Cannon were set up in the market the next day, and two battalions of infantry were kept on alert. More important, the incident was kept out of the newspapers.[104]

Similar events occurred in other cities. In Atlanta, a shoemaker's wife led a raid on a butcher shop; then the mob moved on to other stores as well "and paid their own prices or nothing."[105] Other riots occurred in Macon, Columbus, Augusta, Mobile, and other cities. Occasionally, country-women attacked wagon trains. The reason for this tumult was most likely hunger, although E. Merton Coulter, one of the leading historians of the Confederacy, attributed the violence to inflation and war weariness.[106]

Any thoughtful Confederate had to pause and consider. One can well imagine the reaction of soldiers to their letters from home. Their will was broken and their identity as Confederates undermined – if it ever existed at all – so they acted to protect their families. Frank Owsley summed the result: "The morning sun often shown upon an empty tent, the former occupant of which was far on his way back home, presenting his cocked musket as a furlough, to any who questioned his going."[107]

101 E. Merton Coulter, *The Confederate States of America, 1861–1865*, in Wendell Holmes Stephenson and E. Merton Coulter, eds., *A History of the South* (Baton Rouge, La., 1950), 7:422.
102 Thomas, *Confederate Nation*, 202.
103 Ibid., 203.
104 Coulter, *Confederate States*, 422; Thomas, *Confederate Nation*, 204.
105 Coulter, *Confederate States*, 423.
106 Ibid., 424; Thomas, *Confederate Nation*, 204–5.
107 Owsley, "Defeatism in the Confederacy," 449; see also Hahn, *Roots of Southern Populism*, chap. 3, and *Official Records*, ser . 4, vol . 2:721.

RESIDUAL UNIONISM

Therefore, Southerners, like Northerners, went to war divided, but it was not only danger, hungry families, and parochialism that robbed them of their unity. "The Confederacy was weakened also," says Charles P. Roland, "by the persistence of an open unionism among many Southerners and a latent unionism among an indeterminable number of others."[108] In western Virginia, eastern Tennessee, Northern Alabama, northwestern Arkansas, the mountain counties of Georgia, parts of North Carolina, the German section of Texas, and even here and there in Mississippi, there were men who were Unionist from the beginning and would never be Confederate in their hearts regardless of what they might be forced to say and do. Some of these men sooner or later volunteered to fight in the Union army. Those who remained in the South and found themselves in the army or militia frequently refused to obey orders or went over to the Union at the first opportunity.[109] After Confederates passed the conscription law in the spring of 1862, stubborn Unionists would naturally feel even more resentment at being forced to fight. After the war had calmed passions somewhat, a former member of the Confederate Senate tried to analyze Confederate difficulties and trace their long-term effect in helping to bring about defeat. Defeat was not due, wrote Williamson S. Oldham of Texas, to lack of men and material, failure of Congress to support the president, excessive desertion, or lack of patriotism – of the last he was especially certain. "I do not believe," he wrote, that

the people of the Confederate States possessed less endurence [sic] than did the people of Prussia, who fought seven years for liberty against much greater odds, than that with which we had to contend, nor less than the French, who for twenty five years from the commencement of their revolution to the overthrow of Napoléon at Waterloo fought the combined powers of Europe, nor less than the Dutch, who maintained their war of independence against Spain for fifty years, nor less than our fathers of 1776.[111]

The difficulty was lingering attachment to the Union. Citizens who had followed certain party leaders "could not in the course of a few days, surrender up sentiments, they had entertained all their lives and change in favor of secession with their leaders, whom they regarded as traitorously inconsistent. The union speeches of 1860," Oldham claimed, "made many a Southern traitor."[112] Once the break was made, it was hard to change allegiance instanta-

---

108   Roland, *American Iliad*, 259.
109   Tatum, *Disloyalty in the Confederacy*, 5–6, 8, 10–12.
110   Williamson Simpson Oldham Reminiscences, The Center for American History, The University of Texas at Austin, 137–8, 140
111   Ibid., 141   112   Ibid., 143.

neously. Excessive zeal drove many Southerners into opposition "who by a prudent course on our part might have been brought to think and to act with us."[113]

There was much sense in what Oldham wrote, and he could well have been referring to an ad hoc military commission held in his own state at San Antonio that tried alleged Unionists on the slightest suspicion. One defendant noted that those who testified against him had formerly held the same political opinions he held. "Do they try, by accusing me, to make their antecedents forgotten?" The poor German immigrant defendant confessed to the charge that he had repeated news unfavorable to Confederate fortunes, but he pointed out that "at the time, there was no other news to communicate."[114] Many Confederates simply could not get over their feeling for the old Union. What else are we to make of those Texans, mostly Germans, "who preferred to defend their homes on the frontier rather than fight in the Civil War against the government to which they still felt strong ties," and who only enrolled Unionists in state troops in their area so as to be sure that the defenders of their homes would be friendly?[115] How are we to explain Mississippians, North Carolinians, and others who thought the best way to evade Confederate conscription was to enlist in the Union army? Such men identified themselves as Southerners but not as Confederates.[116]

In Washington County, North Carolina, for example, the presence of Union naval forces encouraged antagonism between pro-secession large planters, on the one hand, and "men of middling means – yeoman farmers and their sons" on the other. The latter were Unionists. The fall 1861 elections for militia officers were won by Unionists (one of the candidates avowed he was a Lincoln man and claimed that he would do his fighting at home), and by June 1862, they had raised several companies of men for Federal service. Guerrilla war eventually followed.[117]

Legislative authorization in February 1862 to suspend habeas corpus and apply martial law was an admission that serious internal dissent was anticipated,[118] especially when the suspensions were applied to areas where there were few military operations at the time.[119] That many Southerners identified themselves as Confederates only by threat of force, rather than by

113 Ibid., 143–4.
114 Alwyn Barr, ed., "Records of the Confederate Military Commission in San Antonio, July 2 to Oct. 10, 1862," *Southwest Historical Quarterly* 71 (Oct. 1967): 257.
115 Barr, "Military Commission," *Southwest Historical Quarterly* 70 (July 1966): 93.
116 Tatum, *Disloyalty in the Confederacy*, 92–3.
117 Durrill, *War of Another Kind*, 52–3, 102–3, 107, 166–85, 229.
118 James M. Matthews, ed., *Public Laws of the Confederate States of America, Passed at the First Session of the First Congress: 1862* (Richmond, Va., 1862), 1.
119 Alexander and Beringer, *Anatomy of the Confederate Congress*, 166–71.

natural inclination, was openly confessed when the writ of habeas corpus was suspended and martial law declared in East Tennessee and western Virginia to counter the threat created by the presence of significant Unionist strength within the borders of the Confederacy.[120] Many of these people evidently had no Confederate identity whatsoever, at least not voluntarily, and even today quite a few "Southern residents… do not think of themselves as Southerners." According to Shelton Reed, these people "come from all age groups, all social classes, and both sexes." Their attitude is based "on ideological grounds that have been around since the Civil War. These people feel that being Southern was 'un-American' in 1860 and still is." Reed's specific reference is to central and western North Carolina, but surely the observation applies as well to other areas that were strongly Unionist in 1860–61.[121]

Whomever most Southerners identified with, it was not with the planter class that led the secession movement. The constant cry of "rich man's war and poor man's fight" indicated that for multitudes of Confederates the planters were a negative reference group. "We used to have certain principles to fight for and now it is the Negro and his master too in fact the thing has shown its self so plain that a great many of the rank and file are becoming very Careless as to the result."[122] By the middle of the war, one of Davis's closest associates warned him that "the day I ever dreaded *has come*. The *enthusiasm* of the masses of the people, *is dead!*"[123] Another Confederate was shocked to overhear a citizen say that "The sooner this damned Government [falls] to pieces the better it [will] be for us."[124]

Many Southerners did not voluntarily identify themselves as Confederates until after the war – and then within a generation, it was sort of a dual nationality. The Confederacy stood for regional identity and nostalgia, even to the point of becoming a civil religion.[125] The United States, on the other hand, represented national pride as the unified country moved on to the international stage. In the end, says John McCardell, the state rights ideology of the South helped to create "a new American nationalist ideology."[126]

---

120 Richardson, ed., *Messages and Papers of the Confederacy*, 1: 219–27.
121 Reed, *Southerners*, 24.
122 "Many Soldiers" to Jefferson Davis, Sept. 7, 1864, Letters Received by the Confederate Secretary of War, roll 118, frames 702–4, JDA.
123 James Phelan to Jefferson Davis, July 29, 1863, Clements Library, University of Michigan at Ann Arbor, microfilm copy, JDA.
124 Frank Myers to T. B. Trout, March 31, 1864, *Official Records*, ser. 4, vol. 3: 413.
125 Charles Reagan Wilson, *Baptized in Blood: The Religion of the Lost Cause, 1865–1920* (Athens, Ga., 1980), 1, 7, 12–13, esp. chap. 8.
126 McCardell, *The Idea of a Southern Nation*, 337–8.

CONCLUSION

Then why did the Confederacy manage to fight for four years, if there was insufficient support for it in the first place? There are a number of answers to this thorny question. The vast geographical extent of the Confederacy gave the defense an immense advantage (the distance between Richmond and Memphis is roughly the same as that between Paris and Berlin, and the Union armies attempting to control all this territory were much smaller than the allied armies that operated in Europe in World Wars I and II). Second, Southern generalship was adequate to the task placed upon it, both sides possessing some generals who were brilliant and others who were anything but. Furthermore, amazing Southern wartime industrialization was effective because the war was waged in an age of cheap, mass-produced weaponry. Weapons were not as complex and costly to manufacture and purchase as they had been in the past or would be in the future; finely crafted suits of armor were useless, and tanks and airplanes were things of the future. The magnitude of the Southern war effort was remarkable and exceeded in efficiency the mobilization of the resource-rich Union. Hence, the Confederacy was able to fight as long and as well as it did.

The lagging rate of modernization in the South was responsible for the relative lack of industrial capacity with which the South began the war. But the war itself was responsible for narrowing the gap between the sections, as the pressures of military need forced the Confederacy into a breathtaking pace of modernization.[127] Not only did the economic system modernize; so too did attitudes. For example, in early 1862, ten Congressmen spread upon the pages of the *Journal* of Congress a statement remarkable for its opposition to modernization. They opposed the construction of railroads by the Confederate government for military purposes as an unconstitutional exercise of power. More to the point, they asserted that such roads would be unnecessary "because armies and munitions and military supplies have been, are now, and probably always will be mainly transported by other means."[128] But in the end, modernization won out, and several lines were built. Luraghi pointed to the end result of the remarkable stimulation of modernization in the South:

[Necessity] amounted for the South to no less than the need to create an industrially effectual apparatus of its own, and to do it out of nothing.... The ordnance Department of the Army created at Augusta, Georgia, the biggest powderworks then existing in America, far better than any Northern counterpart; as for the Navy ... it succeeded in building and contracting for or laying down 150 war vessels, about fifty of which were ironclads. The Navy organized the Marine Engineering Works at

127 Brown, *Modernization*, 22.
128 *Journal of the Confederate Congress*, 1:782.

Charlotte, North Carolina; ... organized ... powder works at Columbia, S.C., which turned out 20,000 pounds of powder per month; [and] created the amazing Selma cannon foundry, in Alabama, in which were cast the big Brooke guns, almost the best in the world.[129]

Ties created by the stress and danger of living in a threatened and invaded land (invaded by one's own army as well as that of the Union), augmented by duty to family, loyalty to one's own back yard, and residual Unionism, all worked to undermine and even preclude Confederate identity. And without much sense of Confederate identity or nationalism, the motivation to fight was confined to a smaller portion of the population than would otherwise have been the case. To many Confederates, the government they were supposed to support simply did not command their loyalty; for many, the Federal government did not command loyalty either, but every able-bodied young man who saw no advantage to being Confederate, who found that "Confederateness" brought only grief, subtracted from the manpower, loyalty, and will necessary to Confederate victory in the Civil War. We cannot come close to quantifying the numbers of men whose will to fight was nonexistent or else destroyed by the fortunes of their family or locality, but that there were enough of them to make a difference seems beyond doubt. A nation had been formed on paper before it took shape in the hearts and minds of enough of its would-be citizens. The Confederate will to fight was perhaps fatally crippled by the weakness of Confederate identity.

---

129 Luraghi, "Civil War and the Modernization of American Society," 244. For extended detail on the amazing and significant development of Confederate war industry, see Raimondo Luraghi, *The Rise and Fall of the Plantation South* (New York, 1978), Thomas, *Confederate Nation*, and Vandiver, *Their Tattered Flags*.

5

Unionism and Abolition:
Political Mobilization in the North

HANS L. TREFOUSSE

At a conference devoted to a comparison of the German Wars of Unification
and the American Civil War, the ideology of nationalism which inspired
both ought to be closely examined. That German, and for that matter, Italian,
unification and the preservation of the Union in the American Civil War
were all the result of this seemingly irresistible ideology has long been recognized. But there were important differences between the nationalism animating European unification movements and the American struggle for the
preservation of the Union, and these distinctions must be stressed as well.

European, and particularly German, nationalism has always had a tribal
basis. It concerned itself with one people, not with the interests of the world.
As the famous "*Turnvater*" Friedrich Ludwig Jahn defined German *Volkstum*
in 1810, "*Volkstum* is the common characteristic of a people, its inner being,
its rules and life, its power of development, its power of progress. All peoples
have their peculiar own thoughts and feelings, loves and hates, joys and
sorrows, hopes and yearnings, ancestors and beliefs. German means national
.... We must return to the lost past and recreate Nation, Germanness,
Fatherland."[1] Johann Gottlieb Fichte, in his *Address to the German Nation*,
agreed. "Liberty to them [the Germans]," he wrote, "meant this: persisting to
remain German and continuing the task of settling their own problems,
independently and in consonance with the original spirit of their race."[2]
And Ernst Moritz Arndt improved on this by stating, "German men, feel
again God, and hear and fear the Eternal, and you hear and feel also your *Volk*;
you feel again in God the honor and dignity of your fathers, their glorious
history rejuvenates itself again in you, the whole German Fatherland stands
again before you in the august halo of past centuries."[3] These effusions of

---

1 Louis L. Snyder, ed., *The Dynamics of Nationalism: Readings in Its Meaning and Development*
   (Princeton, N.J., 1964), 150.
2 Ibid., 148–9.
3 Ibid., 146.

romantic nationalism later enabled Heinrich von Treitschke to state: "There is no mistaking what the German spirit is. The real German is absolutely not to be confounded with any other people, although the frontiers of Germany have undergone so many changes in history."[4] All these definitions were rooted in the tribal idea of a specifically German people and its needs, not in any particular ideal of universal validity.

This type of nationalism, based on romantic notions and hatred of foreign invaders, for Germans and especially the French under Napoléon, was very different from the American spirit.[5] Ever since the eighteenth century, observers found that the New World had ideas that set it off sharply from the Old. Emphasizing the point in his new book, *Disuniting America*, Arthur M. Schlesinger Jr. cites the French traveler Michel-Guillaume-Jean de Crèvecoeur to show that American nationalism has never been tribal but on the contrary, idealistic. As Crèvecoeur pointed out during the American Revolution, the American was a new man. "He is an American," the Frenchman wrote, "who leaving behind all his ancient prejudices and manners, receives new ones from the new mode of life he has embraced, the new government he obeys, and the new rank he holds. The American is a new man, who acts upon new principles. ... Here individuals of all nations are melted into a new race of men."[6] And it was the idea of liberty that united Americans, not their past, an idea that grew stronger with the adoption of the federal Constitution and the subsequent development of the new nation. If in 1815 most Americans were still of British stock, the terms of admission for newcomers, as Clinton Rossiter has explained, were "reasonable and surprisingly mild." Immigrants merely had to pledge allegiance, learn to speak the language tolerably well, and subscribe to America's republican ways.[7] Then, after 1848, Paul Nagel found that talk of American purpose came to stress liberty rather than republicanism. "The Union changed from a procedure to a moral imperative," he has written, and ordinary Americans became imbued with the spirit of Union.[8]

One of these ordinary, but later most extraordinary, Americans was Abraham Lincoln. Animated by the spirit of American nationalism, on July 27, 1838, he delivered his Address to the Young Men's Lyceum of Springfield,

---

4   Heinrich von Treitschke, *Politics*, 2 vols. (New York, 1916), 1:200.
5   Louis L. Snyder, *Roots of German Nationalism* (Bloomington, Ind., 1978), 56–7; Hans Kohn, *The Idea of Nationalism: A Study of Its Origins and Background* (New York, 1961), 276.
6   Arthur M. Schlesinger Jr., *The Disuniting of America: Reflections on a Multicultural Society* (Knoxville, Tenn., 1991), 1–2.
7   Clinton Rossiter, *The American Quest, 1790–1860: An Emerging Nation in Search of Identity, Unity, and Modernity* (New York, 1974), 117.
8   Paul C. Nagel, *This Sacred Trust: American Nationality, 1798–1898* (New York, 1971), 134.

Illinois. As he proudly recalled, the Founding Fathers' ambition "aspired to display before an admiring world, a practical demonstration of the truth of a proposition, which had hitherto been considered, at best no better, than problematical; namely, *the capability of people to govern themselves.*"[9] He never wavered from his belief in this basic fact, and when he was called upon to rally the people in defense of their country, he emphasized this idea from the very beginning as the central issue of the Civil War.

Thus, the maintenance of the Union, which was the slogan for the political mobilization of the North and for which people were asked to give their lives, was always an ideal embracing much more than mere tribalism. It was the idea of democratic governments for which the Union summoned citizens from their homes, an ideal that was considered unique, not merely for the benefit of Americans but for all mankind. Even before the war started, in the midst of the secession crisis, Lincoln phrased it clearly in his inaugural address: "if the minority will not acquiesce," he said, "the majority must, or the government must cease. . . . A majority, held in restraint by constitutional checks and limitations, and always changing easily, with deliberate changes of popular opinions and sentiments, is the only true sovereign of a free people. Whoever rejects it, does, of necessity, fly to anarchy or to despotism." He closed by recalling the "mystic chords of memory" that would "yet swell the chorus of the Union, when again touched . . . by the better angels of our nature."[10]

It was therefore not surprising that when the Civil War broke out and mobilization of popular opinion became necessary in its support, the appeal was primarily to the maintenance of the Union, and thus, popular government. On April 15, in his first call for troops, the president asked all loyal citizens "to favor, facilitate, and aid this effort to maintain the honor, the integrity, and the existence of our national Union, and the perpetuity of popular government"—not just the Union but the Union as a guarantee of democracy.[11]

The response was instantaneous. All were rallying to the flag, reported the Chicago *Tribune.* There were no more Republicans, Whigs, Americans, or Democrats. In fact, the Democrats, "as patriots interested in maintaining the territorial integrity of the Republic, the spotless honor of the old flag, and more than all, the great principle upon which this Government is founded

---

9 Roy P. Basler, ed., *The Collected Works of Abraham Lincoln,* 9 vols. (New Brunswick, N.J., 1953–55), 1:113 (hereafter cited as Lincoln, *Works*).
10 James D. Richardson, *A Compilation of the Messages and Papers of the Presidents, 1789–1907,* 19 vols. (Washington, D.C., 1896–1908), 6: 9–12.
11 Ibid., 6: 13.

– the right of the majority to rule according to the forms and spirit of the organic law," were heading the call. The idea was as important as the country, and the people responded with enthusiasm, so that more troops than the president had demanded were immediately made available.[12]

Lincoln continued his appeal for safeguarding the Union and the principle it represented in his effort to whip up sentiment for the war. "This issue embraces more than the fate of these United States," he said on July 4 in his message to Congress. "It presents to the whole family of man, the question, whether a constitutional republic, or a democracy, – a government of the people, by the same people – can, or cannot, maintain its territorial integrity against its own domestic foes." He called the war "essentially a People's contest … a struggle for the maintaining in the world, that form of, and substance of government, whose leading object is, to elevate the condition of men, to lift artificial weights from all shoulders; to clear the path of laudable pursuit for all; to afford all, an unfettered start, and a fair chance, in the race of life." It was an experiment, an experiment of popular government. Two points concerning it had already been settled, the successful establishment and the successful administration of it. One still remained – the successful maintenance of it against a formidable internal attempt to overthrow it. It was now for the people to demonstrate "that ballots are the rightful, and peaceful successor of bullets; and that when ballots have been fairly, and constitutionally decided, there can be no successful appeal back to bullets."[13] This was his philosophy, his understanding of the nature of the war, and it fell upon receptive ears.

This democratic appeal continued throughout the following years. In his first annual message in December 1861, the president stated that the insurrection was "largely, if not exclusively, a war upon the first principle of popular government – the rights of the people."[14] On May 13, 1862, in response to visiting Evangelical Lutherans who presented resolutions of support for the suppression of rebellion and the maintenance of the Constitution, he said: "I accept with gratitude this assurance of sympathy … in an important crisis which involves, in my judgment, not only the civil and religious liberties of our own dear land, but in a large degree the civil and religious liberties of mankind in many countries and through many ages." And in October, in Frederick, Maryland, he expressed the hope that "our children's children to a thousand generations" might "continue to enjoy the benefits conferred

---

12   *Chicago Tribune*, April 16, 1861; Phillip Shaw Paludan, *"A People's Contest:" The Union and the Civil War, 1861–1865* (New York, 1989), 15.
13   Richardson, *Messages and Papers*, 6: 23–30.
14   Ibid., 56.

upon us by a united country and have cause yet to rejoice under these glorious institutions bequeathed to us by Washington and his compeers."[15]

In spite of this constant appeal to the maintenance of the Union as the embodiment of popular government, everybody was aware of the fact that the issue of slavery had been the primary cause of the war. In addition, the continued existence of the "peculiar institution" marred the example of democracy in America as a beacon to the world, and the radical faction of the ruling party was anxious to turn the struggle into a crusade against slavery. Again, however, it was an idea, or rather the greater inclusiveness of this idea, that constituted the gist of the radicals' argument.

Lincoln himself detested slavery; he had been one of two members of the Illinois legislature in 1837 to enter a protest against proslavery resolutions and had repeated this condemnation of the institution in many speeches since that time. He was also fully aware of the mockery that slavery made of America's claim of being a model for other nations; as he said in 1854 at Peoria: "This deliberate indifference to the spread of slavery I cannot but hate. I hate it because of the monstrous injustice of slavery itself. I hate it because it deprives our republican example of its just influence in the world – enables the enemies of free institutions, with plausibility, to taunt us as hypocrites."[16] Yet he was aware of the constitutional limitations upon the executive and the federal government. Legislation concerning slavery, according to the Constitution, was a matter for the states to decide, and the federal government had no jurisdiction over it. There were exceptions to this rule; Republicans had long insisted, and Southerners as well as Democrats had denied, that Congress could outlaw slavery in the territories and in the District of Columbia, but at the beginning of the conflict, Lincoln felt constrained to assure his listeners that he had no intention of interfering with human bondage. In view of the fact that the slaveholding border states had not seceded, that they were strategically located, and that the president was convinced he needed their support, his caution is understandable and was probably necessary. At first, his appeal simply had to be to the ideal of the Union and of popular government narrowly defined, if only to maintain the loyalty of the largest number of citizens. "I think to lose Kentucky is nearly the same as to lose the whole game," he wrote in September 1861, and he was reputed to have said that he hoped God was on his side but he had to have Kentucky. Maryland, too, was important; its fall would have isolated the capital, which was surrounded by the state on three sides. And Missouri was the

---

15   Lincoln, *Works*, 5: 212, 450.
16   Ibid., 1: 74–5, 2: 225; Benjamin Quarles, *Lincoln and the Negro* (New York, 1962), 19–38.

key to the trans-Mississippi West; it contained many Unionists who certainly deserved the support of the government without being embarrassed by an
antislavery policy calculated to infuriate their neighbors.[17]

In addition to the border states, the administration had to pay attention to
the large number of Democrats in every Northern commonwealth. Lincoln
was well aware of the fact that he had been chosen by only 39 percent of the
popular vote, even though he had garnered a clear majority in the electoral
college. That it was crucial to keep this opposition loyal and to mobilize it for
the great struggle was axiomatic. With Democratic members of the Congress
resisting every measure only remotely touching on the subject of federal
interference with slavery, the administration had to be circumspect. It could
hardly disregard the fact that in July 1861 both houses passed the Johnson-
Crittenden Resolutions asserting that the war was not being waged in any
spirit of oppression, nor for any purpose "of overthrowing or interfering with
the rights or established institutions" of the rebellious states, "but to defend
and maintain the supremacy of the Constitution and to preserve the Union,
with all the dignity, equality and rights of the several States unimpaired, and
that as soon as these objects are accomplished, the war ought to cease."[18]

And yet, the question of slavery and the idea of freedom that it challenged
had a way of intruding upon the public. In fact, the idea of democracy and
popular government that the people were asked to defend would be significantly strengthened by steps leading to emancipation, whether they were
popular or not, and Lincoln knew it.

He was soon to be given an opportunity to act upon this knowledge. When
in May 1861 troops under the command of Gen. Benjamin F. Butler at Fort
Monroe captured several blacks who had been used by the Confederates in
building fortifications, an emissary from the enemy under a flag of truce,
according to Butler's recollections, demanded their return under the Fugitive
Slave Act. Upon the general's objection that Virginia had seceded and no
longer recognized the laws of the Union, the Confederate replied that his
opponents did and therefore ought to live up to their constitutional obligations. Butler knew how to parry this trust. Declaring the captives "contraband of war," he confiscated them and effectively set them free. Thereafter,
fugitives were generally referred to as *contrabands*; Butler's action was
upheld by the secretary of war, and in August 1861, Congress passed the first

---

17 Lincoln, *Works*, 4:532; James M. McPherson, *The Battle Cry of Freedom: The Civil War Era* (New
    York, 1988), 284–5.
18 Edward McPherson, *The Political History of the United States of America during the Great Rebellion,
    1860–1865* (New York, 1972), 286; Joel Silbey, *A Respectable Minority: The Democratic Party in the
    Civil War Era* (New York, 1977), 32ff, 62ff.

Confiscation Bill declaring all slaves used against the federal army confiscated and therefore free. Lincoln promptly signed the measure.[19]

Cleverly utilizing every opportunity to advance the notion of freedom, in spite of Democratic misgivings, the president gradually moved toward a more positive antislavery stand. To be sure, he did so with care. Anxious to retain the conservatives' support, he revoked Gen. John C. Frémont's proclamation of August 31, freeing all slaves of insurgents in the Department of Missouri, but in November he made overtures to the lone representative of Delaware, George P. Fisher, for gradual, compensated emancipation in that border state.[20] And although in his first annual message in December 1861 he again stressed the importance of maintaining the Union and with it popular government, by March 1862 he reiterated, this time in public, his previous offer to Fisher by asking congress to invite all the border states to participate. In spite of his own antislavery predilections, he continued to emphasize the importance of maintaining the Union; it was for this purpose that he made his proposal as the most efficient step for the country's self-preservation.[21] That it would also strengthen the idea of an all-inclusive American nationalism could not have escaped him.

Although the representatives of the border states, despite the president's urging, refused to move, the administration accelerated its antislavery course. In April 1862, Lincoln signed a bill freeing all slaves in the District of Columbia. To sweeten the pill for the conservatives, the measure again contained provisions for compensation and in addition voluntary colonization. But no matter how much the Democrats and their allies protested, the antislavery policy had been inaugurated, and inaugurated in such a form as to maintain the loyalty of much of the opposition. In signing the measure, Lincoln stated succinctly that he had never doubted the constitutional authority of Congress to abolish slavery in the District and had always desired to see the national capital freed from the institution in some satisfactory way. Moreover, he expressed his gratification that the principles of compensation and colonization had both been recognized.[22] The idea of freedom and Union, and thus of a more powerful American example to the world, was making progress.

But the president was still cautious. The loyalty of the border states, to say nothing of that of the Democrats, had to be maintained, and so in May he revoked Gen. David Hunter's order freeing the slaves in the Department of

19 Benjamin F. Butler, *Butler's Book* (Boston, 1892), 256–64; Hans L. Trefousse, *Ben Butler: The South Called Him Beast* (New York, 1956), 78–9, 83.
20 Lincoln, *Works*, 5: 29–31; Hans L. Trefousse, *The Radical Republicans: Lincoln's Vanguard for Racial Justice* (New York, 1969), 176–7, 209.
21 Richardson, *Messages and Papers*, 6: 55–8, 68–9.   22 Ibid., 73–4.

the South. The government had had no knowledge of the proclamation, he wrote; nor had any general been authorized to set free the slaves in any state. Nevertheless, after successfully insisting that the operation of the legislation be limited to the lifetime of the offenders, he signed the far-reaching second Confiscation Bill freeing slaves of insurgents and authorizing their employment in the armed forces. He also agreed to a measure ending slavery in the territories.[23]

It was obvious that the president was coming to a crucial decision concerning slavery. And he continued to invoke the universal nature of American freedom. Repeating his call upon the border states to inaugurate emancipation, he admonished them, "as you would perpetuate popular government for the best people in the world, I beseech you that you in no wise omit this. Our country is in great peril, demanding the loftiest views, and boldest action to bring it speedy relief. Once relieved, it's [sic] form of government is saved to the world," and he again suggested compensated emancipation in loyal states as a fit measure for Congress to enact.

The basic problem of inaugurating abolition and maintaining popular support for the war, however, remained. The radicals constantly urged him to act; the conservatives entreated him to desist. That the danger of foreign intervention, more particularly international recognition of the Confederacy, might well be averted by a bold call for emancipation was also manifest.[25] For these reasons, Lincoln went ahead in his own ingenious fashion. Framing an emancipation proclamation that would free slaves only in states still in rebellion on January 1, 1863, and invoking his powers as commander in chief of the army and navy, he submitted his proposal to the cabinet on July 22. Upon Secretary of State William H. Seward's objection that the measure would better be postponed until some federal victory might give it greater plausibility, the president shelved it until a more appropriate time.[26]

His decisions remained hidden from the public. In fact, when in August Horace Greeley in his Prayer of Twenty Millions demanded that the president carry out the antislavery provisions of the Confiscation Act, Lincoln, far from revealing his purpose, published the oft-quoted reply,

I would save the Union. I would save it in the shortest way under the Constitution. The sooner the National authority can be restored, the sooner the Union will be

23 Ibid., 84, 91–2; J. G. Randall, *Lincoln the President*, 4 vols. (New York, 1945–55), 2:136.
24 Lincoln, *Works*, 5:317
25 Trefousse, *Radical Republicans*, 223ff; John Hope Franklin, *The Emancipation Proclamation* (Garden City, N.Y., 1963), 31ff; Hans L. Trefousse, *Lincoln's Decision for Emancipation* (Philadelphia, 1975), 6.
26 Lincoln, *Works*, 5:336–38; F. B. Carpenter, *Six Months at the White House with Abraham Lincoln* (New York, 1866), 20–2.

"the Union as it was." If there be those who would not save the Union unless at the same time they could *save* slavery, I do not agree with them. If there be those who would not save the Union unless they could at the same time *destroy* slavery, I do not agree with them. My paramount object in this struggle *is* to save the Union, and it is *not* either to save or destroy slavery. If I could save the Union without freeing *any* slaves, I would do it; and if I could do it by freeing *all* the slaves, I would do it; and if I could do it freeing some and leaving others alone, I would also do that. What I do about slavery and the colored race, I do because I believe it helps to save the Union; and what I forbear, I forbear because I do *not* believe it would help save the Union. I shall do *less*, whenever I shall believe what I am doing hurts the cause, and I shall do more whenever I shall believe doing *more* will help the cause. I shall try to correct errors when shown to be errors; and I shall adopt new views as fast as they shall appear to be true views. I have here stated my purpose according to my view of *official* duty, and I intend no modification of my oft-expressed *personal* wish that all men, everywhere, could be free.[27]

Union and its democratic significance was still the main source of popular appeal. That it was rapidly changing to include antislavery was not yet fully apparent.

But it was soon to become obvious. On September 22, following the Battle of Antietam, Lincoln issued the Preliminary Emancipation Proclamation promising freedom to slaves in rebellious states. The measure gave the South a respite of one hundred days before it would go into effect, one hundred days in which the insurgents could return to their allegiance and thus avoid emancipation.[28] Widely attacked by conservatives – "The Government, by act of the president, is itself in rebellion," commented the Chicago *Times* – the measure resulted in heavy pressure upon the president to revoke it, but he remained steadfast. He would rather die than take back a word of it, he told a group of visiting Kentuckians in November, and he kept his word.[29]

Yet he continued to cater to conservative opinion; if he wanted the country to keep supporting the war effort, he had to do so. In his annual message in December, he not only repeated his firm belief in colonization but offered a plan of gradual emancipation, which, if adopted, would have kept some blacks in bondage until 1900. Even this concession, however, was coupled with a call for action. "In *giving* freedom to the *slave*," he insisted, "we assure freedom to the *free* – honorable alike in what we give, and what we preserve. We shall nobly save, or meanly lose, the last best hope of earth."[30] American nationalism was again part of an ideal for the entire world.

27 Lincoln, *Works*, 5:338–9.
28 Richardson, *Messages and Papers*, 6:96–8.
29 Quotes in Chicago *Tribune*, Sept. 24, 1862; Franklin, *Emancipation Proclamation*, 58ff; Lincoln, *Works*, 5:503–4.
30 Richardson, *Messages and Papers*, 6:136–42.

On January 1, 1863, Lincoln promulgated the final Emancipation Proclamation. Couched in careful language invoking his powers as commander in chief of the army and navy in times of actual armed rebellion and as a "fit and necessary war measure" for the suppression of the rebellion, it promised freedom to all slaves in areas still in rebellion and authorized the acceptance of blacks into the armed services.[31] As could be expected, there was a lot of opposition, the legislature of Illinois going so far as to pass resolutions deploring the document as "a gigantic usurpation, at once converting the war, professedly commenced by the administration for the vindication of the authority of the Constitution, into a crusade for the sudden, unconditional and violent liberation of 3,000,000 Negro slaves; a result of which would not only be the total subversion of the Federal Union, but a revolution in the social organization of the Southern States."[32] Democratic newspapers denounced it; Democratic politicians thundered against it; but the administration succeeded in keeping the main part of the nation loyal.[33] As Lincoln, in justifying his action, explained to Gen. John A. McClernand, he struggled for nearly a year and a half to get along without touching the institution, and when he finally conditionally determined to touch it, he gave a hundred days' notice of his intention. Again and again he reiterated his determination never to retract it, and eventually, even the recruiting of black troops was grudgingly accepted by the army and the people alike. "The colored population is the great *available*, and yet *unavailed* of force for restoring the Union," the president wrote to Governor Andrew Johnson of Tennessee. "The bare sight of fifty thousand armed, and drilled black soldiers on the banks of the Mississippi, would end the rebellion at once."[34]

And soldiers were needed. It was in 1863 that Congress passed the first national draft law in the history of the Union, and resistance to it degenerated into riots in various cities, resulting in a three-day period of lawlessness in New York in July 1863. To rally the North, various publication societies became active, distributing pamphlets and propaganda material throughout the country. The New England Loyal Publication Society, the National War Committee of the Citizens of New York, and the Union League of Philadelphia indefatigably printed their material; aided by the victories at

31 Ibid., 157–9.
32 *Illinois State Register*, Jan. 7, 1863, in Henry Steele Commager, ed., *Documents of American History*, 6th ed. (New York, 1958), 421–2.
33 See, e.g., New York *World*, Jan. 8, 1863; New York *Herald*, Jan. 20, 1863; Stephen B. Oates, *With Malice Toward None: The Life of Abraham Lincoln* (New York, 1977), 339; Franklin, *Emancipation Proclamation*, 119 ff.
34 Lincoln, *Works*, 6:48–9, 146, 358–9, 364; Dudley Taylor Cornish, *The Sable Arm: Negro Troops in the Union Army, 1861–1865* (New York, 1966), 95.

Gettysburg, Vicksburg, and Chattanooga, these efforts showed results.[35] The national resolution did not falter, and even though the average Northern soldier was still fighting for the Union and the idea it represented rather than for emancipation, his ideal of the Union also embraced notions of universal republican liberty. That this would eventually be strengthened by freeing the slaves could hardly be denied. And no one could express the American ideal better than the president, who in his Gettysburg Address so magnificently characterized the issue of the struggle, and of American nationalism, as a contest to see whether a nation based on the principle that all men are created equal could long survive. As far as he was concerned, "government of the people, by the people, for the people" in the end included the blacks.[36]

Lincoln acted upon this conviction by continuing to put pressure on individual states to inaugurate measures of emancipation. The Proclamation had not only exempted the border states but also areas in Virginia and Louisiana under Union control. He now sought to remedy these omissions. Thus, in his proposal for reconstruction announced in December 1863, except for a few high-ranking and prominent secessionists, he offered amnesty to all insurgents who would take an oath renewing their allegiance to the constitution and promising to abide by the various measures concerning slavery passed by Congress or announced by the president. In consequence of this proclamation, which authorized the inauguration of new governments if 10 percent of the voters of 1860 took the oath, Louisiana was reconstructed in March 1864 and abolished slavery. Arkansas took similar steps; the new state of West Virginia had already introduced gradual emancipation as the price of its entry into the Union, and the loyal Restored Government of Virginia at Alexandria followed suit.[37] The national will to fight had been sustained in spite of the gradual transformation of the war into a crusade against slavery, and the national ideal of liberty became one of universal freedom.

Of course, the opposition never relented. Attacks on the administration, and particularly its emancipation policy, became ever more fierce. In 1863, Clement C. Vallandigham, the leading Copperhead (as the Peace Democrats were called) in Congress, was arrested for an antiwar speech in his Dayton home district. He was convicted and banished to the Confederacy but

---

35 McPherson, *Battle Cry of Freedom*, 600–1, 610–11; George Weston Smith, "Union Propaganda in the American Civil War," *Social Studies* 35 (Jan. 1994): 26–32; Frank Freidel, "The Loyal Publication Society: A Pro-Union Propaganda Agency," *Mississippi Valley Historical Review* 26 (1939): 359–76.

36 Lincoln, *Works*, 7:22–3; LaWanda Cox, *Lincoln and Black Freedom: A Study in Presidential Leadership* (Columbia, S.C., 1981), 24ff.

37 Richardson, *Messages and Papers*, 6: 213–15; McPherson, *Political History*, 321–2, 377–8.

reappeared to wage a vigorous campaign for the Governor of Ohio from Canadian soil. Democratic newspapers and pamphlets continued to denounce the administration,[38] and should the opposition win the election of 1864, all the gains of the war might be in question. Thus, Lincoln and the Union Party, as the Republicans now called themselves, included a plank for a constitutional amendment abolishing slavery in their 1864 platform. The president was renominated, and it became clear that if his opponent, Gen. George B. McClellan, the Democratic candidate, were to win, a total reversal of national goals would result.[39] Consequently, the rifts that had developed in the party – some wanted to replace Lincoln with a more radical candidate – were healed; the propaganda agencies went all out to urge the president's reelection; ethnic leaders such as Carl Schurz were pressed into service to influence their constituencies, and with the help of timely victories in Mobile Bay, Georgia, and the Valley of Virginia, the Union party achieved a great success in November.[40]

Fresh from this triumph, in his last annual message in December, Lincoln repeated what he had said many times before. He would not yield his determination to save the Union, but he also heartily recommended to Congress to reconsider its action concerning the antislavery amendment, which had failed to receive the necessary two-thirds in the House the previous spring. As he did so often, he couched his appeal in the idealistic language of American nationalism. The people had endorsed the change in the recent elections, he said; the most reliable indication of public purposes in this country was derived through popular elections, and thus the people's resolution to maintain the Union was never more clear.[41]

And he went further. Using all the powers of patronage and persuasion at his disposal, he saw to it that the votes necessary for passage of the amendment were forthcoming, and in the following January, the House accepted the constitutional change. The president had every reason to welcome the victory; he had succeeded in fusing the ideal of maintaining the Union with the cause of emancipation. "He could not but congratulate all present, himself, and the whole world upon the great moral victory," Lincoln told serenaders on February 1, 1865. Now the free republic could really serve as a model for all mankind.[42]

38 Frank L. Klement, *The Limits of Dissent: Clement L. Vallandigham and the Civil War* (Lexington, Ky., 1970); Benjamin F. Thomas, *Abraham Lincoln* (New York, 1952), 379–80; Frank Freidel, ed., *Union Pamphlets of the Civil War, 1861–1865*, 2 vols. (Cambridge, Mass., 1967), 2: 697–738, 752–65.

39 McPherson, *Political History*, 406–7; Lincoln, *Works*, 7: 514.

40 William Frank Zornow, *Lincoln and the Party Divided* (Norman, Okla., 1954), 105–221.

41 Richardson, *Messages and Papers*, 6: 252–5.

42 J. G. Randall and Richard N. Current, *Lincoln the President: Last Full Measure* (New York, 1955), 298–321; Lincoln, *Works*, 8: 254–5.

In the meantime, acting under presidential and radical pressure, all the border states except Kentucky and Delaware had ended their systems of slavery.[43] The country had attained a goal unimaginable in 1861, and when on March 4, 1865, Lincoln was inaugurated for a second term, he fittingly expressed the sentiment that had long animated him, again couching it not in narrowly nationalistic American terms but in religious expressions of universal application. "On the occasion corresponding to this four years ago...," he said,

One eighth of the whole population were colored slaves. ... These slaves constituted a peculiar and powerful interest. All knew that this interest was somehow the cause of the war. To strengthen, perpetuate, and extend this interest was the object for which the insurgents would rend the Union even by war, while the Government claimed no right to do more than to restrict the territorial enlargement of it. Neither party expected for the war the magnitude or the duration which it has already attained. Neither party expected that the *cause* of the conflict might cease with or even before the conflict itself should cease. ... If we shall suppose that American slavery is one of those offenses which, in the providence of God, must needs come, but which, having continued through his appointed time, He now wills to remove, and that He gives to both North and South this terrible war as the woe owing to those by whom the offense came, shall we discern therein any departure from those divine attributes which the believers in a Living God always ascribe to Him? Fondly do we hope, fervently do we pray, that this mighty scourge of war may speedily pass away. Yet, if God wills that it continue until all the wealth piled by the bondsmen's two hundred and fifty years of unrequited toil shall be sunk, and until every drop of blood drawn with the lash shall be paid by another drawn with the sword, as was said three thousand years ago, so it still must be said, "The judgments of the Lord are true and righteous altogether"[44]

It was a fitting conclusion to a war to vindicate the American idea of nationalism, a sentiment, now free from the taint of slavery, appealing to the world, and not merely to a single people.

43 McPherson, *Political History*, 227, 332.
44 Richardson, *Messages and Papers*, 6:276–7.

6

The Prussian Triangle of Leadership in the Face of a People's War: A Reassessment of the Conflict Between Bismarck and Moltke, 1870–71

STIG FÖRSTER

THE PROBLEM

In modern history, conflicts between political leadership and military command over the conduct of war, more often than not, have tended to occur wherever there was a distinction, at least in theory, between a civilian government and the top echelons of the armed forces. This problem characterized the civil-military relations in Germany in the period from 1870 to 1945. As early as the 1820s, the Prussian general Carl von Clausewitz provided an almost prophetic analysis of this issue. In fact, the relationship between politics and war was central to his famous book On War,[1] and his thorough investigation came to a seemingly clear-cut conclusion. Following earlier suggestions by Christian von Massenbach dating back to 1795,[2] Clausewitz demanded in time of war a well-defined hierarchy that put political leadership unquestionably above military command. It could not reasonably be otherwise, as Clausewitz's theory had demonstrated that war was nothing but an instrument of politics, "only a branch of political activity," possessing its own "grammar" but not its own logic. It was policy that gave war its aim and determined its character. Hence, it appeared absurd to Clausewitz to suggest that

---

1 See the introduction to Carl von Clausewitz, *Vom Kriege*, ed. Werner Hahlweg, 16th ed. (Bonn, 1952), 33–4. It should be noticed, however, that Clausewitz was not just interested in the relationship between political leadership and military command. Far beyond that, he focused on the character of war in general. According to him, war was always an act of policy, and this was the basis of any understanding of the history of warfare. See Panayotis Kondylis, *Theorie des Krieges: Clausewitz-Marx-Engels-Lenin* (Stuttgart, 1988), 19, 31–9.

2 Gerhard Ritter, *Staatskunst und Kriegshandwerk: Das Problem des "Militarismus" in Deutschland*, 4 vols. (Munich, 1954–68), 1: 210–11.

the military commander in chief be allowed autonomy in decision making in order to run the war according to purely military considerations.[3]

Logical as this would seem, Clausewitz's deliberations did not, however, provide an altogether convincing theoretical solution to the problem. After all, Clausewitz himself admitted that policy must not demand the impossible of war, that, in fact, it had to understand the use of war as its instrument. To act against the grammar of war could only lead to disaster and was a sign of bad policy.[4] This left a gray area between the logic of policy and wartime grammar. Who was to decide whether governments were demanding the impossible of their generals? In the "darkness of war," when decision making was ultimately a dangerous gamble, whose expertise should determine the limits of political reason and military necessity, particularly if the enemy changed the character of warfare? It was precisely in this gray area of uncertainty, decades after Clausewitz's death (1831), that the struggle between political leadership and military command in Germany began.

In this decades-long conflict, the German generals, not satisfied with asking that meddling politicians leave them alone, increasingly demanded total control of the war effort. This culminated during World War I, when Paul von Hindenburg and Erich Ludendorff established a virtual military dictatorship. The German historian Gerhard Ritter defined this tendency to reverse the dominance of political leadership over military command as "militarism." According to Ritter, an overemphasis on military virtues led to a disturbed relationship between "the art of policy" and the "craft of warfare" and thus to "militarism."[5] Certainly, modern historiography since Ritter has demonstrated that this definition of militarism is both far too narrow and, in a sense, almost empty. It lacks any reference to the sociological background, to those groups in society that foster and shape militarism, and it also says very little indeed about the tendency of militarism to transform society into a vast garrison.[6]

For the sake of argument, however, it will be useful in the context of this chapter to adhere to Ritter's old-fashioned definition, because it neatly describes the tendency of military command to extend its powers at the

---

3 Carl von Clausewitz, *On War*, ed. and trans. Michael Howard and Peter Paret (Princeton, N.J., 1976), 605–12.
4 Ibid., 86–7, 608–9.
5 Ritter, *Staatskunst*, 1:13.
6 See the criticism of Ritter's definition in Hans-Ulrich Wehler, *Das Deutsche Kaiserreich, 1871–1918* (Göttingen, 1973), 158, and Volker Berghahn, *Militarism: The History of an International Debate, 1861–1979* (Leamington Spa, 1981), 53–7, 105–7. For a broader definition of militarism, incorporating the dimension of society, see Stig Förster, *Der doppelte Militarismus: Die deutsche Heeresrüstungspolitik zwischen Status-quo-Sicherung und Aggression, 1890–1914* (Stuttgart, 1985), 3–8.

expense of political leadership.[7] Moreover, Ritter's monumental four-volume oeuvre on *Staatskunst und Kriegshandwerk* provides perhaps the most influential analysis of the topic at issue here.[8] To Ritter, militarism was the scourge of German history from 1890 (the year of Chancellor Otto von Bismarck's dismissal) to 1945. It first peaked during World War I, found its classical formulation in Ludendorff's *Der totale Krieg* (Total War),[9] and was fully put into practice under Adolf Hitler–with disastrous consequences.[10] This argument has found widespread acceptance, and one of the main purposes of this chapter is to test its validity by investigating the origins of the tendency toward militarism in German history.

Ritter himself claimed that the "classical" conflict between political leadership and military command in Germany occurred during the Franco-Prussian War in 1870–71, when Bismarck and the chief of the Prussian General Staff, Helmuth von Moltke, clashed.[11] According to the historian Rudolf Stadelmann, Moltke attempted at this juncture to prevent Bismarck from influencing military operations and thus to defend the autonomy of the General Staff vis-à-vis the chancellor during wartime.[12] Historians Werner Hahlweg and Ulrich Marwedel therefore accuse Moltke of having decidedly deviated from the path prescribed by Clausewitz.[13] Ritter again, who came to the same conclusion, saw here the beginnings of the claim to supremacy by the German military and thus ultimately of militarism.[14] Finally, Ritter and Stadelmann agreed that it was the strains of people's war in France that triggered the conflict between Bismarck and Moltke.[15]

In the context of this volume's general subject, it will therefore be interesting not only to analyze afresh the origins of militarism in Germany but also to take a closer look at the impact of people's war on the relationship between civilian government and military high command. It will be useful in particular to raise the question of whether people's war was indeed only

---

7 However, in order to avoid misunderstandings, the word *militarism* will be put in quotation marks whenever I use it in Ritter's sense.

8 "The Art of Policy and the Craft of Warfare" would be a more literal but not necessarily more catching translation than *The Sword and the Sceptre: The Problem of Militarism in Germany*, 4 vols. (London, 1972–73).

9 Erich Ludendorff, *Der totale Krieg* (Munich, 1935).

10 Ritter, *Staatskunst*, 1:14.

11 Ibid., 238. A similar argument is made in the stimulating article by Peter Paret, "Military Power," *Journal of Military History*, 53 (1989): 239–56, esp. 249–52.

12 Rudolf Stadelmann, *Moltke und der Staat* (Krefeld, 1950), 204–6.

13 See Hahlweg's introduction to Clausewitz, *Vom Kriege*, 20–23, and Ulrich Marwedel's *Carl von Clausewitz: Persönlichkeit und Wirkungsgeschichte seines Werkes bis 1918* (Boppard/Rhein, 1978), 134–5.

14 Ritter, *Staatskunst*, 1: 247–50.

15 Stadelmann, *Moltke*, 210–11, 260–1; and Ritter, *Staatskunst*, 1: 281, 329.

the trigger to the conflict between chancellor and general or whether it was in itself a main issue of that clash. After all, the problem of finding a new strategy in the face of the changing character of warfare may have been at least as important as the quest for supremacy in the royal headquarters. Finally, this article will discuss to what extent the conflict between Bismarck and Moltke mirrored the process that brought Germany on the road to total war.

Hence, it is necessary first of all to define briefly the meaning of "people's war." In modern history, it all began with the French Revolutionary Wars after 1792. Before that, the military history of the eighteenth century had been characterized by a series of "cabinet wars," in which small armies of professional soldiers had fought limited campaigns for limited aims of dynastic rulers, limiting civilians to the roles of paying taxes and, in combat zones, suffering collateral damage. Under no circumstances were civilians to join the fighting. The states at war truly retained their monopoly on the use of force (*Gewaltmonopol*), which they had acquired in the seventeenth century, thereby creating the preconditions of modern warfare.[16]

All this changed when the Revolution overturned the ancien régime in France and the country of the *citoyens* became involved in war with its neighbors. Because politics had become a public affair and a national issue, so had war. The French increasingly mobilized their human, economic, and financial resources for the war effort, and as their mass armies swept through Europe, they revolutionized warfare itself: "Suddenly war again became the business of the people—a people of thirty millions, all of whom considered themselves to be citizens," wrote Clausewitz three decades later.[17]

Again Clausewitz was the first to analyze this momentous change in the character of modern warfare. He clearly understood that the mobilization of the people for war was the main reason for the stunning victories of Napoléon Bonaparte, as well as for the almost incredible radicalization of warfare during that period, particularly after the peoples of Spain, Russia, Prussia, and Austria began to fight back. Thus, people's war in the modern sense was born, and to Clausewitz's mind, it tended to approach "pure war," "absolute war."[18]

But even if conservative régimes, like the Austrian (1808) and Russian (1812) governments, were in the moment of greatest danger ready to experiment with people's war, they did not really like what they had to do. After

---

16   For a stimulating modern view of this subject, see Ekkehard Krippendorff, *Staat und Krieg: Die historische Logik politischer Unvernunft* (Frankfurt/Main, 1985). On the beginnings of the state's monopoly on the use force, especially during the Thirty Years' War, see Johannes Burkardt, *Der Dreissigjährige Krieg* (Frankfurt/Main, 1992).

17   Clausewitz, *On War*, 592.

18   Ibid., 592–3. For an excellent overview of the revolutionary and Napoléonic wars, see Geoffrey Best, *War and Society in Revolutionary Europe, 1770–1870* (London, 1982), 63–190.

all, to arm the people meant to put the state's monopoly on the use of force at risk. Perhaps the most promising way out of this dilemma was to channel the unruly power of people's war into regular armies, led by reliable and conservative officers. The means to achieve this were conscription and extensive military training, as partially demonstrated by Prussia. But this was already too revolutionary a device for most European conservatives of the time, particularly if it included the creation of a bourgeois *Landwehr* or militia, as in Prussia.

Thus, after Waterloo, the victorious conservative governments of Europe tried by other means to put the genie back into the bottle. For more than three decades, the great powers abstained from large-scale wars altogether and did their best to suppress their greatest enemy: nationalism. Even as the revolutions of 1848–49 shattered many restorationist régimes and brought about a new surge of nationalism, major wars could still be avoided for the next few years. But dramatic change was soon in the offing. With the Crimean War (1854–56), the war between Sardinia, France, and Austria (1859), the German-Danish War (1864), and the war between Austria and Prussia (1866), all major European powers at one time or another got involved in extensive fighting. It is important to note, however, that none of these wars were people's wars in the true sense. Despite certain nationalistic undertones, these wars remained essentially cabinet wars, as Moltke later put it.[19] They were coolly managed by the inner circles of governments, and, with the notable exception of Prussia and partially France, they were fought by relatively small professional armies. War aims and combat zones remained limited, and only the Crimean campaign took longer than a few weeks.

But in at least one respect, the series of wars fought in the mid-nineteenth century were decidedly different from the cabinet wars of the eighteenth century. Improvements in arms technology, arms production, and transportation marked them as the first industrialized wars in Europe. Never mind the rather traditionalist political character of these wars, the age of industrialized warfare had begun.[20] This allowed far more rapid and more violent campaigns, and it opened up the potential for warfare on a much larger scale, involving far greater numbers of troops. Under these circumstances, the return of people's war threatened Europe with a major catastrophe, bringing the vastly improved resources of whole industrialized nations to bear.

19 See, e.g., Helmuth von Moltke, "Über den angeblichen Kriegsrath in den Kriegen König Wilhelms I," *Gesammelte Schriften und Denkwürdigkeiten des Generalfeldmarschalls Grafen Helmuth von Moltke*, 8 vols. (Berlin, 1891–93), 3: 415–28, esp. 426.
20 For Germany, see Dennis E. Showalter, *Railroads and Rifles: Soldiers, Technology, and the Unification of Germany* (Hamden, Conn., 1975).

To a large extent, this occurred for the first time in Europe during the second half of the Franco-Prussian War. Employing industrialized warfare, mobilizing the population and resources of their nonoccupied territory, and even using guerrilla tactics, the French faced Germany's well-equipped and well-trained conscript armies, thus fighting an industrialized people's war.[21] Once again the state's monopoly on the use of force was threatened, as poorly trained citizens took up arms to fight a regular army. Certainly, the vast majority of Frenchmen fought in regular forces themselves. But the improvised manner in which they were made ready for the front gave them the appearance of people's armies. Moreover, the national guards and particularly the guerrilla forces of the franc-tireurs had a distinct revolutionary character. This was no longer regular warfare. The Germans were suddenly confronted with a new phenomenon, which reminded many of their conservative leaders of the French revolutionary wars.

THE BACKGROUND

The specifically German aspects of the conflict between political leadership and military command originated in Prussia's peculiar constitutional history. Their roots reach back into the age before industrialized people's war. At their core lay the vexed relationship between monarch, government, and military, complicated since 1848 by their embattled position vis-à-vis the Prussian parliament.

Until their fall in 1918, the Hohenzollern monarchs claimed the right to ultimate personal authority, at least in foreign and military affairs. The ideal role model for this policy was Friedrich the Great, who during his reign had indeed successfully unified political leadership and military command in his person, keeping ministers and generals merely as his advisers.[22] But such an enormous task could only be undertaken by exceptional rulers like Friedrich and Napoléon. Even worse, since the beginning of the age of industrialized warfare, if not already during the French Revolutionary Wars, it had become utterly impossible for just one person to run the increasingly complicated state administration and military machinery single-handedly. Thus, a division of labor had become unavoidable, delegating much power of decision making to the cabinet and the military commanders. The monarch remained merely the ultimate arbiter, in whose name orders were given, and who only

---

21 As overviews for the period from 1815 to 1871, see Best, *War and Society*, 191–308; Brian Bond, *War and Society in Europe, 1870–1970* (London, 1984), 13–39; and Michael Howard, *War in European History*, 5th ed. (Oxford, 1974), 94–100.
22 Ritter, *Staatskunst*, 1:207.

rarely had the knowledge and the willpower to issue general guidelines or even to impose his will in specific matters without the advice and consent of his departmental chiefs.[23]

During the period of the Restoration, the kings of Prussia refused to accept the unavoidable. They did not appoint a prime minister and split the military command into several departments, directly responsible to the king. This, however, left only the illusion of personal rule, as the kings came under the influence of cliques without responsibility, and it created an administrative chaos of competing and jealous ministries and departments.[24]

Much of this changed as a result of the revolutionary events of 1848. Prussia became a constitutional monarchy that guaranteed civil rights to its citizens and gave parliament a voice and some authority, particularly in financial matters. The government, too, was reorganized on a more clearly defined basis, especially when King Friedrich Wilhelm IV appointed a prime minister answerable to parliament. However, according to article 48 of the revised constitution of January 31, 1850, the king and through him the prime minister were almost solely responsible for the conduct of foreign affairs, particularly for the declaration of war and peace. In addition, the king retained the *Oberbefehl* (supreme command) of the armed forces, as stipulated by article 46.[25] Thus, in war and peace the king and his ministers might be influenced by public opinion and limited in their freedom to act by the clout of parliament in financial matters, but they possessed sole sovereignty in foreign affairs and military matters.[26] This was the basis for the emergence of the Prussian triangle of leadership, which ran Prussia's and later Germany's security policy, at least in theory, until 1918.

It became a triangle because of the relative weakness of the prime minister vis-à-vis the military. After the death of Prime Minister Prince Karl von Hardenberg in 1822, the refusal of King Friedrich Wilhelm III to appoint a successor also served the purpose of freeing the military from the control of the head of the civilian government. Even when Friedrich Wilhelm IV finally appointed a prime minister in 1848, he did not give him the right to interfere in military matters. The heads of the army remained directly responsible

---

23 For a general analysis of this problem, see Martin Van Creveld, *The Transformation of War* (New York, 1991), 43. Even Napoléon had difficulties keeping control just by himself of the political apparatus and the military machinery. His refusal to delegate power contributed much to his ultimate downfall. See Russel F. Weigley, *The Age of Battles: The Quest for Decisive Warfare from Breitenfeld to Waterloo* (Bloomington, Ind., 1991), 308–534.

24 Ernst Rudolf Huber, *Deutsche Verfassungsgeschichte*, 8 vols., 3d ed. (Stuttgart, 1988), 2 : 21–3, 477–80.

25 The Prussian Constitution of Jan. 31, 1850, quoted in Ernst Rudolf Huber, ed., *Dokumente zur deutschen Verfassungsgeschichte*, 3 vols., 3d ed. (Stuttgart, 1978), 1 : 501–14.

26 Ritter, *Staatskunst*, 1 : 226–30; and Thomas Nipperdey, *Deutsche Geschichte, 1800–1866: Bürgerwelt und starker Staat* (Munich, 1983), 679–83.

to the king, and the prime minister had no control over them. Thus emerged the dualism between civilian government and the army.[27]

During the Prussian Constitutional Conflict (1859–66), when the majority of parliament challenged the king's unrestricted *Oberbefehl* over the army, this dualism became enshrined once and for all. In 1862, King Wilhelm I appointed Bismarck prime minister, who committed himself to save the throne and to keep the army free from any parliamentary control. Because he was answerable to parliament, Bismarck had to agree to give the heads of the army the right to report directly to the king without the presence, knowledge, or interference of the prime minister. Hence, Bismarck never gained control over the army, although he held fast to his promise to defend the king's unrestricted supreme command at any cost.[28]

The army, however, lacked a clear command and control structure. Since the minister of war, as a member of government, had to answer to parliament, the king and his military advisers tried to deprive him of as much influence as possible. In 1859, Wilhelm I restricted him to financial and administrative matters, while at the same time strengthening the right of the army corps commanders (*Kommandierende Generale*) and the head of the military cabinet to report directly to the king (*Immediatrecht*). From now on, the king issued orders directly to the army, without the assistance of his minister of war. As a result, the army's leadership consisted of several high-ranking officers on equal footing, whose only arbiter was the king himself. This led to administrative chaos, which served Prussia badly during the war of 1864 against Denmark, because Wilhelm I was in no position to assume direct control for the conduct of war.[29]

Hence, there was room for a new institution to take over the leadership of the army in times of war. Since his appointment in 1857 as chief of the General Staff, Moltke had impressed Wilhelm I with his astute memoranda concerning strategic planning. In 1864, after having been finally sent to the front, Moltke had helped to bring the war to a successful conclusion. When war against Austria and its German allies loomed in the spring of 1866, it was Moltke who devised the strategic plan for the operations against the enemy. Wilhelm I had finally found his wartime commander. It was only logical for the king to issue an order on June 2, 1866, giving Moltke the right to direct, in the name of the supreme commander, the movements of the troops. With

---

27 Ritter, *Staatskunst*, 1: 223–6, 260.
28 Ibid., 1:234–5; and Nipperdey, *Geschichte*, 754–5, 757.
29 Ritter, *Staatskunst*, 1:231–4. For a general assessment of the structure of supreme command in Prussia, see Eckart Busch, *Der Oberbefehl: Seine rechtliche Stellung in Preussen und Deutschland seit 1848* (Boppard/Rhine, 1967).

this decision, Moltke became equal to the minister of war and, more importantly, to the prime minister while commanding the Prussian army in time of war.[30]

The Prussian triangle of leadership in wartime was now complete. At the helm stood Wilhelm I, the first soldier-king in Prussia since Friedrich the Great.[31] But he had neither the ability nor, under pressure from parliament, the power to run things himself. Instead, he depended on the two other corners of the triangle and increasingly served as a "lightening rod" for conflicts between them rather than controlling them.[32]

Bismarck, the brilliant and aggressive prime minister, more often than not succeeded in bullying the king to follow his lead. But he had to suffer the independence of the military, particularly the chief of the General Staff, in whose affairs he had little right to meddle. Still, Bismarck was in charge of foreign policy, which could not always be separated from military matters. The quiet but resolute Moltke himself only occasionally interfered with Bismarck's domain. But he certainly guarded jealously over his rights as the king's leading military commander in wartime, who had a duty to keep the army aloof from the politicians in order to preserve the monarch's unrestricted *Oberbefehl*. This triangle contained enormous potential for trouble.

But in 1866, things went well. The Prussian triangle had heeded Clausewitz's advice that a team of leadership should keep together in war and stay close to the action.[33] The royal headquarters, which included Wilhelm I, Bismarck, and Moltke, moved with the army into Bohemia, and together they watched the Austrian rout at Sadowa. Prime minister and chief of General Staff cooperated closely thereafter in preventing the overenthusiastic king from prolonging the war. They forced him to give up the idea of a conquest of Vienna, as well as demands for widespread annexations from Austria. Instead, they brought the war to a rapid close by refraining from exploiting victory to the full and by setting mild conditions for peace.[34]

---

30 Ritter, *Staatskunst*, 1: 235–7; and Ernst Engelberg, *Bismarck: Urpreusse und Reichsgründer* (Berlin, 1985), 603–4. For the rise of Moltke and the General Staff, see Eberhard Kessel, *Moltke* (Stuttgart, 1957), 222–458. The constitution of the General Staff is extensively analyzed in Günther Wohlers, *Die staatsrechtliche Stellung des Generalstabs in Preussen und Deutschland* (Bonn, 1920).
31 Michael Howard, *The Franco-Prussian War: The German Invasion of France, 1870–71*, 4th ed. (London, 1968), 19.
32 Dennis E. Showalter, "German Grand Strategy: A Contradiction in Terms?," *Militärgeschichtliche Mitteilungen* 48, no. 2 (1990): 78.
33 Clausewitz, *On War*, 608–9.
34 Poor Hanover, however, and other German states that suffered annexation by Prussia certainly did not regard the terms of peace as mild. See Kessel, *Moltke*, 488–91, Engelberg, *Bismarck*, 610–14, Heinz Helmert and Hansjürgen Uszeck, *Preussisch-deutsche Kriege von 1864 bis 1871: Militärischer Verlauf*, 5th ed. (Berlin, 1984), 123–35.

In fact, the war of 1866 came close to the ideal of the Prussian mode of warfare: rapid victory for limited political aims. Under those circumstances, it was only natural that Bismarck and Moltke should work well together. After all, they both shared similar objectives: a short and decisive campaign to avoid the hazards of extended warfare and to keep the neutral powers out of the conflict. From the outset, Bismarck pursued very limited war aims vis-à-vis Austria. He wanted to push the Austrians out of a Germany that he intended to unify under Prussian leadership. But he had no wish to humiliate them, for he regarded Austria as a potential partner for the future. Hence, the prime minister refrained from any excessive demands. Moreover, Bismarck feared that if the war were protracted, Napoléon III would interfere. He therefore needed a general who would give him the maximum military success in the shortest possible time.[35]

For this, Moltke was the right man in the right place. He abhorred the brutal slaughter and unspeakable human suffering of prolonged warfare. As with Bismarck, Moltke was aware that Prussia could not afford a war against Austria that dragged on for months, if not longer. He therefore devised a strategy of rapid overthrow, which made full use of Prussia's superior means of transportation (railroads) and vastly increased firepower of the infantry. Perhaps most important of all, he aimed at concentrating almost all of his forces in one decisive battle, in order to annihilate the Austrian army in a swift campaign. In this, he succeeded nearly completely.[36] This was the birth of the modernized version of the Prussian mode of warfare: rapid victory in the age of industry.[37]

Having achieved their main objectives, Moltke and Bismarck would not allow Wilhelm I to ruin their plans. In fact, under the strains of the brief campaign against Austria, the Prussian triangle of leadership had worked reasonably well, as prime minister and chief of staff protected the king from himself. The looming conflict between political leadership and military command had not erupted, because both sides pursued similar aims and almost everything had gone according to plan. But the underlying problems remained.

THE ORIGINS OF THE CONFLICT

First of all there was departmental rivalry. The division of labor under the semblance of personal rule by the monarch did not foster a spirit of cooper-

---

35 Lothar Gall, *Bismarck: Der weisse Revolutionär* (Frankfurt/Main, 1980), 361–5.
36 See, esp., Moltke's memoranda of April 2, 14, and 20, 1866, *Moltkes militärische Werke*, ed. Grosser Generalstab, Abtheilung für Kriegsgeschichte, 17 vols. (Berlin, 1892–1912), 1/2:74–7, 119–28, 130–4. For an assessment of Moltke's strategy in 1866, see Kessel, *Moltke*, 446–88, 507–8.
37 On the Prussian mode of warfare in general, see Showalter, "Grand Strategy."

ation. Instead, it created constant conflicts. Each department jealously guarded its position in government and before the monarch, if it did not actually attempt to widen its influence at the expense of other departments. This was particularly true of the military, which still lacked a unified command structure. The war ministry, the military cabinet, and increasingly the General Staff were time and again at loggerheads with each other. The power struggle within the military leadership became an unhappy Prussian tradition, which, after 1871, continued in Imperial Germany. Between 1856 and 1865, and again in 1883, the military cabinet strengthened its role at the expense of the war ministry.[38] During the 1860s, the General Staff, formerly subservient to the war ministry, emerged as a new power center, equal, and in time of war even superior to the ministry. This led to a bitter rivalry, which, between 1897 and 1914, erupted several times into heated disputes between the war ministry and the General Staff over armament policy.[39]

Such rivalries did not remain confined to the army. They were just as strong between the military leadership and the civilian government, particularly between the General Staff and the prime minister. Besides the traditional arrogance of the Prussian officer corps vis-à-vis civilians, one of the main reasons for these rivalries was professionalism. Moltke was probably the first modern professional soldier in a high-ranking Prussian command. He reorganized the General Staff according to strictly bureaucratic principles, where efficiency and matter-of-factness reigned supreme. His only aim was to carry out his duties perfectly. But in this task, he was not prepared to allow any outsider to interfere. Hence, despite Ritter's assertion to the contrary,[40] and despite the fact that he certainly did not take a narrow-minded view of the world, Moltke was clearly a professional soldier in the sense of historian Morris Janowitz's analysis,[41] who in his official capacity judged matters from a purely military standpoint.[42]

Bismarck, however, was just as much a professional, albeit a first-rate professional politician. He was certainly as dedicated to his job as Moltke. But his appetite for power knew almost no bounds, and politics to him meant to be in control. This was particularly true in time of war. Bismarck was not very keen to wage war, but he did not shy away from employing war as a means of policy if he deemed it necessary. His foreign policy, however, aimed only at

---

38   See Ritter, *Staatskunst*, 1 : 231–4, and Wehler, *Kaiserreich*, 152–3.
39   Förster, *Militarismus*, 108–296.   40   Ritter, *Staatskunst*, 1 : 246.
41   Morris Janowitz, *The Professional Soldier: A Social and Political Portrait* (New York, 1960).
42   For a neat characterization of Moltke as a professional soldier, see Alfred Vagts, *A History of Militarism: Civilian and Military*, 2d ed. (London, 1959), 201. For Moltke's bureaucratization of the General Staff, see Arden Bucholz, *Moltke, Schlieffen, and Prussian War Planning* (New York, 1991), 39–43.

limited changes in Europe, not at revolutionary upheavals that could threaten Prussia with a disastrous all-out conflict. Hence, to Bismarck, war was a rather confined means to obtain limited aims, and the political leadership, therefore, had to remain firmly in control of its instrument. He fought to the point of physical exhaustion against the opposition of Wilhelm I in 1866 and of Moltke in 1870–71 to keep matters in hand.[43]

Long before 1870, there had been tensions between Moltke and Bismarck. For political reasons, the chief of the General Staff always favored a war against the "archenemy," France, who stood in the way of German unity. Moltke regarded such a war as unavoidable. For military reasons, he demanded a preventive war as soon as possible in order to exploit France's weakness, either because the French were engaged elsewhere or because French armament was lagging behind Prussia's. Already in spring 1859, Moltke had asked Wilhelm I to attack France while it was fighting against Austria in Italy.[44] In 1860, 1866, and 1867, he repeated his demands for a preventive action. But each time he was refused. Moltke grew bitterly resentful over the "timidity" of the government and particularly Bismarck, who in 1866 and 1867 had forcefully rejected his proposals.[45] Perhaps without realizing it, however, Moltke had clearly transgressed his domain, thereby arousing Bismarck's suspicion. It is important to note that in extending the limits of his professional position to the full, the general had meddled with politics, an early example of "militaristic" behavior.

Bismarck also did not hesitate to interfere in Moltke's affairs. In the winter of 1865–66, the general had prepared a strategic plan for a war against Austria and its German allies. Moltke intended to denude Prussia's provinces in western Germany of troops almost completely and to concentrate most available forces for an invasion of Bohemia.[46] Bismarck did not like this plan, because he feared adverse political consequences if the Rhineland should be overrun by Austria's allies. Supported by War Minister Albrecht Count von Roon, he therefore demanded a change of strategy, leaving more troops in the west. Only the king's intervention saved Moltke's plan, but the officers in the General Staff did not forget the meddling of the civilian prime minister in military matters.[47] Hence, when war broke out in 1870, there was already tension in the Prussian triangle of leadership.

43 Gall, *Bismarck*, 366–7.
44 Moltke's memorandum of Feb. 26, 1859, and notes for an interview with Wilhelm I of May 19, 1859, *Moltkes militärische Werke*, 1/4:41–50, 103–9.
45 Stadelmann, *Moltke*, 120–41, 179–93, 197–203; and Kessel, *Moltke*, 352.
46 Moltke's strategic plan of winter 1865–66, *Moltkes militärische* Werke, 1/4:31–45.
47 Prince Friedrich Karl von Preussen, *Denkwürdigkeiten aus seinem Leben*, ed. Wolfgang Förster, 2 vols. (Stuttgart, 1910), 2: 12.

THE CLASH

From the very beginning of the war, high-ranking officers tried to make life difficult for Bismarck, who after 1866 had been elevated to the position of chancellor of the newly founded North German Federation. Once again, the king, important members of the cabinet, and top military officials formed a royal headquarters, traveling jointly to the front. During the journey, Bismarck in his rail compartment overheard a conversation between War Minister Roon and Quartermaster General von Podbielski in which Podbielski boasted that this time the chancellor would be prevented from meddling in military affairs.[48] Indeed, on their arrival in Mainz on August 2, 1870, the officers in charge of quartering made sure that the fuming Bismarck was housed as far away as possible from the king.[49] It stayed that way for the rest of the campaign.

But in the first four weeks, there was no serious trouble, as Prussia's winning team once again raced from success to success. First of all, it certainly helped their relationship that both Bismarck and Moltke had finally agreed on the desirability of war against France. When Bismarck in the presence of Roon and Moltke had falsified the king's cable from Bad Ems on July 13, thus making war unavoidable, Moltke exclaimed joyfully: "If I am to live to lead our armies in such a war, then the devil may come immediately afterward to take my old carcass."[50] Moreover, the shining victories of the German allies over the French, culminating in Wimpffen's surrender at Sedan and the capture of Napoléon III on September 2, glossed over most ill feelings. The war appeared to be won.

Once again, Moltke's strategy of rapid overthrow, on which Bismarck's policy depended, seemed to have worked. But Moltke's strategic planning had not really solved the problem of how to convert initially stunning successes over the French into a rapid victorious end of the war. In fact, as late as January 1867, Moltke had feared that "due to the patriotism of that nation," even a heavy defeat in battle would not convince the French to give in. Instead, they would mobilize their considerable resources for a continuation of the war.[51] Only in his final strategic plan of winter 1868–69 had Moltke

---

48 Bismarck made this allegation during an interview with the military historian Fritz A. Hoenig on March 3, 1895. See Eberhard Kolb, "Strategie und Politik in den deutschen Einigungskriegen: Ein unbekanntes Bismarck-Gespräch aus dem Jahre 1895," *Militärgeschichtliche Mitteilungen* 48, no. 2 (1990):131.

49 Heinrich Otto Meisner, ed., *Denkwürdigkeiten des General-Feldmarschalls Alfred Grafen Waldersee*, 3 vols. (Berlin, 1923), 1:83.

50 Quoted from Kessel, *Moltke*, 544.

51 Moltke's memorandum of Jan. 1867 on a war against France and Austria, *Generalfeldmarschall Helmuth von Moltke: Ausgewählte Werke*, ed. Ferdinand von Schmerfeld, 4 vols. (Berlin, 1925), 3:62.

deluded himself with the notion that after a few decisive battles peace could be made quickly, "since we do not want anything from France."[52]

But this argument was bogus, because the political and military leadership as well as public opinion of the newly emerging Germany did indeed want something from France. Since 1859, Moltke himself had always demanded the annexation of Alsace in case of war against the French.[53] Now, in the face of his glorious victories, he pressed Bismarck hard to punish the "archenemy" and to seize this formerly German province as insurance against future aggression. Moltke did not find it difficult to convince Bismarck. Not believing in the possibility of reconciliation with the French, the chancellor himself had, since the outbreak of war, contemplated the annexation of Alsace and the fortress of Metz. Since pressure from public opinion and from high-ranking personalities within the royal headquarters pointed in the same direction, Bismarck stuck by his intention. On September 18 at Ferrières, he presented the French foreign minister, Jules Favre, with his brutal demands, thereby making it impossible for Favre to agree to a settlement. The French were forced to continue the war.[54] Thus, the German campaign against France ceased to be another cabinet war and became what underlying tendencies in public opinion and leadership had driven it toward from the outset: a war with nationalistic aspirations. Following their own nationalistic instincts and alleged military necessities of the future, the Prussian triangle of leadership had decisively deviated from their own recipe for success: short, intense wars for limited aims. In doing so, they opened a Pandora's box of people's war.

There is no need here to analyze in detail the people's war of 1870–71. This is done by other contributions in this book. Instead, this chapter concentrates on Bismarck's and Moltke's actions under the new challenge. On September 2, 1870, half an hour after the signing of the French surrender at Sedan, Moltke directed his troops to march on Paris in order to enforce the demands for widespread annexations. Bismarck disliked this order, as he wrote to his son Herbert on September 7. He would have preferred that the German armies stay put and allow the French to remain anxious and fearful.[55] And

---

52 Moltke's memorandum of winter 1868–69, *Moltkes militärische Werke*, 1/1: 116.
53 See, e.g., Moltke's memorandum of Feb. 26, 1859, *Moltkes militärische Werke*, 1/4: 42.
54 On Bismarck's early readiness to annex Alsace-Lorraine, see Josef Becker, "Baden, Bismarck und die Annexion von Elsass und Lothringen," in Alfons Schäfer, ed., *Oberrheinische Studien*, 2 vols. (Karlsruhe, 1973), 2: 133–73. In general terms, see Howard, *Franco-Prussian War*, 227–33. As a failed attempt to justify the annexation as the result of a complicated decision-making process and the understandable wish for greater security vis-à-vis France, see recently Eberhard Kolb, *Der Weg aus dem Krieg: Bismarcks Politik im Krieg und die Friedensanbahnung, 1870–71* (Munich, 1989), esp. 168–93.
55 Howard, *Franco-Prussian War*, 229.

he was probably right. Moltke, believing the war won and the French broken, overestimated the military importance of Paris and underestimated the strength of unoccupied France to continue the war effort.[56] In fact, the Germans had to face twelve more pitched battles before the war was finally over.[57]

Indeed, according to Alfred Count von Waldersee's memoirs, as late as October 7 Moltke did not grasp the severity of the situation and stated that the war was basically over, that one witnessed only the death throes of the French, and that no major action was to be expected anymore.[58] But on November 23, he complained in a letter to his brother Adolf about the horrors of people's war, and on December 18, he wrote to his friend, Privy Counselor Scheller, that nobody knew when this horrible war would end, as "A whole people in arms must not be underestimated."[59] Since the French continued to fight even after their defeat in the battle of Orléans on December 5, people's war had become an undeniable reality, and Moltke grew increasingly nervous about this.

If Moltke grew nervous, Bismarck panicked. His hopes for a rapid victory were shattered, and he had nightmares about an intervention by neutral powers. The continued resistance of the regular French armies was bad enough, but Bismarck was even more outraged by the guerrilla warfare of the franc-tireurs, which cost the Germans more than 1,000 men and forced them to deploy more than 120,000 men in the rear to defend their lines of communication.[60] Hence, Bismarck was very impressed with the advice of the American Gen. Philip H. Sheridan, who stayed with the royal headquarters, until the siege of Paris, to employ the tactics he had used during the American Civil War by burning down enemy villages.[61] In mid-December, therefore, an angry Bismarck proposed to Wilhelm I to take hostages, employ systematic terror against civilians, and take fewer prisoners in battle. But the king and Moltke did not follow this brutal and foolish advice. Instead, Moltke bitterly resented this and other unwarranted interference in his domain by the chancellor.[62]

By this time, the clash between Bismarck and Moltke was already fully under way. Bismarck became increasingly incensed by the refusal of most

56 Kessel, *Moltke*, 572; and Helmert and Usczeck, *Preussisch-deutsche Kriege*, 228–31.
57 Moltke, "Geschichte des Krieges, 1870–71," *Ausgewahlte Werke*, 2: 446.
58 Meisner, *Denkwürdigkeiten Waldersee*, 1:100–1.
59 Moltke to his brother Adolf, Nov. 23, 1870 and to Geheimrat Scheller, Dec. 18, 1870, *Gesammelte Schriften*, 4:199–204, 5:179.
60 Walter Laqueur, *Guerrilla: A Historical and Critical Study* (London, 1977), 84–6.
61 Meisner, *Denkwürdigkeiten Waldersee*, 1:100–1.
62 Bismarck's memorandum of Dec. 14, 1870, published in his *Die gesammelten Werke* [Friedrichsruh edition], 15 vols. (Berlin, 1924–32), 6b:632–7; see also Engelberg, *Bismarck*, 742; and Ritter, *Staatskunst*, 1: 280–2.

army authorities to work with him. As early as September 9, he had been angered by the General Staff's decision to assume control over the chancellor's appointee as commander of the military police, in charge of dealing with civilians in occupied France.[63] On October 17, he wrote a harsh letter to the chief of the General Staff of Prince Friedrich Karl, who, despite an order by the king, had refused to allow the French general Bourbaki to reenter the beleaguered fortress of Metz.[64]

Worse from Bismarck's point of view was the fact that the General Staff was not prepared to discuss future military operations with the chancellor, or even to keep him informed about the military situation. Bismarck had to rely on newspapers(!) and a few more easily accessible officers, such as Waldersee,[65] to learn the latest news from the fronts. Clearly, the "demi-gods in uniform" wanted to prevent Bismarck from meddling in military matters, and Moltke personally intended in such a way to remain on equal footing with the chancellor, since the chief of the General Staff was not consulted in political affairs either.[66]

On October 22, Bismarck protested directly to Moltke, and when this action was to no avail, he wrote the king on December 5.[67] As foreign minister and chancellor, he demanded to be consulted on military reports "which touch and influence political problems." He also asked to be allowed to approach the General Staff directly in order to obtain military information which he required to fulfill his duties. In his letter to Wilhelm I, Bismarck used as a pretext for his demands the allegation that he had not been informed about a communication between Moltke and General Trochu, the commander of Paris. But this was not true, as Moltke had sent Colonel Bronsart von Schellendorf to consult the chancellor on that matter. Thus, Bismarck was even ready to lie to have his way, which further enraged his military adversaries.[68]

Wilhelm I was clearly impressed by Bismarck's forceful demands, and on December 17, he ordered the General Staff to inform the chancellor in advance of planned military operations. But a disgruntled von Schellendorf refused to obey, since he feared for Moltke's unrestricted command.

63 Meisner, *Denkwürdigkeiten Waldersee*, 1:95.
64 Bismarck to Major General von Stiehle, chief of the General Staff with Prince Friedrich Karl, Oct. 17, 1870, Bismarck, *Werke*, 6b:551–3.
65 Waldersee was apparently flattered by regular invitations to dine with Bismarck and Bismarck's offer to make him military governor of an occupied Paris. Meisner, *Denkwürdigkeiten Waldersee*, 1:96–7, 117.
66 Ritter, *Staatskunst*, 1:258–9.
67 Bismarck to Moltke, Oct. 22, 1870, and his memorandum to the king of Dec. 5, 1870, Bismarck, *Werke*, 6b:558, 615–17.
68 Engelberg, *Bismarck*, 743–4.

Threatening to resign, he convinced the wavering king to rescind the order.[69] Bismarck was outraged, and on January 9, 1871, he repeated his demands to Wilhelm I even more forcefully.[70]

The real issue of the clash, however, ran much deeper than the mere question of whether Bismarck was to be kept informed about military decisions. In fact, Bismarck and Moltke battled over the further conduct of war against France in general. Their first point of disagreement was how to force the surrender of Paris.

On September 19, 1870, 150,000 German troops completed their encirclement of heavily fortified Paris, thereby trapping 350,000 badly trained but highly motivated French troops and threatening the city with starvation. The French commander, General Trochu, believed that the only way of avoiding the ultimate surrender of the capital lay in an outright German attack, in which the enemy would suffer heavy casualties.[71] But Moltke had no intention of doing Trochu such a favor. Instead, he stated as late as October 20 that he wanted to wait until hunger had forced Trochu's hand.[72]

Such a strategy required time, however, something that Bismarck firmly believed the Germans did not have because of continued warfare in the provinces and pressure by the neutrals. The chancellor now held Moltke personally responsible for the alleged feeble manner in which the siege of Paris was conducted. Clearly ignorant of military realities, Bismarck would have loved to see a direct assault on Paris by late September, as he wrote maliciously to the king on December 28.[73] When this "chance" was missed, Bismarck in October forcefully demanded an immediate bombardment of Paris to hasten the city's surrender.[74] But Moltke refused, since, as he probably justly claimed, the meager lines of communication to Paris prevented the speedy transport of a viable siege train containing heavy artillery and sufficient ammunition for the German forces.[75] Still, preparations for a bombardment were made, but if anything painfully slowly. It may even well be that Moltke deliberately held up these preparations in order to teach Bismarck a lesson.[76]

But Bismarck was in no mood to allow any further delay. On November 28, he approached Wilhelm I directly and demanded an immediate

---

69 Ibid., 744, and Ritter, *Staatskunst*, 1 : 258.
70 Bismarck's memorandum to Wilhelm I, Jan. 9, 1871, Bismarck, *Werke*, 6b : 658–60.
71 Howard, *Franco-Prussian War*, 318–22.
72 Ibid., 329.
73 Bismarck's memorandum to Wilhelm I, Dec. 28, 1870 (submitted on Jan. 1, 1871), Bismarck, *Werke*, 6b : 648–51.
74 See, e.g., Waldersee's diary note of Oct. 23, 1870, Meisner, *Denkwürdigkeiten Waldersee*, 1 : 102–3.
75 Helmert and Usczeck, *Preussisch-deutsche Kriege*, 235–44. See also Moltke's self-justification, Moltke, "Geschichte des Krieges, 1870–71," 405–8.
76 Stadelmann, *Moltke*, 234.

bombardment, because from a political point of view there was no time to wait for a surrender brought about by starvation.[77] On December 14, in combination with the aforementioned proposal, Bismarck repeated his request to intensify warfare in the provinces by terrorizing civilians and taking fewer prisoners. He justified these demands by stating that such a strategy would ultimately be humane even for the enemy: "Every means which hastens the end is beneficent to both warring parties."[78]

By then, the question of if and when to shell Paris had deeply divided the German political and military leadership. The crown prince and most high-ranking officers supported the General Staff on military or humanitarian grounds or because they despised Bismarck's interference. But War Minister Roon, jealous of Moltke, sided with Bismarck. Hence, there was no generally clear-cut division between civilians and the military. It was rather a confrontation between the General Staff and Bismarck, the two lower ends of the Prussian triangle of leadership in wartime.[79]

In mid-December 1870, however, pressure was mounting for Moltke to commence shelling. After the fall of most French fortresses to the east, the lines of communication to Paris had been restored, and the artillery was ready for action. Perhaps even more important was the fact that Wilhelm I now came down on Bismarck's side. On December 17, therefore, a military council, presided over by the king, decided to begin with an experimental shelling of Mount Avron in preparation for an all-out bombardment of Paris. The officers in command of the artillery attack were confidants of Bismarck.[80] Indeed, shelling began on December 27 and was so successful that the Germans could take the important positions on Mount Avron the following day. On January 5, 1871, the German guns opened fire on the French forts outside Paris and soon afterward on the city itself.[81] Bismarck had scored a major victory over Moltke.

Their conflict, however, was far from over. The continued staunch resistance of Léon Gambetta's armies in the French provinces had, in the course of December, finally convinced Moltke that this was no ordinary war. He now came to the conclusion that the only way to deal with the French *guerre à outrance* was to respond in kind. Moltke believed that any negotiations with the enemy had become futile. The war could only be fought until the complete occupation of France. Then the German governments could dictate

---

77 Bismarck's memorandum to Wilhelm I, Nov. 28, 1870, Bismarck, *Werke*, 6b:602–4.
78 Bismarck's memorandum to Wilhelm I, Dec. 14, 1870, ibid., 623–7.
79 For details, see Howard, *Franco-Prussian War*, 350–5.
80 Meisner, *Denkwürdigkeiten Waldersee*, 1:117–19.
81 Howard, *Franco-Prussian War*, 355–63; and Helmert and Usczeck, *Preussisch-deutsche Kriege*, 240–76.

the harshest conditions for peace. But until that moment, the politicians had to desist from interfering and leave it to the military commanders to lead the war to total victory.[82]

This stance was the main issue that led to yet another confrontation with Bismarck. On January 13, the crown prince invited the two adversaries to a meeting, hoping to achieve a reconciliation. But the endeavor turned into a disaster. Bismarck severely criticized the conduct of the war so far and then went on to propose that after the surrender of Paris, the city should not be occupied by German troops. Moltke flatly rejected such a notion and angrily insisted on occupation. It now became clear that Bismarck sought a rapid compromise with any French government, preferably one of Bonapartist nature, whereas Moltke aimed at breaking France completely by totally destroying all its means of resistance.[83]

From that point forward, Moltke was even more determined not to cooperate with Bismarck and to leave the final decision to the wavering king. On January 14, he wrote to Wilhelm I demanding the harshest conditions for Paris, including military occupation and the imprisonment of the whole garrison.[84] All this was designed not to make a rapid end to the war possible but to provide a military basis for the continuation of warfare until the complete occupation of France and thus until total victory. Bismarck protested on the same day, claiming that it was necessary to make compromises in order to gain peace quickly.[85]

Once again, Bismarck's argumentation won the day. Although Wilhelm I, who had been proclaimed emperor on January 18, sided emotionally with Moltke, he had to give in to Bismarck's more reasonable course. On January 25, the emperor issued two strongly worded orders, commanding the General Staff once and for all to keep Bismarck fully informed about military operations and to consult with him before communicating with French officials. Moltke was on the verge of resigning, but upon second thought he decided grudgingly to accept defeat.[86]

Meanwhile, on January 23, Bismarck had opened secret negotiations with Favre to secure the surrender of Paris. This new turn of events helped him to bring Wilhelm I over to his side. More important, it led to his final triumph. The emperor entrusted him with the sole authority to continue the negotiations, and on January 26, he accepted Bismarck's relatively moderate stance

---

82 Stadelmann, *Moltke*, 237–9.
83 Friedrich III, German Emperor, *Das Kriegstagebuch von 1870–71*, ed. Heinrich-Otto Meisner (Berlin, 1926), 319, 322, 325.
84 Stadelmann, *Moltke*, 246; and Ritter, *Staatskunst*, 1:283.
85 Bismarck's memorandum to Wilhelm I, Dec. 14, 1870, Bismarck, *Werke*, 6b:665–6.
86 Howard, *Franco-Prussian War*, 438.

regarding the terms. The disgruntled Moltke was only able to limit the scope
of the negotiations to Paris in order to allow Gen. Edwin von Manteuffel to
smash Bourbaki's army in the south. Bismarck did indeed succeed in convincing Favre to surrender quickly by not demanding a German occupation of Paris.[87]

In the following weeks, the chancellor even managed to bring the whole
war to a close. On February 26, a preliminary peace was signed. But its
conditions were still rather brutal. France had to pay reparations, to suffer
temporary occupation of its eastern territory, and, worst of all, to cede
Alsace as well as parts of Lorraine, including the fortress of Metz.

Moltke, who had asked for even more (for example, Belfort), regarded
these terms as the minimum acceptable to make Germany's future military
situation vis-à-vis France safer. And this time, he had the emperor on his side.
Bismarck, therefore, did not dare to challenge Moltke once again, despite
the fact that the chancellor had become uneasy about the prospect of incorporating the French population of Lorraine into the new Reich. Thus,
the German terms for peace, by giving Moltke some consolation, were
partially the result of "militaristic" influence. At least as far as Metz was concerned, military considerations prevailed over political reason. Moltke had
managed, through the back door, to salvage a bit of his concept of total
victory.[88] The people's war in France, therefore, came to its logical conclusion: a harsh peace based on nationalistic instincts and militaristic aspirations.

THE SIGNIFICANCE OF THE CONFLICT

From a superficial point of view, there can be little doubt that the conflict
between Bismarck and Moltke was a battle for supremacy in time of war
between political leadership and military command. The widely accepted
assessment by Ritter, Hahlweg, Peter Paret, and others – that this was a
classical conflict between policy and strategy in a Clausewitzean sense – seems
therefore to be justified. Just as correct appears to be the analysis that the
impact of people's war brought matters to a head.

Indeed, the Prussian triangle of leadership, with its relatively modern
division of labor on the basis of professionalism, which had worked so well
in 1866, proved insufficient in 1870–71. When the war against France
intensified and showed no signs of abating, the already strained relationship
between Bismarck and Moltke cracked, and each of them tried to force
through his own professional point of view. Wilhelm I was too weak to

---

87   See Bismarck, *Werke*, 6b: 676–8; and Howard, *Franco-Prussian War*, 438–43.
88   Ritter, *Staatskunst*, 1: 323–9; and Howard, *Franco-Prussian War*, 432–47.

impose his own ideas on the conduct of war, that is, if he had any cogent ideas at all. Instead, he wavered between the two other points of the triangle, thereby prolonging and aggravating the conflict. But at least he had the sense to support Bismarck at the decisive moment, when an end to the war became a real possibility.

From the outset, Bismarck had been hampered by the constitutional peculiarities of Prussia and his own promise to defend the royal supreme command over the army at all costs. He therefore had little say in military matters. But nevertheless, when the General Staff failed to provide him with another rapid victory, he attempted to influence German strategy. Put together, his demands amounted indeed to nothing less than a claim to general supremacy over the army, giving him the right to issue political guidelines as to what was militarily desirable. Two decades later, Bismarck justified his stance by referring expressly to Clausewitz's ideas concerning the relationship between political leadership and military command.[89] But it was certainly no coincidence that a major issue for the conflict between Bismarck and Moltke lay exactly in that gray area of Clausewitz's theory, where the politician was not supposed to make any militarily impossible demands. Bismarck did precisely that when he asked for a rapid bombardment of Paris and even criticized Moltke for not having taken the city by storm. At this point, Bismarck clearly overstepped his bounds and gave Moltke every reason to fight back.

Moltke, in contrast, was not satisfied with just defending his constitutionally guaranteed autonomy vis-à-vis the chancellor. Already before the war he had meddled with politics by demanding a preventive attack on France for military reasons. This would have meant giving the army a say in the profoundly political question, namely, if and when war should be declared. Now, during the war and particularly in January 1871, Moltke wanted to keep Bismarck out of the picture altogether, especially in the pursuit of total victory. Only a few months after the war, Moltke, while deceptively using Clausewitzean terminology, justified his position in an essay "On Strategy" as follows:

Policy uses war to achieve its aims. It influences decisively the beginning and the end of war, but in such a way as to increase or lower the aims during its course. Owing to this uncertainty, strategy can only go after the greatest possible achievement. In such a way, strategy helps policy best, for the latter's aim only, but acting completely independent of it.[90]

89 Bismarck during his interview with Hoenig in 1895, Kolb, "Strategie," 128–9.
90 Moltke, "Über Strategie," *Moltkes militärische Werke*, 2/2: 291-3.

In other words: Since politicians were unpredictable anyway, the generals had to go it alone until total victory. In reality, however, as events during the Franco-Prussian War had demonstrated, this also meant that Moltke claimed the right to set terms for negotiations with the enemy on armistice and peace as the only way to win total victory in the face of the machinations of too lenient politicians. This was a clear-cut intervention into the domain of policy and put Moltke and his supporters on the road to militarism, according to Ritter's narrow definition.

In this contest, the generally accepted argument states that Bismarck scored a temporary victory particularly by asserting his exclusive authority to conduct negotiations with the enemy and to bring the war to an end. This victory, however, important as it was, was marred by the General Staff's success in forcing the annexation of Metz. Moreover, Bismarck had not established his supremacy in principle, which left room for the generals in later years not only to regain their autonomy but also to establish "militaristic" rule in the end.

But this rather traditional argumentation, which has been slightly revamped here, is not sufficient to grasp the whole significance of the conflict. Its main shortcoming is the underestimation of the impact of people's war as such. In fact, the people's war in France did not just trigger the clash between Bismarck and Moltke; rather, it was the main issue of their conflict. Or to put it more precisely, the chancellor and the general did not merely struggle over the relatively formalistic question of supremacy or autonomy. More importantly, they also fought over the very concrete problem of the most suitable political and military strategy in people's war.

Bismarck himself had contributed to the emergence of the first industrialized people's war on European soil. But he was horrified when the French reacted to his demand to cede large chunks of territory by waging *guerre à outrance*. The new character of warfare at the very least threatened his system of diplomacy, and Bismarck therefore became determined to bring this war to an end as quickly as possible. But under the pressure of public opinion at home, the military, and the royal headquarters, Bismarck could not retreat from the demand for annexations, even had he wanted to. Hence, the only way left open to him was a return to the previously highly successful Prussian mode of warfare, that is, the application of extreme force in order to achieve rapid victory, while pursuing still relatively moderate war aims. Under the prevailing circumstances, however, a complete return to the old ways of industrialized cabinet war was impossible. The chance for a brief and decisive military campaign was gone, and the stakes were too high now for the French to simply give in.

After October 1870, Bismarck therefore pushed for a strategy that would put the Prussian mode of warfare on a more intensive level. All means were to be employed to bring a rapid victory, but at the same time, the French were not to be confronted with even more brutal and dishonoring demands, in order to allow them a way to compromise. All of Bismarck's proposals for the continuation of the war went in this direction. He demanded the immediate shelling of Paris, including civilian targets, and he proposed the most reckless application of force in the provinces in order to break the resistance of the enemy quickly. But he was also ready to accept relatively lenient terms for the surrender of Paris, and in the subsequent peace negotiations, he resisted any temptation to crush France once and for all.

Basically, Bismarck still regarded war as a matter between states and their legitimate governments. In this context, war was to him a justifiable tool of European power politics.[91] But it was only to be waged by responsible institutions—not by the people. The monopoly of the state in the use of force had to remain intact. Those who acted against this principle were to be punished severely. This stance explains Bismarck's outrage over the people's war in France and his occasionally wild demands for harsh measures. In general, however, Bismarck's solution to the dangerous problem of people's war consisted of finding a rapid and relatively moderate closure to the war, thereby restoring order in Europe. To this end, Bismarck was also ready, as subsequent events demonstrated, to lend a helping hand to the French government in crushing the Commune of Paris. Bismarck's policy during the war can be therefore best described as a conservative strategy to restore law and order in the wake of people's war.

Moltke was just as horrified as Bismarck when the war turned into a *guerre à outrance*. As an institution, the General Staff had been created to plan for military campaigns, not for an all-out war. For the latter, it would have required the close cooperation of at least the war ministry and the chancellor, which, if only for reasons of departmental egoism, was not forthcoming.[92] Moltke was therefore not prepared for things to come, and he was literally flabbergasted by the turn of events. Only in December did he begin to find a new strategy. But in January when he confronted the amazed crown prince and Bismarck with his ideas, he had indeed come up with a radical solution. His answer to people's war was the quest for total victory, the complete and

---

91 See Michael Salewksi, "Krieg und Frieden im Denken Bismarcks und Moltkes," in Roland G. Foerster, ed., *Generalfeldmarschall von Moltke: Bedeutung und Wirkung* (Munich, 1991), 67–88.

92 For a more detailed analysis of this point, see Stig Förster, "Helmuth von Moltke und das Problem des industrialisierten Volkskriegs im 19. Jahrhundert," in Roland G. Foerster, ed., *Generalfeldmarschall von Moltke*, 116–17.

lasting defeat of France. He wanted to conquer the whole country, allowing no compromises with the vanquished, and during the peace negotiations, he pressed Bismarck for ever harder terms. Thus, Moltke left behind the Prussian mode of warfare and took a decisive step toward the radicalization of war, where no mercy was to be shown, and not only the regular army, but the whole basis for resistance in the state and society of the enemy, was to be annihilated. Unlike Bismarck, therefore, Moltke did not only aim at containing this people's war by bringing it to a speedy end, but he planned to eradicate the social basis for this dangerous attack on the state's monopoly for the use of force once and for all. France and the French people, whom he regarded not without reason as the traditional hotbed of revolution in Europe, were to be forever deprived of the means to pose a meaningful threat to other states.

This was not a conservative strategy anymore. Instead, by intending to use a regular and well-trained conscript army under the firm control of its traditional military leadership for the attempt to crush a whole people, Moltke planned for a new level of destruction, a new level of modern warfare: total war. Total war at this point appeared to represent a dialectical answer to people's war. It was the attempt to defend the state's monopoly of the use of force (*Gewaltmonopol*) against the revolutionary power of people's war by destroying the latter's bases of support. To this end, however, it required the mighty force of a regular conscript army, the domesticated form of the people in arms under firm leadership. In this sense, the concept of total war was in its origins a further developed form of people's war: better organized, firmly controlled from above, and tending to be even more radical in its aims. It certainly went far beyond the traditional practice of cabinet war, since the concept of total war was deeply rooted in nationalistic aspirations and prejudices like Moltke's notion of France as the archenemy, and it could be carried out only by a modern conscript army, which was backed by powerful nationalistic public opinion at home. But the concept of total war, in a paradoxical way, also tended to deprive the Prussian triangle of leadership of its exclusive clout in matters of war by making it dependent on the support of public opinion. Thus, limiting war, the only way to make the use of military force a rational means of conservative cabinet policy, became extremely difficult. Moreover, since Moltke did not trust France's politicians, never mind their political stance, there would be no room for compromise with the enemy's government. Under these circumstances, the war could drag on for a very long time, wreaking chaos, perhaps making the restoration of law and order in France impossible, thereby threatening the existing order in Europe and endangering the position of the Prussian triangle of leadership at home, which had only just been salvaged from the constitutional conflict with parliament. All this made Moltke's radical plans unacceptable to Bismarck's conservative policy.[93]

The clash of these two concepts was the climax of the confrontation between Bismarck and Moltke. Since Bismarck won and Moltke failed, people in subsequent generations have tended to forget how close Europe came in the winter of 1871 to the brink of catastrophe. But for a couple of weeks, in fact, the Germans and the French stood at the verge of total war, and no one knows how the neutral powers would have reacted if total war had become a reality. In any case, this confrontation was a sincere warning of things to come.

The problem of militarism therefore was not the only legacy of the conflict between Bismarck and Moltke. In fact, after 1871 Bismarck managed quite well to keep Moltke in check, in particular when the chief of the General Staff in 1875 and 1887 once again demanded preventive war.[94] The ascendancy of the generals only gained momentum after 1900 under the weak leadership of Chancellor Bernhard von Bülow.[95] During World War I, however, under Ludendorff's virtual dictatorship, when the Prussian triangle of

---

93 Moltke himself, after all a conservative too, was not sure whether this was indeed a desirable strategy. His suggestion to embark on total war was rather an act of desperation than a rational program. He would have preferred to stick with a strategy of cabinet war, but the experience of people's war, to his mind, left him with no other choice. Still, he abhorred people's war and, by implication, the notion of total war. In his later years, with hindsight, he warned the German public of the terrible danger of just another, even bigger war of this sort. In his last speach in the *Reichstag*, he outlined the origins of this development and almost prophetically described its possible consequences:

> The age of cabinet war is behind us – all we have now is people's war, and any prudent government will hesitate to bring about a war of this nature with all its incalculable consequences.
>
> No, gentlemen, the elements that endanger peace are to be found among the people: domestically, the covetousness of the classes that are less favored by fate, externally, certain national and racial aspirations, everywhere a dissatisfaction with the existing state of affairs. This can lead to the outbreak of war at any time, without the will of the rulers or even *against* their will because, gentlemen, a government that is not strong enough to oppose the passions of the people and the ambitions of the parties – a weak government – is a constant threat of war.
>
> Gentlemen, if the war that has been hanging over our heads for more than ten years like the Sword of Damokles – if this war breaks out, then if its duration and its end will not be foreseeable. The greatest powers of Europe, armed as never before, will be going into battle with each other; not one of them can be crushed so completely in one or two campaigns that it will admit defeat, be compelled to conclude peace under hard terms, and will not come back, even if it is a year later, to renew the struggle. Gentlemen, it may be a war of seven years' or of thirty years' duration – and woe to him who sets Europe alight, who first puts the fuse to the powder keg!

Moltke's speech in the *Reichstag*, May 14, 1890, *Stenographische Berichte über die Verhandlungen des Reichstags 1890–91*, 114:76-7. For an interpretation, see Stig Förster, "Facing People's War: Moltke the Elder and Germany's Military Options after 1871," *Journal of Strategic Studies* 10, no. 2 (1987): 222–5.

94 See Förster, "Facing People's War," 218–22.

95 Showalter, "German Grand Strategy," 78–9.

leadership collapsed altogether, the army did indeed take over.[96] Neverthe-less, militarism was not the only scourge in Germany's modern history. This became apparent, if anything, during World War II, when the ideolog-ical dictatorship of the Nazis, often against the advice of rather subdued generals, embarked on the most total war to date.[97]

The Prussian mode of warfare, which Bismarck had barely reinstated in the second phase of the Franco-Prussian War, had vanished. Not only did the Schlieffen Plan fail in 1914, but it also lacked the corresponding limited war aims.[98] Thereafter, Ludendorff propagated total war, and Hitler went even further in this direction. Herein lay the most awesome legacy of 1870–71. What had been just barely avoided at the time became a terrible reality in two world wars of the twentieth century. Catastrophe came true, when Germany, either led by generals or by politicians, traveled the entire road to total war.

96   Van Creveld, *Transformation of War*, 43–5.
97   See the interesting analysis in Kondylis, *Theorie des Krieges*, 114–15.
98   Showalter, "German Grand Strategy, " 82.

7

Union Generalship, Political Leadership, and Total War Strategy

EDWARD HAGERMAN

The American Civil War introduced modern total war. For the first time, politicians and generals organized the total human and material resources of a mass industrial society for war and turned them to the total destruction of the resources, as well as the social and political system, of another society. For the first time, modern technology combined with modern ideology to realize Carl von Clausewitz's prognosis that the ideological currents of modern nationalism, carried on the backs of citizen armies, would intensify the totality of warfare.

This analysis assumes a definition of total war taken from Clausewitz and ultimately from the convergence of the ideas of Kant and Hegel in his thought. It assumes that pure total war is a logical abstraction, useful as a reference to pure logical limits along a plane from limited to total war. But we pursue military analysis within the real world of practical reason, where historically bound actors make decisions about changing technology, society, and culture, employing a practical balance of critical and intuitive levels of understanding. From this perspective, total war exists as a process of moving toward totality and away from the countervailing tendency toward limitation. This perspective rejects any definition of total war as a static mechanistic construct that requires all of its parts in place before the definition of totality is applied. Conceding the failure of any attempt to change the language usage from the mechanistic term *total war*, this analysis defines total war as this process of the balance shifting toward the totalizing of warfare.

From this perspective, the Civil War was the first total war within the particular historical circumstances of modern warfare. And modern warfare was grounded in the attempt to define the limits of military force, while integrating modern industrial technology, the ideologies of nationalism and liberal democracy, and the techniques of mass organization.

The form that Civil War strategy assumed was to a surprising degree shaped by a politician and two generals. Abraham Lincoln and the composite

141

personality and generalship of Ulysses S. Grant and William Tecumseh Sherman came close to representing Hegel's "world-historical individuals": leaders who acted with an intuitive sense of the historical moment to bring about changes beyond their full comprehension. The context within which Lincoln, Grant, and Sherman changed warfare was driven by ideology in an environment shaped by the transition of mid-nineteenth century America to a mass industrial democracy. Lincoln used the Republican Party and the presidency to provide both a radical reading of ideology and the political vision and organization to advance it. Grant and Sherman used the Union armies to implement a radical reading of military strategy essential to Lincoln's goals. Their combined impetus pushed the modern form of total war across the historical threshold.

James McPherson's thoughtful study of Lincoln as a war president analyzes how he came to his political grand strategy of total war by an ideological route.[1] He arrived when he resolved the basic contradiction in his political world view. Lincoln was a moral man, bound by his covenant with God and by the principles embodied in the Declaration of Independence. He was torn between a Christian and democratic commitment to liberty for all, embodied in his egalitarian reading of the Declaration of Independence, and his duty as president, sworn to uphold the constitution of a slaveholding nation. Whereas Lincoln believed in the principle of individual freedom, he also believed in the social contract embodied in the Declaration of Independence. By this contract, the individual delegated authority to government to prevent social anarchy. In this respect, Lincoln both followed and led the shift of opinion in the North away from an individualistic democracy toward a concern with social order, in which individual rights would be reconciled with institutional authority.[2]

Lincoln seized upon the secession of the Confederate states and their refusal to negotiate on the slavery issue as a violation of the social contract. Since the dispute over slavery was the stated cause of secession, Lincoln saw it as the root of the anarchy that threatened society. The Emancipation Proclamation of September 22, 1862, in the immediate aftermath of victory at Antietam, was the instrument that reconciled Lincoln's view of liberty for all with his oath to preserve the Union. It was the ideological route to a national strategy of total war to destroy the social and political system that threatened the United States.

1 I am indebted to James M. McPherson's *Abraham Lincoln and the Second American Revolution* (New York, 1990) for much of the material on Lincoln's ideological and political road to total war; see esp. chap. 5, which focuses on Lincoln as a war president.
2 For the shift of the Union's intelligentsia to a primary concern for institutional authority and order, see George W. Fredrickson, *The Inner Civil War* (New York, 1965).

When Lincoln with the Proclamation abandoned the limited strategic objective of persuading the South to negotiate on slavery and secession, he declared total war ideologically, politically, and militarily. His objective was the total defeat and unconditional surrender of the Confederacy. Through the Proclamation, Lincoln and the Republican Party harnessed the intellectual and emotional potential contained in the convergence of democratic nationalism and Christianity to support a doctrine of total war. By keeping the Republican Party in power, he achieved part of his goal. And the Republican heir to the Hamiltonian and Whig commitment to use centralized national power to achieve its ends had no hesitation about using the government to organize for total war. Within a year, Lincoln and his party responded to the imperatives of total war with laws, to quote McPherson, that "did more to reshape the relation of government to the economy than any comparable effort except perhaps the first hundred days of the New Deal."[3]

Lincoln and the Republicans easily reconciled the ideological push to total war with the centralizing and modernizing tendencies of the Party. Both the ideological and interest orientation of the Republicans relished being the instrument of modern industrial and commercial capitalism in league with strong executive authority. And the Republican Party rode a rising crest of national feeling in the North that coincided with its goals. Charles Royster documents the imagery of an intense national feeling that from the beginning pushed rather than followed politicians and the generals.[4] Once Lincoln decided on a strategy of total war, Lincoln and his Party, as argued by Jörg Nagler in his accompanying essay, effectively propagated this national feeling.[5] In the scholarly debate over family and local versus national loyalties, in and out of Civil War armies, evidence suggests a complex layering of family, local, religious, and national loyalties. Allowing for diverse motives, it appears that at times this layering fused the motives of the individual and the "people" to fight a war of growing intensity for the North against the

---

3 McPherson, *Lincoln*, 40. In his much quoted argument that the Civil War was not a total war, Mark E. Neely Jr. contends as part of his argument that Lincoln always held open the possibility of a negotiated settlement. Hence, he argues, it is an exaggeration to say that Northern political strategy was total to the extent that Lincoln demanded unconditional surrender. But even Neely acknowledges that Lincoln's preliminary conditions for a negotiated peace were so extreme as to be unacceptable, and that the Confederate leadership interpreted the terms to be, in fact, unconditional surrender. I believe that the emphasis of the argument should fall on the conditions being in fact unacceptable because they would amount to total defeat, with the Confederate leadership correctly interpreting this to be the case. See Mark E. Neely Jr., "Was the Civil War a Total War?" *Civil War History* 37 (Mar. 1991): 5–28.
4 Charles Royster, *Destructive War: William Tecumseh Sherman, Stonewall Jackson, and the Americans* (New York, 1991).
5 See Richard E. Beringer's essay in this volume (Chapter 4), in which he argues that Southern loyalties were local.

South and the Confederacy. Lincoln and the Republicans, critically or intuitively, were able to grasp and to use this developing ideological base. This combination of ideology and interest gave institutional push to Lincoln's singleminded intensity in pursuing his ends. It also provided the context for the imperatives of war pushing Lincoln's world view and that of the enemy into irreconcilable solitude. The first total war derived much of its energy from the confrontation of true believers. The improvised nature of Union military organization and decision making, as McPherson notes, broke down the distinctions between Lincoln's grand strategy of total war and the development of an operational strategy to achieve it. Lincoln as grand strategist went to war without an effective modern staff organization. The highly competent Edwin Stanton, appointed secretary of war in January of 1862, improvised a bureaucratic infrastructure to meet the developing organizational needs of total war. His creation of the short-lived War Board, under Gen. Ethan Allen Hitchcock, was a move to integrate the bureaus and to make recommendations on operational strategy. The Board functioned well under the impetus of some competent bureau chiefs and the drive of Stanton. But Hitchcock lacked the qualities necessary to become a modern chief of staff.[6]

When Gen. Henry Halleck was brought from the western command to Washington in July 1862 as general in chief, he was able to benefit from the War Board precedent. Although the Board officially was discontinued with the revival of the position of general in chief, which had been discontinued after Gen. George B. McClellan, it in fact continued informally. Halleck stepped into the chief of staff function, adding to the War Board his own staff as general in chief.

In the ad hoc experiments to create a modern staff organization, Lincoln had dropped the nebulous position of general in chief following McClellan's dismissal and replaced it with the War Board. The general in chief historically got lost between the political power of the president and the secretary of war, the bureaucratic independence of the staff bureaus, and the operational independence of field command. In the tradition where the president controlled the armies and the secretary of war controlled the organization to put them in the field, the general in chief, who historically had no statutory authority, fought for whatever authority might spill over. That spill came with the Civil War need for some semblance of a modern chief of staff.

When Lincoln brought Halleck to Washington as general in chief, Halleck fitted into Lincoln and Stanton's improvised staff organization as the functioning chief of staff. Halleck grew with the job, continuing to perform the

---

6   For Union staff organization at the level of high command, I am heavily indebted to Herman M. Hattaway and Archer Jones, *How the North Won* (Urbana and Chicago, Ill., 1983).

same function even when Grant replaced him as general in chief. Their relationship became that of chief of staff and commanding general of the armies, which Halleck never was. Prior to Grant, Lincoln was his own commanding general, exercising his prerogatives as commander in chief with increasing confidence and skill.

Lincoln's wielding of his authority as commander in chief reflected how a traditional system of command continued, propped up and sustained by an improvised staff system. At the level of strategic development, the process remained traditional: Leadership for improvising political grand strategy fell to the president; leadership for improvising the operational strategy to achieve it reverted to the field command. The dialogue relating the development of grand strategy and operational strategy flowed primarily between the president, as commander of his armies, and his field commanders. Although Lincoln was always more active in exercising his authority in the East, the pattern, though more controlled by the operational commanders, was essentially the same in the West. One reflection of this relation between Lincoln and his field commanders was how Lincoln's general in chiefs acquired their authority from their successes as field commanders.

Lincoln haunted the War Department's telegraph office, advising and pushing his generals in the field. A diligent student of war, Lincoln let his generals know that he expected a military dialogue. The fact that two of his general in chiefs at the same time commanded armies in the field, and a third came to Washington from the western command, further ensured that the dialogue remained close to field operations and did not get diverted to high-command staff issues. Stanton's energy and competence further shielded Lincoln from the latter. Not until Grant emerged did Lincoln recede somewhat, though by no means completely, into the background, confident that he had found a general to direct the operational strategy of total war.

Lincoln's dismissal of McClellan was the most dramatic instance of Lincoln as commander in chief exercising the vision of total war that accompanied the Emancipation Proclamation. Regardless of the case for McClellan as an operational commander, his political and military world views, as well as predilections of personality, disqualified him for command when Lincoln changed his objective from limited to total war. In an improvised decision-making structure, where the relationship between the president and his most conspicuous general was of necessity so close and immediate, Lincoln had to see McClellan as a poor risk to implement the total destruction of the South. And Lincoln did not fall into the trap of letting the Union's most politically powerful soldier impose an operational strategy that might thwart the president's national strategy.

With his shift of grand strategy from limited to total war, Lincoln also shifted the locus of operational strategy to the West. One must give its due Lincoln's political and military concerns about a Peninsula strategy that left Washington exposed. But suspicion of the Army of the Potomac as indelibly stamped by McClellan must have crossed his mind as he shifted the war to the West. And the specter of McClellan was no doubt present in Lincoln's mind when he brought to Washington as general in chief Halleck, the commander of the successful western armies, and the only general with the prestige to rival McClellan.[7]

Lincoln's transition from limited to total war pushed his generals to develop an accompanying operational strategy. They faced the challenge of penetrating and occupying the South so as to exhaust its resources, its people, and its armies. To meet this challenge, Lincoln and his generals ran against the current of modern strategy that had developed out of the revolutionary and Napoléonic wars. In so doing, they took modern operational strategy in a new direction.

To locate the historical place and significance of their achievement, it is necessary briefly to recount the origins of modern operational strategy. Although total war has very old precedents, the particular form that we define as modern emerged during the American Civil War. It was part of the larger development of modern strategic thought and organization that first took shape during the revolutionary and Napoléonic era. Two currents of modern strategy flowed out of the period from the revolutionary wars and Napoléon through the Civil War. One carried the stamp of Napoléon; the other that of Ulysses Grant. These diverse currents dominated large-scale organized warfare through World War II.

The very concept of strategy as Antoine-Henri Jomini and Clausewitz, the most important formulators of modern strategic thought, understood it arguably had its origins in the era of military reform that preceded the French revolutionary wars. The term *strategy* in its modern sense first appeared in the English language around 1800.[8] Growing out of the study of military geography, the concept addressed problems of moving and maneuvering against enemy armies in time and space, with an emphasis on time. Prior to the revolutionary and Napoléonic wars, there was little possibility of systematic maneuver. But by the late eighteenth century, western European geography was being tamed. Growing populations, urbanization, commerce, and travel produced a fairly extensive road system and logistical base. The Enlightenment

---

7 Hattaway and Jones develop a strong and interesting case for the nature of Halleck's importance and continuing prestige, ibid.
8 Martin van Creveld, *Technology and War* (New York, 1989), 49.

encouraged the application of mathematics and science to practical problems of war.

Two of these applications were particularly important to the development of modern operational strategy. By the revolutionary and Napoléonic era, modern triangulated maps, invented in 1617, were making their way belatedly into usage that could benefit military strategy. The first country to be mapped by triangulation was France during the 1740s. And the first topographical atlas of Prussia was completed in 1780. Reproduction, however, was slow and expensive. And although Napoléon belonged to the dawn of the era of modern maps and did derive some of the benefits, his armies generally marched without them. They did, nevertheless, march with the knowledge of modern mapping.

Napoléon made better use of another mechanical invention: the mechanical timekeeper. This invention, as Martin van Creveld observes, made its appearance in Europe at the same time as gunpowder. Good portable watches were available from the early seventeenth century; by the late eighteenth century, they were almost equal to the quality of contemporary mechanical watches. But Napoléon was the first to use them for strategic maneuver, frequently formulating his orders in relation to time. It was part of the means by which Napoléon was able to disperse and reassemble his armies to affect surprise.[9]

The Napoléonic origins of modern operational strategy was typical of Enlightenment thought in reducing strategy, in part, to a mathematical problem of time. Victory went to the first with the most. Strategy became the art and science of moving large armies faster and more precisely than the enemy. Napoléon's frequent frustrations with timing, with running his armies by the clock, and with getting his generals and marshals precisely to date and time their orders and dispatches, all indicated the novelty of the procedure. This was a good strategic system as long as: (1) European armies fought over the restricted and familiar military geography of western Europe, and (2) total war did not dominate national or operational strategies.

---

9 Ibid., 117–19. A current school of semiotic political theory, based in France, emphasizes the development of the concept of speed in western military strategy as fundamental to the historical development of modern political power and authority. Although it is an aside to this study, their work is an interesting case of how European thought reflects on the complex and far-ranging cultural scope of the strategic concept of speed and movement. For the semiotically innocent, such as myself, the most accessible of these studies are Paul Virilio, *Speed and Politics*, and *Popular Defense and Ecological Struggles*, and Paul Virilio and Sylvere Lotringer, *Pure War*. Giles Deleuze and Felix Guattari, *Nomadology: The War Machine* also produces some startling historical signposts. Their *On the Line* is less penetrable. All are translated from the French for the Semiotext[e] Foreign Agents series published by Columbia University. All were published in French in the period from the late 1970s through the late 1980s.

Napoléon's strategic thinking fell within this context of victory through maneuver. Victory on the field of battle would achieve his political goals. He not only hesitated to wage war against the enemy's human and material resources; he disturbed the enemy population as little as possible so as not to turn it against his armies. When Napoléon took his army to Russia and the Iberian Peninsula, enemy armies in conjunction with partisans and a hostile population turned him to the operational realities of total war. These campaigns also took him deep into uncharted territory, away from the road systems and populations that provided the logistical base for movement in the heartland of western Europe.

It was in the context of this early development of modern strategic thought that Clausewitz and Jomini, in the early and mid-nineteenth century, expressed reservations about moving into hostile territory. Although they did not completely reject the strategy, they gave it a low priority. Although Clausewitz would not be influential outside Prussia until after the Franco-Prussian War, Jomini would interpret Napoléon for the generation of Civil War officers.

But antebellum thought went beyond Jomini. And one of the theorists who took it there was Halleck. His influential antebellum treatise, *Elements of Military Art and Science* (1846), while continuing the orthodox emphasis on movement against the enemy's armies, gave more prominence to the occupation of enemy territory. Although it never became a textbook at West Point, Halleck's book reputedly was the most widely read military work by the antebellum officer corps. Halleck may have been influenced by his West Point teacher, Dennis Hart Mahan. West Point's most influential teacher and the most important theorist of the antebellum period, Mahan emphasized the occupation of the enemy's space. He argued that "carrying the war into the heart of the assailant's country ... is the surest way of making him share its burdens and foiling his plans."[10] The Archduke Charles of Austria, Napoléon's military opponent and a widely read and respected military theorist, made the same arguments. Halleck listed him among his references. Mahan and Halleck also had the American experience of moving armies deep into enemy space during the War with Mexico.[11]

Changing tactical and strategic realities also may have tempered Mahan's and Halleck's appreciation for maneuver against the enemy's armies in favor of movement into the enemy's space. The reorganization of armies during

10 Quoted in John Keegan, *The Mask of Command* (London, 1987), 181.
11 With respect to the thinking of Halleck, Mahan, and the Archduke Charles on strategy and the occupation of space versus the emphases of Jomini and Clausewitz, see Hattaway and Jones, *How the North Won*, 46–7, and Edward Hagerman, *The American Civil War and the Origins of Modern Warfare* (Bloomington, Ind., 1988), 9, 13–14.

the Revolutionary and Napoléonic era into divisions and corps for greater strategic mobility benefited the retreat as much as the attack. Although an army might be defeated, there was little prospect of it being destroyed or captured unless incompetently led. With the Civil War addition of the railway and the telegraph, these prospects grew dimmer.

If the failure of maneuver forced a tactical confrontation, Mahan and Halleck were even more pessimistic. Both agreed that the introduction of the rifled musket had turned the tactical advantage over to the entrenched tactical defense, especially with a green militia-based army. Moreover, Mahan was opposed to wasting in open assaults both American soldiers, whom he saw democratically as valuable members of civilian society and as voters, and the small, hence not to be wasted, professional officer corps.

Halleck's operational strategy in the West was true to the ambivalence of his writings. He both concentrated against the enemies armies and occupied enemy territory. But Halleck got caught up in a traditional strategic maxim that restricted his movements down the river systems of the West and, where necessary, overland. A nervous commander in the face of the enemy, Halleck was somewhat rigid in his respect for the maxim that you move against the enemy with a base of operations secured on interior lines. He grew especially irate with his subordinate commander, Ulysses Grant, for ignoring this maxim.

Grant, during the Fort Henry and Fort Donelson campaign took his supply with him down the rivers and, when necessary, lived off the land. This innovation broke the Confederate defensive line and supported an operational strategy for total war. Grant expressed his philosophy of constant movement in a letter to his wife Julia after Donelson. "I want to push on as rapidly as possible to save hard fighting. These terrible battles are very good things to read about for persons who loose [sic] no friends but I am decidedly in favor of having as little of it as possible. The way to avoid it is to push forward as vigorously as possible."[12]

By orthodox maxims, Confederate strategy made sense. A line of defense against the penetration of Union armies combined with raids against offensive buildups and to win battles held promise. If the line of defense held, or at worst a hostile population supported partisans and the main armies in the case of a deep penetration into Confederate territory, then according to orthodox thinking, a Union army probably could not sustain itself. Chances of prolonging the war for a favorable peace, either through the external

---

12 Letter to Julia Dent Grant, Feb. 24, 1862, Ulysses S. Grant, *Memoirs and Selected Letters* (New York, 1990), 986. For Grant's postwar reflections on his conflict with Halleck on this issue of strategy, see ibid., 255–7, 328.

pressure of foreign recognition or the internal pressure of war weariness and a Democratic election victory, were good. Or so read the dominant strains of European military thought. But at Fort Donelson and Vicksburg, Grant served notice that he was changing the nature of operational strategy.

To seek the source of Grant's knowledge is to balance precariously between impressionistic and more measurable sources. It is to look at what Grant might have known from his experience and education. It is to place experience and education beside technological and organizational developments in mid-nineteenth-century warfare that for the first time made an operational strategy of total war a reasonable option. It is to weight the convergence of beliefs that held Grant, his armies, and Lincoln together in their commitment to national and operational strategies of total war. Finally, it is to weave the historical process by which all of these elements came into play in the first modern total war.

One of the more speculative, yet one of the more important, sources of Grant's intuitive knowledge was his spatial sense of the land. Perhaps this understanding raised him above his contemporaries in developing the other side of modern operational strategy—namely, total war against the enemy's space. Both Grant and his partner in total war, Sherman, matured in the expanses of the early and mid-nineteenth-century American West. They may have shared an intuitive and practical awareness of land as space, a mammoth and moving frontier falling to human effort and technology.

By the mid-nineteenth century, the area between the Appalachians and the Mississippi was sufficiently well organized to be a theater for large-scale military operations. At the same time, it was sufficiently primitive to be a challenge that orthodox strategic maxims would consider a poor risk for a strategy of occupation. Benjamin Cooling, in his careful study of the Fort Henry and Fort Donelson campaign, observes how the Northern world view along the Mississippi and other western river systems saw the region as an expanding geographical space, organized around river commerce. The Southern view along the shared river systems by contrast remained grounded in local community and tradition. These contrasting outlooks, Cooling believes, carried over into the respective western military strategies early in the war.[13]

Grant and Lincoln shared this understanding as they turned their respective strategic visions to the western rivers and the land beyond. Grant in his memoirs made a telling statement on how modern transportation technology changed the nature of American commercial space from local to national. In the process, his view of the new national space and its technological

---

13   Benjamin Franklin Cooling, *Forts Henry and Donelson* (Knoxville, Tenn., 1987).

and economic foundation rejected the right of Southern localism to impose slavery on a commercially unified society through the Fugitive Slave Law.

In the early days of the country, before we had railroads, telegraphs and steam-boats – in a word, rapid transit of any sort – the states were almost a separate nation-ality. At that time the subject of slavery caused but little or no disturbance to the public mind. But the country grew, rapid transit was established, and trade and commerce between the States got to be so much greater than before, that the power of the National government became more felt and recognized and, there-fore, had to be enlisted in the cause of this institution. This (the Fugitive Slave Law) was a degradation which the North would not permit any longer than until they could get the power to expunge such laws from the statute books. Prior to the time of these encroachments the great majority of the people of the North had no particular quarrel with slavery, so long as they were not forced to have it them-selves. But they were not willing to play the role of police for the South in the protection of the particular institution.[14]

Grant built his operational strategy of total war in part through blending this large spatial picture created by modern industrial transport with the reorganization of traditional animal-drawn field transportation for mid-nineteenth-century warfare in America. But his understanding of space extended to the field of operations in more basic ways. Grant had a comfort level with western geography that removed any fear of the land when mov-ing, maneuvering, or fighting troops. This security grew in part from his knowledge of topography combined with an exceptional memory. He developed a reputation for remembering every detail of past battles and campaigns with respect to the disposition of troops and topography. Grant was an avid map collector, and during the War with Mexico, Winfield Scott, Zachary Taylor, and Robert E. Lee used maps from his collection not avail-able elsewhere. Grant had a reputation, while campaigning, for remembering every detail of a map, not referring to it again. His memory for detail with respect to the movement of armies in space contributed to his ability even-tually to direct the operations of both the eastern and western armies. When he came East, he already had been following the fighting in Virginia in close detail.[15]

This intuition of the land that he grew up in, reinforced by youthful curi-osity about the formal exploration of space as cartography, was one possible source of his later confidence in command. His intuitive sense of cartogra-phy perhaps gave to him that edge that accounted for such habits as taking shortcuts in uncharted country. Sherman observed in admiration that Grant

14 Grant, *Memoirs and Letters*, 773–4.
15 Keegan, *Command*, 212–13.

never worried about where the enemy was or what he was doing. Sherman admitted that he always worried. Grant, commenting on this calm, in a statement that captured the essence of Clausewitz's sense of generalship, said: "The way to reach ultimate victory was to develop a stronger sense of war's rhythm than that possessed by the enemy."[16] Grant seemed especially confident of the rhythm of war in the large spaces of western operations. Not until he entered the cramped quarters of the eastern theater did Grant lose his sense of adventure. Until then, there is room for speculation that Grant perhaps acquired some of his feel for the friction and fog of war from his sense of the geography of the West.

By the time Grant came to western field command, he had filtered whatever intuition and youthful knowledge he had of the land through a formal education at the United States Military Academy at West Point. He had filtered both through subsequent experience as a regular officer in the War with Mexico and in service on the frontier. At West Point, Grant had acquired useful formal knowledge and intellectual discipline for his natural strengths. Any dismissal of his student days or general intellectual experience and ability is to miss the whole person. As his biographer, William McFeely, observes, Grant was certainly a diffident personality who would on occasion go mischievously out of his way to perpetuate an image of his intellectual limitations. But his reports and dispatches, to say nothing of his correspondence and graceful and justly celebrated memoirs, revealed a disciplined intellect ordering a thoughtful as well as a practical mind.

Any in his command who thought Grant intellectually slow only had to experience his writing the detailed orders for the disposition of his army in battle. Forbidding any interruption, as an aide observed, Grant wrote clear, precise, and detailed orders, rapidly without pause, hesitation, or revision, pushing each piece of paper off his table as he completed it, gathering the papers from the floor, sorting them quickly, then handing them to a staff officer to distribute without a further glance. West Point likely was due some credit for these displays of trained intelligence.[17]

Grant was an independent student who used the Academy to pursue his interests and strengths. Although he eventually graduated twenty-first in his class of thirty-nine, Grant stood tenth of fifty-three in his second year, when he still managed some modicum of interest in a rote curriculum that increasingly bored him. By his third year, he was badly neglecting this curriculum to read on his own in the library, particularly in literature. Grant excelled in mathematics, the Academy's most rigorous subject. His only ambition at

16   William S. McFeely, *Grant* (New York, 1981), 103.
17   Keegan, *Command*, 199–200.

West Point was, as he put it, "to secure a detail for a few years as assistant professor of mathematics at the Academy, and afterward obtain a permanent position as professor in some respectable college."[18]

Starting with mathematics, we get a picture of intellectual inclinations and strengths that eventually could benefit Grant's strategic thinking. His bent for mathematics complemented his aptitude for cartography. A military academy and an army dominated by the Corps of Engineers and the Corps of Topographical Engineers was a good place to develop both inclinations. Grant was also a skilled artist in a military academy with excellent art instruction. And art instruction was intended to enhance the charting of military geography. Add to these intellectual inclinations Grant's skill as a horseman, perhaps his one personal vanity, and the practical knowledge with working teams that he acquired in his youth, and of which he was proud, as well as his assignment as a quartermaster during the War with Mexico and after. You are left with an intellectual, practical, and organizational background that helps to explain Grant's strength as a logistician and strategist in the transition to modern industrial warfare.[19]

There also is evidence that Grant did not learn everything as a practical exercise in trial and error and that he did pay some attention to military literature. At the time that he received his first Civil War command in Ohio, for instance, he was reading McClellan's report as a member of the Delafield Commission to Europe, with particular interest in the Crimean War. His prodigious memory no doubt added this to detail accumulated from the War with Mexico. And the memory for the detail of Napoléon's campaigns that he displayed after the war probably came from knowledge acquired before or during the war.[20]

Grant admitted to serious gaps in his knowledge. He seemed almost proud of bringing up the bottom of his West Point class in tactics. He admitted that he needed McPherson, later commander of Grant's old Army of the Tennessee and first assigned to Grant as an engineering officer, to fill his deficiencies in military engineering. He admitted training his troops in tactics while only partially familiarizing himself with the contents of the tactical manual.[21] And it was in tactics that Grant's performance was most questionable, filled with inconsistent acts and utterances. He was ambivalent toward the application of the new industrial technology in all areas but logistics. He remained ambivalent about the impact of the rifled musket and the role of field fortifications. And early in the war, he was hesitant about

18 McFeely, *Grant*, 14–18; Grant, *Memoirs and Letters*, 32.
19 McFeely, *Grant*, 17–19.   20 Ibid., 79; Keegan, *Command*, 213.
21 Grant, *Memoirs and Letters*, 32–3, 166–7.

accepting the new military telegraph and the signals organization that came with it.[22] But Grant used Sherman and McPherson, both theoretically grounded officers, to tutor him in his deficiencies. Grant credited them with having taught him more than any others.[23] One is left to wonder whether his close relationship with both officers, the only such relationships he developed with subordinate officers other than his personal staff, was based in part upon their usefulness in his areas of deficiency.

Sherman's observation that Grant knew little of the formal principles of war is probably true. But the formal principles that Sherman referred to were no doubt the mechanistic and geometric maxims of strategy and tactics embodied in prevailing theory and doctrine. Sherman knew this world well and tended to use its language. Grant never did. But Grant did understand the basic strategic principles and objectives of warfare, and he early began to work out a system to realize them.

He particularly understood moving and maneuvering troops through the western spaces of the Confederacy. He understood logistics. He knew how railroad and steam-powered transportation technology affected logistics. He also reorganized animal-drawn field transportation to move and maneuver in the American countryside. And he put animals and the steam engine together to break preindustrial era rules and maxims about movement and maneuver deep into hostile enemy country. Grant's genius as a strategist was a balance of his sense of geography in the western theater of operations and his talents as a logistical organizer and manager in the field.

Grant developed his understanding of organization and maneuver in a military culture that offered little guidance. With no incentive to innovate, antebellum military thought did not, as noted, develop a modern staff system that coordinated operational strategy and planning with grand strategic planning and bureau organization. An ad hoc system, as noted, grew out of the Civil War. Union strategic organization did benefit from some early industrial development in the North. Two major benefits were the railroad and the telegraph. The telegraph was an American invention. Although not invented until 1844, there were 50,000 miles of wire by the time of the Civil War. The country had 31,000 miles of rail, all but 9,000 of this in the North. Civil War armies were the first to wage war with the railroad and telegraph fully integrated into field operations.

With respect to both railroads and telegraph, there was an understanding in the North that war was total. Lincoln and his War Department quickly centralized both for military needs. The War Department also established the

---

22   Hagerman, *Civil War.*
23   Letter to Sherman, March 4, 1864, Grant, *Memoirs and Letters*, 1046–7

U.S. Military Railroads to organize and administer captured enemy railroads. Early railroad promoters helped to raise awareness by supplementing their commercial arguments for westward railroad expansion with arguments for the strategic value of railroads. This subordination of railroads to military usage gave the North a major organizational and strategic advantage over the South, which never adequately integrated railroads into its logistical system.[24]

Yet Northern railroadlike military organization was not prepared for modern war. To a degree, early railroad and military organization had some linkages that reinforced their mutual failure to develop a modern organizational concept. Both railroad and military staff organization at the outbreak of war shared in a limited concept of hierarchical organization for distributing authority and responsibility, largely with respect to financial accountability. The Civil War forced the War Department to improvise modern centralized systems and to integrate them with the field organization of Union armies.[25]

The part of the logistical system most crucial to moving and sustaining armies in the field was quartermaster organization. And early improvisation was impressive, from the Quartermaster Department under the able Montgomery Meigs through the quartermaster organization of field armies.[26] But different styles emerged from the eastern and western armies. Owing to the early emphasis on eastern strategy, organizational efforts focused on moving and maneuvering the enormous Army of the Potomac. By 1863, a modern staff structure integrated logistical planning from the general in chief, Halleck, functioning as chief of staff, through Meigs's Quartermaster Department, through Rufus Ingalls, the talented quartermaster of the Army of the Potomac, down through brigade quartermasters. The system analyzed logistical problems, experimented with solutions, and implemented its findings. Logistical organization successfully moved supplies to the army in the field by rail and water. Most impressive was the way it worked out a system of field transportation to move the Army of the Potomac overland away from its base of supply.

Part of the price paid for early logistical concentration in the East, however, was early neglect in the West. By the time that Lincoln and Halleck shifted strategic emphasis to the West, the neglected western armies had

24 Hattaway and Jones, *How the North Won*; Richard D. Goff, *Confederate Supply* (Durham, N.C., 1969).
25 I have attempted to synthesize briefly the conflicting debates on the linkages between early railroad and military organization in Hagerman, *Civil War*, 35, 306 fn 5.
26 The following material on logistics and strategy is from ibid. For an abbreviated version, see Hagerman, "Field Transportation and Strategic Mobility in the Union Armies," *Civil War History* 34 (1988): 143–71.

developed their own style. There was little, if any, transfer to the West of either eastern staff organization or the knowledge that it generated. Ingall's development of a staff organization for the order of march of the Army of the Potomac during the Maryland campaign, for instance, was not emulated in the western armies until almost a year later. Left more to their own devices, the western armies developed a pattern of local improvisation and resourcefulness. The early division of command in the West, and the raising of the various armies locally, accentuated this pattern. Logistical organization in the western armies developed an independent aloofness to Washington and the Quartermaster Department that continued even after Lincoln shifted strategic emphasis to the West. Sherman's independence in logistical improvisation as western commander would cause Meigs to complain, on occasion, that Sherman was fighting his own private war, and the Quartermaster Department did not know what was going on.[27]

The western field commanders were able improvisers. From the beginning, they displayed a Yankee flair for combining steam-powered river transportation, rail transportation, and animal-drawn field transportation. All field commanders, East and West, North and South, immediately abandoned the Napoléonic standard of field transportation, which was twelve wagons for 1,000 men. Meigs, in a case of tradition ignoring reality, continued to advocate the Napoléonic standard, while acquiescing to the higher demands of the field commanders and their quartermasters.

Field commanders, adapting to American foraging conditions, tripled, quadrupled, and, in the case of Gen. William S. Rosecrans's important Tullahoma campaign in the summer of 1863, exceeded by six times the Napoléonic standard. McClellan began the Peninsula campaign with a standard of forty-five wagons for 1,000 for men. Grant worked out a standard of forty wagons per 1,000 men when in command of the Army of the Tennessee. He then imposed this standard on the Army of the Potomac when he came East. Despite the exasperation of his old friend and West Point roommate Ingalls, the quartermaster of the Army of the Potomac, Grant overruled the streamlining of transportation during 1863 which had reduced that army's standard to twenty wagons per 1,000 men in the aftermath of Gettysburg. This reorganization probably played a role in the army's improved speed of movement during the Gettysburg campaign, when it marched with a standard of thirty wagons for 1,000 men. Sherman began his Atlanta campaign with fifty

27   Sherman's relationship with Meigs was soured by what Sherman considered Meigs's misrepresentation from the scene of Sherman's part in the Battle of Chattanooga and its aftermath. Stanton published Meigs's letter on the matter as semi-official. Meigs's failure to retract his position exacerbated the problem. Letter to John Sherman, Dec. 29, 1863, *The Sherman Letters*, ed. Rachel Sherman Thorndike (New York, 1969), 216–17.

wagons per 1,000 men. He marched to the sea at Savannah and through the Carolinas with forty wagons per 1,000 men, thus bringing the principle armies of the Union to the same standard by the end of the war.

Rosecrans's Tullahoma campaign and subsequent move to Chattanooga with an army of 60,000 were important logistical experiences behind the preparation of Grant's and Sherman's western strategy for 1864–65. Rosecrans's considerable achievement was the only precedent for overland maneuver with an army the scale of Sherman's for his march to Atlanta and beyond. Earlier maneuvers in the West had been with small armies, with river and rail transportation frequently a logistical component. As Sherman organized the Armies of the Tennessee, Cumberland, and Ohio into an army group of 100,000 men for the march on Atlanta, it is significant that he appointed Rosecrans's quartermaster for the Army of the Cumberland during the Tullahoma and Chattanooga campaigns, Colonel L. C. Easton, as his chief quartermaster.

Sherman, who shared the tendency of the command tradition that he inherited to overcentralize command in his own hands, made an exception for Easton. He gave Easton independent authority to organize logistics, including cooperation with the U.S. Military Railroads Construction Corps, which laid rail to give Sherman a moving railhead for his advance on Atlanta. Easton also had the authority to make strategic decisions if called for by logistical considerations.

It is appropriate to note, in this respect, the contrast in command and control styles between Sherman and Grant. One expression of Grant's organizational and managerial talent, which benefited logistics as well as other areas of command and control, was his improvisation of a modern staff to assist him in the command and control of his army. Rather than using his staff in the traditional way as mere specialized and personal aides, Grant used them to implement and coordinate plans of operation. Grant developed a procedure whereby he freely discussed the details of orders with his staff. He then disbursed them, as an aide quoted Grant's explaining the procedure to him, to "critical points of the line to keep me promptly alerted of what is taking place, and in cases of great emergency, when new dispositions have to be made on the instant, or it becomes suddenly necessary to reinforce one command by sending to its aid troops from another, and there is not time to communicate with headquarters, I want you to explain my views to commanders and urge immediate action, looking to cooperation, without waiting for specific orders from me."[28]

---

28 Keegan, *Command*, 198.

Sherman and Easton refined their logistics for the task at hand. They experimented throughout the Atlanta campaign with long forays away from the moving railhead provided by the U.S. Military Railroads Construction Corps, using field transportation to live off the land. Sherman had his own experience living off the land, alone and with Grant, to complement what Easton had to offer. Although, unlike Easton, he had never lived off the land with an army approaching this size, he had been converted to the possibilities with Grant at Vicksburg. Opposed to Grant's plan and proven wrong, he thereafter followed Grant's lead and example.

Sherman, in conjunction with Grant, experimented further with living off the land in the aftermath of Vicksburg, and during the fall and winter leading to the Atlanta campaign. Sherman's first movement overland was his move against Joseph Johnston's army at Jackson, Mississippi, following the fall of Vicksburg. Reorganizing his field transportation, subsistence, and baggage on a light standard set by Grant, Sherman arrived before Jackson with the intention of dislodging the enemy not by attacking his entrenchments but by a combination of siege and the destruction of communications and the countryside. The strategy was a trial run for the 1864–65 campaign against Atlanta and through the Carolinas in that the intention was to live off the enemy's resources while denying them to the enemy. Sherman tore up over 100 miles of the railroad upon which civilians and the Confederate army alike depended. He stripped the land of food and forage. With his communications thus threatened, Johnston withdrew into the interior of Mississippi, destroying the railroad along which he retreated.

In the autumn of 1863 Sherman marched more than a corps some 250 miles actually traveled to help relieve the Union army besieged at Chattanooga. He then continued on to relieve Knoxville and back, a round trip of another 250–300 miles. He lived off the land while being resupplied en route to Chattanooga by rail and river steamers, and by river steamers en route to Knoxville and back. He also planned with Grant his spectacular December 1863 raid on Meridian, Mississippi. Living off the land, with Grant dispersing forces to disguise his intentions with several feints, Sherman destroyed the resources and communications in the area, while Johnston failed to figure out where he was headed. Sherman covered some 150–175 miles actually traveled in eleven days.

Beginning with Vicksburg, we begin to get an answer to the question of the relationship of Grant and Sherman in the development of western strategy. The Vicksburg campaign appears to have solidified the military relationship and merged it with a close personal bond between the two men.

Sherman's resistance to Grant's logistical plan that made the Vicksburg campaign possible came from the same theoretical direction as the opposition by Sherman's friend Halleck to Grant's breaking of the logistical rules at Donelson. After Vicksburg one senses from Sherman's correspondence that he realized that in Grant he had found a general who was redefining the rules of modern warfare.

A relationship developed that Sherman, by the end of 1863, described as one in which "with him I am as a second self. We are personal and official friends."[29] That perhaps captured the closeness of the two generals as well as any statement could. But there was also an intellectual compatibility generally overlooked in the underestimation of Grant's and overestimation of Sherman's intellectuality. Sherman, as with Grant, was a well educated soldier with great practical intelligence. A professor under Sherman at the Louisiana Seminary, where Sherman was president before the war, noted that Sherman had great intelligence and was well educated in his profession, but he was not a scholar or even a general reader. Like Grant, he lived in a world of practical applied knowledge.[30] And he found his practical calling in military command. The two generals were perfectly matched. They had a relationship of mutual trust and thought in which Grant from Vicksburg led and Sherman followed.

Grant was also Sherman's strategic and logistical teacher. Grant was impressed with Sherman's early display of organizational skill in keeping Grant's army supplied while Sherman was commanding the military District of West Tennessee, with headquarters at Memphis. But Grant was the operational teacher during their early relationship in command. The basic strategic plans of operation continued to be either Grant's or were worked out in a process of consultation between the two. Particular plans, like the particulars of movement and maneuver for the march to Atlanta and beyond, were Sherman's responsibility. But the knowledge of operational logistics that Sherman marched on had its origins at Donelson and Vicksburg in the mind of Grant. When Sherman departed for Atlanta, he marched on the accumulated wisdom of western command.

The advance on Atlanta was a slow and conservative holding and turning movement, contrasted to the Meridian raid, the Vicksburg campaign, and Sherman's subsequent march to the sea and through the Carolinas.[31] Several considerations could have shaped Grant's and Sherman's thinking. On the

---

29 Letter to John Sherman, Dec. 30, 1863, *Sherman Letters*, 220.
30 Charles Edmund Vetter, *Sherman: Merchant of Terror, Advocate of Peace* (Gretna, Ill., 1992), 61–2.
31 The following material on logistics and strategy for the Atlanta, Savannah, and Carolinas campaigns is from Hagerman, *Civil War*, chap. 5.

side of a more radical deep maneuver was the Tullahoma campaign; against it was the near disaster that followed, with Rosecrans besieged at Chattanooga. Sherman and Grant also respected the defensive abilities of Johnston, especially with an army of some 60,000 men, the size of which they overestimated. Also, neither Sherman nor Grant had commanded an army the size of the combined western forces in battle, let alone moving so large an army deep into enemy country with a formidable foe on its front. In a theater of operations where improvisation from army to army, campaign to campaign was the pattern, both Grant and Sherman worked their way through the challenge. Caution was in order. And it was a cautious and nervous Sherman who made his way to Atlanta.

By the time he reached Atlanta, Sherman had gained his confidence. He also acknowledged that he could not threaten, by holding and turning maneuvers, a large well-led army on the defensive in its own back yard. The advance to Atlanta had proceeded at the rate of about a mile and a half a day. Johnston withdrew before each turning movement, refusing to leave his trenches. Sherman in turn determined not to bloody his army in what he considered useless assaults on Johnston's entrenchments. The one time he launched a major frontal attack, the Battle of Kennesaw Mountain, the Confederates beat him back with heavy losses. Sherman maintained that he launched the attack so as not to lull Johnston into thinking he would not attack him. But he acknowledged that the attack was a mistake. And the heavy losses accumulated by his army in lesser battles and general skirmishing did not sit well with Sherman. By the time Sherman reached Atlanta, both he and Grant were ready to return to the alternate strategy of diversion and deep maneuver while living off the land. The opportunity came when Johnston's successor before Atlanta, Gen. John Bell Hood, moved from Sherman's front to maneuver against his communications.

The march to the sea at Savannah and on through the Carolinas would be the most remarkable campaign of dispersion, diversion, and surprise while living off the land in modern warfare. The combination of animal-drawn field transportation overland, with resupply by water and rail, would be the organizational key to one face of the operational strategy necessary for Lincoln's grand strategy of total war. As Sherman and Grant discussed by telegraph the strategic timing and the implications of breaking for the coast, Sherman thought that diversion and surprise would be a major part of his campaign. He surmised that Hood would follow once he headed for the sea and that he would have to take diversionary action to avoid him. As Sherman put it in his exchange with Grant at the time, Hood "will be forced to follow me. Instead of being on the defensive, I would be on the offensive; instead of guessing at what he means to do, he would have to guess at my plans. The difference in war is full twenty-five percent. I can take Savannah, Charleston, or the mouth of the Chattahoochie."[32] At the same time, he would lay waste to the land and communications while subduing the population.

Grant told Sherman that he did not think Hood would follow but would head for Nashville instead.[33] And Grant was correct. Sherman was free to do his damage largely unobstructed, having dispersed part of his army to deal with Hood. He now dispersed his army on the march for foraging and destruction. He divided it into from four to seven independent columns kept in communication by cavalry, since the terrain and speed of continuous movement eliminated the telegraph. These columns swept up all resources and destroyed all Confederate communications between them across a sixty-mile swath of countryside. The destruction ensured that no army could follow in his path. Sherman controlled partisan activity as before by making the population dependent on his largesse.

To emphasize the convergence of the operational means of movement and maneuver, and the strategic objective of destroying the enemy's resources, Sherman carried the agricultural statistics for every county in his path. What his army did not use, Sherman either sent behind his lines or destroyed. Sherman repeated the strategy through the Carolinas, again moving to resupply by water. Only at the end of his journey of destruction did he turn his attention to the Confederate army in the Battle of Bentonville.

The campaign was in part a classic Napoléonic maneuver, using diversion, dispersion, and surprise – except the object was not the enemy's army, but the enemy's space. And the devastation of the enemy's space was also the means to sustain the invading army. As Herman M. Hattaway and Archer Jones observe, by so totally exhausting the enemy's resources, communications, and will, Sherman's deep raid had the effect of a strategy of occupation through denying to the enemy the use of its territory, even though no army occupied it. It was a new face to operational strategy and organization; it was one face of the shifting strategic balance from limited to modern total war.

While emphasizing the coincidence of the grand strategic objectives and operational strategy of total war, Sherman's marches at the same time raised the question of the primary motivation of field commanders, pushed from one side by the ideological and political motives behind grand strategy, and pulled from the other by how best to organize and strategically to employ their armies. Grant's remaining in the field while general in chief, as de facto

32 Grant, *Memoirs and Letters*, 816.
33 Telegraphic communication, Oct. 11, 1864, ibid., 815–16.

commander of the Army of the Potomac, while closely following Sherman with the eyes of a field commander, enhanced the operational context of decision making in East and West. Yet the ideological and grand strategic consensus between the president, Grant, and Sherman, and Lincoln's confidence in Grant and his commanders, appear to have melded the operational and political faces of total war strategy.

Both Grant and Sherman were ideologically as well as militarily motivated in their operational strategy of total war. Both shared Lincoln's liberal constitutional view of secession and war. Although they came to their view of the ideological correctness of the war from somewhat different emphases and experiences, secession and Southern intransigence on slavery made militant nationalists of both. Neither was an abolitionist, and both favored compromise that would have avoided secession and war. Grant even regretted that there was no constitutional provision for secession and indicated that secession would have been acceptable to him if the South had agreed to disagree and turned away without attempting to expand slavery into the remainder of the nation. But both Grant and Sherman agreed that the South must bend on what they considered its attempt to impose slavery on the nation.

Grant's earlier noted argument against slavery was the voice of expanding commercial and industrial capitalism in the Northwest. Sherman's antebellum experience living and working in the South bred more empathy if not more sympathy for Southern society. The egalitarian inclination in Grant, by contrast, found repugnant an exploitative class system built on slavery. Sherman layered his liberal nationalism, as Charles Royster observes, with a fatalistic evolutionary naturalism. This intellectual tendency reinforced Sherman's growing fatalism about the inevitable totalization of modern war fought with industrial technology and citizen armies. Their convictions made the operational imperatives of total war against the Southern people more palatable.[34]

Both, in fact, found themselves pushing for total war measures at a political level in support of strategic operations before Lincoln's administration was willing to move. The issue was Union trade with the South on the Mississippi River. On July 22, 1862, the day after he assumed command of the District of West Tennessee, with headquarters at Memphis, Sherman wrote to his brother, Republican Senator John Sherman: "It is about time the North understood the truth. That the entire South, man, woman and child are

---

34   For Grant's political views, see his letter to Frederick Dent, April 19, 1861, ibid., 955–6; and ibid., 145–51, 419. For Sherman, see letters to John Sherman, Sept. 1859; Dec. 12, 1859; Jan. 16, 1860; April 4, 1860; June 1860; Jan. 18, 1861, *Sherman Letters*, 76–9, 82, 84, 105–6.

against us, armed and determined."[35] As he witnessed Southern profits from Union commerce going to support the armies that faced him, Sherman recognized that war against civilians and their resources was necessary to win.

Grant, similarly, on July 31, 1862, wrote to Secretary of the Treasury Salmon P. Chase, critical of the government's liberal trade policy with the Confederacy. Like Sherman, Grant saw that it was financing military operations against his armies. He again lobbied Chase in July 1863. Upon leaving Memphis in the early spring of 1863, Grant took matters into his own hands as far as he could, prohibiting trade below Helena, the point to where the Union permitted it. To further let the civilian population know that its liberties were restricted, Grant, in orders of April 9, 1863, suppressed the press of Memphis for publishing information relevant to his operations. He arrested the offending editor of the *Memphis Bulletin*.[36]

At the basic operational level of total war, both Grant and Sherman, as well as Halleck in western command, indicated early that they were willing to wage war against the civilian population to protect their armies. Grant and Sherman revealed some sensitivity to waging war against civilians, but both could be harsh when their armies encountered the least resistance. Grant on the one hand was a strict disciplinarian against his armies interfering with civilians who were not actively hostile. At times, he was generous with civilian transgressions on the principle that punishing everybody to get the guilty few only increased civilian hostility to his army.[37] He maintained in his memoirs that it was Halleck who first ordered him, on August 2, 1862, to handle Southerners "without gloves" and to live "on the resources of citizen's [*sic*] hostile to the government."[38] But there is evidence that Grant was easily provoked and that he helped to establish the new spirit of total war against civilians much earlier than Halleck's prodding. On January 11, 1862, Grant, from his headquarters for the District of Cairo, wrote to Brig. Gen. E. A. Paine, commanding Bird's Point, Missouri:

I understand that four of our pickets were shot this morning. If this is so, and appearances indicate that the assassins were citizens, not regularly organized in the rebel army, the whole country should be cleaned out, for six miles around, and word given that all citizens making their appearance within those limits are liable to be shot. To execute this, patrols should be sent out in all directions, and bring into camp at Bird's

35 Letter to John Sherman, Oct. 1, 1862, ibid., 165–6. On Sherman and total war, see John Bennett Walters, *Merchant of Terror: General Sherman and Total War* (Indianapolis, Ind., 1973); Royster, *Destructive War*; Vetter, *Sherman*; and Hagerman, *Civil War*.
36 Letters to Secretary of the Treasury Salmon P. Chase, July 31, 1862 and July 21, 1863; letter of April 21, 1863; order of April 9, 1863, Grant, *Memoirs and Letters*, 1010–11, 1021, 1023, 1028–9.
37 See, e.g., general orders, Jan. 13, 1862, ibid., 979–98. See also ibid., 256–7, 265, 289, 291, 387–8.
38 Ibid., 265.

Point all citizens, together with subsistence, and require them to remain under pain of death and destruction of their property until properly relieved."[39]

Grant noted that during his subsequent march to Fort Donelson, his army obviously aroused great fear on the part of the population.[40] Grant also noted the shock of the civilian population when, during operations following the Fort Donelson campaign, he responded to the destruction of his supply base at Holly Springs not by retreating, as the population expected, but by living off the land in the vicinity of Oxford, Mississippi, leaving the distressed population to survive off his sparse leavings.[41] In communications surrounding the first incident in particular, one detects that his growing distaste for the society that he is fighting is pushing the military motive.

Sherman, as well, when he was in command at Memphis, quickly adopted a total war policy to cope with partisan activity along the Mississippi. He burned down the village of Randolph, Tennessee, for harboring partisans, thus sending a message through any territory where his army might march. The nonbeliever Sherman even invoked the Christian imagery of the devil to reinforce the nationalist justification for the cause of total war. In a communication with Grant in October 1862, he wrote: "We cannot change the hearts of the people of the South, but we can make war so terrible that they will realize the fact that however brave and galant [sic] and devoted to their country, they are still mortal." He added that for those who submitted "to rightful law and authority, all gentleness and forbearance, but for such as would rebel against a government so mild and just as ours was in peace," Sherman predicted the doom of "Satan and the rebellious Saints of Heaven."[42]

During Sherman's advance on Johnston's army at Jackson, Mississippi, following the Vicksburg campaign, Grant, in a more generous mood, opted for the "carrot and stick" strategy. He ordered that Sherman's troops take nothing not absolutely necessary for their subsistence, so "they should try to create as favorable an impression as possible upon the people."[43] Arriving before Jackson, Sherman wielded the stick. For the first time, as noted before, he practiced the strategy of wasting the countryside that he would use to make his way through Georgia and the Carolinas. As he turned fields of corn into pastures for his animals, his trains hauling away what food and

---

39 Ibid., 978–9.   40 Letter to Mary Dent Grant, Feb. 9, 1862, ibid., 981–2.   41 Ibid., 291.
42 Quoted by Phillip Shaw Paludan, *A People's Contest* (New York, 1988), 291. For the role of religion as an aspect of the world view behind total war, see Richard E. Beringer et al., *Why the South Lost the Civil War* (Athens, Ga., 1986). The authors ably relate the convergence of religious and political world views.
43 Quoted by Grant from his orders, Grant, *Memoirs and Letters*, 387–8.

forage his army could not eat, Sherman made his famous remark: "The whole destruction to which this country is now being subjected is terrible to contemplate, but it is the scourge of war."[44]

Beginning with operations around Jackson, Sherman's actions went beyond his rhetoric. At Jackson, Sherman for the first time unleashed his disciplined army to follow its own lead. Charles Vetter and Royster both paint chilling pictures of Sherman tacitly supporting his army's escalated burning and looting. While his troops devastated the countryside, Sherman rationalized its acts with his fatalistic contention that it was the natural momentum of a people's army. In the subsequent and jointly planned raid on Meridian, Mississippi, Sherman and Grant reinforced the removal of all restraints short of the direct killing of civilians. The subsequent destruction and impoverishment blurred the distinction between the direct and indirect killing of civilians. Grant's and Sherman's total war strategy caught the spirit of Gen. Philip H. Sheridan's later strategic insight that what people most fear is poverty not death.

Both Royster and Vetter effectively contribute to the argument that Sherman and Grant adopted the strategic view that there were no innocent civilians. They knowingly accepted indirect civilian deaths from the intensified total war strategy as inevitable and just. To complete the military circle of total war thinking among Union strategists, Halleck congratulated Sherman for the Meridian raid by way of telling him that it was almost the first execution of "the severe rules of war that I have endeavored to impress upon our community for the past two years."[45] Vetter further observes that Sherman's army, left to follow its own lead, wrought greater destruction in the Southern states that the troops held responsible for the war than elsewhere, thus reinforcing the argument that ideology at least contributed to the destructive momentum of citizen armies. And Royster documents the popular imagery of humiliation, annihilation, vengeance, and vindication that lays the basis for speculation about the emotional and psychological sources of ideological and other overt expressions of motive.

Sherman brought the rapidly totalizing nature of strategy fully to national attention and into the Union political dialogue when he evacuated Atlanta. Without the troops to garrison the city following its capture, he enhanced the humiliation by asking his adversary, Gen. John Bell Hood, to assist in the evacuation. In response to cries of barbarism and worse from Hood and the Mayor and City Council of Atlanta, Sherman had the local press publish

---

44 Hagerman, *Civil War*, 208; Sherman's quote is from U.S. War Department, *War of the Rebellion: A Compilation of the Official Records of the Union and Confederate Armies*, 128 vols. (Washington, D.C., 1880–1901), ser. 1, vol. 24, pt. 2, 526.   45 Vetter, *Sherman*, 187.

two chilling responses, presenting the realities and rules of total war. "War is cruelty," he wrote in part, "and you cannot refine it, and those who brought war into our country deserve all the curses and maledictions a people can pour out."[46] These letters caught the public imagination and became part of the ideological battle waged by Lincoln and the Republicans both North and South. The subsequent burning of Atlanta, regardless of its cause, merely engraved the ideological and military picture of the growing totality of the Civil War more deeply in the consciousness of all.

The fall of Atlanta and events surrounding it may have been the catalyst that finally brought the North to accept Lincoln's political strategy of total war and the operational strategy necessary to achieve it. Atlanta revived the emotionally charged nationalism that Royster documents as present in Northern public opinion from the beginning. Nationalistic expression declined in late 1862 and 1863 with military defeat, the Emancipation Proclamation, and the suspension of civil liberties. But the fall of Atlanta and the accompanying imagery of the total destruction of the South stirred its emotional and ideological roots. The imagery of this revived nationalism, fortified by religious certitude, was by now moving both the Northern population and its citizen-soldiers (1) to a more realistic picture of the brutality and sacrifice of modern total war, and (2) to a willingness to see it through to the end. And Lincoln with his skilled party propagandists, as presented by Nagler, exploited the symbolism of Atlanta and the imagery of total war to the end of Southern destruction or surrender.

The impact of the fall of Atlanta in reelecting Lincoln and defeating the Democratic candidate, McClellan, was evidence of the changing mood. To underscore the mood, only 29 percent of McClellan's old Army of the Potomac voted for their once idolized creator and commander. This was less than the national return. Even allowing for turnover in the army, this was significant, considering that the army at this time was suffering horrible casualties under Grant. This fact reinforced the election results as a vote for both the president and general in chief and their respective political and military strategies of total war.[47]

Having sermonized the South on the ideological and military realities of total war, the nonbeliever Sherman let loose his hymn-singing army on the

---

46 Quoted by Paludan, *A People's Contest*, 301. Sherman gives a lengthy treatise on his philosophy of total war in a letter to the adjutant of his Army of the Tennessee, written Jan. 31, 1864, in response to the adjutant's request for guidelines on how to treat the civilian population of Huntsville, Alabama. The adjutant claimed that the letter, when printed, had a powerful effect on the citizenry. Sherman, on April 11, 1864, called for the letter to be more widely distributed to inform the areas of the South through which Sherman intended to pass, *Sherman Letters*, 228–32.

47 Paludan, *A People's Contest*, 312–13.

countryside of Georgia and the Carolinas. He estimated that he cost the state of Georgia $100 million, with $20 million accruing to the Union and "the remainder simple waste and destruction."[48] Together with General Sheridan on Grant's orders laying waste to the Shenandoah Valley, it indicated how far Grant and his commanders would move during 1864–65 in totalizing the nature of the war. Vetter extends the picture of destruction with his sociological observation that both Grant and Sherman acted with the awareness that one purpose of total war was to break up the social organization of a region. They were aware that local social disorganization also would separate one region of the South from another.[49]

While Sherman exhausted the will and resources of Georgia and the Carolinas, another face of modern total war was emerging in Virginia: attrition.[50] The strategy that Grant pursued when he took to the field with the Army of the Potomac in 1864 was in sharp contrast to that which he developed and continued to coordinate in the West. The western campaign through 1864–65 remained consistent with Grant's stated preference, after the fall of Donelson, for a war of maneuver that successfully occupied the enemy's territory without the bloodletting of major battles. But in the East, Grant appears to have developed a deliberate strategy of attrition against Robert E. Lee's Army of Northern Virginia. This may have reflected in part, as Hattaway and Jones suggest, Grant's lack of confidence in the will of the Army of the Potomac's command and staff to fight a war of maneuver. It may have reflected in part a prudent respect for the experience and success of his opponent in leading a large army, while he was new to commanding an army the size of the Army of the Potomac. With Lee in front of him, fighting on his own ground, Grant also may have taken more seriously the same strategic awareness that Sherman expressed as he pushed Johnston back to Atlanta – namely, that it was increasingly difficult in modern warfare for one large army to turn the flank of another.

Grant eventually attempted the deep turning movement that ended in the siege of Petersburg and scenes of static trench warfare that anticipated World War I. But he never moved more than ten miles a day or for more than five days at a time. Stripped down during 1863 to the standards of a flying column, the Army of the Potomac, as noted, had displayed its potential to move quickly and efficiently. One might think that Grant would have taken more

48 Hagerman, *Civil War*, 285.
49 Vetter, *Sherman*, 166, 181, 184.
50 For Grant's strategy with the Army of the Potomac, see Hagerman, *Civil War*, chap. 10. See also
    the analysis of Grant's strategy by Hattaway and Jones, *How the North Won*, to which I am indebt-
    ed, and which concludes that Grant did not develop a strategy of attrition.

chances at turning Lee's weary and depleted army. But Grant immediately abandoned the logistical structure of the flying column. He replaced it, as noted, with the transportation standard of forty wagons per 1,000 men that he had developed for his Army of the Tennessee, a standard twice what the Army of the Potomac achieved after Gettysburg. Grant's old friend and West Point roommate, Rufus Ingalls, quartermaster of the Army of the Potomac, was not party to Grant's motives, though he guessed that Grant simply gave in to the creature demands of a pampered army.

And it well may have been that Grant wanted as contented an army as possible for the task ahead. That task was to wear down Lee's army by attrition, as Grant cautiously but surely pushed it back to Richmond. Maneuver was not forgotten. That was Sherman's task in a concentric or coordinated two-theater strategy of exhaustion through maneuver and attrition. Grant in the East added to the weight of purely military considerations the political need to shield Washington, while he gave to Lincoln the tests of battle that the politics and public mood of 1864 increasingly demanded.

One can wonder whether the diffident and fearless soldier who could not stand the sight of blood drifted during his Virginia campaign into the psychological space of the war lover or avenger. Total war certainly gave to political and military leadership the potential to work out violent fantasies for themselves and for the collective unconscious of their culture. There is perhaps enough suggestive data to merit exploring in Grant and Sherman the psychological motives of the war lover that Thomas L. Connelly sought in Lee.[51] The approach to aggression and war pursued in the various strains of psychoanalytical theory, whether following Sigmund Freud, Melanie Klein, or the more recent work of Alice Miller, might help to explain the language and the reality of humiliation, vindication, violence, and annihilation present in the Civil War.[52] During 1864–65, the total war culture of Union politicians, generals, citizen soldiers, media, and public may have taken on a psychological face necessary to complete the explanation of Union strategy. Royster's excellent development of the emotional imagery of public, political, and military opinion, which Vetter compliments, invites a psychohistorical analysis of the emotional push to modern total war. We are overwhelmed with the language of aggressive social pathology projected onto another

51   Thomas L. Connelly, *The Marble Man* (New York, 1977).
52   Two interesting probes into the psychology of war from these perspectives are Alice Miller, *For Your Own Good: Hidden Cruelty in Child Rearing and the Roots of Violence* (New York, 1984); Sam Keen, *Faces of the Enemy: Reflections on the Hostile Imagination* (San Francisco, 1986). I am indebted to conversations with Prof. Claudio Duran of York University, Toronto, concerning his psychoanalytical study of public crisis and media response in Chile surrounding the election of the Salvador Allende government and its overthrow by the military coup of Gen. Augusto Pinochet.

society in the crisis of war. Such an analysis might help us to understand the psychological processes that bind together varying loyalties to culture, nation, state, locality, and family in the impulse to destroy the enemy. Such an analysis might extend our understanding of Sherman, Grant, Lincoln, and the bond that held them together as historical agents of modern total war strategy.

Union political and military strategy was the most deliberate and deepest plunge by western military culture into the depths of total war until World War II. It was so encompassing and unambiguous in part because it was out of necessity so spontaneous and so improvised. Emerging unexpectedly out of the moment, the war ran in directions difficult to anticipate. Out of the events of 1861–65 came an integrated ideological, political, and military world view constructed around the convergence of the ideological, social, and technological upheavals of mid-nineteenth-century America. Without developed political and military structures to moderate the course of an extended and unanticipated major war, the strategic response was more true to the realities of change than it might otherwise have been. Once set on their course, everybody did what they had to do next to win.

The purposeful leadership of Lincoln and Grant assured few checks in exploring and exploiting the possibilities of total war. The legacy of more than a half million dead (equal to the toll of all other American wars combined), the loss to the Confederacy, as McPherson notes in his accompanying essay, of a higher proportion of its population than any country in World War I, and greater than any area in World War II other than the region between the Rhine and the Volga, as well as the loss of two-thirds of its assessed wealth, the unconditional surrender of its armies, and finally the destruction of its political system and the social-economic structure that it represented, all constituted a sobering introduction to the course of modern total war strategy. The horrible loss of life emphasized that even without the systematic killing of civilians, the imperatives of modern war blurred distinctions between civilians and combatants. The range of human, institutional, social, and economic destruction in the South emphasized the process by which Union strategy engulfed the whole of the enemy's existence. This process in turn emphasized the importance of the whole picture of totalizing strategy in any explanation of the Civil War as a total war. The ominous legacy was the common purpose of modern nationalism and mass democracy-shaping strategy organized around the destructive potential of modern industrial society. Not until World War II would there again be such a convergence in western society of political and military commitment to total war as an ideological, organizational, and strategic concept.

PART THREE

Mobilization and Warfare

8

The Civil War Armies: Creation, Mobilization, and Development

HERMAN M. HATTAWAY

The United States Civil War eventually would compel both North and South to create, mobilize, and develop armies far larger and more complex than ever before had existed in the Western Hemisphere. In the process, armies ultimately were molded which in potency and in modernity would become fully equal to those of the great military nations of Europe—but not until after considerable development, which was accomplished only gradually. The Confederacy initially patterned its military system exactly after that of the Union. In both, as the war progressed, some evolutionary changes occurred— and this is important, really, as *the key* to understanding how much more crucial was *development* than was *creation* or *mobilization* in rendering the Civil War armies as the potent entities they became.

Since its earliest days, the United States had maintained two separate military forces: one, an active, regular organization of professionals; the other, the militia, a volunteer, civilian force to be swelled in size commensurate with any emergency. Various reports on file in the War Office indicated that there existed 3,163,711 militia: 2,471,377 in Union states and 692,334 in Confederate states. But these figures in essence were meaningless, for some of the returns dated back as far as 1827. A major conflict, such as the Civil War quickly proved to be, had to be fought largely by volunteers—later augmented by draftees. These forces were raised and maintained only for the duration of the conflict. West Point graduates dominated the key command and managerial positions, but their numbers necessarily had to be augmented by volunteer officers.[1]

---

1 See Marvin A. Kreidberg and Merton G. Henry, *History of Military Mobilization in the United States Army 1775–1945* (Washington, D.C., 1955), 83–90. Although caustically criticized by some of its reviewers, quite useful, long in the making and magnificently researched, is George T. Ness Jr., *The Regular Army on the Eve of the Civil War* (Baltimore, Md., 1990); much of the material in the immediately ensuing paragraphs is drawn from Herman M. Hattaway and Archer Jones, *How the North Won* (Urbana, Ill., Chicago, and London, 1983), chap. 1.

I

On the eve of the American Civil War, the nation's regular army consisted of 1,105 officers and 15,259 enlisted men – the majority of whom were foreign-born (and some 700 were sick or on detached duty). This widely scattered entity was organized into ten regiments of infantry, four of artillery, two of cavalry, two of dragoons, and one of mounted riflemen. Of 197 extant com-panies, 179 occupied seventy-nine isolated posts in the western territories and the remaining 18 manned ten garrisons east of the Mississippi River, mostly along the Canadian border and on the Atlantic coast. Each state had an elaborate – though typically very ill-trained, ill-equipped, poorly organ-ized, and poorly managed – militia system. Extant scholarship on these militia is still quite inadequate; we could use some good new works to shed more light upon precise numbers of available personnel and relative soldierly capability. But it would not be primarily militia that comprised the bulk of the fighting forces; instead, it would be masses of freshly recruited men with absolutely no prior military experience.

The 1860 census indicated that the U.S. population stood at 31,443,321. The eleven states that officially seceded encompassed 9,103,332 of this num-ber: 5,449,462 whites, 3,521,110 slaves, and 132,760 free Negroes. Some whites who resided in the states that remained in the Union, approximately 600,000, also cast their sympathies and efforts in behalf of the South, bring-ing the white population in support of the Confederacy to about six million. The North's population therefore stood at 22,339,989 less the 600,000 esti-mated Southern sympathizers, or an effective 21,739,989.

From the Southern totals should be subtracted (1) those people who lived in what during the war became the new state of West Virginia and in areas such as East Tennessee, which contributed substantial support to the Union, and (2) the Southern blacks who eventually were liberated and subsequent-ly saw service in the Union army. Black soldiers ultimately became a major factor of significance in the Northern war effort (but not until after mid-1863). For the South, and from the first, the labor provided by masses of blacks (mostly in impressed gangs) was of inestimably great military value.

Another crucial demographic statistic, aside from population totals, is relative "military population" – in other words, white (because neither side initially used, nor at the outset intended ever to use, any black soldiers) males between the ages of eighteen and forty-five. Absolutely accurate data on this cannot be attained,[2] but careful estimates suggest that the Confederacy had approximately 1,000,000 potential soldiers, while the North possessed

2   See E[verette] B[each] Long, *The Civil War Day by Day* (Garden City, N.Y., 1971), 704.

perhaps slightly under 3,500,000. To that last number could be added the eventual acquisitions of liberated Southern blacks, as well as the surprisingly high number of more than 100,000 white Southerners who chose to be "loyalists" (the Confederates called them "Tories") and fought for the Union. Civil War scholars long have been relatively ignorant about this group – save for the fraction of them known as "the galvanized Yankees," written about by Dee Alexander Brown – until the recent path-breaking book by Richard N. Current closed a major gap in our understanding.[3]

I I

When secession came, regular officers who wished to vacate their commissions were allowed to do so, and some were dismissed under suspicion of disloyalty. A total of 296 officers left the federal army; 270 of this number eventually joined the Confederate military forces. A rather effective effort was made to retain in federal service all regular enlisted personnel, but at least 70 – and possibly nearly 400 – enlisted men managed to get out of United States service and go south.[4] During the time span of but a few months, in late 1860 and early 1861, eleven states officially seceded from the Union. Both sides later claimed two additional states (Kentucky and Missouri), and the entire border region between the two sections was severely strained with division; many persons in each of the border states choosing to support one side and many persons choosing the other side.

Initially, both sides relied upon the state governments as the medium for recruiting and equipping the needed manpower. Both eventually would shift, though only gradually, toward centralized control over the mobilization process. Ironically perhaps, given its espousal of the state rights concept, the Confederacy inclined first toward centralization. On March 6, 1861, the Confederate Congress passed two major military laws. The first authorized the President to call out the Militia for six months and to accept 100,000 volunteers for one year in the Provisional Army of the Confederate States. Some 27,200 were inducted prior to the firing on Fort Sumter. The second act authorized the establishment of a regular army of 10,600 men. Five days earlier, President Jefferson Davis had named the first general officer, Pierre Gustave Toutant Beauregard, the former United States major of engineers

---

3 Dee Alexander Brown, *The Galvanized Yankees* (Urbana, Ill., 1963); Richard N. Current, *Lincoln's Loyalists: Union Soldiers from the Confederacy* (Boston, 1992).

4 This number was asserted by Emory Upton to have been only twenty-six; his assertion long was accepted as correct, and that number appears in a great many works on the Civil War. The higher estimate is proven by Richard P. Weinert Jr. in his *The Confederate Regular Army* (Shippensburg, Pa., 1991).

and a West Point graduate whose last assignment had been the superintendency of West Point.

Much controversy has raged about whether or not the South garnered a disproportionate share of West Point–trained officers. (Also, it is of some significance that initially the regular army was somewhat demoralized by the fact that so seemingly large a portion of its officers chose either to resign or to accept dismissal in order to join the Confederate forces.) At the outset, West Point graduates on the active duty list numbered 824; of these, 184 became Confederate officers. Of the approximately 900 military academy graduates then in civilian life, 114 returned to the Union army and 99 others acquired Southern commissions. Thus, the North enjoyed the services of 754 West Pointers while the South had 283; the North possessed two-and-two-thirds times as many West Point–trained personnel.

Another (and closely related) controversy has to do with an allegation that, the proportions notwithstanding, the South attracted "the cream" of the old officer corps. A plausible argument in support of this notion can be made, to be sure, and it is strengthened by the obvious high level of quality in command and leadership achieved by the South, early on, and particularly in the eastern theater of the war. But there are other possible explanations for how and why this occurred; furthermore, the posit has been inflated and badly distorted, not least by the development of a so-called "Myth of the Lost Cause" and the winning of the war – retroactively – by Virginia.[5] I could not possibly settle this issue in so brief an essay as this, if indeed anyone could settle it at all, but suffice it to say that I assert that the argument is moot in the present context.

During the crisis between Abraham Lincoln's election as President of the United States and his inauguration, the seceded states formed a joint government, the Confederate States of America. This new government proceeded to seize federal property, forts, and arsenals within the borders of the territory it claimed. Until formation of the Confederate government on February 4, 1861, South Carolina – the first state to secede, and the site early in April of the first significant exchange of hostile gunfire – purported to function as a separate nation. Even for a brief period following the creation of the Confederacy, South Carolina maintained its own army, comprising state militia, cadets from the Citadel (a Charleston military college), and numerous other volunteers. This polymorphous group was rapidly transformed and much of it absorbed, following the Fort Sumter episode, into

---

5   See the relevant works by Thomas Lawrence Connelly, Barbara Bellows, Charles Reagan Wilson, Gaines Foster, William Garrett Piston, John A. Simpson, Lloyd Hunter, and myself.

the Confederate army. Even at this point in time, the various Southern states probably had larger numbers of men under arms than did the Confederate government, but the speed of national mobilization rapidly increased. On April 16, 1861, President Davis called for another 32,000 volunteers. All of the early calls for manpower were met enthusiastically. A greater problem than getting numbers of men was how to supply them; and still greater was the problem of organization, administration, and training.

The United States potentially possessed an advantage at the outset for it could have used the regular army as a cadre to train the volunteers. This was not done, however, for several reasons; hence, the United States kept its regular army intact. Lincoln did not foresee a long war, the regulars seemed needed on the frontier, and it was politically expedient to appoint new high-ranking officers to command and lead the volunteers. The Confederacy, of course, initially possessed no regular army at all, and the creation of one never got much beyond the blueprint stage, although six full generals were appointed.

The Union used a departmental system of regional responsibility, initiated in the 1820s by Secretary of War John C. Calhoun and modified in 1850 by Davis when he held the same office. In each department, a senior colonel or general officer by brevet (there were no non-brevet general officers at all on active duty on the eve of the Civil War) commanded whatever officers and men were stationed therein. The system continued into the Civil War, and this same department system, although with some significant twists of difference in practice, would be used by the Confederacy as well.

Since neither the regular nor the militia organizations provided a suitable base for the huge new armies, the belligerents were obliged to build them from scratch. Both the Union volunteer forces and the Confederacy's provisional army were modeled on the regular army and relied for leadership on a mixture of regular and militia officers, Mexican War veterans, men of political significance, and assorted prominent citizens. When a nation so construed, as was the United States, finds itself in a large war, it will have to rely much upon volunteer officers. The mass of these will, to be sure, remain at company grade levels, but the better of them may rise to field grades, and some even might – as *was* the case in the Civil War – attain general grade ranks. The topic of the Civil War volunteer officer, in a general sense, still awaits a good scholarly treatment.[6]

---

6 My late major professor, T. Harry Williams, was much interested in this, and intended his *Hayes of the Twenty-third: The Civil War Volunteer Officer* to be a case study. Rutherford B. Hayes, incidentally, did not hanker for a star on his collar (although he eventually got one), preferring instead – as he put it – "to be one of the good colonels to being one of the poor generals." T. Harry Williams, *Hayes of the Twenty-third: The Civil War Volunteer Officer* (New York, 1965), the quotation comes from 18.

Many of the volunteer officers, the future President Hayes among that number, had no prior military knowledge whatsoever. But rather significant is the fact that many other nonsoldiers at least had attended one of the numerous private and state military schools that had proliferated since the Mexican War. The great majority of these were located in the South. But one very important private military school in the North was Norwich University in Vermont, which furnished 523 Northern officers and 34 Confederate subalterns. The important thing in general about this is: If a volunteer attained high rank, there was some good reason underlying the reality.

Only a small fragment of the volunteer officers who attained very high ranks, such as the North's Alexander Schimmelfennig, made real asses of themselves – and most of the incompetents were weeded out rather effectively, or reassigned to some job where they were not terribly dangerous. I will venture one "shoot-from-the-hip" speculation concerning the relative collective merit of the North's and the South's pool of potential volunteer officers. Since the South had a greater number of men with some prior military schooling, the pool probably provided for better leadership at company grade and staff positions. But at general grade ranks, *if* it is fair to posit that two quintessentially representative samples from each side were, say, Joshua Lawrence Chamberlain and Rutherford B. Hayes for the North, and Nathan Bedford Forrest and James Johnston Pettigrew for the South, we see a significant contrast. The South's better volunteer general officers tended more to be eccentric geniuses or brooding intellectuals, often with an aristocratic bent, while the North's were more likely to be professional men with more universally applicable managerial skills.[7]

III

Initially, state and individual initiative played a large role in the formation of regiments, the basic units of the armies. The voluntary infantry regiment comprised ten companies with no battalion organization intervening between the colonel and the ten captains and their companies, each numbering between fifty and one hundred men. Usually four to six regiments, grouped together, formed a brigade under a brigadier general. The next higher unit, the division, commanded by a major general, was quite unstandardized as was the next larger unit, the corps. Once the fighting commenced

---

7   See the following interesting and illuminating biographical studies: Williams, *Hayes*; Alice Rains Trulock, *In the Hands of Providence: Joshua L. Chamberlain and the American Civil War* (Raleigh, N.C., 1992); Clyde N. Wilson, *Carolina Cavalier: The Life and Mind of James Johnston Pettigrew* (Athens, Ga., 1990); and Brian Steel Wills, *A Battle from the Start: The Life of Nathan Bedford Forrest* (New York, 1992).

in earnest, battle losses often made organizational ideals something of a mockery. Sometimes a division might have been reduced to a size that rendered it hardly as large as a proper regiment.

The "esprit" of any regiment was of crucial significance during the Civil War. Men had an intense affinity with their regiment, and regiments typically were formed from men who came from the same area and who often had known each other in civilian life. Whatever other loyalties one might espouse, one's pride depended most upon his regimental identity. The Union created 3,559 separate units, while the Confederacy spawned probably 1,526.[8]

Armies usually were named for the geographic department in which they operated or, when initially formed, were expected to operate. Military Departments tended to be named by the Union for rivers, while the Confederacy typically named them for states or for regions. There eventually were sixteen Union and at least twenty-five Confederate field armies—the latter number is unclear because the varying complexity of the Confederate Military Department System renders it impossible to say with certainty, in some cases, what was and what was not a field army. Official records indicate that the total enlistment in the Federal forces were 2,778,304, but scholars dispute the figures. Of course, many thousands of individuals enlisted more than once, and some troops served only for very short periods. Estimates of how many *individuals* served run from 1,550,000 to 2,200,000. The greatest student of Civil War minutiae who ever lived, E. B. Long, suggested that "probably something over 2,000,000 would be as accurate a figure as possible on total individuals in the Federal armed forces."[9] Confederate totals are even more in dispute. Numerous scholars believe that the Southern forces comprised no more than 600,000 individuals; other estimates range upward to 1,400,000. Long judiciously asserted that "perhaps 750,000 individuals would be reasonably close."[10] James M. McPherson, however, puts the number at 900,000 and thinks that even this may be too low because of uncertainty as to precisely how much Southern militia might, for brief episodes, actually have gotten into combat.[11]

The armies, alike in their personnel—at least until after the mid-war Northern augmentation of black troops—and also alike in their organization, resembled each other in doctrine. Again, this was because of the domination of the highest commands on both sides by West Point graduates. Modeled on

8 See Long, *The Civil War Day by Day*, 716-17.
9 Ibid., 705.
10 Ibid.
11 James M. McPherson, *Ordeal by Fire* (New York, 1982), 181; and *Battle Cry of Freedom* (New York, 1988), 30n. See also Maris A. Vinovskis, *Toward a Social History of the American Civil War: Exploratory Essays* (Cambridge, Mass., 1990), 11.

the Ecole Polytechnique in France, the West Point curriculum emphasized engineering. It provided an excellent technical education, the best graduates being selected for service in the engineers. Its military education instilled a good understanding of weapons and of army routine, making the graduates adept at map reading, drill, and small-unit tactics. Thereafter, service in the regular army had provided West Pointers with a knowledge of troop leading, logistics, and small-unit staff duties.

I V

In the months that followed the fall of Fort Sumter, both sides steadily groped toward full mobilization. Two days after the fort's capitulation, President Lincoln issued a proclamation declaring the existence of an insurrection in the then only seven Confederate states, called out 75,000 militia for three months service, and scheduled a special session of Congress to convene on July 4, at that time more than six weeks away. On April 29, Davis sent a lengthy message to his Congress, meticulously detailing the history of the establishment of the Southern government, and terming Lincoln's proclamation a presidential declaration of war, which indeed it was.[12]

The strongly pro-Union Northern states immediately wired their acceptance of the call for troops, but the border states balked. Virginia seceded on April 17 and promptly raised forces to protect her borders. North Carolina state troops mustered and seized Fort Caswell and Fort Johnson. Meetings of patriotic groups stirred attention in both the North and the South, and efforts everywhere were concentrated upon mustering and organizing militia. To Lincoln's great relief, because he was intensely worried about the possibility of a rebel incursion in Washington, on April 18, 1861, five companies of Pennsylvanians numbering about 460 men (known thereafter in tribute as the "First Defenders") reached the capital, the vanguard of troops to defend the District.

On the same day, General in Chief Winfield Scott—himself too old and infirm to take the field—held a conference with his former engineer staff officer from the Mexican War, brevet Col. Robert E. Lee, and offered him command of the Union army. But Lee declined, resigned his commission two days later, and within a week became major general in command of all of Virginia's military forces. Lee, of course, ultimately would emerge as the preeminent Southern general—but not until after a lackluster early performance in western Virginia, coastal defense duty in South Carolina, and staff

---

12 Much in the immediately ensuing paragraphs is drawn from Hattaway and Jones, *How the North Won*, chap. 2.

work in Richmond. The North placed first reliance for major field command upon a former major elevated to major general, Irvin McDowell ... and, after McDowell's debacle at the Battle of Bull Run, upon thirty-six-year-old George B. McClellan. First in the West Point class of 1846, McClellan had resigned from the army in 1857, still a captain, to become chief engineer of the Illinois Central Railroad.

The early, and subsequent, swelling size of both opposing armies forced Lincoln and Davis to elevate numerous individuals to general grade ranks. Lincoln could select almost two-thirds of his general officers from numbers of regulars because, contrary to a traditional supposition, he had three times as many as Davis from whom to choose. Yet Lincoln, without Davis's regular military background, sometimes yielded to temptation to give less recognition to military professionalism. His nation suffered from far more division than Davis's, and the appointment of general officers constituted a valuable resource for the use of patronage in enlisting support for the war among the various political, ethnic, and other interest groups.

Actually, for a variety of reasons, the South had a keener appreciation for military professionalism than did the North. It has been asserted that early in the Civil War the South did a better job than the North in identifying its more able officers, and getting them sooner into high levels of command. More to the point is that the South much more, and from the outset, welcomed its military professionals and capitalized upon their talents. Sixty-four percent of the regular army officers who went South became generals, while less than thirty percent of those who stayed with the Union did so.[13] But *all* of this was something that came *after* the war had commenced.

In appointing generals, Lincoln sought a broad base of support for the war, drawing appointees from the hard-core abolitionists, the high-tariff advocates, the War Democrats, and the foreign-language immigrant groups. In 1861 alone, he made generals of two Dutchmen, two Germans, a Hungarian, an Irishman, and a Pole. Yet Lincoln also recognized the professional expertise of the regulars and appointed, proportionally, half again more career soldiers than did Davis, handicapped as Davis was by a far smaller number from whom to choose.

V

We do not know nearly as much about Civil War basic training as might be useful for us; here is still another great topic awaiting its student, but for a good start, see William J. Miller's *The Training of an Army: Camp Curtin and the North's*

---

13   Samuel P. Huntington, *The Soldier and the State* (New York, 1957), 213.

Civil War.[14] While it is true that masses of soldiers got no basic training at all, and learned on-the-job (even sometimes being committed to combat literally from the first moment of their service), basic training did take place for some troops. The Confederacy, for example, at least early in the war, maintained a number of basic training camps, the most notable one being located on the fairgrounds just outside of Richmond, Virginia. Another, and ill-fated, Confederate basic training facility was Camp Moore, near Kentwood, Louisiana, where the hapless entire garrison was wiped out by a deadly epidemic of measles. Following the first Battle of Bull Run in July 1861 and the commencement of the Peninsula in May 1862, the principal Union army remained so long in garrison near Washington, D.C., that the experience, in large measure, constituted an extensive and convoluted episode of basic training. The commander of that force, the Union Army of the Potomac, McClellan—called by Williams, my major professor, and other detractors "the problem child of the Civil War"—his many egregious flaws notwithstanding, was, students usually agree, the most keenly able organizer and administrator that the war produced.[15] Aside from McClellan, no other high-level Union officers, with the notable exceptions of William Tecumseh Sherman and George G. Meade—on certain occasions—accomplished much in the way of setting up practical training programs.[16]

Training camps followed no normative standard. There was no prescribed length of training. For some men, their time in training camp was measured in hours, but some others spent months in one training camp or another. The vast majority of training camps existed only early in the war. They might spring up anywhere, in North or South, on fairgrounds, vacant lots, train yards, parks, or village greens. Some of them remained in existence only a few weeks or months. Nearly all of them that were developed with much in the way of physical facility, especially those in the North, ultimately were converted into places of incarceration for prisoners of war. Camp Curtin, located about a mile north of Harrisburg, Pennsylvania, was a notable exception. Remaining in operation as a training center throughout the war, more than 300,000 troops from Pennsylvania, Maryland, Michigan, Minnesota, New Jersey, New York, Ohio, and Wisconsin spent some time there during the conflict.

Some lower-level officers took the initiative and, during lulls between battles, instituted training programs on their own. We know in some detail

14 Weinert, *The Confederate Regular Army.*
15 Many useful insights can be gleaned from Stephen W. Sears, *George B. McClellan: The Young Napoleon* (New York, 1988), and from the much older but still unsupplanted Fred A. Shannon, *The Organization and Administration of the Union Army, 1861–1865,* 2 vols. (Cleveland, Ohio, 1928).
16 Kreidberg and Henry, *Military Mobilization,* 121–2.

about the activities of a few such noteworthy individuals; for example, I have written much about the training activities of the Confederate Stephen D. Lee during the nearly year-long period that he was a field grade officer. While he often was compelled through circumstance to go into battle at the head of green troops, he never left himself in so unfortunate a position as to have to commit *raw* troops to a fight, because he insisted upon some training from the first instant that they came under his purview.[17] Doubtless there were an uncounted number of other similarly judicious-minded officers. Here again is an underworked topic awaiting a good synthesizer. But whatever limited amount of training in the field that was prescribed, the most effective training in most cases came from the experience of combat itself.

V I

When it comes to studying particular armies, there are a number of different initial approaches possible: investigations of personnel from the bottom ranks up, or from the top-ranking people down, institutional delineations (especially regimental histories), or some combination. Probably the best-known and best-loved study of a single army is Bruce Catton's vivid and emotionally moving memorial to the Federal Army of the Potomac: *Mr. Lincoln's Army* (1951), *Glory Road* (1952), and the Pulitzer Prize–winning *A Stillness at Appomattox* (1953). Catton uses to some extent all four of the variant approaches, but – more than any other – his is primarily an institutional one. While justly and endearingly popular, Catton was somewhat opinionated, always slightly pro-Northern in viewpoint, and much of his work is only lightly documented, being based largely on regimental histories.

The Northern armies have not yet been compared and contrasted with each other at the macrocosmic level nearly to the same degree as have, at least two, of the Southern armies. Douglas Southall Freeman in the mid-1930s made a magnificent pioneering study of the Confederate Army of Northern Virginia, albeit through a complex delineation of its commanders.[18] (I particularly point out Freeman's approach because, in all fairness, it is probably true that any army can be studied effectively – certainly to a significant degree – by studying the biographies of its leaders.) Thomas Lawrence Connelly, in the late 1960s and early 1970s, set a new standard for histories

---

17 See Herman M. Hattaway, *General Stephen D. Lee* (Jackson, Miss., 1976) but even more on this specific point in my "Stephen D. Lee and the Guns at Second Manassas," to be in a forthcoming book edited by Roman Heleniak and Lawrence Hewitt, the proceedings of the Third Annual Deep Delta Civil War Symposium held at Hammond, Louisiana.
18 Douglas Southall Freeman, *R. E. Lee: A Biography*, 4 vols. (New York, 1934–35); and *Lee's Lieutenants: A Study in Command*, 3 vols. (New York, 1946).

of Civil War armies with his two volumes on the Confederate Army of Tennessee.[19] But Richard M. McMurry accomplished a transcending achievement in comparative analysis, probing these same two armies from an entirely fresh perspective in his 1989 book, *Two Great Rebel Armies*.[20]

McMurry intended his short book to be "a philosophical and historiographical introduction"[21] to his projected lifetime magnum opus: a history of the Civil War in the West. This is a worthy goal, one on which I wish him well. Far too much emphasis has, until rather recently, been exclusively put upon study of the war in, and the armies of, the eastern theater. Connelly was something of a modern harbinger of a proper and more balanced perspective, much added to by a handful of other like-minded zealots: especially Archer Jones, Albert Castel, myself (I hope I am not being unduly pompous with this personal citation), the Reverend Larry J. Daniel, and Connelly's great student William Garrett Piston.

McMurry has shed edifying new light on the perplexing contrast between the accomplishments of the two principal Confederate armies, the Army of Northern Virginia and the Army of Tennessee. The former, under Robert E. Lee for nearly all of the war, enjoyed much success; the latter, under six different (and relatively incompetent) commanders, enjoyed almost no successes at all. This was not, as previous students typically surmised, because of the huge difference in operational area. McMurry posits that "the Army of Tennessee was not unsuccessful because it campaigned over a vast area; it campaigned over a vast area because it was unsuccessful."[22] But why?

Many factors apply: boundary amorphousness, effect of waterways and of railroads, and differences in quality and availability of command and leadership, as well as organization and execution. Most significant was the truth that far more personnel who found their way into the Army of Northern Virginia had some previous military experience or training than did those who served in the Army of Tennessee. Ultimately, the Army of Northern Virginia was far superior to the Army of Tennessee because of the latter's disparate underpinnings. This affected leadership at all levels, but it had greatest impact with respect to commanding generals. Robert E. Lee and Virginia Governor John Letcher made a good team, as did Lee and President Davis. Lee was

---

19 Thomas Lawrence Connelly, *Army of the Heartland: The Army of Tennessee, 1861–1862* (Baton Rouge, La., 1967); and *Autumn of Glory: The Army of Tennessee, 1863–1865* (Baton Rouge, La., 1971). These two volumes eclipsed Stanley Horn's rather well-written and competently documented *The Army of Tennessee* (Norman, Okla., 1941), which remains popular because of its readability.

20 Richard M. McMurry, *Two Great Rebel Armies: An Essay in Confederate Military History* (Chapel Hill, N.C., and London, 1989).

21 Ibid., xiii.

22 Ibid., 150.

self-effacing, cooperative, and communicative. He constantly tinkered at improving administration, organization, and articulation. For much of the war, he faced inferior opposite numbers in the Federal army. In *every way* was the reverse true in the West.

V I I

It is also possible to begin the study of an army not from the top down – via looks at the lives of the commanders – but rather from the bottom up – by investigating the common soldiers.[23] The great pioneer of this technique was Bell I. Wiley, whose classic works on the common soldier include *The Life of Johnny Reb* and *The Life of Billy Yank*.[24] Wiley's able student James I. Robertson Jr. offered a good supplement to the master's work in 1988 with *Soldiers Blue and Gray*,[25] but a new and higher level of achievement in this regard has been reached by Reid Mitchell with his much superior 1990 book, *Civil War Soldiers*.[26]

Mitchell began by depicting the North and the South as much more alike than different. But shared national identity does not necessarily prevent violent conflict, and, assuredly, it did not. Hatred for the enemy became a reality; it either existed at the outset, or it developed. Soldiers projected stark differences upon the individuals and culture of the other side, and that helped them not only to nurture hatred but also to be fomenters of depravity and destruction. And, too, the war itself engendered and fed an ensuing mythology. If, for example, at the outset the South did not possess any internal force powerful enough to tie its whites together, it did have that by 1865.

Brave deeds, and above all a shared military experience, bred a potent brotherly affinity. The war profoundly changed its participants. More than anything else, it welded the loyalties of combatants to each other and alienated them from society at large. The war was hell. But those who endured it tended to internalize a certain indifference to brutality and savagery. Further, any individual's own virtue and courage, and that of his fellows, in contrast to the evil cruelty (real or not) of those on the other side, also provided a sustaining element. Mitchell concludes that "fraternizing between the armies

<hr />

23 In "Have Social Historians Lost the Civil War?" which is the lead essay in his *Toward a Social History of the American Civil War*, Vinovskis cites, among others, the good pioneering work in this regard already done, and being done, by Earl J. Hess and W. J. Rorabaugh. There are, here and there, elsewhere in the Vinovskis book a few tidbits that refer to and reinforce the concept, but they are too arcane and tentative to warrant being taken into account within the scope of this essay.

24 Bell E. Wiley, *The Life of Johnny Reb: The Common Soldier of the Confederacy* (Indianapolis, Ind., 1943); and *The Life of Billy Yank: The Common Soldier of the Union* (Indianapolis, Ind., 1952).

25 James I. Robertson Jr., *Soldiers Blue and Gray* (Columbia, S.C., 1988).

26 Reid Mitchell, *Civil War Soldiers* (New York, 1990).

was not as prevalent as postwar myth would have it."[27] On the other hand, Civil War soldiers usually were willing to give quarter, to take prisoners and not to abuse them. But brutality, especially in the prisons, apparently increased toward the war's end.

The most significant of all puzzles concerning the Civil War are the questions of loyalty, tenacity, and will. Mitchell is fascinated with these matters and deals much with them. His interesting conclusion is that "the North had a superior will to fight the war it had to fight than the South had to fight its war."[28]

VIII

We know a good deal about the black soldiers thanks to two outstanding books: Dudley T. Cornish's 1956 classic, *The Sable Arm*, and Joseph T. Glatthaar's prize-winning 1990 work, *Forged in Battle*.[29] The black troop units mostly were outstanding outfits. This resulted in part because blacks were highly motivated and strove mightily to be good soldiers and also because generally their officers – almost all of them white – were particularly well qualified. White men were drawn as candidates for commissions in the United States Colored Troops by a variety of motivations: "I would drill a company of alligators for a hundred and twenty a month,"[30] confessed one; some were what we might call "turkeys" (for example, men whose previous units wanted to "dump" them); but the mass were keenly able. One famous institution that helped many of them to qualify was the Free Military School for Applicants for Commands of Colored Troops, in Pennsylvania, a precursor of Officer Candidate School.

More than 34,000 Northern blacks served in the Union Army, over 15 percent of the 1860 free black population. The precise total of all black troops cannot be ascertained. An officially recorded number is 178,892; hence, some 80 percent of the black troops were former slaves. Donning the Federal uniform was rather an esoteric experience for blacks, "This is the biggest thing that ever happened in my life,"[31] commented one. They encountered all manner of trial, exacerbated by racism, prejudice, negative stereotype, doubts about their worth, and myriad hostility. They persevered; and they turned in a collective war record well marked by honor and valor. They also

---

27 Ibid., 37.   28 Ibid., 183.
29 Dudley T. Cornish, *The Sable Arm: Black Troops in the Union Army, 1861–1865* (New York, 1956; new ed. with introduction by Herman M. Hattaway: Lawrence, Kan., 1987); and Joseph T. Glatthaar, *Forged in Battle: The Civil War Alliance of Black Soldiers and White Officers* (New York, 1990)
30 Glatthaar, *Forged in Battle*, 41.
31 Ibid., 79.

provided an ultimate psychological blow: In the end—because of such appalling rates of Confederate battle casualties combined with egregious numbers of desertions—there were about as many blacks serving in the Union army as there were whites still remaining on active duty in the Confederate forces.

I X

Until recently, rather little has been done to delineate any specific differences, *as groups*, between common soldiers who comprised the various different armies spawned by the two sides. In this regard, a step in the desired direction has been taken by the Reverend Daniel, whose *Soldiering in the Army of Tennessee*[32] has done much, as Gary Gallagher has put it, to bring "these western Confederates out from the shadow of their more famous counterparts in Lee's army."[33] It is striking that the western army retained cohesiveness despite its lack of strong leadership and its frustrations on the battlefields. This resulted, Daniel concludes, from fear of punishment, a fortuitous religious revival that stressed commitment and sacrifice, and a strong element of comradeship that was engendered in large part by the common experience of serving for so long under losing generals. Nevertheless, the ultimate reality is that the Civil War was decided in the western theater, and there the principal Union army came to far outclass *any* of the Confederate forces.

X

A crucial reality with respect to the ongoing development of the opposing principal forces in the western theater is that, with the passage of time, the Confederate forces did not improve as much as the Federal forces, which continued to evolve and became quintessentially effective—*this*, really, is the key, as I see it, to the topic of this essay! Late in the war, even Confederate Gen. Joseph E. Johnston asserted of his adversarial force that "there had been no such army since the days of Julius Caesar ... [and] it is not likely that one equal to it will be seen again in the country in our day and generation."[34]

Two recent books tell much about this process. The first is Charles Royster's complex and very stimulating long essay, entitled *The Destructive War*, in which he attempts to explain (1) how the war came to be so violent,

32   Larry J. Daniel, *Soldiering in the Army of Tennessee: A Portrait of Life in the Confederate Army* (Chapel Hill, N.C., 1991).
33   Gallagher, probably in his evaluation of the book for the University of North Carolina Press, quoted in advertising.
34   Quoted in Joseph T. Glatthaar, *The March to the Sea and Beyond: Sherman's Troops in the Savannah and Carolinas Campaigns* (New York and London, 1985), 15.

and (2) how the people who waged it, both soldier and civilian, became able to accept that level of violence. In the process, Royster winds up describing within a sociocultural context quite a bit about Americans of the Civil War era in general, and in particular Thomas J. "Stonewall" Jackson and Sherman.[35]

Rather more pertinent to the subject of this chapter is Glatthaar's superb *The March to the Sea and Beyond*, which delineates much about the internal and institutional development of Sherman's army—really an "army group" comprised of three field forces.[36] I perhaps have yielded too much to the temptation (I hope not to a culpable degree) to quote in the remainder of this chapter much from this intriguing work by Glatthaar. I am attracted, I think, by the *artfulness* of his approach. And it is through an artful approach, I feel convinced, that one can best grasp the significance and impact of Sherman's achievement. To that end, I highly recommend Keith F. Davis's *George N. Barnard: Photographer of Sherman's Campaign*.[37]

Sherman's march to the sea in late 1864, and his subsequent campaign in early 1865 into the Carolinas, was an integrated part of the grand strategy formulated by the Union's general in chief, Ulysses S. Grant, a strategy aimed at overcoming a significant twofold advantage enjoyed by the Confederacy: of being on the defensive, and being able to use interior lines. Grant envisioned army-sized raids (rather than penetrations, for example, invasions and occupations) of enemy territory. Concomitantly, in order to preclude the South's ability to redeploy to meet and counter any significant threat of the moment (as it had managed to do, rather spectacularly on several previous occasions), Grant prescribed something that Abraham Lincoln long had advocated: simultaneous advance along several fronts. Any, or even all but one, of such simultaneous advances could in effect become holding actions—in favor of the one advance that would become the Union's principal hammer blow against the South's will to continue making war. *This* one advance, this will-breaking venture, became Sherman's march!

It was a march conducted by an army of veterans. This "army had more actual experience than any other Federal command,"[38] for it was a group of men who had learned the art of soldiering through several years of actual, often hard, campaigning. Nearly all the troops had received their training

---

35 Charles Royster, *The Destructive War: William Tecumseh Sherman, Stonewall Jackson and the Americans* (New York, 1991); and see my review of this book in *The Washington Times* (March 22, 1992).
36 Much material in the ensuing paragraphs is based on Glatthaar's *The March to the Sea* and on John G. Barrett, *Sherman's March Through the Carolinas* (Chapel Hill, N.C., 1956); and Richard E. Beringer et al., *Why the South Lost the Civil War* (Athens, Ga., 1986).
37 Published in 1990. It was personally and professionally gratifying to me to have had the opportunity to assist in the preparation of this work, by serving as editorial advisor.
38 Glatthaar, *The March to the Sea*, 17.

in the western theater, where prolonged campaigns, lengthy marches, supply shortages, and Northern success in battle were the rule rather than the exception.

It was a march destined to have amazing psychological impact upon the Southern people! The famed Civil War historian Frank E. Vandiver once said with tongue-in-cheek that communities from Texas to Virginia swear that Sherman's army marched through them. As Glatthaar observes, "beneath the lighthearted side to that statement, however, is a very powerful message which clearly indicates the enormous effects of total war as implemented by Sherman's army. This was both an element of actual devastation and the inducement of *fears into the hearts and minds* of the civilian populace."[39] Resolved to "make the march and make Georgia howl," Sherman's object was not only to destroy resources but also, as Sherman himself put it, to "illustrate the vulnerability of the South. They don't know what war means; but when the rich planters of the Oconee and Savannah see their fences, and corn, and hogs, and sheep vanish before their eyes, they will have something more than a mean opinion of the 'Yanks'."[40]

It is worthwhile to remember that Sherman's men not only were experienced veterans; they also were citizen soldiers and for the most part intensely patriotic. Southerners anxiously had awaited the coming of the November 1864 Union presidential election, hoping for Lincoln's defeat as a sign of the failure of the North's determination to triumph over the Confederacy. But not among Sherman's men did those who hoped for a Lincoln defeat find much reason to hope: Sherman's men overwhelmingly favored Lincoln's reelection, and, when they voted, a staggering 86 percent of them so cast their ballots. It seems, too, significantly, that – as Glatthaar says – "in a sense, the 1864 Lincoln victory at the polls, coupled with the fall of Atlanta, renewed the commitment of Sherman's troops to the Union cause."[41]

Sherman wisely had "realized from the start that in the campaigns [ahead] the burdens were going to shift [markedly] from headquarters to lower-grade officers and even upon the initiative that might be shown by enlisted men." And here was "one key element in the success of Sherman's army ... the astonishing amount of experience in the officer corps. Nearly all the officers had served for several years, many of them having worked their way up from the enlisted ranks ... Ninety-six percent of the regimental commanders had served previously in companies, with one in six coming from the enlisted ranks. More revealing are the statistics on company-grade officers [captains and lieutenants], the men who dealt directly with the rank and file.

39 Ibid., xiii.   40 Beringer et al., *Why the South Lost*, 329.
41 Glatthaar, *The March to the Sea*, 28, 49.

Almost 50 percent of the captains and over 90 percent of the lieutenants served at one time as enlisted men. The result, then, was the formation of a body of ingenious young officers with a wealth of experience who, Sherman insisted, 'accomplished many things far better than I could have ordered'."[42]

Sherman also carefully limited the *kind* of men who would make up his expedition: He keenly believed that he had to have soldiers who knew what to do and how to care for themselves, and he was willing to take "only the best fighting material," experienced soldiers accustomed to hardship and disease. All others had to remain behind. Before the march to the sea commenced, Sherman ordered his senior officers and medical staff to undertake what one soldier called "a rigorous weeding-out process." And, as Glatthaar observed, "from a medical standpoint, the results were astounding": During the campaign to Savannah, "Sherman's entire army averaged less than two percent of its men unfit for duty owing to sickness on any given day, and on the much more demanding [subsequent] march through the Carolinas, the average was a fraction over two percent. In comparison with all other Union troops, Sherman's army suffered 46 percent fewer illnesses per 1,000 men during the campaign months." As the campaigns unfolded, Sherman's "army began to believe itself invincible, and with each day's march confidence in its … abilities grew." One veteran recorded in his journal: "We have weeded out all the sick, feeble ones and all the faint hearted ones and all the boys are ready for a meal or a fight and don't seem to care which it is." And they were men who *wanted* to go on the campaign! "I wouldn't miss going on this expedition for 6 month's pay," jotted an ecstatic officer in his diary.[43]

And Sherman himself was quite a remarkable man! Sherman's nickname, "Uncle Billy," signified both familiarity and respect. Like some quintessential precast Boy Scout leader, Sherman himself had become "the premier veteran, a man who awed his troops with his vast knowledge of the terrain of Georgia and the Carolinas and all aspects of campaigning. Whether it was showing a soldier how to mend a harness, teaching several drummer boys how to light a fire in pouring rain, or guiding his army through innumerable swamps … without suffering heavy losses, Sherman always seemed to know exactly what to do and how to do it. The end result was unfailing confidence in his generalship."[44]

X I

The operation was unprecedented: No longer did Sherman have any communications to protect, nor any for his principal adversary, Confederate Gen.

---

42 Ibid., 15, 21.   43 Ibid., 19–20, 44.   44 Ibid., 16.

John Bell Hood, to threaten. Sherman led his army-group of more than 60,000 men unmolested to the coast and reached Savannah, Georgia, in time to present it to President Lincoln as a "Christmas gift." On the way, Sherman had created such ambiguity about his route that he had no difficulty avoiding the meager forces available to oppose him. His army moved rapidly, easily living off the country, and destroying in its path anything of value to the Confederate war effort. Sherman's raid was aimed as much at Confederate morale and will as it was at her railroads and granaries.[45]

Sherman's march presented the Confederates with a serious dilemma: What could possibly be done in effective response? Southern General Hood chose to march into Middle Tennessee while Sherman moved toward the coast. But General Hood, unlike General Sherman, planned not a raid but a reconquest of Middle Tennessee. The two regions, the one into which General Hood moved, as opposed by the one General Sherman moved into, did not have equal value! Middle Tennessee could not possibly contribute as much to sustain Confederate armies as the railways in Georgia, severed by Sherman, had provided throughout the war. As a raider, Sherman had the goal and the opportunity to avoid the enemy's army. But Hood, aiming to conquer territory, had to engage Union forces in his path. The advantage of the defense thus accrued – and thereafter continued to belong to the Union![46]

Hood seemed determined to help the Union make the most of its advantage. After first turning back the Federal army opposing him almost to Nashville, on November 30, 1864, Hood made a costly frontal attack against his entrenched opponent at Franklin, Tennessee. Hood had an army roughly the same size as that of his opponents, but the power of the defense (here enjoyed by the Union!) proved decisive as Hood lost 15 percent of his force, including six generals killed or mortally wounded. His capable adversary, the seasoned Union Maj. Gen. John M. Schofield, withdrew even though he had resisted Hood's attacks successfully and his casualties numbered barely a third of his opponent's. Schofield fell back to Nashville, where he joined his superior, Gen. George H. Thomas, in well-entrenched positions protected from turning movements by the Cumberland River, patrolled by Union gunboats. And very soon thereafter, in freezing weather, on December 15 and 16, Thomas, in an essentially frontal battle, easily defeated Hood's already demoralized army and drove what was left of it into Northern Mississippi. Superior in numbers, morale, and cavalry, Thomas conducted a damaging pursuit. Discredited and disgraced, Hood resigned as army commander; his army had lost so heavily in numbers and morale that it effectively had ceased to exist.[47]

X I I

It was not just Confederate armies that had to be vanquished, however, for as Sherman wrote Union chief of staff Maj. Gen. Henry Halleck: "We are not only fighting hostile armies, but a hostile people, and must make old and young, rich and poor, feel the hard hand of war, as well as their organized armies. I know that this recent movement of mine through Georgia has had a wonderful effect in this respect. Thousands who had been deceived by their lying papers into the belief that we were being whipped all the time, realized the truth." President Davis succinctly summed up the nonmaterial impact of this significant march: "Sherman's campaign has produced [a] bad effect on our people. Success against his future operations is needed to reanimate public confidence." By this point in time, Grant and Sherman both had come to envision a second thrust to be made by Sherman's army: northward, through South Carolina.[48]

Sherman's men had by now come to reflect in their appearance the kind of life they had been leading... and Sherman intended for them to continue to lead. At first glance, the men looked more like a mob than an army. Yet Sherman's men were an army, superbly skilled in both marching and fighting. Other Union commands might take pride in their spit-and-polish dress and expertise in marching drills, but Sherman's men cared little for that. Again, I quote Glatthaar: "Instead, they took extra pride in their ability to endure all hardships and still achieve in battle and on the march. The sinewy frames, bronzed skin, scraggly beards, and dilapidated clothing all there trophies from the just-concluded successful campaign. They were an unkempt, boisterous, seemingly unruly lot, in no way resembling the stereotypical professional army of the mid-nineteenth century or even their counterpart then besieging Petersburg, Virginia, under the leadership of generals Meade and U. S. Grant."[49]

---

47   Ibid., 330–1.
48   Glatthaar, *The March to the Sea,* 135; Hattaway and Jones, *How the North Won,* chap. 19.
49   Meade, the final, and successful, commander of the Union's principal field force, the Army of the Potomac, remains still something of an enigma. My friend, the eminent military scholar Russell Weigley, and I have discussed on several occasions how intrigued we are about the still unsolved puzzle: the Grant–Meade command relationship. Furthermore, however, as Weigley and I observed together in conversation at the conference when this essay was first presented (April 2, 1992), Grant really had "an army group" too (and his situation was made still more complex by his also being in command over *all* the Union armies. Until it can be eclipsed, the best biography is Freeman Cleaves, *Meade of Gettysburg* (Norman, Okla., 1960; reprinted with a foreword by Herman M. Hattaway, 1991).

"Upon their arrival in Beaufort, South Carolina, one member of Sherman's army overheard a black soldier in a shiny, new uniform, comment, 'they alls are about as black as we alls.' [The hearer further recorded], 'though not very complimentary [it] told something how we did look.' "[50] Contrary to how the hearer of the remark assessed it, perhaps the black man had meant to utter the greatest compliment he could! One of the things that Sherman and his army did was to bring about the de facto emancipation of many thousands of blacks from slavery. On one occasion, Sherman measured *in miles* the blacks who trailed behind the raiding infantry of his army.[51]

It is interesting, I believe, and somewhat counter to popular myth that Sherman's "troops had surprisingly infrequent contact with Southern whites on the march. . . . It was not unusual, particularly in South Carolina where thousands throughout the state evacuated to 'safer' areas, for some troops to go several days without seeing any white inhabitants. Only in the larger towns and cities of Georgia and the Carolinas did Sherman's men find Southern whites in sizable numbers."[52]

"Rumors of mistreatment by Sherman's troops, whether or not they had any basis, had spread throughout Georgia and the Carolinas and left the people frantic . . . South Carolinians were particularly susceptible to such tales, for they had good reason to fear Sherman's army, especially after they learned of the fate of Columbia and other towns." Sherman's men had entered Columbia, the state capitol of South Carolina, on February 17, 1865. Not far outside of that place, Sherman spent one cold night sleeping on the floor of an abandoned country mansion. The fire burned low, and he awakened uncomfortably cold. He arose and renewed the flames with an old, wooden mantel clock and a bedstead, "the only act of vandalism," he later asserted, "that I recall done by myself personally during the war."[54] About one-third of the city of Columbia was destroyed by fire before Sherman pushed on. In a brilliant piece of historical detective work, Marion B. Lucas, in 1976, demonstrated that the fire had not been the fault of Sherman nor his troops. But Southerners, then and since, have typically equated the fire with Sherman's willful policies of war making.[55]

But, as Glatthaar observes, the fear of terror and destruction was always a key element: "A handful of Union soldiers went out of their way to propagate the myths of Yankee ferocity by telling South Carolina women stories intended to terrorize them. At Barnswell two soldiers told some women that

50 Glatthaar, *The March to the Sea*, 37.
51 Ibid., 52, 57.
52 Ibid., 66.
53 Ibid., 70–1.
54 Hattaway and Jones, *How the North Won*, 666.
55 Marion B. Lucas, *Sherman and the Burning of Columbia* (College Station, Tex., 1976).

there were no gentlemen in Sherman's army, . . . [and] that convicts released solely to subjugate the South constituted the entire enlisted population." Of course, not all Southern women cowered; some defiantly displayed their anti-Union sentiments at every opportunity and, at times, without regard to the consequences. "A South Carolina woman tried to drive away some foragers by throwing scalding water in their faces but instead got a dunking in a barrel of molasses to sweeten her temper . . . Many of these women possessed a bitter hatred of Union soldiers . . . Wartime propaganda at home intensified their burning hatred for the Union Army . . . One North Carolina woman told a soldier that she would not give a cup of water to a dying Yankee. Later, after becoming better acquainted with the man, she admitted, 'I would give you a cup of water to soothe your dying agonies, and, as you are a Yankee *I wish I had the opportunity to do so.*'"[56]

In general, [however] Sherman's army treated southern civilians well. [In fact] three prominent Confederates – Lt. Gen. William J. Hardee, Maj. Gen. Gustavus W. Smith, and Col. Edward C. Anderson – left their wives to the care of Sherman's occupation forces in Savannah . . . Time after time, members of Sherman's army performed acts of kindness for southerners, especially the poor . . . Many of Sherman's troops were eligible bachelors, and since there were very few southern men outside the Confederate Army, they found in Georgia and the Carolinas a considerable number of unattended and unspoken-for women. Soldiers of every rank commented on the attractiveness of southern women and once both parties got over their initial hesitancy, all sorts of relationships blossomed, from lifelong friendships to marriages.[57]

X I I I

Because Confederates *now* were concentrating fragments of forces – mostly remnants of the bedraggled and battered Confederate Army of Tennessee – *and* the next raid would bring Sherman toward Lee's army in Virginia, the situation was significantly different than it was during Sherman's march to the sea. Grant prepared for the probable use of the Confederates of interior lines to achieve dangerous concentration against Sherman. Wanting Sherman this time to have a supply line so he could remain stationary and hold his ground if attacked, Grant sent General Schofield with part of General Thomas's army by rail and water to land on the North Carolina coast, take Wilmington, and establish a line of communications with which Sherman could connect if necessary. Fort Fisher – the principal Confederate defensive emplacement at Wilmington – fell to a combined assault in the middle of

56   Glatthaar, *The March to the Sea,* 71–2.
57   Ibid., 74–5.

January 1865. Schofield's Twenty-Third Corps reached the North Carolina coast on February 9 and, along with the troops of Maj. Gen. Alfred Terry, occupied Wilmington eleven days later. The Union force, some 30,000 effectives, then prepared to move up the Cape Fear River and secure Fayetteville, North Carolina, for Sherman's approaching army.[58]

XIV

By the winter of 1865, Federal efforts to improve their cavalry, which had been markedly inferior to the Confederate cavalry earlier in the war, at last had created a well-led force, numerically superior and better armed than its Confederate counterpart. Grant used this force to make several minor and two major cavalry raids. Both major raids began in March 1865. One, under Philip Sheridan, went from Winchester, Virginia, through that state to the Federal army at Petersburg. This raid successfully disrupted Richmond's rail and canal communications with the western part of Virginia.[59]

The other raid, under James H. Wilson, an 1860 West Point graduate and now a brevet major general, moved from Tennessee into Alabama and captured Selma, an important war industrial center on a rail route connecting Georgia and Mississippi. In the desperate defensive operations, the famed genius Nathan Bedford Forrest at last met his match. Thanks to Wilson's insistence and perseverance in the matter, almost all of the Federal cavalrymen were armed principally with Spencer seven-shot repeating carbines. In addition, the men carried a six-shot revolver as well as a light cavalry saber. Each division was equipped with a battery of horse artillery. And most significantly, Wilson had a pontoon train outfitted with enough equipment to enable his pontonier battalion to build a 400-foot bridge. Forrest was outmaneuvered as well as outfought, for Wilson's compact force of 13,480 moved with a swiftness not achieved by any of Forrest's previous foes. Not depending upon the land for food or forage, the Federal troopers each carried on their mounts five days' light rations, twenty-four pounds of grain, one hundred rounds of ammunition, and a pair of extra horseshoes. It is not without good reason that a standard book on this campaign is entitled *Yankee Blitzkrieg*.[60] After defeating Forrest and smashing the industrial installations at Selma, Wilson's men continued on to take Montgomery, Alabama; Columbus and Macon, Georgia, and eventually to capture the fleeing Davis near Irwinville, Georgia, on May 10, 1861.

---

58 Beringer, et al., *Why the South Lost*, 330–1.
59 Ibid., 331–2.
60 James Pickett Jones, *Yankee Blitzkrieg: Wilson's Raid through Alabama and Georgia* (Athens, Ga., 1976).

And, all the while, prior to the final capitulation of the Western Confederate army late in April, Sherman's men had continued their march. "By the time Sherman's army reached Goldsboro, North Carolina, it was all in its glory. Hatless heads, frazzled pants, threadbare shirts, torn shoes or barefoot, faces blackened by Carolina pine smoke, they looked, as a member of General Schofield's army noted, 'very hard.' "[61] By the end of March, Sheridan had completed his destructive raid and had joined Grant at Petersburg, the army from the trans-Mississippi was besieging Mobile, the Selma cavalry raid was in full swing, and Sherman and Schofield had united in North Carolina. Sherman had beaten off a feeble attack at Bentonville on March 19–21, 1865, by a small patchwork Confederate army under General Johnston. Grant was clearly attaining the object of his raids – to "leave the rebellion nothing to stand upon."[62]

Sherman's Savannah and Carolina campaigns ... [were] very different from *any other* campaign in the war ... Success had not depended upon victory in combat; and the enemy was *not just* the Confederate Army. Sherman's objective ... [had been] *to demonstrate* [to the South] that the Confederate armies were *no longer capable* of protecting its citizens and that life outside the Union was much worse than life within the Union. The march itself, then, determined the success of the campaign, and *its primary enemies were the mud and hunger* rather than the Confederate troops ... For the most part, ... the campaigns were arduous at best and frequently very dangerous. As Sherman's army marched to Savannah and through the Carolinas it had to deal with an increasingly larger and highly mobile Confederate force ... The Confederates had little success delaying Sherman's army with gunfire, but they did slow the march somewhat through the use of other tactics. One practice was to fell trees across the roads ... another was to light fires using barrels of turpentine or pine trees to block the roads and scare the horses and mules as the air filled with pitch pine smoke [making] it almost unbearable to breathe ... and the Confederates emplaced land mines.... These subterranean explosives, had a crippling, sometimes fatal effect on their unsuspecting victims, prompting Sherman – [ironically and] strangely enough – to declare them a violation of civilized warfare."[63]

XV

The capitulation of the Confederacy was but a symptom of the *defeatism* that had by this time triumphed throughout the South. Grant's strategy of raids had provided a useful solution to the military stalemate. But a broken stalemate dictates only that military activity, if it continues, becomes more fluid;

61 Glatthaar, *The March to the Sea*, 38.
62 Beringer et al., *Why the South Lost*, 332.
63 Glatthaar, *The March to the Sea*, 101, 108.

it does *not* dictate the defeat of one side or the other. Even when the Union armies accepted the surrender of the Confederate armies, the latter had still other alternatives open to them.[64] Few Southerners wished to continue the fight. For now, even if the Confederacy did continue to exist, slavery was gone. The preservation of slavery was not precisely and openly what the Confederacy had come into being primarily to protect; but it certainly had not come into being with any expectation that the institution soon would be demolished! Neither had the Union had the extinction of slavery as its *original* war aim; *that* had been preservation of the Union. But "as the war progressed," most Union troops did come "to see emancipation as a powerful tool in crushing secession." Indeed, "as Sherman's troops passed through Georgia and the Carolinas, opposition to slavery grew stronger and stronger."[65]

And, meanwhile, somewhere along the way, just as the Union officially had added the extinction of slavery to its original war aim, so too had the Confederate leadership altered the concept of the political goal of the war. And, beyond the loss of slavery, much else previously dear to Confederates seemed now to have been demolished. State rights appeared to be gone. Soul-searing casualty lists indicated the loss of many young men. Even God seemed to be turned against the South. In the late summer of 1864, one Confederate citizen had prayed: "Oh God, wilt thou hear the prayers of Thy people who daily say, Lord, give us peace."[66] But he had meant peace with a tinge of satisfaction; peace at least in part on the South's terms. The *depression* of the Southern people, and their desires for peace (perhaps, more and more, unadulterated peace, peace on any terms) deepened after the fall of Atlanta and the start of the siege of Petersburg. By 1865, Southern morale was beyond recovery. The armies had not yet surrendered, but the people were beaten. At last, in April 1865, the days of sacrifice ended.

---

64 Beringer et al., *Why the South Lost*, 334.
65 Glatthaar, *The March to the Sea*, 41–2.
66 Beringer et al., *Why the South Lost*, 335.

9

African-Americans and the Mobilization for Civil War

JOSEPH T. GLATTHAAR

On a dreary, drizzling night in mid-October 1859, fanatical abolitionist John Brown and his party of eighteen loyalists descended on the sleepy little village of Harpers Ferry, Virginia. Furtively, the raiders slipped into town, overpowered the lone guard, and seized the United States Arsenal there. Some followers then cut telegraph lines and barricaded the wagon and railroad bridges across the Potomac River against any approaching militiamen, while a handful of others slipped out to nearby farms, alerting slaves that salvation was at hand and taking hostages back to the arsenal for security.

Yet it did not take long for the bizarre scheme to unravel. Months before, Brown had crafted a fanciful plan to wrest control of the prized arsenal from federal authorities and use the weapons to create a military force from slaves flocking to his banner. With the Appalachian Mountains as an auxiliary shield, he would drive deep into the South, disrupting plantations and gathering more "soldiers" for his army of freedom. Success would build upon success, Brown believed, and soon the dreaded institution of slavery would crumble beneath the weight of his mighty ranks. Unfortunately, no one thought it necessary to notify slaves in advance; thus, none rallied to their self-appointed savior. Nor could Brown and his party keep their enterprise a secret for very long. Shortly after securing the arsenal, Brown's henchmen fired on a relief watchman and then on two workers from an eastbound train that halted to clear the obstruction on the railroad bridge. The gunshots alerted townsfolk to the commotion around the arsenal, and it was not long before church bells rang out a warning signal. By morning, armed locals and Brown's force were exchanging gunfire, with the invaders suffering eight killed. Incredibly, Brown's men negated the work of severing the telegraph lines when they let the train pass after a few hours' delay, which in turn enabled passengers and crew to spread word of the uprising to neighboring communities. Brown also had made no provision for retreat, and when the Maryland and Virginia militiamen arrived late in the morning, they quickly sealed all escape routes. Even the hostages proved valueless, as Virginians deemed the threat to slave uprisings more important than the lives of a few friends and neighbors. During the night, a company of marines under the command of a U.S. Army colonel named Robert E. Lee arrived on the scene. By this time, locals had Brown and his survivors holed up in the engine house, perhaps the most secure structure on the arsenal grounds. Lee, making short shrift of the entire affair, ordered the marines to batter down the doors and assault with fixed bayonets. Brown's exhausted force resisted feebly. One marine and two more of Brown's crew died in the melee, while Brown, who suffered a saber wound in the fray, surrendered with the others.[1]

After the initial shock subsided, most Northerners and Southerners reacted to Brown's plot with either astonishment at its hopelessness and desperation or with indignation. Certainly the idea of arming blacks to overthrow slavery appalled them, but the plan was so short-sighted that most categorized it as the work of lunatics. "Nothing but a wild fanaticism, amounting to almost insanity, could account for twenty men combining together in such a foolhardy enterprise," averred the *Baltimore American*.[2] The *Charleston Mercury*, a hotbed of secessionist opinion, reacted with considerable restraint. While its editor downplayed the "magnitude" of the insurrection, he warned readers that the event "fully establishes the fact that there are at the North men ready to engage in adventures upon the peace and security of the Southern people, however heinously and recklessly."[3] In the North, too, the press opposed Brown's transgression of law and order, even those periodicals that regarded his motives as honorable. The *Chicago Press and Tribune* called the scheme the product of "addled brains" and insisted that Brown and his comrades "are guilty of the most incomprehensible stupidity and folly as well as unpardonable criminality in all these acts."[4] More circumspect was the moderate Republican *New York Times*. Its editors described the plan as one of a "crazed fanatic, who in his eagerness for vengeance lost all sense of proportion between means and ends." This was not a widespread plot to destroy the institution of slavery. "*The people of the North*," the editors reassured their Southern brethren, "*have neither agency in this movement, nor excuse, apology, or an instant's toleration for it.*"[5] When the trial and Brown's execution evoked

---

1 See Stephen B. Oates, *To Purge This Land with Blood: A Biography of John Brown* (New York, 1970), 243–301; James M. McPherson, *Battle Cry of Freedom: The Civil War Era* (New York, 1988), 202–6.
2 *Baltimore American*, Oct. 18, 1859, quoted in *The Charleston Mercury*, Oct. 21, 1859.
3 *The Charleston Mercury*, Oct. 21, 1859.
4 Quoted in Richard Warch and Jonathan F. Fanton, eds., *John Brown* (Englewood Cliffs, N.J, 1973), 119–20.
5 *New York Times*, Oct. 20.

sympathy across the North, the *New York Times* again defended public sentiments: "We do not believe that one-tenth of the people of the Northern
States would assent to the justice of Brown's views of duty, or deny that he
merited the penalty which has overtaken his offense. But we have just as little doubt that a majority of them pity his fate and respect his memory as that
of a brave, conscientious and misguided man."[6]

Despite overwhelming disapproval throughout the North for Brown's
raid, less than three years later the Federal government adopted as its official
policy the destruction of slavery and the recruitment and arming of blacks as
soldiers. This momentous shift in attitudes indicates the stunning transformation that the war wrought on Northern society. After fifteen months of
fighting and tens of thousands of casualties, the government of Abraham
Lincoln determined that it had to employ harsher methods to subdue the
rebellion. At first hesitantly and later vigorously, the Union implemented
controversial programs such as conscription, the systematic destruction or
confiscation of private property, and black enlistment to jack up the war
effort to a higher level of mobilization, ruthlessness, and efficiency, approaching total war against secessionists.

At the time of Lincoln's election in 1860, approximately four and one-
half million blacks lived in the United States. Ninety percent, or nearly four
million, endured the hardships, indignities, and repression of slavery. Another
one-half million, scattered throughout the North and South, had severely
restricted rights and were, therefore, free only in comparison with slavery.
Genuine equality with whites, the goal to which blacks aspired, simply did
not exist.

In fact, at the beginning of the war, both sides attempted to keep the issue
of blacks and slavery in the periphery. Soldiers on both sides denied that
blacks had anything to do with the cause or object of the war. Northern
enlistees, even those who sympathized with the plight of slaves, donned
the blue first and foremost to restore the Union. Only a minority of the
Federal "Men of 1861" sought the destruction of slavery. Among secessionists as well, the role of blacks appeared incidental. Northerners threatened
their rights as free men. They attempted to deprive Southerners of their right
to own property, to take that property anywhere in the United States, and
to protect themselves, their families, and their friends from attempts to
undermine local security by inciting servile discontent and insurrection.
Once Northern armies advanced into the South, then the war over rights
also became a war for the defense of home and hearth. From the Confederate vantage point, oppression was the root cause of the conflict.

6 Quoted in Warch and Fanton, eds., *John Brown*, 125–6.

Nevertheless, with the onset of hostilities, blacks North and South ten-
dered services to their respective sections. One black physician from
Michigan offered to raise 5,000 to 10,000 blacks in sixty days, while others,
not quite so ambitious, vowed to organize individual regiments for Federal
service. Free blacks in the South, too, formed several militia units and volunteered to work on behalf of their states. At the time, few Southern blacks
imagined that this would be a war against secession and slavery; on the contrary, blacks and whites alike viewed the conflict as one over the Union. For
blacks, the best means of gaining favor and enhancing their position in
society appeared to be through military service in this moment of crisis. "No
matter where I fight," announced a black man who had volunteered to
fight for the Confederacy and a year later extended his services to the
Federals, "I only wish to spend what I have, and fight as long as I can, if only
my boy may stand in the street equal to a white boy when the war is over."[7]

Neither Union nor Confederate governments had any intention of permitting blacks to serve under arms, though. Initially, more whites stepped
forward than the Lincoln administration could handle, as Northern governors pleaded with the president and the War Department to increase their
manpower quotas. Lincoln, keenly aware of the divisiveness of the war in
the North and his tenuous hold on the border states, had no intention
of adopting such a controversial policy as black enlistment when the Federal
government turned away thousands of able-bodied whites.

To the South, Confederate President Jefferson Davis dismissed the notion
of black enlistment peremptorily. Like Lincoln, he had more white volunteers at the beginning of the war than his nation could arm and equip properly, and the elevation of blacks to military service was even more
objectionable to his constituency. As Vice President Alexander Stephens
had argued in 1861, the "corner-stone [of the new government] rests upon
the great truth, that the Negro is not equal to the white man; that slavery –
subordination to the superior race – is his natural and normal condition."[8]
Acknowledgment by the Confederacy that blacks could make credible
soldiers would shake the very foundations of Southern society.

To be sure, blacks continued to be an extraordinarily valuable resource for
the Confederacy, as they had been to Southerners in peacetime. On farms and

---

7   Quoted in Joseph T. Glatthaar, *Forged in Battle: The Civil War Alliance of Black Soldiers and White
    Officers* (New York, 1990), 3. See also G. P. Miller to Simon Cameron, Oct. 30, 1861; W. T. Boyd
    and J. T. Alston to Hon. Simon Cameron, Nov. 15, 1861; William A. Jones to Hon. Simon
    Cameron, Nov. 27, 1861. Ira Berlin, Joseph P. Reidy, and Leslie J. Rowland, eds., *Freedom: A
    Documentary History of Emancipation, 1861–1867*, ser. 2 (New York, 1982), 79–81.
8   Robert F. Durden, *The Gray and the Black: The Confederate Debate on Emancipation* (Baton Rouge,
    La., 1972), 7–8.

plantations, blacks cultivated the crops, cared for the livestock, and maintained the property. In factories, black workers helped to manufacture clothing, weapons, ammunition, and accouterments. Labor gangs composed of blacks erected fortifications, laid and repaired railroad track, and built and restored roads and bridges. For the army, they even cooked meals, drove wagons, and cared for the personal property of soldiers. But in the eyes of Southern whites, the distinction between service for the military and military service was clear. "Use all the Negroes you can get, for all the purposes for which you need them, but don't arm them," urged Georgian Howell Cobb to the secretary of war late in the war. "The day you make soldiers of them is the beginning of the end of the revolution. If slaves will make good soldiers our whole theory of slavery is wrong."[9]

While whites sought to arrest the influence of blacks on the war, blacks themselves tried to thrust the issue onto center stage. In an editorial after the firing on Fort Sumter, Frederick Douglass asserted that "The American people and the Government at Washington may refuse to recognize it for a time; but the 'inexorable logic of events' will force it upon them in the end; that the war now being waged in this land is a war for and against slavery; and that it can never be effectually put down till one or the other of these vital forces is completely destroyed." Four months later, Douglass went one step farther and demanded the use of black soldiers to crush the rebellion. "This is no time to fight only with your white hand, and allow your black hand to remain tied," he taunted the Lincoln administration. "Men in earnest don't fight with one hand, when they might fight with two, and a man drowning would not refuse to be saved even by a colored man."[10]

Despite such evident logic, the Lincoln government and the Northern white populace were not swayed easily. Many believed that this was a white man's war and that blacks, owing to their innate inferiority, could contribute little toward subduing the Confederates. Others anticipated the value of black soldiers but hesitated to advance the idea. Black military service was a highly controversial notion, and the loss of white support in the prosecution of the war might override all benefits from increased manpower.

As Northern authorities procrastinated, three Virginia slaves and a Union general took matters into their own hands. The bondsmen, laboring on Confederate fortifications, fled to Union lines late one night. The next morning, when a Confederate officer under flag of truce sought their return under the fugitive slave laws, Federal Brig. Gen. Benjamin Butler declined. If

9   Durden, *The Gray and the Black*, 184.
10 James M. McPherson, *The Negro's Civil War: How American Negroes Felt and Acted During the War for the Union* (New York, 1965), 17–18, 162.

Virginia had seceded, Butler reasoned, then United States laws did not apply to its inhabitants. And since Confederates had employed the slaves on military projects, such slaves were subject to confiscation as contraband of war, according to international law. Later that day, Butler hired the three men to construct a bakery for Federal troops. With these decisions, Butler had in effect freed the runaways and employed them to work for the Union army. The secretary of war endorsed Butler's decisions, and four months later, Congress passed an important piece of legislation known as the First Confiscation Act. The bill permitted Federal officials to seize Confederate property, including slaves, used "in aid of the rebellion."[11]

Butler's decision, made with little forethought or knowledge of its extraordinary ramifications, initiated the process of emancipation and black military service and set the Union on a course toward total war. Not only did he force the government to formulate a policy on "contrabands," but at the very same time that Congress was debating the First Confiscation Act, Butler was pressing the secretary of war to broaden the interpretation of his ruling. Male slaves, who had labored on Confederate military projects, had fled to his lines with women and children in tow. "What shall be done with them?," Butler wondered. "What is their state and condition?"[12] By empowering military authorities to confiscate slaves who worked for the Confederate army, the Federal government also had obliged them to cope with a whole host of unusual cases of runaway slaves. Each time that officers resolved those matters on humanitarian grounds, they widened the breach that Congress had created and took the nation closer to complete emancipation. By permitting Butler to hire blacks for military projects, the War Department paved the way for use of blacks in all sorts of military capacities. From Butler's bakery to the construction of fortifications, to service as teamsters and stevedores, blacks handled sundry jobs that soldiers usually performed, which freed troops for their primary mission–combat.

Throughout the remainder of 1861 and well into 1862, slaves fled to Union lines in ever-increasing numbers. Some Yankee officers insisted upon their return to bondage unless the runaways could prove that they had worked for the Confederate army. Other officers and men found such duties morally reprehensible or downright annoying. In either case, they had joined the army to fight for the Union, not to return slaves to secessionists. Deluged with complaints, the War Department finally responded by directing that military personnel were no longer to involve themselves in the return of runaway bondsmen. The army, then, was not to serve as an instrument for the preservation of slavery.

11 Quoted in McPherson, *The Negro's Civil War*, 28 .
12 Benjamin F . Butler to Hon. Simon Cameron, July 30, 1861. *New York Times*, Aug. 6, 1861.

Once Federal commands began penetrating into Confederate territory, masses of black refugees sought sanctuary among the blue coats. In the eyes of blacks, they were the armies of freedom, safe havens from enslavement. An estimated 500,000 to 700,000 chattels endured the hardships of the journey and the risk of recapture to find safety behind Union lines. Some arrived in wagons or on horseback, with family and assorted household goods to ease their transition into freedom. Others completed the dangerous trek alone, barefoot and penniless, and dressed only in rags. All their loved ones remained behind in bondage.[13]

The economic impact of this mass exodus on the Confederate war effort was immense. These refugees from slavery were conservatively valued at $1.5 billion prewar and, more importantly, composed between 15 and 20 percent of the black labor force in the Confederacy. During the war, Confederates had to feed and clothe the same number of people as before, but on a drastically reduced work force. Between 600,000 and 1,000,000 white men left the fields and factories to serve in Rebel gray. The war, moreover, consumed enormous quantities of materiel, much of which the Southern states had not produced before the war and could import only sparingly owing to the Federal blockade. White women filled part of the labor void, but Confederates had to depend on their black workers to increase output. Instead, hundreds of thousands ran off or fell into Union hands, creating shortages and a skyrocketing inflation that undermined morale at home and in the field. They left crops and livestock untended, railroads and homes in disrepair, mineral resources untapped, factory machines unused, and the war effort diminished.[14]

Along with the economic chaos, runaway slaves caused considerable psychological distress among whites. Dating back to the eighteenth century but taking hold in the antebellum era, Southern whites justified the enslavement of blacks with the "positive good" thesis. Slavery, they argued, was a natural condition for blacks, which provided the chattels with comfort and contentment. It removed them from savagery and offered them an opportunity to develop to their fullest, albeit limited, capacities. When thousands upon thousands of slaves abandoned their homes in search of freedom, they challenged whites' core beliefs and threatened a social order based on slavery.

13 James McPherson estimates the number at 700,000. Leslie Rowland maintains the figure at approximately 500,000.

14 In the Victory Plan before World War II, Maj. Albert C. Wedemeyer ascertained through research on previous wars that a nation could place 10 percent of its total population in military service without causing serious harm to the economic or social life of that nation. After that, conditions began to deteriorate. The Confederacy lost 700,000 slave laborers to the Union and had a total military force of 600,000–1,000,000 out of a population of 9 million. That equaled between 14.4 percent and 18.8 percent of the total population.

The mere thought of bands of slaves wandering throughout the countryside in search of Union lines and resisting authority terrified the citizenry. Southern whites, it seemed, were losing control of their world.

Slaves who remained at home, too, augmented this anguish among whites in and outside of the army. They recognized the dramatic diminution of the controlling force, white males, and reacted with greater assertiveness. Broken tools and equipment, work slowdowns, a general lack of cooperation, and insolence increased as slaves reacted to the power vacuum. Such behavior horrified whites, who more than ever feared servile insurrections. One woman in North Carolina wrote her husband in the army, asking him to come home. She despaired of her plight, with nearly all men in the community absent and the folks at home fearful that the slaves "will kill us all up." Blacks, she complained, were "cursing the Ladies and abusing some of them now and after all the men leave, it will be worse."[15] Evidently upset by the report, her spouse could only suggest that she shoot any slaves who got sassy with her. But the matter, fairly commonplace among Confederates, continued to gnaw at the soldier, diverting his attention from the war effort and amplifying his uneasiness about the family's welfare.

By acting on their own behalf, slaves also challenged Federal authorities to reexamine their approach to the war. The unanticipated black response compelled Northern officials to adapt their policies to meet wartime exigencies. First, they authorized the seizure of slaves employed in Confederate military projects, and later the Northern government prohibited military personnel from retrieving runaway bondsmen. By July 1862, Congress had decided to go one step farther. The masses of slaves who sought refuge and freedom behind Union lines, the significant contributions that enslaved blacks were making to the Confederate war effort, and the slow progress of the Union armies convinced Congress that effective prosecution of the war required bolder measures. In the Second Confiscation Act, Congress awarded freedom to all slaves of Confederates upon entering Federal lines.

Previously, the Lincoln administration had waged economic warfare solely with a naval blockade and attempts to block foreign loans to the Confederate government. The Second Confiscation Act struck a blow at the heart of the Confederate economic system by stripping away invaluable producers and promising them freedom as an inducement for flight. "So long as the rebels retain and employ their slaves in producing grains &c., they can employ all the whites in the field," expounded Maj. Gen. Henry W. Halleck

---

15   R.F. Evans to husband, Jan. 1, 1864. Eleanor Brockenbrough Library, Museum of the Confederacy.

to subordinate Maj. Gen. Ulysses S. Grant. "Every slave withdrawn from the enemy is equivalent to a white man put *hors de combat*."[16]

As black refugees poured into Union lines and armies penetrating deep into the Confederacy rescued even more chattels, authorities directed these masses to labor for Northern benefit. Officials put women, children, and elderly and unfit males to work on abandoned plantations to raise cotton and foodstuffs. The able-bodied men went to work for the army, performing support duties and freeing more soldiers for combat. The needs of war were drawing blacks slowly but steadily into military service.

Yet to Northern blacks, progress seemed to come more slowly than steadily. Throughout the first fifteen months of the war, they had persevered in their efforts to place men of African descent in military service. Entreaties streamed steadily into the War Department requesting permission to raise black troops or seeking "the poor priverlige of fighting – and (if need be dying) to suport those in office who are our own choise."[17] Editorials in newspapers that serviced a black readership pleaded for an opportunity to fight, as their ancestors had done in previous wars. "Colored men were good enough to fight under Washington," charged Frederick Douglass with biting sarcasm. "They are not good enough to fight under [Gen. George B.] McClellan. They were good enough to fight under Andrew Jackson. They are not good enough to fight under General Halleck. They were good enough to help win American independence, but they are not good enough to help preserve that independence against treason and rebellion."[18]

In its official position, the Lincoln administration staunchly refused to budge. Lincoln had a chance to endorse efforts to raise black troops; in that instance, he declined to lift a hand to aid the venture. Maj. Gen. David Hunter had organized freed slaves from the South Carolina coastal islands into companies, some by point of bayonet, and proceeded to bombard the War Department with requests for uniforms, rifles, and accouterments. The flippant, even condescending, tone to his justification report so alienated Congress that Lincoln wanted no part of the enterprise. The Northern public was not quite ready for black enlistment, Lincoln concluded, and such a controversial policy required extensive planning and delicacy in its implementation.

---

16 Halleck to Grant, Mar. 31, 1863. *The War of the Rebellion: A Compilation of the Official Records of the Union and Confederate Armies* (Washington, D.C., 1880–1901), ser. 1, vol. 24, pt. 3, 156–7. Hereafter *OR.*

17 W. T. Boyd and J. T. Alston to Hon. Simon Cameron, Nov. 15, 1861. Berlin et al., eds., *Freedom,* II, 80.

18 McPherson, *The Negro's Civil War,* 163.

But in his own mind, Lincoln was moving toward a decision in favor of black military service and emancipation. An opponent of slavery for decades, Lincoln viewed the institution as the fundamental cause of the war. Less than two weeks before he announced his decision to emancipate the slaves, Lincoln admitted to an abolitionist delegation that "slavery is the root of the rebellion, or at least its *sine qua non*. The ambition of politicians may have instigated them to act, but they would have been impotent without slavery as their instrument."[19] Public opinion and constitutional obligations had constrained him from acting against it. But as the war dragged into its second year, Lincoln sensed a shift in the minds of many soldiers, civilians, and politicians that suggested a more receptive reaction to these policies.

The first fifteen months of the war had not gone well for the Union. Tens of thousands of Northern boys had been laid to rest, and thousands more had suffered debilitating wounds, injuries, and illnesses. The army that citizens had once battled to enter was now an army that soldiers begged to leave. Recruits dwindled to a trickle, and the number of desertions soared. Letters home complained of bad food, boredom, sickness, and hardships. Combat offered far less glory than enlistees had anticipated; rather, it was a horrible place where the lifeblood of the Northern states – its finest, most promising young men – lost their lives. And the Union appeared only marginally closer to victory.

The dismal performance of Federal armies, and the difficulties and sacrifices of military personnel and their families, forced advocates of reunion to reexamine their commitment to further prosecution of the war. Some determined that the price of victory, if at all achievable, was too great, and they resigned, deserted, or began counting the days until their service commitment expired. Many others, however, emerged from the process with renewed resolve to fight on to the war's conclusion. "I don't like the Service & the war & shall be glad enough when peace shall be proclaimed & I can return again to my books & peaceful pursuits," wrote a Connecticut sergeant, "for all that I am in it to the end."[20]

With this fresh commitment came a new approach to the war. It evolved gradually, taking hold in some individuals well before others, and it altered the entire Northern war effort. Along with the glamor of military service, the realities of war removed misconceptions that Federals had about their

19   Roy P. Basler et al., eds., *The Collected Works of Abraham Lincoln* (New Brunswick, N. J., 1953), 5 : 420. See also Basler et al., eds., *The Collected Works of Abraham Lincoln*, 8: 332.
20   Hen. [Marshall] to Hattie, Dec. 13, 1863. Schoff Collection, Clements Library, University of Michigan. For more on this transformation, see Gerald Linderman, *Embattled Courage: The Experience of Combat in the American Civil War* (New York, 1987); and chap. 2 in Glatthaar, *Forged in Battle*.

enemies and what victory demanded. Not only were they fighting hostile armies but also a hostile people. Unionists had to make war against the entire Confederate nation, its people, and its property—in fact, anything that aided the Rebels' ability to wage war. "The character of the war has very much changed within the last year," Halleck explained to Grant in March 1863. "There is now no possible hope of reconciliation with the rebels. The Union party in the South is virtually destroyed. There can be no peace but that which is forced by the sword. We must conquer the rebels or be conquered by them."[21] Northerners had to augment their military forces at the expense of certain traditional values. Volunteerism and conventional methods of taxation could no longer provide the manpower or funds to expand the war effort; conscription and income taxes replaced them. Racial attitudes, too, had to take a back seat to the demands of war, with the government hiring black laborers by the thousands to free white soldiers for combat duty. In this changing atmosphere, Lincoln was able to amass support beyond the abolitionist ranks for emancipation and black military service.

Lincoln concluded that when hostilities reached such a magnitude, peaceful reconciliation was impossible, and he had to strike a permanent blow against slavery. The peculiar institution was the critical, divisive issue between the North and South; it lay at the heart of the war. Whereas the North had become a region of abundance and opportunity, slavery had stifled Southern economic development and impeded mobility. For a reunited nation to grow and prosper, it must, as he had written back in 1858, "place it where the public mind shall rest in the belief that it is in the course of ultimate extinction."[22] Otherwise, once Southern whites regained their full rights and privileges, the two sections would fight the same political battles all over again, and the South would continue to stagnate by comparison with the North.

In both content and legality, Lincoln's declaration generated extensive controversy. Technically, the Emancipation Proclamation freed no one. The document stated that all slaves in areas of the rebellious states that Federal troops did not occupy on January 1, 1863, were free. Lincoln, then, granted freedom to individuals beyond his control. The force of the Emancipation Proclamation rested in Lincoln's unwavering commitment to restore the Union. As slaves in these areas fell under Federal control, the bondsmen would receive their freedom. Its justification derived from Lincoln's wartime powers as commander-in-chief. He could order the seizure of anything that aided the Confederate war effort, and surely, slaves did.

21 Halleck to Grant, Mar. 31, 1863. *OR*, 1:24, pt. 3, 56–7.
22 Basler et al., eds., *The Collected Works of Abraham Lincoln*, 452–3. See Gabor S. Boritt, *Lincoln and the Economics of the American Dream* (Memphis, Tenn., 1978), 163–4.

Although the initial reaction to the Emancipation Proclamation in and out of the army was mixed, in the long run it provided a great morale boost. Among antislavery advocates, the decision reconciled their awkward position of fighting for the Union under a constitution that tolerated bondage. Most supporters of reunion, too, came around and eventually endorsed the proposal. Slavery had enormous military value. Lincoln's proclamation deprived the Confederate war effort of a mighty resource, and its controversial nature indicated how Lincoln would do anything in his power to aid Federal soldiers in the field.

The Emancipation Proclamation also blunted Confederate efforts to gain recognition and support from Great Britain and France. Since the outbreak of the war, the Confederacy had sought aid from the two European powers, and in the late summer of 1862, they had come close to achieving it. France wanted to assist the Confederacy, but would not do so without the cooperation of Great Britain. British officials were hesitant to act without a consensus at home, which did not exist. During August and September, as Robert E. Lee's army drove Union troops out of Virginia and invaded Maryland, the movement for British recognition of the Confederacy gained momentum. Just as quickly, though, it collapsed. Federal forces checked Lee's advance at Antietam, and the Emancipation Proclamation secured the high moral ground for the Union. Never again did the Southern Confederacy come so close to recognition and, perhaps, foreign assistance.[23]

Emancipation was only a part of Lincoln's sweeping decision to use blacks as a weapon against the Confederacy; the other component was black military service. Blacks were a tremendous undeveloped resource, and when white enlistment began to fall off, Congress and the president looked toward them. In July 1862, Congress passed a law that authorized the president to employ blacks in any military or naval service "for which they may be found competent."[24] Lincoln construed that as authorization to enlist blacks in the army. It was a stroke of brilliance. Not only would the Union deprive the Confederacy of a valuable source of labor, but it would convert those workers into soldiers to help subdue their former masters. As Lincoln aptly maintained, "It works doubly, weakening the enemy & strengthening us."[25]

Apparently, Lincoln decided on emancipation and black enlistment at the same time. On the recommendation of his secretary of state, Lincoln delayed the announcement of emancipation until after a major Union victory,

23 See Howard Jones, *Union in Peril: The Crisis over British Intervention in the Civil War* (Chapel Hill, N.C., 1992).
24 Quoted in Glatthaar, *Forged in Battle*, 7.
25 Lincoln to Grant, Aug. 9, 1863. *OR*, 1: 24, pt. 3, 584.

Antietam in mid-September, so that he could issue the proclamation from a position of strength. When the opportunity arose for black enlistment, however, he moved ahead, albeit with care.

The honor fell to Maj. Gen. Benjamin Butler, commander of the Department of the Gulf, to organize the first black regiments. After the fall of New Orleans to Union forces, local black militiamen, many of whom had volunteered for Confederate duty one year earlier, offered their services to Butler. At the time, Butler had no authorization to enlist blacks and respectfully declined to accept them. Several months later and still short of manpower, Butler received word from the secretary of the treasury that the administration would accept blacks, and he promptly swore into national service the First, Second, and Third Louisiana Native Guards. These were primarily free blacks, with a longstanding tradition of military service. They entered the Union army with dozens of black company-grade officers and one black major.

Breaking the color barrier in the Army was a monumental event for blacks. Although the Navy already had accepted them for duty (10,000 or more enlisted during the war), this was predominantly a ground war, and if blacks were to leave a mark, it had to be in the Army. Military service, particularly in the Army, offered blacks a chance to strike a monstrous blow for freedom, to aid in the destruction of slavery. "We are fighting for liberty and right," proclaimed a black sergeant, "and we intend to follow the old flag while there is a man left to hold it up to the breeze of heaven. Slavery must and shall pass away."[26] Moreover, only through effective wartime service, many blacks believed, could they win postwar political gains. "Once let the black man get upon his person the brass letters, U.S., let him get an eagle on his button, and a musket on his shoulder and bullets in his pocket," Douglass professed, "and there is no power on earth which can deny that he has earned the right to citizenship in the United States."[27]

By accepting blacks for wartime service, the Northern government was admitting that in times of crisis it needed blacks. Once the Federal government placed uniforms on their backs and weapons in their hands, it elevated blacks to a level with whites and acknowledged that blacks could make genuine contributions in this moment of need. For many, particularly those who had toiled all their lives in slavery, enlistment was their moment of glory. "This was the biggest thing that ever happened in my life," recalled a freedman. "I felt like a man with a uniform on and a gun in my hand."[28] Runaway slave

26 John W. Pratt to Sir, Nov. 30, 1864. *Christian Recorder*, Dec . 24, 1864 .
27 Quoted in McPherson, *The Negro's Civil War*, 161.
28 Quoted in John Cimprich, *Slavery's End in Tennessee, 1861–1865* (University, Ala., 1985), 90.

Elijah Marrs probably described it best when he wrote of his first roll call, "I felt freedom in my bones."[29]

Blacks enlisted in substantial numbers, and it was not long before the Union felt their impact. After the fall of Vicksburg, Grant assessed the value of the new policy: "I have given the subject of arming the Negro my hearty support. This, with the emancipation of the Negro, is the heavyest blow yet given the Confederacy." He insisted that "by arming the Negro we have added a powerful ally" and predicted, "They will make good soldiers and taking them from the enemy weaken him in the same proportion they strengthen us."[30]

To those who opposed emancipation and black enlistment, Lincoln simply argued that he was employing all means at his disposal to restore the Union. "I thought that in your struggle for the Union, to whatever extent the Negroes should cease helping the enemy, to that extent it weakened the enemy in his resistance to you," he declared. "Do you think differently? I thought that whatever Negroes can be got to do as soldiers, leaves just so much less for white soldiers to do, in saving the Union. Does it appear otherwise to you?" Whites need not feel as though they were fighting for emancipation; the ultimate objective, Lincoln contended, was still reunion.

> You say you will not fight to free Negroes. Some of them seem willing to fight for you; but, no matter. Fight you, then, exclusively to save the Union. I issued the proclamation on purpose to aid you in saving the Union. Whenever you shall have conquered all resistance to the Union, if I shall urge you to continue fighting, it will be apt time, then, for you to declare you will not fight to free Negroes.[31]

Still, whites were not wholly won over to the concept of blacks in the Army. Opposition was strong and remained so throughout much of the war. To make black military service more palatable to the white population, the War Department decided that whites should officer black troops. By 1864, whites had driven all black officers in the Butler regiments from the service, and with few exceptions, men who received commissions in the United States Colored Troops, as these black units were called, were white.

In mid-1863, Lincoln foresaw emancipation and the enlistment of blacks as the policy that would eventually win the war. "I believe it is a resource which if vigorously applied right now, will soon close out the contest," he

---

29   Elijah P. Marrs, *Life and History of Rev. Elijah P. Marrs* (Louisville, Ky., 1885), 22.
30   Grant to Lincoln, Aug. 23, 1863. John Y. Simon et al., eds., *The Papers of Ulysses S. Grant* (Carbondale, Ill., 1967–), 9:196.
31   Lincoln to James C. Conkling, Aug. 26, 1863. Basler et al., eds., *The Collected Works of Abraham Lincoln*, 6:409.

commented to Grant.[32] Thirteen months later, the contributions of blacks to the war effort had only reinforced Lincoln's views. "Any different policy in regard to the colored man," he wrote, "deprives us of his help, and this is more than we can bear. We can not spare the hundred and forty or fifty thousand now serving us as soldiers, seamen, and laborers. This is not a question of sentiment or taste, but one of physical force which may be measured and estimated as horse-power and Steam-power are measured and estimated. Keep it and you can save the Union. Throw it away, and the Union goes with it."[33]

Nearly 179,000 blacks served in the Union army during the war, and at one time over 20,000 were in uniform. They participated in 41 major battles and 449 smaller engagements. Among the many battlefields where black soldiers sacrificed their lives for the Union and freedom were Port Hudson, Milliken's Bend, Fort Wagner, the Crater, Hatcher's Run, Chaffin's Farm, Nashville, and Fort Blakely. When they were not fighting, black troops dug trenches, guarded critical bridges and railroads, manned fortifications, guarded prisoners, loaded and unloaded supplies, and performed sundry other tasks, all essential to the cause. Over 20,000 blacks joined the Union Navy and some 200,000 freedmen labored for Union forces in all sorts of capacities. Lincoln was right to measure them as horsepower and steampower.

Blacks made good soldiers and sailors, no better nor worse than whites. Their performance in hundreds of engagements and the twenty Medals of Honor that black soldiers and sailors received for wartime accomplishments testify to their valiant service. They came in vast numbers when the need was greatest, the final two years of the war. Their absence damaged the Confederate economy and war effort, and their presence elevated the Union army to its highest level of efficiency and effectiveness.

Late in the war, the Confederacy paid black Union soldiers the ultimate compliment when it decided to raise black troops of its own. Despite slavery's centrality to secession, a handful of high-ranking Confederate officers by early 1864 began to perceive slavery as no longer a strength but "in a military point of view, one of our chief sources of weakness."[34] European nations were reticent to assist the Confederacy in its struggle for independence because of slavery. Once bountiful producers for the Confederacy, bondsmen had run off to labor for the Union or to serve in its armed forces. Meanwhile, Confederate armies narrowly staved off defeat against

---

32   Lincoln to Grant, Aug. 9, 1863. *OR*, 1:24, pt. 3, 584.
33   Lincoln to Isaac M. Schemerhorn, Sept. 12, 1864. Basler et al., eds., *The Collected Works of Abraham Lincoln*, 8:2.
34   P. R. Cleburne et al., Circular Letter, [Jan. 2, 1864]. Quoted in Durden, *The Gray and the Black*, 55.

overwhelming numbers of Federals, as able-bodied black males, an enormous military resource, were unusable in the ranks according to Confederate law. At the time, the proposal generated little support, but one year later, as the Confederate nation tottered on the brink of collapse, politicians formally proposed black military service. The debate was heated, but with the endorsement of Gen. Robert E. Lee, who believed blacks would make "efficient soldiers,"[35] the legislation passed. The war ended before the Confederate government could raise and train black troops for combat. Nevertheless, it indicates how strongly the war and the performance of black soldiers in the Union army had affected Confederate attitudes.

From the misguided notions of warfare that dominated the thought of Yankee soldiers as they deployed for the Battle of First Manassas, to the extensive, deliberate destruction of Sherman's veterans on their march through Georgia and the Carolinas, the war forced dramatic changes on its participants. Just as the Union soldiers had to cast aside naive ideas of military service and harden themselves emotionally and physically to endure the brutalities of war, so the government of Abraham Lincoln had to adapt its policies to meet the exigencies of a long and bloody struggle. Like its soldiers, the Lincoln government had to recommit to the cause of unification, recognize the Confederate nation, not just its armed forces, as the enemy, and launch war against property in order to inflict hardships upon Southern civilians as well as soldiers. It also had to introduce revolutionary policies, however unpopular, to escalate the Union war effort. When enlistments slowed and the armies required manpower, the Union government conscripted. When funds to pay for the war grew scarce, Federal authorities printed greenbacks and imposed an income tax. Both were important components of an expanded policy that took the Union toward total war.

Yet at the nucleus of Northern military expansion were emancipation and black enlistment. By targeting the institution of slavery, Lincoln attacked the bedrock of Southern society. More than any other single factor, slavery influenced economics, politics, and social standing in the region. Slavery was the primary reason that Southerners seceded. With hundreds of thousands of Southern whites away in the armed forces, the fledgling Confederate nation depended more than ever on the cooperation and productivity of its slave labor. Early in the war, with the ruling that slaves employed on Confederate military projects were contraband of war and subject to confiscation, the Federal government initiated a conscious policy of undermining the peculiar institution. The decisions to issue the Emancipation Proclamation

35   Lee to Ethelbert Barksdale, Feb. 18, 1865. Quoted in Durden, *The Gray and the Black*, 206.

and to enlist blacks in the Union army culminated that process. They were the critical blows that struck directly at the Confederacy's heart. During the war, emancipation welcomed an estimated 500,000 or more slave laborers into the Union; as free men and women, some 200,000 then accepted employment from the U.S. government, cultivating fields or working on behalf of the military. Additionally, 179,000 blacks, at least 144,000 of whom came from slave states, donned the Union blue to help destroy the slave system and topple the rebellion. They were, as Lincoln had argued, indispensable to Federal success.

Less than three weeks after John Brown's raid on Harpers Ferry, the Athens, Georgia, *Southern Watchman* lectured the Northern public on its flawed understanding of the peculiar institution: "It shows them that the slaves their misdirected philanthropy would relieve are so well satisfied with their condition that they will not join them in their rebellion."[36] As four years of war proved, nothing could have been further from the truth.

36   Warch and Fanton, eds., *John Brown*, 123.

10

The Civil War Economy: A Modern View

STANLEY L. ENGERMAN AND J. MATTHEW GALLMAN

I. INTRODUCTION: WHEN IS THE CIVIL WAR A TOTAL WAR?

Perhaps more so than any other episode in American history, the main lines of the Civil War story are familiar to Americans. Insofar as today's discussion of total war is concerned, that conventional wisdom proceeds through three logical stages. First, we all recognize that this war was a tremendously destructive war. Second, accounts of the conflict often characterize it as the world's first excursion into *total war* or *modern war*, terms sometimes, although not necessarily, used interchangeably. Some approach that conclusion more gingerly, suggesting that this was a transitional war, with one foot in modern, total war and the other in some sort of traditional world. The third stage in this common analysis acknowledges the North as the side most ready to engage in total war. This conclusion builds on the North's industrial superiority, emphasizing the link between the Industrial Revolution and the global transition to a new kind of warfare. The North was the more modern, industrialized state and thus best prepared to win a total war.

Although this chain of logic makes some sense, it blurs distinctions and can lead to imprecise conclusions. The first point—the Civil War was tremendously destructive—is certainly true.[1] But before we take the next step and locate the Civil War on war's grand evolutionary scale, we should define our terms more clearly. When we do so, we are left with a paradox: The industrial North may have adopted fewer of the trappings of total war than its more agrarian opponent.

---

1 America's Civil War casualties far surpassed those of any other war, both in absolute terms and—even more dramatically—as a share of the total population. See Claudia D. Goldin, "War," in Glenn Porter, ed., *Encyclopedia of American Economic History: Studies of the Principal Movements and Ideas*, 3 vols. (New York, 1980), 3:935–57; and Maris Vinovskis, "Have Social Historians Lost the Civil War? Some Preliminary Demographic Speculations," in Vinovskis, ed., *Toward a Social History of the American Civil War: Exploratory Essays* (Cambridge, 1990), 1–30.

Our intention in this essay is to hone the issues a little more sharply, particularly as they relate to economic concerns. The first step will be to distinguish between *modern war* and *total war* in preparation for considering how each side approached the conflict. We also hope to examine the various assumptions concerning the relationship between industrialization and the Civil War. Specifically, this will involve distinguishing between, on the one hand, industry's role in the fighting of the Civil War and, on the other, the importance of the Civil War in the United States' subsequent industrial development.

II. TOTAL AND MODERN WAR

The literature touching on these terms is certainly vast, although often the discussions seem to be running at cross purposes. Our first task is to sketch out some generalizable definitions. We begin with a simple observation. *Modern war* generally implies specific characteristics associated with a modern, or modernizing, society and economy.[2] Conversely, the measurement of a nation's movement toward total war is relative rather than absolute.

The progress toward modern war reflects changes in three areas: (1) the behavior of the state; (2) the pattern of economic growth; (3) and the level of military technology. A nation engaged in modern war will see an expansion in the government bureaucracy and a concomitant shift of powers toward the central state. This political process is accompanied by industrial development, reflected in economic shifts such as an expanded manufacturing output and movement toward an urban economy. On the battlefield, modern wars feature an increased reliance on new military technologies in the form of munitions, transportation, and the like. These new technologies, in turn, spur on strategic innovations. These characteristics are certainly connected. The military technology required to sustain modern war depends on a strong industrial base and the governmental mechanisms necessary to bring that power to bear on a military objective. Similarly, the military demands of a strong central state may spur technological and industrial adjustments.

Whereas modern warfare is generally best seen as a post–Industrial Revolution phenomenon, some scholars have treated total war in more relative terms. Thus, total war may be viewed as the opposite of *limited war*. Or, if we shift from hard dichotomies to a seamless continuum, various characteristics may place a particular war effort on a spectrum between the most limited war and full total war. Three broad questions are commonly

---

2   For a discussion on the use of "modernity" in describing wars, see Mark E. Neely Jr., "Was the Civil War a Total War?" *Civil War History* 37 (March 1991): 5–28.

associated with total war. First, what is the magnitude of the nation's commitment to the conflict? That is, what share of productive manpower and economic output are mobilized to fight the conflict? The second question—or cluster of questions—concerns military strategy. What are the strategic intentions? How are those intentions enacted in battlefield strategy? We associate total war with attacks on civilians, destruction of property, and the strategic aim of destroying the enemy's "will to fight." In this sense, the totality of a war effort could be described either by the declared goals of the actual effect of that strategy on the enemy. Third, moving beyond matters of mobilization and strategy, we may ask about the nature of the nation's war aims. A country engaging in limited war may have quite circumscribed objectives in mind, whereas total war might emerge out of a broader array of conflicts in which at least one combatant insists on the right to reshape dramatically the future of its opponent if victory is won.

These three questions really identify different, although certainly related, aspects of what historians have described as total war. In discussing the American Civil War, many scholars have emphasized strategic considerations, particularly William Tecumseh Sherman's famed march to the sea.[3] Others add a focus on the North's war aims, pointing to Lincoln's insistence on unconditional surrender.[4] Still others place the Civil War in the long-term development of warfare by concentrating on the movement toward heavy mobilization of resources.[5]

Each of these approaches concentrates on events during the war years, perhaps linking them to long-term patterns of military development. A further measure of total war could look beyond the conflict to gauge the lasting effects of wartime measures. In the political arena, this would encompass the long-term shifts in the balance of powers among branches. If wartime mobilization led to an expanded central government, did this shift last into the postwar decades? Similar questions could be asked about the legacy of military and economic policies. Did the nation continue to support an expanded military into the peacetime decades? Did the economic

---

3   The classic statement on Sherman is John Bennett Walters, "General William T. Sherman and Total War," *Journal of Southern History* 14 (Nov. 1948): 447–80. See also Edward Hagerman, *The American Civil War and the Origins of Modern Warfare: Ideas, Organization and Field Command* (Bloomington, Ind., 1988), xiii–xiv, 207–9; and Charles Royster, *The Destructive War: William Tecumseh Sherman, Stonewall Jackson, and the Americans* (New York, 1991). For an excellent review of the literature on the Civil War, see Neely, "Was the Civil War a Total War?"(Chapter 2, this volume).

4   James M. McPherson, "Lincoln and the Strategy of Unconditional Surrender," in *Abraham Lincoln and the Second American Revolution* (New York, 1990), 69–91. Mark E. Neely Jr. disagrees with this reading of Lincoln's war aims in his "Was the Civil War a Total War?" See also Richard A. Preston, Sydney F. Wise, and Herman O. Werner, *Men in Arms: A History of Warfare and Its Interrelationships with Western Society* (New York, 1956), 243.

5   Raymond Aron, *The Century of Total War* (Garden City, N.Y., 1954), 19.

mobilization associated with war yield long-term sectoral shifts within the economy?

Let us shift now from the general to the specific. How can we build the case for the Civil War as either a modern war or a total war? The case for the war's modernity can be made both in terms of economic patterns and governmental initiatives. By the eve of the Civil War, the United States could—by most measures—be described as in the midst of modern economic growth. The previous half-century had witnessed high rates of growth in total output and in output per capita, accelerated by a post-1840 shift toward industrial production in the North. This economic growth was built in part on a steady pattern of development in transportation and communications so that by mid-century the major urban areas were linked by rail and telegraph. And as the nation's economic infrastructure matured, America's financial network emerged as one of the world's leaders. At a bureaucratic level, there is ample room to argue that the North, at least, had achieved the status of a modern state. As the conflict progressed, the Union demonstrated the capacity to collect taxes and issue bonds to fund the effort while developing the institutional apparatus to direct a region-wide conscription system. Moreover, although the Civil War dwarfed all previous American military ventures, the North did have a military in place that had won the Mexican War barely a decade before. In short, the nation that had divided in Civil War could certainly be treated as a modern nation capable of engaging in modern war.

But we are really more concerned with fitting our discussion of total war to the Civil War case. On the face of it, there is room to argue that the conflict was a total war (or at least toward that end of the total war — limited war spectrum) according to any of the three aforementioned criteria: commitment, strategy, or objectives. The commitment to war, or mobilization, could be measured in manpower terms or by military expenditure. About 2.1 million soldiers fought for the Union, and between 850,000 and 900,000 fought for the Confederacy. Taken together, roughly 40 percent of military-aged whites served in the war, including over 60 percent of Southerners.[6] The direct costs of the Civil War can be presented in a variety of ways, all pointing to the heavy mobilization of resources. The Northern government spent roughly $3.4 billion during the war years; the direct costs of the Union war effort were an estimated $2.3 billion, of which the federal government paid $1.8 billion. In the four prewar years (1857–60), the entire federal budget only totaled about $274 million. Or, to phrase the point in a different way, the Northern war expenditures over

---

6 James M. McPherson, *Battle Cry of Freedom* (New York, 1988), 306–7; Vinovskis, "Have Social Historians Lost the Civil War?" 9.

the four years amounted to nearly three-fourths (74.4 percent) of the region's 1859 output, while the Confederacy—at all government levels— actually spent more ($1.03 billion) than the value of its 1859 output.[7]

Both the scale and organization of this vast mobilization are central to our understanding of the economic aspects of total war. The lively debate over wartime strategy in general, and on General Sherman in particular, is perhaps best left for others to continue. But at the very least, the record offers substantial ammunition to support the claim that numerous tacticians on either side recognized the military benefits of destroying enemy resources and undercutting the "will" of civilians.[8] When we turn to war aims, we enter another battlefield that is beyond our present purview. If we take prewar claims at face value, the North simply sought to preserve the Union, and Jefferson Davis insisted in April that "all we ask is to be left alone." Neither goal seems particularly dramatic until they are set side by side. After Lincoln's Emancipation Proclamation, the recognized aims of the North had shifted and with them the stakes had risen, guaranteeing that a Northern victory would have a tremendous impact on the South.

We have also suggested that a proper understanding of total war should take us into the postwar period. The pursuit of the elusive "economic impact of the American Civil War" requires that we follow several of the aforementioned threads beyond Appomattox. In institutional terms, many of the most centrist aspects of mobilization failed to survive into the postwar years. Nineteenth-century Americans, it seems, were quick to take advantage of their "peace dividend." Similarly, the quantitative data do not support the conclusion that the war's economic demands launched the United States into a period of accelerated economic growth. One of the strongest cases for the war's economic legacy emphasizes the lasting impact of the wartime financial legislation. But even if we can identify such an impact, we must mull over the relationship between such acts and our understanding of total war. What, for instance, do we make of the passage of Republican initiatives that predated the conflict and were only tangentially related to the war's economic needs? Finally, the war's economic impact must consider the varied effects on the

---

7   On the direct and indirect costs of the war, see the estimates in Claudia D. Goldin and Frank D. Lewis, "The Economic Costs of the American Civil War: Estimates and Implications," *Journal of Economic History* 35 (June 1975): 299–325. For a broader comparison, see Goldin, "War." On federal government expenditures, see U.S. Bureau of the Census, *Historical Statistics of the United States, Colonial Times to 1970*, 2 vols. (Washington, D.C., 1975), 2:1114.

8   In addition to the aforementioned sources on Sherman, see Michael Fellman, *Inside War: The Guerrilla Conflict in Missouri During the American Civil War* (New York, 1989). Of course, some of the strategies commonly associated with total war—the destruction of resources on the home front, for instance—were staples in traditional warfare as well.

South, ranging from physical damage to the emancipation of slaves, to the shift in political dominance to the North.

The discussion that follows will concentrate on those aspects of our definition of total war that are most closely tied to economic concerns. The first section examines the economic evidence itself, which is followed by a discussion of the various mobilization policies and their ramifications. It becomes evident in each section that the conclusions are largely dependent on the particular measure selected. Moreover, as we shall see, a separate analysis of each region yields the rather surprising conclusion that the South–the less "modern" of the two combatants–became more fully committed to total war than the North.

III. THE CIVIL WAR AND ECONOMIC CHANGE

As with many historical questions, the debate on the economic aspects of the Civil War includes a number of distinct but related issues. Their analysis rests upon various assumptions both as to the causes of what did happen and as to the probable patterns of change that could have occurred in the absence of the war. While the full set of issues and arguments cannot be dealt with adequately in this limited space, some distinctions may usefully be made at the start. Of particular concern are separating those changes that occurred in the period of the war itself from those long-run changes that reflect subsequent developments attributable to the war.

In describing the war's immediate effects, attention is paid to various measures of aggregate economic activity – as indicators of the nature of economic change in the wartime period – and to their implications for those other economic, political, and social changes that had continuing effects. The links between the short-run and long-run effects relates the latter to specific changes introduced in pursuing the war, and the nature and magnitude of the effects may appear quite different depending on the particular time span analyzed. While it may seem relatively straightforward to describe the aggregate economic change in the war interval, it is rather difficult in the absence of annual censuses of production. The data that are generally available for the war years are limited to partial indicators, which are difficult to interpret as indicators of aggregate behavior. Since there may be offsetting movements in different sectors, and sectors often may change at different rates, partial data make any projection somewhat uncertain. Moreover, some traditionally used indices are based on inferences derived from presumed economic connections that may not be appropriate. To use real wages as an index of profits has limitations, while the use of date on changing prices to indicate changes in real outputs can also be misleading. In short, use of partial indicators and theoretical inferences cannot provide as definite an answer to the question of the nature of the Civil War economy as would be possible with the more complete data available for the twentieth century.

The basic problems in analyzing long-term changes are of a rather different nature. The problems are in the drawing out of the precise relations to explain the causes and consequences of specific changes over time. One aspect of the complexity arises from the need to differentiate several possible forms of relationship between the war and the subsequent changes, meaning that the specific questions asked may be quite diverse. There are (at least) three possible relations. First, basic changes may have resulted from particular wartime operations and patterns of change, with the implication that the specific circumstances of the war led to changes that otherwise would not have occurred. Second, basic changes may have resulted from the outcome of the war, and the policies imposed upon the losing side by the winners, whether to the subsequent benefit of the winners, of the losers, to both, or to neither. Third, is the introduction of policies implemented as a result of the political changes brought about by the war and its outcome, policies that might have been sought earlier and possibly accomplished within a reasonable time, even without the military conflict? To Charles and Mary Beard, the triumph of the industrial economy was inevitable, even without a war.[9] Thus, many post–Civil War changes might be argued to have been the result of basic trends that had earlier emerged, changes that no doubt would have occurred in the absence of the war. These trends were not, it can be argued, directly related to the war and to wartime needs. The presence of similar developments of economic, social, and political patterns in other countries might suggest that the links drawn, in the American case, to the Civil War do not reflect necessary conditions. All of these variants have been argued for, and all have some plausibility. We, therefore, shall examine some of the posited mechanisms.

While we would obviously prefer data for the war years themselves to describe short-run changes, it will be easiest to set the context by using decadal estimates comparing 1860–70. We will generally compare the antebellum years with the decade 1860–70 – a comparison that is, however, sensitive to business cycles, since the 1850s were generally a period of rapid growth, particularly in the South (with the cyclical downturn of 1857 being particularly sharp in the North).

Thomas Cochran was one of the first historians to question the contention that the Civil War period had been one of significant economic expansion

9   Charles A. Beard and Mary R. Beard, *The Rise of American Civilization* (New York, 1930), 2:115.

to the Northern economy.[10] But it was only in the late 1950s, with the presentation of Robert Gallman's estimates of commodity output from 1839 to 1899, that a systematic analysis of the war decade become possible.[11] Gallman presented estimates based on the decadal censuses, with various production series used to interpolate output levels, but no estimates were presented for years in the period between 1859 and 1869. Nevertheless, the pattern found for the war decade was sufficiently dramatic that it permitted some clear interpretations of the earlier years of the decade.[12]

First, at the national level, overall economic growth was relatively low during the Civil War decade, the slowest nineteenth-century growth subsequent to the onset of economic expansion after the War of 1812. The pattern of the Civil War decade thus differed quite dramatically from the rapid expansion seen during World War II, with the latter's coming out of a prolonged depression, but it resembled more closely the experience of most other American wars. By using the census data and Richard Easterlin's regional income estimation, Stanley Engerman pointed out the extent to which the national change was influenced by the decline in output in the Southern economy in the decade.[13] The Southern decline was attributed to the wartime destruction and, more importantly, the dramatic effects of the ending of slavery and the virtual disappearance of the plantation system in Southern agriculture. Yet, looking at the North alone, this decade was a period of relatively slow growth, compared to that in prior and subsequent decades. Thus, unless there was a severe postbellum depression, the war years were a period of relative economic stagnation in the North.

There are two basic economic aggregates for which we have recently obtained more reliable measures for the nineteenth century. Gallman has presented detailed estimates of capital stock, and Thomas Weiss has modified

10 Thomas Cochran, "Did the Civil War Retard Industrialization?" *Mississippi Valley Historical Review* 48 (Sept. 1961): 197–210. Cochran had, however, raised this same point in earlier writings. For a recent survey of the debate on the effects of the Civil War, see Patrick K. O'Brien, *The Economic Effects of the American Civil War* (London, 1988).
11 Robert E. Gallman, "Commodity Output, 1839–1899, "in Conference on Research in Income and Wealth, *Trends in the American Economy in the Nineteenth Century* (Princeton, N.J., 1960), 24: 13–71.
12 We should note that Robert E. Gallman has subsequently presented national income estimates for the non Civil War years after 1834 and that these provide some modest revisions to the basic commodity output pattern. The newer estimates, nevertheless, indicate the same basic patterns and conclusions pointed to in earlier writings. Robert E. Gallman, "Gross National Product in the United States, 1834–1909," in Conference on Research in Income and Wealth, *Output, Employment, and Productivity in the United States after 1800*, Studies in Income and Wealth, vol . 30 (New York, 1966), 3–76.
13 Richard Easterlin, "Regional Income Trends, 1840–1950," in Seymour Harris, ed., *American Economic History* (New York, 1961), 525–47; Stanley L. Engerman, "The Economic Impact of the Civil War," *Exploration in Economic History* 3 (Spring/Summer 1966): 176–99.

and extended Stanley Lebergott's labor force estimates.[14] The growth pattern of the capital stock at the national level mirrors that of national income for the decade between 1860 and 1870. The war decade was one of slower growth of the overall capital stock, as well as of each of its major subcategories: structures, equipment, land, inventories. Suggestive of the impact of the war on the Northern economy was the slow growth of structures and equipment, components of capital considerably more important in the Northern than the Southern capital stock. There was an accelerated growth of capital stock in the subsequent decade, but the overall growth of the national capital stock in the period 1860–80 was below that of 1840–60, suggesting that any impact of debt finance and repayment in increasing the savings rate of the postbellum period may not have offset the shortfall generated during the period of the war itself.

Weiss's recent labor force estimates also suggest a marked slowing down in growth in the decade 1860–70, with possibly an overall decline in measured Southern labor input. Even for the North, however, the labor force growth slowed down. In part, this reflected a decline in immigration in the war period, reductions in the manpower pool owing to wartime deaths and injuries, an increased mortality for civilians in this decade, which was probably related to the circumstances of the Civil War and, for the South and some border states, the loss of control over slave labor, with slave runaways (often to fight for the North), and then legal emancipation.[15] Deaths were high in this war, equal, in the North, to about 10 percent of white males aged 18–45 in 1860, while for the South, deaths were equal to about 25 percent of all white males in that age bracket. During the war, the male labor force was reduced owing to military needs. At any given moment, about 10 percent of the total labor force was lost in each region owing to military service, with the South suffering even greater losses owing to the loss of slave labor.[16]

14 Robert E. Gallman, "American Economic Growth before the Civil War: the Testimony of the Capital Stock Estimates," in Robert E. Gallman and John Wallis, eds., *The Standard of Living in Early Nineteenth-Century America* (Chicago, 1993), 79–115; Thomas Weiss, "Long-Term Changes in U.S. Agricultural Output per Worker, 1800–1900, " *Economic History Review* 46 (May 1993): 324–41; and Thomas Weiss, "U.S. Labor Force Estimates, 1800-1860, " in Robert E. Gallman and John Wallis, eds., *The Standard of Living in Early Nineteenth-Century America*, 19–75. Some of the discussion on the labor force is based on worksheets underlying Weiss's published estimates, and we wish to thank Weiss for permission to use them at this time.

15 For data on these issues, see Thomas L. Livermore, *Number and Losses in the Civil War in America 1861–65* (Boston, 1901); Goldin and Lewis, "The Economic Cost of the American Civil War," Clayne L. Pope, "Adult Mortality in America before 1900: A View from Family Histories," in Claudia Goldin and Hugh Rockoff, eds., *Strategic Factors in Nineteenth Century American Economic History: A Volume to Honor Robert W. Fogel* (Chicago, 1992), 267–96; and U.S. Bureau of the Census, *Historical Statistics of the United States*, 2:1140.

16 See Livermore, *Numbers and Losses*; Weiss, "U.S. Labor Force Estimates," and underlying worksheets.

There was some increased participation of women and children in the labor force during the war, but this increase apparently did not continue to affect significantly the postbellum situation.

Nor did the Civil War decade lead to dramatic changes in the basic occupational structure of the labor force.[17] For the South, there was little change in the share of the labor force in agriculture between 1860 and 1870 – indeed, little change until after 1880. For the Northern regions, there was some decline in the agricultural share in the labor force, but the decline was less than in the preceding decades (although greater than in the next decade). Thus, the pattern of change in the decade was not unique, nor was it continued. Nevertheless, the maintenance of the share of agricultural output in the North, combined with a reduction in the agricultural share in the labor force, did mean a sharp increase in measured labor productivity in agriculture in that region – and for the national average as well. The South did experience some relative growth in manufacturing output over this decade, since the war led to a more rapid expansion and ensuing smaller decline in manufacturing than in agriculture. Nevertheless, the Southern manufacturing sector did not experience a continued postbellum increase, nor, when Southern manufacturing subsequently developed, was it on the basis of industries whose growth was accelerated by military needs or wartime exigencies.

While the decadal estimates suggest that it is doubtful that the war period itself, even in the North, could have been one of rapid economic expansion, it is possible to use some recent economic observations as well as some of the available fragmentary measures to isolate the changes within the years 1861–65. One of the major reasons for the belief in economic expansion during the war years was the reliance on a specific economic model to infer the relation between the known changes in prices and the unknown movement in the level of output. Reflecting patterns generally observed in the expansion phase of business cycles, it was widely argued that the price rises indicated output increases. We now have more recent information on the price–output relationship, and a useful set of models with which to interpret this period. Our recent experience with inflationary periods demonstrates that these can yield price rises with limited output growth. Evidence of rising prices, of some individuals getting wealthy, and of some sectors expanding, all can occur without there necessarily being increases in the overall level of output for the economy. Vietnam was a war with periods of

---

17 See Weiss, "U.S. Labor Force Estimates," and underlying worksheets. See also the claims in Lee A. Craig and Thomas Weiss, "Agricultural Productivity Growth During the Decade of the Civil War," *Journal of Economic History* 53 (Sept. 1993): 527–48, who argue that the growth reflected increases in labor impact more than the increases in conventionally measured productivity.

sharply rising prices and relatively slow output growth, while the oil shock of the 1970s similarly led to rising prices with slow growth. Unexpected shocks to the economy (as in the Civil War) can lead to such patterns of behavior. We should be more cautious than in the past in the arguing for economic growth from price changes. Indeed, we are quite aware for the South that rising prices occurred with falling output, and while the Northern pattern was not so dramatic, the price increases by themselves need not imply rapid economic growth.

It is also useful to remember that part of any increase in Northern output after the start of the war may not have reflected only new demands from prewar levels but were in part offsets to the disturbances to the Northern economy that came with the loss of Southern markets at war's start.[18] Frequently discussed by contemporaries were problems owing to the inability to collect financial debts from Southerners, and in various industries, particularly textile and shoe manufacture, there were believed to have been increased levels of unemployment owing to the removal of Southern demand. Within agriculture, some losses also resulted from the ending of Southern markets, and the shifting patterns owing to the war also affected various commercial and service industries. Thus, some of the North's subsequent output growth marked the replacement by new Northern demand sources for disappearing Southern demands.

Much of the fragmentary data available for the war years in the North suggest that the output of those sectors measured either declined in the North or else grew less rapidly than it had in prior or subsequent periods. Censuses of manufacturing for New York and Massachusetts indicate declines in output over the war period, as do the overall data for the manufacturing center of Philadelphia.[19] The decline in cotton textile production with the loss of its raw materials is quite clear, but it should be noted that this decline was greater than the marked expansion of woolen textiles that the war brought about. Shoe output fell – as did the level of patent activity in the industry.[20] The production of pig iron declined early in the war, but

18   Victor S. Clark, *History of Manufacturers in the United States*, vol. 2: *1860–1893* (Washington, D.C., 1929), 7–53; Paul Gates, *Agriculture and the Civil War* (New York, 1965), 10, 224; and J. Matthew Gallman, *Mastering Wartime: A Social History of Philadelphia During the Civil War* (Cambridge, 1990), 251–328.

19   Engerman, "The Economic Impact of the Civil War"; J. Matthew Gallman, *Mastering Wartime* and Philip Scranton, *Proprietary Capitalism: The Textile Manufacture at Philadelphia 1800–1885* (Cambridge, 1983). See also Raymond H. Robinson, *The Boston Economy During the Civil War* (New York, 1988); and James A. Huston, *The Sinews of War: Army Logistics 1775–1953* (Washington, D.C., 1966), 176–87, for a description of wartime purchasing.

20   Ross Thomson, *The Path to Mechanized Shoe Production in the United States* (Chapel Hill, N.C., 1989), 161, 183.

even after recovery, this five-year span represented the slowest growth of any period after the War of 1812, with slower growth for the overall industry as well as for the newly emerging sectors using coal fuel.[21] DuPont's production of explosives also grew less rapidly in the war period than previously, and the employed labor force did not increase.[22] Thus, for many of the key sectors of industry producing military output, decline or slowed growth was the general pattern, not rapid expansion. This pattern is consistent with the suggestion of the one index of overall manufacturing production for the period.[23]

While less is known about the pattern of output within agriculture, by linking the decadal censuses with the data collected after 1866 by the Department of Agriculture, some inferences are permitted. The expanded output of wheat and corn in the North was generally post-1866 rather than during the war years.[24] The pattern of change within agriculture thus resembles that in manufacturing, with a postwar boom developing after some wartime declines in output.

In what way did the Civil War economy of the North differ from that of the South, and why did the wartime demands have an apparently limited measured effect on Northern production? In regard to the latter question, there are two considerations to discuss. First, in the period prior to the start of the war, the Northern economy was at a near full-employment level, with output at peak amounts. There was relatively little unemployment or excess capacity, and with limited amounts of new entrants into the labor force or enhanced ability to invest in the private sector after the war started, the rising war demands for military purposes to a large extent meant primarily some diversion of output and investment from other uses rather than increased outputs. The ability to accelerate technical change in such a short period in order to increase productivity was limited, as was the ability of innovations to have a substantial effect on the economy. Second, the military demands in many ways were not those of what we have come to regard as those of a modern war, requiring production of a set of new goods or greatly expanding the output of goods earlier produced by simpler means of technology. Rather, in the Civil War, the primary goods purchased by the army were foodstuffs,

21 Peter Temin, *Iron and Steel in Nineteenth-Century America: An Economic Inquiry* (Cambridge, Mass., 1964), 264–6; and Clark, *History and Manufactures*, 2 :15–16.
22 Harold B. Hancock and Norman B. Wilkinson, "A Manufacturer in Wartime: DuPont, 1860–1865," *Business History Review* 40 (Summer 1966): 213–36.
23 Edwin Frickey, *Production in the United States, 1860–1914* (Cambridge, Mass., 1947).
24 U.S. Department of Agriculture, Agricultural Marketing Service Statistical bulletin no. 56, "Corn: Acreage, Yield, and Production by States, 1866–1943" (Washington, D.C., 1954); and U.S. Department of Agriculture, Agricultural Marketing Service Statistical bulletin no. 158, "Wheat: Acreage, Yield and Production by States, 1866–1943" (Washington, D.C., 1955).

textiles (for uniforms), and boots and shoes, and even those purchases of arms and explosives involved limited amounts of new materials relative to prewar uses. The closing down of Southern exports of cotton did mean that textiles would need to be produced with woolens, but woolen output had been about three-fifths that of cotton textiles in 1860, wool textiles already being a large producing sector.

Thus, while there were considerable military purchases, these generally replaced civilian demands for the same commodities, limiting any overall net increase in the demand for these products. The demand for iron for military uses was only a small part of total iron output, and these increases did not fully offset the declining growth in demand for iron for railroad construction, for agricultural implements, and for use in construction.[25] Similarly, the military use of explosives needed to offset changing demands from railroad construction and mining. It is this similarity in demand patterns and amounts from the prewar pattern that limited the magnitude of overall change in both the war period itself and then in the postwar era. The changing magnitudes of demand and the imposed degree of standardization did not lead to the dramatic changes in size of firms and in methods of production that some later wars did.

The similarity in Northern demand patterns before and during the war had one further set of implications, pointing to a major difference in the nature of the necessary economic readjustments that the war generated in the two regions. Given the nature of military goods demanded, and the antebellum pattern of relatively limited imports of manufactured goods, there remained a greater compatibility of goods demanded and goods produced within the North than was possible in the Southern economy of that period. The Northern military needs did not require a dramatic change from the normal prewar production pattern. There was little need to develop new industries to fight the conflict. Thus, it was possible to acquire more of the necessary goods by budget policies and increased expenditures. The existing production structure provided the possibilities of rapid response with basic financial incentives, and the North could make use of taxes, borrowing, and money creation to pay for the goods. In addition, it was possible to place primary reliance upon contracting with already existing firms, and there was little need to provide specific aids to create new firms or new productive technologies. There was some flexibility in choosing among alternative suppliers. Despite these advantages, however, it should be noted that there

25   Richard Wacht, "A Note on the Cochran Thesis and the Small Arms Industry in the Civil War," *Explorations in Entrepreneurial History* 4 (Fall 1966): 57–62.

were frequent charges of scandal and corruption in procurement and contracting, particularly in the conflict's early years (these not being a characteristic separating the Civil War from any premodern or modern war).

For the South, however, the situation of meeting wartime needs was somewhat different. These wartime demands required a quite different production structure from that previously existing, which had been based on expectations of ongoing trade with the Northern states and with England – trading patterns that had yielded a high level of consumption to the Southern states over the previous decades. The South was not, however, backward in the magnitude and nature of its manufacturing output prior to the Civil War, and it ranked high among the developed world in the production of some basic industrial goods.[26] Once the war began, it was clear that the North would not remain a major supplier of needs to the South, meaning either that there had to be increased imports from England or increased production of manufactured goods within the South. Given the time required to reorganize the Southern production structure, it is not surprising that the initial focus was upon increased imports from England.[27] The South attempted to influence England to provide more exports by measures made more familiar and (done more successfully) in recent years – by restricting the export of its key commodity.[28] The fact that King Cotton diplomacy was less successful than was to be King Oil diplomacy led to a Southern need for foreign borrowing to finance its import needs, a tactic that met with only limited success. It was not only in manufacturing that structural reorganization was required. The Southern strategy meant that the output of cotton would be reduced in the interest of greater production of foodstuffs, but with food production still primarily based upon the slave labor on plantations.[29] All of this dictated a larger governmental role in the war for the South, with more direct controls and a larger use of subsidies to encourage

26 Robert William Fogel and Stanley L. Engerman, *Time on the Cross: The Economics of American Negro Slavery* (Boston, 1974).
27 See Richard D. Goff, *Confederate Supply* (Durham, N.C., 1969); and Raimondo Luraghi, *The Rise and Fall of the Plantation South* (New York, 1978). See also Richard E. Beringer et al., eds., *Why the South Lost the Civil War* (Athens, Ga., 1986).
28 On the failure of this policy, argued for quite different reasons, see, most recently, Stanley Lebergott, "Why the South Lost: Commercial Purpose in the Confederacy, 1861–1865," *Journal of American History* 70 (June 1983): 58–74; Douglas Ball, *Financial Failure and Confederate Defeat* (Urbana, Ill., 1991); and David G. Surdam, "A Case of Regicide: The Strange Demise of King Cotton," unpublished paper, University of Chicago, 1991.
29 See Stanley Lebergott, "Through the Blockade: The Profitability and Extent of Cotton Smuggling, 1861–1865, "*Journal of Economic History* 41 (Dec. 1981): 867–88; and Gates, *Agriculture and the Civil War*, on Southern wartime agriculture. On the antebellum Southern economy, see Fogel and Engerman, *Time on the Cross*, and the subsequent debates in the *American Economic Review* between 1977 and 1980. See also Robert William Fogel, *Without Consent or Contract: The Rise and Fall of American Slavery* (New York, 1989).

industry.[30] However, with the major conflicts regarding the role of the central Confederacy in contrast with the rights of state governments, this enhanced governmental role was undertaken with a weakened tax system. Yet the fact that the South was able to produce sufficient materials to fight for four years does suggest that there was sufficient flexibility in adjusting the production structure when necessary, as well as enough direction to ensure the flow of goods to the appropriate segments of the military. There had been some iron furnaces in the South prior to the Civil War, and these expanded production to meet military needs, while the textile sector required considerable expansion. The war demands led to what the historian Raimondo Luraghi has described as a form of "state socialism" in the South, which permitted a prolonged war, relative, at least, to some post-dictions of Southern capacity, but this type of industrial expansion did not have any carryover into the postwar period.

While the war may have led to a slowing of the rate of Northern economic expansion, the war period and the outcome of the war led to actual declines in the regional income of the South. The weakening and then ending of slavery meant a fundamental change in the nature of the Southern economy, leading to the effective disappearance of the system of plantation agriculture that had been the principal basis of Southern production and economic growth in the antebellum period. The losses in the productive efficiency that had been achieved with plantation production led to a sharp decline in production, particularly by black labor, and it took decades for the Southern economy to recover.[31] These declines had been foreshadowed during the war, with slave runaways, slaves held captive by the North, and a weakened ability to control the remaining slave population. Thus, the effective input of labor from the slave population fell during the war, even before the granting of legal freedom at the end of the war.

In addition to the losses in labor input because of the reduced number of effective slave laborers, the military drain of white adult males also lowered the available labor supply within the South. Further, the impact of the Northern army, particularly in the latter part of the war, was to force losses

30 See, e.g., Mary A. DeCredico, *Patriotism for Profit: Georgia's Urban Entrepreneurs and the Confederate War Effort* (Chapel Hill, N.C., 1990); Luraghi, *The Rise and Fall of the Plantation South*; and Emory M. Thomas, *The Confederate Nation: 1861–1865* (New York, 1979). On Confederate financing of the war effort, see Richard Cecil Todd, *Confederate Finance* (Athens, Ga., 1954).

31 Roger L. Ransom and Richard Sutch, *One Kind of Freedom: The Economic Consequences of Emancipation* (Cambridge, 1979); Jon R. Moen, "Changes in the Productivity System of Southern Agriculture between 1860 and 1880, " in Robert William Fogel and Stanley L. Engerman, eds., *Without Consent or Contract: The Rise and Fall of American Slavery; Technical Papers* (New York, 1992), 1:320–50; and Robert William Fogel, Ralph A. Galantine, and Richard L. Manning, eds., *Without Consent or Contract: The Rise and Fall of American Slavery: Evidence and Methods* (New York, 1992).

upon the capital and land used by Southerners. Railroads were destroyed, land and machinery were ruined, and livestock were killed, which, with the reductions in labor, meant that considerable amounts of land were withdrawn from production. While the destruction of land and capital did not necessarily lead to prolonged postwar problems, recovery to earlier levels not always taking a very long time, it did serve to set back the wartime economy. Neither agriculture nor manufacturing can easily be undertaken in an area when military action is taking place.

The South also suffered in the wartime from the disruption of its trading patterns. The limits, ill-conceived as they now seem, on cotton production and sales reduced import possibilities, even while they permitted increased production of foodstuffs within the South.[32] While the causes of the decline in cotton production remain debated, given the absence of any centrally enforced prohibitions, the sharpness of the wartime decline is quite clear.[33] The total cotton output of years 1862 through 1865 was below that of 1861 (which had been planted at the very start of the war), a clear sign of the adjustments in agricultural production to the changing needs and possibilities of war. The Northern blockade appears to have been generally successful, but some merchandise did squeeze through. Nevertheless, the interference with Southern trade did have an impact, lowering Southern incomes. While the Northern states experienced difficulties in their trade with Europe and suffered from a deterioration in the terms of trade, their problems in international trade were not as severe as those confronted by the South.[34]

Thus, the costs to the white South of the Civil War were large, as were the long-term consequences of the major institutional changes coming out of the war – the ending of slavery and the plantation system. By the end of 1865, the Southern economy was severely weakened. Yet this decline in the war and with slave emancipation was a once-and-for-all change in the position of the South vis-à-vis the North. Over the next three-quarters of a century, the per capita income of the South grew about as rapidly as did the Northern, and Southern manufacturing also expanded. Despite the late nineteenth-century impacts of racism, colonialism, and sharecropping, the Southern economy was able to expand as rapidly as did the North and, after 1880, did so with significant declines in the importance of the agricultural economy and increases in manufacturing. And to argue that the South should have had a higher income and grown more rapidly than did the North after the

32 See Ball, *Financial Failure and Confederate Defeat.*
33 See Lebergott, "Why the South Lost."
34 See Reuben A. Kessel and Armen A. Alchian, "Real Wages in the North during the Civil War: Mitchell's Data Reinterpreted," *Journal of Law and Economics* 2 (Oct. 1959): 95–113.

war overlooks the basic factor that had permitted high incomes in the antebellum era – the slave plantation. Whatever difficulties the war caused the South, it did not mean, once the initial adjustment was made, that prospects for continued economic growth did not persist.

Discussions of the long-term effects of the Civil War on the economy usually focus on the Northern states, with the arguments that the North was the source of modern development as well as the locus of political power for the nation. Yet, in many ways, the most dramatic changes occurred within the Southern states, and the postbellum Southern economy differed more dramatically from that of the antebellum years than did the Northern.

In the North, the postbellum structural changes in output, capital, and the labor force represented a basic continuation of the prewar patterns. The war neither initiated nor accelerated these changes, although, in many cases, the actual growth or changes over the period 1860 to 1880 were lower than that in the last two antebellum decades. There was no unusual expansion in the size of firms or the structure of industries for over a decade – certainly none that seems directly linked to the wartime economy. The large firms of the late nineteenth century were not those uniquely affected by wartime military needs. Clearly, it is possible to visualize alternative events that might have occurred post-1860 without the war, so that even this slower growth might seem to represent a major economic step forward (such visualizations are always possible), but we wish to avoid such conjectures for the present.

It was in the relation of the federal government to the overall economy that the wartime Northern changes were most dramatic. It was not because of any introduction of direct controls, since these were limited. Rather, the major changes were in the increased share of resources taken by the Northern government, and the tax, expenditure, money, and debt policies that led to this. There were also significant new policies regarding tariffs, land, and immigration passed early in the war, but these were generally not war related, in terms of its financial and military needs, and will be discussed later. (The revenue effect of the tariff was itself small. Tariffs fell from over 90 percent of tax revenues in 1861 to about 25 percent by 1865, changing little in real terms during the war.) These changes could, presumably, have had longer-term impacts upon the centralized operation of the economy, and the development of a military-industrial complex, through their effects on debt policy and subsequent financial market and investment behavior.

While the increased federal budget during the war meant a rise to nineteenth-century peaks, the postbellum reaction was quite different from that experienced in the twentieth century, particularly after World War II. With the ending of the Civil War, there was a sharp decline in the size of the federal budget, absolutely and as a ratio to gross national product (GNP).[35] There was a dramatic decline in military expenditures (and in the size of the military as measured by dollar expenditures and by manpower), while federal civilian expenditures as a share of GNP soon began to decline from post-bellum levels. Within the expenditure categories, there were few changes in expenditures on resource-using components relative to prewar, and the main structural changes in federal expenditures came in the category of transfers among taxpayers not in government purchases of goods and services. The primary categories of expenditure growth were veteran's payments (which, however, increased greatly in amount only several decades after the war), interest payments to holders of the debt, and debt repayments. The revenues to pay for these items came in part from tariffs but also from various excise taxes introduced during the war. The net effects of this system of taxes and transfers is still not clear, but it is probable that its overall effects on savings and investment were limited. Indeed, in the post–Civil War decades, as in the antebellum years, most resource-using governmental expenditures occurred on the state and local, not the federal, level.[36] The direct impact upon government, as measured by the federal budget, did not point to an accelerated increase in the degree of governmental centralization. Several decades were to pass before the expansion of those various federal agencies and commissions that were to influence so strongly the economy in the twentieth century.

Similarly, the impact of debt issues during the war and their retirements after the war, and of the overall postbellum tax and expenditure system, were somewhat mixed.[37] To determine their effects requires consideration of the circumstances both at the time of debt issue and debt retirement, as well as the incidence of taxes and of the transfers upon their recipients. While government debt retirement may promote further capital formation, this might not offset the impact of its creation in "crowding-out" private investment.

---

35   M. Slade Kendrick, *A Century and a Half of Federal Expenditures*, NBER Occasional Paper no. 48, revised (New York, 1955); and U.S. Bureau of the Census, *Historical Studies*, 2:1106–15. On the costs of the war, see Goldin, "War," and Goldin and Lewis, "The Economic Costs of the American Civil War." See also Bert W. Rein, *An Analysis and Critique of the Union Financing of the Civil War* (Amherst, Mass., 1962).

36   Paul Studenski and Herman E. Krooss, *Financial History of the United States: Fiscal, Monetary, Banking, and Tariff including Financial Administration and State and Local Finance*, 2d ed. (New York, 1963), 6–8; and Lance E. Davis and John B. Legler, "The Government and the American Economy, 1815–1902: A Quantitative Study," *Journal of Economic History* 26 (Dec. 1966): 514–52.

37   Jeffrey G. Williamson, "Watersheds and Turning Points: Conjectures on the Long-Term Impact of Civil War Financing," *Journal of Economic History* 34 (Sept. 1974): 636–61; and John A. James, "Public Debt Management Policy and Nineteenth-Century American Economic Growth," *Explorations in Economic History* 21 (April 1984): 192–217.

There might be to some redistribution of the pattern of investment over time, but with possibly limited effects on the magnitude of long-term capital formation. And the net impact of the system of compulsory bond sales via the National Bank Act's creation of new banks is not clear. We now know more how well financial and bank systems have operated in the absence of such centralized controls as imposed by the National Banking System (as well as how poorly centrally controlled banking systems can operate). The specifics of National Bank Act measures, designed to support the Civil War bond issue for the North, need not have done much to promote investment in the private sector. Further, while it is clear that its terms were used to favor Northern banking after the Civil War, the manner of its operation was not costless to the Southern economy and its attempts at financial recovery to its antebellum levels.[38]

The effects of the Civil War on the overall tax system were somewhat limited in their economic consequences. While income taxation was introduced to a limited extent during the war, it did not survive one decade and thus had no permanent impact on the nature of taxation. The introduction of excise taxes, primarily on alcohol and tobacco, did lead to increased revenues relative to tariffs; indeed, their presence may have helped to maintain a lower tariff structure than might otherwise have existed if tariffs had remained the primary source of federal revenues. The full effect of tariffs on income distribution and relative output structures remains uncertain, both because of their limited quantitative magnitude and because, for many manufactured and agricultural goods, the United States was already a net exporter in the world markets.

There were a number of significant policies introduced by the Northern Congress after the Southern secession, policies that had been previously discussed in Congress and whose passage apparently reflected nothing specific to the economic *needs* of war. The war permitted the Northern Republicans to implement their prewar agenda, and the outcome of the Civil War permitted its maintenance – at least for some limited period of time. There remains some question, however, as to whether these measures did much to promote growth, and if they did so in a desirable manner for the long-term development of the economy. In some cases, policies had diametrically opposing effects: For example, the raising of tariffs to promote industry offset the greater availability of land via the Homestead Act, which drained labor from the eastern manufacturing centers. Some policies were

---

38   Larry Schweikart, *Banking in the American South: From the Age of Jackson to Reconstruction* (Baton Rouge, La., 1987); and Richard Sylla, "Federal Policy, Banking Market Structure, and Capital Mobilization in the United States, 1863–1913," *Journal of Economic History* 29 (Dec. 1969): 657–86.

of limited importance and were terminated before the end of the century – the contract labor laws were inessential, used primarily for union-busting, and ended in 1885; land grants to transcontinental railroads apparently served primarily to subsidize investors and came to a scandal-ridden end in 1871.[39] And, as always, banking and financial matters are difficult to disentangle. While praise by some is given to the limitations on note issues that, in part, led to the price fall prior to Resumption by 1879 (thus returning the United States to the gold standard), others complain that the slow monetary growth permitting this price fall restricted output growth and had perverse distributional effects. None of this is meant to deny the political importance of the passage of wartime measures nor the significant symbolic effects that they may have had. Rather, it is meant to suggest that the nature and magnitude of their presumed growth effects remain somewhat uncertain. (For example, what percent of the governmental economic measures of the past decades would we believe were significantly growth-promoting and of a large magnitude, despite the promises at the time of passage that they would have such an impact?)

It was in the South, of course, that the social, political, and economic changes were most pronounced, starting with the pivotal change of the ending of legal slavery – immediate and with no compensation to either former slaveowners or ex-slaves. Whatever the limitations to a more complete freedom then, and with the more virulent racism after the 1890s, there was a dramatic reduction in the ability to control and coerce the black population.[40] Similarly, with the outcome of the war, there was a loss in Southern political power nationally and an increased inability to restrict Northern policy preferences. While much legislation favorable to Southern elites emerged in postbellum decades, particularly in regard to racial matters, these were, generally, at the sufferance of the North. The South lacked the political opportunity to independently set pro-Southern policy.[41]

In some ways, there was modernizing economic change within the South after the Civil War. Nevertheless, the share of the labor force in agriculture did not decline until after 1880, and cotton remained the primary crop in Southern agriculture. Indeed, cotton accounted for a higher share of

39 Lloyd J. Mercer, *Railroads and Land Grant Policy: A Study of Government Intervention* (New York, 1982).
40 Stanley L. Engerman, "The Economic Response to Emancipation and Some Economic Aspects of the Meaning of Freedom," in Frank McGlynn and Seymour Drescher, eds., *The Meaning of Freedom: Economics, Politics, and Culture After Slavery* (Pittsburgh, 1992), 49–68.
41 How these North – South compromises evolved, and the extent to which the coalition of Northern and Southern whites served to limit the power of Southern blacks and poorer whites – North and South – will not be discussed here.

Southern agricultural output in the postbellum than in the antebellum era. Yet the end of slavery had led to dramatic changes in the level and efficiency of Southern production. The decline of the plantation system (a characteristic of almost all areas where slavery had ended) meant a sharp reduction in the output per black agricultural worker. While there may have been some declines in black labor force participation and in hours worked, clearly the decline in efficiency in the production of cotton, as well as the sharper reduction in the output of sugar and of rice, led to a lowered measured Southern output (but with obvious, albeit unmeasured, gains in utility to those now freed and able to avoid gang work.)

The maintenance of Southern cotton output, even with the reduced output from ex-slave labor, resulted from major changes in the production pattern of white yeoman farmers. Unable to compete with the more efficient slave plantations before the Civil War (except perhaps during boom periods such as the 1850s), white farmers in the postbellum period came to dominate cotton production. This movement meant that Southern staple production could continue to expand, without the need for contract labor from Asia or Africa that characterized those areas of the Caribbean in which sugar production expanded in the late nineteenth century or for the subsidized southern European migrants that accounted for continued coffee production in Brazil once slavery there had been ended.

In describing the economic effects of the Civil War on Southern growth, it is useful to remember that the Southern decline, steep as it was, was basically a one-time decline resulting from wartime damage and the ending of slavery. This decline was then followed by what was, by American and world standards, a relatively rapid rate of long-term economic growth. It did take some years for the South to achieve the levels attained when the economy was dominated by the economically productive slave plantation system, but it does not seem that the institutions in the South in the postbellum era precluded economic expansion, either within agriculture or later when, after several decades, there was a shift out of agriculture into manufacturing.

IV. THE NORTHERN ECONOMY: HOW CENTRALIZED IS CENTRALIZED?

Although the Civil War did not dramatically reshape the American economy, it may still meet our larger understanding of *total war*. Let us shift our emphasis from matters of economic impact to questions of economic policy. We start with the assumption that the totality of a nation's war effort may be

gauged by considering two variables: (1) the degree of economic mobilization of the population, and (2) the level of centralized direction imposed by
the state. Thus, a nation moves toward total war as it shifts economic production to the war effort and as the direction of that war effort moves into the
hands of a centralized government. In this sense, the relative modernity of a
nation's military is not necessarily the best measure of the totality of its war
effort. Nor does the movement toward total war imply a concomitant shift in
political ideology.

In the antebellum decades, divisions over the role of the federal government in national development repeatedly broke along regional lines, with
Northern congressmen supporting legislation aimed at stimulating growth
and development while their Southern counterparts, carrying the banner
of states' rights, resisted such statist initiatives.[42] Following secession, the
Confederate states – far from rejecting the Constitution – claimed to be the
Founding Fathers' proper heirs.

Soon the Southerners discovered that their dedication to individual
liberties and states' rights, which may have served them well in peacetime,
presented major obstacles to the developing war effort.[43] Less than a year
following the firing on Fort Sumter, Davis asked the Confederate Congress
for a military draft. Many Rebels resented this federal imposition; state
governors undercut its effect with wholesale exemptions; and poorer
Southerners, objecting to the legislation's class biases, actively resisted. But
despite the controversies and inefficiencies, the Confederate draft proved a
much heavier – and earlier – imposition than did the North's version.[44]

Similarly, the cost of supporting the war effort led Confederate Secretary
of the Treasury Christopher Memminger to issue repeated calls for taxation
legislation. In the war's first months, the Confederates had passed a modest
tax on real estate and personal property, but the government relied on the
individual states to collect their quotas; only South Carolina did so by enforcing the legislation. Rather than accept the impositions of taxation,
Southerners preferred to turn to the sale of bonds; when the sources of funds
dried up, the government eventually joined cities and states in relying on

42 Richard Bensel argues that the South's antebellum states' rights rhetoric was largely tactical rather
    than ideological, designed to protect their own legislative agenda, but it is not clear that such a dis-
    tinction does not apply more widely in the political arena. Richard F. Bensel, *Yankee Leviathan: The
    Origins of Central State Authority in America, 1859–1877* (Cambridge, 1990).
43 For a comparison of the Confederate and Union political systems, see Eric L. McKitrick, "Party
    Politics and the Union and Confederate War Efforts," in William Nesbet Chambers and Walter
    Dean Burnham, eds., *The American Party Systems* (New York, 1967), 117–51.
44 Thomas, *The Confederate Nation,* 152–254, 260–1; McPherson, *Battle Cry of Freedom,* 430–2; see also
    Armstead Louis Robinson, "Day of Jubilo: Civil War and the Demise of Slavery in the Mississippi
    Valley, 1861–1865, " Ph.D. diss., University of Rochester, 1976.

printed notes, which quickly depreciated in value. Finally, in April 1863, with Southern finances in turmoil, the Confederate Congress levied heavy taxes on agricultural products, bank deposits, commercial paper, and various other goods.[45]

The Confederate government proved particularly aggressive in taking on the task of providing materiel for its army. At the outset of the war, the South supplemented its inadequate manufacturing sector with imports from abroad. But soon unpaid foreign debts and the Union blockade forced the Confederacy to seek internal solutions. Where possible, the War Department turned to indigenous Southern businesses. But apart from Richmond's Treadegar Iron Works, there were few Southern factories able to answer the call for heavy industrial goods, forcing the Confederate War Department to open up government manufactories. The war industry system that emerged combined equal parts private enterprise and government armories, with both halves under the centralized control of a handful of military officials. By 1863, Josiah Gorgas was able to report that his Ordnance Bureau was able "to respond to all calls made upon it."[46]

In its zeal to supply the military, the Confederacy did not stop at issuing government contracts and opening new establishments. In the name of military necessity, planners directed the movements of Southern railroads. And time and again the Confederates took advantage of the 1863 Impressment Act to seize goods to support the war effort. The military authorities even periodically impressed slaves – who stood at the heart of the South's commitment to private property – for government labor. And in the war's waning months the Confederacy nearly turned to the unthinkable policy of offering slaves their freedom in exchange for taking up arms for the government.[47]

In the United States Congress, Northern Republicans – long-time advocates of a more aggressive central government – suddenly found the seats of their most persistent opponents vacant and the call of patriotism providing new support for their larger agenda.[48] The best case for the Civil War's long-term economic effect emphasizes the legislation passed by the Republican-

---

45 Thomas, *The Confederate Nation*, 196–8; Mcpherson, *Battle Cry of Freedom*, 437–42, 615–17.

46 Frank E. Vandiver, *Ploughshares into Swords: Josiah Gorgas and Confederate Ordnance* (Austin, Tex., 1952), 207; Thomas, *The Confederate Nation*, 206–17; Roger L. Ransom, *Conflict and Compromise: The Political Economy of Slavery, Emancipation, and the American Civil War* (Cambridge, 1989), 200–1; and Raimondo Luraghi, "The Civil War and the Modernization of American Society: Social Structure and the Industrial Revolution in the Old South Before and During the Civil War, " *Civil War History*, 18 (Sept. 1972): 230–50.

47 Thomas, *Confederate Nation*, 196, 209–10.

48 Allan G. Bogue, *The Earnest Men: Republicans of the Civil War Senate* (Ithaca, N.Y., 1981), 330. For the antebellum debates, see McPherson, *Battle Cry of Freedom*, 193–5.

dominated War Congress. While the Confederacy relied on inflationary currency to finance most of its war expenditures, the Union raised 21 percent
of its funds through taxation, including the revolutionary federal income
tax passed in 1861 and expanded in subsequent years.[49] In February 1862,
Congressional Republicans overwhelmed Democratic resistance to push
through the Legal Tender Act, allowing for the printing of greenbacks.[50]

This early financial legislation expanded the government's economic
role while furthering the war effort. In the war's second year, Congress went
well beyond military necessity in passing a series of bills distributing public lands. The May 1862 Homestead Act, granting 160 acres of public land
to settlers who stayed on the property for five years, fulfilled a long-term
Republican goal. A few months later, Justin Morrill successfully steered
legislation through Congress legislation that paved the way for the establishment of state land-grant colleges. And in a series of measures, Congress
granted 120 million acres of public land to various transcontinental railroad
companies.[51]

Perhaps the Civil War Congress's most important piece of financial legislation was the National Bank Act of February 1863. This act, which created
a national banking system, also established a mechanism for the distribution
of federal war bonds. But in a larger sense, it answered the longstanding
Whig (and then Republican) call for effective regulation of banking. The roll
call on the Bank Act revealed a clear partisan split, with nearly all Democrats lining up against the Act and three-fourths of Republicans voting
for its passage.[52]

Taken together, this array of economic legislation—taxation, currency,
banking, land, land grants – suggests a newly active Congress expanding the
role of the federal government in everyday life.[53] Such legislation certainly
supports the view that the war led to long-term economic change. But, as
suggested earlier, many of these measures—the land grants, for instance—
owed less to military goals than to political opportunity. Others, such as the
National Bank Act and the Internal Revenue Act, were important precedents
but not necessarily vital to the war years. What of the larger matter of wartime

49 The use of an income tax was new for the Americans but not unheard of. The British had intro-
    duced an income tax in 1799 to help finance the Napoléonic Wars. On the history of the income
    tax, see John F. Witte, *The Politics and Development of the Federal Income Tax* (Madison, Wis., 1985).
50 McPherson, *Battle Cry of Freedom*, 442–8.
51 Ibid., 193–5, 450–3.
52 Ibid., 593–4. Although we have questioned (earlier in this chapter) the economic value of this
    financial legislation, its passage was certainly a victory for major forces within the Republican
    Party.
53 For a detailed analysis of wartime voting patterns, see Bogue, *Earnest Men*. On wartime politics in
    general, see Allan G. Bogue, *The Congressman's Civil War* (Cambridge, 1989).

mobilization? Let us consider three aspects of Northern mobilization: recruitment, military contracting, and voluntarism.

The North's controversial conscription system, and the series of mid-war draft riots, tends to distract attention from the larger reality: The vast majority of Union soldiers served as volunteers. Fewer than 10 percent of the Union army was made up of draftees and hired substitutes; one in five Confederate soldiers followed one of these two routes.[54] Of course, this may distort the larger point. The draft laws were designed to be spurs to recruiting; as such, they were a critical component in the North's manpower policies.

On the one hand, the conscription legislation points to a growing federal presence in daily life. This is particularly marked when we note the transition from the state military drafts of 1862 to the four federally administered call-ups following the 1863 Enrollment Act. Still, the North's manpower policies essentially relied on local initiatives and free-market principles. Throughout the North, the approach of draft day drove communities to frenzied recruiting campaigns aimed at filling local quotas. The quota system assured energetic grassroots recruiting. A successful effort enabled a ward or community to relax as draft day passed; those who had failed to meet the quotas faced tense public drawings and the specter of violent rioting. After the war's first year, recruiting efforts relied not so much on appeals to patriotism or federal imposition as on the baser and more privatized pull of cash bounties. Thus, even in the midst of heavy military demands, the North pursued policies based on market principles.[55]

If the mobilization of men depended on local initiatives and market forces, what of the mobilization of materials? Once again, the case for total war seems to weaken under close inspection. As we have seen, the war left only a modest impact on long-term patterns of manufacturing output. The organization of that output also revealed a continued reliance on the private sector and market forces rather than on the sort of government control regularly employed in the Confederacy. Several observations point to this conclusion. First, the Union consistently chose to contract with private firms rather than engaging directly in war-related production. The most prominent exception

---

54   McPherson, *Ordeal By Fire*, 182–3, 357.
55   The quota system imposed governmental coercion on the community rather than on the individual. The communities, in turn, relied on the market-based strategy of aggressive bounty fund raising. Meanwhile, the federal policy of accepting substitutes allowed draftees to enter a different market–for hired replacements–in order to avoid service. The Northern legislation allowing draftees to pay a $300 commutation fee in lieu of furnishing a substitute may have placed a ceiling on the market price for substitutes, but public outcry over commutation led to its repeal in 1864, removing this one modest government infringement on free market principles. On recruitment and conscription, see J. Matthew Gallman, *Mastering Wartime*, 11–53; and James W. Geary, "Civil War Conscription in the North: A Historiographical Review," *Civil War History* 32 (Sept. 1986): 208–28.

to this pattern was probably the federally administered arsenals that produced goods such as tents and uniforms. But even these establishments contracted out portions of the work and ran at below capacity when local entrepreneurs could fill the military's demands.[56]

Second, even those policy areas with a strong government presence did not reveal a commitment to centrally directed mobilization. Lincoln had a hand in policies ranging from recruitment and emancipation to battlefield strategy, but he generally left economic policies to the legislature.[57] The nation's railroads, often cited as one of the most prosperous and strategically important sectors of the wartime economy, responded largely to market demands rather than to official controls. Only rarely did the government step in and take over Northern lines threatened by labor strife. And even when the military engaged in its own transportation construction, it relied on the direction of key experts from the private sector, such as Herman Haupt.[58]

The example of the railroads underscores the distinctions between a war that is strategically modern and one where heavy mobilization suggests total war. The North's superior railroad system is often portrayed as an important key to its military success. Moreover, the demands on that system stimulated important technological modernization in the midst of the conflict.[59] Yet despite the military importance of railroads, the war years saw a decline in the annual production of new mileage; and in their dealings with military officials, the railroad officials tended to play the role of profit-minded partners rather than helpless cogs in a government-controlled military machine.

Third, the contracting system that men like Edwin Stanton and Montgomery Meigs perfected was based on open bidding rather than ongoing relationships between private business and military purchasers. And whereas other economic forces may have accelerated the wartime concentration of capital, the contracting system does not appear to have favored large manufacturers.[60] The result was that the military procurement system was grafted

---

56 In Philadelphia, sewing women petitioned Lincoln to get the arsenal to run at capacity because they preferred the higher federal wages to working for private subcontractors. J. Matthew Gallman, *Mastering Wartime*, 245.

57 Phillip S. Paludan, *"A People's Contest": The Union and the Civil War 1861–1865* (New York, 1988), 107.

58 Paludan, *"A People's Contest,"* 139–42. The Union did run a substantial railroad operation in conquered portions of the Confederacy. See Bensel, *Yankee Leviathan*, 151.

59 Long-distance movement of men and materials encouraged competing railroad companies to move toward a standardized gauge. The heavy wear on iron rails accelerated the transition to steel. Paludan, *"A People's Contest,"* 140.

60 This is in direct contrast to America's contracting experience in World War II, when two-thirds of the government's $240 billion in military spending went to roughly 100 corporations, with nearly 18,000 smaller companies splitting the remainder. James L. Abrahamson, *The American Home Front: Revolutionary War, Civil War, World War I, World War II* (Washington, D.C., 1983), 149. See also Harold G. Vatter, *The U.S. Economy in World War II* (New York, 1985), 57–66.

onto an existing world of small manufactories with only minimal adjustments. Thus, the wartime procurement system left the Northern economy largely in the hands of small entrepreneurs who responded to market incentives rather than government directives.

A final case for the widespread mobilization of total war can be made by shifting our attention to private initiatives. Perhaps the Northern war effort fueled the emerging forces of centralization but simply outside of the realm of governmental controls. The strongest support for this argument can be found in the workings of the two national benevolent bodies: the United States Sanitary Commission (USSC) and the United States Christian Commission (USCC). Both bodies spanned the entire North, far outstripping the South's most ambitious voluntary societies. And at least the founders of the USSC claimed to be pursuing rational organizing goals while bringing comfort to the soldiers at the front.[61]

As a mobilizing force, the two national bodies were certainly quite important: Thousands of volunteers, mostly women, labored under their banners throughout the North. But two factors argue against the importance of these efforts as episodes in total warfare. First, the rank and file in these bodies had only tenuous connections with the national leadership. Thus, the mobilization may have been under a single name, but it is best seen as an upsurge of localized activism. And second, the national bodies in each locality competed with a host of entirely local groups engaged in similar pursuits. Although benevolence certainly became a rallying cry that mobilized an enormous portion of the Northern population, their actions did not reveal the centralized direction that we would expect out of true total warfare.[62]

What can we conclude about the North's wartime experience? Certainly mobilization was extraordinary, if measured by the proportion of citizens who became wrapped up in some aspect of the war effort.[63] But if the test for total war includes some consideration of the level of governmental direction, the case weakens. After examining a wide array of wartime legislation, Richard Bensel concluded that in most areas "the Union relied on an unregulated capitalist market to supply resources and manpower."[64] Federal activism definitely grew during the war, but private efforts remained dominant. Similarly, the evidence for the war as a centralizing force in the private

61   See George M. Frederickson, *The Inner Civil War: Northern Intellectuals and the Crisis of the Union* (New York, 1965), 98–112.
62   J. Matthew Gallman, *Mastering Wartime.*
63   Of course, even by this measurement, the Northern mobilization was much less than that in the South.
64   Bensel, *Yankee Leviathan*, 233.

world is not convincing, either if measured by wartime voluntarism or economic activity. Northerners became heavily involved in the war effort, but much of what they did fit within antebellum patterns of behavior.[65]

Perhaps in institutional developments, as in economic growth, the best way to understand the Civil War as a total war is to contemplate the conflict's postwar legacy. Certainly some pieces of wartime legislation—banking, currency, taxation, land—left an impact on patterns of economic development. But many of these developments should be viewed as a legacy of secession, which left the Republican forces guarding the nation's economic chicken coop (and the successful outcome of the war), rather than as true war measures. Moreover, the postwar history of these legislative initiatives does not suggest a steady growth in the government's role. For instance, as described earlier, the expansion of the federal debt and the growth of taxes and expenditures only lasted until the war's conclusion. During Reconstruction, Congress reduced taxes while striving to bring down the (to them) disturbing debt.[66] Similarly, whatever relationships developed between government and business during the war did not leave behind a formidable military-industrial complex.[67]

And while the costs of the Civil War did remain a persistent budget item long into the postwar years, as Congress worked to retire the debt while taking on the costs of dramatically expanded military pensions, most of these involved taxes and transfers among individuals, not government provision of goods and services.[68] But even if the government's role shrank with peace, the organizational skills developed during the conflict may have left their mark. The leaders of the USSC, for instance, went on to remain active in public life. And several Union generals, such as George B. McClellan,

65 For a discussion of these continuities in Philadelphia, see J. Matthew Gallman, *Mastering Wartime*.

66 Ransom, *Conflict and Compromise*, 267; and Morton Keller, *Affairs of State: Public Life in Late Nineteenth Century America* (Cambridge, Mass., 1977), 107. See preceding discussion in this chapter of the economic legacy of these measures.

67 Although Northern manufacturing prospered during the war years, it appears that the effect of military contracting was broad, with many businesses sharing in the profits. Moreover, the immediate postwar years saw a wave of business failures, particularly among firms most closely tied to military contracting. J. Matthew Gallman, "Entrepreneurial Experiences in the Civil War: Evidence from Philadelphia," in Thomas Weiss and Donald Schaeffer, eds., *American Economic Development in Historical Perspective* (Stanford, Calif., 1994), 205–22.

68 Ransom, *Conflict and Compromise*, 287–8. As late as 1893, 40 percent of the federal budget was devoted to pensions for Civil War veterans and their dependents with interest on the debt accounting for another 7 percent. (To retire two-thirds of the Civil War debt, the federal budget was in surplus every year from 1866 through 1893). See Vinovskis, "Have Social Historians Lost the Civil War?" 21–8. See also Amy E. Holmes, "'Such Is the Price We Pay': American Widows and the Civil War Pension System," in Vinovskis, ed., *Toward a Social History*, 171–95. For a discussion of the postbellum medical experience, see Dora L. Costa, "Height, Weight, Wartime, Stress, and Older Age Mentality: Evidence from the Union Army Records," *Explorations in Entrepreneurial History* 30 (Oct. 1993): 424–49.

took their expertise from the field and applied it to postwar political and economic challenges.[69]

Where does all this leave us? Despite casual references to the Civil War as a "turning point", military history has no such right angles. For instance, the Spanish-American War over a generation later seems in many senses more "traditional" than its predecessor. That conflict certainly required a much more limited commitment of men and resources, triggering fewer economic or political adjustments.[70]

If we turn our gaze in the other direction, we can find ample evidence that the Civil War was, if not a watershed, at least a major departure from earlier experience. The casualties alone – whether measured by the bloodiest days, the harshest campaigns, or the awesome totals spanning four years – place the war in a distinctive place in our (and any nation's) history.[71] Similarly, the enormous cost of the war and the legacy of debt left an enduring mark on federal fiscal policies. To these weighty effects, we must add the dramatic changes accompanying the destruction of slavery and the damage – both economic and psychological – that the defeated South suffered. It comes as no surprise that so many participants looked back on the war as the nation's formative episode.

Nonetheless, we have seen that the Civil War left only a modest mark on long-term patterns of economic and political development, arguing against the notion that it was the first modern war. Many aspects of the war effort remained entirely or partially in private, voluntary hands. And where military purposes expanded the government's role, demobilization allowed private citizens to reclaim most of their lost autonomy.[72] While the costs of outfitting the armies was unprecedented, those business consolidations that marked the late nineteenth century were not clearly linked to the early military spending or to the ensuing financial policies.

69 For instance (and whether to be regarded as a plus or a minus), many of the Northern "carpetbaggers" who rose to political and economic power in the postwar South had served in the Union army. Richard Current, "Carpetbaggers Reconsidered," in *A Festschrift for Frederick B. Artz* (Durham, N.C., 1964), reprinted in Kenneth M. Stampp and Leon F. Litwack, eds., *Reconstruction: An Anthology of Revisionist Writings* (Baton Rouge, La., 1969), 223–40.
70 The five-month-long Spanish-American War had a direct cost of only $270 million, or roughly 2 percent of the GNP. But even this relatively minor war absorbed roughly 60 percent of federal expenditures for the year. Goldin, "War," 938.
71 Vinovskis, "Have Social Historians Lost the Civil War?" 3–7.
72 See Keller, *Affairs of State*, 1–33.

Let us return to our initial paradox: How can a conflict of this scale leave such a modest mark on the nation's political and economical world? Three observations may help to explain this problem. First, if we are interested in the war's economic impact, we should look at the *nature* of the demand as well as the quantity. Even if the Civil War foreshadowed a modern emphasis on heavy military technology, we have seen that much of the expenditure on this war went for more traditional items—animals, wagons, clothing, food— that differed little from peacetime products. Thus, much of the military needs could be met by the private sector, with only modest adjustments to meet government specifications. Even that proportion of military spending that went into heavy industrial products—arms, railroads, ships—did not necessarily require the sort of enormous military factories that characterized later conflicts.[73] The war's economic impact was broad rather than deep, involving thousands of entrepreneurs while leaving the shape of the economy largely unchanged.

Our second observation builds from the first. There is no reason to believe that Americans would have welcomed the changes that we have associated with total war. For generations, they had prospered in a world of limited government encroachment that valued localism, privatism, and market forces over centralized control or public management. This is not to suggest that such values would have blocked the successful prosecution of the war, but they certainly informed the way that policy makers on both sides went about their tasks. Conscription is an excellent case in point. The initial objective, particularly in the North, was to provide incentives for rigorous local recruiting efforts. Those efforts, in turn, hinged on cash bounties rather than forced service. Similarly, by emphasizing open bidding for government contracts, the North took advantage of established market forces rather than relying on the existing federal arsenals. Even the national benevolent organizations prospered by working within familiar local associational patterns. In 1862, Lincoln declared that he would free no slaves, some slaves, or all slaves in order to preserve the Union. He could have made a similar pronouncement about localism and privatism. Such values would be sacrificed if necessary, but only if they did not serve the cause.

This leads, finally, to our third observation. The key to unraveling the war's modest impact may rest in the differences between the two combatants. Whereas Charles and Mary Beard claimed the Civil War as a victory for the modernizing industrial North, it may be that the war exerted stronger modernizing forces on the Confederacy. If so, perhaps the direct legacy of change – as caused by war measures – was muted by the Northern victory

73   Abrahamson, *The American Home Front*, 48–9, 91, 148–9.

(leaving us with the indirect effects resulting from the victory of the more modern North). Thus, we have traded one paradox for another. The South – the bastion of tradition – embraced the techniques of modern warfare more fully than did the industrializing North, which engaged in a more familiar form of limited war.[74]

Consider the war measures passed by the two competing governments. The South turned to conscription and taxation before the North. Southerners, much more so than Northerners, suffered from federal impressment of their property. While Union officials worked largely with private manufacturers, the Confederacy relied heavily on government-run manufactories. Despite states' rights rhetoric, the Confederate government entered the daily lives of its citizens more than did its Northern counterpart.

The reasons for these differences are clear. The Confederacy was forced to fight a long war with far fewer usable men and only a fraction of the North's resources and industrial might. Moreover, the antebellum South lacked the industrial, transportation, and financial infrastructure necessary to support such a huge war effort. Thus, Confederate policy makers had to become more directly involved in munitions making, railroad building, and the like.[75] Union officials could work through an existing industrial and financial system.

In April 1861, the term *total war* had yet to enter the military lexicon. But the ideas that we associate with the phrase – complete mobilization, centralization, federal control – would not have been welcomed in Washington or Richmond, and certainly not in the state capitals, North and South. On the other hand, as the first armies began drilling, neither side recognized the scale of the conflict to come. In the years that followed, the Union and the Confederacy turned to various controversial policies – conscription, taxation, arbitrary arrests, impressment – in the pursuit of victory.

The North's economy and society was certainly the more modern of the two. And the eventual Northern success owed much to that modernity. But it was that modernity, coupled with the obvious numerical advantages, that allowed the North to carry on the war without fully turning to total war. The South – although more resistant to such changes – took on more of the trappings of total war, grafted onto a traditional agrarian economy. In short, the North fought a technologically modern war but organized around traditional assumptions and limitations. It did not embark upon total war because it did not have to. The South, on the other hand, moved toward total war because it had to.

---

74 Bensel argues that the requirements of war pushed the Confederacy to much more substantial centrist legislation than the North. *Yankee Leviathan*, 94–237.

75 Ransom, *Conflict and Compromise*, 200–1. See also Thomas, *The Confederate Nation*; and Vandiver, *Ploughshares into Swords*.

11

Industry and Warfare in Prussia

ULRICH WENGENROTH

If the totality of war is to be measured by the involvement of private industry and the degree to which its potential is used, Prussia in 1870–71 was most certainly at the very beginning of the road to total war. It continued to be vital to the military leadership that it remain in full control over every material aspect of warfare and would not have to compromise with private industry. Previous wars had been short and could largely be conducted on the basis of the inventories and the output of the military's own armories. To a large extent, this was still the case in the Franco-Prussian War. Losses of material were modest even more so since the victorious German armies controlled the battlefield and could easily recoup arms of their own troops as well as of the enemy. The total consumption of artillery guns on the German side was not more than 116 barrels (92 Prussians, 23 Bavarians, and 1 Württemberger). The total loss of rifles is not known, but the Twelfth Army Corps, for example, did not have to receive more than 33 needle-guns and 39 breechloaders (*Hinterlader-Karabiner*) during the campaign.[1]

The nonprofit character of the army's own factories, the full control over costs and quality, and the greatly reduced risk of labor unrest had made this arrangement very attractive in the eyes of most officers. After all, the growing discontent with the performance of private entrepreneurs, high prices, and low quality of the weapons that they produced had led to the establishment of state-owned and state-run rifle factories in the early 1850s.[2] If control of labor was the raison d'être of concentrating the work force in

1 *Der deutsch-französische Krieg 1870–71*, ed. Preussischer Generalstab, Abteilung für Kriegsgeschichte, vol. 3, pt. 2 (vol. 5 of the entire work) (Berlin, 1881), 1527. See also appendix in ibid., Anlage Nr. 198, "Zusammenstellung des der Deutschen Armee von Beginn des Krieges bis Anfangs März 1871 nachgeschickten Ersatzes," 866.
2 August Genth, "Die preussischen Heereswerkstätten, ihre Entwicklung, allgemeine volkswirtschaftliche Bedeutung und ihr Übergang in privatwirtschaftliche Betriebe," Ph.D. diss., Universität Berlin, 1926, 24. Dennis E. Showalter, *Railroads and Rifles: Soldiers, Technology, and the Unification of Germany* (Hamden, Conn., 1975), 92.

factories, the army out of tradition certainly did better than private enterprise. In view of tight budgets, which had been the most hotly debated issue in the much despised parliament, "profit-hungry" capitalists who dominated this institution were only entrusted with modifications of existing ordnance or covering peak demand.[3] Army and industry did not get along well in the 1850s and 1860s. Values held were too different, and there was more mutual disdain than efforts to cooperate.

Much of this, however, did change in the years immediately preceding and following the Franco-Prussian War. And if this war did not yet call for a "total effort" of industry, it most certainly turned the tide to industry-based warfare and more particularly to a modern armament industry, the capacity of which was deeply rooted in the scale and scope of civilian production. One could exactingly argue that if the king had waged war at the expense of the industrial taxpayer in the 1860s, industry itself would be prepared to go to war in the 1870s.

FROM ARMY FACTORIES TO MASS PRODUCTION

The technological rationale behind this shift was modern mass production, its exigencies and opportunities. Whereas the methods of mass production per se were known to both the army's own factories and private industry, the ability to reallocate resources from civilian to military uses was the sole privilege of multiproduct companies operating in the market. In not tying their investment to arms production exclusively, private companies, unlike the king's armories, acquired both the innovative scope and economies of scale of a growing manufacturing sector. The most striking example in the case of Prussia, to which this chapter is dedicated, was the production of guns and rifles. In both cases, the new technologies of mass production that were to constitute the backbone of high-volume industries had come out of military demand.

CASE I: STEEL GUNS

The heroic tale of Alfred Krupp's dogged perfection of cast steel artillery and its stunning effect in the Franco-Prussian War was the delight of every patriotic engineer in the Wilhelmine Empire: With only the support of the prince regent against a generally ignorant officer corps and a particularly shortsighted inspector general of the artillery, Krupp unselfishly had honed

---

3 Manfred Messerschmidt, *Die politische Geschichte der preussisch-deutschen Armee*, [= *Handbuch zur deutschen Militärgeschichte, 1648–1939*, vol. 4, pt. 1: *Militärgeschichte im 19. Jahrhundert (1814–1890)*] (Munich, 1975), 367–9.

the tools for German military superiority over two decades before it won him the well-deserved place in the Empire's hall of fame. That Krupp did not hesitate for a minute to sell the same weapons to Prussia's potential enemies and after 1875 to export over 80 percent of his guns did little to harm Krupp's heroism in this piece of edifying folklore.[4]

Not surprisingly, when seen from an industrial point of view, the Krupp story looks somewhat different. Krupp was one of the few steel companies to master the very difficult process of crucible steel production, which gave the best steel quality for casting tools and guns before electric furnaces came into operation around 1900. The chemistry of the smelting of crucible steel – the metal that made Krupp's guns superior to any other – was not fully understood at the time of the Franco-Prussian War. Only in 1873 was the first scientific analysis of this process undertaken without making it wholly transparent to would-be users.[5]

Crucible steel making for most of the nineteenth century was surrounded by an aura of secrecy. The outcome of the process was very dependent on the raw materials used and their preprocessing. Refining crude steel in crucibles required substantial experience, which was acquired on the job. The selling price of crucible steel was about ten to twenty times higher than the price of ordinary wrought iron, which was used for most iron products until well into the 1880s.[6]

The high price of crucible steel very much limited demand. A market developed only for top-of-the-line cutlery, some parts of machines, and wheels for locomotives. Given the high technological barriers to entering the market for crucible steel, producers earned handsome profits, although on the basis of very limited production. Since raw materials were abundant – it was rather the judicious mixture of readily available ores and fireproof material for the crucibles that made the process difficult – there were no other effective limitations to production than demand at what were prohibitive prices for most purposes.

Whereas the Sheffield steel makers had a good outlet with the world's greatest engineering industry in their backyard, Krupp was faced with a rather underdeveloped market. To benefit fully from his technological headstart, he had to develop a product for his process, even more so since a competing

---

4 Messerschmidt, *Die politische Geschichte*, 374.
5 L. Troost and P. Hautefeuille, "Recherches sur la dissolution des gaz dans la fonte, l'acier et le fer," *Comtes rendus Hebdomadaires des Séances de l'Academie des Sciences* 76 (1873): 482–5. On the various steel-making processes discussed in this essay, see my brief introduction to nineteenth-century steel technology in Ulrich Wengenroth, *Enterprise and Technology: The German and the British Steel Industries, 1865–1895* (Cambridge, 1994), 11–30.
6 William Fairbairn, *Iron: Its History, Properties, and Processes of Manufacture*, 3d ed. (Edinburgh, 1869), 156.

company in his vicinity, the Bochumer Verein, had also mastered the crucible process in the 1850s. While Bochum soon specialized in manufacturing cast steel bells in the place of bronze bells, Krupp took up the other major product of bronze casting – namely, guns, for which consumption was likely to increase once the military could be convinced of their superiority. Producing cast steel guns – first rifle barrels and, only as a second attempt, cannons – on his own account and presenting them to the artillery and the prince regent was an effort to develop a market for an underutilized production process for which there was little competition. In the 1850s and early 1860s, the Bochumer Verein was a much smaller company, one that lacked the comparable market position regarding product-specific raw materials for cast steel. To check the only serious competitor's growth, however, Krupp had to create and defend a monopoly in the greatest potential market, that is, guns. This was ever-more urgent since the Prussian ministry of trade wanted to bring other manufacturers of cast steel, among them the Bochumer Verein, into the arms deal for the single purpose of preventing Krupp from gaining a monopoly position.[7]

This situation took a dramatic turn when Krupp learned about Henry Bessemer's successful demonstration in 1856 of turning iron into steel by simply blowing air through the molten metal. All of Krupp's comparative advantages were now at stake. If steel could be made cheaply for big castings, his secret cast steel process would be worthless, and everyone could produce guns at low prices. This, after all, had been Bessemer's motivation for investigating new processes of steel making.

Bessemer was a professional inventor and had already made a fortune with a process to grind bronze into bronze powder. He was familiar with the metal that most guns were made of and knew its limitations all too well. In the wake of the Crimean War (1853–56), and more particularly the annihilation of the Turkish fleet through heavy shellfire, Bessemer developed an interest in heavy, rotating, elongated projectiles. Emperor Napoléon III and the French army were attracted to Bessemer's designs and in December 1854 invited him to run trials on the polygon of the Vincennes fortress, where Krupp's cast steel guns were also tested one year later. Both of these trials were supervised by Commander Minié, who was thoroughly impressed by the performance of Bessemer's thirty-pound rotating projectiles. However, his major concern was: "Could any guns be made to withstand the shock of firing such heavy projectiles?"[8] There was no question that cast steel would be the one material to meet these criteria, but it was outrageously expensive.

7 Messerschmidt, *Die politische Geschichte*, 372. Showalter, *Railroads and Rifles*, 175.
8 Henry Bessemer, *Sir Henry Bessemer: An Autobiography* (London, 1905), 135.

From the beginning, Bessemer had ruled out bronze or any other copper alloy as well as cast iron. He set out to produce a wrought iron that could be cast into big molds for guns. Wrought iron was already used for guns in a way similar to the manufacture of Turkish muskets, where a strip of wrought iron was wound in a spiral and shrunk on an iron barrel. William Armstrong's Elswick Company in England manufactured such big guns with one important difference—namely, the gun was made of many separate pieces of wrought iron shrunk on a steel barrel that yielded a great number of dangerous seams. At the time, wrought iron was the result of a very tedious so-called puddling process involving highly skilled manual labor. Since men could handle iron pieces only up to a certain weight, there was no way around this patching together of what still were heterogeneous pieces of handicraft. Meanwhile, Armstrong had been made superintendent of the Royal Gun Factories at Woolwich Arsenal in 1859 and from there successfully blocked outsiders' innovations in the manufacture of ordnance.[9]

Bessemer had already succeeded in producing a liquid "wrought iron" (that is, a decarbonized iron), which everyone within the trade immediately called "steel" because of its outstanding homogeneity. This killed two birds with one stone: Unlike wrought iron, the "Bessemer steel" was homogeneous and could be cast from a converter holding two to five tons, which was more than enough for artillery horses to drag around on the battlefield. If more capacity was required, two converters could easily be cast simultaneously. Bessemer's process was the first that could justifiably qualify as mechanized mass production, the output depending on the size and power of the plant and not on the number and craft-skills of laborers. Most important, Bessemer steel could be sold profitably for only twice the price of the cheapest wrought iron or, what impressed Krupp, for a fraction of what first-rate cast steel cost.

Not surprisingly, Krupp was among the first iron masters to arrive at Bessemer's steel plant and buy the patent rights for all of Prussia to guard his much-threatened monopoly.[10] Since he was already well known among arms producers, his move induced others to follow suit. John Brown of Sheffield, who had planned to erect a steel works similar to Krupp's with puddling furnaces to produce the input for the crucibles, changed his mind when he saw Krupp approaching Bessemer and did the same to become the first Bessemer steel manufacturer in England, that is, in addition to Bessemer

9   See the biting remarks in *Scientific American* a few years later. *Scientific American*, Nov. 7, 1863, 403.
10   On the early history of the Bessemer process and its shortcomings, see Wengenroth, *Enterprise and Technology*, 31–3.

himself. The next Englishman to follow suit was Charles Cammell, another specialist for ordnance steel.

They all were misled, however, by the first reports and samples of Bessemer steel, since eventually it turned out to be no serious threat to crucible steel. It was not hard enough and did not have the same tensile strength. The threat of cheap mass-produced cast steel had passed, since the ultimate step, melting down the crude steel in crucibles and letting it soak there for two days, was not made redundant. The Bessemer steel works then turned to the manufacture of steel rails opening the age of mass steel production with steel prices falling below those of wrought iron, since the few cast steel makers could now use cheap and mass-produced Bessemer steel instead of "handmade" puddled iron to charge their crucibles. Bessemer himself quickly lost interest in producing elongated projectiles and grew rich from royalties from steel rails production. Krupp waived all his German rights for the process, which were difficult to defend anyway. He built a huge steel rail mill and a big new crucible furnace next to each other. Krupp continued to call his Bessemer converters "crucibles," although other iron masters no longer did so.

A second drama over cheap cast steel played itself out in the industry only a few years after Bessemer's invention, when, in the early 1860s, Wilhelm Siemens and Pierre Martin developed the open-hearth furnace. Together with the Bessemer converters, this furnace formed the backbone of mass steel production until the 1960s. The outcome was similar: Krupp acquired the process immediately only to find out again that the steel, although very good and indeed better than Bessemer steel, was still not equal to cast steel from his crucibles.[11] Like Bessemer steel, however, it was an excellent or even better input for the crucibles and, moreover, the heating system of the open hearth was the most efficient that one could think of. Even more open-hearth steel than Bessemer steel went into the crucibles, which were heated by an open-hearth regenerative heating system.

Although these two efforts to produce cheaply first-rate gun steel eventually failed, the important outcome remained that, on the eve of the Franco-Prussian War, all of the inputs to the crucible process were characteristically modern and oriented toward mass production. What remained was the secrecy of how the melting process was carried out and the composition of crucible linings, which were made of a complex mixture of materials including silicon and very precious and pure graphite. Typically, the crucibles were responsible for about half the cost of the whole process.[12] Since they were used only once for high-quality ordnance steel, consumption of these

11   Wengenroth, *Enterprise and Technology*, 203.
12   Bernhard Osann, *Lehrbuch der Eisenhüttenkunde* (Leipzig, 1921), 2 : 503.

materials and the price of this steel had to be very high. Crucibles could be used a second and even a third time, however, if employed for making tool steel or railway wheels. A large demand for ordnance steel would consequently provide the works with great numbers of "free" crucibles, which would greatly enhance the competitiveness of civilian production and give an arms supplier a clear edge over the competition. In short, the more cast steel guns Krupp could sell, the cheaper was his tool steel and the famous seamless wheels that became his trademark. The company, if rather obliquely, recognized the importance of this linkage in its centenary publication.[13]

Arms production in this respect was a linchpin of cost reduction. In other words, the peculiar mix of civilian and military steel products made high-quality steel cheaper. Krupp, as with Schneider, Vickers, Harvey, Skoda, Schwab, Carnegie, and others after him, combined the economies of scale of nonmilitary industry with more limited arms production.[14] This extended well into raw materials markets, where a dozen different iron ore, clay, and graphite mines, which were all necessary metallurgically to provide the delicate blend of steel alloys and crucible linings, would not pay for a few thousand tons of ordnance steel. Thus, the claim by the historian Manfred Messerschmidt – that it was an inability of the royal armories to handle cast steel that made steel guns the product of private industry by the 1860s – does not bear up under closer scrutiny.[15] The armories were perfectly capable of manufacturing guns from cast steel. It was rather Krupp's need for economies of scale that pushed him into an aggressive sales policy for cast steel products such as guns.

After a first strategic purchase of a German iron works with ores particularly suited for crucible steel,[16] in 1871 Krupp acquired a major interest in what was probably the best iron ore mine in Europe.[17] The vast majority of the ore from this mine was transformed into rails and plates. Some open hearths, however, would use it to produce the best possible input for crucibles. Krupp's main competitor, the Bochumer Verein, also had to rely on these ores, which were available on the market at a price well above Krupp's initial costs.

13 *Krupp, 1812–1912: Zum 100 Jährigen Bestehen der Firma Krupp und Gussstahlfabrik zu Essen-Ruhr* (Essen, 1912), 146.
14 Eckart Kehr, "Krieg und Geld im Zeitalter der Maschinenrevolution, Fragmente," in Hans-Ulrich Wehler, ed., *Primat der Innenpolitik: Gesammelte Aufsätze zur preussisch-deutschen Sozialgeschichte im 19. und 20. Jahrhundert* (Berlin, 1965), 211.
15 "Mit der Entscheidung für das Gussstahlrohr war zugleich angebahnt, dass die Artillerieproduktion nun im wesentlichen von der privaten Rüstungsindustrie geleistet wurde." Messerschmidt, *Die politische Geschichte*, 358.
16 It was the Sayner Hütte on the Rhine. *Krupp 1812–1912*, 163–4.
17 Wengenroth, *Enterprise and Technology*, 190–1, 195.

In spite of Krupp's intensive exports of ordnance, which certainly improved his company's economies of scale, gun steel was not a mass product, such as rails; but since the 1870s, its manufacture rested qualitatively and economically on the resources for mass production, which were never available to the army's own Spandau gun factory. It made good economic sense for both sides, therefore, that Krupp would send steel castings to Spandau, where the calibers were drilled and honed into the semiproducts. As a result, the armories became an ancillary workshop of Krupp's rather than the reverse.[18] Eventually, this division of labor was only the first step on the way to a private industry that turned out finished weapons under the inspection of army and navy artillery experts.

CASE 2: RIFLES

A somewhat different case was the balance of power between army and private industry in the production of rifles. Here, too, however, a notable shift toward reliance on the resources of private industry took place in the wake of the Franco-Prussian War. Whereas the performance of Krupp's cast steel guns had been second to none, and the production facilities at the Essen works were among the most advanced in the world, the manufacture of rifles in the army's own workshops still had the air of a sectarian brotherhood of artisans' secret trade (zünftlerisches Geheimhandwerk).[19] And it was meant to be so since secretiveness about its rifles had been one of the army's obsessions in the decades preceding the Franco-Prussian War – a secretiveness, however, that was as quickly abandoned in the wake of the military contest as the unsuccessful needle-gun itself. Although Krupp's cannons had won the war, the Prussian rifle was clearly outperformed by the French chassepot rifle and had to be replaced as quickly as possible if the German armies were not to compromise their effectiveness. With the very limited output of the army system and the Dreyse gun factory, which had taken more than two decades to equip the troops with the needle-gun, there were no viable alternatives to bringing modern mass production to the gun factories and resorting to the productivity of private industry.[20] This produced not only a new rifle, the Mauser breechloader, which was introduced by a cabinet order of March 1872,[21] but also the final breakthrough to the full-scale industrialization and engagement

18   Kehr, "Krieg und Geld," 205.
19   Bertold Buxbaum, "Der deutsche Werkzeugmaschinen- und Werkzeugbau im 19. Jahrhundert,"
     Beiträge zur Geschichte der Technik und Industrie 9 (1919): 100.
20   Messerschmidt, Die politische Geschichte, 352–3. Showalter, Railroads and Rifles, pt. 2, esp. 81–2, 90,
     95–9.
21   Messerschmidt, Die politische Geschichte, 355.

of private business in German armaments production. For the army's part, tight control was traded in for rapid output, and big industry was eventually mobilized.

The problems of the old system had been apparent before the unfavorable contest with the French *chassepot* rifle. In May 1867, a meeting of the German Association of Engineers in Berlin raised this issue.[22] At this meeting, a former director of a rifle factory maintained that, owing to the outdated way of manufacture in the Prussian armories, rifles would cost the army more than twice what was possible with modern methods of mass production. The model he held up was the United States, where, "helped by big political events and the blessings of freedom," the highest degree of perfection was achieved. He gave a vivid account of the "American way of manufacture" in army ordnance as we know it from Merrit Roe Smith's and David Hounshell's books and articles.[23] Interestingly enough, he strongly advocated the employment of girls to do the delicate drilling of the calibers and to check for accuracy and smooth functioning of locks and bolts, which had always been a problem for the needle-gun.[24]

Modern American machine tools for arms production had first been shown in Europe at the 1867 World Exhibition in Paris. The radical new design of these lightweight milling machines and turret lathes for the mass production of small parts had fascinated engineering companies all over Europe, more than the most recent British exhibits. The newly converted critics of the Prussian armories had these machines in mind. Long-overdue reform of rifle production, however, occurred only after the Franco-Prussian War. But once reforms were carried out, they were radical and very much along the lines of the Berlin proposals of 1867.

The army renounced all of its own research and development in manufacturing and instead imported turnkey factories from the United States, particularly from Pratt & Whitney of Hartford, Connecticut. An agent of the American company had already visited the royal armories in 1870 as well as a few private gun factories in Germany, scouting around for business. Like many other American engineering companies whose plant and operations had grown tremendously during the American Civil War, Pratt & Whitney was in desperate need of new orders. This business trip of its agent turned into one of the greatest sales successes that the company celebrated before World War I.[25]

---

22 "Mittheilungen aus den Sitzungsprotokollen der Bezirks- und Zweigvereine–Berliner Bezirksverein," *Zeitschrift des Vereines Deutscher Ingenieure* 12 (1868): cols. 93–6.

23 David Hounshell, *From the American System to Mass Production, 1800–1932* (Baltimore, Md., 1984); Merrit Roe Smith, *Harpers Ferry Armory and the New Technology* (Ithaca, N.Y., 1977).

24 "Mittheilungen aus den Sitzungsprotokollen," cols. 94–5.

25 Pratt & Whitney Company, *Accuracy for Seventy Years, 1860–1930* (Hartford, Conn., 1930), 29.

Before taking up production of the new model no. 71 in 1872, a Prussian commission was sent to the United States, and American experts, among them Mr. Pratt himself, had been invited to Prussia to evaluate German rifle production. The outcome of these investigations was a contract between the army and Pratt & Whitney that stipulated that the American company should supply the armories of Spandau, Erfurt, and Danzig with the necessary machine tools, jigs, and gages to manufacture rifles with interchangeable parts.[26] A price of $350,000 was agreed upon for the first shipment of equipment to be delivered. Eventually, with a great number of additional orders from the armories and from private manufacturers working under license, the total sales of Pratt & Whitney tools and machinery amounted to $1,250,000.[27] This sum was equivalent to the cost of five modern American Bessemer steel plants and certainly one of the greatest industrial contracts of that time.[28]

Once set on industrializing its rifle production, the Prussian army moved toward creating the largest conceivable scale. Within a year, the proud artisans of the armories had been converted into machine operators. The shock of the new situation had been somewhat mitigated by allowing these workers to share in the benefits of increased productivity through higher wages.[29] Still, the overall economic results of the "American way of manufacture" were decidedly in favor of the army and, eventually, the taxpayer. Outright military control and discipline gave way to equally efficient control of operations through automatic and semiautomatic machine tools.

The war ministry was so satisfied with the company's performance that it sent a letter expressing its gratitude to Hartford:

The Pratt & Whitney Company has furnished the Royal Armories of Spandau, Erfurt, and Danzig with machinery that execute the work with such nicety and precision as to save one half of the wages, and to render the government in no small degree independent of the power and skill of the workmen.[30]

By 1874, the higher productivity of the American system increased the annual production of a royal rifle factory from around 10,000 rifles to between 40,000 to 50,000 rifles in each of the establishments.[31] Still, this level was regarded as insufficient, since the arrival of the French indemnity of 5

---

26   Ibid., 29–31.
27   Ibid., 31.
28   The secretary of the British Iron and Steel Institute, J. S. Jeans, quoted a price of $220, 000 for the exemplary 1877 Bessemer plant of the Edgar Thomson Steel Company. See J. S. Jeans, *Steel: Its History, Manufacture, Properties and Uses* (London, 1880), 834–5.
29   Buxbaum, "Der deutsche Werkzeugmaschinen, " 118.
30   Pratt and Whitney, *Accuracy for Seventy Years*, 31.
31   Genth, "Die preussischen Heereswerkstätten," 25.

billion francs provided an abundant source of capital. Consequently, private industry had to be mobilized.

Earlier and parallel to the army's commission, German industrialists had also gone to America to investigate the "American way of manufacture." The most influential of these, Ludwig Loewe of Berlin, was very impressed with New England machine tools, the manufacture of sewing machines, and Colt's factory, which he had seen in early 1870.[32] As with the army commission, he returned back home with Pratt & Whitney machine tools plus a design for a sewing machine factory. Since the American machine tool makers could not satisfy European demand in the early 1870s, Loewe, under license, started copying their machines and adapting them to the somewhat different properties of German iron. Among his first customers were the Prussian armories, which ranked "German" American machines equal to the original.

With the economic crisis of 1873, however, Loewe's dreams of selling hundreds of thousands of sewing machines vanished. As with Krupp twenty years before, Loewe was looking for a product to keep his modern plant running. With the army pushing hard to replace the old Dreyse needle-gun with the new rifle model no. 71, an agreement was quickly reached in 1873 stipulating that Loewe would manufacture parts of the rifle on the same kind of Pratt & Whitney machines used by the armories. What was meant to be the greatest German factory for sewing machines eventually turned into the greatest private ordnance manufacture.

In the first year of this contract, 282 of Loewe's 503 machine tools were turning out rifle parts, while 92 were used in the production of machine tools and the remainder of 129 solely for sewing machines, the production of which was eventually ended in 1879.[33] Emil Rathenau (1838–1915), who in the 1880s founded the Allgemeine Elektrizitäts-Gesellschaft (AEG) and who had also tried to win the contract that went to Loewe, reckoned in his autobiography that this deal with the army amounted to several million marks in profits.[34]

The production of model no. 71 had started out along the old-fashioned lines of concentrating production in the army's own factories. The Mauser brothers, who had developed this model at their rifle factory in Württemberg, were not awarded a major contract for the manufacture of their very own weapon – to their great disappointment. Only when it became obvious that the Prussian armories would not be able to keep up with the army's demand

32 Conrad Matschoss, "Geschichte der Ludw. Loewe & Co. A.-G.," in *Ludwig Loewe and Co.*, ed., *Ludwig Loewe & Co., Aktiengesellschaft Berlin, 1869–1929* (Berlin, 1929), 9.

33 Buxbaum, "Der deutsche Werkzeugmaschinen," 120.

34 Alois Riedler, *Emil Rathenau und das Werden der Grosswirtschaft* (Berlin, 1916), 26–7.

did the Royal Inspection of Rifle Manufacture give additional orders to private industry. The policy then was first to give these contracts to companies that the army would have some influence over, and easy access to, and then, if this was still insufficient, to go to the best-equipped and most powerful producers.

Step one was the cooperation with Loewe and a contract with three rifle factories in Suhl, which got an order for 180,000 rifles. This went together with an interest-free advance of 100,000 marks for the purchase of American machinery. The three rifle manufacturers of Suhl closely cooperated with the Schilling & Krämer machine tool company, also in Suhl, which, much like Loewe, took up the production of Pratt & Whitney-type machines.[35] In this policy, the army was clearly strengthening the private industrial base of arms manufacture. The next step involved going to the Austrian Waffenfabrikgesellschaft in Steyr with a contract for 600,000 rifles. The economically rather weak Württemberg rifle factory, which had become a private company owned by the Mausers after the Franco-Prussian War, had to be content with an order for a modest 28,000 minor components.[36] The desire for tighter control by the Prussian army had given way to the desire for a maximum capacity to guarantee fast and abundant supplies.

The buildup of capacity needed for the quick replacement of the needle-gun was aided most by giving orders to private industry and supporting it in the acquisition of suitable mass-production machinery, if necessary through interest-free loans. Army contracts, unlike sewing machines, turned out to have been the most efficient way for the introduction to German industry of the "American way of manufacture" and its revolutionary machine tools. As in the case of Krupp, however, this greatly increased capacity had to look for an outlet greater and more evenly spread over time than the demand of the Prussian army alone. This goal could be achieved through both variations of the product mix in shifting to the production of more civilian goods or high-volume exports. In the late 1870s, for example, Loewe manufactured American Smith & Wesson revolvers for the Russian army after the contract for the Prussian model no. 71 rifle had expired.[37] At the same time, these renewed contracts put Loewe's machine tool department into a position to offer what Pratt & Whitney had in 1872—namely, complete turnkey workshops for the mass production of small iron and steel components, since they were widely used in the manufacture of bicycles and, as happened in the 1880s and 1890s, sewing machines.

35   Buxbaum, "Der deutsche Werkzeugmaschinen," 121.
36   Friedrich Hassler, Geschichte der Mauser-Werke (Berlin, 1938), 31–3.
37   Matschoss, "Geschichte der Ludw. Loewe & Co.," 231–4.

DUAL-USE INDUSTRY:
THE BACKBONE OF MODERN WARFARE

The privatization of arms production as it occurred at the time of the Franco-Prussian War owed as much to the benefits of mass-production technology as it did to its constraints. To utilize fully the economies of scale available through modern mass-production techniques, arms production in the 1860s and 1870s had to be integrated into the wider framework of the steel and mechanical engineering industries, respectively.

By the late 1860s, the output of an efficient steel plant eclipsed the demand of the army for ordnance steel. Limiting gun production to the armories under these conditions would either have resulted in dramatically higher costs or would have greatly reduced control over the quality of raw materials used. Steel technology, with the buildup of vertically integrated high-volume plants, had by that time outgrown the limited demand of the royal gun factories. Not even a single modern plant such as Krupp's in Essen could be kept running at full capacity through the army's demands for gun steel. Yet, turning to the private steel industry instantly opened up productive capacities that were far beyond the scope of the army's own. The army was fully aware of the advantages of having these industrial potentials at their disposal and, therefore, did not categorically object to Krupp's extensive arms exports, since they were essential to the company's ability to supply the German armies at short notice with any desired weapon.[38] A kind of official recognition of this new form of army-industry relationship was the huge credit that the Prussian state bank gave Krupp in 1874 to save him – by then the Empire's most important arms supplier – from impending bankruptcy. The survival of the private company of Krupp had become an issue of national security.[39]

At first glance, the situation looked somewhat different in the case of rifle manufacture, where many companies supplied the army with the new model no. 71 rifle. But here, again, the introduction of American mass-production technologies created production capacities beyond even the long-term needs of the army. Exports, as in the case of Krupp, were an important way out for these private companies. But just as important was the possibility of using the same skills and technologies in civilian production and developing its potential in this field. The underlying technology – the high-volume cutting of metal – was much improved and spread throughout the industry in products such as sewing machines, bicycles, and electrical equipment in the

38   Messerschmidt, *Die politische Geschichte*, 371.
39   Ibid., 374.

decades to come. It was in this industry that women mass-produced arms and ammunitions during World War I.

In turning to private industry for its arms supplies in the 1860s and 1870s, the Prussian army acknowledged the superior productivity of new processes of mass production in steel and mechanical engineering, the scope of which extended beyond its immediate needs. It was a tacit mobilization of a rapidly growing potential and a first step toward industrialized rather than artisanal warfare. It had an effect similar, one could argue, to conscription, although firms such as Krupp or Loewe did not have to be coaxed into cooperation.

12

The Prussian Army from Reform to War

MANFRED MESSERSCHMIDT

Bismarck's wars with Austria and the greater part of the German Confederation (1866) and with France (1870–71) led to German unification. The army that had decided the outcome of these wars was the army of the so-called Roon Reform, carried out between 1859 and 1863. It is no exaggeration to argue that the army reform was pushed through by Wilhelm, prince regent since 1858 and king since 1861, Albrecht von Roon as minister of war, and Bismarck, using procedures that dragged the country into its greatest political and constitutional crisis since the revolutionary era (1848– 50).

After the wars, there was a widespread belief in Germany that during the constitutional conflict, the army, by being steadfast and farsighted, had laid the foundation of the Empire, thus fulfilling the dream of the German people. Today, we have many reasons to doubt the existence of such a red line in Prussia's policy and German history. There is, of course, a connection between army reform and German unification, because there is an obvious nexus between reform and military successes. This is not to say that the reformers did not expect political gains by improving the army's strength and organization. But one can infer from these leaders' expectations that they pursued rather general ideas about strengthening Prussia's position in Germany and, of course, the monarchic order at home.

The prince regent must be regarded as the driving force behind the reform project. His education and professional experiences had been connected primarily with the military. When he became king, he looked back on nearly fifty years of military service. For him, the army was the very embodiment of kingship, a credo that he had derived from the lessons of history, which he had learned in the days of Napoléon and during the following revolutionary events of 1830 and 1848–50. During the constitutional crisis, Wilhelm's thinking had not wandered very far from his belief in the 1830s, when he was convinced of the dangers inherent in liberal "false" doctrines. In those days, he had developed that idea that was to govern his political philosophy for the rest of his life:

The tendency of the revolutionary or liberal party in Europe is to gradually tear down all the pillars affording the sovereign power and prestige and thereby, in moments of danger, security. That the armies are the principal pillars is natural–the more a true military spirit pervades this pillar, the more difficult it will be to get the better of it.[1]

Thus, it was a syndrome of monarchical convictions, domestic policy strategy, and professional military considerations that led him to tackle the question of army reform. Foreign policy intentions played a rather vague role in his approach. Even historians of the Prussian school of historiography agree with this evaluation. The historian Otto Hintze's remark seems a just characterization when he says that King Wilhelm I was convinced that Prussia would take the lead in Germany one day, but he himself would not witness this in his own lifetime; hence, he had left the "German question" aside during the first years of his reign, that is, during the reform era.[2]

The king's main military adviser turned out to be General von Roon, who viewed reform problems as his master did but differed from Wilhelm I's views in some important aspects. The differences not only applied to budget questions or the role of parliament but also to military matters as such. There was no generally accepted plan for army reform except for the intention to move two or three younger age groups from the Landwehr, the territorial militia, over to the field army and to replace older age groups. These ideas were not new. Military experts recalled imperfections during the mobilizations in 1850 and, especially in 1859, when Prussia had mobilized different army corps during the Franco-Sardinian War with Austria. These imperfections were owing to the neglect of the *Landwehr* system, which had always been criticized by the active army, the so-called line. But the *Landwehr* was in a way a citizens' branch of the military constitution, a national militia. Its elimination would have meant nothing less than constitutional quarrels with the liberals, who were far from being convinced that an army reform pushed through by conservative generals could serve national ends. They suspected bad intentions, and they would doubtless have felt their fears confirmed if they had seen Roon's memorandum "Observations on and Outlines for the Fatherland's Military Constitution" from July 21, 1858,[3] which had received

---

1   Letter to War Minister from von Hake, April 9, 1832, in *Kaiser Wilhelm des Grossen: Briefe, Reden und Schriften*, vol. 1: 1797–1860, 4th ed. (Berlin, 1906), 89.
2   Otto Hintze, *Die Hohenzollern und ihr Werk: Fünfhundert Jahre vaterländischer Geschichte*, 7th ed. (Berlin, 1916), 565–6.
3   Königlich Preussisches Kriegsministerium, ed., *Militärische Schriften weiland Kaiser Wilhelms des Grossen Majestät*, vol. 2: 1848-1865 (Berlin, 1897), 344–78.

Wilhelm's principal approval. As far as Prussia's position in Europe was concerned, von Roon mentioned no specifics. He argued, like his royal master, in general terms: Prussia's mission was the basis of her "claims to power." She had to have the best army possible. But that was not the case. The double system of line and *Landwehr*, both of which were to form the field army in time of war, was founded on illusions, for the *Landwehr* was an inappropriate institution from a political and military point of view: It did not impress other countries and was of doubtful importance for foreign and domestic policy. When the *Landwehr* became part of the regular forces in 1814, von Roon argued, nobody had expected revolutionary troubles.

Yet the *Landwehr* was not that bad. It could have been much better had it not been neglected for years, despite the fact that numerous line officers had been assigned to its peace cadres. What von Roon, who after Bonin's resignation became war minister at the beginning of December 1859, really wanted was to abolish the popular *Landwehr* and to have its younger classes incorporated into the line. This was also the king's view. It meant new line regiments, more discipline, and effective mobilization, but not necessarily more manpower, because the reform centered on shifting age cohorts.

Parliamentary resistance threatened these plans. The king came close to resigning, and conservative generals were ready to stage a coup d'état. It was Bismarck – finally called to power by a king who had long hesitated to appoint him prime minister – who mastered the situation, and on his terms. The reform was completed without a budget law.

RESULTS OF THE ROON REFORM

The reform's main achievement was the abolition of the military organization introduced by Boyen's military law of 1814. The reform work of 1808–14 was thus deprived of its main institution. This represented a full triumph of the "spirit of the line" of the officer corps. An "armed part of the people" was no longer one of the pillars of Prussia's military strength. But this was not a conservative success per se. The king and Roon differed in their aims from Wilhelm's predecessor and his advisors, the men of the so-called *Kamarilla* (camarilla). Prussian power policy seemed necessary to the new leaders, though they had no plans for the future. Their new army was simply a precondition for backing Prussia's interests in Germany and Europe. The Prime Minister had strengthened the king's and the army's position at home. The king's control over the army – his *Kommandogewalt* – was firmly established beyond parliamentary influence. Bismarck had indeed acted as

"stabilizer of the *Kommandogewalt*."[4] He had combined his own political existence with that of the army, as von Roon had expected he would when he
had urged the king to call Bismarck into office.[5]

The new army organization added greatly to Prussia's strength. These were
the results in figures (war strength):

	Before 1859	After the reform
Field army	335,300	354,400
Replacements	52,200	106,100
Occupation forces	145,200	155,400
Total	532,700	615,900

Peacetime strength in 1862 with 7,814 officers and 202,420 soldiers surpassed the former figures by 1,202 and 58,550, respectively. Time of service,
set by the law from September 1814, was as follows:

Regular army	3 years
Reserve	2 years
Landwehr I	7 years
Landwehr II	7 years
Landsturm	until the age of 50

The latter was reduced and lasted now from 20 to 42, namely:

Regular army	3 years
Reserve	4 years
Landwehr	5 years
Landsturm	until the age of 42

The field army consisted only of seven-year classes, against twelve before
the reform. This "loss" was compensated by the establishment of thirty-nine
new infantry regiments and ten new cavalry regiments. This way it was possible to raise the annual recruiting figure from about 40,000 up to 63,000.
Better promotion possibilities attracted many young men. Cadet schools and
the newly established war schools introduced shorter courses to meet the
demand for more officers.

This army was imbued with what the king called the true military spirit.
Soldiers had to serve three years for this reason. To come to terms with parliament, even military advisors had proposed conceding two year's service.

---

4 Manfred Messerschmidt, "Die Armee in Staat und Gesellschaft–Die Bismarckzeit," in Michael
   Stürmer, ed., *Das Kaiserliche Deutschland: Politik und Gesellschaft, 1870–1918* (Düsseldorf, 1970), 95.
5 *Denkwürdigkeiten aus dem Leben des General-Feldmarschalls Kriegsministers Grafen von Roon*, 4th ed.
   (Breslau, 1897), 2–81, 87, 93, 304.

But the king did not budge.[6] For him, the three-year period of service was the keystone of the whole reform edifice, in his eyes a guarantee for loyalty and a defense against revolutionary sedition. Another important aspect of the military spirit of the army was the idea of having a higher percentage of volunteers who served more than three years—in the regular army the so-called *Kapitulanten* (reenlistees), later the famous *Zwölfender* (twelve-month enlistees). They indeed formed the nucleus of the units, being attracted by special advantages such as small pensions or lower posts in local administrations after their military service. Since 1814, this institution had become a normal feature of the army. The reformers planned to have one-third of the peacetime strength of an infantry battalion serving as *Kapitulanten*, that is, 159 out of 476 soldiers. This meant a direct correlation between numerical strength and "military spirit." The king made his opinion on this very clear in a memorandum from October 10, 1862, in which he said, "reduction in the number of heads and reduction in the period of service destroys the spirit of every army and generates sullenness."[7]

One of the results of the reform was a better application of the principle of universal conscription. Between 1814 and the 1850s, there was no improvement in numerical peacetime strength. The numbers varied between 120,000 and 140,000 soldiers, whereas the population grew from 10 to 18 million. In July 1857, a report from the General War Department, the main branch of the War Ministry, had already pointed out that many more young men could have been called up, giving the following figures: 1852 – 27,601; 1853 – 27,108; 1854 – 28,390; 1855 – 24,453; 1856 – 27,525.

By raising the annual number of recruits from about 40,000 to 63,000, the reform achieved a much higher degree of equal treatment. In principle, this was also an ideal cherished by the liberals, who found it easy after the campaign with Austria to hail the military reforms and to grant the government parliamentary indemnity for what had been executed during the constitutional crisis.

The financial consequences of the reform are shown by the following figures:

	Total expenses in millions of marks
1816	66.95
1822	79
1840	75.6

6 See, e.g., his statement given during the council session of Jan. 7, 1860, in *Militärische Schriften Kaiser Wilhelms*, 2:320–1.
7 Ibid., 488.
8 Ibid., 329.

Total expenses in millions of marks (cont'd.)

1850	81.6
1859	96.9
1860	97.9
1861	121.08
1862	118.8

A comparison of the figures from 1859 and 1862 shows the greatest increase in expenditures since the introduction of compulsory service. The share of the military budget in the general budget in 1859 was 24 percent (a ratio of 96.9 : 403.30 in millions of marks); in 1862, it was 27.6 percent (118.8 : 431.17).[9]

ARMAMENTS

Manpower was one decisive factor of the army reform, but it alone was not responsible for the military successes to come. Historians look at army reform mainly because it provided the background to the constitutional crisis. The change in the military constitution made it necessary to bring Bismarck to the helm, who then practiced greater Prussian policy, which led to German unification, thereby serving national longings, and, because this caught the spirit of the time, making the reform look like a wonderful national inspiration.

But it is doubtful whether the new army organization could have achieved this national success had there not been other, less-noted changes. Curt Jany, one of Prussia's leading military historians, was certainly right when he said the importance of the reform was exceptional because it coincided with new developments in warfare induced by new weapons.[10]

Generally, it must be said that Prussia did not use its industrial and technical know-how for armament purposes during the first half of the nineteenth century. Artillery guns and infantry weapons were behind the Austrian and French models even in the mid-1850s.

As for Prussia's infantry, in 1855 only ninety battalions were equipped with the needle-gun, which had already satisfied army requirements around 1835. It had proved its superiority in street fighting during the 1848–49 revolution, whereupon the king had decided to replace defective guns with needle breechloaders. But the process turned out to be rather slow. Experiences in the Crimean War had shown the superiority of rifled guns, so Prussia planned

9 *Das Königlich Preussische Kriegsministerium 1909, 1. März 1909* (Berlin, 1909), statistics on the development of the military budget, 147–53.

10 Curt Jany, *Geschichte der Königlich Preussischen Armee*, vol. 4: *Die Königlich Preussische Armee und das Deutsche Reichsheer 1807 bis 1914* (Berlin, 1933), 230.

to reconstruct the old percussion rifles. This was deemed necessary because the Dreyse-Zündnadel factory could only deliver 30,000 weapons annually, which seemed unsatisfactory in view of the fact that the bulk of the infantry had only the old percussion gun, which was inferior to the French Minie gun and did not equal the ballistic quality of the Austrian model.[11]

Only technical developments and the reformers' resolution enabled the army to equip the infantry with the needle breechloaders before Bismarck initiated a military solution to German unification. The main progress was the use of cast steel barrels, which allowed industrial mass production. But it must be remembered that this was done only a couple of years before 1866. In the mid-1850s, things looked quite different as a generals' commission called by the king voted ten to eight in favor of the Minie system as a transitional solution.

In the war with Austria, the Prussian infantry was completely equipped with an improved type of needle-gun. Nearly 270,000 weapons of this kind, together with highly improved ammunition, allowed for a greater rate of fire compared to the Austrian muzzleloaders with their better ballistic profile. The time of army-owned gun workshops was over. Private industry had become indispensable for armaments. The industrial revolution and the army reform acted together.

Artillery equipment underwent a similar development.[12] The war ministry and influential generals showed no special sympathy for Krupp's offers. They feared encroachments of private interests on army matters, higher costs, and the danger of monopolization. It took some time for the generals to understand the possible influence of industrialization and technological progress on armed forces. George W. F. Hallgarten was perhaps right when he characterized the technical progress in the 1860s and the growing influence of private firms as "preliminary exercises,"[13] but it represented an important example of cooperation that in the twentieth century finally made armaments a sphere of activity involving society in general.

Prussian artillery pieces were essentially inferior to the French and Austrian models. General von Hahn, Inspector General of the Prussian artillery (1853–64), was a decided opponent of the employment of cast steel guns. He always preferred bronze barrels. Tests by the *Artillerieprüfungskommission* (Artillery testing commission) with rifled breechloader guns in 1851 therefore had no

11   The development is described in *Das Königlich Preussische Kriegsministerium*, 158–76.
12   See August Genth, "Die preussischen Heereswerkstätten: Ihre Entwicklung, allgemeine volkswirtschaftliche Bedeutung und ihr Übergang in privatwirtschaftliche Betriebe," Ph.D. diss., Universität Berlin, 1926.
13   George W. F. Hallgarten, *Das Wettrüsten: Seine Geschichte bis zur Gegenwart* (Frankfurt/Main, 1966), 15.

impact on modernization. It was a direct decision by the prince regent in 1859 that marked the change. The new Krupp rifled cast steel breechloader had convinced him, so instead of 100, he ordered the purchase of 300 guns. It was a rather long way from Krupp's prototype of 1847 to the acceptance of his model, and without Wilhelm's interference, he might have stopped the project.[14] The subsequent progress of artillery equipment design was very much directed by Hahn's successor, General von Hindersin. In the Danish War, the army corps had only four batteries each with rifled Krupp six pounders. In the war between Prussia and Austria, the number had risen to ten batteries per artillery regiment.

From now on, artillery production became a matter of private industry. Already in 1858, the Inspection of the Artillery Workshops was replaced by the Inspection of the Technical Institutes of the Artillery, which had at their disposal test institutions that gained increasing importance in cooperation with private firms. Since 1859, Prussia's and Germany's forces kept up more closely with technological progress. But on the side of the army, even in Roon's views, there remained residual distrust of the profit-oriented thinking and price calculations of private enterprise. Although dependency on private industries became increasingly the norm, army agencies attempted to maintain control over industrial activities and to regain lost ground by reorganizing and modernizing state-owned plants and arsenals. Prussia's artillery possessed powder factories, ammunition factories, gun foundries, pyrotechnic workshops, various metallurgical institutes, and planning bureaus.

It seemed clear that the face of battle would be changed decidedly by the effectiveness of the new type of guns. Experiences of other powers were studied. Hindersin did much to improve the tactical efficiency of his troops. In a study, he compiled the experiences of the Austrian campaign. Finally, the year 1867 saw the founding of the Berlin Artillery Firing School, where new methods of artillery field training, tactical employment, and cooperation with infantry units were introduced.[15]

One of the surprises of the Franco-Prussian War was the superiority of the German field artillery, which had been brought about by the measures previously discussed. At the beginning of the war, the Germans disposed of a

---

14 For Krupp's policy, see Wilhelm Berdrow, *Alfred Krupp*, 2 vols. (Berlin, 1927); Gert von Klass, *Die drei Ringe: Lebensgeschichte eines Industrieunternehmens*, 6th ed. (Tübingen, 1966); Ernst Schröder, *Krupp: Geschichte einer Unternehmerfamilie* (Göttingen, 1957); Willi A. Boelcke, *Krupp und die Hohenzollern in Dokumenten: Krupp-Korrespondenz mit Kaisern, Kabinettschefs und Ministern, 1850–1918* (1956; Frankfurt/Main, 1970).

15 E. von Hoffbauer, *Entwicklung des Massengebrauchs der Feldartillerie und des Schiessens in grösseren Artillerieverbänden in Preussen* (Berlin, 1900); H. von Müller, *Die Entwicklung der Feldartillerie*, vol. 1: *Kriegsgeschichtliche Einzelschriften des Preussischen Generalstabes*, no. 7 (Berlin, 1886).

considerable superiority in numbers: roughly 1,260 German against 924 French field pieces.[16] This superiority outweighed the advantages of the French *chassepot* infantry gun. Nevertheless, very often the German artillery had to operate within the range of French infantry fire, the range of Krupp's field gun being only 3,800 meters. It follows then that a general assessment of the effectiveness of Germany's artillery after the reform should not forget the heavy German losses in the battles from Weissenburg until Sedan.[17] Thus, the most important experience gained by the Germans was the impact of infantry guns on artillery tactics; the French, in contrast, learned the lesson of what artillery superiority on the enemy side meant in modern warfare.

German successes, of course, owed much to the military reforms, but there was also the factor of personalities who were able to handle the improved technology. The outstanding figure in this respect was the chief of the Prussian general staff, Helmuth von Moltke.

STRATEGIC LEADERSHIP

Ironically, Moltke was unable to exert any influence on the whole reform process. Before the Wars of Unification, the chief of the general staff was dependent on the war minister. The general staff, as a department of the war ministry, had not yet reached the position of an *Immediatstelle*; in other words, its chief had no direct access to the king. Things began to change when Moltke became chief of the general staff in 1857. During the mobilization against Austria in 1850, which turned out to be somewhat of a fiasco, the general staff did not play a prominent role. Mobilization and deployments were war ministry business. But in 1866, mobilization and movements proceeded completely according to Moltke's plans. Moltke had won the king's appreciation during the Danish War. He was able to obtain undisputed authority in operative matters and mobilization planning. This meant that in times of war he took the position of commander in chief in the name of the king, who was *Oberster Kriegsherr* or supreme commander. This important change in Prussia's top military organization was introduced by royal order on June 2, 1866,[18] which entitled the chief of the general staff to issue orders directly to army commanders independent of the war ministry. The order said:

16   Hoffbauer, *Entwicklung des Massengebrauchs*, 92–120.
17   See, e.g., Eberhard Kaulbach, "Der Feldzug 1870 bis zum Fall von Sedan: Zur deutschen militärischen Führung in heutiger Sicht," in *Entscheidung 1870: Der deutschfranzösische Krieg*, published by the Militärgeschichtliches Forschungsamt (Stuttgart, 1970), 47.
18   See Gerhard Ritter, *Staatskunst und Kriegshandwerk: Das Problem des "Militarismus" in Deutschland*, vol. 1: *Die altpreussische Tradition*, 2d ed. (Munich, 1959), 237; Manfred Messerschmidt, *Die politische Geschichte der preussischdeutschen Armee*, vol. 2 of the *Handbuch zur deutschen Militärgeschichte*, ed. Messerschmidt (Munich, 1979), 2:316.

Enclosed I send you my order issued today to the War Minister, according to which from now on my orders regarding strategic movements of the concentrated army and its individual parts will be issued to the commanders through the chief of the general staff of the Army; however, simultaneously the War Ministry is to be informed of events by you.

Already in June 1862, Moltke had placed general staff officers in army and army corps staffs. They were under the command of their respective generals as well as under the command of the chief of the general staff of the army, an arrangement that secured effective operational management.[19] Moltke's ideas in this regard made use of modern transportation facilities. He was the first systematically to base mobilization plans and deployments on strategic railway lines. For that purpose, he institutionalized cooperation with the Ministry of Commerce. Railway transportation for the Danish War was already prepared by the general staff and executed by a special railway section established by Moltke in 1859. And in 1866, the Prussian army introduced "railroad troops" or "field railroad sections" consisting of mixed civilian-military units. Together with 3,600 railway personnel, engineer units assisted these military organizations in 1870–71. In addition, the great east-west railway line was built to military specifications. Yet the different German railway systems grew together only slowly, so France was temporarily able to catch up with Germany in the 1850s.

Bringing huge masses of troops into position according to operational schemes by railway transport helped the Prussian and German armies to secure victories during the initial battles and, likewise decisive, to achieve numerical superiority at the beginning of the war. The North German Confederation, which was Prussian dominated and militarily organized northern Germany, had mobilized nearly 400,000 men. Together with the troops of the southern German states, the German forces comprised a total of 450,000 men, whereas France, in Moltke's eyes, could only mass 250,000 to 350,000 troops on the border when the Germans arrived. What was to follow was the result of training and firepower. Moltke put it this way: "Clearly it is important to take advantage of the superiority that we have right at the beginning."[20] One of the means that he used to exploit initial success was the solid general staff training and the special authority of command that linked

---

19 Ritter, *Staatskunst und Kriegshandwerk*, 1: 237.
20 *Moltkes Militärische Korrespondenz: Aus den Dienstvorschriften des Kriegs, 1870–1871* (Berlin, 1897), 121. For a comparison of the two adversaries, see Michael Howard, *The Franco-Prussian War: The German Invasion of France, 1870–1871* (London, 1962).

army staffs directly with the chief of the general staff, whereby extravagances of army commanders could be checked or minimized in their effect.[21]

Moltke's role in the education of the general staff must also be seen as a continuing effort to form a corps of highly efficient experts, to integrate staff officers coming from the forces of the other states of the North German Confederation and from the Hanoverian army, which became part of the Prussian military when Hanover was swallowed by Prussia after the defeat in 1866. It must also be seen in connection with the new tasks of the Prussian general staff after Prussia had concluded the "offensive–defensive alliances" with the southern German states in August 1866. In this way, Prussia gained a foothold in the south. A period of standardization followed, connected with the broader planning facilities for the general staff.

Developments in military matters after 1866 showed a direct application of Prussian organization, equipment, regulations and education to the forces in northern Germany and the beginning of their application in the south. The Prussian king as *Bundesfeldherr* (commander of the federated troops) became *Oberster Kriegsherr*, although Bavaria was able to preserve special rights.[22] Whereas Saxony, Württemberg, and Bavaria had been conceded their own war ministries and general staffs, the Bavarian king retained direct control of his army. But in wartime, things changed. The king of Prussia, after 1871 the emperor of Germany, was the supreme commander, and the Prussian chief of the general staff was in fact commander-in-chief of the German forces. This can be seen as a consequence of the reform era: In all practical matters, the German forces represented a "Greater Prussian" military power.

POSITION IN STATE AND POLITICS

The army's position in state and politics has aroused great interest among historians and the public in general. The story of the evaluation of these phenomena is controversial, but there has been some consensus on the impact of the reform era and the military successes in the wars of unification on that position.

---

21 As to the realization of tactical and operational experiences in guidelines for staff education, see, e.g., Grosser Generalstab, ed., *Moltkes taktisch-strategische Aufsätze aus den Jahren 1857 bis 1871* (Berlin, 1900), 165, "Aus den Verordnungen für die höheren Truppenführer vom 24. Juni 1869." For operational ideas, see Volkmar Regling, "Grundzüge der Landkriegführung zur Zeit des Absolutismus und im 19. Jahrhundert," *Handbuch zur deutschen Militärgeschichte* (Munich, 1979), 5: 379–425; Eberhard Kessel, *Moltke* (Stuttgart, 1957); Wiegand Schmidt-Richberg, *Die Generalstäbe in Deutschland, 1871-1945: Aufgaben in der Armee und Stellung im Staat* (Stuttgart, 1962).

22 In accordance with the treaty concluded on November 23, 1870, with the North German Confederation, *Bundesgesetzblatt* (1871): 9.

Adherents and critics of the army's role in society agree that the period between 1859 and 1871 had strengthened greatly the position of the military in Germany.[23] It was, above all, the general staff that claimed control over politics in time of war. Moltke's authority, based on the military successes of 1866 and 1870–71, paved the way for his successors. He had his quarrel with Bismarck over the Paris bombardment question. In his essay "On Strategy" (1871), he wrote:

Politics uses war to achieve its goals; it decisively influences war's beginning and end in such a way that it reserves the right during the war's course to increase its claims or on the other hand to be satisfied with a lesser success. In light of this uncertainty, strategy can only aim its efforts steadily at the highest goal, which the necessary means make at all achievable. In this way strategy best helps politics, only for this purpose, but in its actions [remain] independent.

The growing self-confidence of the general staff and the strengthening of its chief in the military hierarchy – already the case before he was given direct access to the king in 1883 – was clearly promoted by the personal authority of Moltke. Very soon it was to become the credit of the institution, and it developed ultimately into an extraordinary position until, during World War I, the chief of the general staff stood de facto at the helm of the Reich.

During the reform era until 1866–70, Moltke had had little influence on foreign policy. As with the king and Roon, he was originally not in favor of a war with Austria. On the contrary, he hailed the weight of the two German powers in Europe. As soon as he saw Austria as a future adversary, he dismissed foreign policy considerations as obstacles to his strategic plans. In his opinion, the deployment of the Prussian armies as envisaged in his strategy asked for the elimination of every diplomatic deliberation that might hamper the offensive. Strategy claimed the role of the most certain guarantee of success that no other device could offer. Moltke emphasized this dogma in a memo from April 1866 when he said that once mobilization has been decided upon, one must not be afraid of being accused of aggression. We find similar demands shortly before the war with France. Politics had to secure the operative advantage. Moltke talked about the "fiction" of aggression.[24] The

23   E.g., Ritter, *Staatskunst und Kriegshandwerk*; Kessel, *Moltke*; Hans-Ulrich Wehler, *Das Deutsche Kaiserreich 1871–1918* (Göttingen, 1973); Ludwig Dehio, "Um den deutschen Militarismus," *Historische Zeitschrift* 180 (1955): 43–64; Friedrich Meinecke, *Die deutsche Katastrophe: Betrachtungen und Erinnerungen*, 2d ed. (Wiesbaden, 1946); Fritz Fischer, *Griff nach der Weltmacht: Die Kriegszielpolitik des kaiserlichen Deutschland, 1914–18*, 3d ed. (Düsseldorf, 1964); Fritz Fischer, *Bündnis der Eliten: Zur Kontinuität der Machtstrukturen in Deutschland, 1871–1945* (Düsseldorf, 1979).
24   For his position in the war council in August 1870, see Eberhard Kolb: "Der Kriegsrat zu Herny am 14. August 1870," *Militärgeschichtliche Mitteilungen* 1 (1971): 5–13.

war itself did not convince him of the dubious value of an exclusively military assessment. The idea of the decisive battle as part of a "preventive war,"[25] which would stabilize and develop Germany's position, began to dominate the strategic wisdom of the "demigods" in the general staff. Obviously, the victories had aroused a feeling of superiority as well as apprehension: Not only Bismarck was haunted by a *cauchemar de coalitions*; the general staff developed numerous plans for a war on two fronts. Never had Germany been in a stronger position than after 1871, and never was there stronger strategic dissatisfaction. Without Bismarck, the generals would probably have launched a "preventive war" in the 1870s or 1880s.[26]

Moltke had some feeling for what a future war would look like when he reflected on possible solutions in 1871. "We have just experienced," he said, "how difficult it is to conclude even a victorious war with France. One must not hope to be able to quickly eliminate one enemy by a successful offensive." But in the planning studies of the general staff, the "demigods" counted on a new Königgrätz or Cannae and considered only enemy regular and mobile forces as having dangerous potential. Armies, not nations, figured in their calculations. It was a world seen through Prussian eyes. And it was War Minister von Roon who refused to send *Landwehr* troops to fight against the French *levée-en-masse* after the defeat of the Imperial army: King Wilhelm was to win the war with his regular army only; he did not want to rely on popular elements for the establishment of the Reich.

What is important to show here is this: the well-known and often described role of the general staff in foreign policy, more precisely, the impact of its strategic schemes on the options of German policy, was one of the results of the military reforms, and it was intrinsically connected and intertwined with the position of the military in general, which at this point had been nationally accepted, and the general staff in particular. The position of Prussia's military in domestic policy and constitutional matters was likewise strengthened by the reforms and the wars. In military matters, the budget prerogative of the North German Confederation's parliament was

---

25 See Rudolf Stadelmann, *Moltke und der Staat* (Krefeld, 1950); Ritter, *Staatskunst und Kriegshandwerk*, 1.
26 On the "Krieg-in-Sicht-Krise" of 1875, see Ritter, *Staatskunst und Kriegshandwerk*, 1; Andreas Hillgruber, "Die 'Krieg-in-Sicht-Krise' 1875: Wegscheide der Politik der europäischen Grossmächte in der späten Bismarck-Zeit," in Ernst Schulin, ed., *Gedenkschrift Martin Göhring: Studien zur Europäischen Geschichte* (Wiesbaden, 1968), 239–53; for preventive war plans, see Konrad Canis, "Bismarck, Waldersee und die Kriegsgefahr Ende 1887," in Horst Bartel and Ernst Engelberg, eds., *Die grosspreussisch-militärische Reichsgründung 1871* (Berlin, 1971), 2: 397–435; Karl Ernst Jeismann, *Blick auf die Bismarckzeit* (Freiburg, 1957); Peter Rassow, *Der Plan des Feldmarschalls Grafen Moltke für den Zweifrontenkrieg, 1871–1890* (Breslau, 1936); Helmuth von Moltke, *Die deutschen Aufmarschpläne, 1871–1890*, ed. Ferdinand von Schmerfeld, Forschungen und Darstellungen aus dem Reichsarchiv, no. 7 (Berlin, 1929).

reduced: Until 1871, the peacetime strength of the army was fixed at 1 percent of the population for five years; the war ministry's draft had even proposed ten years.

The king's "power of command" worked as an unshakable barrier between the military and parliament. Despite universal conscription and the general franchise, the king's army resided outside of society. During the constitutional crisis, von Roon had managed to suppress the soldiers' franchise. In this he cooperated with the chief of the military cabinet, Edwin von Manteuffel. Both of them suspected that liberal views might disintegrate the army. Manteuffel asked the king to abolish the soldiers right to vote. For him this was simply a military question, namely, "no civilian minister can judge what the army can bear or what is a condition for its cohesion."[27] In September 1863, von Roon was informed of the king's decision. Soldiers were forbidden to go to the polls and vote. This became the definitive solution as settled by the election bill of the North German Confederation. Moltke said in the parliamentary debate:

> We should be happy that we in Germany have an army that only obeys. We look at other countries, where the army is not a defense against the revolution, where instead, this revolution comes from the army.[28]

Meanwhile, social democracy had replaced liberalism as the main enemy and critic of the military state. The results of the army reform played an important role in this context, because the reform had provided for a disciplined integration of the nation into the old Prussian military state. In this system, the army performed an eminent political task: it was supposed to be the educator of the people, but in reality, it helped to divide the nation into patriots and enemies of the state. The army of universal conscription fostered suspicion and developed all kinds of control measures and plans for civil war. In the synchronization of the industrial revolution, the irresistible growth of a socialist party and the shaping of a greater Prussia, the army became the decisive factor even in the eyes of the bourgeoisie, which had lost its liberal impetus and became an important advocate of empire. After all, the reformers' army had realized their political dreams by delivering the military solution to the problem of German unity.

THEORY AND REALITY IN MODERN WARFARE

This solution to the German national question, together with unanticipated economic progress, conditioned the new German feelings of strength, which

27   Cited in Messerschmidt, *Politische Geschichte der preussisch-deutschen Armee*, 164.
28   Cited in ibid., 165.

was imbued with political recklessness and the formation of new concepts of the enemy. Ideas about how to fight the enemy at home—that is, social-ism—corresponded with those prepared for foreign adversaries. Experiences with the French levée-en-masse combined with post-Hegelian doctrines and social Darwinism.[29] The outcome resulted in the devaluation of internation-al law, which was no longer seen as a binding authority but simply as a tool of foreign policy that could be ignored at will. The new formula was "mili-tary realism," "military war aim."[30] General von Hartmann argued, "The mili-tary war aim lies in the immediate aims of the act of violence in war itself."[31] "Military realism" could allow the forcible suppression of a people's patrio-tism and sense of justice in occupied territories. The belief that war followed laws of its own corresponded with the strategic dogma of the battle of annihilation but surpassed it in so far as it went far beyond the aim of utterly destroying the enemy on the battlefield. It was the enemy nation that was to be overpowered. The war was to develop into a "war of extermination," as the crown prince described Moltke's position during the war with France.[32] Moltke underlined his view later in a letter to Johann Bluntschli (1880).[33] War could not only aim at "wearing down the armed forces" but was a fight for existence and must be directed against the vital resources of the enemy, including the prestige of government. Apparently, Moltke developed this view especially with France in mind. Already before 1870, he expected a national war of this kind.[34] After 1870–71, the general staff dominated polit-ical thinking so strongly with its idea of war aims and necessities of war that no change could be effected. Even Bismarck could not interfere here. In 1902, a publication issued by the general staff compiled these opinions on war and law for the purpose of officer education.[35] Thus materialized the guidelines for a radicalization of warfare, which had already seen an early realization in the treatment of the franc-tireurs.

The fighting methods of the franc-tireurs—sudden attacks on patrols,

---

29 Gen. Julius von Hartmann, "Militärische Notwendigkeit und Humanität," in *Prinzip und Zukunft des Völkerrechts*, (Berlin, 1871); Max Seydel, *Grundzüge einer allgemeinen Staatslehre* (Würzburg, 1873).

30 Manfred Messerschmidt, "Völkerrecht und 'Kriegsnotwendigkeit' in der deutschen militärischen Tradition seit den Einigungskriegen," *German Studies Review* 6 (1983): 237–69, and *Revue de droit pénal militaire et de droit de la guerre* 22, nos. 3–4 (1983): 211–41.

31 Hartmann, "Militärische Notwendigkeit," 21.

32 Friedrich III, German Emperor, *Das Kriegstagebuch von 1870–1871*, ed. Heinrich O. Meisner (Berlin, 1926), 325. See also Lothar Gall, *Bismarck: Der weisse Revolutionär* (Frankfurt/Main, 1980), 441–2.

33 *Briefe des General-Feldmarschalls Grafen Helmuth von Moltke*, 2d ed. (Berlin, 1892); *Gesammelte Schriften und Denkwürdigkeiten*, 5: 193–7.

34 Ritter, *Staatskunst und Kriegshandwerk*, 1: 252, 275–7.

35 Kriegsgeschichtliche Abteilung des Grossen Generalstabs, ed., *Kriegsbrauch im Landkriege*, Kriegsgeschichtliche Einzelschriften, no. 31 (Berlin, 1902).

ambushes, cooperation with the rural population, maiming of individual soldiers, and so forth–were upon closer examination anything but a "people's war" of threatening proportions. Only in connection with the *garde mobile* and *garde nationale* could they have become an operational challenge for the Prussian-German army. But the volunteer corps lacked adequate training, weaponry, and organization for that. In his diary, Captain Count Maurice d'Hérisson, a member of General Trochu's staff, probably expressed the opinion that the majority of the French officer corps had of the franc-tireurs: "One would have to be completely mad to believe that with the volunteer corps one could harm the masses of Prussians even a little, with franc-tireurs, with highway men, who they did not even bother with, and who only harmed the French farmers."[36]

Yet even if the franc-tireurs did not represent an operational danger, they still forced the German troops to take measures in order to protect their communication and supply lines. There were repeated smaller engagements. At the end of September 1870, the Third Army Corps was forced to relocate the Third Brandenburg Infantry Regiment along the Orne River, in order to "protect" the rear of the army "from franc-tireurs bands."[37] Large strips of land, especially in terrain that was not open such as the Argonne, were systematically combed through, and the troops there were billeted according to special measures.[38] Bloody engagements with franc-tireurs and the population in individual villages lead to especially harsh repressive measures.[39] Incidents of this sort remained etched on the memory of both sides; on the German side, they led to grave consequences for the debasement of the international law of war, and they produced on both sides an extreme image of the other as "enemy."

This special character of the war is reflected in the accounts of German officers and soldiers in a way that shows that they had no doubts that the Germans were in the right, or at least that such excesses were understandable or emotionally justified. An impression of this is provided by the report on events in the village of Bazeille near Sedan in the beginning of September 1870, written by the Bavarian officer Friedrich Koch-Breuberg:

36 At the time, General Trochu was governor of Paris and commander of the troops in the French capital. Graf Maurice von Hérisson, *Tagebuch eines Ordonnanz-Offiziers: Juli 1870–Februar 1871* (Augsburg, 1885), 58.

37 Kirchhof und Brandenburg, *Das 3. Brandenburgische Infanterie-Regiment Nr. 20 in den Feldzügen 1866 und 1870–71* (Berlin, 1881), 165.

38 Braun, *Das Rheinische Ulanen-Regiment Nr. 7 im Deutsch-Französischen Kriege, 1870–71* (Berlin 1909), 112–13.

39 See the one-sided and exaggerated account from Gustave Isambert, *Combat et Incendie de Chateaudun (18 Octobre 1870), avec Notes et Pièces Justificatives* (Paris, 1871), 27, and esp. the "Rapport du maire de Chateaudun à M. le ministre de l'intérieur, sur la journée du 18 octobre," 73–80.

Two Blusenmänner, probably farmers, who had fired on soldiers, are led before a major.

"Shoot them! On the spot!" ordered the major.

"Our people should have killed them immediately," said a calm comrade to me. Now they actually belong before a military court. …

The rage of the soldiers in Bazeilles was such, however, that everything that happened there must be excused. Those who escaped honest battle with their lives, were threatened with treacherous murder; those who fell wounded could expect that a hate filled woman or farmer would send them to kingdom come in a hideous way. The Bavarian soldiers were completely justified in seizing equally cruel counter-measures.[40]

From a bivouac, a soldier of the Fourth Thuringian Infantry Regiment no. 20 wrote to his brother at the end of August 1870:

Here in this village there is not even any water to be had, for some of the wells have been poisoned, and others have had rotten meat dumped in them. The French civilians are nasty people; they have fired on the wounded.[41]

In a letter written on Christmas day, he tells of a franc-tireur attack on the same day:

We fell on those treacherous murderers with a "Hurrah," but we could not get hold of them because ten minutes away from this attack there was a very big forest, where further pursuit was impossible. From us there were 2 dead, 3 wounded; we also found a patrol from the 60th regiment, 6 men, which had been sent out at 6 o'clock in the morning, two shot, the other 4 murdered, their throats cut. We took 8 prisoners; besides that perhaps 15 men were shot and 5 men were beaten to death. …

The next village, Bricon, was set on fire, because it was believed that those horrible scoundrels had their hiding places there.[42]

From the French side, the German reprisals, or methods of prosecuting the war, were described thus:

Breaking into homes with axes, pillage, plunder, murder, and especially arson. –All these atrocities continued during the whole night and the following day under the orders of a disciplined organization, which places the responsibility for this as high as the Prussian government. …

Long after the fighting, during the night and the following day, peaceful inhabitants, elderly people, the sick have been killed by the blows of guns and revolvers in their homes and at their doors. Some have been burned in their beds which had been set on fire; wounded people were thrown alive into the flames where they were burned to such an extent that it became impossible to recognize them.[43]

40 Friedrich Koch-Breuberg, *Drei Jahre in Frankreich: Erinnerungen eines Truppenoffiziers aus dem Feldzug, 1870–71 und der Occupation, 1871–1873* (Munich, 1891), 37–80.
41 Hermann Radestock, *Acht Feldpostbriefe aus dem deutsch-französischen Kriege, 1870–1871*, ed. Hans-Joachim Radestock (Hanover, 1967), August 27, 1870, 5.
42 Radestock, *Acht Feldpostbriefe*, Dec. 25, 1870, 8.
43 Isambert, *Combat et Incedie de Chateaudum*, 75–6.

Such reports give the impression of a war fought by both sides in a cruel manner that went beyond all rules and customs of international law. The haphazard attacks of the franc-tireurs – typically ambushes – led to radical countermeasures on the part of the German authorities in command. Many innocent people were caught up in the process, in which soldiers often practiced a sort of personal revenge. The overall picture is of an invading army that accepted these kinds of excesses, and even later theoretically summed them up in a system of "terrorism" without, however, sanctioning wild individual actions of soldiers. On the other side, the French army did not see itself in a position to integrate the franc-tireurs into its defense concept in the sense of disciplined coordination. The army appears to have assessed the value of the "volunteer corps" with some skepticism. Some officers felt the German reprisals were understandable – excepting the excesses. D'Hérisson was, however, probably an exception when he expressed the opinion:

> If I were a General and I came to Prussia, I would do it exactly as the Prussians – I would have all disorderly warring people who fell into my hands killed. There is no other way to prosecute a war orderly, that is, humanely, so humanely at least, as it brings with it immediate oblivion, which should still of course be regulated according to the general rules of humanity.[44]

Soldiers' excesses after franc-tireurs activities – mostly shootings of captured *Blusenmänner* – were manifold, but these stood next to the orders for retaliation by the troops.[45] Spontaneous reactions of soldiers often came because of rumors or exaggerated news.[46] Officers frequently ordered executions without following proper military legal procedure. On December 26, 1870, a company commander recorded in his diary, "yes, it is an evil task of this war, that one often must tear the farmer from his home, have him shot, and his house set on fire, and yet through their behavior they force one to resort to these methods."[47] The murder of peaceful civilians was threatened with the death penalty, which before military engagements was disregarded and replaced instead with a prison sentence.[48]

---

44   Von Hérisson, *Tagebuch eines Ordonnanz-Offiziers*, 59.
45   More in Braun, *Ulanenregiment Nr. 7*, 123.
46   Tilla Ris, ed., *Kriegserlebnisse meines verstorbenen Mannes Richard Ris, Oberstleutnant a.D. während des Feldzuges 1870–71: Premierelieutenant und Kompagnieführer im (1.) Badischen Leibgrenadier-Regiment* (Auerbach, 1911) 47. Ris remarks: "One only has to have been there oneself in order to understand the feelings of the soldier, when he hears 'shot in ambush,' 'one of us murdered,' 'eyes poked out,' etc., and all the other exaggerated rumours that fall on the troops ears mostly one hundred times enlarged."
47   Ibid., 157.
48   Koch-Breuberg, *Drei Jahre in Frankreich*, 62. Thus, we could take the example of the two soldiers who murdered an old woman because of a piece of cheese.

The most common reprisal of the units was the burning down of villages and farms, such as in Chablis. A soldier of the Grand Ducal Mecklenburg Grenadier Regiment no. 89 remarked in his memoirs: "since the night of the 7th to the 8th of October when a squadron of the 16th Hussars was murdered in their sleep, there was only a heap of rubble were the place [had] stood."[49] Death sentences passed by military courts on captured franc-tireurs and accomplices were often supplemented by financial contributions levied against towns, not just as punishment, but also because of an order from the Versailles headquarters issued with the intent of making the French population war-weary.[50]

The war of the franc-tireurs was, for all its national psychological effect, which lasted for decades, only one facet of the war, both before and after the capitulation of Sedan. The other face of the war showed itself in the officers of the invading army, who were often comfortably quartered in bourgeois houses or on nobles' estates. In many cases, this resulted in social encounters where champagne was served and the family held a reception.[51] Experiences of this kind have been reported from officers billeted with priests and nobles. "In general," writes a reserve officer, "one got on well with the providers of quarters, and people of the educated classes behaved irreproachably, and also were not afraid of officers."[52] Contacts in restaurants were not infrequent, and political conversations often were held.[53] The division chaplain of the First Garde Infantry Division, later the royal court chaplain in Potsdam, reports of common religious services with members of the community and a good relationship to the Catholic clergy.[54] There were accordingly personal experiences that were suited to convey a less emotionally charged picture of the French neighbors and thereby call into question the self-evidence of the enemy image. This was the case on both sides. The hate campaigns of some newspapers, like *Journal de Paris*, *Gaulois*, and *La Liberté*, by no means reflected the opinion of everyone in France.

49 Hermann Stier-Herzwolde, *Erinnerungen aus dem letzten Kriege* (Neustrelitz, 1897), 53.
50 Bernhard Stürtz, *Mit den 25ern vor 42 Jahren vom Rhein zur Küstenwacht und an die Lisaine: Erinnerungen eines ehemaligen Reserve-Offiziers des heutigen Infantrie-Regiments v. Lützow, 1. Rhein. Nr. 25, aus dem Feldzuge von 1870–71* (Aachen, 1912), 26, 39.
51 Hugo Dinckelberg, *Kriegserlebnisse eines Kaiser Alexander Garde-Grenadiers im Felde und im Lazarett 1870–71* (Munich, 1909), 79; Koch-Breuberg, *Drei Jahre in Frankreich*, 56, 136. Similar from Chablis, the report from Hermann Freiherr von Meysenburg, *Erinnerungen eines alten Fünfundfünfzigers aus der Zeit des deutsch-französischen Krieges der Jahre 1870–71* (Berlin, 1910), 93–6.
52 Stürtz, *Mit den 25ern*, 42.
53 Fritz Ehrenberg, *Kleine Erlebnisse in grosser Zeit: Aus dem Tagebuche eines Kriegsstudenten von 1870–71* (Strasbourg, 1890), 91.
54 Bernhard Rogge, *Bei der Garde: Erlebnisse und Eindrücke aus dem Kriegsjahre 1870–71* (Berlin, 1912), 78.

Thus, Gambetta's use of troops in the war did not, with the exception of the franc-tireur war, correspond with the conclusions that the Prussian military leadership had drawn with respect to the prosecution of the war and treatment of the civilian population in the future. The long tradition of the military state, which prevented a coming together of military and civilian or even democratic interests at home, also stood in the way of any understanding of the feelings of a nation that continued to fight in the face of awful defeats under a new government, and that anticipated the role of nation and society in future wars. Tyranny and "military terror" were no solution to the problem, that is, if the achievements of the humanitarian international law of war were not to be devalued.

The army of the Roon Reform probably could have mastered a genuine "people's war" only with the greatest of difficulties. At home, the "democratic" aspects of military organization, as conceived in Scharnhorst's *Landsturm* plans, did not materialize because the monarchy did not want to arm the people. That smelled too much of the revolutionary spirit. Von Roon then did away with the remains of Boyens *Landwehr*, thereby dispensing with the rest of the reforms of 1808–14, excepting universal conscription. This "king's army" was everything but a people's or citizens' army. With this army, it was possible to prosecute wars such as the one of 1870–71, in which it then reached its limits. World War I saw the armed nation constrained within the framework of this military organization, and in the end disintegrating tendencies proved that the concept of the king's army had failed. The Franco-Prussian War was, in spite of the feelings of triumph which victory had brought, the first hint of such an outcome.

The military reforms and the Wars of Unification – won with an instrument that had been shaped by this very reform process – produced strength and efficiency in the Reich but allowed little leeway for democratic progress and the creation of a social and international equilibrium. This was not only owing to the extension of the Prussian military system to all of Germany but also to the military momentum gained in terms of society's feelings and thinking, which was perceived as something similar to a normal consequence of the massive accumulation of power. Prussia and Germany had given birth to their Procrustean bed, in which it was so inconvenient to rest in the twentieth century. One may or may not call it the result of a special path in German historical development. In any case, this development had a lasting impact on what was to come: Germany's burden of reconciling efficiency, discipline, and a technocratic approach – which was indeed representative of the activities of general staff – with democracy, parliamentary compromise, tolerance, and individual constitutional rights.

13

French Mobilization in 1870

WILLIAM SERMAN

In 1870, the French were unaware of the distinction between mobilization (*Mobilmachung*) and concentration of forces (*Strategischer Aufmarsch*).[1] They carried out both operations simultaneously, calling the former the "conversion from a peacetime footing to a wartime footing" and the latter the "formation of the army."

On July 11, 1870, when he decided to take personal command and organize a single army out of the twenty-six divisions of eight different corps, Napoléon III was convinced that he could have 400,000 men at the ready within a fortnight. His optimism belied the fact that his secretary of war, Field Marshal Edmond Leboeuf, had informed him that it would be difficult to form an army of 250,000 men within two weeks time, that it was overly optimistic to expect 350,000, and that it was virtually impossible to hope for any more.

At this particular time, the Imperial Army consisted of 350,000 noncommissioned officers (NCOs) and enlisted men, including soldiers on leave but not counting the gendarmes. Part of the French armed forces was stationed outside of the country, particularly in Algeria (approximately 80,000 men) and Rome (8,000). It is true that, as early as July 8, the governor-general of Algeria received orders to prepare the troops of the African army for redeployment. The decision to recall the occupation corps in Rome was not made until August 2; actual troop movement did not take place until the beginning of September. In contrast, the regiments from Africa arrived fairly quickly and were able to take part in the battles in Alsace and Lorraine.

---

1 A. Martinien, *La mobilisation de l' armée: Mouvements des dépôts (Armée active) du 15 juillet 1870 au ler mars 1871* (Paris, 1911), 463; Général Thoumas, *Les transformations de l' armée française* (Paris. 1887) 1: 545–68; P. Leehautcourt, *Histoire de la guerre de 1870–1871*, vol. 2: *Lee deux adversaires, Premières opérations* (Paris, 1902); Michael Howard, *The Franco-Prussian War* (London and New York, 1988), 63–76, 233–56; Stéphane Audoin-Rouzeau, *1870: La France dans la guerre* (Paris, 1989), 75–87, 183–95, 253–60, 420; Colonel P. Rocolle, "Anatomie d'une mobilisation," *Revue historique des armées* 2 (1972): 35–68.

Still on a peacetime footing during the first few days of July, the Imperial army consisted of 49 percent draftees, 16 percent volunteers, 17 percent reenlisted soldiers, 15 percent substitutes, 3 percent gendarmes, and assorted musicians.

The Niel Act – passed by the French parliament or *Corps législatif* on January 14, 1868, by the senate on January 28, and promulgated by the emperor on February 1 – mandated that men over the age of twenty-one, measuring at least 5 foot, 1 inch tall, and who had drawn an "unlucky number" were obliged to serve in the regular army for five years, followed by four years in the reserves. The majority were of working-class origin, too poor to escape the obligation of personal service by paying the exoneration fee (before 1868) or the price of a substitute (after 1868).

Substitutes and reenlisted soldiers generally came from the same social class. Together with the volunteers from mixed social backgrounds, they formed the professional part of the Imperial army. As a whole, it would be improper to consider this a professional army in view of the fact that the draftees were compelled to carry out a long military service.

The strength of the contingent to be recruited was fixed annually by a vote of the *Corps législatif*. Generally set at 100,000 men, this number was reduced to 90,000 in June 1870. This annual draft of able-bodied men was divided into two groups by an appropriations bill. The first group of men was drafted into the regular army for five years; the second was assigned to the reserve, where it should, in theory, have received minimal military training. However, in practice, this training was rarely provided.

On July 14, 1870, the secretary of war ordered the call-up of reservists for active duty, starting with the most recent contingents (and consequently the least prepared). Out of a potential pool of 400,000 men, the ministry expected approximately 163,000 to arrive at army depots within two weeks, not including the sick, the exempt, and the provisionally exempt conscripts. These expectations were, however, far from being fulfilled – by July 30, only 39,000 reservists had joined their regiments, and by August 6, barely 85,000 had done so.

The main reason for such a delay was the recruiting method, which was national rather than regional. Reservists from different *départements* were assigned to the same regiment. At first, they were mustered in the capital of their *département*, where detachments of 60 to 200 men were formed. They sometimes had to travel several hundred miles to join their unit, where they received their uniforms and were equipped and armed. They were then dispatched to their war battalions and squadrons, which had already left for the northeastern frontiers. Thus, within a few days, reservists from ten *départements* (Vendée, Charente-Inférieure, Mayenne, Finistère, Côtes-du-Nord, Manche, Loir et Cher, Dordogne, Gard, and Aude) arrived at the depot of the Fifty-fourth Infantry Regiment, situated in Napoléon-Vendée (La Roche-sur-Yon). They then were moved gradually to the front where, over the course of several days in late July, they joined their war battalions in Condé (Nord), Thionville (Moselle), and elsewhere. The wanderings of reservists from the Nord, drafted into the Second Zouaves, are worth mentioning in particular. By train and then by boat, they were transported from Lille to Oran (Algeria), where their depot was situated. From there, they traveled back to Alsace where the regiment was incorporated into the First Corps.

Approximately 2,000 detachments crossed France in a similar manner, from the *département* capitals to the infantry or cavalry unit depots, then from the depots to the main regiment body. Even when regiments were still in their peacetime garrison, they were often located at a considerable distance from their depots: The depot of the Eighty-sixth Infantry Regiment, garrisoned in Lyon, was situated in Saint-Malo; the Thirteenth was in Béthune with its depot in Romans; the Sixteenth was in Setif (Algeria) with its depot in Le Puy.

Occasionally, the depots lacked arms and indispensable gear, horses, horseshoes, and harnesses. Consequently, either extra supplies were awaited at the risk of delaying reservist mobilization even further, or the newly incorporated soldiers were dispatched with incomplete gear, without mess kits or camping equipment, and without ammunition or pistols.

The consolidation of active units was carried out in such great haste that mobilization was delayed, confused, and deficient. On July 15, the infantry regiments were ordered to form three war battalions composed of six companies (instead of eight), and a depot battalion was formed with the six remaining companies. The colonels had to send the three active battalions of their regiment to the assigned mustering point without waiting for the arrival of the remaining manpower, provisions, and equipment. The necessary reinforcements of men, horses, arms, ammunition, vehicles, and provisions were to be delivered in the field.

Following July 18, the majority of the infantry regiments set out for the front with varying strengths of between 950 and 1,300 men, instead of the usual minimum of at least 1,900 (or sometimes 2,100 if each company was comprised of the regulation manpower of 112 men). It took more than a month for the average strength of a battalion to increase from approximately

450 to approximately 750 men. An equal amount of time was necessary for the cavalry to supply mounts for all its men—by the end of July, only 110 horses were available for each squadron instead of the usual 150.

The remount, transport, and quartermaster corps did their best to supply the animals, vehicles, arms, ammunition, equipment, and provisions, which, with little notice, they were asked to requisition, buy, or release from the arsenals, depots, and stores. In the absence of previously articulated plans, except for depot sully, they had to improvise the logistic organization of the Imperial army according to the delayed data communicated to them concerning the nature, quantity, dates, and places of the deliveries required. Under such conditions, it is hardly surprising that there were numerous delays, mistakes, and shortages, which gave many soldiers of all grades cause for complaint on the eve of battle.

This exceptionally high volume of rail traffic created congestion on the tracks and platforms and at the stations, particularly within the rail network in eastern France. Transportation problems were exacerbated by the fact that Leboeuf had not convened the railway committee—created by the Niel Act—since January 1870. However, the manager of the Eastern Railway Company, Jacqmin, and his technicians managed to compensate for the French army's lack of preparation for the entraining and detraining of troops as well as for evacuation operations. Within ten days—that is, between July 16 and July 26—the Eastern Railway Company sent 594 military trains carrying more than 186,000 men, 32,000 horses, 1,500 vehicles, 500 guns, and 1,000 wagonloads of ammunition from Paris to Metz and other towns close to the border with Germany.

The fact remains that, by the end of July, Napoléon III's hopes for gathering sufficient offensive strength were dashed. Instead of the 400,000 men he anticipated, in Alsace and Lorraine he had only 250,000 men and 912 guns at his command. There had been sufficient time to form the army staff and corps, but it had not been an easy undertaking. The officers were informed of their assignment only on July 14, and, in spite of their haste, it took several days before they could assume their posts and organize their work. Although Leboeuf, the chief of the general staff, Generals Lebrun and Jarras, assistant chiefs of staff, and General Dejean, acting secretary of war, filled their positions quickly, the emperor's aides-de-camp only arrived on July 18. Field Marshal MacMahon, recalled from Algeria on July 12, embarked from Algiers on July 18, arrived in Paris on July 21, and then traveled to Strasbourg on July 23, where he took command of the First Corps. On July 20, the staff of the Fourth Corps (Ladmirault) had neither a secretary nor any paper. Almost all the other corps complained about the lack of horses, vehicles, and detailed maps of France, not to mention accurate information concerning the different units or commanding officers under their command. Once again, they had to improvise, and, despite poor organization, they managed to overcome numerous obstacles.

It was nonetheless extremely difficult to compensate for the shortage of available manpower. The government and the *Corps législatif* hoped to increase the size of the regular army and the reserves by adding hundreds of thousands of men, as a result of a series of measures taken between July 15 and 28. The majority of these measures, however, proved to be disappointing, either because they were unfavorably received by the population or because they required several months to produce the desired effect.

The first of these supplementary measures was an act, passed by the *Corps législatif* on the night of July 15, authorizing voluntary enlistments for the duration of the war. In view of the patriotic enthusiasm that Leboeuf – like the Empress Eugenie, the Duc de Gramont, and most of the ministers and right-wing members of parliament – had observed among the public, he had hoped for 100,000 volunteers. In reality, between July 19 and 31, barely 4,000 volunteers enlisted, whereas at the beginning of the wars against Russia in 1854 and Italy in 1859, there had been between 12,000 and 15,000 enlistees. However, German successes on the battlefield raised the stakes, bringing the total number of volunteers to around 20,000 men by August 31. Leboeuf's optimistic expectations remained nevertheless far beyond his reach. The aggressive patriotism of many Frenchmen did not translate into action. How many of the demonstrators who shouted "On to Berlin!" in the streets of Paris actually took up arms?

The second supplementary measure, taken on July 16 and 17, placed the *Garde Nationale Mobile* on active duty. This move no doubt contributed to the reduction of the potential number of volunteers, since it affected approximately 450,000 men destined by decree on July 18 to form provisional regiments (six were created on July 24).[2]

The news of the mobilization of the *Garde Nationale Mobile* was met with little enthusiasm by the general population. Requests for exemption were common. Recrimination by the individuals affected and their families against such an unusual decision grew increasingly frequent. The agitation of public opinion was particularly high in the *départements* of the Creuse, Dordogne, Drôme, Orne, and Pas-de-Calais. Nevertheless, resignation finally prevailed over consternation, and the majority of the *Garde Nationale Mobile* complied with the orders they received.

---

2 Colonel J. Chabanier, "La garde nationale mobile on 1870–1871," and Commandant H. Lachouque, " Résistance de 1870–1871," *Revue historique des armées* 1 (1971): 43–67.

Virtually nothing had been arranged, however, for the organization, officering, equipping, arming, training, feeding, and quartering of such a body of men. There was a lack of qualified officers and experienced noncommissioned officers, rifles and ammunition, clothing and camping gear, horses and carriages. The lack of foresight of the military administrative services jeopardized the rapid formation of the provisional regiments, delayed their deployment, and created discontent among the soldiers, who had minimal training and were too often deprived of basic necessities. The lack of discipline among the *Gardes Nationaux Mobiles* from the *département* of the Seine in the camp at Chalons was more the result of the inefficiency of the command and quartermaster corps responsible for their installation, supplies, and equipment than of the insubordination or subversive spirit of the Parisians. Their return to the capital, ordered by General Trochu on August 17, would have been politically absurd were it only justified by fear of their revolutionary tendencies. However, it was militarily necessary for a commander anxious to avoid the premature engagement of a hastily raised and insufficiently prepared army in battle.

Although they were less speedily mustered and organized than those from the Seine, by the beginning of August, the *Gardes Nationaux Mobiles* from other parts of the country were eager to complain about insufficient clothing and improper armaments. Until October, many of them advanced against the enemy with only a cap and a blue cotton blouse for a uniform and a muzzle-loading rifle as sole armament. Instead of a modern chassepot rifle, they used a model dating from 1857 that had been modified to enable breech-loading.

The *Corps législatif* and/or the imperial government undertook additional measures that aimed to increase the number of mobilized Frenchmen. On July 18, the contingent mustered in 1870 was set at 140,000 men, and its mobilization date was brought forward from July 1 to January 1, 1871. On July 26, the decision was made to place customs officers and foresters under the orders of the secretary of war. On July 28, the organization of commando units was authorized. With regard to financing the war effort, on July 16, members of parliament provided emergency funds amounting to 50 million francs; on July 21, a second sum of 500 million was granted. Both of these sums were to be added to the national debt. Along with the normal war and navy budget (approximately 420 million francs), these supplementary funds proved insufficient to cover the expenses of the armed forces, which had tripled or quadrupled in size. As operations developed and events unfolded, the financial needs of the armed forces increased dramatically. As a result, an act of parliament from August 12 set the amount of supplementary funds at 1 billion francs. In order to obtain such a sum, a loan of 750 million francs was floated on August 19. Within ten days, investments in 3-percent government bonds brought more than 800 million francs into the treasury. Although once underway, the mobilization of capital proceeded at a satisfactory speed, it was initiated belatedly and barely followed the call to arms of the men, instead of preceding or accompanying it.

Following the first disastrous battles along the front (Wissembourg, Wörth/Fröschwiller, Forbach), on August 7, 1870, the French minister of justice, Emile Ollivier, decreed the drafting of all able-bodied citizens between the ages of 30 and 40 years into the *Garde Nationale Sédentaire*. On August 10, his successor, the Comte de Palikao, who headed a 26-day ministry, pushed for the conscription of all bachelors or widowers, ages 25 to 35, not belonging to the *Garde Nationale Mobile*.

On September 2, when Napoléon III, MacMahon, and their army surrendered at Sedan, the mobilization of French manpower was still incomplete. However, the National Defense Government, formed in Paris on September 4, decided to continue and, if possible, accelerate it.

The politician Léon Gambetta exerted himself with the energy of a second Danton. As secretary of the interior, he decided to increase the number of Seine *Garde Nationale Mobile* battalions from 50 to 120 (September 6) and allocate to each *garde nationale* 1.50 francs per day, plus 0.75 francs if married and 0.25 francs per dependent child (September 12). As a result, by September 30, 194 new battalions had been formed, instead of the 60 originally planned. Paris therefore had more than 300,000 *Gardes Nationaux Sédentaires*, to whom 280,000 rifles were issued.

In addition, Gambetta and his colleagues in the National Defense Government reverted to some of the decisions decreed prior to September 4 by the Imperial authorities, widening their scope of application, and speeding up their implementation. From the day after Napoléon III's overthrow, it was decided to call up all young men in the contingent of 1870 (not only 140,000 of them) and advance their mobilization date from January 1, 1871, to October 1, 1870. The review boards were, however, unable to operate in eleven départements occupied by the Germans. Elsewhere, they examined the conscripts between September 5 and 19. Once their work was completed, they sent a total of 120,000 men to the regular army depots.

Furthermore, on September 29, in accordance with the Palikao Act of August 10, it was decreed that all men from 21 to 40 years of age with no dependents and belonging to the *Garde Nationale Sédentaire* should form units named *Gardes Nationaux Mobilisés* at the rate of one battalion per canton, one legion per arrondissement, and one brigade per *département*.

On October 10, Gambetta, assisted by the civil engineer Charles-Louis Freycinet, took up his duties as secretary of war, first in Tours and then after December 9 in Birdhouse.[3] On November 2, 1870, he also ordered the mobilization of married men into the *Garde Nationale Mobilisée*. Thus, three and a half months after the declaration of war, theoretically, and according to the different methods used, mobilization finally involved all able-bodied men between 21 and 40 years of age. Because the country was in danger, the concept of compulsory military service for all citizens became imperative. In practice, however, the number of men actually drafted proved to be considerably lower than what had been anticipated. The number amounted to 260,000 instead of a potential force of at least 600,000. Moreover, the twenty-three *départements* occupied by the Germans were unable to levy their contingent. By December 31, out of the 579,000 men drafted, only 500,000 had responded, and the induction of almost half was postponed owing to the fact that these draftees failed to meet the requirements. The shortage of 79,000 men registered by the military administrative services did not, under these circumstances, imply serious consequences for the army but did indeed create a problem. It remains unclear who or what was to blame. Errors in orientation? Transportation bottlenecks? A wave of insubordination?

In view of the evolution of voluntary enlistment alone, care must be taken not to jump to the conclusion that the French fighting spirit or the will to defend the country decreased. The number of volunteers reached a maximum of 30,500 in September, then dropped to 17,000 in October, 10,000 in November, 5,700 in December, and 4,000 in January 1871. But, during these four months, the categories and number of drafted citizens multiplied to such an extent that sources of potential volunteers were reduced considerably.

In similar fashion, we must not overestimate the attraction exerted by specialized commando units, some of which had exotic names and were permitted to wear civilian dress. Despite the difficult conditions that they had to endure, and the nature of their work, these units do not deserve to be categorized along with thugs or lawless brigands.

Three hundred of these units were officially registered with a total manpower of 57,800, including several thousand Italians who came with other foreigners to fight for the French Republic. In addition, hundreds of formerly papal Zouaves and *volontaires de l'Ouest* joined the battle determined, under the emblem of the cross and the sacred heart, to defend France with as much devoted courage as the republican nonbelievers who formed the franc-tireurs

---

3   Charles de Freycinet, *La guerre en province pendant le siège de Paris, 1870–1871: Précis historique*, 10th ed. (Paris, 1872).

battalion from the Seine. Since all the troops did not belong to the so-called "regular" army, these units were incorporated into the auxiliary army, created on October 14, and then joined with the regular army in the heterogeneous body referred to as the "army of national defense."

Twelve new army corps were formed from the volunteers and mobilized servicemen of all categories, but to equip them took time. The Fifteenth and Sixteenth Corps were organized by September; the Seventeenth, Eighteenth, and Twentieth in November; the Twenty-first, Twenty-second, and Twenty-third in December; and the Nineteenth, Twenty-fourth, Twenty-fifth, and Twenty-sixth in January 1871. There were numerous difficulties to overcome.

At first improvised, then organized by a ministerial decision from November 25, the eleven regional training camps established in Conlie (Sarthe), Toulouse, Birdhouse, La Rochelle, Cherbourg, Saint-Omer (Pas-de-Calais), Nevers, Clermont-Ferrand, Montpellier, Sathonay (near Lyon), and in the Alpilles or Alipines (to the northwest of Bouches du Rhône) lacked space, water, rudimentary sanitary arrangements, and regular supplies. Each had to accommodate more than 20,000–25,000 men, although Freycinet had anticipated the billeting and training of 60,000 to 250,000 soldiers per site.

When they finally reached the front, the guardsmen lacked appropriate shelter, that is, tents. They were equipped with only light blankets and were insufficiently clothed and shod. By the end of 1870, not all had benefited from the efforts made by Freycinet and the *intendant* Lahaussois to increase the productive capacity of military workshops. Between October 15 and January 31, these workshops managed to produce the supplies and footwear necessary to equip at least 600,000 men, including approximately 780,000 blankets, more than 670,000 greatcoats, 380,000 sheepskins, 700,000 jackets, 600,000 woolen vests or jumpers, 1,800,000 shirts, 950,000 pairs of trousers, and 1,800,000 pairs of shoes.

As far as armaments were concerned, the National Defense Government had to cope with a catastrophic shortage of rifles. Most of the chassepots made during the Empire had been seized by the enemy or were stockpiled in besieged locations, particularly in Metz. About 300,000 chassepots remained available to the national defense troops. The state workshops could only produce between 15,000–18,000 chassepots per month and, between September 17 and February 28, supplied scarcely more than 120,000 in total. The government was therefore forced to resort to other resources. Thousands of old muzzle-loading rifles were collected from all over France. Several kinds of arms available on the international market had been procured: in particular,

Remingtons, Sniders, Springfields, and Enfields. Thus, the number of rifles available gradually rose to 1,500,000 but consisted of about fifteen different models. This variety of rifle types greatly complicated the procurement of ammunition. The supply of ammunition was sufficient only for those units armed with chassepots, which received an abundant quantity of rifle cartridges produced at the rate of 2,800,000 per week in September, 4, 500,000 per week in December, and 7,000,000 during the first week of February 1871.

As far as artillery was concerned, guns were cast not only in the state-run factories situated in the unoccupied *départements*, for example, in the Nièvre (Imphy, Guérigny) or in the lower Loire (Indret). But they were also produced in factories belonging to private firms located in the central regions of the country as well as in the Midi–for example, the Forges et Chantiers de la Méditerranée cast 340 guns, and the Schneider workshops in le Creusot cast 250. Between October 10 and February 9, the artillery directorate, consigned to Colonel Thoumas, delivered a total of 1,400 guns of all calibers to the different army corps.

Raising armies and supplying them in the field created one set of problems; paying for all of this activity created another. In addition to the original arrangements made to finance the war, discussed previously, the government soon had to draw from state funds in the Banque de France, request donations from citizens, and float another loan of 250 million francs, of which 94 million came from French sources and a large part of the remainder from the Morgan Bank in the United States.[4] Despite all of these efforts, the government continued to fail to raise sufficient funds to cover its war expenses. The National Defense Government budget, deprived of many sources of tax revenues, showed an increasing deficit as early as December 1870. Wartime deficits would have been even greater had the authorities of the *départements* not taken over a large portion of the expenses of equipping the new army corps.

In addition to these material problems, there existed another particularly serious handicap for an improvised army designed to take the field rapidly–the shortage of officers. By the beginning of September, most of the regular army officers and NCOs still active–that is, not seriously wounded or taken prisoner–were bogged down in Metz or at some other defensive location. Officers still in Algeria, such as Antoine Chanzy, were recalled. Generals from the *cadre de réserve* and former retired or resigned senior or subaltern officers were returned to active duty. Promotions were granted to a

4   A. Duchene, Guerre et finances: Dépenses et liquidation d'une guerre, 1867–1873 (Paris, 1943), 47–67, 227.

large number of NCOs, but the positions to be filled were so numerous that Gambetta sought radical solutions better suited to the urgency of the situation. The decree of October 13 suspended customary promotion rules for the duration of the war. The decree of October 14 enabled the auxiliary army to be assigned officers of all ranks suitable for command, without regard to nationality or social class. In this manner, a number of temporary or auxiliary, French or foreign, republican or monarchist, generals and colonels were commissioned, regardless of whether they descended from noble, middle-, or working-class families. Among the seventy-three generals posted in sole command of a division, brigade, or commando by the National Defense Government were: the Italian brothers Giuseppe, Riccioti, and Menotti Garibaldi; the Pole Bossack (an ex-colonel in the Russian army); the American Trevis; the Native American chiefs Charette and Cathelineau; and a prince from Polignac; along with Cremer, Pélissier, and eighteen naval officers, three of whom distinguished themselves as generals; and the corps commanders Rear Admiral Jauréguiberry (Sixteenth Corps), Captain Jaurès (Twenty-first Corps), and Rear Admiral La Roncière-Le Noury (Fourteenth Corps).

It was, however, impossible to find an adequate number of majors, captains, lieutenants, and sublieutenants since too many former soldiers lacked the minimum educational requirements and too many educated young men had no military experience whatsoever. Before 1870, they had either drawn a "lucky number," had been exempted, or had paid sub-stitutes. In order to solve the problem of an insufficient number of officers, the number of soldiers in each unit was increased—a company was expanded to 200 men and a temporary regiment to 3,600. The exact opposite, how-ever, would have been preferable in order to compensate for the recruits' lack of experience: The officering rate for companies and battalions should have been increased, not reduced. The National Defense Government was well aware of this fact but had little choice in the matter. The rush of events at the front forced them to respond in any way they could. The German in-vasion pressed toward Paris. Thousands of cities and towns fell into enemy hands. Few dared to resist the occupying force for fear of reprisal, although many hoped for a quick reversal of their fortunes. Paris, which was then under siege, called for help. It became imperative for the French to advance without delay, even at the risk of exposing the numerous but minimally trained, green, and poorly commanded troops to excessive danger, waves of panic, or the temptation to commit insubordination or mutiny.

What remains surprising is that the French army, mobilized and organ-ized under such conditions, could have managed to prolong the struggle for almost five months and valiantly fight against an undeniably superior army, both in number and quality. The perseverance of the French was mainly the result of the effort put forth by Gambetta and Freycinet. The political authority of the former and the organizing activity of the latter succeeded in transforming the semiprofessional Imperial army into a massive people's army. Their joint willpower boosted the defensive spirit of the nation, energized the civil administration, raised the morale of the soldiers, and increased industrial production, the mustering of the troops, and the collection of capital.

Yet they had to improvise everything within a short period of time. The Empire had scarcely prepared for the mobilization of 500,000 men. As in 1854 and 1859, Napoléon III had declared war before his army was ready, even though he had contemplated fighting the Germans since at least 1866. In four months, the National Defense Government tried to carry out what the Empire had not accomplished in four years. It failed, however, owing to a lack of time. The government did manage to raise a force of 600,000 men, but it was unable to clothe, arm, command, and train them properly. Moreover, it failed to carry out the adequate economic mobilization of the country's resources. It failed to convince the military commanders, the leading citizens of France, and the majority of the rural population to wage guerrilla warfare against the enemy. Forced by circumstances, the government attempted to fight a war in a conventional manner but with means far superior than those available in times of peace. In any case, it would be wrong to refer to the 1870 war as a total war since the majority of French believed that neither the existence of the nation nor the independence of the state were at stake in this conflict. They clearly demonstrated this opinion on the occasion of the elections on February 8, 1871.

14

From Limited War to Total War in America

JAMES M. McPHERSON

A few years after the Civil War, Mark Twain described that great conflict as having "uprooted institutions that were centuries old, changed the politics of a people, transformed the social life of half the country, and wrought so profoundly upon the entire national character that the influence cannot be measured short of two or three generations."[1] This profound transformation was achieved at enormous cost in lives and property. The 620,000 soldiers who lost their lives almost equaled the number of American soldiers killed in all the other wars this country has fought combined. If the same proportion of soldiers to the total American population were to be killed in a war fought today, the number of American war dead would be *five million*.

Fully one-quarter of the white men of military age in the South lost their lives. And that ghastly toll does not include an unknown number of civilian deaths, nearly all in the South, victims of malnutrition, disease, and exposure resulting from the destruction of resources and the uprooting of hundreds of thousands of people who became refugees. Altogether nearly 4 percent of the Southern people, black and white, civilians and soldiers, died as a consequence of the war. This percentage exceeded the toll of any country in World War I and was outstripped only by the region between the Rhine and the Volga in World War II. The amount of property and resources destroyed in the Confederate States is almost incalculable. It has been estimated at two-thirds of all assessed wealth, including the market value of slaves.[2] As a proportion of national wealth in 1860, the abolition of slavery alone confiscated the equivalent of $3 *trillion* of property in the United States today.

---

1 Mark Twain and Charles Dudley Warner, *The Gilded Age*, New American Library Edition (New York, 1969), 137–88.
2 James L. Sellers, "The Economic Incidence of the Civil War in the South," *Mississippi Valley Historical Review* 14 (1927): 179–91; Stanley Engerman, "Some Economic Factors in Southern Backwardness in the Nineteenth Century," in John F. Kain and John B. Meyers, eds., *Essays in Regional Economics* (Cambridge, Mass., 1971), 291, 300–2.

These are the negative statistics of that radical transformation described by Twain. The positive side included preservation of the United States as a unified nation, the liberation of four million slaves, and the abolition by constitutional amendment of the institution of bondage that had plagued and divided the nation since the beginning, inhibited its progress, and made a mockery of the libertarian values on which it was founded. No other society in history freed so many slaves in so short a time at such a cost in violence.

The Civil War also mobilized human resources on a scale unmatched by any other event in American history except, perhaps, World War II. For actual combat duty, the Civil War mustered a considerably larger proportion of American manpower than did World War II. And, in another comparison with that global conflict, the victorious power in the Civil War did all it could to devastate the enemy's economic resources as well as the morale of its home front population, which was considered almost as important as enemy armies in the war effort. In World War II, this was done by strategic bombing; in the Civil War, it was done by cavalry and infantry penetrating deep into the Confederate heartland.

It is these factors – the devastation wrought by the war, the radical changes it accomplished, and the mobilization of the whole society to sustain the war effort – that caused many historians to label the Civil War a *total war*. Recently, however, some analysts have questioned this terminology. They maintain that true total war – or in the words of Carl von Clausewitz, "absolute war" – makes no distinction between combatants and does not discriminate between taking the lives of enemy soldiers and those of enemy civilians; it is war "without any scruple or limitations," war in which combatants give no quarter and take no prisoners.[3]

Some wars through history have approached this totality – for example, World War II, in which Germany deliberately murdered millions of civilians in eastern Europe, allied strategic bombing killed hundreds of thousands of German and Japanese civilians, and both sides sometimes refused to take prisoners and shot those who tried to surrender. In that sense of totality, the Civil War was not a total war. Although suffering and disease mortality were high among prisoners of war, and Confederates occasionally murdered captured black soldiers, there was no systematic effort to kill prisoners. While soldiers on both sides in the Civil War pillaged and looted civilian property,

---

3 Mark E. Neely Jr., "Was the Civil War a Total War?" *Civil War History* 37 (1991): 5–28; Eric T. Dean Jr., "Clausewitz and the American Civil War: The Theory of 'Total War' Reconsidered," seminar paper, Department of History, Yale University Graduate School, June 1991; quotation from the *Oxford English Dictionary's* definition of total war in *OED*, 2d ed., 18:286–7.

and several Union commanders (notably William Tecumseh Sherman and Philip H. Sheridan) systematized this destruction into a policy, they did not deliberately kill civilians. Mark E. Neely Jr., the chief critic of the notion of the Civil War as a total war, maintains that "the *essential* aspect of any definition of total war asserts that it breaks down the distinction between soldiers and civilians, combatants and noncombatants, and this no one in the Civil War did systematically."[4]

Even Sherman, widely regarded as the progenitor of total war, was more bark than bite according to Neely. Sherman wrote and spoke in a nervous, rapid-fire, sometimes offhand manner; he said extreme things about "slaying millions" and "repopulating Georgia" if necessary to win the war. But this was rhetorical exaggeration. One of Sherman's most widely quoted statements— "We are not only fighting hostile armies, but a hostile people, and must make old and young, rich and poor, feel the hard hand of war, as well as their organized armies"—did not really erase the distinction between combatants and noncombatants, for Sherman did not mean it to justify killing civilians.[5]

To note the difference between rhetoric and substance in the Civil War is to make a valid point. The rhetoric not only of Sherman but also of many other people on both sides was far more ferocious than anything that actually happened. Northerners had no monopoly on such rhetoric. A Savannah newspaper proclaimed in 1863: "Let Yankee cities burn and their fields be laid waste," while a Richmond editor echoed: "It surely must be made plain at last that this is to be a war of extermination." A month after the firing on Fort Sumter, a Nashville woman prayed that "God may be with us to give us strength to conquer them, to exterminate them, to lay waste every Northern city, town and village, to destroy them utterly."[6] Yankees used similar language. In the first month of the war, a Milwaukee judge said that Northern armies should "restore New Orleans to its native marshes, then march across the country, burn Montgomery to ashes, and serve Charleston in the same way. ... We must starve, drown, burn, shoot the traitors."[7] In St. Louis, the uneasy truce between Union and Confederate factions that had followed the riots and fighting in May 1861 broke down a month later when the Union commander Nathaniel Lyon rejected a compromise with pro-Confederate elements, which included the governor, with these words:

---

4   Neely, "Was the Civil War a Total War?" 27.
5   Ibid., 14–15, John B. Walters, "General William T. Sherman and Total War," *Journal of Southern History* 14 (1948): 463.
6   Charles Royster, *The Destructive War: William Tecumseh Sherman, Stonewall Jackson, and the Americans* (New York, 1991), 35, 37–8, 211–12.
7   Ibid., 79–80.

"Rather than concede to the State of Missouri for one single instant the right to dictate to my Government in any matter...I would see you...and every man, woman, and child in the State, dead and buried."[8]

These statements certainly sound like total war, war without limits or restraints. But, of course, none of the scenarios sketched in these quotations literally came true – not even in Missouri, where reality came closer to rhetoric than anywhere else. Therefore, those who insist that the Civil War was not a total war appear to have won their case, at least semantically. Recognizing this, a few historians have sought different adjectives to describe the kind of conflict that the Civil War became: One uses the phrase "destructive war"; another prefers "hard war."[9]

But these phrases, though accurate, do not convey the true dimensions of devastation in the Civil War. All wars are hard and destructive to some degree; what made the Civil War distinctive in the American experience? It *was* that overwhelming involvement of the whole population, the shocking loss of life, The wholesale devastation and radical social and political transformation that it wrought. The war accomplished the extinction of a nation-state – the Confederacy. It also extinguished a social system of property relations – slavery. Few other wars in history have achieved such total results. Thus, conceding the distinction between combatants and noncombatants, the concept of total war remains a useful one for understanding the American Civil War. It is what the sociologist Max Weber called an "ideal type" – a theoretical model used to measure a reality that never fully conforms to the model but that nevertheless remains a useful tool for analyzing the reality.

This is the sense in which I shall try to analyze the evolution of the Civil War from a limited to a total war. Despite that fierce rhetoric of destruction quoted a page or two earlier, the official war aims of both sides in 1861 were quite limited. In his first message to the Confederate Congress after the firing on Fort Sumter by his troops had provoked war, Jefferson Davis declared that "we seek no conquest, no aggrandizement, no concession of any kind from the States with which we were lately confederated; all we ask is to be let alone."[10] As for the Union government, its initial conception of the war was of a domestic insurrection, an uprising against national authority by certain lawless hotheads who had gained temporary sway over the otherwise

---

8   Thomas L. Snead, *The Fight for Missouri from the Election of Lincoln to the Death of Lyon* (New York, 1886), 199–200.

9   Royster, *The Destructive War*; see also Mark Grimsley's dissertation prospectus, Ohio State University, 1990.

10 Dunber Rowland, ed., *Jefferson Davis Constitutionalist: His Letters, Papers and Speeches*, 10 vols. (Jackson, Miss., 1923), 5: 84 .

lawabiding citizens of a few Southern states – or as Lincoln put it in his proclamation calling out 75,000 state militia to put down the uprising, "combinations too powerful to be suppressed by the ordinary course of judicial proceedings." This was a strategy of limited war – indeed, so limited that it was scarcely seen as a war at all, but rather as a police action to quell a large riot. It was a strategy founded on an assumption of residual loyalty among the silent majority of Southerners. Once the national government demonstrated its firmness by regaining control of its forts and by blockading Southern ports, those presumed legions of Unionists would come to the fore and bring their states back into the Union. To cultivate this loyalty, and to temper firmness with restraint, Lincoln promised that the federalized ninety-day militia would avoid "any devastation, any destruction of, or interference with, property, or any disturbance of peaceful citizens."[11]

None other than Sherman echoed these sentiments in the summer of 1861. Commander of a brigade that fought at Bull Run, Sherman deplored the marauding tendencies of his poorly disciplined soldiers. "No curse could be greater than invasion by a volunteer army," he wrote. "No Goths or Vandals ever had less respect for the lives and properties of friends and foes, and henceforth we should never hope for any friends in Virginia … My only hope now is that a common sense of decency may be infused into this soldiery to respect life and property."[12]

The most important and vulnerable form of Southern property was slaves. The Lincoln administration went out of its way to reassure Southerners in 1861 that it had no designs on slavery. Congress followed suit, passing by an overwhelming majority in July 1861 a resolution affirming that Union war aims included no intention "of overthrowing or interfering with the rights or established institutions of the States" – in plain words, slavery – but intended only "to defend and maintain the supremacy of the Constitution and to preserve the Union with all the dignity, equality, and rights of the several States unimpaired."[13]

There were, to be sure, murmurings in the North against this soft-war approach, this "kid-glove policy." Abolitionists and radical Republicans insisted that a rebellion sustained *by* slavery in defense *of* slavery could be crushed only by striking *against* slavery. As Frederick Douglass put it: "To fight against slaveholders, without fighting against slavery, is but a half-

---

11 Roy F. Basler et al, eds., *The Collected Works of Abraham Lincoln*, 9 vols . (New Brunswick, N. J., 1953–55), 4: 332.
12 William Tecumseh Sherman to his wife, July 28, 1861, and undated, probably August 1861, in Mark A. DeWolfe Howe, ed., *Home Letters of General Sherman* (New York, 1909), 209, 214.
13 *Congressional Globe*, 37 Congress, 1 session, 222–3.

hearted business, and paralyzes the hands engaged in it…Fire must be met with water…War for the destruction of liberty must be met with war for the destruction of slavery."[14] A few Union soldiers and their officers, some with no previous antislavery convictions, also began to grumble about the protection of the property of traitors in arms against the United States.

The first practical manifestation of this sentiment came in Missouri. Thus began a pattern whereby events in that state set the pace for the transformation from a limited to a total war, radiating eastward and southward from Missouri. The commander of the Western Department of the Union army in the summer of 1861, with headquarters at St. Louis, was John C. Frémont, famed explorer of the West, first Republican presidential candidate (in 1856), and now ambitious for military glory. Handicapped by his own administrative incompetence, bedeviled by a Confederate invasion of southwest Missouri that defeated and killed Nathaniel Lyon at Wilson's Creek on August 10 and then marched northward to the Missouri River, and driven to distraction by Confederate guerrilla bands that sprang up almost everywhere, Frémont took a bold step on August 30 toward total war. He placed the whole state of Missouri under martial law, announced the death penalty for guerrillas captured behind Union lines, and confiscated the property and emancipated the slaves of Confederate activists.[15]

Northern radicals applauded, but conservatives shuddered and border-state Unionists expressed outrage. Still pursuing a strategy of trying to cultivate Southern Unionists as the best way to restore the Union, Lincoln feared that Frémont's edict would "alarm our Southern Union friends, and turn them against us – perhaps ruin our rather fair prospect for Kentucky.…To lose Kentucky is nearly the same as to lose the whole game. Kentucky gone, we can not hold Missouri, nor, as I think, Maryland. These all against us, and the job on our hands is too large for us. We would as well consent to separation at once, including the surrender of this capitol."[16]

Lincoln thus revoked the confiscation and emancipation provisions of Frémont's edict. He also ordered the general to execute no guerrillas without specific presidential approval. Lincoln feared that such a policy would only provoke reprisals whereby guerrillas would shoot captured Union soldiers, "man for man, indefinitely." His apprehensions were well founded. One guerrilla leader in southeast Missouri had already issued a counter

---

14   *Douglass' Monthly*, May, Sept. 1861.

15   *War of the Rebellion … Official Records of the Union and Confederate Armies* (hereafter cited as *OR*), 128 vols. (Washington, D.C., 1880–1901), ser. 1, vol. 3, 466–7.

16   Basler et al., eds., *Collected Works of Abraham Lincoln*, 4: 506, 532 .

proclamation declaring that for every man executed under Frémont's order, he would "HANG, DRAW, and QUARTER a minion of said Abraham Lincoln."[17] Lincoln had the Missouri situation very much in mind when he told Congress in his State of the Union message in December 1861 that "in considering the policy to be adopted for suppressing the insurrection, I have been anxious and careful that the inevitable conflict for this purpose shall not degenerate into a violent and remorseless revolutionary struggle."[18] But that was already happening. The momentum of a conflict that had already mobilized nearly a million men on both sides plus an incalculable number of guerrillas was becoming remorseless even as Lincoln spoke, and it would soon become revolutionary. Nowhere was this more true than in Missouri. There occurred the tragedy of a civil war within the Civil War, of neighbor against neighbor and sometimes literally brother against brother, of an armed conflict along the Kansas border that went back to 1854 and had never really stopped, of ugly, vicious, no-holds-barred bushwhacking that constituted pretty much a total war in fact as well as in theory. Bands of Confederate guerrillas led by the notorious William Clarke Quantrill, Bloody Bill Anderson, and other pathological killers, and containing such famous desperadoes as the James and Younger brothers, ambushed, murdered, and burned out Missouri Unionists and tied down thousands of Union troops by hit-and-run raids. Union militia and Kansas Jayhawkers retaliated in kind. In contrapuntal disharmony, guerrillas and Jayhawkers plundered and pillaged their way across the state, taking no prisoners, killing in cold blood, terrorizing the civilian population, leaving large parts of Missouri a scorched earth. In 1863, Quantrill's band rode into Kansas to the hated Yankee settlement of Lawrence and murdered almost every adult male they found there, some 180 in all. A year later, Bloody Bill Anderson's gang took twenty-four unarmed Union soldiers from a train, shot them in the head, then turned on a posse of pursuing militia and slaughtered 127 of them including the wounded and captured. In April 1864, the Missourian John S. Marmaduke, a Confederate general (and later governor of Missouri), led an attack on Union supply wagons at Poison Springs, Arkansas, killing in cold blood almost as many black soldiers as Nathan Bedford Forrest's troops did at almost the same time in the more famous Fort Pillow massacre in Tennessee.[19]

17 Ibid., 506; Jay Monaghan, *Civil War on the Western Border 1854–1865* (Boston, 1955), 185.
18 Basler et al., eds., *Collected Works of Abraham Lincoln*, 5: 48–9.
19 Monaghan, *Civil War on the Western Border*; Richard S. Brownlee, *Gray Ghosts of the Confederacy: Guerrilla Warfare in the West, 1861–1865*; Stephen Z . Starr, *Jennison's Jayhawkers: A Civil War Cavalry Regiment and Its Commander* (Baton Rouge, La., 1973); Albert E. Castel, *A Frontier State at War: Kansas 1861–1865* (Ithaca, N.Y., 1950); Michael Fellman, *Inside War: The Guerrilla Conflict in Missouri during the American Civil War* (New York, 1989) .

Confederate guerrillas had no monopoly on atrocities and scorched-earth practices in Missouri. The Seventh Kansas Cavalry – "Jennison's Jayhawkers" – containing many abolitionists including a son of John Brown, seemed determined to exterminate rebellion and slaveholders in the most literal manner. The Union commander in western Missouri where guerrilla activity was most rife, Thomas Ewing, issued his notorious Order No. 11 after Quantrill's raid to Lawrence. Order No. 11 forcibly removed thousands of families from four Missouri counties along the Kansas border and burned their farms to deny the guerrillas the sanctuary they had enjoyed in this region. Interestingly, Ewing was Sherman's brother-in-law. In fact, most of the Union commanders who subsequently became famous as practitioners of total war spent part of their early Civil War careers in Missouri – including Ulysses S. Grant, Sherman, and Sheridan. This was more than coincidence. What they saw and experienced in that state helped to predispose them toward a conviction that, in Sherman's words, "we are not only fighting hostile armies, but a hostile people," and must make them "feel the hard hand of war."[20]

That conviction took root and began to grow among the Northern people and their leaders in the summer of 1862. Before then, for several months in the winter and spring, Union forces had seemed on the verge of winning the war without resorting to such measures. The capture of Forts Henry and Donelson, the victories at Mill Springs in Kentucky, Pea Ridge in Arkansas, Shiloh in Tennessee, Roanoke Island and New Bern in North Carolina, the capture of Nashville, New Orleans, and Memphis, the expulsion of organized Confederate armies from Missouri, Kentucky, and West Virginia, the occupation of much of the lower Mississippi Valley and most of the state of Tennessee, and the advance of the splendidly equipped Army of the Potomac to within five miles of Richmond in May 1862, all seemed to herald the Confederacy's doom. But then came counteroffensives by Stonewall Jackson and Robert E. Lee in Virginia and by Braxton Bragg and Kirby Smith in Tennessee, which took Confederate armies almost to the Ohio River and across the Potomac River by September 1862.

Those deceptively easy Union advances and victories in early 1862 had apparently confirmed the validity of a limited-war strategy. Grant's capture of Forts Henry and Donelson, for example, had convinced him that the Confederacy was a hollow shell about to collapse. When the rebels regrouped and counterpunched so hard at Shiloh that they nearly whipped him, Grant changed his mind. He now "gave up all idea," he said, "of saving the Union except by complete conquest." Complete conquest meant not merely the

20   Walters, "General William T. Sherman and Total War," 463.

occupation of territory but also the crippling or destruction of Confederate armies. For if they remained intact, they could reconquer territory, as they did in the summer of 1862. Grant's new conception of the war also included the seizure or destruction of any property or other resources used to sustain the Confederate war effort. Before those Southern counteroffensives, Grant said that he had been careful "to protect the property of the citizens whose territory was invaded"; afterward, his policy became to "consume everything that could be used to support or supply armies."[21]

This included slaves, whose labor was one of the principal resources used to support and supply Confederate armies. If the Confederacy "cannot be whipped in any other way than through a war against slavery," wrote Grant, "let it come to that."[22] Union armies in the field as well as Republican leaders in Congress had been edging toward an emancipation policy ever since May 1861 when Gen. Benjamin Butler had admitted three escaped slaves to his lines at Fort Monroe, labeled them contraband of war, and put them to work for wages to help support and supply *Union* forces. By the summer of 1862, tens of thousands of these contrabands had come within Union lines. Congress had forbidden army officers to return them. Legislation passed in July 1862 declared free all of those belonging to masters who supported the Confederacy. Frémont in Missouri turned out not to have been wrong, but a year ahead of his time.

By the summer of 1862, Lincoln too had come to the position enunciated by Douglass a year earlier: "To fight against slaveholders, without fighting against slavery, is but a halfhearted business." Acting in his capacity as commander-in-chief with power to seize property used to wage war against the United States, Lincoln decided to issue a proclamation freeing all slaves in those states engaged in rebellion. Emancipation, he told his cabinet in July 1862, had become "a military necessity, absolutely essential to the preservation of the Union ... We must free the slaves or be ourselves subdued. The slaves [are] undeniably an element of strength to those who [have] their service, and we must decide whether that element should be with us or against us. ... Decisive and extensive measures must be adopted. ... We wanted the army to strike more vigorous blows. The Administration must set an example, and strike at the heart of the rebellion."[23] After a wait of two months for a victory to give the proclamation credibility, Lincoln announced it on September 22, 1862, to go into effect on January 1, 1863.

21 *Personal Memoirs of U.S. Grant*, 2 vols. (New York, 1885), 1: 368–9
22 Ulysses S. Grant to Jesse Root Grant, Nov. 27, 1881, in John Y. Simon, ed., *The Papers of Ulysses S. Grant*, 16 vols. to date (Carbondale, Ill., 1967–95), 3: 227.
23 Gideon Welles, "The History of Emancipation," *The Galaxy* 14 (1872): 842–3.

With this action, Lincoln embraced the idea of the Civil War as a revolutionary conflict. Things had changed a great deal since he had promised to avoid "any devastation, or destruction of, or interference with, property." The Emancipation Proclamation was just what the *Springfield Republican* pronounced it: "the greatest social and political revolution of the age." No less an authority on revolutions than Karl Marx exulted: "*Never* has such a gigantic transformation taken place so rapidly."[24] Gen. Henry W. Halleck, who had been called from his headquarters in St. Louis as commander of the Western Department to Washington to become general-in-chief, made clear the practical import of the Emancipation Proclamation in a dispatch to Grant at Memphis in January 1863. "The character of the war has very much changed within the last year," he wrote. "There is now no possible hope of reconciliation with the rebels. . . . We must conquer the rebels or be conquered by them. . . . Every slave withdrawn from the enemy is the equivalent of a white man put *hors de combat.*" One of Grant's field commanders explained that the new "policy is to be terrible on the enemy. I am using Negroes all the time for my work as teamsters, and have 1,000 employed."[25]

The program of "being terrible on the enemy" soon went beyond emancipating slaves and using them as teamsters. In early 1863, the Lincoln administration committed itself to a policy that had first emerged, like other total-war practices, in the trans-Mississippi theater. The 1st Kansas Colored Volunteers, composed mostly of contrabands from Missouri, were the earliest black soldiers to see combat, in 1862, and along with the Louisiana Native Guards the first to take shape as organized units. Arms in the hands of slaves constituted the South's ultimate revolutionary nightmare. After initial hesitation, Lincoln embraced this revolution as well. In March 1863, he wrote to Andrew Johnson, military governor of occupied Tennessee: "The bare sight of fifty thousand armed, and drilled black soldiers on the banks of the Mississippi, would end the rebellion at once. And who doubts that we can present that sight, if we but take hold in earnest?" By August 1863, Lincoln could declare in a public letter that "the emancipation policy, and the use of colored troops, constitute the heaviest blow yet dealt to the rebellion."[26]

Well before then, the conflict had become remorseless as well as revolutionary, with Lincoln's approval. Two of the generals he brought to Washington from the West in the summer of 1862, John Pope and Halleck,

24 *Springfield Republican*, Sept . 24, 1862; Karl Marx, *On America and the Civil War*, ed. and trans. Saul K. Padover (New York, 1972), 272.
25 Halleck in *OR*, ser. 1, vol. 24, pt. 3, 157; Dodge quoted in Bruce Catton, *Grant Moves South* (Boston, 1960), 294.
26 Basler et al., eds., *Collected Works of Abraham Lincoln*, 6: 149–50, 408–9.

helped to define and enunciate the remorselessness. Both had spent the previous winter and spring in Missouri, where experience with guerrillas had shaped their hard-war approach. One of Pope's first actions upon becoming commander of the Army of Virginia was a series of orders authorizing his officers to seize Confederate property without compensation, to execute captured guerrillas who had fired on Union troops, and to expel from occupied territory any civilians who sheltered guerrillas or who refused to take an oath of allegiance to the United States. From Halleck's office as general-in-chief in August 1862 went orders to Grant, now commander of Union forces in western Tennessee and Mississippi. "Take up all active [rebel] sympathizers," wrote Halleck, "and either hold them as prisoners or put them beyond our lines. Handle that class without gloves, and take their property for public use.... It is time that they should begin to feel the presence of the war."[27] With or without such orders, Union soldiers in the South were erasing the distinction between military and civilian property belonging to the enemy. A soldier from St. Louis with his regiment in west Tennessee wrote home that "this thing of guarding rebels' property has about 'played out.'" "The iron gauntlet," wrote another officer in the Mississippi Valley, "must be used more than the silken glove to crush this serpent."[28]

Inevitably, bitter protests against this harshness reached Lincoln from purported Southern Unionists. A few months earlier, the president would have rebuked the harshness, as he had rebuked Frémont, for alienating potential Unionist friends in the South. But in July 1862, Lincoln rebuked the protesters instead. He asked one of them sarcastically if they expected him to fight the war "with elder-stalk squirts, charged with rose water?" Did they think he would "surrender the government to save them from losing all"? Lincoln had lost faith in those professed Unionists. "The paralysis – the dead palsy – of the government in this whole struggle is, that this class of men will do nothing for the government ... except [demand] that the government shall not strike its open enemies, lest they be struck by accident! ... This government cannot much longer play a game in which it stakes all, and its enemy stake nothing. Those enemies must understand that they cannot experiment for ten years trying to destroy the government, and if they fail still come back into the Union unhurt." Using one of his favorite metaphors, Lincoln warned Southerners that "broken eggs cannot be mended." The rebels had already cracked the egg of slavery by their own rash

27   *OR*, ser. 1, vol. 12, pt. 2, 50–2 (Pope's orders), vol. 17, pt. 1, 150 (Halleck' s dispatch).
28   A. Fisk Gore to Sister Katie, Aug. 5, 1862, A. Fisk Gore papers, Missouri Historical Society (St. Louis); officer quoted in Catton, *Grant Moves South*, 294.

behavior; the sooner they gave up and ceased the insurrection, "the smaller will be the amount of [eggs] which will be past mending."[29]

Sherman became the foremost military spokesmen for remorseless war and the most effective general in carrying it out. Sherman too had spent part of the winter of 1861–62 in Missouri where he stored up impressions of guerrilla ferocity. Nevertheless, as late as July 1862, as commander of Union occupation forces around Memphis, he complained of some Northern troops who took several mules and horses from farmers. Such "petty thieving and pillaging," he wrote, "does us infinite harm."[30] This scarcely sounds like the Sherman known to history. And indeed, his command problems in western Tennessee soon taught him what his brother-in-law Ewing was also learning about guerrillas and the civilian population that sheltered them across the river in Arkansas and Missouri. Nearly every white man, woman, and child in Sherman's district seemed to hate the Yankees and to abet the bushwhackers who fired into Union supply boats on the river, burned railroad bridges and ripped up the tracks, attacked Union picket outposts, ambushed Northern soldiers unless they moved in large groups, and generally raised hell behind Union lines. Some of the cavalry troopers that rode with Forrest and John Hunt Morgan on devastating raids behind Union lines also functioned in the manner of guerrillas, fading away to their homes and melting into the civilian population after a raid.

This convinced Sherman to take off the gloves. The distinction between enemy civilians and soldiers grew blurred. After their warning, Sherman burned houses and sometimes whole villages in western Tennessee that he suspected of harboring snipers and guerrillas. The Union army, he now said, must operate "on the proper rule that all in the South *are* enemies of all in the North.... The whole country is full of guerrilla bands.... The entire South, man, woman, and child, is against us, armed and determined."[31] This was the philosophy that governed Sherman's subsequent operations, which left smoldering ruins in his track from Vicksburg to Meridian, from Atlanta to the sea, and from the sea to Goldsboro, North Carolina.

When Mississippians protested, Sherman told them that they were lucky to get off so lightly: A commander "may take your house, your fields, your everything, and turn you all out, helpless, to starve. It may be wrong, but that don't alter the case. In war you can't help yourselves, and the only possible remedy is to stop the war.... Our duty is not to build up; it is rather

---

29   Basler et al., eds., *Collected Works of Abraham Lincoln*, 5: 344–6, 350.
30   *OR*, ser. 1, vol. 17, pt. 2, 85–9.
31   Quoted in John Bennett Walters, *Merchant of Terror: General Sherman and Total War* (Indianapolis, Ind., 1973), 57–60

to destroy both the rebel army and whatever of wealth or property it has founded its boasted strength upon."[32] When Confederate Gen. John Bell Hood charged him with barbarism and cruelty for expelling the civilian population from Atlanta, Sherman gave Hood a tongue-lashing. Accusations of barbarity, he said, came with a fine irony from "you who, in the midst of peace and prosperity, have plunged a nation into war … who dared and badgered us to battle, insulted our flag … turned loose your privateers to plunder unarmed ships, expelled Union families by the thousands [and] burned their houses. … Talk thus to the marines, but not to me, who have seen these things." Sherman vowed to "make Georgia howl" in his march from Atlanta to Savannah; afterward, he expressed satisfaction with having done so, estimating the damage to Confederate resources "at $100,000,000; at least $20,000,000 of which has inured to our advantage, and the remainder is simple waste and destruction."[33] And this turned out to be mere child's play compared with what awaited South Carolina.

Sherman was convinced that not only the economic resources but also the will of Southern civilians sustained the Confederate war effort. His campaigns of devastation were intended to break that will as much as to destroy the resources. This is certainly a feature of modern total war; Sherman was a pioneer in the concept of psychological warfare as part of a total war against the whole enemy population. Sherman was well aware of the fear that his soldiers inspired among Southern whites. This terror "was a power," he wrote, "and I intended to utilize it … to humble their pride, to follow them to their inmost recesses, and to make them fear and dread us. … We cannot change the hearts and minds of those people of the South, but we can make war so terrible … [and] make them so sick of war that generations would pass away before they would again appeal to it."[34]

This seemed to work; Sherman's destruction not only deprived Confederate armies of desperately needed supplies but also crippled morale both on the home front and in the army. Numerous soldiers deserted from Confederate armies in response to letters of despair from homes in the wake of Sherman's juggernaut. One Southern soldier wrote after the march through Georgia: "I hev conckludud that the dam fulishness uv tryin to lick shurmin Had better be stopped, we have been gettin nuthin but hell & lots uv it ever since we saw the dam yankys & I am tirde uv it … thair thicker than lise on a hen and a dam site ornraier." After the march through South Carolina, a civilian in that state

32 *OR*, ser. 1, vol. 30, pt. 3, 403.
33 William Tecumseh Sherman, *Memoirs*, 2d rev. ed., 2 vols. (New York, 1886), 2: 119–21, 125–7; *OR*, ser. 1, vol. 44, 13.
34 Sherman, *Memoirs*, 1: 368, 2: 249, 254.

wrote: "All is gloom, despondency, and inactivity. Our army is demoralized and the people panic stricken. To fight longer seems to be madness."[35]

Sheridan carried out a similar policy of scorched earth in the Shenandoah Valley. Interestingly, Sheridan too had spent most of the war's first year in Missouri. There, as well as subsequently in Tennessee and Virginia, he saw the ravages of Confederate guerrillas and responded as Sherman did. If guerrilla operations and Union counterinsurgency activities in Virginia during 1864 were slightly less vicious than in Missouri, it was perhaps only because the proximity of Washington and Richmond and of large field armies imposed some restraint. Nevertheless, plenty of atrocities piled up in John Singleton Mosby's Confederacy just east of the Blue Ridge and in the Shenandoah Valley to the west. In retaliation, and with a purpose similar to Sherman's to destroy the Valley's resources, which helped to supply Lee's army, Sheridan carried out a campaign of devastation that left nothing to sustain Confederate armies or even to enable the Valley's inhabitants to get through the winter. In little more than a week, wrote Sheridan in one of his reports, his army had "destroyed over 2,000 barns filled with wheat, hay, and farming implements; over seventy mills filled with flour and wheat; have driven in front of the army over 4,000 head of stock, and have killed and issued to the troops not less than 3,000 sheep." This was just the beginning, Sheridan promised. By the time he was through, "the Valley, from Winchester up to Staunton, ninety-two miles, will have little in it for man or beast."[36]

Several years later, while serving as an American military observer at German headquarters during the Franco-Prussian War, Sheridan lectured his hosts on the correct way to wage war. The "proper strategy," said Sheridan, consisted first of "inflicting as telling blows as possible on the enemy's army, and then in causing the inhabitants so much suffering that they must long for peace, and force the government to demand it. The people must be left nothing but their eyes to weep with over the war."[37]

Abraham Lincoln is famed for his compassion; he issued many pardons and commuted many sentences of execution; the concluding passage of his second inaugural address, beginning "with malice toward none; with charity for all," is one of his most familiar utterances. Lincoln regretted the devastation and suffering caused by the army's scorched-earth policy in the South. Yet he had warned Southerners in 1862 that the longer they fought, the more eggs would be broken. He would have agreed with Sherman's

35 Quotations in E. Merton Coulter, *The Confederate States of America* (Baton Rouge, La., 1950), 549–50, and John G. Barrett, *Sherman's March Through the Carolinas* (Chapel Hill, N.C., 1956), 96.
36 *OR*, ser. 1, vol. 43, pt. 1, 30–1.
37 Michael Howard, *The Franco-Prussian War* (New York, 1989), 380.

words to a Southerner: "You brought all this on yourselves." In 1864, after the march to the sea, Lincoln officially conveyed to Sherman's army the "grateful acknowledgments" of the nation; to Sheridan he offered the "thanks of the nation, and my own personal admiration, for [your] operations in the Shenandoah Valley." And while the words in the second inaugural address about malice toward none and charity for all promised a generous peace, the victory that must precede this peace could be achieved only by hard war – indeed, by total war. Listen to *these* words from the second inaugural address:

American Slavery is one of those offenses which, in the providence of God … He now wills to remove [through] this terrible war, as the woe due to those by whom the offence came. … Fondly do we hope – fervently do we pray – that this mighty scourge of war may speedily pass away. Yet if God wills that it continue, until all the wealth piled by the bond-man's two hundred and fifty years of unrequited toil shall be sunk, and until every drop of blood drawn with the lash, shall be paid by another drawn with the sword, as was said three thousand years ago, so still it must be said "the judgments of the Lord, are true and righteous altogether."[38]

The kind of conflict that the Civil War had become merits the label of *total war*. To be sure, Union soldiers did not set out to kill Southern civilians. Sherman's bummers destroyed property; Allied bombers in World War II destroyed hundreds of thousands of lives as well. But the strategic purpose of both were the same: to eliminate the resources and break the will of the people to sustain war. White people in large parts of the Confederacy were indeed left with "nothing but their eyes to weep with." This was not pretty; it was not glorious; it did not conform to the image of war held by most Americans in 1861 of flags waving, bands playing, and people cheering on a spring afternoon. But as Sherman himself put it in a speech fifteen years after the Civil War, the notion that war is glorious was nothing but moonshine. "When … you come down to the practical realities, boys," said Sherman, "war is all hell."[39]

---

38 Basler et al., eds., *Collected Words of Abraham Lincoln*, 8: 8, 73–4, 182, 333.
39 Quoted in James Reston Jr., *Sherman's March and Vietnam* (New York, 1984), xi.

15

Remarks on the Preconditions to Waging War in Prussia-Germany, 1866–71

WILHELM DEIST

I

The war between Austria and Prussia in June and July 1866 and the Franco-Prussian War of 1870–71 have already been examined and recounted hundreds of times with respect to military planning, the specifics of the operational and tactical course of the war, and their concomitant military problems.[1] In the 120 to 125 years since the events took place, the battles of Königgrätz, Weissenburg and Wörth, Vionville/Mars-La-Tours and Gravelotte/St. Privat, as well as the victory of the German army at Sedan and the successful sieges of Metz and Paris have been described in detail and from differing perspectives by participants on both sides, by officers, and by historians. Hence, the historian today can scarcely expect to stake out new ground in this area.[2] The same is also true for those areas that still are being treated more marginally, such as the supply and medical systems as well as the significance of railroads for operational activities and for supplying the armies.[3] Consonant with the times, the literature in recent decades in Germany has been almost exclusively concerned with the tensions between political and military thinking.[4] Therefore, in the aforementioned areas, it

---

1   Here, I will forgo giving an exhaustive catalog of recent literature and refer instead to the bibliographical information contained in the *Handbuch zur deutschen Militärgeschichte, 1648–1939* (Munich, 1979), 5:620–3.
2   See the study of Stéphane Audoin-Rouzeau, *1870: La France dans la guerre* (Paris, 1989).
3   See, esp., *Der Sanitätsdienst bei den Deutschen Heeren im Krieg gegen Frankreich, 1870–71* (Berlin, 1884–91), vols. 1–8; Hermann Budde, *Die französischen Eisenbahnen im deutschen Kriegsbetriebe, 1870–71* (Berlin, 1904); Gustaf Lehmann, *Die Mobilmachung von 1870–71* (Berlin, 1905); *Heeresverpflegung: Studien zur Kriegsgeschichte und Taktik,* ed. Great General Staff (Berlin, 1905), vol. 6; Martin L. Van Creveld, *Supplying War: Logistics from Wallenstein to Patton* (Cambridge, 1977).
4   See, esp., Eberhard Kolb, ed., *Europa vor dem Krieg von 1870: Mächtekonstellation. Konfliktfelder, Kriegsausbruch* (Munich, 1987); Eberhard Kolb, *Der Weg aus dem Krieg: Bismarcks Politik im Krieg und die Friedensanbahnung, 1870–71* (Munich, 1989); as well as the classic study by Michael Howard, *The Franco-Prussian War: The German Invasion of France, 1870–1871,* 4th ed. (London, 1968), and the two collections: *Entscheidung 1866: Der Krieg zwischen Österreich und Preussen,* published by the Militärgeschichtliches Forschungsamt and edited by Wolfgang von Groote and Ursula von

311

might be useful to pay greater attention to the literature from the years prior to World War I, a literature rich in factual presentation for the issues and topics in question.

This historiographic situation encourages one to divert primary focus away from the events and their course and toward certain factors regarding the conduct of war that lent these two conflicts their peculiar character. Even the reports and accounts of contemporaries emphasize the large size of the opposing armies, the surprisingly rapid deployment – at least of the Prussian-German armies – and the increased destructive power of the weaponry. With respect to the Prussian army, it will be important to understand and interpret the structural changes underlying these phenomena.

There are three areas on which the following observations concentrate. First, I look at how universal conscription based on the Prussian military reform was administered, and I examine, above all, the military consequences of this organizational system. Second, I discuss the use of new technical aids and developments and their consequences for the conduct of the war. Here, attention must be directed first and foremost to the qualitative leap in the mobility of the armies through utilization of the railroads and also to the consequences of new, technically improved weapons development. Finally, I discuss whether German conduct of the war actually evolved from cabinet war (1866) to war between whole peoples (*Volkskrieg*), or whether it evolved instead more in the direction of total war. Clarification of conceptual issues also appears necessary and helpful, even with respect, for example, to World War I. Only then is it possible to make assertions about which stage of development had been reached by the end of the Franco-Prussian War.

II

Universal conscription was initially introduced in Prussia on February 9, 1813, as an emergency measure, through the "Directive on Suspending Prior Exemptions from *Kanton* [district] Obligations for the Duration of the War."[5] With the "Law on the Obligation to Perform Military Service" of September 3, 1814, the regulations were laid down that determined the structure of the Prussian army for decades to come.[6] This stipulated that every (male) Prussian between the ages of twenty and fifty was fundamentally obligated to perform military service "for the defense of the Fatherland." If drafted, he first served

---

Gersdorff (Stuttgart, 1966); and *Entscheidung 1870: Der Deutsch-Französische Krieg*, published by the Militärgeschichtliches Forschungsamt and edited by Wolfgang von Groote and Ursula von Gersdorff (Stuttgart, 1970).

5   Ernst R. Huber, ed., *Dokumente zur deutschen Verfassungsgeschichte*, 8 vols. (Stuttgart, 1961), 1:48–9.
6   Ibid., 53ff.

for a period of three years, after which he belonged to the reserves of the standing army for two additional years; then he was turned over to the first and second levy of the *Landwehr* (militia) between the ages of twenty-six and thirty-nine, and finally, between forty and fifty, he rounded out his military service in the *Landsturm* (home reserves). Quite apart from political opposition and conflicts, this well-ordered system of military obligation was never realized to its fullest extent, if only as a result of financial considerations. Generally speaking, it can be observed that political argumentation based on the principle of universal conscription is distinctly more rigorous than the practical implementation thereof, even today. In this regard, the idea that universal conscription implies a democratization of the armed forces played a role then and continues to do so at the present time. Yet historical development refutes this myth; universal conscription is nothing more than one among many possible instruments available to a state to organize national defense. And its practical implementation is exclusively determined by the respective political forces within the state and the society.

In practice, implementation in Prussia was characterized by the fact that as the population increased, the percentage of men bearing arms sank from 1.25 percent in 1816 to 0.79 percent in 1850, and that the actual peacetime strength of the army, and with it the annual quota of recruits, scarcely changed over three decades. The strength of the army fluctuated between 120,000 and 130,000; the annual contingent of recruits was about 30,000 men.[7] Determination of who was to be drafted from the group of those found to be fit took place by lottery or according to the date of birth, with those born in December having the best chances of not being drafted.[8]

Minister of War Albrecht von Roon's military reform from 1859 onward has been termed the "Prussian revolution" by the military historian Michael Geyer.[9] Apart from the well-known political implications, it aimed at greater exploitation of the conscription potential and – it should be emphasized – at imposing unlimited power of organization and authority by the military leadership and its monarchical head over the armed forces as a whole. Universal conscription in the framework of the standing army thus effected an "equality of the dominated and dependent" manpower resources of the nation.[10]

7 With respect to the figures, see Manfred Messerschmidt, "Die politische Geschichte der preussisch-deutschen Armee," in Messerschmidt, ed., *Handbuch zur deutschen Militärgeschichte, 1648–1939*; *Militärgeschichte im 19. Jahrhundert: 1814–1890* (Munich, 1975), 2(IV/1):61; Ernst Engel, "Kritische Beiträge zur vergleichenden Finanzstatistik der Gross- und Mittelstaaten Europas, mit besonderer Berücksichtigung ihrer Militärbudgets," *Zeitschrift des Königlich Preussischen Statistischen Bureaus* 2 (1862): 160.
8 Cf. Messerschmidt, *Die politische Geschichte*, 62.
9 Michael Geyer, *Deutsche Rüstungspolitik, 1860–1980* (Frankfurt/Main, 1984), 25.
10 Ibid., 29.

The annual quota of new soldiers was raised to more than 60,000 men, with the result that the army's actual peacetime strength rose to about 212,000 men.[11] The percentage of men bearing arms, however, still did not reach the figure for the year 1816 (1861 = 1.12 percent); the exploitation of conscription potential was temporarily enhanced by the growing numbers in the pertinent annual age cohorts. After all, out of a pool of 69,933 fit for service in 1861, 59,431 were actually drafted. Every year from 1860 to 1868, between 59,000 and 93,000 recruits were called up.[12] More important, however, was the fact that with the breakup of the "old style" *Landwehr*, the standing army now had five more age groups of reservists at its disposal, and that in case of war, the remaining eleven age groups of the *Landwehr* were to be used in rear areas and forts, and for garrison duty. An officer trained and formed by his service in the "line" took the place of the original *Landwehr* officer. The subsequent changes, comprising primarily a reduction in the duration of compulsory military service, did not alter the political and military aims of this system. It strengthened significantly the military might of Prussia in peace and in war with the help of universal conscription and thus at the same time assured the extraconstitutional command authority of the crown and the military leadership to a not precisely measurable but very real preponderance within the domestic political power structure.

This newly formed army withstood its first real probationary test in the war against Austria in 1866. Its opponent, the Austrian army, was recruited from conscripts who had to complete an eight-year period of service, followed by two years in the reserves. In 1866, this army of men who had already served several years found itself involved in war on two fronts; but it was still in a position to confront the Prussian enemy in Bohemia with a force of about 240,000 men.[13] Through mobilization, the Prussian leadership had more than 440,000 men available. Four armies with a strength of about 310,000 soldiers launched the offensive against Austria and its allies in the German Confederation (*Deutscher Bund*).[14] The course of the war, the operational development up to the decisive battle at Sadowa on July 3, 1866, has often been recounted and is not a subject of debate here. Only one detail is of interest in this context. Although no sufficiently reliable information is available about the exact number of soldiers taking part in the decisive battle, it does

11   Cf. Messerschmidt, *Die politische Geschichte*, 183ff.
12   See *Zeitschrift des Königlich Preussischen Statistischen Bureaus*, 9: (1869), 254; (1862): 69513/62517; (1863): 68718/62281; (1864): 70782/65940; (1865): 65133/59217; (1866): 103290/93616; (1867): 90232/81920; (1868): 97888/83371.
13   Cf. Heinrich von Sybel, *Die Begründung des Deutschen Reiches durch Wilhelm I.* (Leipzig, 1889), 5:9ff.
14   See *Zeitschrift des Königlich Preussischen Statistischen Bureaus* 7 (1867): 158; Sybel, *Die Begründung*, 24.

seem quite clear that the Prussian army maintained numerical superiority on this battlefield. General Field Marshal Helmuth von Moltke, chief of the General Staff, was thus not only successful in uniting the Prussian armies at the right point in time on the intended terrain but also in confronting the enemy with superior numbers. Prussia's victory is commonly ascribed to Moltke's genius and to the planning achievements of the Prussian General Staff, as well as to the technical superiority of the Prussian percussion pin rifle (*Zündnadelgewehr*) and the resulting military consequences. A further element should not, however, be overlooked, namely, the organized availability to the military leadership of fit conscripts achieved by the reform of the army. The implementation of universal conscription within the framework of the standing army after 1860 contributed significantly to Prussia's overwhelming military success. Moreover, this instrument of the military executive had to prove itself under what initially were adverse conditions: Public opinion in Prussia was quite divided with respect to a possible war with the Austrian monarchy.[15] Nonetheless, the uncertainty that this provoked remained without perceptible influence on the attitude of those subject to conscription and on the reservists. The discipline shaped by the military institution (*Anstalt*–Geyer's term) and secured by the three-year active duty requirement proved to be an effective and indispensable instrument in both the political as well as military spheres.

The fundamental political importance of army reform for the Prussian state can also be inferred from the debates in the French parliament on restructuring the French army along the lines of the Prussian model. This project foundered on the vehement protests of precisely those bourgeois and peasant groups that had hitherto supported the Empire.[16] In Prussia, in contrast, Bismarck finally obtained the agreement of the Prussian *Landtag* (state parliament) for the Indemnity Act of September 1866 as a result of military success.

The military importance of the reform of the army was demonstrated to its fullest in the war against France in 1870–71. Under the leadership of Prussia, the North German Confederation, with a population of about twenty-nine million, mobilized some 880,000 men on the basis of the Prussian military law, and in August 1870 assembled a field army of about 560,000 on the border to France, whose movable army assembled with about 300,000

---

15 Sybel, *Die Begründung des Deutschen Reiches*, 7:357–69; *Handbuch der europäischen Geschichte*, ed. Theodor Schieder (Stuttgart, 1981), 5:567ff.
16 Ibid., 313.

men from a population of some thirty-seven million.[17] This numerical relationship reflects the Germans' greater and more consistent exploitation of the potential pool of conscripts for a period of ten years. The military result of the army reform becomes even clearer when we remember that in the spring of 1870, the North German Confederation had in addition to the standing army – with a strength of 12,924 officers and 299,704 regulars – also the reservist age groups with 1,647 officers and 315,283 men, as well as the *Landwehr* with 4,495 officers and 415,860 men.[18] Thus, from these three categories, the military leadership had at its disposal a total of 19,066 officers and 1,030,845 men. The system offered the added advantage that the formations of the movable field army could be replenished in graduated phases with reservists and members of the *Landwehr*. Thus, about 40 or 50 percent of the army corps consisted of reservists when it marched to the front.[19] On the one hand, it was really quite typical of the professional, rational organization of this army that the proportion of volunteers in the group of formations headed to the front was exceptionally low. On the other hand, it speaks for the enthusiasm for war and the acceptance of the military institutions that, apart from regional exceptions and those owing to seasonal factors, the rate of reservists and *Landwehr* men who did not respond when called up was very low.[20]

A considerable role, both in military and political respects, was played by the group of one-year volunteers. This special arrangement, which had existed since the "Law on the Obligation to Perform Military Service" of 1814 and which was designed to reconcile the educated and property-owning bourgeoisie to universal conscription,[21] gained particular importance for the military leadership under the changed and more hostile conditions of the conflict over the army in the 1860s. In the years 1862–68, there were between 15,000 and 23,000 in each age cohort who had obtained the right to serve as one-year volunteers, of which only a tenth met their military obligation in this way. The figures of the one-year volunteers on active duty decreased between 1863 and 1865 compared with the level attained in 1862, and it was not until 1867 that they rapidly increased; in 1868, there were about 4,800 one-year volunteers serving in the army, and in the Franco-Prussian War,

17 For the actual figures, see *Handbuch der europäischen Geschichte*, 5:302; Lehmann, *Die Mobilmachung*, 154; Hermann Rahne, *Mobilmachung: Militärische Mobilmachungsplanung und - technik in Preussen und im Deutschen Reich von der Mitte des 19. Jahrhunderts bis zum Zweiten Weltkrieg* (Berlin, 1983), 61ff; V. Regling, "Grundzüge der militärischen Kriegführung zur Zeit des Absolutismus und im 19. Jahrhundert," *Handbuch zur deutschen Militärgeschichte, 1648–1939* (Munich, 1979), 5:409.
18 Lehmann, *Die Mobilmachung*, 217, 227.
19 Ibid., 287.
20 Ibid., 47, 280; Rahne, *Mobilmachung*, 62.
21 Messerschmidt, *Die politische Geschichte*, 87–8.

some 9,000 members of this group participated.[22] In political respects, this development is no doubt an indication of increasing acceptance of the reformed army in bourgeois circles since 1866–67. For the military leadership, the politically desired result combined with military necessity. The active officer corps was not in a position to lead the gigantic wartime army at all levels. Among other things, attempts were made to accomplish the necessary supplementation of the officer corps from the group of one-year volunteers. This necessity is also expressed in the increasing numbers of one-year volunteers. Generally, more than 40 percent of this group completed their one-year service qualified to become officers, and about 15 percent qualified as noncommissioned officers.[23]

It was on the basis of this differentiated organization of the conscription potential, which sought to combine quantity and quality, that the mobilization of the wartime army and the assembling of the field army took place in 1870. An analysis of the course of the campaign to the battle of Sedan (September 1–2, 1870) shows as well that the victories of the Prussian-German army were not determined by numerical superiority, which did obtain in the majority of cases, but that the army was also able to defeat a numerically superior enemy.[24]

Troops on the offensive often sustained heavy casualties. In the battle at Gravelotte/St. Privat (August 18, 1870), in which 109,000 men were involved on the German side, for example, the number of German casualties (dead and wounded) amounted to 20,173 – almost a fifth of the combat strength. The military institution had also made provision for this eventuality: "On the battlefield," it was said, there were twenty medical detachments and twenty-four military field hospitals with a total of 260 "budgeted" physicians on hand to care for the wounded. Although in this war private volunteer charitable activities still played a role – a Herr von Hoenika even made two military hospital trains available[26] – here, too, the state via the military institution took matters into its own hands. The military's organizational talents extended into areas that hitherto had been considered marginal. The medical system, organized and administered along military lines, mastered the task assigned to it, that is, to provide for maintaining the combat strength of the army by medical means, with great skill and admirable success. For instance, military doctors were successful in drastically reducing the number of deaths from

22 With respect to the figures, see *Zeitschrift des Königlich Preussischen Statistischen Bureaus* 9 (1869): 249–57; see also Lehmann, *Die Mobilmachung*, 281ff.
23 *Zeitschrift des Königlich Preussischen Statistischen Bureaus* 9 (1869): 255.
24 *Kriegsgeschichtliche Einzelschriften*, ed. Grosser Generalstab, no. 12 (Berlin, 1889), 836ff.
25 Ibid., 841; *Der Sanitätsdienst*, 1:219.
26 Ibid., 269.

diseases and epidemics compared with previous campaigns. Medical care of the soldiers was improved considerably and made easier by the deployment of a total of thirty-six military hospital trains that could accommodate some 40,000 wounded and sick men.[27]

Military planners faced greater problems in replacing fallen or wounded military personnel and in strengthening the field army as operations progressed, especially for the purpose of securing conquered territory. The demands placed on the military institution demonstrated its limits, since the potential pool of conscripts that had been organized and trained was clearly being exhausted. By January 31, 1871, more than 120,000 men had been added as replacements. Essentially, this involved parts of the recruitment group from 1870, as well as reservists and militiamen from the *Landwehr*.[28] At the beginning of February 1871, there were approximately 32,500 noncommissioned officers and men in the reserves, 68,000 so-called replacement reservists, and 23,000 recruits still available in the territory of the North German Confederation. By the beginning of May, an additional 25,000 of these men were put at the disposal of the field army.[29] Even then there still remained a reserve of more than 90,000 men, although these essentially involved recruits still undergoing training or age groups that were older and poorly trained. If one considers that in the area of the North German Confederation a total of 1,226,218 men served as officers, doctors, and enlisted men in the war of 1870–71,[30] then a replacement contingent of more than 90,000 men might well be deemed sufficient, at least in terms of quantity. How then are we to interpret the well-known conflict between Roon and Moltke on this issue?

It was not solely the expanded activity of the franc-tireurs after the battle of Sedan that presented growing difficulties for Roon and the Prussian Ministry of War. Moltke's increasingly radical demands were, of course, occasioned by the growing threat to the rear area, particularly to the railroad lines, in the autumn and winter of 1870, as well as by the unexpectedly successful efforts of the French leader Léon Gambetta in forming new armies. Thus, for example, on December 8, while referring to France's ability "to create countless troop units out of nothing," Moltke demanded the immediate dispatch of fifty-seven *Landwehr* battalions to France, only to raise this demand a few days later on December 14 to one hundred battalions "as a preliminary minimum."[31] Theoretically, these forces were certainly

27 Ibid., appendix 81; see also *Der Sanitätsdienst* (Berlin, 1886), 2: table 167.
28 Lehmann, *Die Mobilmachung*, 364–5.
29 Ibid., 361ff.
30 *Der Sanitätsdienst*, 2: vi.
31 Lehmann, *Die Mobilmachung*, 103, 105.

available, but practically, they were tied up with various tasks in the interior. In particular, the provisioning and guarding of the relatively large number of prisoners of war caused problems for the army. Roon's proposal to utilize smaller French forts as prisoner of war camps was rejected. Thus, in November, there were some 260,000 men to care for and to guard in numerous camps in the territory of the North German Confederation. This number grew to about 320,000 men by mid-February 1871.[32] As has already been suggested, there was no lack of soldiers in the interior for these and other tasks, especially since the men of the *Landsturm* (conscripts aged seventeen to forty-two who had not served) were still available as the last reserves under special circumstances. What was lacking was commissioned and noncommissioned officers. On November 24, 1870, the War Ministry stated that in the replacement troop units approximately a fourth of the officer positions could not be filled and that there were "no dispensable officers available on reserve status, and only a very small number of noncommissioned officers."[33] Not a "nation in arms" but the availability of potential conscripts for the political and military leadership had been the aim of Roon's army reform; and this could only be achieved with a correspondingly trained officer corps. It was therefore only logical that the minister of war was not willing to assent to any improvisations in this field. In Roon's system of army reform, the implementation of general conscription was tied to the framework of the standing army. The limits of the system had been reached when the shortage of officers and noncommissioned officers became apparent. Nevertheless, Roon and the War Ministry succeeded in accommodating the demands of the general staff, albeit with clear reductions. Thus, in the end, 129 of the 162 Prussian *Landwehr* battalions were deployed in the French theater of war, 16 other field battalions were made available, and only 17 were not mobilized.[34] Still, in spite of this great organizational achievement, Roon was aware that the limits of the system had been reached and should not be transgressed. Hence, responding to another urgent demand from Moltke to transfer *Landwehr* battalions to the Paris front, he replied

Terribly sorry! Not before the garrison troops have attained their full complement and consolidation. After the fall of Paris, I think it would be better to send the *Landwehr* home, rather than bring them in. Conducting a war that leads us to the foothills of the Pyrenees without overexerting our strength is a task that will take years.[35]

32   Ibid., 137ff.
33   Ibid., 101; see also Rahne, *Mobilmachung*, 66.
34   Lehmann, *Die Mobilmachung*, 108.
35   Ibid., Feb. 11, 1871.

Neither Roon nor Moltke was prepared to abandon the framework of the standing army, which guaranteed that the manpower resources of the nation made available by universal conscription were used according to orders of the Prussian king, who possessed extra-constitutional command authority, and structure of his officer corps. With this, Roon and Moltke, reinforced in their views by the fate of Gambetta's armies, did not move in the direction of a people's war but instead experienced the first steps on the path to total war.

III

The military results of a goal-oriented organization of manpower resources comprised one factor that characterized Prussia-Germany's conduct of the wars of 1866 and 1870–71. Another factor was the degree to which contemporary technical developments were utilized in conducting these wars. Two such developments were central: the railroads, by means of which the army's mobility was enormously increased, and the guns, the perfecting of which also greatly boosted the firepower of the army. Both developments had far-reaching consequences, some of which can already be pointed out in the Wars of Unification.

In the three decades between 1850 and 1881, the length of the railway network in the territory of the North German Confederation expanded from 6,470 to 34,305 km. In 1861, Prussia had a railway network of 7,353 km, which, a mere ten years later, comprised 12,672 km, more than half of which was under the auspices of private enterprise.[36] In view of such figures and also in light of the fact that other European armies had already gathered experience regarding the possibilities of military rail transportation, it would have been highly unusual had the Prussian army leadership not concerned themselves with this issue. The question is rather how they integrated this new means of transportation into their planning.

The railroad offered the possibility of transporting large masses of troops over long distances in a relatively short period of time. Mobilizing and deploying the army were therefore the phases of future warfare in which the utilization of the railroad promised the greatest advantages. In the war against Austria in 1866, in which mobilization and deployment were very much subordinate to Bismarck's political calculations, these advantages did not bear as much fruit as they did in the initial phase of the Franco-Prussian War, in which there was at least a chance for the experience of 1866 to be taken into account.

---

36 *Jahrbuch für die Amtliche Statistik des preussischen Staates* 5 (1883): 330–1

Moltke's decisions in the spirit of the motto "March separately, attack together," which finally culminated in the battle of Sadowa (July 3, 1866), have been analyzed and recounted repeatedly. What has often been overlooked, however, is that the plan of operations was determined to a great degree by the actual situation of the railroads in the deployment zone. The five existing railway lines with their unloading points, to no small degree, predetermined the further course of events.

The launching of the war against France in July 1870 was determined in its military course by how rapidly the Prussian-German side could mobilize and deploy troops, and rigorous planning and railroad efficiency proved decisive.[37] On July 15, 1870, the decision to mobilize the army of the North German Confederation was made, and July 16 was designated the first day of mobilization. In contrast to 1866, the transports that were to deploy the troops began as soon as marching readiness had been achieved by the units and did not await the completion of mobilization. The transports began on July 24; by August 3, the greatest part of the field army had already been transported into the assembly area; and by August 12, the transport movements on the whole had been completed.

The transport of 18,134 officers, 531,237 men, 150,755 horses, and 15,585 vehicles within this three-week period was possible solely as a result of detailed planning. The transports took place on a total of six rail lines, only two of which had double tracks and could therefore carry eighteen transport trains a day, whereas the four single-track stretches handled twelve trains per day. The years of prior planning covered not only precautions in terms of construction at the loading and unloading rail stations and the time required for loading and unloading but also for provisioning troops during the transport, and especially the disposition of rolling stock and the creation of schedules. The organization of this task was managed by rail line commissions, in which military officers and railroad officials worked together on each transport line. A ministry official and an officer from the Great General Staff, Major von Brandenstein, were responsible for the entire operation. The planning, worked out in peacetime, continually reexamined, and frequently modified in accordance with operational arrangements, could be put into effect only by implementing the so-called military schedule for the selected rail lines as soon as mobilization was announced. This meant excluding all other traffic on these particular rail lines. In accordance with the binding plan, the rail line commissions alone had unrestricted authority over the lines and over the rolling stock. Authority over this modern means of transportation,

---

37   See Lehmann, *Die Mobilmachung*, 57ff, 295ff, esp. 312–13.

the railroad, had been recognized as decisive for campaigns, and the military executive had appropriated this instrument in an exemplary manner for mobilizing and assembling troops; this was all the more remarkable in that the railways were largely privately owned.

But the emphasis on mobilization and on the assembling of troops to serve the conduct of operations resulted in the organization of campaign logistics being neglected. In this regard, the same problems arose as in the Austrian campaign: Because absolute priority was given to the deployment transports of combat troops, the logistically essential supply columns did not reach their destinations until relatively late, with the result that the supply trains could not be unloaded quickly enough. The ensuing slowdown eventually reached gigantic proportions. The historian Martin L. Van Creveld gives as an example the bottleneck with the 2d Army on September 5, 1870, which immobilized 2,322 freight cars with 16,830 tons of supply goods on five rail lines.[38] Utilization of the French railways was also made difficult because, although the German leadership had blockaded a whole series of forts, it had not placed any particular emphasis on capturing them. Hence, important railway lines remained blocked. For example, Mezières did not fall until January 2, 1871, and therefore the important rail line Metz-Rheims-Paris was not available until then.[39] Defense of the railroad lines from destruction by the franc-tireurs presented additional problems. Not until December 1870 was the situation finally sorted out, thus allowing the railroad gradually to assume its role as an indispensable instrument of logistics as well.

A survey of how the modern means of transportation of the railroad was utilized in the German Wars of Unification leads to a contradictory result: The Prussian military leaders had developed organizational concepts and structures for optimal utilization of the railways during the opening phases of the war that permitted and assured them unlimited powers. As a result, operational planning for the launching of the war could be calculated. Ironically, this ability to control the resources of traffic and transportation nearly became a liability when the actual fighting began. A few of the specific reasons have already been cited. What was decisive was the attitude of military leaders who regarded the war as essentially a series of operational events. To be sure, the consequences of such an attitude were serious. Supplies for the troops could initially be secured to some degree only through extensive requisitioning. Repeated requisitions and high contributions, however, without doubt

38 On all of this, see Creveld, *Supplying*, 89–108; Wolfgang Petter, "Die Logistik des Deutschen Heeres im deutschfranzösischen Krieg von 1870–71," in Militärgeschichtliches Forschungsamt, ed., *Vorträge zur Militärgeschichte* (Herford, 1986), 7:109–33; *Heeresverpflegung*, 134ff.

39 See Budde, *Die französischen Eisenbahnen*, 39.

rather heightened than hindered the preparedness of the French civilian population to resist. The spiral of violence began to turn. The French "people's war"–irrespective of how its significance is judged[40]–is to no small extent the result of the failure of the Prussian military leadership to pay sufficient attention to logistics. The necessary supply goods did exist but were unavailable owing to imperfect planning.

In addition to the railways, technical developments in the field of firearms had a decisive impact on the forms and consequences of warfare. The story of the Prussian percussion pin rifle and its triumph over the Austrian front-end loader in the war of 1866 is as well-known as the dispute over Krupp's cast steel cannon, which formed the basis of the superiority of the Prussian artillery in the war against France. In both cases, the outcome was shaped by technical intelligence and by a series of rather accidental decisions, namely, four decades of developing the percussion pin rifle and Prince Wilhelm's order for 300 Krupp cannons, respectively. The military's armaments policy was, in any case, not goal-oriented; neither did it encompass the organization of industrial resources.[41] Instead, one has the impression that it was more important to the military leadership–seen as the various commissions–to demonstrate its absolute control over the process of arming the troops rather than to exploit the possibilities of modern technologies and the means of industrial production. To be sure, the first stage of development, which would finally permit this relationship to be turned around, was reached in the wars of 1866 and 1870–71. The triumph of the percussion pin rifle was only short-lived, however, before the chassepot rifle and the repeating rifle determined further developments. In short, the arms race had begun, and even at this point in time it was doubtful whether the military leadership possessed or could develop the ability to retain control over it.

IV

When characterizing the wars of 1866 and 1870–71, historians frequently stress those features that distinguish these two conflicts from each other. Whereas the war of 1866 was at first conducted without the support of public opinion, as previously mentioned, the war against France was extraordinarily popular from the outset and was understood as a national war, that is, a war

---

40   See, esp., the study by Audoin-Rouzeau, *1870*, 175ff, 261ff; and the dissertation by Bernhard Winterhalter, "Die Behandlung der französischen Zivilbevölkerung durch die deutschen Truppen im Kriege 1870–71, " Ph.D. diss., University of Freiburg, 1952.

41   Cf. Messerschmidt, *Die politische Geschichte*, 351–9; Dennis E. Showalter, *Railroads and Rifles: Soldiers, Technology, and the Unification of Germany* (Hamden, 1975); as well as Georg Ortenburg, *Waffe und Waffengebrauch im Zeitalter der Einigungskriege* (Koblenz, 1990).

between nations. From this perspective, the war against Austria is seen as a classic cabinet war, one that remained firmly within the control of the political and military leadership. The Franco-Prussian War, in contrast, is seen as having taken a course after Sedan that included elements of an industrialized *Volkskrieg*, as already cruelly manifested in the American Civil War of 1860–65.[42]

It should be emphasized, however, that the essential elements of German warfare scarcely changed from the beginning of each war to its armistice, even though in reaction to the appearance of the franc-tireurs, in the case of 1870–71, the extent of violent reprisals indeed expanded. Just as before, the conduct of the war still remained under the exclusive control of the military leadership, and its instrument of war remained the conscript army, operating according to the principles of command and obedience. Without doubt, the *guerre à outrance* posed extraordinary problems for German military leaders, but they reacted with the exploitation of all the available resources subject to their control; their action continued to be in accordance with their plan and avoided improvisation whenever possible. It is true that Gambetta's formation of new armies won the respect of the Prussian military, yet his actions embodied a principle that contradicted their own basic ideas. For the Prussian military, the monopoly of power lay solely in the hands of the army, which exclusively commanded its organization and disposition. A people's war on the German side would first have had to be waged against the Prussian military.

In making resources available and appropriating them to a greater extent, this pointed the way to total war, which then became reality on the German side in World War I under the leadership of the Supreme Army Command. In the war of 1870–71, mobilization of manpower resources remained limited, and one cannot speak of a general mobilization of materiel resources. On the Prussian-German side, it is difficult to find recognizable forms of an industrialized *Volkskrieg*.

This conclusion seems to contradict some of the results of the extensive research on the thinking and mentalité of the dominant military figure of the

---

42 See Stig Förster's essays: "Optionen der Kriegführung im Zeitalter des 'Volkskrieges': Zu Helmuth von Moltkes militärisch-politischen Überlegungen nach den Erfahrungen der Einigungskriege," in Detlef Bald, ed., *Militärische Verantwortung in Staat und Gesellschaft* (Koblenz, 1986), 83–107; "Facing 'People's War:' The Elder Moltke and Germany's Military Options after 1871," *Journal of Strategic Studies* 10 (1987): 209–30; "General-Feldmarschall Helmuth von Moltke und die kriegsgeschichtlichen Folgen des deutsch-französischen Krieges," in Philippe Levillain and Rainer Riemenschneider, eds., *La guerre de 1870–71 et ses conséquences* (Bonn, 1990), 86–96; and, in particular, "Helmuth von Moltke und das Problem des industrialisierten Volkskrieges im 19. Jahrhundert," in Roland G. Foerster, ed., *Generalfeldmarschall von Moltke: Bedeutung und Wirkung*, Beiträge zur Militärgeschichte (Munich, 1991), 33: 103–15.

Prussian-German army, General von Moltke.[43] Persuasive evidence has been uncovered that, since the beginning of the 1850s, Moltke repeatedly asserted the view that the "German question" could only be resolved by war; and since the end of the 1850s, he had maintained the idea that the decisive battle over the future European order would have to be fought with France. For him, France was the "hereditary enemy" itself. To what extent did this fundamental political and ideological conviction influence his actions as the chief of the general staff? It has been pointed out that the "destruction" of the enemy, which Moltke declared to be the aim of every campaign, was equivalent to rendering the hostile armed forces incapable of fighting, and this was consonant with the goal of swiftly ending the war and in this respect was certainly within the framework of a cabinet war. When in the wake of Sedan the French began to wage what looked like *Volkskrieg*, Moltke, who had anticipated the war against France and who had regarded it as a necessity, at first reacted hesitantly. He responded with traditional measures, that is, destruction of the newly formed armies and reinforcement of the field army by *Landwehr* battalions. He abhorred the *Volkskrieg* and remained the king's chief of general staff, who through military reform had placed the army under his individual direct control. In his military conduct, Moltke did not follow political principles; rather, he calculated as precisely as possible, using the concrete given realities, and repeatedly forced his imagination to be constrained by reason—that is what made him great. Moltke is indeed the ideal representative of the Prussian-German military state, a state in which the conduct of war remained the exclusive prerogative of the military. It was a state that endeavored as well to place the resources that would be needed to conduct war under the sole control of the military. That was the German path to total war.

---

43   See the contribution in this volume by Stig Förster as well as the standard works by Rudolf Stadelmann, *Moltke und der Staat* (Krefeld, 1950) and Eberhard Kessel, *Moltke* (Stuttgart, 1957).

PART FOUR

The Home Front

16

Loyalty and Dissent:
The Home Front in the American Civil War

JÖRG NAGLER

I

In the turbulent and challenging year of 1863, when morale was low and disillusionment high in the North, an anonymous pamphlet writer expressed for many Americans, both in and out of uniform, a deeply rooted concern about the meaning of the paramount social, political, and military conflict facing the nation.

Loyalty. What is it? To whom or what due? These are questions vital to the American people, and if properly understood, may yet exercise a wholesome influence on the momentous issues of the day.[1]

This pamphlet writer realized that the meaning of loyalty was central to the conflict, and this held true for both the North and South. In every modern war, the inclusion of the civilian population is essential for the war effort, and loyalty becomes the psychological touchstone on which to base national cohesiveness and the ability to motivate civilians to become soldiers, to leave their families, homes, friends, and communities, and to risk the ultimate sacrifice—death—for a cause, a nation, or both combined. Without the home front, loyal and committed to a cause, politicians in a democratic state hesitate to support a war, and ultimately the battle front collapses. The question of loyalty is intimately connected to patriotism, nationalism, and ideology. Disloyalty—or dissent—endangers the national consensus on the home front and is detrimental to the war effort.

Before examining the specific ramifications of loyalty and dissent in the context of the American Civil War and how this subject relates to the overall methodological and thematic framework of this volume, let me attempt to

---

1 Anonymous, *Loyalty: What is it? To Whom or What due?* (n.p., 1863).

define loyalty and its significance.[2] Political scientists have located loyalty between patriotism and obligation. Political loyalty is a devoted attachment to the political ideals and institutions established in a community; hence, it is itself a foremost component of them. In most of its manifestations, political loyalty is a complex mixture of tradition and sentiment, choice and reason. Most of our loyalties are acquired in the course of social conditioning and are "integrated into the character structure without conscious thought."[3] National attachment and loyalty per se are neither innate nor congenital. Loyalties are qualitatively different, depending on their sources.[4]

It is loyalty that defines the community and preserves its integrity in the face of changing conditions, such as wars. The terms *loyalty*, *allegiance*, and *patriotism* are inherently interconnected, and the difference in meaning is defined by the differences in their object of attachment. Since the object of loyalty is often ambiguous, it allows the inclusion of a variety of emotions, ideologies, and symbols. Loyalty is also both a response and an attitude.[5] One of the foremost historians of total war and its social effects, Arthur Marwick, links the psychological dimension of war with loyalty.

War is an enormous emotional experience, during which loyalty towards one's own group, or those with whom one comes to identify in wartime (one's trade union, the working class, other women, the entire nation) intensifies, as does hostility to "out groups" (principally, of course, the enemy). Considerable force is also given to the notion... that such appalling slaughter must be *for* something, that change in many spheres, including the cultural, must eventuate.[6]

---

2 *Webster's... Unabridged* dictionary defines loyalty as: "The faithfulness or faithful adherence to a person, government, cause, duty, etc." The *Encyclopedia Britannica* describes the term as: "signifying a person's devotion or sentiment of attachment to a particular object, which may be another person or group of persons, an ideal, a duty, or a cause." *Encyclopedia Britannica* (1970 ed.), 14:378A. Social psychologist Harald Guetzkow has written a useful general definition of this term: "An attitude predisposing its holder to respond toward an idea, person, or group, with actions perceived by the holder to be supportive of, and/or with feelings which value the continued existence of the object toward the attitude is directed." Harold Guetzkow, *Multiple Loyalties: Theoretical Approach to a Problem in International Organization* (Princeton, N.J., 1955), 8.
3 See John H. Schaar, *Loyalty in America* (1957; reprinted: Westport, Conn., 1982), 19–20.
4 Guetzkow, *Multiple Loyalties*, 15.
5 Sociologists and psychologists almost share the same definitions of loyalty in this respect. For some sociologists, loyalty is a "sense of solidarity and a feeling of attachment to a particular social order and the codes that regulate it." For some psychologists, loyalty means "an attitude of firm attachment or allegiance on the part of an individual to a single individual, a group, a symbol, or (figuratively) an ideal." Both definitions quoted in Guetzkow, *Multiple Loyalties*, 9.
6 Arthur Marwick, ed., *Total War and Social Change* (New York, 1988), xvi. In his classic work, *War and Social Change in the Twentieth Century: A Comparative Study of Britain, France, Germany, Russia, and the United States* (London, 1974), Marwick developed a four-dimensional model of the interrelationship between war and society. The four dimensions are the destructive, test, participation, and psychological aspects. See his *Total War and Social Change*, 11–13.

Applied to the American Civil War, it is indeed interesting to look into the political, cultural, and psychological foundations of loyalty and disloyalty.[7] Revolutions and civil wars could be described in general terms as the absence of shared loyalties within a society. Once war breaks out, these loyalties have to be redefined.[8]

The modern nation-state requires loyalty from its citizens, especially in times of war when the whole nation is in danger – self-inflicted or not – of losing its actual identity, which is strongly connected to the territory, culture, and language. Civil wars are, of course, an exceptional case (*Sonderfall*) in the histories of wars. The external enemy does not exist – except in the case where a civil war becomes an international conflict by the intervention of a foreign force. It is the internal "war between brothers" (*Bruderkrieg*) that changes the perspectives of loyalty. I would suggest that revolutionary and civil wars evoke even stronger attachments and loyalties than external conflicts. This could be an explanation as to why most civil wars are fought with such intensity. I think the answer lies in the genuinely deeper roots of this kind of social conflict. The conflict of loyalties runs deeper through families and communities. On the individual level, loyalty to the family and the community are also very strong and might interfere with the demands of national loyalty. On the societal level, class cleavages may lead to class loyalty that again may cause friction between national loyalty.[9] Dissent, hence, occurs when different loyalties collide, and the individual decides for one loyalty, which is considered by the majority at a specific time and place as disloyal. The main question, then, is: When dissent appears, how is it countered by the state authorities? The fostering of loyalty is on the one hand a positive preventive streamlining, and on the other hand a counterreaction against already existing dissent. In a civil war, society is in conflict with itself, and the interpretation of loyalty can lead us to a deeper understanding of the complexities of this kind of war.[10] I have consequently organized this chapter in two major parts. The first examines the positive promotion of loyalty and attempts to identify what I call the "agents" of loyalty enforcement. The second part

---

7 See Vincent William DeCoursey, "Loyalty and Disloyalty," Ph.D. diss., University of Chicago, 1974. For a discussion of loyalty and disloyalty – although in the twentieth-century context, but still interesting in its possible application for the nineteenth century – see Morton Grodzin, *The Loyal and the Disloyal: Social Boundaries of Patriotism and Treason* (Chicago, 1956).

8 See Schaar, *Loyalty in America*, 20–1.

9 "Since wars in one way or another involve the whole population, they have been highly significant tests of national loyalty," Merle Curti, *Roots of American Loyalty* (New York, 1946), 148.

10 Historian George M. Fredrickson thinks that the reevaluation of basic concepts such as loyalty is one of the most "intellectual products of the war." See his *The Inner Civil War: Northern Intellectuals and the Crisis of the Union* (New York, 1965), 132. See also his chapter on loyalty in the Civil War, ibid., 130–50.

examines the negative enforcement of loyalty – for example, the repression of dissent and the mechanisms involved. My primary interest lies in the extent to which the nation-state intervened and developed its organizational structure in order to intervene effectively. Such analysis is relevant for understanding if, and to what extent, the American Civil War became total or not. It is then interesting to ask the question: Did the enforcement of loyalty and the suppression of dissent lead to an even greater increase in the mobilization of the civilian population, thus enabling the belligerents to wage a devastating war that lasted four years?

The domestic front is crucial in sustaining a war. It is thus all the more surprising that the historiography on the home front during the Civil War is not yet as rich as military history.[11] The socioeconomic dimension is one aspect of this question; in addition, the political, cultural, religious, and psychological experiences of citizens are also crucial in analyzing the home front. We need to understand the complexities of this subject in order to understand the mechanism of total warfare, because the interplay between the battle front and the home front is dialectical. Disloyalty and dissent on the home front

---

11 Compared to the flood of historical literature on military and political leaders, military campaigns, etc. Social historians are slowly developing an interest in the Civil War itself and the experience of ordinary soldiers and civilians. The "new military history," however, has been more productive in examining the fate of ordinary soldiers than the "new social history" has been in researching civilians. It is probably not surprising that an encompassing work on the home front does not exist yet. The terrain to cover is just too great and diverse to come up with a "synthetic" work on this subject. My interest for the home front experience is primarily orientated toward the ideological and mental framework of the civilian population during the Civil War. For that aspect, see George W. Smith and Charles Judah, eds., *Life in the North During the Civil War* (Albuquerque, N.M., 1966); Carl Degler, *The Other South: Southern Dissenters in the Nineteenth Century* (New York, 1974); Emory M. Thomas, *The Confederacy as a Revolutionary Experience* (Englewood Cliffs, N.J., 1971); Randall C. Jimerson, *The Private Civil War: Popular Thought During the Sectional Conflict* (Baton Rouge, La., 1988); Earl J. Hess, *Liberty, Virtue, and Progress: Northerners and Their War for the Union* (New York, 1988); Phillip S. Paludan, "*A People's Contest": The Union and the Civil War, 1861–1865* (New York, 1988); Reid Mitchell, "The Northern Soldier and His Community," in Maris A. Vinovskis, ed., *Toward a Social History of the American Civil War* (New York, 1990), 78–92. The more traditional home front historiography primarily orientated toward the economic situation in the North is Emerson D. Fite, *Social and Economic Conditions in the North* (New York, 1910); David Gilchrist and W. David Lewis, eds., *Economic Change in the Civil War Era* (Greenville, Del., 1965); Ralph Andreano, ed., *The Economics of the Civil War* (Cambridge, Mass., 1967); for the South, see Charles W. Ramsdell, *Behind the Lines in the Southern Confederacy* (Baton Rouge, La., 1944); John C. Schwab, *The Confederate States: A Financial and Industrial History of the South during the Civil War* (New York, 1901); Richard C. Todd, *Confederate Finance* (Athens, Ga., 1954); there are numerous articles in historical journals covering specific aspects of the home front experience during the Civil War. For a brief examination of both home fronts, see James L. Abrahamson, *The American Home Front: Revolutionary War, Civil War, World War I, World War II* (Washington, D.C., 1983), 43–85; for a somewhat outdated historiographical overview on the Confederacy's home front, see Mary Elisabeth Massey, "The Confederate States of America: The Home Front," in Arthur S. Link and Rembert W. Patrick, eds., *Writing Southern History: Essays in Historiography in Honor of Fletcher M. Green* (Baton Rouge, La., 1965), 249–72. Most recently, see J. Matthew Gallmann, *The Northern Homefront in the Civil War* (Chicago, 1994).

weaken the spirit on the front line. Once battles are lost, dissent on the home front increases, and this again has an impact on the battlefield. Politicians have to ensure military leaders of the undivided loyalty of the home front. In the American Civil War, the communication between the domestic and the battle front was well developed. Soldiers were informed about the political struggles in general and the situation in their communities in specific. Sometimes tensions arose between the two fronts when combatants felt that civilians did not sufficiently support the effort for which they risked their lives.[12]

Moreover, when industrialized nations go to war, they have to rely on a constant flow of supplies transported to the front. War-related industries are the vital center of production.[13] The laborers in these vitally important industries and in other industries now are part of the war effort. The different interests between capital and labor have to be suspended temporarily, and governments are easily convinced by entrepreneurs or employers that strikes should be viewed as treasonous.

Once aroused, loyalty in wartime makes it hard to compromise with the enemy, as the population becomes actively involved in defining and enforcing patriotism. All the sacrifices on the battlefield and on the home front should have an ultimate teleological purpose. We need to ask if loyalty and its enforcement ultimately led to a more destructive war than anybody anticipated before Fort Sumter. The populace is not only a passive receiver of loyalty propaganda; it also actively generates this sentiment.[14] The historian Charles Strozier has emphasized that the modern state requires "unconditional surrender as a necessity correlative of its total war."[15] But how modern were the two states in the American Civil War? The answer to this question is key to an understanding of total war, since only a centralized nation–state is capable of concentrating all its economic, technological, and psychological power for the final purpose of winning a victory over his adversary. The historian Leonard P. Curry has rightly emphasized that during the Civil War, the "blueprint for modern America" was drafted.[16] In this chapter, I accordingly use loyalty and dissent also as a lens to look at the emerging nation-

---

12 See Mitchell, "Northern Soldier and His Community," 88.
13 For the interdependence between armed forces and the productive forces in modern warfare, see Hans Speier, *Social Order and the Risks of War* (Cambridge, Mass., 1952), 254–5.
14 See Charles Royster's interesting final remark in the preface to his *The Destructive War: William Tecumseh Sherman, Stonewall Jackson, and the Americans* (New York, 1991), xii: "The people who made it [the Civil War] surprised themselves, but the surprise consisted, in part, of getting what they had asked for."
15 Charles Strozier quoted in Mark E. Neely Jr., "Was the Civil War a Total War?" *Civil War History* 37 (1991): 5.
16 Leonard P. Curry, *Blueprint for Modern America: Nonmilitary Legislation of the First Civil War Congress* (Nashville, Tenn., 1968).

state during the Civil War. Dissent within this framework is used as a process of deviation and to illuminate aspects of loyalty. Since in a democratic society political parties are (ideally) the expression of the will of the people and reflect cultural and regional trends, the history of political parties during this conflict and their different functions within the Union and within the Confederacy—with respect to the question of loyalty—is central. By applying a comparative methodology to examine the actions of the Union and the Confederacy in fostering loyalty among their populations and, at the same time, their reactions toward dissent, light may be shed on the commonalities and the differences in the two state systems.

The American Civil War was fought between two social systems that each faced internal divisions of a social, political, cultural, and regional nature. Creating loyalty became one of the central political and emotional tasks. Spontaneous demonstrations of patriots on both sides of the Mason-Dixon Line occurred after news of the bombardment of Fort Sumter reached the North and the South. Loyalty became a keyword in these demonstrations. Two days after Fort Sumter, an editorial in the *New York Times* commented on these demonstrations: "The incidents of the last two days will live in History. Not for fifty years has such a spectacle been seen, as that glorious uprising of American loyalty." The editorial added that party dissensions and political differences were instantly forgotten in the face of "common fears and hopes."[17] Although this statement was probably a true sentiment, it was more wishful thinking than reality. North and South faced a variety of internal social, political, ethnic, cultural, religious, and regional divisions that erupted in open dissent after the euphoria had vanished. But let me first concentrate on the aspects of loyalty enforcement in the North and South before I examine the aspects of dissent and its suppression.

During the era of the American Revolution, "patriots" had enthusiastically tormented disloyal American "loyalists"; after independence, the social pressures of legally enforced and formalized loyalty increased. In antebellum America, the strong tradition of exceptionalism conflicted with the sense of loyalty thus established. The Declaration of Independence and the Constitution had created an ideological framework to accommodate broad political differences, and loyalty and allegiance to the nation were based on the principle of individual freedom. Americans had considered their new nation unique in its foundation based not on common culture, history, blood, or religion of its people. In the exceptionalist tradition, loyalty to the nation

17 *New York Times,* April 16, 1861, quoted in Smith and Judah, eds., *Life in the North during the Civil War,* 38.

meant loyalty to the principle of individual liberty, the bond between people and a nation.

The American Civil War demonstrated that shared national loyalties could not mediate between different sectional loyalties formed by distinct cultural and ideological developments. But it also made clear that transsectional or local loyalties were in conflict with sectional and local ones.[18] Early enthusiasm for the war on both sides of the Mason-Dixon Line indicated regional or state pride rather than true nationalism or sectional identification. The South Carolinian Randal C. Jimerson expressed the point well when he said: "I go first for Greenville, then for Greenville District, then for the up-country, then for South Carolina, then for the South, then for the United States, and after that I don't go for anything."[19] Despite these strong regional loyalties, however, the reality and organizational necessities of warfare consolidated the nation-state and the idea of a nation. According to the historian Eric Foner, this was accomplished at least for the North "via emancipation, with the interests of humanity in general, and, more prosaically, with a coalition of diverse groups and classes."[20] Loyalty was thus projected to the larger abstract entity of a cause that came to be identified with liberty as the moral goal of a nation.[21] One should also add to the catalog of nationalizing values the principle of free labor versus unfree labor and the ideology of republicanism in general.[22] Neither complete sectional loyalty nor national loyalty was achieved during the war. Hence, the borderlines for either loyalty for the Union or the Confederacy were not clear-cut by geographical factors. Among the 22.5 million civilians in the North, there were loyal Southerners or people in sympathy with the South; among the 5.5 million whites in the South, there were elements loyal to the North or at least in support of it.[23]

In both the Union and Confederacy, there were attempts by ideologists to establish a national loyalty-consensus among the population without which the successful continuation of the conflict was endangered. Loyalty became the vehicle for either reaffirming or evoking nationalism on both sides.

18 See Schaar, *American Loyalty*, 80.
19 Cited in Randall C. Jimerson, *Private Civil War*, 181; see also ibid., 182.
20 Eric Foner, *Reconstruction: America's Unfinished Revolution, 1863–1877* (New York, 1988), 30.
21 See, e.g., Merle Curti's remark: "The identification of the nation with moral principle, moral will, moral struggle and regeneration, led to the conviction that only through the nation can the individual realize his own moral freedom." Curti, *Roots of American Loyalty*, 177.
22 See Eric Foner, *Free Soil, Free Labor, Free Men: The Ideology of the Republican Party before the Civil War* (New York, 1970).
23 See Paludan, *A People's Contest*, 238. On the eve of the Civil War, 33.5 million civilians, men and women, resided in the United States. The Confederacy encompassed approximately 9 million persons, among them 3.5 million slaves and over 100,000 free blacks. Out of the total population, over 4 million (13 percent) were foreign-born with the Irish and Germans as the greatest proportion. Less than 10 percent of the immigrant population lived in the South. For population figures,

I I

Clausewitz's dictum–"War is merely the continuation of politics by other means"–applies well to the American Civil War.[24] In this context, *loyalty* is a key term for understanding the political culture that underlies the political process. The American Civil War was a highly politicized conflict; indeed, politics was the driving force behind the war effort. But there is always a dialectic relationship between the political and the military situation involved. Politics might be the primary driving force, but the military situation is often crucial for changing the course of politics. The Union victory at Atlanta in September 1864, for example, paved the way for President Abraham Lincoln's reelection that same year.

Political forces and channels were differently structured in North and South. In the conclusion to his essay, "Party Politics and the Union and Confederate War Efforts," the historian Eric McKitrick emphasizes the significance of the elections during the Civil war: "Every election…was a step in nationalizing the war."[25] He also stresses the linkage between party politics and loyalty: "The extension of local and state loyalties into national loyalties during this period was something of a revolution," and he rightly continues that "it did not occur easily."[26] Even more important perhaps is the thesis–originally propounded by the historian David M. Potter and further developed by McKitrick–that the defeat of the Confederacy was caused by a lack of a two-party system.[27] This now well-established thesis revised the traditional interpretation that the Confederacy actually benefited from this lack of a two-party system. This meant for the political situation in the North that the Democrats served as an essential identifiable "disloyal" political target at which to direct the unified energies of the Republican Party. Hence, political dissent when it occurred could be channeled in one direction rather than looking for dissent everywhere, as was the case in the Confederacy. In identifying a scapegoat for disloyalty and dissent, the Democratic

see *Historical Statistics of the United States: Colonial Times to 1970* (Washington, D.C., 1975), pt. 1, ser. A: 91–104; Walker Page, "The Distribution of Immigrants in the United States Before 1870," *Journal of Political Economy* 20 (July 1912): 679–80; see also J. G. Randall and David Donald, *The Civil and Reconstruction*, 2d ed. (Boston, Mass., 1961), 5.

24 Carl von Clausewitz, *On War*, ed. and trans. Michael Howard and Peter Paret (Princeton, N.J., 1984), 87.

25 Eric McKitrick, "Party Politics and the Union and Confederate War Efforts," in William N. Chambers and Walter D. Burnham, eds., *The American Party Systems: Stages of Political Development* (New York, 1975), 117–51.

26 McKitrick, "Party Politics and the Union and Confederate War Efforts," 151.

27 See David M. Potter, "Jefferson Davis and the Political Factors in Confederate Defeat," in David H. Donald, ed., *Why the North Won the Civil War: Essays by Richard N. Current and Others* (Baton Rouge, La., 1960), 91–114.

Party increased unity among the ranks of the Republicans, so badly needed because of its internal divisions. The slogan that "every Democrat may not be a traitor, but every traitor is a Democrat," was an essential strategy for political unity for the party in power, namely, the Republicans.[28] Repression of dissent channeled into party politics and established a middle-ground for Republican politicians to cope with this problem. There they could demonstrate to the public that they were neither paralyzed by dissent nor were they establishing a dictatorial state, since they simply followed the rules of party politics within the constitutional framework. In this process, they could focus more sharply on policy and strategy and on improving their partisan skills. They were largely able to smooth over the inner-party struggles between the conservatives and the radicals,[29] and they consequently, as historian John L. Thomas has phrased it, "however unintentionally, contributed to the winning of the war."[30] The two-party system was advantageous for the Republican Party, since they could convince the public that dissent stemmed primarily from within the ranks of the Democrats. Partisanship also helped to draw clear distinctions between supporters of a vigorous prosecution of the war and advocates of peace.

Jefferson Davis, in contrast, lacked this political instrument to channel internal dissent into party politics, since there were no formal political parties in the Confederacy. The collapse of the Whigs in the 1850s and the Democratic Party in 1860 left the South devoid of a viable political party system.[31] Consequently, dissent in the South was much more damaging to the general morale. In the Union, the Republican Party during the Civil War became almost identical with the state and embodied the emergence of a nation-state. It was hence recently even compared—in a study on the origins of central state authority in America—with the Bolsheviks of the early years of the Soviet Union.[32] Although this comparison might be overdrawn, the fusion of the Republican Party and the state during the Civil War was indeed nearly complete. The elected Republican administration was instrumental

---

28 See McKitrick, "Party Politics and the Union and Confederate War Efforts," 141; Earl J. Hess, *Liberty, Virtue, and Progress*, 95.

29 On the "ultra radical" side was the Radical Democracy Party, with Charles C. Fremont as its presidential candidate in the election of 1864. On this campaign, see Jörg Nagler, *Fremont contra Lincoln: Die deutschamerikanische Opposition in der Republikanischen Partei während des amerikanischen Bürgerkrieges* (Frankfurt/Main, 1984); Jörg Nagler, "The Lincoln-Fremont Debate and the Forty-Eighters," in Charlotte L. Brancaforte, ed., *The German Forty-Eighters in the United States* (New York, 1989), 157–78.

30 John L. Thomas, ed., *Abraham Lincoln and the American Political Tradition* (Amherst, Mass., 1986), 8.

31 See McKitrick, "Party Politics and the Union and Confederate War Efforts," 123; McPherson, *Battle Cry of Freedom*, 689; Hess, *Liberty, Virtue, and Progress*, 95.

32 See Richard Franklin Bensel, *Yankee Leviathan: The Origins of Central State Authority in America, 1859–1877* (New York, 1990), x.

in organizing the war and was thus capable of mixing political loyalty with national loyalty. American parties were a manifestation of the political culture at this time and "served as answers to the question of public identity."[33] In this way, the paradigms of public identity and loyalty are thematically connected, since loyalty in political as well as in psychological terms leads to an individual identity and consequently to the identity of a community, and to a nation. In other words, when we turn from the formal function of party politics to the informal patterns and structures, we will find at the bottom issues related to loyalty. Then we also could come to a better understanding of why the North (and the South?) was willing to endure four years of hardship and death. One example may suffice to illustrate the will to prosecute a vigorous war. When Andrew Johnson spoke at a "Loyal Meeting of the People of New York" at the Cooper Institute on March 6, 1863, he expressed this sentiment:

> Compromise? Let the last life be lost, the last dollar spent, the last drop of blood shed, but the Star and Stripes shall remain triumphant. Compromise? No, if need be, let us, testing our sincerity, come forward and pour out the blood that now warms our existence, as the last libation upon Freedom's altar.[34]

This kind of rhetoric on both sides – whether taken at face value or not – makes more understandable the idea of waging a war to the bitter end and with all means. The crucial question in this context, then, is: To what degree did the Confederacy and the Union instrumentalize the concept of loyalty to sustain the will to fight? Loyalty propaganda was channeled in the Union through the parties, and again the Republican Party was a master of this technique, creating a patriotic "loyalty crusade" that called for conformity.[35] Compared with the well-known propaganda efforts of the twentieth-century nation-state, the propaganda efforts of the Civil War might seem amateurish.

The ebbs and flows of military success were reflected in the changing moods on the home front. Loyalty was put to a decisive test, and dissent developed after battles were lost and public support for the war soured. A war of words attempted to counterbalance the negative military situation. But who were the carriers/agents of loyalty propaganda, and in what respect did

33 Amy Bridges, "Becoming American: The Working Classes in the United States before the Civil War," in Ira Katznelson and Aristide R. Zolberg, eds., *Working-Class Formation: Nineteenth-Century Patterns in Western Europe and the United States* (Princeton, N.J., 1986), 193.

34 Andrew Johnson at a meeting at the Cooper Institute, March 6, 1863, in *Loyal Meeting of the People of New York to Support the Government, Prosecute the War, and Maintain the Union* (New York, 1863), 79.

35 See Frank Klement, *Dark Lanterns: Secret Societies, Conspiracies, and Treason Trials in the Civil War* (Baton Rouge, La., 1984), 3.

they advocate certain elements of total war, such as the utter destruction of the enemy, including attacks on civilians and property? It is worthwhile to emphasize that demand for total war is probably never fully expressed in detail in propaganda efforts. It is also possible that civilian propagandists had something different in mind than the military when they finally confronted the enemy. In other words, loyalty propaganda on the home front and the appeal to the will to fight may lead to a popular consensus that is subsequently transmitted by the administration to the military, which can continue to wage a total war.

Where there is an appeal to loyalty, there is also a lack of loyalty. In the North, there was a crisis of loyalty in late 1862 and early 1863. The seemingly successful gains of the Democrats in the 1862 elections encouraged them to maintain their separate identity and to continue with their political dissent. The Democrats could build on popular dissent that rose in face of the repression of civil liberties, the threat of a national conscription act, and the new directions of Lincoln's emancipation policy.[36]

In the North, the discussion of loyalty, or what George Fredrickson has called the "doctrine of loyalty," and with it all the ramifications of nationalism and ideology, reached a high peak in the first months of 1863.[37] This public discourse found its expression in numerous pamphlets, which continued the pamphlet tradition of the American Revolution. In these pamphlets, the central issues of the Civil War were brought into focus: What was the struggle all about, by what means should it be finished, and under what circumstances should the war continue? Loyalty versus dissent were very intensely debated. Pamphleteering became a public discourse and reflected the military and political situation facing the North.[38]

The founding of publication societies tremendously increased the output of pamphlets, since they republished and distributed them widely. Both Republican and Democratic publication societies tried to shape the opinion of soldiers and civilians. The leitmotiv of the Republican pamphlets was to bolster morale and loyalty, whereas the Democratic pamphlets tried to take advantage of certain waves of public anxiety, caused by the military situation and by Lincoln's political measures. Obviously, the Democratic pamphlets had their greatest effective impact on the soldiers, a fact noted by Francis

---

36 See James A. Rawley, *The Politics of Union: Northern Politics during the Civil War* (Lincoln, Neb., 1974), 89.

37 See George M. Fredrickson, *The Inner Civil War: Northern Intellectuals and the Crisis of the Union* (New York, 1965), 130–50. This chapter is dedicated to the role of Northern intellectuals in fostering loyalty during the Civil War.

38 For a good collection of Union pamphlets, see Frank Freidel, ed., *Union Pamphlets of the Civil War, 1861–1865*, 2 vols. (Cambridge, Mass., 1967).

Lieber, a German political émigré of the 1830s and political science professor at Columbia College in New York. Lieber drafted the famous General Orders, no. 100, in which he defined the laws of war.[39] On his return to New York from Washington in February 1863, Lieber heard from discharged soldiers "loud, nasty, infernal treason."[40] In order to counterbalance the "disloyal" Democratic pamphlets, especially those published by the Society for the Diffusion of Political Knowledge, written by New York Democrats and Southern sympathizers, several publication societies were founded by Republicans in early 1863.[41] The most influential organization of its kind was the Loyal Publication Society founded in February 1863, whose membership consisted mainly of intellectuals, financiers, and merchants from New York City.[42] The resolutions of the first meeting clearly indicate the purpose of the Society: "distribution of journals and documents of unquestionable and unconditional loyalty" throughout the Union; materials were also to be sent to the troops to counteract the activities of the government enemies who talked about peace.[43] The pamphlets were carefully selected to appeal to a broad audience, including recent Irish and German immigrants and minority groups in the North. Thematically, they were structured along similar lines and advocated the improvement of morale and the continuation of loyalty.[44] Probably the most famous of the ninety pamphlets published by the Loyal Publication Society was Lieber's "No Party Now But All for the Country," in which he defined the criteria for loyalty. Loyalty had to transcend party lines, the unconditional support of the government policies of conscription, the suspension of the writ of habeas corpus, the distinction of slavery, and the total conquest of the South.[45] The distribution of over 900,000 Loyal Publication Society pamphlets was indeed impressive and undoubtedly had considerable political impact. In the South, Davis only very rarely considered the opinions of civilians to be worthwhile.[46]

39   See Richard Shelly Hartigan, *Lieber's Code and the Law of War* (Chicago, Ill., 1983); Frank Freidel, "General Orders 100 and Military Government," *Mississippi Valley Historical Review* 32 (1946): 541–56. A good example of how different loyalties separated families is Francis Lieber's son Oscar, who fought and died for the Confederacy. See James O. Breeden, "Oscar Lieber: Southern Scientist, Southern Patriot," *Civil War History* 36 (1990): 226–49.
40   Quoted in Frank Freidel, *Francis Lieber: Nineteenth-Century Liberal* (Baton Rouge, La., 1947), 345.
41   For the various organizations, see Freidel, ed., *Union Pamphlets*, 1: 4–5.
42   Frank Freidel, "The Loyal Publication Society," *Mississippi Valley Historical Review* 26 (1939):361.
43   Freidel, "The Loyal Publication Sooty," 360; Robin Brooks, "Domestic Violence and America's Wars, and International War and Domestic Turmoil," in Hugh D. Graham and Ted R. Gurr, eds., *The History of Violence in America* (New York, 1969); Harold M. Hyman, *Era of the Oath: Northern Loyalty Tests during the Civil War and Reconstruction* (New York, 1954; reprinted: New York, 1978).
44   Freidel, "Loyal Publication Society," 364.
45   See "No Party Now But All for Our Country," *Loyal Publication Society*, no. 16 (New York, 1863); Freidel, *Francis Lieber*, 347.
46   See Richard E. Beringer et al., *Why the South Lost the Civil War* (Athens, Ga., 1986), 323.

But not only politically motivated loyalty propaganda helped to bolster home front morale. Religion and its administrative structure – the churches – became instrumental in the propagation of loyalty. The function of religion and church in fostering loyalty to the cause in this struggle is often neglected in historiography, but, besides politics, it is essential for our understanding of loyalty during the war.[47] The numerous sermons for the purpose of encouraging loyalty and patriotism in the Union and in the Confederate states hint at the essential function that religion and the church played in supporting the war effort.[48] The synthesis of religion and politics was especially evident in the case of the Republican Party. The historian Victor B. Howard has emphasized that the "Northern Protestant church was the conscience of the Republican Party." The justification for this view was the conviction that the Republican Party was morally superior to any other political organization and, as one Congregational layman remarked during the war, was "brought into being by Almighty God himself."[49] Churches legitimized the government's use of force – internally as well as externally – to obtain its goals; and success in war was interpreted as a sign of providence.[50]

There is an abundance of sermons that reflect this synthesis of religion and politics and emphasize loyalty. The reemergence of pre-Lockean views of the divine origins of governments was noticeable among some of them. Probably the most radical sermon of this type was Horace Bushnell's "The Doctrine of Loyalty," which was widely published in the Union in 1863.[51] In it he emphasized that "there is a relation so deep between true loyalty and religion that the loyal man will be inclined toward religion by his public devotion, and the religious man rised in the temper of his loyalty to his country, by his religious devotion."[52] Henry W. Bellows's "Unconditional Loyalty" was also based on the divine right theory of government, and Bellows warned oppositional voices that they were undermining the strength of a government "that is to save us."[53]

Protestant groups in the North also believed in a strong federal government that was to enable the Union to become victorious over the "evil

---

47   Gerald F. Linderman has rightly emphasized that "Religious faith was another buttress of the war's moral framework for both soldiers and civilians." See Gerald F. Linderman, *Embattled Courage: The Experience of Combat in the American Civil War* (New York, 1987), 102.

48   For the role of religion in the North, see James H. Moorhead, *American Apocalypse: Yankee Protestants and the Civil War, 1860–1869* (New Haven, Conn., 1978).

49   Quoted in Victor B. Howard, *Religion and the Radical Republican Movement, 1860–1870* (Lexington, Ky., 1990), 1.

50   See Fredrickson, *The Inner Civil War*, 146.

51   Horace Bushnell, "The Doctrine of Loyalty," *New Englander* 22 (1863): 560.

52   Quoted in Fredrickson, *The Inner Civil War*, 139.

53   Henry W. Bellows, *Unconditional Loyalty* (New York, 1863), 15, quoted in Fredrickson, *The Inner Civil War*, 136.

powers" of the Confederacy, which was interpreted as the embodiment of the Antichrist. The war itself was consequently perceived by many Protestants as the continuation of the fight between Christ and Antichrist as prophesied in the Book of Revelation.[54] Unconditional loyalty in religious terms also added to the justification of the war's cause. Religion played a key role in the legitimation of the Confederacy's mission in that respect.[55] As Drew Faust has recently emphasized: "The most fundamental source for legitimation for the Confederacy was Christianity. Religion provided a transcendent framework for Southern nationalism."[56]

Southern churches were evidently more radical in their support of the war effort and interested in sustaining the morale and loyalty of civilians on the home front. The interpretation that God was on their side rapidly became problematic, however, once the South began to lose battles.[57]

III

When the first wave of patriotic enthusiasm gave way to a more realistic assessment of the situation, the Union as well as the Confederacy faced internal dissent. For a variety of reasons, dissent affected the South more dramatically, among them the different interests of the nonslaveholding white majority in comparison to the minority of slaveholding planters and the strained economic situation, partly caused by the Union's blockade. The bread riots in the Confederacy were but one example of eruptive violence reflecting the social turmoil in the South.[58] After the fall of Vicksburg in July 1863, civilians in the Confederacy increasingly feared that their government was no longer able to guarantee them protection from enemy forces, and their willingness to remain loyal dwindled accordingly.[59]

Disaffection with the conscription led to open resistance, both in the Confederacy and in the Union, where the New York City and Boston draft

---

54 See Thomas Curran, "'Resist Not Evil': The Ideological Roots of Civil War Pacificism," *Civil War History* 36 (1990): 198.

55 One of the best books on the functions of churches in the Confederacy is James W. Silver, *Confederate Morale and Church Propaganda* (New York, 1957). For the function of religion in bolstering morale in the Confederacy, see Beringer, *Why the South Lost the Civil War*, 82–102.

56 Drew Gilpin Faust, *The Creation of Confederate Nationalism: Ideology and Identity in the Civil South* (Baton Rouge, La., and London, 1988), 22.

57 See Beringer, *Why the South Lost the Civil War*, chap. 5.

58 For the bread riots in the Confederacy, see Susan Barber, "The Quiet Battles of the Home Front War: Civil War Bread Riots and the Development of a Confederate Welfare System," M.A. thesis, University of Maryland, 1986; Faust, *Confederate Nationalism*, 52–5.

59 See Lawrence N. Powell and Michael S. Wayne, "Self Interest and the Decline of Confederate Nationalism," in Harry P. Owens and James J. Cooke, eds., *The Old South in the Crucible of War* (Jackson, Miss., 1983), 33; Beringer, *Why the South Lost the Civil War*, 263.

riots in the summer of 1863 revealed the potential for social upheaval.[60] Gradually, Americans on both sides of the Mason-Dixon Line saw the effects of an overzealous federal state creeping into their lives. In an unprecedented way, they saw censorship, the suspension of the writ of habeas corpus, tax legislation, and the draft permeating their private lives. All of these state measures seriously tested the loyalty of most citizens. In addition, everyone accused the federal government of despotism, and pamphlets such as the "Four Acts of Despotism" appeared throughout the North.[61]

Considering that the North was much more diversified than the South in social and economic terms, it is rather surprising that no more such expressions of dissent occurred there. The potential of internal dissent was great. Parts of the society were still skeptical about emancipation, some were openly racist in their attitudes, and in some parts of the Union, the population had mainly Southern origins or at least close ties with the South. The overwhelming presence of immigrants had created tensions with the nativist movement in the antebellum period and continued to threaten the social and national consensus.[62] The war environment added complexity and passion to these issues, and Lincoln's government could not anticipate in which direction and to what degree this potential for dissent would be realized. Except perhaps for the experience of the American Revolution and of the quasi-war with France, when the Federalist-dominated Congress passed the Alien and Sedition Acts, there was no precedent on how to deal with opposition and dissent in a situation of war. Where was the line between a "loyal opposition" and open dissent against a legislation that was supposed to be instrumental for successfully concluding the war? Which acts and words were unlawful, which were protected? How literal should the First Amendment be interpreted and applied to opponents?[63] When did civilian dissent against the national war effort become treason, the only criminal offense specifically defined in Article III, Section 3, of the U.S. Constitution? At the time of the Civil War, there was no statutory sedition law. Some acts, however, were considered

---

60 See Iver Bernstein, *The New York City Draft Riots: Their Significance for American Society and Politics in the Age of Civil War* (New York, 1990); William F. Hanna, "The Boston Draft Riot," *Civil War History* 36 (1990): 262–73. For disaffection with the draft in the South, see Albert Burton Moore, *Conscription and Conflict in the Confederacy* (New York, 1924); Marc W. Kruman, "Dissent in the Confederacy: The North Carolina Experience," *Civil War History* 27 (1981): 293–313; James Marten, *Texas Divided: Loyalty and Dissent in the Lone Star State, 1856–1874* (Lexington, Ky., 1990), 94–101; McPherson, *Battle Cry of Freedom*, 432.

61 See, e.g., the pamphlet by D. A. Mahony, *The Four Acts of Despotism: The Tax Bill, the Finance Bill, the Conscription Act, the Indemnity Bill* (New York, 1863). For the South, see McPherson, *Battle Cry of Freedom*, 435.

62 See William G. Carleton, "Civil War Dissidence in the North: The Perspective of a Century," *South Atlantic Quarterly* 65 (1966): 390–402.

63 See Paludan, *A People's Contest*, 238.

treasonous, although they did not fall within the constitutional definition of treason.[64] In this respect, it is important to emphasize that the administration not only acted on its own; it also responded to popular sentiments.

The perennial concern in the Union that "traitors" might disrupt the domestic front, and subsequently the war effort, reflected ideological discords that threatened the consensus and the Union cause. Dissenters such as the Copperheads—Northerners who sympathized with the South—served as identifiable scapegoats and symbols for Unionists, who projected their uncertainties about the war, and their lack of ideological unity, onto this group. The "fifth column" syndrome, a typical phenomenon of the home front of modern warfare, affected many both in and out of uniform.[65] Soldiers were very much aware of dissent and inner conflict "at home," and when the war dragged on without much success, they directed their anger against "disloyal" elements who allegedly had delayed the victory over the Confederacy. An Illinois soldier wrote home in a typically vindictive spirit:

You may tell every man of Doubtful Loyalty for me up there in the north that he is meaner than any son of a bitch in hell. I would rather shoot one of them a great deal [more] than one living here . . . ther [sic] may be some excuse for the one but not for the other.[66]

The longer the war lasted, the more soldiers became impatient and angry with dissent at home, and they wanted to punish those responsible.[67]

How did the governments of the Union and Confederacy deal with the problem of internal dissent and disloyalty? The North responded to this challenge in a much more centralized fashion than did the South, where internal security measures more or less resembled local police functions.[68] After Fort Sumter, both the Union and the Confederacy faced the problem of how to deal with uncontrollable groups of patriots and vigilantes that accused fellow citizens of treacherous activity and disloyalty. In public opinion, the notion prevailed that every community was infested by traitors and dissenters. It was lawlessness in the name of loyalty that led to terror in some communities. Lincoln asked Secretary of State William Seward to implement a program to prevent disloyalty and suppress dissent on the home front. This task also had

---

64 See Shirley Burton and Kelee Green, "Defining Disloyalty: Treason, Espionage, and Sedition Prosecutions 1861–1946," *Prologue* 21 (1989): 215–16. Sedition, unlike treason, could be punished with measures less than death.

65 See Jimerson, *The Private Civil War*, 226.

66 Quoted in Bell Irvin Wiley, *The Life of Billy Yank: The Common Soldier of the Union* (1952; Baton Rouge, La., 1989), 286. For the attitude of Union soldiers toward dissenters on the home front, see Jimerson, *The Private Civil War*, 223–6.

67 See Linderman, *Embattled Courage*, 3.

68 See Harold M. Hyman, *To Try Men's Souls: Loyalty Tests in American History* (Berkeley, Calif., 1959), 139-42.

its direct political partisan function: Many of those subject to surveillance and arrest were Democrats. The employment of federal marshals and federal attorneys, as well as city mayors, county sheriffs, and policemen for internal security deviated from the theoretical norm of the separation of powers. Seward's group of loyalty enforcement agents was enlarged by the addition of private detectives, among them the notorious Allan Pinkerton.[69] In addition, General George B. McClellan employed Pinkerton's services for the surveillance of dissident groups, as, for example, the Knights of the Golden Circle, the Order of American Knights, and the Sons of Liberty, Democrats, and other allegedly dissident civilians.[70] Seward also took advantage of the eagerness of civilians to enforce loyalty, and he subsequently employed their services as spies.[71]

In the summer of 1861, Seward felt in the position to state: "I can touch a bell...and order the arrest of a citizen of Ohio...and the imprisonment of a citizen of New York, and no power on earth, except that of the President of the United States, can release them."[72] Some of the "disloyal" acts for which federal officials and even civilians hired by Seward arrested American citizens during a three-week period in 1861 included:

having secessionist tendencies, being an intimate friend of someone arrested for disloyalty, expressing gratification over a rebel victory, habitually leaving home early and coming home late, and saying that the U.S. government was oppressive, displaying Confederate buttons and emblems, selling Confederate songs, refusing to take an oath of allegiance to the Union.[73]

But judging from the actual number and nature of arrests, one cannot argue that there was a "totalitarian" police state apparatus crushing dissent. As indicated in a recent study on civil liberties in the Civil War, the prisoners were mostly "Confederate citizens and blockade runners."[74] The Lincoln administration soon realized that clemency was the more effective policy. Prisoners were set free when they agreed to take a loyalty oath. In addition, the more prominent and vocal prisoners caused public debate and concern that was eventually heard in Congress.

In February 1862, Lincoln subsequently responded to his critics in Congress, shifting responsibilities of internal security from the State Depart-

69 See Hyman, *To Try Men's Souls*, 142.
70 See Joan Jensen, *Army Surveillance in America, 1775–1980* (New Haven, Conn., and London, 1991), 25.
71 See ibid., 26.
72 Quoted in Alvan Sanborn, ed., *Reminiscences of Richard Lathers* (New York, 1907), 229.
73 See Hyman, *To Try Men's Souls*, 143–4.
74 See Mark E. Neeley Jr., *The Fate of Liberty. Abraham Lincoln and Civil Liberties* (New York, 1991), 28.

ment to the War Department. Edwin Stanton, the new secretary of war, followed the practice of releasing political prisoners by requiring a loyalty oath from them and their promise that they would not sue the government for false arrest.[75] Behind this practice stood the government's fear that public opinion would be aroused even further by political martyrdom.

Dissent and internal security became an important national issue, and Congress reacted accordingly. Starting in the summer of 1861, federal employees had to swear their future devotion to the Union by taking a loyalty oath.[76]

Both Confederate and Union governments exercised their authority by suspending the writ of habeas corpus. In fact, during the Civil War, this instrument of power was noted for its potential for repression and arbitrary manipulation by the executive in charge. The Union used the suspension of the writ, along with martial law, to detain close to 14,000 civilians, who posed a security threat to the government, whether real or imagined, and to shut down dissident newspapers or influence their editorial decisions.[77]

Much has been written on the suspension of the writ of habeas corpus and its ramifications—more so for the situation in the Union than in the Confederacy. On both sides, however, the suspension of the writ can be interpreted as "an expansion of central state authority."[78] In Article I, Section 9 of the Constitution, the possible conditions under which the writ of habeas corpus might have been suspended are clear: "when in cases of rebellion or invasion the public safety may require it." On August 8, 1862, Secretary of War Stanton published two unprecedented orders at Lincoln's request. They directed U.S. marshals and chiefs of police to "arrest and imprison" any persons "discouraging volunteer enlistment" or "giving aid and comfort to the enemy" or for "any other disloyal practice."[79] These were the first orders authorizing political arrests to apply nationwide. Thus, it was the secretary of war rather than Lincoln who suspended the writ nationwide in General Order no. 104.[80] The main object of the orders, Stanton explained to the press, was to "compel every citizen of the United States subject to military duty to bear his share in supporting the Government."[81] Judging from the

---

75 See Jensen, *Army Surveillance*, 27; Paludan, *A People's Contest*, 239; McPherson, *Battle Cry of Freedom*, 436.

76 See Harold Hyman, *Era of the Oath: Northern Loyalty Tests during the Civil War and Reconstruction* (Philadelphia, 1954), 13–20.

77 See Neeley, *The Fate of Liberty*, 234; Bensel, *Yankee Leviathan*, 141.

78 See Bensel, *Yankee Leviathan*, 140.

79 Robert J. Chandler, "Crushing Dissent: The Pacific Coast Tests Lincoln's Policy of Suppression," *Civil War History* 30 (1984): 235; U.S. War Dept., ed., *War of the Rebellion: Official Records of the Union and Confederate Armies*, 128 vols. (Washington, D.C., 1880–1901), ser. 2, 4:359; and ibid., ser. 3, 2:321.   80 Neely, *Fate of Liberty*, 53.   81 Quoted in ibid.

amount of arbitrary arrests made after the order was put into effect, the North reached what the historian Mark E. Neely Jr. has called, "the lowest point for civil liberties in U.S. history to that time, and one of the lowest for civil liberties in American history."[82] In his blanket proclamation of September 24, 1862, Lincoln put the military courts in charge of trying and punishing all rebels, disloyal persons, and draft resisters owing to his belief that "civil courts were incapable of coping with the political arrest necessary in a time of insurrection."[83] Federal detention of civilians under suspension of the writ and arrests of citizens under martial law were one and the same. The implementation of this proclamation required a network of officials such as provost-marshals, whose duty was to report acts of disloyalty and dissent, such as the distribution of disloyal literature and the forming of secret societies. According to the evidence, the main voices of dissent derived from the Democratic Party.[84] The prosecution of disloyal citizens by military tribunals instead of civil courts was contested in a landmark case. In this case, Clement L. Vallandigham, Democratic leader of the Copperhead movement, was arrested by General Ambrose E. Burnside for defiance of his General Order no. 38 from 1863, which prohibited the declaration of sympathies for the enemy.[85] From the autumn of 1862 until the end of the war, people who discouraged enlistment, impeded the draft, or afforded aid and comfort to the enemy were theoretically subject to martial law: arrest, trial, and punishment by the U.S. Army. The restriction of civil liberties in the North was now geographically complete.[86] But the government primarily used the suspension of the writ to enforce conscription rather than as a weapon against the home front. The effort to counter dissent was strong and widespread, but the North was far from a rigid and closed society during the Civil War.[87] The restriction of civil liberties prompted a vehement public debate in Northern society, and the relatively few cases of political prisoners that became public caused enough uproar to change the official policy.[88]

The situation in the South differed slightly from that in the North in that Davis did not exercise his authority as sweepingly or with as much obvious

82. Ibid.

83 Quoted in Roy P. Basler, ed., *The Collected Works of Abraham Lincoln* (New Brunswick, N.J., 1953), 5:436–7.

84 See Nathaniel Weyl, *Treason: The Story of Disloyalty and Betrayal in American History* (Washington, D.C., 1950), 275; Bensel, *Yankee Leviathan*, 141; McKitrick, "Party Politics and the Union and Confederate War Efforts," 137.

85 See Frank L. Klement, *The Limits of Dissent: Clement L. Vallandigham and the Civil War* (Lexington, Ky., 1970); McPherson, *Battle Cry of Freedom*, 596–8.

86 See Neeley, *The Fate of Liberty*, 65.

87 See Hess, *Liberty, Virtue, and Progress*, 91.

88 See Paludan, *A People's Contest*, 238.

political purpose as did his compatriot Lincoln. Davis never suspended the writ without first receiving congressional approval, and then the suspension was only in effect for thirty-day intervals, that is, between meetings of congress. During the period 1862–64, Davis and the Southern congress enacted four separate suspension acts.[89] In the South, there was also strong opposition to the suspension of the writ, organized mainly by the states. At a conference of Confederate governors held in October 1864, the suspension of the writ of habeas corpus was denounced as a dictatorial measure.[90] Consequently, the war effort was seriously hampered by this opposition. Draft evaders or deserters were issued writs of habeas corpus by judges in many Southern states. Even in areas where, under the pressures of wartime, local governments collapsed with increasing frequency, civilians accused of trading with the enemy or supporting disloyal secret societies, such as the Order of the Heroes of America, the Peace Society, and the Peace and Constitution,[91] were released based on habeas corpus.[92] Indeed, Davis was keenly aware of the crucial role that the suspension of the writ played in the "successful conduct of the war."[93]

In the North, the context for the implementation of the suspension of the writ and the repression of dissent and disloyalty was strikingly different. For an explanation, we have to look, once again, to the viable two-party system. Since the Republican Party was the driving force behind the initial war mobilization, and also had a very well-organized party apparatus under the control of the Republican governors, it did not face opposition from the states, in contrast to the South. Quite on the contrary, Republican governors constantly pressed the administration in Washington for a more rigorous policy against dissent. By doing so, however, they delegated more power and initiative to Lincoln. Federal repression of dissent was thus a complex process of state-federal relations that in a way took on a life of its own.[94] In the North, the suspension of the writ tightened the Republicans' hold on the local as well as the national state political apparatus. In the Midwest in particular, the mostly Republican governors were instrumental in implementing the

89 The first law was approved Feb. 27, 1862, which, after a second act passed April 19, was set to expire on Oct. 1862 (30 days after the next meeting of Congress). On that date, Congress approved a third suspension act, which again was set to expire 30 days after the next meeting of Congress. On Feb. 13, 1863, the authority expired, only to be renewed one year later, on Feb. 15, 1864, under a fourth and final law. See Bensel, *Yankee Leviathan*, 142, and ibid., n. 93.
90 See William M. Robinson Jr., *Justice in Grey: A History of the Judicial System of the Confederate States of America* (Cambridge, Mass., 1941), 191.
91 Georgia Lee Tatum, *Disloyalty in the Confederacy* (Chapel Hill, N.C., 1934), 3.
92 See McKitrick, "Party Politics and the Union and Confederate War Efforts," 139.
93 Quoted in McKitrick, "Party Politics and the Union and Confederate War Efforts," 139; U.S. War Dept., ed., *War of the Rebellion: Official Records of the Union and Confederate Armies*, 4. ser., 3 : 660, 1134.
94 See McKitrick, "Party Politics and the Union and Confederate War Efforts," 139.

president's proclamation of September 24, 1862. After the Democratic-controlled state legislature refused to enact war measures, for example, Indiana Governor Oliver Morton exercised virtual dictatorial authority – under martial law and suspension powers – from 1863 to 1865.[95]

The enforcement of centralization, authority, and internal control triggered resentment and disillusionment in Southern communities. They were somewhat beleaguered by the rigors of war and the impingement on their personal freedoms, embodied by the omnipresence of provost-marshals to enforce martial law. The confiscation of supplies also strained their loyalty to the Confederacy. In the eyes of one disillusioned Southern politician: "Secession seems not to have produced the results predicted by *iotas sanguine* friends. There was to be no war, no taxes worth prating about, but an increase of happiness, boundless prosperity, and entire freedom from Yankee annoyance."[96] The realties of warfare, however, had changed these expectations into a sober assessment. The intrusion of the central government into the private lives of Southerners was deeply felt, and "Yankee annoyance" became almost as bad a nuisance as the annoyance caused by the Confederate government. Internal dissent was a danger to both the Union and the Confederacy, and generally threatened the existence of the latter. Both governments handled dissent rigorously although with different approaches and different efficiencies. The North was much more successful in establishing an administrative structure to counterbalance dissent.[97] Southern localism prevented an efficiently organized internal security structure. Already aroused patriotic emotions, elevated even more by loyalty crusades, led to grass-roots violence directed against alleged disloyalty and dissent in the communities and without control from the central government. In general, the Southern social order was based on communal and kin relations. In such a social order, loyalty would be enforced locally by communal violence.[98]

There were excesses almost everywhere in the South, and a passport and loyalty test system became a permanent part of Southern wartime life. Superficially, the South used the same loyalty-testing methods and procedures as its Northern enemies. Certain factors, however, made tests of loyalty in the North and the South markedly different. Nonetheless, judges continued to appeal to the citizens in the name of loyalty and its sacredness, reminding them of Southern loyalty tests along the way, while the citizens successfully turned in their neighbors for acts of treason or sabotage. But the South never

95 See Bensel, *Yankee Leviathan*, 144, n. 99.
96 Quoted in Beringer, *Why the South Lost the Civil War*, 286.
97 Harold Hymn, *To Try Men's Souls*, 219.
98 On Southern "folk culture," see McPherson, "Southern Exceptionalism," 236.

created a central agency to coordinate work on the level of the Provost-Marshals General Bureau in the North. Without an agency to oversee the vigilantism involved in security work, the arbitrary imprisonment of political dissenters became an embarrassment by early 1863. Thousands of men were engaged in internal security work behind the lines in order to preserve the dream of victory. In the South, defeatism became synonymous with disloyalty.[99]

Dissent also manifested itself in protests against conscription, and many Northerners shared Horace Greeley's view on the draft: "Drafting is an anomaly in a free state; it oppresses the masses."[100] Any conscription system impacts all sectors of a society.[101] Within two years after the firing on Fort Sumter, both the Union and the Confederacy had enacted draft laws. In the spring of 1862, the Confederacy introduced the first national draft in American history; the Union took this step in March 1863 (Enrollment Act). Together, these governments had established the principle of national conscription for their generation and for those to follow. Other influences notwithstanding, from that point on, the state possessed the unequivocal right to take a citizen from hearth and home and subject him to military discipline under national authority.[102] The Enrollment Act of 1863 was necessary to pursue the war, and opposition to conscription was consequently interpreted as "disloyal."[103]

A historical study on the draft in the North indicates that more than 270,000 men deserted.[104] Desertions increased by 63 percent during the last months of the war, and high competitive bounties were partly to blame. By May 1865, 37 percent of males of military age were or had been in the federal forces. Besides state militia call-ups, 2,653,062 men had entered the national army in total.[105] Depending on the locale, the motives for the draft riots were a mixture of racism, political partisanship, a distaste for military service, and a rejection of the centralizing nature of conscription laws. Common to all of the studies regarding draft evasion is that the overwhelming resistance to the draft existed in principally Democratic areas with high ratios of foreign-born and working-class men.[106] The historian Peter Levine,

99   See Hyman, *To Try Men's Souls*, 219, 221, 228, 238, 233, 236.
100 Quoted in Rawley, *The Politics* of Union, 127.
101 See James W. Geary, *We Need Men: The Union Draft in the Civil War* (DeKalb, Ill., 1991), xc.
102 See ibid., ix.
103 For the opposition against conscription, see Grace Palladino, *Another Civil War: Labor, Capital, and the State in the Anthracite Regions of Pennsylvania, 1840–1868* (Urbana, Ill., and Chicago, 1990), 95–120; Geary, *We Need Men*, 44, 71, 73, 105, 107.
104 See Geary, *We Need Men*, 14–15.
105 See Montgomery, *Beyond Equality*, 94.
106 See Geary, *We Need Men*, 107.

however, has convincingly argued that, only in the first conscription, draft evaders were predominantly Catholic, non-Republican, and from areas of high immigration. Evasion in the subsequent drafts was so numerous that no clear pattern can be established.[107] Workers were also upset by employers' enforcement of federal authority against their interests.[108] In Pennsylvania, for example, ethnic tensions in the anthracite mining regions compounded draft resistance,[109] and German Catholics in Ozaukee County, Wisconsin, created the most serious draft disturbance of 1862.[110] Besides Wisconsin, opposition to the draft was most violent in Maryland, Pennsylvania, Ohio, Indiana, and Illinois. The governors of Maryland and Pennsylvania had to ask for federal troops to maintain social order. However, it is important to note that the opposition to conscription did not question the government's authority to institute a draft but rather opposed injustices in the process, or resentment toward local authorities.[111] But draft resistance is just one facet in the overall framework of dissident behavior against the war measures and was deeply interwoven with class-related problems. The Copperheads took full advantage of the seemingly class nature of the Conscription Act.[112] Dissent had its roots in class divisions and conflicts in North and South that diminished sectional unity. As in every modern war, class-conscious common soldiers and civilians alike denounced the war as a "rich man's war and a poor man's fight." For most wage-earners, the economic effects of the war had been devastating and led them to criticize vehemently the radical Republican war measures. For them, conscription appeared to reconfirm their suspicion of the class character of the war, since enough dollars could pay for commutation. The imagined threat of labor competition and subsequent decrease of wage levels, caused by the influx of freed blacks in Northern industries, inspired many workers to oppose Lincoln's emancipation policy. Taxation posed a great burden on them, and greenbacks became a symbol of inflation. Dissent among workers against the measures of the Lincoln administration coincided in some areas with the outspoken protests of Peace Democrats and rendered the impression that labor was shifting away from the Republicans. The Democrats, with their genuine ideology of decentralization, exploited the political situation by targeting the roots of

107 See Peter Levine, "Draft Evasion in the North During the Civil War, 1863–1865," *Journal of American History* 67 (1981): 816–34.
108 See Geary, *We Need Men*, 107–8.
109 See Palladino, *Another Civil War*, 95–120.
110 See Rawley, *The Politics of Union*, 94.
111 See Geary, *We Need Men*, 44.
112 See Philip S. Foner, *History of the Labor Movement of the United States* (1947; reprinted: New York, 1982), 1: 322.

worker dissent, namely, distrust of the increasing influence of the central government, as embodied in the suppression of strikes by the military, conscription, inflation, and the emancipation policy.[113] On the Southern home front in particular, food shortages, extortion, and inflation were interpreted as the results of undemocratic class distinctions and led to vigorous protest actions.[114]

These protests escalated into a longstanding and growing strike movement that was organized by workers, especially the unskilled who were witnessing a decline in their real wages.[115] But employers maintained the upper hand, for the strikes were a definite nuisance to the war effort. Union generals rushed in to establish order in the workplace, and in April 1864, Major General William Rosecrans issued General Order no. 65, which outlawed the organization of unions, picketing by men engaged in war production, and guaranteed military protection for scabs. But labor leaders struggled to convince the government that every action taken against them would incite Copperhead propaganda within the working classes.[116] Despite the fact that many workers in the North were critical of governmental policies, they remained ardently devoted to the cause of preserving the Union. As the historian David Montgomery has expressed it: "This devotion was rooted in the intense nationalism of the working classes—their commitment to the world's only political democracy."[117] The presidential election of 1864, one of the most crucial in American history, demonstrated that the intensity of political conflict was indeed high. A year after the violent draft riots, voters turned out in numbers considerably greater than those of 1860, and much of this increase went to McClellan.[118]

In the South, the industrial labor force was small compared to the North. But still the industrial expansion caused by the necessities of warfare "called

---

113 See Montgomery, *Beyond Equality*, 91, 102. The wartime pressures increased the demand for labor, and the Union explicitly endorsed increased immigration for revitalizing the labor market. See Heather Cox Richardson, "Forging 'a Liberal and Just Policy': The Republican Party's Changing Attitude toward Immigration during the Civil War," paper read at the American Historical Association annual meeting, Chicago, 1991.

114 See Jimerson, *The Private Civil War*, 190.

115 In addition to the standard labor history works by John R. Commons and Philip S. Foner, there are still too few studies on the labor movement during the Civil War. For a partial treatment of this subject, see James Matthew Morris, "The Road to Trade Unionism: Organized Labor in Cincinnati to 1893," Ph.D. diss., Princeton University, 1980, 109–33; Steven J. Ross, *Workers on the Edge: Work Leisure and Politics in Industrializing Cincinnati, 1788–1890* (New York, 1985), chap. 8; Palladino, *Another Civil War*, chaps. 5–7; see also my paper "German-American Labor and the Republican Party during the Civil War," read at the American Historical Association annual meeting, Cincinnati, 1988.

116 See Philip Foner, *History of the Labor Movement*, 328–9.

117 See Montgomery, *Beyond Equality*, 91–2.

118 Ibid., 107.

into being a genuine, if incipient, urban proletariat."[119] Workers in the South in war-related industries used their positions to their greatest advantage. Although they were exempt from the draft, they organized and struck to improve their wages and their working conditions. As historian Emory M. Thomas has rightly remarked in this regard:

> This is not to imply that the Confederate South seethed with labor unrest; it is rather to say that working people asserted themselves. Public opinion was hostile to any movement which impeded war production, and the government adopted the practice of drafting the strikers into the army and ordering them to go back to work.[120]

The biggest class conflict in the South, however, existed between planters and poor farmers. This was reflected in the Southern draft law that exempted owners of more than twenty slaves. Dissent caused by class cleavages and by workers' unrest haunted both the Confederacy and the Union, but never to a point that became critical to continuation of the war itself. Dissent in this social group did, however, markedly increase as the war dragged on. Again, it found its expression more in popular dissidence rather than in structured party politics. Social unrest could not be channeled into prefigured outlets that offered a political and thus social identity, as was the case for the North.

IV

At the end of the Civil War, the American poet and essayist James Russell Lowell concluded that loyalty for the first time in American history had become identical with patriotism. It had become a virtue instead of a sentiment.[121] And, indeed, loyalty on both sides of the Mason-Dixon Line was deeply rooted, and popular passion in this "people's war" prevailed. The question of loyalty and dissent on the home front brought into focus the central issues of the war: attitudes toward states' rights, communal ties, individual liberty, liberty as a republican virtue, and, above all, the principle of freedom. Loyalty and dissent derived from complex social, political, and cultural origins. Class, ethnicity, race, religion, and sometimes gender were denominators. In the process of industrialization, the North had slowly replaced gemeinschaft with gesellschaft. The political parties were the central expression of this development and consequently were able to absorb the overwhelming proportion of the public discourse about loyalty and dissent. In

---

119   The South proved to be more effective than the North in mobilizing labor resources by extending its central state authority. See Bensel, *Yankee Leviathan*, 135.
120   See Thomas, *The Confederacy as a Revolutionary Experience*, 102.
121   James Russell Lowell, *Writings* (New York, 1890), 5:211-12.

the South, however, the gemeinschaft character still prevailed and with it the emphasis on more local traditions.[122] Issues of loyalty and dissent addressed the question of the relationship between civilians and their national government. Americans on both sides of the Mason-Dixon Line realized that only the national government was capable of orchestrating the war effort, and they accepted its coercive powers during the war.[123] The majority did in fact support this discipline and accepted the legitimacy of the state, assuming that this was the best way to secure the safety of their families and communities. There was a dialectic relation between the enforcement of discipline by a nation-state on its civilians and simultaneous acceptance of this discipline. Even beyond acceptance, civilians now and then even asked for increased enforcement of the war measures. The restriction of civil liberties in the North—although it caused political dissent—was accepted as a means for the greater achievement of freedom once the war had changed its character after the Emancipation Proclamation. Unconditional loyalty was another expression for this quest and led to the support of a vigorously committed war.

A question that remains is: How widespread was dissent, and what was its character? Looking at the quantitative side of dissent—by counting political prisoners—is rather one-dimensional. It is true that the overwhelming majority of the prisoners was captured in border states, but the government's threats of legal enforcement against dissenters at home probably prevented many potentially "disloyal" activities. As in every modern war, the term *loyalty* became painfully misused during the American Civil War, and it served as a transmission belt for increased nationalism or the milder form of it, namely, patriotism. But under the name of loyalty and its ideal of conformity, dissent was suppressed through sanctions, in the attempt to maintain social control.[124] Compared with the wars of the twentieth century, the government policies in the Civil War were indeed rather benign. It was, however, a point of departure for the ongoing development of relations between civilians and their state in future wars. In World Wars I and II, the psychological mobilization of civilians under the name of loyalty reached a climax. Revealingly enough, there was no Committee on Public Information in the American Civil War, and Francis Lieber was no George Creel, the

---

122 For the *Gesellschaft-Gemeinschaft* debate and its application for North and South, see McPherson, "Southern Exceptionalism," 236.

123 For the acceptance of coercion in war, see Michael Walzer, *Just and Unjust Wars* (New York, 1977), 35.

124 In this context, David W. Blight has rightly observed: "Loyalty is an often distorted and an over-dosed concept in time of war. It often serves the ends of conservative nationalism while causing inherent conflict over dissent and individual liberty." David W. Blight, *Frederick Douglass' Civil War: Keeping Faith in Jubilee* (Baton Rouge, La., and London, 1989), 154.

noted American journalist from the first half of the twentieth century. In World War I, American society had to be convinced of the war effort, and this was done through a federally sponsored agency to foster patriotism and loyalty. The external enemy far across the Atlantic was almost unknown. This geographically distant enemy was projected into a psychologically close enemy. Again a "fifth column" syndrome prevailed, and pacifists, Wobblies, German sympathizers, and socialists were treated as dissenters with a "stern hand of repression" in President Woodrow Wilson's words. In contemporary press releases, the references to the Civil War home front were numerous, especially the suspension of the writ of habeas corpus by Lincoln. Dissenters, such as the Wobblies and pacifists on the American home front in World War I, stirred the same emotions in American patriots as did Copperheads and Southern sympathizers during the Civil War.[125] Historian Michael Walzer has emphasized that in revolutionary wars "Democracy is a factor only as it increases the legitimacy of the state and then the effectiveness of its coercive power."[126] Applied to the Civil War as a revolutionary event, it is indeed a challenging thought that democratic societies might be more capable than other politically structured societies to wage a totally committed and vigorous war. Loyalty behind democracies with their ideal of freedom is easier to achieve, since the individual feels the congruence between him and the ideals that the nation represents. Strict, hierarchical structures of totalitarian governments tend to crumble, when the system is about to collapse.

As the anonymous writer at the beginning of this chapter postulated, loyalty had indeed a "wholesome influence on the momentous issues" of the American Civil War.

---

125 In the wake of World War I, William A. Dunning concluded in an essay in the *American Historical Review* that "among the many interesting comparisons that now can and will be made between the war of 1861 and that of 1917 in respect to the policies and achievements of the American government, none is likely to be more striking than that concerned with the treatment of disloyal civilians." William A. Dunning, "Disloyalty in Two Wars," *American Historical Review* 24 (1919): 625.
126 Walzer, *Just and Unjust Wars*, 35.

17

"The Better Angels of Our Nature": Lincoln, Propaganda, and Public Opinion in the North during the Civil War

PHILLIP S. PALUDAN

It is no longer possible to believe in the original dogma of democracy: that the knowledge needed for the management of human affairs comes up spontaneously from the human heart. Where we act on that theory we expose ourselves to self-deception, and to forms of persuasion that we cannot verify.   – Walter Lippman

We approach the fifty-first election in our nation's history. As with the fifty that preceded it, the election is a defining moment. We will once again discover who we are and what we stand for. But we need to recognize that such definitions do not simply emerge spontaneously – they are created by men and women who tell us who we are and what our ideals should be. It is important that we have the best instruction possible. To discover what that might be, I want to talk about the fundamental aspect of that instruction – propaganda, the shaping of public opinion. My focus is the efforts of Northerners to shape public opinion during the Civil War era. I want to do four things here: (1) to explain the value of talking about propaganda in the Civil War era; (2) to define the term and place that definition within the context of American society; (3) to show how Northern opinion makers propagandized during the war; and, most importantly, (4) to discuss Abraham Lincoln, who deserves much more than any recent American leader the term "The *Great* Communicator." I argue that Lincoln was self-consciously a propagandist and that, although his activities in that realm occasionally revealed a dark side, he ultimately provided propaganda that shaped an American society that was far better able to achieve its goals than it had been.[1]

It may seem surprising to consider Lincoln a propagandist. He seems so much the quintessential great and good man, so much the embodiment of

---

1   This essay was published in 1992 under the title "'The Better Angels of Our Nature': Lincoln, Propaganda, and Public Opinion in the North during the American Civil War," as the Fifteenth Annual Gerald R. McMurty Lecture of The Lincoln Museum, Fort Wayne, Indiana.

what the nation and its polity are at their best, that we Americans may find it difficult to link him with a term that carries much negative feeling.[2] But the problem is not just applying it to Lincoln; it is becoming aware of the vast amount of propaganda in this nation, and becoming aware that the United States has probably been the most propagandized nation in the world at least from the beginning of the nineteenth century.[3] This is something that may be hard to accept about ourselves. For at the foundation of our democratic faith is the idea that we are a people capable of understanding our national needs, able to weigh and assess the options presented to us, that "We the people" can make objective, rational judgments based on a weighing of the facts in the light of "self-evident truths." Discovering that we are a propandized and manipulated people raises serious issues.

But our effort to confront and understand the nature and power of propaganda is impeded not just by Lincoln's goodness and our own self-image but also by his deception on this point. Part of being a propagandist in the United States involves denying it, and Lincoln downplayed his own influence. He would say that "Public opinion is everything in this country" and thus obscure his own responsibility for making that public opinion. His claim that "events have controlled me" again pointed the finger in the direction of outside forces and not on Lincoln himself for defining what those events meant. Denying that one is a propagandist of course plays into the vision we have of the freely deciding citizenry. It encourages a faith that the people themselves are decent and wise enough to generate their own solutions to the crises they face. But citizens should never accept such denials, no matter how flattering, no matter where they come from. We need to understand, and let our leaders know we understand, that they (as well as we) are responsible for the form and the content of political discussion. If we can treat Lincoln this way, surely no other politician can escape challenge and scrutiny.

2 Historians have been sensitive to the fact that Lincoln tried to shape public opinion, but they have not been sensitive enough to explore self-consciously what is involved in propagandizing. Believing that propaganda is *res ipsit loquitor* bad, it has been hard for Lincoln apologists, who currently dominate Lincoln scholarship, to think in terms of his propagandizing [see my "Toward a Lincoln Conversation," *Reviews in American History* 16 (March 1988): 35–42]. They thus miss exploring the extent of his responsibility for shaping the nature of the war and the society he led. Lincoln has helped them. He was at pains to deny his own influence; "events have controlled me," he said. "And the war came," he proclaimed, the subjunctive form hiding his role in bringing it on, understandable in terms of the hundreds of thousands of dead young men but misleading as well, for not only had his firm stand in the face of secession provoked the conflict; he could, himself, alone, decide when and if the war stopped.

3 Daniel Walker Howe, "The Evangelical Movement and Political Culture in the North during the Second Party System," *Journal of American History* 77 (March 1991): 1216–39. Howe observes: Without considering the propaganda aspects "at a minimum, the evangelical agenda, media, and institutions provided models showing how to influence people, how to involve them, and how to get things done."

All countries – totalitarian, democratic, and constitutional – use propaganda. It is more important in a democracy, which relies predominantly on persuasion, on shaping opinion, than in a totalitarian state, which can coerce its citizens. As Walter Lippman knew as far back as 1922, there is no way to dispense with shaping opinion by providing ways to think about the complex series of facts and opinions that compete for attention. The so-called "omnicompetent citizen" making rational, objective judgments based simply on the facts is a myth, perhaps imperative in theoretical democracies, but nonexistent in practice. "We do not first see, and then define, we define first, and then we see," Lippman said. A democratic polity demands definers, people who give shape to our feelings and impressions; people who give meanings for our "facts." It demands propagandists who will shape the ways that we think about means and ends. Much as B. F. Skinner argued in another context, we cannot choose between being shaped by our environment or not; we must choose between kinds of influence. Self-consciousness of that influence is the first step in making the wisest choice. The choice is not between propagandists and nonpropagandists; it is between those who act for the best values and opportunities in a society and those who constrict opportunities and appeal to our worst prejudices.[4]

The concept of propaganda thus allows self-conscious study of how leaders define and mold the nation. Lincoln will claim our attention now, but in looking at his actions, we learn that all of our leaders are responsible *for* and not just *to* public opinion. Using the concept of propaganda helps us to look at the conscious efforts of leaders to make us into who we are as a people. To use a recent example, the concept helps us understand that campaign propagandists and not the American people gave us "Willie Horton."[5]

What do we mean when we speak of propaganda? Most authorities accept Terence H. Qualter's definition: "the deliberate attempt by the few to influence the attitudes and behavior of the many by the manipulation of symbolic communication."[6] Please note that there is no moral judgment in that definition. Propaganda here is not good or bad. It is an attempt to shape people's perceptions. If we begin with a neutral definition, we gain the ability

4 Walter Lippman, *Public Opinion* (New York, 1922), 248–9; Ronald Steel, *Walter Lippman and the American Century* (Boston, 1980), 180–5, 212–16; B. F. Skinner, *Beyond Freedom and Dignity* (New York, 1971).
5 Lee Atwater and Todd Brewster, "Lee Atwater's Last Campaign," *Life* 14 (Feb. 1991).
6 Terence H. Qualter, *Opinion Control in the Democracies* (London, 1985), 124; see also *Encyclopedia Britannica* (1991); *Encyclopedia Americana* (1989); *Webster's Third New International Dictionary* (1986); *Oxford English Dictionary* (1990). Philip Davidson, *Propaganda and the American Revolution 1763–1783* (Chapel Hill, N.C., 1941), xiii, accepts the definition of Leonard W. Doob in *Propaganda: Its Psychology and Technique* (New York, 1935), 89: "Intentional propaganda is a systematic attempt by an interested individual (or individuals) to control the attitudes of groups of individuals through the use of

to analyze before we judge. We can ask, for example, whether and how the great and good Lincoln propagandized without immediately denying that he could do such a questionable thing. I want us here to keep that neutral definition in mind, because our concern is very much how Lincoln and his age did it, not whether it was wrong. At the same time, it is important also to follow our instincts and apply a moral standard. Without it, we might end up with an argument that says that if "Saint Lincoln" propagandized, then we all who aren't saints get to do it too.

So we must now note that there are degrees and types of propaganda. Writers have distinguished between "white," "gray," and "black." White propaganda is generally overt as to its source; it stays reasonably close to the truth, and it associates the sender with positive ideals and goals. Gray is more obscure as to the source – a speaker may hide who s/he really is, and the information used may not be accurate. Black is deceptive in every aspect – it lies about its source and the subjects it talks about.[7]

These distinctions rest on a moral idea. A fundamental question is who benefits from the propaganda. Dark propaganda is characterized by the fact that it is consciously employed by the propagandist to serve his/her own purposes. Thus, the audience's wishes, ideals, and goals may be irrelevant except insofar as the propagandist wants to know which of their "buttons" to push. In the propaganda situation, the moral element is much like Kant's moral ideal of treating people as ends rather than as means. The immoral propagandist does not treat the audience as people with their own ends, with their own capacities. He does not treat them as capable or worthy of rational discussion. He tries to produce effects rather than seeking agreement. The dark propagandist not only hides his motive; he tries to influence people rather than to reason with them – he treats them as things to be influenced rather than humans with whom to communicate. And he does not describe reality; he tries to deceive so that people will see the world as he wants them to. Keeping such distinction in mind, it is time to turn to the Civil War.

suggestion and, consequently, to control, their actions." Davidson continues, "Intentional propaganda arises, therefore, from interested motives, is consciously and systematically carried on, and its primary purpose is to obtain public support for a particular idea or course of action. ... It is not necessary for propaganda to be false or for the propagandist to conceal himself or his motives. Whether the suggestions are to be true or false, whether the activities are to be open or concealed, are matters for the propagandist to decide."

7   Victoria O'Donnell and Garth S. Jowett, "Propaganda as a Form of Communication," in Ted J. Smith III, ed., *Propaganda: A Pluralist Perspective* (New York, 1989), 49–63. The importance of propaganda in a positive sense is suggested in Thomas Engeman, "Utopianism and Preservation: The Rhetorical Dimension of American Statesmanship" in Ralph Rossum and Gary McDowell, eds., *The American Founding: Politics, Statesmanship, and the Constitution* (Port Washington, N.Y., 1981), 143–56. Engeman says that leaders who proclaim the best ideals of the nation show that their superior qualities [are] a public resource, not a public danger, 155.

The Civil War was a war of words as well as of weapons and men. Public opinion was the target of both. Both Lincoln and Jefferson Davis knew that they had to build and sustain morale and thus retain the capacity to raise armies and the desire to continue fighting. They had to define what their nations were fighting for and defend their governments against opposition behind the lines as well as on the battlefield. Soldiers and generals knew that their victories and defeats shaped the hopes and fears of their societies. Soldiers' letters are filled with reassurances to loved ones not only about personal safety but about the values that were worth fighting for. Generals knew that they had to fight and win battles according to popular timetables as well as their own. George B. McClellan's obstinacy on this point helped to cost him his command. Ulysses S. Grant's and William Tecumseh Sherman's awareness of this fact ensured their continuing support by president and Congress.

Sherman especially was conscious that the public, North and South, was watching, that his target was opinion and not just rebel warriors. To see his activities in the context of propaganda helps to provide a more balanced picture of him than prevails in much writing. Sherman's most common image is captured in the vision of his march to the sea, a vision so horrible that one writer linked that march with the war in Vietnam. Certainly, some of Sherman's rhetoric was terrifying. When he commanded in Memphis, Sherman threatened to shoot anyone who tried to ambush his troops. "To secure the safety of the navigation of the Mississippi River," he proclaimed, "I would slay millions. On that point I am not only insane but mad.... For every bullet shot at a steamboat, I would shoot a thousand 30 pound Parrots into even helpless towns." But Sherman was barking, not biting. He never executed his threat and accepted Grant's reminder that Union armies could also gain by examples of leniency and restraint on the march. When Sherman had his well-known debate with John Bell Hood before Atlanta, both men knew they were speaking to the whole country, not just man to man, general to general. Hood protested that Sherman's decision to expel civilians from Atlanta "transcends in studied and inglorious cruelty, all acts of war ever brought to my attention in the dark history of war." He sent his letter to Southern newspapers as well as to Sherman. Sherman returned the favor. When he replied to Hood, and to the Atlanta city council, who had joined Hood's protest, he recited cases where rebel armies had expelled Unionists, included a lecture on who had started the war by attacking "the finest government in the world," and then threatened that he would be unrelenting in war but when peace came "you may call upon me for anything." Sherman published this broadside in Northern newspapers that he knew would be read by the enemy as well as friends in the North. It was a propaganda blitzkrieg that inspired Northerners and frightened Dixie.[8]

There was also, of course, more obvious propaganda. The Civil War produced a huge outpouring of pamphlets both promoting and opposing the Union war effort. For the first two years of the war, pamphlets were private efforts, supported on a one-time basis by a range of individuals and groups. But by early 1863, groups had been organized specifically to promote the viewpoints of contending Democrats and Republicans. The Democrats were first in the field in the Northeast with their Society for the Diffusion of Political Knowledge (SDPK) established on February 13, 1863. But the defenders of the administration were more prolific, backed as they were by deeper pockets and the better position of defending a war rather than opposing it. Two most important Northern organizations defending the administration goals were Philadelphia's Board of Publications of the Union League and New York City's Loyal Publication Society. From Philadelphia came over four million copies of 104 different pamphlets defending Republican policy from 1863 to 1868. The New York Society printed 90 different pamphlets; 900,000 total copies were sent out. In 1863, the New York Society sent pamphlets to 21,160 private individuals, 744 editors, 649 Union Leagues, and 474 "Ladies Associations." Equally effective was the New England Loyal Publication Society, which clipped articles from newspapers and other sources, printed them on newspaper-sized broadsheets, and sent them out to over 860 newspapers throughout the country, where busy editors often simply inserted them in their papers.[9]

These pamphlets and broadsides circulated wherever there was opinion to be shaped. "You can hardly go into a public office or store," one Democrat protested, "but you will see ... [Union League] documents on tables, counters, and even *posted* as handbills." And the publications reflected the diversity of the society that their authors were trying to persuade. Robert Dale Owens's "Future of the Northwest" circulated especially well in the Old Northwest. Irish-Americans were treated to Daniel O'Connell's 1843 attack on slavery. German Americans and Dutch Americans read "Lincoln or McClellan?" in

8 Phillip S. Paludan, "A People's Contest": *The Union and Civil War, 1861–1865* (New York, 1988), 300–9. On Sherman and Vietnam, see James Reston Jr., *Sherman's March and Vietnam* (New York, 1984); John Bennett Walters, *Merchant of Terror: General Sherman and Total War* (Indianapolis, Ind., 1973). Mark E. Neely Jr., "Was the Civil War a Total War?" *Civil War History* 37 (March 1991): 5–28. See Charles Royster, *The Destructive War: William Tecumseh Sherman, Stonewall Jackson, and the Americans* (New York, 1991), 357–9, and passim for further discussion of Sherman and war.

9 George Winston Smith, "Broadsides for Freedom: Civil War Propaganda in New England, "*New England Quarterly* 21 (Sept. 1948): 291–312; Frank Freidel, "The Loyal Publication Society," *Mississippi Valley Historical Review* 26 (Dec. 1939): 359–76; Edith Ware, "Committees of Public Information, 1863–1866, "*Historical Outlook* 10 (Feb. 1919).

their own languages. Mechanics and manual laborers were warned in Loyal Publication Society pamphlet No. 30 that if the rebels won, workingmen and women would be treated like slaves. "A Few Words in Behalf of Loyal Ladies of the United States by One of Themselves" urged them to sustain the war effort as decent and virtuous women, shunning the example of brutal Confederate women who, like the Parisian women gathered around the guillotine, called for blood, and asked their soldiers to bring home a Yankee "hand" or "a thumb at least."[10]

Atrocity stories were part of the campaign to rally people round their flag. After the first battle of Bull Run, the New York *Herald* told of ambulances being intentionally fired on and of wounded men purposely trampled by rebel horsemen. The New York *World* spoke of "helpless prisoners stripped and tortured." Other papers occasionally spoke of scalping and hearts being cut out. In 1863, John Bartlett Marshall offered readers *The Brutality of the Rebels, As Shown by Their Cruelty to the Federal Wounded Prisoners; in Their Outrages on Union Men; in the Murder of Negroes, and in Their Unmanly Conduct Throughout the Rebellion* (Providence, 1863). Even Edward Everett when he spoke at Gettysburg used some of his two hours to accuse Confederates of atrocities. As late as September 1864, the Chicago *Tribune* filled a whole page with varied atrocity tales. When true atrocities did come to light – the Fort Pillow massacre of surrendering black soldiers, the horrible conditions in Andersonville prison – newspapers broadcast their outrage, and the Lincoln administration threatened retaliation.[11]

Pamphlets joined the huge stream of editorials and news articles in the thousands of newspapers around the country in explaining and cajoling and inspiring and provoking policies and opinions. They served as supplement to the constant campaign oratory and general "speechifying" that entertained and instructed Americans in the mid-nineteenth century. They built upon a tradition of pamphleteering that went back to the Revolution and to the 1820s and 1830s, when first revolutionaries and then home missionary societies such as the American Tract Society spread their gospels to free and then purify the nation.[12] Soldiers in the field, editors at home, voters in

10 Frank Freidel, "The Loyal Publication Society: A ProUnion Propaganda Agency," *Mississippi Valley Historical Review* 26 (Dec. 1939): 364–71; Frank Klement, *Dark Lanterns: Secret Political Societies, Conspiracies, and Treason Trials in the Civil War* (Baton Rouge, La., 1984), 56.

11 Bernard Weisberger, *Reporters for the Union* (Boston, 1953), 298–9; Albert Castel, "The Fort Pilow Massacre," *Civil War History* 4 (March 1958): 37–50; James M. McPherson, *Battle Cry of Freedom*, 791–8; Gary Wills, "The Words That Remade America: Lincoln at Gettysburg," *Atlantic Monthly* 269 (June 1992): 64.

12 See Bernard Bailyn, ed., *Pamphlets of the American Revolution 1750–1776* (Cambridge, Mass., 1965–); Clifford S. Griffin, *Their Brothers Keepers: Moral Stewardship in the United States, 1800–1865* (New Brunswick, N.J., 1960) .

every election—in short, every citizen, every person, in the most literate and politically vital society in the world—had access to some communication which told him or her what to think, how to vote, and what to do to bring victory to their cause.[13]

People of the age thought such that opinion shaping mattered. New Yorker George T. Strong thought that the antiwar newspapers circulating in army camps were "demoralizing." Many influential Republicans blamed the valleys of falling morale that followed battlefield defeats more on antiwar newspapers and speeches than on the losses themselves. The Union League of New York was organized the *day* after the Democrats created their Society for the Diffusion of Political Knowledge, a Democratic National Committee organization, and within four days, the Philadelphia organization was born. Republicans were determined that the opposition would not steal a march on them in this vital campaign.[14]

While all parties recognized the importance of persuasion in reinforcing materials and men, and while atrocity stories had their days, it is striking how much wartime propaganda was focused away from such horrors of war. Many of the pamphlets, for example, contained constitutional arguments that justified presidential power to emancipate the slaves, or to fight secession, or to suspend the privilege of the writ of habeas corpus. Over fifty pamphlets appeared to debate the latter subject alone.[15] Political parties used the pamphlets to charge each other with dangerous doctrine. Democrats warned of tyranny and the suppression of civil liberty, and especially of miscegenation. Republicans predominantly accused their foes of disloyalty, thus causing needless deaths or inspiring continued rebel resistance. But this rhetoric was similar in many ways to prewar charge and countercharge that Republicans were racial egalitarians and consolidators, "the meddling party" that Horatio Seymour called them, while Democrats had sold out to the "slavocracy" or were obstructionists to progress. Ironically, in the midst of war, the underlying tone of political debate was "business as usual." The electoral process that never stopped throughout the war also demonstrated in day-to-day

13 Jean Baker, *Affairs of Party: The Political Culture of Northern Democrats in the Mid-Nineteenth Century* (Ithaca, N.Y., 1983); William Gienapp, "Politics Seem to Enter into Everything," in Stephen Maizlish, ed., *Essays on Antebellum American Politics* (Arlington, Tex., 1982); Walter Dean Burnham, "The Changing Shape of the American Political Universe," *American Political Science Review* 59 (1965).

14 Frank Freidel, "Introduction," in Freidel, ed., *Union Pamphlets of the Civil War, 1861–1865*, 2 vols. (Cambridge, 1967); George Templeton Strong, *The Diary of George Templeton Strong*, ed., Allan Nevins and Milton Halsey Thomas, 4 vols. (New York, 1952; reprinted: New York, 1974), 3 :300.

15 Sydney G. Fisher, "The Suspension of Habeas Corpus during the War of the Rebellion," *Political Science Quarterly* 3 (1888): 454–88; Harold M. Hyman, *A More Perfect Union: The Impact of the Civil War and Reconstruction on the Constitution* (New York, 1973); Phillip S. Paludan," *A Covenant with Death": The Constitution, Law and Equality in the Civil War Era* (Urbana, Ill., 1979); Freidel, "Loyal Publication Society," 364–5.

experience the principle of self-government that Lincoln kept asserting the war was about.[16]

Propaganda and persuasion thus were entwined during the war, and the level of both remained reasonably elevated. The reason in part was that in this society, political persuasion encompassed almost every subject of political discussion. What they were being propagandized about were things that mattered to them: a vital constitutional system, and the interconnection between slavery and ideals and institutions that they treasured. They were being propagandized about what democratic government meant.

No one had greater responsibility for defining and directing democracy than the president, and Abraham Lincoln may have been the most qualified man in the nation for the job. For over a quarter century, as both lawyer and politician, Lincoln had been in the persuading business in the most democratic society in the world. And what especially had prepared him was the fact that Lincoln had a particular attitude about and relationship toward the democracy that Andrew Jackson helped to spawn in the 1820s.

There is an old saying that says, "No one is sure who discovered water, but we can be pretty sure it wasn't a fish." Lincoln is so consistently linked in public and scholarly thought with democracy that few people have wondered what he meant by the term. The most recent Lincoln book, a collection of his writings intended for a popular audience (edited by former New York governor, Mario Cuomo) is called *Lincoln on Democracy*. His most well-known phrase is arguably "government of the people, by the people and for the people" from the Gettysburg address. The most respected of the older Lincoln scholars, James G. Randall, mused on the meaning of that phrase by wondering if Lincoln emphasized "the *people*" or the prepositions, *of, by,* and *for*. Benjamin Thomas calls the Civil War "A War for Democracy." Yet the most recent collection of Lincoln scholarship contains eight meager references to the word, and Mark E. Neely Jr.'s authoritative *Abraham Lincoln Encyclopedia* refers readers to a short discussion of "representative government." In that brief discussion, however, Neely does insist on "Lincoln's democratic faith that the common man did not need elites to govern him."[17]

16   On prewar political dialogue, see Baker, *Affairs of Party*; Eric Foner, *Free Soil, Free Labor, Free Men: The Ideology of the Republican Party before the Civil War* (New York, 1970); William Gienapp, *The Origins of the Republican Party, 1852–1856* (New York, 1987). Wartime Democrats are studied in Joel Silbey, *A Respectable Minority: The Democratic Party in the Civil War Era* (New York, 1977). Paludan, "*A People's Contest*," chaps. 4, 10.

17   Gabor Boritt, ed., *The Historian's Lincoln: Pseudohistory, Psychohistory, and History* (Urbana, Ill., 1988); Benjamin P. Thomas, *Abraham Lincoln: A Biography* (New York, 1952); James G. Randall, *Lincoln the President* (New York, 1955), 2: 304; Mark E. Neely Jr., *Abraham Lincoln Encyclopedia* (New York, 1982), 81, 261–2; Robert Weibe's fascinating "Lincoln's Fraternal Democracy," in John Thomas, ed., *Abraham Lincoln and the American Political Tradition* (Amherst, Mass., 1986) is about Lincoln's private feelings toward comradeship among men in his age rather than the president's public philosophy.

And yet there are many reasons to wonder if Lincoln was as devoted to pure democracy as that statement suggests. The former president is pretty quiet on what he means. While Lincoln spoke extensively about the meanings of liberty and equality and government, he provided posterity with a thirty-three word definition of democracy: "As I would not be a *slave*, so I would not be a *master*. This expresses my idea of democracy. Whatever differs from this, to the extent of the difference, is no democracy." Certainly, this is an intriguing definition, but it explains very little about Lincoln's understanding of or hopes for democracy. His background does not suggest unqualified admiration for popular rule. Lincoln grew up in the world of Andrew Jackson, and there were things about it that greatly troubled him. Andrew Jackson had proclaimed his faith in the people by saying, "Never for a moment believe that the great body of the citizens ... can deliberately intend to do wrong." But by the time Lincoln entered politics, it was hard to ignore the "wrongs," real and potential, of the citizens. In 1835 and 1840, Alexis de Tocqueville published his two volumes of *Democracy in America* warning of the "tyranny of the majority." Andrew Jackson was less than a year out of the presidency when Lincoln in his first major speech catalogued the dangers of mob rule, warned of Jackson-like tyranny, and asked that respect for the laws, not for popular will, be made "the political religion of the nation." It is not surprising that Lincoln joined the Whig, not Jackson's Democratic, party.[18]

Lincoln also quarreled with Stephen Douglas's advocacy of "popular sovereignty" in determining whether slavery or freedom should exist in the territories. He asserted instead that the Constitution's solution to territorial government was rule by Congress, not the more direct rule by the people in the territories. When Confederate states seceded, they claimed the right of the people in those states to determine who should be their rulers. But Lincoln answered with a legal argument showing that the Constitutional system for changing government was primary. I think there is good reason to believe that Lincoln's emphasis at Gettysburg was on neither "the people" nor the prepositions. It was on "government."

Lincoln seems not to have believed that simply trusting popular will was the ultimate answer to the meaning of the nation. He believed in legal and constitutional restraints. Despite an occasional bow in the direction of simply registering the voters' wishes, Lincoln believed much more strongly in

18 Jackson quoted in Harry Watson, *Liberty and Power: The Politics of Jacksonian America* (New York, 1990); Abraham Lincoln, *Collected Works of Abraham Lincoln*, ed. Roy P. Basler, Marion D. Pratt, and Lloyd A. Dunlap, 9 vols. (New Brunswick, N.J., 1953–55), 1: 108–15. George Frederickson, "The Search for Order and Community," in Cullom Davis, ed., *The Public and the Private Lincoln: Contemporary Perspectives* (Carbondale, Ill., 1979) is sensitive to Lincoln's devotion to the legal order.

the importance of shaping public opinion. In his major speeches, he emphasizes restraints that ranged from paeans to "all conquering mind" to "making
reverence for the laws, the political religion of the nation" to spending over a
third of his first inaugural explaining the constitutionality of his position on
secession.[19]

Lincoln also revealed his doubts about democracy in his belief that the passage of the Kansas-Nebraska Act and the Dred Scott decision were signs of
the erosion of public morality – a "blow[ing] out [of] the moral lights around
us." Challenging Douglas's appeal to popular rule in the territories, Lincoln
told a tale of lost virtue: "Near eighty years ago we began by declaring that
all men are created equal; but now from that beginning we have run down to
the other declaration that for SOME men to enslave OTHERS is a 'sacred right
of self government.'" Lincoln was appealing to a pre-Jacksonian age to cure
the evils of the world that Andrew Jackson had made.[20]

Lincoln did not act like he believed that he needed direct instruction from
"the people" during the secession crisis. He avoided calling Congress to
Washington for almost three months after Sumter was fired on. He also
denied the allegedly popular act of secession by insisting that people had
to be bound by the constitution, which made changing governments in a
constitutional election the most legitimate way. He spoke of majority rule,
but it was majority rule guided by a constitutional process.

Lincoln's desire to escape the pressures of public opinion in certain instances does not mean that he believed for a moment that he could be insensitive
to it. Throughout the war, Lincoln constantly manipulated public opinion.
The most well-known example is his response to Horace Greeley's "Prayer
of Twenty Millions." In August of 1862, the powerful editor of the *New
York Tribune* scolded Lincoln for his laggard emancipation policy, for revers-
ing the proclamations of Generals Fremont and Hunter that freed slaves
and for upholding generals who opposed emancipation. Lincoln's answer
is perhaps as famous as anything he wrote. "What I do about emancipation
I do to save the union," Lincoln said. "If I could save the union by freeing
all, some or none of the slaves I would do any of these things."[21]

Some authors have insisted that this shows his reluctance to emancipate,
his greater devotion to the Union than to emancipation. However, when
considered as propagandizing, as consciously shaping public opinion,

---

19 See references in Neely's article on "Representative Government."
20 Lincoln, *Collected Works of Abraham Lincoln*, 2:275. See also David Donald, *Lincoln Reconsidered* (New
York, 1956), 231–3, for Lincoln's Whig opposition to majoritarian rule. Donald is arguing for his
idea that "an excess of democracy" brought on the Civil War and includes Lincoln's comments in
that context.
21 Lincoln, *Collected Works of Abraham Lincoln*, 5:388–9.

Lincoln's answer takes on new light—Lincoln knew that Greeley's readers numbered in the hundreds of thousands and that he was not writing to the editor alone. Furthermore, Lincoln had decided, at least a month before his August 1862 letter, to free a very large "some" of the slaves—all those still under rebel control. In addition, he had already gone public in March with a plan to have border states emancipate their slaves. Lincoln's reply to Greeley, Stephan Oates has argued, was an effort to let the Northern people know that when the slaves were freed they would be free in service of a deeply treasured, bloodily purchased ideal. Liberty and Union were being made inseparable.[22]

Lincoln also propagandized in the realm of civil liberties. He took special pains to explain why he suspended the privilege of the writ of habeas corpus in April 1861 and kept on suspending it whenever the safety of the Union demanded it. Historians have, of course, written of Lincoln's defense, but they have not clearly understood how Lincoln was shaping a vision of what was at stake and what their constitutional system meant. Lincoln's defense is an effort to capture the allegiance of potential opponents by showing them how encompassing constitutional questions are and how much they are linked to the survival of the Union. The president spent many hours on his letters to New York and Ohio Democrats explaining the stakes and why the constitution justified what he had done, thus bringing a listening audience to his side and justifying the ongoing fight. In a general sense, Lincoln kept the constitutional debate going throughout the war and thus propagandized to persuade the people that their constitutional system was adequate to survive and prosecute a war.[23]

Lincoln was not only propagandizing in a general sense. He timed his remarks to fit specific circumstances. The president was very sensitive to timing, to issuing his arguments and pronouncements to counteract or to respond to specific incidents as well. He waited, of course, for the "victory" at Antietam before issuing the preliminary Emancipation Proclamation. But in the civil liberties realm, Lincoln acutely watched events as well. This fact is less well appreciated. In his otherwise superb book on Lincoln and civil liberties, Neely provides a very subtle argument to explain the fact that Lincoln in June 1863 defined threats to the nation in a very broad and chilling way for dissent against government policy. Neely's argument rests on

---

22 Stephan B. Oates, *Abraham Lincoln: The Man Behind the Myths* (New York, 1984), 106–7.

23 See Hyman, *A More Perfect Union*, as well as Harold Hyman and William Wiecek, *Equal Justice under Law* (New York, 1982) on the adequacy of the Constitution and an argument for a broadly, not narrowly, construed vision of what constitutional discussion encompasses. Mark E. Neely Jr., '*Fate of Liberty: Abraham Lincoln and Civil Liberties* (New York, 1991), 34, 68, 235, denies that Lincoln was a constitutional theorist but does so from a narrower definition than is offered here.

an idea that Lincoln understood habeas corpus rights as "mythical" and general rather than "legalistic." I do not have time to explore the nuances of that argument, but I think it misses the point, a point that is clarified if we consider Lincoln's words here as propaganda focused on an immediate result.

Lincoln held off replying to his critics against his "attack on civil liberties" until June 1863, although they had written him in early May. There was not a pressing need for an immediate answer then. But by early June, Robert E. Lee, fresh from victory at Chancellorsville, was advancing north. One of the reasons he was doing that was because he believed, as did Davis, that Northern antiwar protest might signal support for the rebellion. In this environment, Lincoln answered his critics with a sweeping and threatening justification of government suppression of dissent. "The man who stands by and says nothing, when the peril of his government is discussed, can not be misunderstood. If not hindered, he is sure to help the enemy. Much more if he talks ambiguously—talks for his country with 'buts' and 'ifs' and 'ands.'" One of the striking things about this statement is that Lincoln in fact arrested very few people for protesting against the war. He allowed Democratic critics a huge amount of latitude to call him a "tyrant," a "dictator," and other things much less attractive. But he knew the value of pressing the button of restraint in a time of crisis, and he knew the value of allowing people to wonder what the limits of dissent might be. Words of propaganda as well as the guns at Gettysburg were part of the Union arsenal.[24]

Lincoln may have worked even more broadly than in his well-publicized open letters to critics and friends. In election campaigns there is evidence to suggest that the president quietly used his influence to implement both dark and brighter forces of Republican Party campaigning. The major instrument used was the Union League. Organized in the early days of the war in the border states, these leagues by 1862 had fallen into lethargy in the aftermath of Democratic electoral successes. But by early 1863, they were reviving again, thanks to energetic efforts by Lincoln supporters and friends. The governor of Illinois, Richard Yates, was especially encouraging, faced as he was with a Democratic majority in the state legislature as of January 1863. He put the authority and resources of the governor's office as well as the Republican Party behind the league and helped to send agents to other midwestern states. Lincoln's old friends and associates began to appear in local leagues. The Springfield branch gained membership and influence when James C. Conkling, a personal friend of Lincoln, became president. Republican governors throughout the midwest began looking to the

24 Lincoln, *Collected Works of Abraham Lincoln*, 6:265 (June 12, 1863); Neely, *Fate of Liberty*, 223–4.

League to counteract democratic legislatures and opposition. Indiana's
Morton organized his state's league from the top down, using a "gift" from a
banker friend to subsidize early recruiting efforts, and the organization soon
spread all over the state. A similar pattern could be seen in activities in Iowa
and Michigan as league popularity grew. Illinois alone boasted over 140,000
members by late 1863.[25]

Meanwhile, another eastern league was very much within the president's
reach in Washington. Under the leadership of Illini James Edmunds, this
group began to build bridges outside the capital city, organized a national
council, and began to issue charters to leagues that neighboring states were
organizing. Edmunds contacted the midwestern group, and the two planned
a national convention that met in Cleveland in mid-May 1863. The convention was dominated by people very close to the president. John Forney,
editor of two newspapers in Philadelphia and Washington, D.C., and a confi-
dant of Lincoln, attended. Postmaster General Blair gave the major address.
Chase sent some of his lieutenants. Stanton had a man there. Edmunds was
chosen national president, and one of Lincoln's personal secretaries, William
O. Stoddard, became corresponding secretary. The national council of the
new organization was given its headquarters in Lincoln's city, and all nine of
the national officers were also from the district. State councils still retained
autonomy, but the network of their activity reached to Washington, where
Lincoln could watch. By 1864, this national league would so correspond to
the Republican Party that it met the day before the party nominating
convention, beat back efforts to nominate a more radical man, and then
endorsed Lincoln. The next day, two-thirds of the members of that convention showed up in the same hall as members of the National Union Convention—the name that the Republicans chose to run under in 1864. Not
surprisingly, these men also nominated Lincoln.[26]

While the Union Leagues propagandized and "politicked" at a relatively
elevated level, emphasizing rational if strong arguments, there was less deco-
rum in state political organizations. There, almost any charge was legitimate,
and conspiracy theories were staples of the campaigns. The president could
not directly control state-level arguments that were used to defeat the Democrats in the election. But what state politicians said and did was not beyond
his knowledge, nor was it beyond his influence. A word of disapproval from
him, and tactics would have been moderated, rhetoric restrained. But he did

---

25 Klement, *Dark Lanterns*, 54–5; Frank Freidel, ed., *Union Pamphlets of the Civil War, 1861–1865*
(Cambridge, Mass., 1967), 1:1–14; Strong, *Diary of George Templeton Strong*, 3: 303–7.
26 Klement, *Dark Lanterns*, chap. 2. Klement does not make as much of the Lincoln connection as I
do here. He also is less critical of the president than I am going to be.

not act to restrain the rhetoric of partisans who manufactured the story of a Democratic conspiracy to organize secret "Dark Lantern" societies. He did nothing to contradict stories that were circulated about the purported strength of the Knights of the Golden Circle and their plots. He did not deny the possibility that there were treasonous groups with plans to help the Confederacy by seizing the Indianapolis arsenal, massacring Union League supporters, and importing 50,000 voters from other states to elect Clement C. Vallandigham in Ohio.[27]

Lincoln may not have been able to influence state-level political campaigns, and he may not have wanted to. He and his supporters benefited from public belief that Democrats were disloyal. But he was one of the shrewdest politicians of his time. Using his 26 years of political experience, he had successfully maneuvered himself into the Republican nomination. As one supporter put it, "One great public mistake ... generally received and acquiesced in, is that he is considered by the people of this country as a frank, guileless, and unsophisticated man. There never was greater mistake ... He handled and moved men remotely as we do pieces upon a chess board." And he continued to control his cabinet carefully and to keep his influence in the Republican Party, to reward friends with office and take them away from apostates. Lincoln was surely watching campaigns and may have been doing more than that, or with similar effect, not doing it.[28]

It seems clear that Lincoln was a propagandist in the ways that he manipulated public opinion during the war and that disposition grew from his belief that the people needed guidance and restraint. But I have said that Lincoln was a good propagandist. He shaped public opinion and the polity itself in ways that permitted it, and the people who were ultimately the foundation of it, to advance toward their goals in liberating ways.[29]

Lincoln's problem simply stated (it is by no means a simple problem) is this: He knew the necessity of making Americans of his age accept his vision of what was wrong with the nation and how to make it right. He also had some immediate instrumental needs to satisfy – he had to keep the people of the North at war, and that meant that he had to rally them around ideals that would define their purposes in ways likely to maintain their support for the cause. They had lost their way in previous decades. They

27 William Hesseltine, *Lincoln and the War Governors* (New York, 1955), 311–36.
28 Richard N. Current, *The Lincoln Nobody Knows* (New York, 1958), 187–213; David Donald, *Lincoln Reconsidered* (New York, 1956), 57–81; Harry Carmen and Richard Luthin, *Lincoln and the Patronage* (New York, 1943).
29 I am here relying on the ideas of how the constitutional system should work at its best as argued by Ronald Dworkin, *Law's Empire* (Cambridge, Mass., 1986); Sortirios Barber, *On What the Constitution Means* (Baltimore, Md., 1984).

had lost their way because they had been propagandized by other voices and perspectives who had used some positive ideals to advance some dangerous causes. Those forces, specifically Andrew Jackson and his party and Roger Taney and the Supreme Court – a court appointed predominantly by Jackson and other Democratic presidents – were telling the people a story of who they were, defining for them the meaning of democratic government. That viewpoint emphasized their least attractive qualities but did so in the name of ideals they treasured. It anointed racism in the name of democracy, protected slavery in the name of self-government, and promoted the expansion of slavery in the name of the constitution. Some of the consequences of this position had been gag rules in Congress, attacks on abolitionist speakers in public, the beating of a United States senator for making a speech, and the silencing of Southern debate over the merits of slavery, the most destructive element in the constitutional system. In addition, of course, the Union itself was constantly in danger from threats of secession.[30]

Lincoln's responsibility was to counteract the arguments that had led to these results. In a world that was very conscious of how language might be deployed to shape public opinion, Lincoln had to point the escape route from the peril of the nation and the failure of its best hopes. As James M. McPherson suggests, Lincoln first caught his audience's attention with metaphors that placed his ideals within their concrete experience.[31] But Lincoln, I believe, was not just mirroring, not just talking to common people in their language to gain their support; he was also shaping their understanding, educating them. Lincoln reached beyond their current frames of reference to change who they were.

He did so by calling on their history. He argued persuasively that the founders of the nation had hopes for an end to slavery. He showed that the Declaration of Independence established the ideals that the Constitution was designed to implement. Lincoln also provided carefully reasoned arguments to reconcile basic contradictions within the Declaration of Independence – conflicts between equality on the one hand and the consent of the governed on the other. The problem was that the people whose government this was were being urged by Douglas and proslavery apologists in Dixie and on the

---

30 Paludan, *A Covenant with Death*; Russell B. Rye, *Fettered Freedom: Civil Liberties and the Slavery Controversy, 1830–1860* (East Lansing, Mich., 1963).

31 Kenneth Cmeil, *Democratic Eloquence: The Fight Over Popular Speech in Nineteenth Century America* (Berkeley, Calif., 1991); Daniel McInerney, "The Fortunate Heirs of Freedom: Abolition and Republican Thought," Ph.D. diss., Purdue University, 1984, chap. 6; James M. McPherson, "How Lincoln Won the War with Metaphors," in *Abraham Lincoln and the Second American Revolution* (New York, 1990), 93–112.

Supreme Court not to consent to the equality of "all men" whom the Declaration said were "created equal."[32]

Lincoln was trying to counteract the local prejudices of his age, to overcome the mindless fears of an age that saw foreigners and blacks as threats to local community traditions. He called on them to overcome the small community-nurtured racism of the day by asking listeners to think beyond those communities in both space and time – to recall a revolutionary generation that opposed slavery, to consider the claims of a transcending and enduring idea of equal liberty.[33] Much like William Lloyd Garrison and other immediatists, Lincoln knew there were "mountains of ice" to melt. He defined the changes that he sought in more conservative terms, but he knew that propaganda was imperative faced with the moral inertia of pre–Civil War democracy.[34]

There were dark moments in Lincoln's propaganda. At times, he tried to reach his audiences by calming and thus sustaining their biases. In debates with Douglas, Lincoln did tell audiences that he shared their prejudice against

32 Harry V. Jaffa, *Crisis of the House Divided: An Interpretation of the Issues in the Lincoln-Douglas Debates, with a new preface* (Seattle, 1959; reissued: Chicago, 1982); Thomas Engerman, "Assessing Jaffa's Contribution," *Review of Politics* 49 (Winter 1987).

33 Jacques Ellul, *Propaganda: The Formation of Men's Attitudes* (New York, 1966), 63–6, 90ff, argues that propaganda is a sociological phenomenon by which a society 'seeks to integrate the maximum number of individuals into itself" and to persuade people that "the civilization representing their way of life is the best." Political propaganda appears when political parties and interest groups seek to modify behavior. Ellul sees the use of propaganda as "intrinsically undemocratic." In a modern world, there are reasons to feel that it is. Ellul's critique rests on his earlier book, *Technological Society,* in which he described a world of isolated individuals cut off from their roots in families and small communities and hence cut off from values that allowed individuals to develop visions of the world with its uniqueness and complexity. In modern society with mass communications, Ellul argues, people are more easily victimized by a media that excludes views outside the "mainstream," which it creates to meet the needs of a consumer society with a national and international market. In addition, the vast amounts of information to which individuals have access to requires them to have frames of reference in which to place disparate data. All of these serve a modern propaganda effort that is itself shaped by a willingness to meet the populace at its most irrational level, its least common denominator.

But Lincoln's world was not modern in many of these senses. Small communities characterized the United States in the mid-nineteenth century. Approximately 80 percent of the people lived in places smaller than 2,500 population. Local newspapers spread community values, as did local churches, local politicians, local government meetings, and locally generated and controlled schools. A few newspapers had at least a regional circulation: Horace Greeley's *New York Tribune* is the best example. Church newspapers spread the faith to parishioners throughout North and South. But the world of Lincoln was one where people's independence of judgment was strengthened by the effects of their personalized local experience and the values with which they had grown up. And yet there is reason to doubt that small-community America meant that propaganda was absent, irrelevant, or weakened. The point here is that Lincoln was challenging the very dark prejudices that had been nurtured by and within those local communities which Ellul admires. Lincoln was using persuasion to liberate people from their prejudices.

34 Leonard Richards, *"Gentlemen of Property and Standing": Antiabolitionist Mobs in Jacksonian Democracy* (New York, 1970); James Brewer Stewart, *"Holy Warriors": The Abolitionists and American Slavery* (New York, 1977) both emphasize the ways in which abolitionists threatened locally based racism.

social and political equality with blacks. He also provoked their fears by alleging a conspiracy by Chief Justice Taney, Presidents Pierce and Buchanan, and Senator Douglas to introduce slavery into Northern states. Yet, at the same time, Lincoln was also providing a propaganda that did not pander to, but promised to change, public discourse by appealing to what he called "the better angels of our nature." He denied Douglas's argument that attacking slavery ultimately implied miscegenation. He insisted that blacks were equal to whites in their right "to keep what they earned by the sweat of their brow," and he showed that that belief also lay deep in their experience by describing and proclaiming the abiding relevance of the Declaration of Independence's promise that "all men are created equal."

But for all the manipulation and control that he exercised, for all the persuasive arguments that he utilized, through all the shaping and building of union support and morale, Lincoln did not succumb very often to the dark possibilities of propagandizing. And what is remarkable is that during war, the time when propaganda historically has become most crude and vicious, Lincoln's messages chose to inspire and not to frighten the public to act. He never rallied Union sentiment to hatred of the Southern enemy. He never targeted rebel leaders as villains, he never pictured the enemy as inhuman or deserving of death. With few exceptions, his propaganda essentially appealed to the best qualities of the Union, and as he faced the prospect of peace and the beginning of his second term, he argued that the North shared Southern guilt for slavery and hence was similarly deserving of God's punishment – the war. Healing persuasion, indeed.

Surely, political calculation can explain some of this reconciling language – the need to restore the Union, the presence in the North of thousands of people born in Dixie. But there was also, I believe, something else – a serious understanding that when leaders spoke to the people, the stakes were high. Political leaders were not just candidates for office and then officeholders. They were not just asking voters what they wanted and then giving it to them. They were opinion makers. They helped to create the people's ideas and showed them how to implement their hopes into laws and into a future. They helped to create the polity by the way that they propagandized. Writing in August 1858, Lincoln, preparing to debate Douglas about the future of the nation and the existence of slavery, noted how powerful was the influence of the senator:

Judge Douglas is a man of large influence. His bare opinion goes far to fix the opinions of others. Besides this, thousands hang their hopes upon forcing their opinions to agree with his. It is a party necessity with them to *say* they agree with him ... If ... he shall succeed in moulding public sentiment to a perfect accordance with his own ... what barrier will be left against slavery being made lawful every-where?[35]

And Lincoln came from a Whig background, which knew that there were both pernicious and positive ways that leaders helped to create the nation, the people they hoped to lead. As one Whig paper wrote:

Put the case that the same multitude were addressed by two orators, and on the same question and occasion; that the first of these orators considered in his mind that the people he addressed were to be controlled by several passions ... – the orator may be fairly said to have no faith in the people; he rather believes that they are creatures of passion, and subject to none but base and selfish impulses. But now a second orator arises, a Chatham, a Webster, a Pericles, a Clay; his generous spirit expands itself through the vast auditory, and he believes that he is addressing a company of high spirited men, citizens. ... When he says "fellow citizens," they believe him, and at once, from a tumultuous herd they are converted into men ... their thoughts and feeling rise to an heroical heights, beyond that of common men or common times. The second orator "had faith in the people"; he addressed the better part of each man's nature, supposing it to be in him – and it was in him.

Thus, Lincoln was thinking of responsibility and education when he spoke of public opinion: "In this age, in this country, public sentiment is everything. *With* it, nothing can fail; *against* it, nothing can succeed. Whoever moulds public sentiment, goes deeper than he who enacts statutes or pronounces judicial decisions. He makes enforcement of these, else impossible."[37]

Lincoln had not learned very well the lesson promoted by modern campaign advisors that people vote their fears. He kept demonstrating a belief that the American people might be appealed to according to "the better angels of our nature." Trained by decades of experience as politician and lawyer, propelled into the public arena by efforts to define the nation's future according to its darkest qualities, Lincoln used his persuasive talents to create a society better than he found it. In war and in peace, he was, usually, the kind of propagandist that the polity profoundly needs.

35   Lincoln, *Collected Works of Abraham Lincoln*, 2:553.
36   As quoted in Thomas Brown, *Politics and Statesmanship Essays on the American Whig Party* (New York, 1985), 10-11. On politics of the era generally, see Robert Kelley, *The Cultural Pattern in American Politics* (New York, 1979). On Whigs, see Daniel Walker Howe, *The Political Culture of the American Whigs* (Chicago, 1979); Rush Welter, *The Mind of America*, 1820–1860 (New York, 1975), 190–218. Writing after the Lincoln Douglas debates had ended, the pro-Republican *Illinois Journal* observed that Lincoln's speeches "are stamped with the impress of a sincerity and candor which appeals at once to the higher and noble faculties of the mind, and wins over the better feelings and affections of our nature. ... They, in effect, are in advance of the age . . . and thus contain those elements which ... [carry] them beyond the present and makes them useful and beautiful in the future." Nov. 14, 1858, 1.
37   Lincoln, *Collected Works of Abraham Lincoln*, 2: 552–3.

18

The Permanence of Internal War:
The Prussian State and Its Opponents, 1870–71

ALF LÜDTKE

Historians relate the totalizing of war to long-term historical transformations. Whereas some stress the impact of commercialization and industrialization, others refer to claims for and the spread of mass participation in politics. This structuralist argument ignores, however, a cultural shift that prepared the ground, namely, an increasing readiness for violence against "others."

Movements claiming missionary goals, in particular, tend to commit unrestricted violence against those on the outside or in the way. Medieval crusades established the precedent. But during the religious wars of the sixteenth and seventeenth centuries, the opposing factions intensified tremendously the brutality used against foes of their respective "good cause."[1] Groups that set out from European "centers" to colonize "the rest of the world," moreover, displayed similar attitudes. They promised religious and cultural redemption. In practice, however, the colonizers resorted to mutilating or killing their audiences, at least when the latter exhibited skepticism toward the new order of things. Colonialist assumptions about the sociocultural inequality of peoples resonated with appeals to "the national," which had been voiced in Europe since the late eighteenth century. As a consequence, religion was not the only basis on which the exclusion, and sometimes the wholesale murder, of others was legitimized.

Violence against "others" may be seen as taking place not only between but also within sovereignties or "states." In one respect, however, this view remains blind: It ignores the perpetual internal "small war," designed by authorities to suppress or keep at bay all those whom they considered "dangerous." In the context of state making, such efforts were expanded under the label of *police* beginning in the late sixteenth century in parts of western and

---

1 For the French "case," see Denis Crouzet, *Les guerriers de Dieu: La violence au temps de troubles de religion, vers 1525–vers 1610*, 2 vols. (Seyssel, 1990).

continental Europe. To be sure, justifications of the *good police* avoided any reference to war. *Policing* was legitimized as a product of the sovereigns' all-encompassing responsibility for and protection of their territories. Concepts of a good police stimulated officials to aim at the strict control of communities and people. Nothing but total surveillance of everyone and a strong hand against presumed violators would guarantee the well-being of both, the individual subjects and the nation as a whole. Accordingly, the nation's prosperity and the contentment of individuals rested upon the "security" of the state. Only provision of the latter would enable the pursuit of the former. Individual efforts were doomed to fail if "public" security was not established and preserved.

From the early eighteenth century onward, the protection and enhancement of "good police" in Prussia had been a permanent concern of the king's servants. Accordingly, officials made a constant effort to maintain order among the state's subjects. To enforce rigorous discipline would propel the commonweal. Those who would not abide by the rules had to be physically removed from the social order, if not expelled from the state entirely. Beggars and other migrant people of apparently no means were forced to turn to a "decent" way to support themselves. However, if such measures as the confinement to a workhouse, for instance, brought no results, the authorities would then expel these *classes dangereuses*. Their treatment followed military patterns of fighting against an enemy. In fact, troops were regularly called on and, thus, participated routinely in searches for internal enemies. This longstanding practice of policing *modo militaire* directly contributed to rendering warfare a legitimate means of state, not only in external but also in internal affairs. Thus, everyday practices of the state gradually undermined notions of a limited war that was common in early modern times. In other words, internal war developed a totalizing drive well before the 1860s and 1870s. The episode of 1870–71, which is to follow here, marks the final stage of this process.

I

On March 1, 1877, Chancellor Otto von Bismarck reported to the Prussian king and German emperor, Wilhelm I, on a case unheard of in the history of the Prussian officer corps, the foundation of this monarchy and state. A retired general, Vogel von Falckenstein, had been fined in a ruling of a Braunschweig civil court. In a public trial, the judges had found this senior officer, then the military governor of the coastal provinces, principally liable for the detention of five Social Democrats during most of the war against France in the fall and winter of 1870–71. The actual amount of the fine still had to be set in a second trial. Bismarck "respectfully" proposed that the *Fiskus* (state finances) should intercede and pay the sum; in addition, the *Fiskus* should also take care of the court fees and Falckenstein's legal counsel, which presently amounted to 340 marks.[2] He argued that Falckenstein had not acted as a private person but in his official capacity as military governor, a servant of the state who had executed royal ordinances during the "state of siege."[3]

An outline of the case follows. On September 9, 1870, Falckenstein had issued the order to arrest five members of the board of the Socialist German Workers' Party (*Sozialistische Deutsche Arbeiterpartei*, or SDAP), headquartered in Braunschweig, and to detain them at the fortress of Lötzen in East Prussia. On September 14, an additional detention was ordered by the military governor, that of the prominent democrat and deputy to the Prussian *Landtag* (state parliament), Johann Jacoby from Königsberg (East Prussia).[4] The five from Braunschweig were held at Lötzen for five months, whereas Jacoby was released after only five weeks.

The reason given by the military governor for ordering these arrests was the danger that the six individuals posed to the security of the state, especially during this time of war. In the case of the five from Braunschweig, the military referred to the publication of a declaration in the SDAP's journal, *Der Volksstaat*. This text fiercely opposed continuation of the war in the wake of Napoléon III's defeat at Sedan (September 2, 1870). Jacoby had voiced similar views in a public meeting. In particular, he had opposed the annexation of Alsace and Lorraine as war aims. To the military, statements such as those criticizing the war effort appeared dangerous or, for that matter, treasonous.

II

On July 19, 1870, immediately after the declaration of war, the king of Prussia released a statement that declared large parts of the North German Confederation to be in a state of siege. Affected were extensive frontier areas, namely, the provinces along the Rhine and the entire coastal district, from the Dutch border to Russia. Regarding the latter, spy reports as well as

---

2   Geheimes Staatsarchiv Preussischer Kulturbesitz, Berlin-Dahlem (hereafter cited as GStA/PK), Rep. 2.2.1 (M), Nr. 32403, fol. 1ff.

3   Two years later, the chancellor reported again on the state of the affair. Meanwhile, it was not only the costs and fees of the counsellors or the courts. Now, the five plaintiffs had succeeded also on the actual compensation: Vogel von Falckenstein would have to pay the total amount of 4,300 marks. To Bismarck, it was out of question that this money would be taken from state funds, see GStA/PK, Rep. 2.2.1 (M), Nr. 32403.

4   August Bebel, *Aus meinem Leben* (Leipzig, 1946), 2:166ff; Paul Kampffmeyer, Bruno Altmann, *Vor dem Sozialistengesetz: Krisenjahre des Obrigkeitsstaates* (Berlin, 1928), 62.

widespread rumors maintained that the French fleet might blockade the ports and, possibly, launch an invasion. At this time, Prussia installed military governors throughout the country.[5] In the coastal provinces, General Falckenstein was charged with safeguarding these areas and protecting the state and its citizens from potential threats.

The state of siege transferred the responsibility for keeping security and maintaining order from the civilian administration and the criminal (or police) courts to the commanding officers of army districts (*Generalkommando* or, as in this case, a military governor, who combined several *Generalkommandos*) and their military courts. These officers were empowered to act wherever and whenever they deemed necessary to establish that somebody or some behavior was interfering with the war effort.

This regulation relied on longstanding traditions of the Prussian monarchy and its army. A law of June 4, 1851, gave the government the right to declare a state of siege under certain conditions.[6] The law's main function was to provide legal cover for preserving the essentials of the military's prerogative in all matters of public security as it had developed during the ancien régime.[7] The necessity to legalize the military's claim to possess the final authority to define what good order meant for the state and society had resulted in the Prussian constitution of 1850.[8] Here, the state had granted Prussians a bill of rights, which included the sanctity of private homes and the right to associate with others. However, specific laws – for example, the laws regarding police, public assembly, and associations – regulated as well as severely restricted basic rights prescribed in the constitution. Yet Prussian citizens had *civil* institutions that could be called upon when they felt hampered or harassed by agents of the state, namely, the courts.[9] Thereafter, conflicts over such situations became matters between the individual and the *Fiskus*, or another administrative state body (the monarch, however, continued to rule "above" the law), and not simply a matter between the individual and the state agent.

It was precisely this feature of the Prussian mode of "rule of law" that ran counter to the *superarbitrium*, or final say in all affairs concerning the order of

---

5 Bundesarchiv Potsdam (hereafter cited as BA Potsdam), RKA, Nr. 1136, fol. 2, cf. the instruction from July 28, ibid., fol. 5ff.

6 Ernst Rudolf Huber, ed., *Dokumente zur deutschen Verfassungsgeschichte* (Stuttgart, 1961), 1:414ff; on the previous (and preparatory) order of May 10, 1849, see Ernst Rudolf Huber, *Deutsche Verfassungsgeschichte seit 1789*, 3d rev. ed. (Stuttgart, 1988), 3:47–8.

7 On the prerogative and its daily execution in the eighteenth century, see Max Lehmann, *Scharnhorst* (Leipzig, 1887), vol. 2; Otto Büsch, *Militärsystem und Sozialleben im alten Preussen, 1713–1807* (Berlin, 1962).

8 Huber, ed., *Dokumente*, 401ff; Huber, *Deutsche Verfassungsgeschichte*, 3:35ff, chap. 2.

9 On another domain of citizens' efforts to establish self-regulation, see Heinrich Heffter, *Deutsche Selbstverwaltung im 19. Jahrhundert* (Stuttgart, 1950), 322ff, 404ff.

state and society, and that the military jealously tried to guard.[10] In fact, a cabinet order from October 17, 1820, prescribed conditions that were to be fulfilled before military officers could take charge of matters in civil life.[11] At issue was the quelling of riots. Contrary to the informal routines as they had been practiced for decades, the order of 1820 generally required a formal request from a civilian authority to the local military officer. However, this new requirement was undermined by another paragraph of the very same text: In cases of "imminent danger," military action was justified without a prior civilian request. Ironically, this order was never officially published (it only appeared in the *Annalen der Preussischen Inneren Staatsverwaltung*, thereby addressing officials but not the wider public).

Thus, the cabinet order of 1820 allowed the military to pursue its practices of intervening in the day-to-day affairs of civil society not only upon the request of civil authorities. Under the umbrella of ascribing new legal restrictions, this order left untouched the military's claim to a general *superarbitrium*. In addition, no further limits would apply after the military had been called in. The troops could discharge their full force, including firearms and ammunition. Consequently, civilian officials at all levels perceived the perpetuation of the "military condominium in all police matters" (Max Lehmann) to be legal and legitimate.

But military involvement in civilian affairs and the treatment of civilians according to military standards was not limited to cases of heated conflict. The experiences of "loyal subjects" and military officers was shaped, to a considerable extent, by daily life in the 200 or so towns housing military garrisons. Thus, a majority of the residents of these towns were accustomed to continuous military involvement in all police matters. In addition, military guards were more numerous and patrolled more frequently than the local police, who often were elderly and sometimes handicapped. As a result, soldiers and noncommissioned officers (NCOs) were responsible for turning abstract regulations into concrete policing "on the spot." For example, soldiers and not *Polizeidiener* (civil police agents) often controlled speeding carriages or prohibited smoking in public spaces. Thus, civilians were accustomed to the arbitrariness of military personnel. Soldiers followed their instructions to enforce "good order" at any cost. However, they had not obtained even the minimum professional training required of civil police agents.

10 Minister of the interior, Otto von Manteuffel, Sept. 14, 1850, in a statement opposing proposals of the minister of war, in the course of the ministerial deliberations of the law on the state of siege, GStA/PK Berlin, Rep. 84a, Nr. 2106, fol. 23.
11 See Alf Lüdtke, *Police and State in Prussia, 1815–1850* (Cambridge, 1989), 180–1; for the text of the order, see ibid., 214.

A so-called "state of siege" might entail the suspension of certain provisions of the Prussian constitution. In July 1870, however, the Prussian government acted reluctantly on this score. For example, government ministers left untouched the competence of criminal and civil courts, as contained in Article VII of the constitution.

In Falckenstein's case, the military governor did not rely on a court order when his troops made the previously mentioned arrests of the five socialists and the democrat Jacoby in September 1870. The Prussian civilian officials who commented on the reports that the general submitted to the king employed solid juridical reasoning and immediately sensed the problem that might be created. Bismarck himself shared their skepticism. In a note to the king, he begged the question and explicitly refrained from commenting on whether or not the detention could be upheld if the detainees appealed to a civilian court. The chancellor remained firm, however, with regard to the general policy toward critics. In a letter sent from the royal headquarters in France on September 13, he instructed the Prussian Ministry of State (*Staatsministerium*) that

wherever similar treacherous activities show up they have to be repelled immediately. Editors of journals who publish such statements have to be indicted. And if it is necessary to declare a state of siege in certain areas, the responsible official or minister should approach His Majesty, the King without hesitation.[12]

In the realm of everyday politics, strong rhetoric and flexible practices were not mutually exclusive. The detention of Jacoby in particular triggered criticism of the government's "illegal" practices, prompting Bismarck to look for tactical relief. The chancellor felt that he had no alternative but to recommend to Falckenstein that he abandon another of his measures—the general and unspecified prohibition of any public assembly of Social Democrats throughout the coastal provinces. The only means by which to achieve this goal would be to issue special decrees that prohibited each and every assembly. The general followed this advice and suspended the ban on assembly, an action that he was not obliged to undertake, since his superior, after all, was the king and not Bismarck. Concomitantly, though, he ordered that police should "immediately report anybody who by public statement supported France in its resistance to German conditions for peace. ... These persons are to be arrested as long as the state of siege is in effect."[13]

12 GStA/PK, Rep. 77 (M), tit. 500, Nr. 42, fol. 33.
13 GStA/PK, Rep. 77 (M), tit. 500, Nr. 42, fol. 67, Oct. 5, 1870; on the range of repressive aspirations of the military governor, see his reports of the following months, BA Potsdam, RKA, Nr. 1130.

I V

The Prussian ministers were quick to take up Bismarck's instruction to expand the state of siege. They concurred with the chancellor that it seemed politically unwise to expand the competences of the military commanders at this point. They gave two particular reasons. The first referred to secret police reports that indicated that about 25,000 draftees in the army were members or sympathizers of the Social Democratic movement. The ministers were unsure whether Social Democratic agitation could in any way resonate with these conscripts, since it was the SDAP's position to denounce all wars, while at the same time avoiding national issues.

The second reason appeared to be more problematic than the potential existence of Social Democrats among the troops. During the first days of the war, when French troops seemed close to invading the western provinces of the Reich as well as attacking the shoreline, the government had not yet extended the competences of the military. If these measures were now granted in September – after the French navy had withdrawn and the Prussians were victoriously marching into France – the general public would neither understand nor support them.

V

On August 16, 1870, the president of the province of Hanover sent a special report to the king.[14] The president was responsible for maintaining security and order in this province, which comprised the former kingdom of Hanover conquered by Prussian troops four years earlier. Provincial administrators had been repeatedly admonished to focus on sympathizers of the Guelph dynasty, that is, individuals striving for the reconstitution of a separate Hanoverian state. Accordingly, the president referred to a previous report in which he had outlined aspects of the increasing activity of that group, which he labeled the "particularistic faction" (*partikularistische Partei*). He contended that agitators might gain wider support, at least among the lower strata of the population. In his view, these people could easily be infused with mistrust and discontent toward the Prussian government. He added that the Guelphs had even hinted at the possibility of war, which appeared to them the only means to regain independence from Prussia. Thus, the president noted, in the wake of the war

---

14   GStA/PK, Rep. 2.2.1. (M), Nr. 15853, fol. 128ff. On the background of the situation in Hanover after 1866–67, see also Heide Barmeyer, *Hannovers Eingliederung in den Preussischen Staat: Annexion und administrative Integration, 1866–1868* (Hildesheim, 1983).

of 1866, this particularistic faction had been extremely active. His majesty, however, could feel secure, the president further stated, because the overwhelming majority of the population demonstrated a strong sense of national patriotism. As a result of this general support for the nation, treasonous utterances and activities were pursued only "in secret."[15]

To his surprise, the provincial president of Hanover witnessed a sweeping wave of friendly if not enthusiastic sentiment toward Prussian troops. Both anti-French (or anti-Napoléon) feelings and aspirations for German unity seemed to overcome the stubborn antipathy toward Prussia, which so many Hanoverians had hitherto displayed.

The government and its administration had not relied solely on uncertain perspectives on the people's consent of (if not support for) the government's policies. The provincial president emphasized the need to move aggressively against those who might undermine patriotic feelings and, thus, the state. He wrote that "as far as the law allowed, [his] administration was active." After the state of siege had been declared, some of the "most fanatic leaders of the particularistic faction" would be taken into protective custody and would be "rendered harmless." Furthermore, the two most important journals of this faction had been suppressed.

Furthermore, the provincial president pointed out that the mood in general was very good and, in some areas, people were "truly enthusiastically patriotic." He observed that this expression of feeling was not just a self-propelled development; he would contribute as much as possible through the distribution of leaflets or through requests that the local newspapers strengthen such patriotic feelings. As further evidence of the intensity of national patriotism, he reported that several well-known people, who were rumored to have made unpatriotic statements, had been harshly attacked "by the people."

15 The president or his officials had either overlooked or decided to conceal that, already in July 1870, the central committee of one of the most prominent Guelph associations, the *Welfische Wahlverein*, had stopped its activities and suspended the whole organization until the war with France had been concluded. The nation as a whole seemed endangered. Even these fierce critics of Prussia were not in doubt that political opposition had to stop precisely at this point; see Hans-Georg Aschoff, *Welfische Bewegung und politischer Katholizismus, 1866–1918: Die Deutschhannoversche Partei und das Zentrum in der Provinz Hannover während des Kaiserreiches* (Düsseldorf, 1987), esp. 86–7. For the Rhenish Palatinate, see the detailed account of public opinion and sentiments in the summer of 1870 by Erich Schneider, "Die Reaktion der deutschen Öffentlichkeit auf den Kriegsbeginn: Das Beispiel der Bayerischen Rheinpfalz," in Philippe Levillain and Rainer Riemenschneider, eds., *La guerre de 1870–71 et ses conséquences* (Bonn, 1990), 110–57; here, suspicion of the "Caesar at the Seine," Napoléon III, increasingly weakened the only antiwar voice among the regional newspapers, the Social Democratic *Pfälzische Volkszeitung*. Finally, after the first military engagements, the Left voiced a similarly strong resentment against "the French" as did the papers representing the other factions of the political specter. Public outrage focused particularly on the participation of black troops on the French side, the "*Turcos*."

Meanwhile, the Prussian government contacted the government of its ally, Saxony, to demand immediate action. The Prussians wanted those persons whom they perceived to be instigators of presumable disloyalty among the troops to be kept under lock and key, including the leading Social Democrats, August Bebel, Wilhelm Liebknecht, and Adolf Hepner – all of whom were living in Leipzig at the time. The Saxon government, however, did not take action at once. The three men, who were also members of the board of the SDAP, were not arrested until December 17. The Leipzig prosecutor indicted them on charges of treason for demanding the immediate end of the war against the French Republic.

V I

Repression of opponents of the dominant classes and elites had been a continuous activity of various Prussian agencies and state officials since the revolutionary movements of 1848–49 (if not since the eighteenth century). In the view of these officials, the government had an obligation to repress those who struggled for fundamental political change, such as the democrat Jacoby, or those who sought to overcome the fundamentals of society – for example, private property – such as the Social Democrats of the Eisenach Program. Most officials, however, saw little difference between the various democratic and socialist groups. To the political and social leaders of Prussian society, critics or opponents were loathsome, despicable, and indistinguishable in their "socialist" utopias.

From this perspective, the dramatic movements of the Paris Commune, March 18 through late May 1871, did not surprise Prussian officials or ministers. On the contrary, the revolutionary actions of the Communards confirmed or even enhanced their suspicions of urban crowds, which had been etched on their mind long before serving with the royal government. Nevertheless, the Commune had an impact on police activity, prompting the fear of further reverberations of "revolution" and triggering international communication and cooperation among political police forces. Contacts that had previously been occasional were intensified and extended.[16] (From the late 1850s to the mid-1860s, half a dozen officials in charge of political surveillance in several German states developed a network for the routine exchange of information.)[17]

---

16   See Hsi-Huey Liang, *The Rise of Modern Police and the European State System from Metternich to the Second World War* (Cambridge, 1992), chap. 2.

In the wake of the Paris Commune, the Prussian police force intensified its cooperation with Austrian authorities throughout the summer of 1871. The "socialists" remained the main targets of surveillance. Repression of socialist and other "red" activities bridged even the gap to the military enemy. In one of the additional agreements accompanying the Frankfurt peace treaty with the French Republic, Prussia lent its direct and effective cooperation to the quelling of the Communards. On several occasions between fall 1871 and spring 1872, the Prussian government or its ambassador complimented the French government for the measures it took against the Communards or any members of the (London-based) First Workers' International. Nevertheless, efforts to turn these various contacts into permanent cooperation and, thus, to establish a permanent "international police" failed.

VII

In 1852, Albert Ballhorn stated that "it is the nature of police to be in a permanent war with everybody in the state and society; thus it serves the common weal." Ballhorn, an official in Berlin's *Polizeipräsidium* (police headquarters), published this statement in a booklet on the newly formed Berlin police force.[18] This metropolitan police force had been totally reorganized following the revolutionary upheaval in spring and summer 1848. In March 1848, rioters had forced the king and his army to flee the capital. During the subsequent weeks and months, the working classes – or, to many contemporary observers, the "unrespectable" and "unruly crowds" – had ruled the public space. Neither the police nor even the army had been able to control their activities. To the adherents of Prussian grandeur as well as to other defenders of law and order, the spatial center of the monarchy and state appeared devoid of any true authority.

Counter-revolutionary efforts started with the reorganization of the Berlin police force. The newly founded royal *Schutzmannschaft* (gendarmerie) replaced the former police and its mostly aged and invalid police officers in the summer of 1848. Regarding organization and code of conduct, the

---

17 Documented in Wolfram Siemann, ed., *Der "Polizeiverein" deutscher Staaten* (Tübingen, 1983); an unabridged edition is available from Friedrich Beck and Walter Schmidt, eds., *Die Polizeikonferenzen deutscher Staaten, 1851–1866*, Dokumente aus geheimen Archiven (Weimar, 1993), vol. 5. In the German context, the first channels of mutual information exchange had been opened when the German Confederation issued the Carlsbad Decrees, which repressed student fraternities (*Burschenschaften*) in 1819; this network of political police was reactivated in 1833, after rioters attacked the guards at Frankfurt am Main, the locus of the boards of the German Confederation. See the careful account in Wolfram Siemann, *"Deutschlands Ruhe, Sicherheit und Ordnung": Die Anfänge der politischen Polizei, 1806–1866* (Tübingen, 1985).

18 Albert Ballhorn, *Das Polizei-Präsidium zu Berlin*, (Berlin, 1852), iii.

Schutzmannschaft strictly adhered to the military model. Established to patrol the countryside, members of this new force unabashedly displayed their military-like uniforms. In daily interactions with the public, they demonstrated their willingness to intervene harshly in street encounters, public inns, or wherever officials suspected threats to the public order.

The *Schutzmannschaft* certainly drew on notions and images of the police that had been employed for decades. According to these ideas, the police fostered and served both security and the common welfare. Since the later part of the eighteenth century – and exacerbated by the French Revolution and the mental shock that it triggered among the majority of the propertied classes – however, concerns for security had moved to the forefront. Observations on the *classes dangereuses*, as they had been published in France in the 1830s and 1840s, had been eagerly discussed if not directly accepted among higher officials.[19] But also rank and file policemen frequently encountered on their beat demands from "respectable" people to engage more forcefully with those migrants or inhabitants who literally smelled of danger and obstinacy.

This broad view of the unlimited potential dangers facing the society and state hindered the articulation of differences between political enemies and social problems. On the contrary, grass-roots experiences and the pressures of lower-level officials had strongly contributed to the inflation of a catch-all notion of politics and political enemies. Even vagrants and beggars who desperately scavenged food for their very survival were increasingly and routinely thought of as potential revolutionaries. Since the early nineteenth century, officials maintained that the vigilant control of every activity and all movement was indispensable for the protection of the state.

The execution of everyday policing of the broad range of suspicious individuals fell to rank and file police officials. Their experiences of months and years of struggling with their unruly clients produced a harsh demeanor while on duty. However, their superiors did little to challenge or correct this attitude. To them, more important and more convincing was the result – quiet streets and no "excesses" of the *classes dangereuses*.

Higher officials and neighborhood policemen applied practices of giving their clients "short shrift" (*kurzer Prozess*), even in mundane cases that paled in comparison to spectacular events such as riots or large-scale strikes. They were inclined to categorize crudely the "administered" individuals as either friends or foes (of the state). Such a Manichaean worldview and view of society focused only on the immediate maintenance of law and order. The

---

19 See Lüdtke, *Police and State in Prussia*, 77ff.

"fortress" of the state had to be defended against all enemies, real and potential; the "others"—that is, the state's prospective enemies—would simply be forced to bear the costs. Diverse expressions of alternative lifestyles, various movements of disobedience or obstinacy, defined as having interests of one's own—all were subsumed under the few crude categories operative in the minds of policemen.[20]

In the 1840s, the Hanoverian Gustav Zimmermann strongly emphasized the need to cultivate police awareness of the dangers that might threaten civil society. According to Zimmermann, police should act as a "flying wedge of modern society" sorting out the "chaos of modern life."[21] F. B. C. Avé-Lallemant, an official from Bremen, elaborated on this point during the second half of the nineteenth century. He argued for intensified study of the refined techniques of the hundreds and thousands of swindlers and scoundrels, which he depicted as *the* growing threat to modern life. In contrast to the plebeian and early proletarian masses, these scoundrels hid themselves among ordinary people. Careful observation and surveillance was needed to detect particular habits and gestures or linguistic forms. Thus, a *scientific* approach that included careful and constant documentation—or scientific observation—should be systematically developed.[22]

From his desk in the Berlin *Polizeipräsidium*, Ballhorn followed a similar approach. He did not stop with his previously mentioned remark on policing as another form of warfare; he elaborated on this idea by emphasizing that the police was "the sword of internal order" and that one had to hinder any "arbitrary or violent police practices" because, as he stated, the police "enforces the law but is not above it." Therefore, it would be necessary "to train and educate every police officer in an academic and scientific way." In this respect, police work should be on a par with the legal profession.

After the revolution of 1848–49, the successive counter-revolutionary Prussian governments did not await a "scientific revolution" within the police. Instead, they continued to think of the police as a means of maintaining domestic order. Accordingly, the ministers of the interior and of justice introduced legal measures to curtail drastically associations and public meetings or gatherings. The restrictions on assembly, association, and all media mandated their registration in advance and declared that any meeting, above a small

---

20   On the gradual internalization of this mode of conduct, see Lüdtke, *Police and State in Prussia*; see also Albrecht Funk, *Polizei und Rechtsstaat: Die Entwicklung des staatlichen Gewaltmonopols in Preussen 1848–1914* (Frankfurt/Main and New York, 1986), chaps. 6, 7.

21   Gustav Zimmermann, *Die deutsche Polizei im neunzehnten Jahrhundert* (Hanover, 1849), 3:161.

22   Peter Becker, "Vom 'Haltlosen' zur 'Bestie': Das polizeiliche Bild des 'Verbrechers' im 19. Jahrhundert," in Alf Lüdtke, ed., *"Sicherheit" und "Wohlfahrt": Polizei, Gesellschaft und Herrschaft im 19. Jahrhundert* (Frankfurt/Main, 1992), 97–132.

number of people, was illegal if it had not been previously licensed. Simultaneously, the law of assembly prescribed the presence of a police official at any meeting where political issues were discussed. The attending police official, moreover, was given the right to suspend the meeting at any point if he decided that the monarch might take offense or if state security had in some way been threatened.[23]

The police administration subsequently undertook the registration and listing of the goals and members of each and every association. Furthermore, the reports written by the police officials who attended meetings of associations were painstakingly evaluated. By the late 1850s, Ballhorn's domestic "permanent war," waged by the police on behalf of the society and the state, had been fully declared.

VIII

To cope with what was perceived to be the "rising tide" of criminality, many contemporaries believed that the state's monopoly on violence, and not self-help or self-control, was the appropriate means. The Prussian establishment viewed all offenses as synonymous to social upheaval and as increasing the likelihood of revolution. Their socialist opponents colluded in a certain way. They shared concerns about the imminent dangers posed to "modern" civilization at large, which the disorderly behavior of riotous males, females, and youths might engender. The police could thus rely on a large consensus that was prepared to accept almost every mode of intervention; in short, the police produced and simultaneously represented "order." In the end, the practices of the police may have invoked widespread longing, even among discriminated classes, to become incorporated into that very order.

The routine application of state force and the sovereign manner of its presentation was accompanied by the silent consent – if not audible applause – of "decent citizens"[24] and the "respectable working class." Its customary victims, in contrast, reacted with overt hostility. The officers on foot patrol could rely on supervisors, who established a framework within which customarily acquired standards of perception, modes of interpretation, and forms of conduct interacted to shape what Pierre Bourdieu has called "a form of habitus"

23　For an intriguing analysis that emphasizes the impact of repressive practices on the socialist labor movement, see Heinz-Gerhard Haupt, "Staatliche Bürokratie und Arbeiterbewegung: Zum Einfluss der Polizei auf die Konstituierung von Arbeiterbewegung und Arbeiterklasse in Deutschland und Frankreich zwischen 1848 und 1880," in Jürgen Kocka, ed., *Arbeiter und Bürger im 19. Jahrhundert* (Munich, 1986), 219–54.

24　See Elaine Glowka Spencer, *Police and the Social Order in German Cities: The Düsseldorf District, 1848–1914* (DeKalb, Ill., 1992), 61ff.

within the bureaucracy that may be termed a "structuring structure."[25] Naturally, this structuring principle of "fortress practice" required regular trial and application: Hence, although fortress practice could function without constant formal reiteration by supervisors, it should not be seen as a spontaneous mechanism. Fortress practice reflected the total spectrum of police and administrative activity. The police, for example, enforced universal education in the form of compulsory school attendance; they intervened in schools as well in urban neighborhoods to implement compulsory medical examinations; and in the 1890s, they systematically searched houses for the mentally ill, who were to be transferred to the growing number of asylums.

Evidently, the demands of bourgeois society for intellectual and moral "hygiene" were inseparable from the exercise of violent policing. The open use of force may well have been seen, both by its practitioners and the educated public, as the only means by which "order" in the state as a whole could be secured. By reflecting the boundaries of social and political inequality, the application of force in turn gave a disciplinary edge to the idea of the "rule of law." Concomitantly, the letter of the law and the pretensions of the police sometimes proved to be more than what the historian E. P. Thompson referred to as "empty rhetoric."[26] Occasionally, propertyless people – for example, maid-servants – also appealed to the police for help. The local lieutenant could execute the power ascribed to the police by the Servants' Order and enforce decent housing inside the master's home.

I X

For a moment, let us turn back to Bismarck and Falckenstein. Bismarck regretted that Braunschweig was not Prussia, which is to say that in Prussia, the state would have been entitled to intervene on grounds of "conflict of jurisdiction." In all cases of criminal or civil matters, state authorities could block a trial if they declared state security to be threatened by further investigation. Since Braunschweig was and remained one of the autonomous states that had joined together in 1871 to reestablish the Reich, Bismarck and his advisers did not see any immediate solution. To prevent further incidents of that sort, an imperial law was to be enacted. A majority of the Reichstag could not be found, however, to support such a law, which would exempt all military personnel from being subjected to civil law and civil courts. The alternative was to allow the Reich to intervene in Braunschweig on the grounds of the presumed disloyal acts of Braunschweig authorities in matters of imperial

25   Pierre Bourdieu, *Entwurf einer Theorie der Praxis* (Frankfurt/Main, 1976), 165.
26   Edward P. Thompson, *Whigs and Hunters: The Origins of the Black Act* (London, 1975), 265.

politics. But here as well, Bismarck did not recommend action. He did not want to attract any more public attention to the matter–thus the recommendation that the *Fiskus* should pay whatever fees or fines were assessed. Bismarck made it very clear that he considered the whole situation fundamentally contradictory. Never before had a Prussian general, who had been motivated only by his concern for monarchical and state security, been accused of having violated the rights of a few subjects of that monarch and state. Moreover, never before had a Prussian general been fined for behavior that, on political grounds, seemed fully justified. The polity of the new Reich, as laid out in the Bismarckian constitution, certainly contained what appeared to be contradictory elements. On the one hand, there was the demonstrative if not revolutionary appeal to the "masses"– the inauguration of the secret ballot and the one-man, one-vote rule (Prussia continued to deny citizens the latter until 1918).[27] On the other hand, monarchical prerogative prevailed with regard to the role of the chancellor and, in particular, all matters of the armed forces. Except for the size of the various state armies and of the imperial navy, neither the Reichstag nor the individual state parliaments were entitled to intervene in matters of the military. The actual spending of the military's budget remained as "off limits" as the often cruel treatment of recruits.

Regarding the future role of the military, however, the conflict over Falckenstein indicated that claims for the special status of the monarch and his army would increasingly come under attack. First, the pretense of an autonomous military domain collided with calls from various groups and segments of the bourgeois "camp" for the unrestricted rule of law. Second, the necessities of military *superarbitrium* in times of emergency were not consistent with a fundamental principle of the Reich's constitution *modo Bismarck* – the preservation of the German states. The Reich was established not to absorb but to sustain and link these given political and monarchical entities. Regarding the case discussed in this chapter, the implication was that regulations that were valid in Prussia were not necessarily binding in other states. In Prussia, the fundamental concession for police arbitrariness comprised the nonliability of officials, whether civilian or military, while on duty. In

---

27   The usual attribution of this "bonapartist" policy solely to Bismarck underrates shifts that had started already in 1858–59 and were related to the successor of Wilhelm IV, Prince Wilhelm, later Emperor Wilhelm I. As *the* symbolic figure of the military counter-revolution of 1848, Prince Wilhelm, nevertheless, accepted a policy of cooperation with those factions of the bourgeois classes that favored a strong Prussia. Accordingly, the Prussian government did not follow suit when other German governments or their leading police officials called for suppression of the Deutscher Nationalverein in fall of 1859; see the detailed account by Wolfram Siemann, *Gesellschaft im Aufbruch: Deutschland, 1849–1871* (Frankfurt/Main, 1990).

the state of Braunschweig, the rule was different, however. Thus, one of the more conservative features of the Reich's constitution could foster the spread of legal and mental *Verbürgerlichung* (embourgeoisification).

Bismarck and his advisers were indeed aware of this irony and acknowledged the implicit limits on political action that it contained. Consequently, the chancellor recommended a symbolic gesture. He proposed that the emperor write a personal letter to his most loyal general, Falckenstein. Since the chancellor's office had already prepared the text, Bismarck "respectfully" enclosed it.

19

French Public Opinion in 1870–71 and the Emergence of Total War

STÉPHANE AUDOIN-ROUZEAU

In the twentieth century, total warfare has not only been a matter of material mobilization for the belligerent countries, but it has also involved psychological mobilization as well as an investment of public opinion in the war itself. From 1914 onward, total warfare has involved culture, attitude, and the phenomenon known as public opinion. Without taking these factors into account in international conflict, one cannot understand, for example, what French historians mean when they write about the "war culture" of World War I. Yet it was precisely this war culture, backed by a patriotism of exceptional intensity that was shared by civilians and soldiers alike, that explains the surprising tenacity of French society between 1914 and 1918.[1]

There is little doubt that French patriotism reached its historical height between these two dates; historians are largely agreed on this point. But how intense was it during the Franco-Prussian War? Did the degree of investment of French society first in the Imperial war and then in the war of the Third Republic herald the unparalleled cohesion of this same society almost a half-century later? Were the seeds of total warfare present in public opinion, *en sentiment*, as early as 1870? In this chapter, I address these questions as part of a broader attempt to understand the relation of French society to war between 1792 and 1945.[2] I place at the center of my analysis the issue that I deem to be the most essential – namely, the question of patriotism, which may be defined as the body of attachments – be they conscious, rationalized, or not – that connects the individual to the community that he belongs to and that forces him to defend it.

1   A version of this chapter has already appeared in French in the journal, *Historiens et Géographes*, no. 338 (Dec. 1992). Abbreviations used in this essay: S.H.A.T.: Service historique de l'Armee de terre. (Historical service of the army); and A. N.: Archives Nationales (National archives).
2   For a general treatment of the war, see Michael Howard, *The Franco-Prussian War: The German Invasion of France, 1870–1871* (London and New York, 1985). For further analysis of the problems of public opinion in France, see Stéphane Audoin-Rouzeau, *1870: La France dans la guerre* (Paris, 1989).

A superficial examination of the Franco-Prussian War might lead one to place undue emphasis on the apparent lack of continuity between the conflict of 1870–71 and the total wars of the twentieth century. Much evidence points toward the absence of an investment on the part of a majority of the French in the earlier war, in the lamentable military defeat, and, above all, in the vote of February 8, 1871, which expressed the rural population's overwhelming desire for peace. The rural population represented nearly two-thirds of French society and was viscerally opposed to the pursuit of a war advocated by the Gambettist republican fringe and the urban far left. It is difficult not to recall here the theses of the historian Eugen Weber, who attributes the republican regime – established in the 1880s – with the growth of patriotism in France and its extension to a rural community heretofore indifferent to the idea of a nation, in his opinion, until the end of the nineteenth century.[3]

I would suggest, however, that a rethinking of the Franco-Prussian War in its general context is in order. In my view, the war of 1870, by creating the necessary conditions, paved the way for World War I. An examination of public opinion at the time of the Franco-Prussian War offers evidence of the nation's psychological and emotional investment in this conflict, an investment that was stronger than it is generally believed to have been and that foreshadowed, in many ways, the great collective mobilization that took place at the beginning of the twentieth century.

FRENCH SOCIETY AND THE BEGINNING OF THE WAR

Such a perspective demands that particular attention be paid to the attitude of French society at the beginning of the war, since the onset of war can represent in itself, as Jean-Jacques Becker has shown for August 1914, the true test of the nation as a whole.[4] Public opinion at the beginning of the war cannot be taken into account without revisiting the chronology of the diplomatic crisis of July 1870, as it was experienced by French contemporaries. Chronologically, the Franco-Prussian crisis lasted for a little under two weeks: Thirteen days elapsed between the announcement in Paris of the Hohenzollern candidacy (July 3) and the vote for military funds in the *Corps législatif* (the night of July 15), which was, as far as public opinion was concerned, equivalent to a declaration of war.[5] The diplomatic crisis that led to

3 Eugen Weber, *Peasants into Frenchman: The Modernization of Rural France (1870–1914)* (Stanford, Calif., 1976).
4 Jean-Jacques Becker, *1914: Comment les Français sont entrés dans la guerre* (Paris, 1977).
5 The official date of the declaration of war (July 19) is insignificant for an examination that focuses on public opinion.

war, however, was experienced by only a small minority of French citizens, those who had access to the greatest amount of and the most reliable information. The vast majority of the French only gradually became aware of the actual existence of the Franco-German dispute. Paris was a special case because it was on July 4 and 5 – that is, *before* the speech delivered on July 6 by the Duc de Gramont, the minister of foreign affairs–that the denizens of Paris learned of the existence of an international crisis. There is no doubt that the press played an important role in the capital–where two million people benefited from a faster and more extensive diffusion of information – than in the provinces. Outside Paris, people were unaware of the crisis before July 6, as can be seen from reports of prefects and public prosecutors that were sent between July 3 and 6.[6] As the public prosecutor of Douai wrote on July 6, "The questions of foreign policy, Concile, Spain, Prussia, do not seem to preoccupy many minds. One hardly even discusses such questions in the upper classes of society."[7]

Even Gramont's bellicose speech of July 6, which caused the crisis to pass a crucial threshold, had no immediate impact on public opinion. In Paris, the contents of the speech were widely known that same evening. But diffusion of this type of information remained slow in the provinces, where awareness of the impending danger of war came much later. The combination of both the special reports that the prefects were asked to write after July 6 (extracts of which were published by the republicans on October 2, 1870) and the reports of public prosecutors written after the foreign minister's speech allow one to draw the following conclusions: In provincial cities, people became aware of the possibility of war on July 8 and 9, although not all social groups were informed at once (on July 9, the working classes of Dijon remained uninformed, for example).[8] In the countryside, this process was even slower, hindered as it was by preoccupation with a worsening drought that affected a large proportion of the rural population. On July 11, for example,

---

6   The reports were for April, May, and June in the case of public prosecutors, and for June only in the case of prefects. As nothing prevented their authors from extending their reports by speculating on the beginning of the following month, prosecutors and prefects thus provide information on public opinion in their *départements* for the beginning of July. This type of document has been analyzed by Lynn M. Case in *French Opinion on War and Dilomacy during the Second Empire* (Philadelphia, 1954). The reports of prosecutors, only some of which survived, had not been used before my study (*1870, La France dans la guerre*) due to an error in classification in the French archives. The same is true for the monthly reports of prefects for the beginning of July and August, also out of order, of which only half, approximately, have been found. The latter should not be confused with the prefects' special reports written after July 6, already studied by Case and of which there remains no trace, save the extracts of men published in the *Journal Officiel* by the republicans on Oct. 2, 1870.

7   Report of the public prosecutor of Douai, July 6, 1870, A. N. BB30 390. The jurisdiction of the public prosecutor of Douai covers the *département* of Nord and Pas-de-Calais.

8   Report on the prefect of Côte-d'Or, July 9, 1870, *Journal Officiel* (Oct. 2, 1870).

the public prosecutors of Caen (Normandy)[9] and of Riom (l'Auvergne) indicated the absence of any interest on the part of the rural population in any external problems. As the latter explained, "the Prussian candidacy does not seem to have moved masses. Only among functionaries and persons of the leisure class do the eventualities that might arise become the object of diverse commentary." Although one can speak of an awareness of the risks of war in Paris ten days before the decisive vote of July 15, this awareness did not reach provincial cities and the countryside until a week or less than a week before the vote, respectively. (There is no question that many people remained completely ignorant of the threat until war was declared.) This explains why the news of the vote for military funds by the *Corps législatif* on the night of July 15 immediately spread throughout the cities and reached the country-side only on the 16, causing a *surprised* and *emotional* reaction. (The latter term comes up repeatedly in the writings of the prefects.) In short, to a large segment of the French public, the crisis of July 1870 appeared to be a *rushed* affair, although to diplomatic historians it lasted a relatively long period of time. Popular reaction to the outbreak of the Franco-Prussian War in France, thus, cannot be understood without taking into account the dimension of surprise in a country that had been, for the most part, caught unawares.

In moving from the problem of *information* regarding the war to the problem of *sentiment* toward the war, one must differentiate between two periods on either side of the turning point of July 15. From July 6 to 15, patriotic fervor overwhelmed the Parisian population. One should not, however, exaggerate the importance of the prowar rallies that took place in Paris between July 7 and 15. Although these demonstrations were perceived as massive by those in attendance, they attracted only a small percentage of the city's population of nearly two million. On the night of July 14, for example, popular excitement in Paris was at its height, following the news of the Ems dispatch. Several rallies took place, but police reports indicate that only small groups – of between 600 and 1,200 people – were involved.[10] In this pre-war period, it was probable that the most boisterous segment of the capital's population obscured the views of those who were less excitable. Paris overshadowed the provinces in the same way. In analyzing the special reports of the prefects following Gramont's famous speech of July 6, the historian Lynn M. Case has shown that a clear majority of *départements* approved of the

9   Report of the prosecutor of Caen, July 11, 1870, A. N., BB30 390. The jurisdiction of the prosecutor of Caen includes the *départements* of Calvados, the Manche, and l'Orne.

10 Only some of the police reports for the city of Paris could be found in the National Archives, and only for the period concerning the second half of July. Those cited here have been published by Emile Ollivier in his memoirs, *L'Empire libéral* (Paris, 1909), 14: 116.

foreign minister's warmongering; that a smaller majority, although they pre-ferred a peaceful solution, would accept war; and that only a minority opposed it outright.[11] Nevertheless, Case's study contains several flaws. Because the original reports were lost, the study only takes into account excerpts from them, which are often very short and scattered over time. In addition, the classification that the author attempts is overly schematic, since he tends to divide the *départements* into those who were "partisans of the war" and those who were "opposed" to it.

It would be more accurate to differentiate among them according to three attitudes: *resolution, acceptance*, and *opposition*. Thus, if one sets aside the twelve undecided cases, it seems that before July 15, feelings of patriotic resolve were in the minority (16 *départements*), as was opposition to the war (12 *départe-ments*), and that acceptance of the war was the clearly predominant feeling (31 *départements*). A subtle analysis of the prefect of Charente-Inférieure is a good example.

The self-righteous and energetic attitude of the government was pleasing at first, but after the initial excitement one begins to perceive concern for security, concern that the idea of war brings in its wake, and one understands that thought and discus-sion about the war will follow. They will not lead this *département* to hostility … but they will bring it to ask that everything that is compatible with the dignity of this country be done to keep the peace. This limit … tried, the population of the Charente-Inférieure will remain devoted to the Empire, even if it must go to war.[12]

Thus, one did not find an aggressive enthusiasm in the provinces, nor did one find an unflinching "pacifism." Resignation predominated, in spite of the existence of urban populations clearly more "decided" than the rural populations. On the basis of this *preliminary acceptance* of the war, a deep-seated certainty of the "just right of the French" emerged in face of the "provocative duplicity" of Prussia, aggravated by a feeling of the necessity of once and for all finishing this serious business with an enemy whose hostile acts toward France had been escalating since 1866.

The state of French opinion changed perceptibly between July 15 and August 2, the date of the first engagements at the border. We know very little about the immediate effect on public opinion of the news of France's entry into the war. Whereas the Parisian crowd exhibited its enthusiasm, the dominant reaction in the countryside, it seems, could be summed up as one of emotion and sadness. The departure of men in arms (soldiers on duty, reservists, and especially guardsmen) is certainly traumatic, but it does not provoke in men, however, an open hostility toward war.

11   Case, *French Opinion on War and Diplomacy*. Some reports remained undecided.
12   Report of the prefect of the Charente-Inférieure, July 10, 1870, *Journal Officiel* (Oct. 2, 1870).

Over the next two weeks, a profound change in public opinion seems to have taken place at the core of French society. A phenomenon of "patriotic conversion" occurred, to which the monthly reports of the prefects written at the end of July and beginning of August testify (48 out of 89 prefects).[13] During this period – that is, between the declaration of war and the first battle – opposition to the war virtually disappeared. Even acceptance of the war became an attitude of the minority (13 *départements*), to the benefit of patriotic resolve (24 *départements*, that is, half of those found). A minority of *départements* (11 according to the prefects) were described as enthusiastic.

The shift in opinion toward the affirmation of national feelings glossed over many internal conflicts: The contrast between cities and countryside persisted, with the latter still more reluctant about embracing the war than the former. A complex contrast between north and south also developed. Southern France comprised, paradoxically, both a majority of the *départements* most reticent about the war and a majority of the *départements* enthusiastic about it. The north was characterized by a greater homogeneity regarding attitudes toward acceptance or resolve, and by the presence of a majority of *départements* whose opinion was one of resolve. The *départements* in eastern France presented a special case: Before July 15, the attitude here was very conflicted, and certain *départements*, such as the Haut-Rhin, the Meuse, and the Moselle, opposed the war. But at the beginning of August, all of the *départements* in the east fell under the category of *départements* expressing resolve or enthusiasm. Throughout the east, one observed the most impressive conversion in favor of war. Antiwar feelings were at first high in those *départements* situated in the east, owing to the security risks they faced. But as strong and deeply rooted frontier patriotism crystallized among them, they grew to accept and embrace the war.

Although their resolve increased during the second half of July, many people were still reticent to express prowar feelings: Dejection was evident as men departed for war, in particular as the mobile guard was called to leave on July 17; rural and urban worries surfaced regarding the economic situation; public opinion became increasingly volatile as demonstrated by the propagation of false news of a "pessimistic" nature. Isolated incidents of opposition to the war, in the form of mobs demonstrating against the emperor and the war, occurred, for which the radical or socialist left was responsible. Although such groups were in the extreme minority, their actions obscured those of others who were reticent but chose to keep quiet. The low rate of enlistment was a further indication of popular reluctance. Although contributions and dona-

13 Series A.N. Fl c111.

tions in kind poured in from all over the country in impressive quantities, only 4,000 voluntary enlistments for the second half of July were recorded.[14] These exceptions, however, do not call into question what I have already said of the general movement of French opinion in July 1870. The factors that explain this palpable patriotism in French society were linked to four elements of a cultural order. French public opinion, as indicated by all administrative reports, saw France as being in the right. In addition, a shift took place quickly from seeing the war as *inevitable* to seeing it as *necessary*, once it was declared. This reinterpretation greatly facilitated the phenomenon of widespread patriotic conversion in support of the war. There was complete confidence in victory – and in a speedy one at that. Despite some concern, there was no doubt as to the immediate success of the "sword of France." Furthermore, the July crisis of 1870 triggered the recollection of historical memories of the nation, and these were highly conducive to mobilization: memories of the heroic venture of the *Grande Armée* of the First Empire, of the severity of the Prussian occupation of 1814–15, and of the regions in France that had suffered under the latter. For the urban republican minorities, the memory of the Great Revolution carried with it the most patriotic force. Despite the Imperial regime, the memory of the "nation at risk" allowed for France's struggle of 1870 to become conflated with the earlier one of 1792–93.

With regard to the concept of total war, there are numerous, even striking, similarities between July 1870 and August 1914: the shortness of the crisis from the standpoint of popular awareness, a similar mitigated reception of the war, and an attitude of resignation and/or acceptance. In addition to these initial reactions, once war had been declared, a patriotic resolve emerged in both cases that occasionally manifested itself in outbursts of enthusiasm in public places, such as train stations. There are also similarities in the explanations given for the war, including the just right of the French, German aggression and premeditation that made war inevitable, confidence in ultimate victory, and flashbacks of historical conflicts.

The sacrifices asked of the French people were undoubtedly greater in 1914, with a mobilization of 3.6 million men as compared to less than 1.2 million in 1870,[15] when there were 2 million fewer French. The mobilization in 1914 threatened almost all families with the possible loss of a

---

14   Telegram from the interim minister of defense to Marshal Leboeuf on Aug. 6, 1870, S .H.A.T., La 7.
15   The number given here is theoretical: The Niel law was supposed to supply 640,000 men for active duty and the reserve and 500,000 mobile guards, but the number of men who were finally mobilized was much lower. When fighting first began, less than 250,000 men had been assembled of the 640,000 active, forcing the Army of the Rhine into a strategic paralysis.

member. Nevertheless, if the entry into war in 1914 constituted the highest point in the history of patriotism and showed that France was a "polished"[16] nation, the experience of 1870 proved that this process was well under way forty years earlier. As the republicans claimed, before July 15, 1870, the war was an Imperial one, but after that date it became a war of the whole nation. One of the cultural components of total war—the deep emotional investment of a society in the conflict—was present in 1870, almost a quarter century before the great trial of World War I.

A "SACRED UNION"?

In the examination of French public opinion with the country at war, a word must be said about the political situation. In addition, an examination must be made of whether a "sacred union" was formed, as in 1914, to erase effectively political differences in the face of the exigencies of patriotism. Appearances are deceptive here, depending on whether one places oneself in the perspective of the leading circles or whether one examines French society as a whole. It is a commonplace in the historiography of this conflict to underscore the chance for political revenge that the war presented the Bonapartist right, which had been considerably weakened since 1869.[17] For the right, the war was an unexpected opportunity to put the government of Emile Ollivier in a difficult position, to intone the concessions of the liberal empire, and to attempt to revitalize the dynasty.

Whatever the role of the right may have been in the process of entering the war, however, it would be wrong to reduce the events that took place in the political arena at the outset of the conflict to this aspect alone. Too little attention has been paid to the effectiveness of the impulse toward a sacred union within the *Corps législatif* in this period. During the vote for funds on July 15, a number of declared opponents to the regime voiced their support for the war—only 10 nays and 7 abstentions were recorded, although there were 25 republicans who had been "irreconcilable" since the elections of 1869. Several partisans of the left, such as Adolphe Thiers, who delivered a "pacifist" speech that very afternoon, relented at this critical moment. Thus, patriotic feelings overwhelmed a good number of the opposition, and support for the war grew even stronger in the next three votes taken that day (funds for the marine, the mobilization of the mobile guard, and the law on voluntary enlistment). Only one republican stood in opposition to these

---

16 René Remond's preface to Becker, *1914*, 8.
17 Pierre de La Gorce, *Histoire du Second Empire* (Paris, 1905), vol. 4; Louis Girard, *Napoléon III* (Paris, 1986).

measures, with abstentions ranging from between 16 and 18. In the end, the left consented to the war, or at least refrained from opposing it. On July 18, when the vote for increasing military expenditures and increasing the number of conscripts to 140,000 took place, there was not one single voice of dissent. By dissociating defense of the country from confidence in the government's domestic policies, the left was able to support the war.

Political consensus appealed to the nation as a whole. Certainly, a number of opponents of the war and of the regime were still to be found, in a fraction of the legitimist movement and among some in the clergy whose opinion was reinforced by the retreat of the French garrison of Rome at the beginning of August. The far left groups and radical republicans (both very small minorities) exhibited their opposition by castigating the war directly or by participating in meager demonstrations that were easily dispersed. Both groups maintained their dual opposition to the Empire and to the conflict in which it was engaged. But the republican camp, already a small minority in 1870 in nonurban France, found itself profoundly divided, and it only rarely achieved organized opposition to the war. The silence into which the most resolved opposition groups were forced reflected, *a contrario*, their isolation and the strong support of public opinion for the war. The prefect of Seine-Inférieure wisely commented that the "demagogic opposition" did not disband but that it was silenced by the "imposing manifestation of opinion."[18] For the nation, the impulse toward a sacred union was largely hegemonic: The prefect noticed its effects in a number of legitimist groups, in the Catholic church, in the modern republican groups, and in the Orleanists (who, it is true, had not constituted a real opposition to the regime since 1869). However optimistic it may be, this judgment of the prefect of Maine-et-Loire on August 4, 1870, is nonetheless revealing: "Legitimists, Orleanists, clericals and moderate democrats, all approve the war."[19] In Alsace, the public prosecutor noted that the "war [had] come and disrupted all of the internal political preoccupations" and that it had "united all parties and classes in the same patriotic fervor."[20] Undoubtedly, the political consensus concerning the war was both relative and temporary: It was nonetheless real, as the attitude of the opposition press (Parisian and provincial) tended to show.

These facts are further evidence of a strong patriotism already present at the beginning of the war and reinforced by the notion of a "war of the nation," when an attempt was made to transcend political differences. French politi-

---

18 Monthly report of the prefect of Seine-Inférieure, Aug. 1, 1870, A.N. F1c111, Seine-Inférieure 9.
19 Prefect of Maine-et-Loire, Aug. 4, 1870, A.N. F1c111, Maine-et-Loire 8.
20 Report of the prosecutor of Colmar, July 21, 1870, A.N. BB30/390.

cal differences were too drastic to have been resolved by four weeks of impending war, but the priority given to the defense of the nation over domestic political conflicts – as was the case in August 1914 – found its precedent in July 1870.

It is interesting to observe that this sacred union, destroyed prematurely by the first defeats in August and the constitution of the Palikao government (August 9), reconstituted itself at the end of the republican revolution of September 4. This revolution paradoxically provoked the crystallization of a second "sacred union" around a republican government, however illegitimate, representative of a minority, and exclusively Parisian. Although the rural world was wary of the news coming from Paris, the Orleanist groups rallied behind the revolution massively, and the legitimists largely supported it. *Le Dimanche des familles*, the Catholic and legitimist propaganda instrument in Puy-de-Dôme, helped in this regard: "France," it stated, "should award the crown of the Immortals to those members of the government of the National defense whose energy and intelligence shall save France. Let no one accuse us of being political. Politics is not our domain."[21] Even the church gave up its opposition to the Republic, as demonstrated by the following lines from the *Revue chrétienne*: "The duty of all citizens is to go along with the new government without hesitation and to work with it to save the country."[22] Even a certain number of Bonapartists switched their positions. On September 6, the *Moniteur du Puy-de-Dôme*, which was considered a progovernment paper in this *département* until the defeat at Sedan, stated that

As for us, we accept the Republic with confidence, because we think that in the unique circumstances in which we find ourselves, it is the only form of government that can best realize measures for the protection of the general public.... Let the republic save the nation, and it will have our loyal support, and that of all good French citizens.[23]

At the other extreme of the political spectrum, the circles on the far left rallied behind the government of national defense. The phenomenon of political truce provoked by the onset of war was thus largely reproduced after the republican takeover. This political truce was indeed fragile and temporary, the support often conditional. However, the support did not immediately dissolve. In Paris and in the Midi, the far left was the first to break off its ties with the republican government before the end of September. The support of the right lasted much longer; only in November did the right,

21   *Le Dimanche des familles*, Sept. 18, 1870.
22   News summary in the Paris press, Sept. 9, 1870, S.H.A.T., Lo 21.
23   The *Moniteur du Puy-de-Dôme,* Sept. 6, 1870.

beginning in the provinces, cease to show its support for the Delegation of Tours – the Parisian government knew how to quell the far left until the very end and escaped criticism for this reason. Outside of Paris, the breaking point was reached on December 24, 1870, when Léon Gambetta decided to dissolve the general council of the *départements*, which had been accused of bad will in the vote for the funds necessary to pursue the fight. The reaction of the right to this move was violent, and Gambetta's decision caused the right to sever its ties to the delegation. Shortly after the war, Paul Leroy-Beaulieu spoke of Gambetta's "incoherent and frenzied dictatorship."[24] Yet, giving the nation's defense priority over internal political battles could not last in the face of the siege of Paris and the military defeats incurred by the republicans. The end of the conflict found the republicans exposed to growing opposition on the left and on the right. Leftist opposition did not truly take shape in the big cities until October, and right-wing opposition congealed only in the last month of the war. The republicans' desire for political revenge, clumsily maneuvered in September 1870 along with their desire to prolong a conflict that looked increasingly hopeless, gradually undermined the initial impulse toward political consensus.

PUBLIC OPINION AND PATRIOTISM IN DEFEAT

Aside from its political dimensions, one of the fundamental questions raised by the conflict of 1870 pertains to the evolution of French public opinion in the wake of the first defeats. Did the war remain "national" as it had been in the beginning, in the context of repeated military setbacks,[25] the capitulation of cities, and the siege of the capital? Answering this question is made all the more difficult by the evolution of the strategic situation that obliges one to look at patriotism in the face of defeat, and not merely before the fighting, as in July 1870, or in the context of stabilized fronts, as in 1914–18. The difficulty becomes still greater owing to the shadow cast by the vote of February 8, 1871, which indicated French society's strong desire for peace.[26] In fact, the ballot was indicative of patriotism at only a very specific point in time – namely, at the end of the war, or, to be more precise, in the immediate postwar period, when the capitulation of Paris demonstrated that defeat was inevitable. This is why a diachronic study is needed to account for the reactions of the armies and the civilian populations.

---

24 Paul Leroy-Beaulieu, "La province pendant le siége de Paris," *Revue des Deux-Mondes* (1871), 325.
25 With the exception of the battle of Coulmiers at the beginning of Nov. 1870.
26 Jacques Gouault, *Comment la France est devenue républicaine: Les élections générales et partielles á l'Assemblée nationale, 1870–1875* (Paris, 1954).

The Rhine army—made up essentially of peasants and recruits from the lowest classes of French society because of the policy of replacement[27]—exhibited a strong sense of patriotism at its core. During August, the "pressure" exerted by French soldiers was demonstrated by the elevated ratio of losses (approximately 23 percent at Wissembourg and Fröschwiller),[28] the small number of prisoners captured, and the significantly higher number of German casualties in absolute terms. These losses reflected the determination of the French soldiers and were further confirmed by their letters and diaries. Those who could write (one-third of the army was either analphabetic or illiterate) showed high morale at the time that they marched off to war and an absolute confidence in victory. This was especially true for officers, for whom patriotism had the force of a veritable cult. In train stations, when soldiers departed for the front, authorities noted their "zeal," "spirit," "enthusiasm," and their "confidence in success."[29] Not a single official report described a lack of determination and will to fight among the troops. Ordinary soldiers testified to much of the same. It could be argued that when the soldiers from the country met up with the soldiers from the city at depots and train stations, they fell in line with the general spirit, and what resulted was a generally heightened morale. This testimony emphasizes the fraternizing of civilians with soldiers at this moment of their departure—another sign of a solid feeling of belonging to the same community.

Nevertheless, French patriotic resolve did not evaporate after the first defeats. A strong feeling of duty persisted, as did the desire to be kept informed of the events and to obtain news of the war, about which there were many illusions as to the strategic situation. In any case, the peasant-soldiers, about whom we know a little, did not appear at the time to be indifferent to the fate of the nation that they were called on to defend. As one of them, a farmer from Brittany, wrote in a letter to his brother:

27 Bernard Schnapper, *Le remplacement militaire en France: Quelques aspects politiques, économiques et sociaux du recrutement au XIXéme* (Paris, 1968).
28 These rates, it is true, fell: 13-14 percent at Forbach, 7 percent at Borny, 12-13 percent at Rezonville, 10 percent at Saint-Privat. The rate of losses of the army of Châlons were approximately 13 percent at Beaumont and 14 percent at Sedan, but in these two cases, a considerable number of prisoners were taken during the battle: This new phenomenon showed how the army of Châlons followed suit with the republican armies, which were much less determined than the armies of the Empire.
29 Monthly report of the prefect of l'Orne, Aug. 1, 1870, A.N. F1c111 Orne 9. Monthly report of the prefect of Hautes-Pyrénées 7. Monthly report of the prefect of l'Aude, Aug. 2, 1870, A.N. F1c111, Aude 6. Monthly report of the prefect of l'Aube, Aug. 4, 1870. A.N. F1c111 Aube 4. Monthly report of the prefect of Côtes-du-Nord, July 5, 1870, A.N. F1c111 Côtes-de-Nord 11, Report on the prefect of Moselle á Intérieur, July 20, 1870, S.H.A.T., La 6. Report of the prefect of Pas-de-Calais à Intérieur, July 20, 1870, A.N. F7 12660.

I think France is in danger. Why aren't the people in the West as patriotic as those in the East? … If the guard is called in, you must march without fear or we will have to serve the Prussians … If the French knew what the situation was, not a single man would be left at home.[30]

During the siege of Metz, during which the largest part of the Rhine army was encircled until the end of October, the determination to fight lasted until the moment of surrender. The patriotism of the soldiers can be explained perhaps by the fact that they remained in contact with their families and village communities that they left behind (hence, the extreme importance of the postal system). Overall, what comes across of their mental and cultural worlds showed that they were more *aware* than one might have thought, and awareness is an important factor in analyzing the fighting spirit in August 1870.

The republican armies were regrouped very differently from the armies of the Empire. Their formation resulted from a general draft at the beginning of September that kept the revision of the 1870 class; the Republic drafted single men aged 21 to 40 to form a "mobilized national guard," which in October combined with the "mobile guard" of the regular army. Thus, the defense of the territory was no longer the sole obligation of troops on active duty. On November 2, all men aged 21 to 40, even those with families, were sent to join the mobilized army: This was the implementation of the "nation at arms," although the war ended before the new recruits could join the line. It is significant that the principle of a general draft was universally accepted by the people and encountered only sporadic resistance. Nominally trained and prepared for war, and thrown into a rigorous winter campaign that required constant movement, the troops of the Republic showed a tenacity far inferior to the troops of the fallen Empire, as indicated by the ratio of losses of 5 to 10 percent and the greater number of prisoners taken before September 4. Until the beginning of December, however, the troops sustained a resolve that was based on the hopes of eventual military recovery.

During the last two months of the war, the armies raised after September 4 reached their breaking point. From December 1870 through January 1871, the will to fight utterly collapsed. From then on, following every battle, enormous numbers of men were taken prisoner (for example, 20,000 at the battle of Le Mans). The phenomenon of collective desertions, a few instances of which appeared for the first time in November, became widespread after the fall of Orléans in the beginning of December. The soldiers left the battlefields by the thousands and attempted to return home in large groups.

30 Correspondence of Y. C. Quentel, Aug. 10, 1870, *Gwéchall* (1979), 2:72.

The prefect of Blois saw 10,000 men pass through Vendôme, deserting the lines at Josnes.[31] There were groups of deserters spotted in the Dordogne area after the fall of Orléans and in Morbihan and Maine-et-Loire after the defeat at Le Mans. In January, there was a veritable dissolution of the armies; mutinies erupted in the boot camps and were followed by pillaging and refusal to board trains. Whatever the concrete reasons may have been for the multifarious crises of insubordination, there is no doubt that significant factions of different armies refused to make a personal sacrifice that they now deemed useless.

One exception to this general pattern is the case of the army of Paris. Its failings appeared more numerous in the beginning of the siege than at the end when the fighting spirit of the Parisian troops was relatively strong. But outside the capital, the two final months of the war were met with a weakened will to resist on the part of the republican armies.

It appeared that the evolution of the attitude of the civilian population paralleled that of the armies. Beginning in December, opposition to the war arose that, having become widespread, finally resulted in a vote for peace on February 8, 1871. But the question of civilian attitudes was complex, owing to the differences in situation between cities besieged, occupied, and spared, and the diversity in social and cultural environments. In the following, I briefly examine the three most important points: the reaction to the defeat, the differences between rural world and urban world, and the evolution in the image of the enemy.

A thorough examination of the reaction of French public opinion to the military defeats attests to the general absence of indifference. From Wissembourg (August 4) to the fall of Paris (January 28, 1871), after the news of the defeat at Sedan (September 2), the surrender of Metz (late October), and the defeat of Orléans (early December), the authorities, first Imperial and then republican, all recorded the same reaction: disbelief upon hearing the news of military collapse (a disbelief that in some cases lasted several days), followed by consternation and dejection. A patriotic reaction followed that exploded in anger (August 9, September 4, and late October/early November) and was itself followed by a demand for weapons by a population that, in its confusion, called for a general draft. This type of Jacobinic impulse, reminiscent of 1792 and Year II, existed mostly in large republican cities, such as Paris, Lyons, and Marseille and implied, in these cases, a clearly subversive meaning. However, a purely defensive patriotism was expressed more often than one might have thought in less important cities and in the countryside.[32]

31 Prefect of Blois à Guerre, Dec. 17, 1870, S.H.A.T., La 16.
32 After Sedan, there are, e.g., demands for weapons in villages close to the combat zones.

Once the shock of the first defeats had passed, the authorities indicated a general recovery of opinion – its "zeal," its "patriotic fervor," its "steadfastness," its "energy."[33] French opinion had yet to yield to defeat, and the war was not over, even after the setbacks of August 4–6. In fact, 36,000 volunteers enlisted that month. The following judgment about the *département* of the Vosges was, in this sense, rather representative: "One is reassured, one is on the alert as before, one appraises the situation more calmly, more confidently, with greater courage. Initiatives reappear, the offers of support are plentiful ... morale is higher."[34]

Conversely, any announcement of victory provoked disproportionate enthusiasm. This was the case after the initial success at Coulmiers on November 9, 1870. Yet, with no known victory, the numerous rumors that circulated during the war served to exorcise the defeat and reveal the hidden hopes of military recovery. At the end of October, in the Dordogne, the point of view of the prefectural authority was characteristic of this type of reaction:

The spirit is still one of resistance. The public receives with disfavor rumors of armistice and could only accept a peace without loss and without concession. The general belief is that when the mobilized national guard is promptly equipped and armed, it will finish the job of saving France.[35]

It was only in December that hope began to fade irremediably. Evidence of the reactions of people to the news of the bombardment of Paris tends to show, however, that in mid-January, acceptance of the war had not yet disappeared, even in the rural heartland. In the Indre, for example, the detailed analysis of the local reaction to this news, recorded by the mayors of a number of districts, showed that most of the people still declared themselves to be in favor of resistance.[36] Around the same time, the prefect of the Gers noted the unexpected reaction of patriotic resistance in this rural community.[37] It was then – that is, during the war and not afterward – that the myth of revenge originated; this myth was the indisputable sign of the acceptance of defeat in the immediate present, but also, paradoxically, of a refusal to acknowledge it as definitive. Here, finally, one must measure the impact on public opinion of the news of the fall of Paris at the end of January 1871. The feeling of disgrace that the surrender provoked in Paris is well known, as is the part

33 Reports of the prefect of Calvados, of Doubs, of l'Aisne, of l'Isère, and of the sub-prefect of Quimper, Aug. 7 and 8, 1870, S.H.A.T. La 7. Reports of the prefect of Cantal, of l'Aube, Aug. 7–8, 1870, A.N. F7 12660.
34 Report of M. Delatour to the Minister of Commerce, Sept. 1, 1870, S.H.A.T., La 10.
35 Prefect of the Dordogne, Oct. 24, 1870, F7 12675.
36 Prefect of the Indre, Jan. 20, 1871, A.N. F1 12676.
37 Prefect of the Gers, Jan. 21, 1871, A.N. F7 1275.

played by patriotic humiliation in the communal explosion of March 18. But it should be pointed out that the fall of Paris did not leave the opinion of the provinces indifferent in the least; the reaction was one of consternation and dejection. Contrary to what Parisians believed, the myth of the capital's resistance was in fact extended to the nation as a whole.

The nation's reaction expressed contradictory feelings that included a strong desire for peace and a conflicting desire to refuse terms that would be too humiliating. The vote of February 8, 1871, was in large measure the result of the decisive jolt caused by the capitulation of Paris. This surrender changed all of the strategic givens and did away with all that was left of the public's resolve or acceptance of the war. All hope for a revival of hostilities seemed, as a result, illusory. Without question, this vote expressed a profound desire for peace within the context of the absence of patriotism, particularly in rural areas. But this does not mean that the desire for peace was present either following the first defeats or even at the beginning of the Republic.

The differences between urban and rural areas, so often emphasized by the historiography of the war, require further examination. The "black legend," which opposed the peasant reaction to the patriotism without reproach of the cities,[38] had some basis in reality; and there were clear differences between town and country when it came to resistance. One should point out that few villages defended themselves with the help of the national guard (only ten districts in a *département* such as the Loiret),[39] and some did not hesitate to give up their weapons at the approach of the enemy.[40] As a last resort, French peasants also opposed the invaders using the "scorched earth" tactic. They were opposed to the draft that the Republic tried to enforce and supplied very few volunteers to the army and few recruits to the companies of franctireurs, who, for the most part, came from the cities.

Moreover, the resistance in the countryside presented difficulties harder to overcome than those in the cities: Without weapons, the defense of villages was not always possible, and, in this sense, the fight against the invader presented far more danger for the villager. In addition, the scorched-earth tactics advocated by city authorities seemed to the peasants ineffective in the short term (the Germans simply requisitioned peasants to rebuild roads) and catastrophic in the long term for agriculture. However, peasant resistance

38 "All the cities, big or small," writes Gambetta on Oct. 24, "are passionately republican and in favor of war. The countryside is lifeless and frightened." (Tours-Bourdeaux-Paris: les dépéches officielles de 1870–1871, S.H.A.T., Li N 111 bis, 42.)

39 Inquiry of the Ministry of Defense, 1912, S.H.A.T., Lv 23–5.

40 Sub-prefect of Meaux, Sept. 9, 1870, F7 12661. Prefect of l'Aube, Sept. 11, 1870, AHAT, Li 1. Prefect of Seine-et-Oise, Oct., 1870, F7 12679.

to direct and personal investment in the conflict was not universal; material in the archives indicates that a rather large number of attacks of enemy divisions were led by peasant communities against fringes of the German occupation forces.[41] At the end of October, in the Haute-Marne, for example, 4,000 national guardsmen from the villages of two districts of the *département* spontaneously mobilized themselves for three days to defend their communities against a phantom Prussian column and then, equipped with scythes and pitchforks, placed themselves at the disposal of the military authority of Langres, which sent them home.[42]

It is useful to color in much the same way the received idea of an urban patriotism above reproach. There is no doubt that the French wished to defend the strongholds of eastern France (for example, Metz or Strasbourg) or Paris. But it must be observed that the defense in question did not rest directly on the people themselves but rather on the garrisons. Furthermore, in Laon and in Soissons, it was the former who pushed the latter to surrender in September. In cases of small unfortified cities with a regular military force, the people did not show more of an inclination to resist than did the neighboring villages. In Bar-sur-Aube, Troyes, Evreux, and Rouen, in fact, the people advocated surrender even before the arrival of the Germans. Active resistance such as that in Saint-Quentin and especially that of Châteaudun remained isolated phenomena. It is therefore better to reject the overly simplistic terms of the traditional separation between town and country in matters of patriotism. Reactions were often less different than is generally thought.

Separate from the phenomena of resistance or surrender, but a determining factor in the future of Franco-German relations, was the dramatic degradation of images of the enemy in French public opinion as the conflict dragged on. The negative and then repulsive connotations associated with the very name of the invaders were absent at the beginning of the conflict. We see no traces of it, for example, in the letters or diaries written by soldiers during the first weeks of war. It is only afterward, in all written sources, that the accusations of pillage, vandalism, and assassination appear. These culminate with the bombardment of Paris, after which the enemy is exclusively viewed in a negative light. This new image of the enemy, as a barbarian, imposed itself with particular force in the occupied regions and in the eastern provinces, where favorable images of the Germans, who were perceived as a homogeneous group and whereby no distinctions were made between

41 This was the case in Seine-sur-Marne and Seine-et-Oise in September; in Eure, Eure-et-Loire, and Seine-et-Marne in October.
42 Prefect of the Haute-Marne, Oct. 27 and 28, 1870, A.N. F7 12677 and S.H.A.T. La 12.

the different regional ethnicities that composed "Germany" in 1870, disappeared for a long time. Especially in the northern half of the country, a fundamental change in the vision of the "other" occurred over the course of the war. This turning point in attitude also marked a fundamental transformation on the cultural level. Anti-German feelings, which represented a real threat to Germany, were the direct result of the war. The Third Republic sustained these feelings, structured and expanded them. As with the spirit of revenge, however, the Republic did not base these feelings on the memory of defeat and the "lost provinces."

CONCLUSION

This general overview of French society and public opinion in wartime has shown that the bedrock of patriotism, without which one cannot understand the French reaction to the war of 1914–18, was already in existence in 1870–71. The strength of this foundation was uneven, however, and clearly more fragile than it was forty-four years later. But the investment of the French in the Franco-Prussian War was a solid investment in war, long before the greater struggles of World War I. Furthermore, the similarity between the reactions of French public opinion at the outset of both wars is striking. The intensity with which people reacted to the outbreak of war in July 1870 evinced the growth of French patriotism from at least the beginning of the nineteenth century. Despite the defeats and a very unfavorable military situation from the beginning of August, the acceptance of the war and the determination to pursue it were sustained for a longer period of time and to a greater extent than historians have been willing to admit. Opposition to the war was not expressed until much later on, mostly in the last two months of the conflict. Thus, the attitude of the French during the war does not reflect the image cast by the verdict of the ballot boxes in 1871.

In this chapter, I have sketched a brief history of the role that the war of 1870 played in the rise of French patriotism. It is now possible to gauge more accurately the exact limits of the "republican success" between 1871 and 1914: compulsory education, the military service that became progressively more equal and universal, the propagation of urban and written culture in the countryside – all of which caused patriotic values to spread considerably, and without which one can understand nothing of the surprising resistance of French society during World War I. But French patriotism was not created by the republican regime; it was only reinforced by it. In this way, the Franco-Prussian War illustrates that the cultural substratum of total war was partially in place from this date forward. The conflict of 1870 thus constituted a decisive step in the "investment of the French in France," which, in achieving its historical heights a quarter century later, created the cultural conditions particular to war in the twentieth century.[43]

43   This is Pierre Chaunu's expression in *La France* (Paris, 1982), 20.

20

Women and War in the Confederacy

DONNA REBECCA D. KRUG

If Confederate women had heard the Civil War referred to as a *total war*, they would have agreed because of the war's immense effect on their lives.[1] Union generals did not intentionally kill or physically harm unoffending women and children. Nevertheless, the pillaging and destruction of private property as a strategy of war was shocking to civilians. They saw such attempts to break the will of the people to resist as violations of codes of war. There was no way that women and children on the home front could avoid the war. Whether or not civilians were in the pathway of troops, the Confederate government required sacrifices that affected each citizen's daily life. Fighting of the war caused the widespread absence of men, which was the most serious problem confronting Confederate women as they attempted to hold their homes and families together amidst unfamiliar duties that had previously belonged to men (see Table 20.1).[2] Most women reluctantly assumed management of homes, families, farms, and businesses after male family heads went away to war. Many women for the first time faced the necessity of making decisions on their own and devising ways to support their families. The shortage of men made old standards impractical. "Before the war," wrote Nell Grey of Virginia, "it was scarcely considered wise or delicate for women to live without the protection of a male relative in the

1 I express my appreciation to Michael P. Johnson, David Rankin, and Cornelia Dayton for their criticism of my dissertation, "The Folks Back Home: The Confederate Homefront During the Civil War," Ph.D. diss., University of California, Irvine, 1990, from which this essay is drawn; forthcoming with the University of South Carolina Press; and to George Rable, Lee Anne Whites, Bertram Wyatt-Brown, Carol Bleser, and Reid Mitchell for critiques of earlier work. Any finishing touches I owe to the participants of the German Historical Institute's conference, "On the Road to Total War: The American Civil War and the German Wars of Unification, 1861–1871," Washington, D.C., April 1–4, 1992 .
2 The tables in this study were derived from a sample of 2,085 complaints in National Archives, Washington, D.C., Letters Received by Confederate secretary of war, 1861–65, record group 109, microcopy 437 (hereafter cited as LR).

Table 20.1. *Confederate States of America – Family Hardship Complaints by Type*[a]

Type Complaint	1861	1862	1863	1864	1865	Total
Hardships from the absence of men at home	133	362	166	150	40	850
(% of N, All Ltrs)	(57.3)	(45.1)	(33.9)	(34.1)	(32.5)	(40.8)
Invasion hardship	17	46	38	57	26	184
(% of N)	(7.3)	(5.8)	(7.8)	(13.0)	(21.1)	(8.8)
Shortage of skilled men	31	293	143	85	11	563
(% of N)	(13.4)	(36.6)	(29.2)	(19.3)	(8.9)	(27.0)
Slave problems/fears	9	100	60	40	5	214
(% of N)	(3.9)	(12.5)	(12.2)	(9.1)	(8.9)	(10.3)
Requests to leave CSA	16	32	53	80	20	201
(% of N)	(6.9)	(4.0)	(10.8)	(18.2)	(16.3)	(9.6)
Hardships from CSA government policies	38	136	192	198	56	620
(% of N)	(16.4)	(17.0)	(39.2)	(45.0)	(45.5)	(29.7)
Law and order problems	12	39	58	42	13	164
(% of N)	(5.2)	(4.9)	(11.8)	(9.5)	(10.6)	(7.9)
Sons too young to fight	39	88	15	4	0	146
(% of N)	(16.8)	(11.0)	(3.1)	(0.9)	(0)	(7.0)
Miscellaneous	15	50	22	30	7	124
(% of N)	(6.5)	(6.3)	(4.5)	(6.8)	(5.7)	(5.9)
Total letters = N =	232	800	490	440	123	2,085
Total letters to secretary of war in sample	5,125	3,869	1,818	1,347	660	12,819
(% of family hardships)	(4.5)	(20.7)	(27.0)	(32.7)	(18.6)	(16.3)
Total letters received by secretary of war	8,856	17,181	9,188	6,344	1,270	42,839
(% of all letters read)	(57.9)	(22.5)	(19.8)	(21.2)	(52.0)	(29.9)

[a]The tables in this study were derived from a sample of 2,085 complaints in National Archives, Washington, D.C., Letters Received by Confederate Secretary of War, 1861–1865, Record Group 109, Microcopy 437 (hereafter cited as LR).

house, and as far as possible they were shielded from the burden of business responsibilities."[3]

More than anything, men fought for honor, but men's duty to fight conflicted with their duty to support and protect their families, especially among common soldiers who owned no slaves. Wartime hardships brought out contradictions that required reshaping the ideal. Honor permitted women to show courage and to assume wider roles, but it also required them to resume their subordinate role when the crisis was over and men returned.[4] Regardless of their social class, women were expected to encourage their men to fight and to accept stoically additional responsibilities.

The absence of men did not bring about instantaneous changes. At first, husbands and wives tried to continue old roles by correspondence. Men were reluctant to relinquish control of their children, homes, and property, but at the same time, they needed their wives to manage their homes without them. Absent farmers and planters made the major decisions and asked for detailed accounts of the crops, while their wives carried out their directions. Warren Akin, a Georgia Representative, wanted to know "how the stable and crib are finished whether my mules and corn, etc. are safe ... how much milk the cow gives, ... how the wheat looks." In January 1863, James Michael Barr, who was unsure of his wife's management, directed Rebecca that "the big wheat, the Watson wheat, not to be mixed with the other wheat. ... After it is thrashed, put it in boxes or barrels in the store house till it can be hauled off. ... When it is cut I want it shocked well." She was to "never loan my buggy unless it was to some one that could and would return the same favor. If the harness gets broke up, you know we cannot replace them. If the buggy gets broken, it cannot be mended to look as well." Like other planters, Barr was pleased by his wife's success, but he tried to retain some control through letters, and he clung to the cultivation of at least some cotton amidst government attempts to get people to change to food crops: "I don't want any thing planted in the cotton patches, but I want a good stand of cotton."[5] Other absent men tried to retain some control over their land and crops.

3 Myrta Locket Avary, ed., *A Virginia Girl in the Civil War, 1861–1865: Being a Record of the Actual Experiences of the Wife of a Confederate Officer* (New York, 1903), 10–11. See also Joseph F. White, "Social Conditions in the South During the War Between the States," *Confederate Veteran* 30 (April 1922): 142–5.

4 Bertram Wyatt-Brown, *Southern Honor: Ethics and Behavior in the Old South* (New York, 1982), 51–2, 230–4; Bertram Wyatt-Brown, "The Antebellum South As a 'Culture of Courage,'" *Journal of Southern Studies* 20 (Sept. 1981): 213–46; and Bertram Wyatt-Brown, "The Ideal Typology and Antebellum Southern History: A Testing of a New Approach," *Societas* 5 (Winter 1975): 1–29.

5 Warren Akin to Mary Akin, Dec. 11, 1864, in Bell I. Wiley, ed., *The Letters of Warren Akin, Confederate Congressman* (Athens, Ga.,1959), 36–8; James Michael Barr to Rebecca Barr, Mar. 8, 1863; June 2, 1863; June 5, 1863; in Ruth Barr McDaniel, comp., *Confederate War Correspondence of James Michael Barr and Wife Rebecca Ann Dowling Barr* (Taylors, S.C., 1963), 62–4, 98–9, 100–1.

John Cotton, a nonslaveowning farmer in Alabama, hired a slave, Manuel, to help his wife and seven children farm after he went to war. His wife, Mariah, who was unaccustomed to managing a laborer and making decisions about farming, sought direction from her husband. He instructed her "to send for par every time manuel crooks his finger til he gets him straight. ... I want the fresh field all sowed in wheat if the fresh part is not two fowl what lay out must bee broken up first then sowed I want the ould field on the creek sowed in rye what lay out rite off as soon as possible and the peech orcherd in rye romane."[6]

As the war progressed, men increasingly came to see that they had to delegate greater autonomy to women. Communications were too slow for solving day-to-day problems. Women had to rely upon themselves rather than wait for their husbands' advice. John Cotton, like many other soldiers, had to delegate direct responsibility to his wife: "I would bee glad to come but I cant so you must make your own arrangement[s] I no you are at a great loss to no what to do but you can see what is needed better than I can and me not nowing how things is going on. ... " Although he urged his wife to act on her own, he tried to remain an influence in the family. He thought of their material well-being through his own agrarian values in case he did not return: "if I never come back again ... I want you to keep your land and such things as you need and raise your children the best you can ... carry on your business as if you never expected me at home. ... "[7]

Major W. J. Mims of Alabama was similarly concerned about his family. Above all, he wanted his wife to uphold his ideas of honor and a good name. She should do the best she could "economizing & trying to pay all our debts mine and yours as I would rather my children live poor than they should have the sneers of people whom their father owed & had not paid."[8]

Sgt. Edwin Fay of Minden, Louisiana, urged his wife to make decisions on her own after the fall of New Orleans and Vicksburg when communication became difficult. In December 1863, he wrote, "About the sale of our house and lot I have written you to do just as you please. ... You must cultivate self reliance to a greater degree and learn to depend upon yourself, for I may not live thro this War and you must take care of your own."[9]

Some women resisted autonomy. For example, in March 1862, after the death of her father, Mrs. Frances J. Brightwell of Virginia requested that

---

6   John Cotton to Mariah Cotton, Sept. 17, 1862, in John Weaver Cotton, *Yours Till Death: Civil War Letters of John W. Cotton*, ed. Lucille Griffith (Tuscaloosa, Ala., 1951), 21–2.

7   John Cotton to Mariah Cotton, Dec. 17, 1862; Oct. 2, 1862; Ibid., 24–5, 38–9.

8   Major W. J. Mims to Kate Mims, Aug. 11, 1862; for a similar idea, Apr. 16, 1863, "Letters of Major W. J. Mims, C.S.A.," *Alabama Historical Quarterly* 3 (Summer 1941): 207–8, 210–11.

9   Edwin Fay to Sarah Fay, Dec. 8, 1863, in Bell I. Wiley and Lucy E. Fay, eds., *"This Infernal War:" The Confederate Letters of Sgt. Edwin H. Fay* (Austin, Tex., 1958), 374–9.

President Jefferson Davis discharge her husband: "My poore bline Farther dide a few weaks back he leaves me a poor orfient child no one to take care of me."[10] Although the majority of women did not express the dependence of Brightwell, most of them were unaccustomed to making farming and financial decisions on their own.

Early in the war, most women were uncertain of their ability to take charge of business. Kate Peddy expressed her uneasiness to her husband in 1862: "I would give anything in my power to be with you now, for all goes well when you are here, but some how I can't do as well when you are gone. I know it is selfish of me to want you here when you are where you can do your country and fellow men so much good, but I am only a woman and a very ordinary one too, not competent or worthy to be your companion."[11] She could look for assistance from her father, a lawyer who was too old for service. Similarly, Mariah Cotton, Rebecca Barr, and Sarah Fay turned to male kinsmen for assistance, which helped them to develop autonomy gradually.

Much of the stability of Southern society and culture came from the strength of kin and community ties.[12] The women who succeeded in the absence of their men sought the assistance of males, not dependence on them. For these women, self-reliance was a gradual growing process while men encouraged, aided, and advised them. In crises, women looked to traditional ties for solutions to holding their families together.

Few women thought that the assumption of wider roles on the home front was anything other than a temporary expedient while their men were away. They sought their husbands' approval or the assurance of other male kin. The roles that women assumed were usually those established by precedent and were related to domestic duties or the expansion of domestic duties to the public.

Although women's domestic duties were valued more from wartime requirements, many women wished to do more than put on a brave front when their men left and then wait for their return. Kate Stone longed to "see and be in it all. I hate the weary days of inaction. Yet what can women do but wait and suffer?" Catherine Edmondston described women's waiting as "a terrible state to live in. Expectations and anxiety unsettle and destroy one's peace of mind to that degree we are ready for anything." Women sat at home

10 Mrs. Francis J. Brightwell to President Davis, Mar. 17, 1862, referred to Confederate secretary of war, LR, no. B167–1862, roll 31, 578–80.
11 Kate Peddy to George W. Peddy, Jan. 25, 1862, in George Peddy Cuttino, ed., *Saddle Bag and Spinning Wheel Being the Civil War Letters of George Peddy, M.D, and Kate Featherston Peddy* (Macon, Ga., 1981), 42–4.
12 Jean E. Friedman, *The Enclosed Garden: Women and Community in the Evangelical South 1830–1900* (Chapel Hill, N.C., 1985), 92–104.

in "a calm of desperation." Ida Dulaney expressed her anxiety after a battle: "When I think that Hal was in that struggle I am nearly wild with fear lest he should have been hurt, yet here I am shut up ... ignorant even of his present position and without the faintest possibility of hearing from him. The anxiety is almost insupportable." William Nugent described to his wife his apprecia- tion of the women of the South who were the ones to "uncomplainingly bear the brunt of privations at home. ... If our men of stout frame had but the staunch hearts of our women, Nell, we would indeed be a nation of heroes worthy of the name."[13]

How much could women do beyond wait? Many women wrote of their desire to fight. Lucy Breckinridge wrote that she "would gladly shoulder" her pistol and "shoot some Yankees if it were allowable." Sarah Morgan said that she "would be fighting if she were a man," and she had "tried on her brother's clothes and felt ashamed."[14] However, like most Southern women, internal- ized notions of a lady's proper role made them unable to cast off the garments of the role that patriarchal society expected.

Women were subject to both admiration and suspicion if they went beyond what was essential to keep their homes and families together. A few extraordinary individuals became female soldiers early in the war. Confed- erate Amazons sought to be near male relatives. Some women such as Mrs. Amy Clark and Madame Loreta Janette Velazquez assumed the attire and names of men, joined the Confederate army, and fought with the male soldiers as legendary women had during the Revolutionary War. Mrs. Clark continued to fight after her husband was killed until she was wounded a second time and captured by Federals. Madame Velazquez claimed that after her husband died fighting for the Confederacy, she assumed the identity of Lt. Harry T. Buford and raised a company. After her second wound and discovery of her sex, a major convinced her "that if regularly enlisted in the secret corps," she could "render assistance of the first value." She resumed

13 Entries, May 16, 1861, and June 11, 1861, Anderson, *Brokenburn: Kate Stone*, 17, 24; Beth G. Crabtree and James W. Patton, eds., *"Journal of a Secesh Lady:" The Diary of Catherine Ann Devereux Edmondston, 1860–1866* (Raleigh, N. C., 1979) , 443–4; entry, June 6, 1863 from " The Journal of Aunt Ida" in Marietta M. Andrews, ed., *Scraps of Paper* (New York, 1929), 17; and William Nugent to Eleanor Nugent, May 26, 1862, in William M. Cash and Lucy Somerville Howorth, eds., *My Dear Dear Nellie: The Civil War Letters of William L. Nugent to Eleanor Smith Nugent* (Jackson, Miss., 1977), 76–8.
14 Entry, Aug. 13, 1863, in Mary D. Robertson, ed., *Lucy Breckinridge of Grove Hill: The Journal of a Virginia Girl, 1862–64* (Kent, 1979), 132–3; Sarah Morgan Dawson, *A Confederate Girl's Diary*, ed. James I. Robertson (Bloomington, Ind., 1960), 118–20. See also E. Culpepper Clark, "Sarah Morgan and Francis Dawson: Raising the Woman Question in Reconstruction South Carolina," *South Carolina Historical Magazine* (Jan. 1980): 8–23; and Mary Katherine Davis, "Sarah Morgan Dawson: A Renunciation of Southern Society," M.A. thesis, University of North Carolina, Chapel Hill, 1970.

the dress of a lady and served the Confederate government as a secret agent in Washington and diplomat to Canada.[15]

When she was a refugee on her way from Memphis to Alabama, Elizabeth Avery Meriwether met Melverina Elverina Peppercorn, who joined the army to be with her twin brother. On her return to Tennessee, Elizabeth learned from Melverina's mother that she fought only once in a battle because after her brother was shot in the leg and sent to the hospital, she quit the army to nurse him until he was well, and then it was too late to return to the army as General Lee had "gone and surrendered."[16] Melverina put the traditional female duty of nursing a wounded family member before fighting for the Cause.

Men and women alike were uncomfortable with radical departures from established roles. Theodore Fogle of Georgia was shocked when he saw a drunken woman, dressed in an army shirt, with a short skirt, a pistol and sword at her waist. "I don't like her looks. She is too free and easy," he wrote.[17]

Other ladies rendered services as spies, couriers, and blockade runners that were just as risky. Reactions were ambivalent. Mrs. Rose O'Neal Greenhow led a female spy ring in Washington, D.C., that passed Union secrets to the Confederacy.[18] After Mrs. Greenhow's capture, Mary Chesnut described women's suspicion of her risks as "a ruse de guerre. She has all her life been for *sale* & we will trust her better & she can do us more injury if they pretend to distrust her." Mrs. Chesnut herself was discontent sitting on the sidelines: "With *men* it is on to the field – glory, honour, praise, and power. Women can only stay at home – & every paper reminds us that women are to be *violated* – ravished & all manner of humiliation. How are the daughters of Eve punished?"[19]

15 Francis B. Simkins and James W. Patton, *The Women of the Confederacy* (Richmond, Va., 1936), 75–81; Mary Elizabeth Massey, *Bonnet Brigades* (New York, 1966), 75–86; Janet E. Kaufman, "'Under the Petticoat Flag': Women Soldiers in the Confederate Army," *Journal of Southern Studies* 23 (Winter 1984): 363–75; and George C. Rable, *Civil Wars: Women and the Crisis of Southern Nationalism* (Urbana, Ill., 1989), 151–3; Katharine M. Jones, *Heroines of Dixie: Confederate Women Tell Their Story of the War* (New York, 1955), 290–8; Katharine M. Jones, *Ladies of Richmond: Confederate Capital* (New York, 1962), 136–60; and C. J. Worthington, ed., *The Woman in Battle: A Narrative of the Exploits, Adventures, and Travels of Madame Loreta Velazquez* (Hartford, Conn., 1876); the Velazquez story has been neither proven nor disproven.

16 Elizabeth Avery Meriwether, *Recollections of 92 Years, 1824–1916* (Nashville, Tenn., 1958), 102–5, 161–4; and Kaufman, "Under the Petticoat Flag," 305–6.

17 Theodore Fogle to his parents, Sept. 11, 1861, in Mills Lane, ed., *"Dear Mother: Don't Grieve About Me: If I Get Killed, I'll Only be Dead:" Letters from Georgia Soldiers in the Civil War* (Savannah, Ga., 1977), xxx.

18 Ishel Ross, *Rebel Rose: Life of Rose O'Neal Greenhow, Confederate Spy* (New York, 1954); and John Bakeless, *Spies for the Confederacy* (Philadelphia and New York, 1970), 14, 27, 53–7.

19 Entry, Aug 29, 1861, in C. Vann Woodward and Elisabeth Muhlenfeld, eds., *The Private Mary Chesnut: The Unpublished Civil War Diaries* (New York, 1984), 145–6, with other references to Greenhow on 144, 147, 212. See also, entry, Aug. 29, 1861, in C. Vann Woodward, ed., *Mary Chesnut's Civil War* (New Haven, Conn., 1981), 171–2, in which she wrote years later: "The Manassas men swear she was our good angel."

A more notorious female spy was Belle Boyd of the Virginia Shenandoah Valley. She gleaned military secrets from Yankee admirers and carried the information to Confederate officers. Belle and other lady spies conveyed coded messages by methods such as sewing them in riding habits or coiling them in their hair. Belle smuggled weapons under her hoop skirts from the Union to the Confederacy.[20] Many people were shocked because Belle consorted freely with the enemy. Lucy Rebecca Buck thought that she was "all surface, vain and hollow, false an heartless." Kate Sperry wrote that "of all the fools I ever saw of the womankind, she beats all – perfectly insane on the subject of men."[21]

Greenhow and Boyd were resourceful spies who outwitted Yankees for a time, but early in the war, both women were captured and banished to the Confederacy. Yankees did not believe female spies would be dangerous if they were far behind Confederate lines. President Davis respected their courage, and he employed them as agents in Canada and Europe. The wider roles that most women assumed were related to caring for their families and to applying domestic duties to the public through voluntary associations for soldiers.

Women had to hold their homes together against greater obstacles than their men had before the war. The blockade created shortages of many essential items and led to hoarding, inflated prices, and the greed of profiteers. Confederate, state, and local governments were unable to develop an effective policy for dealing with shortages, speculating, or poverty. Many localities, private individuals, and organizations tried to tackle poverty, but it proved too widespread for their resources.

When their families needed financial assistance more than ever, formerly self-sufficient family heads often earned only $11.00 or $12.00 per month as privates. Soldiers' families suffered even more because the Confederacy paid them slowly. David Golightly Harris noted in his journal that his pay as a private "was $11 per month and my expense is about $15.00." It cost him more to serve his country than he could earn as a soldier.[22]

---

20 Bakeless, *Spies for the Confederacy*, 64–5, 141–72; Massey, *Bonnet Brigades*, 96; Ruth Scarborough, *Belle Boyd: Siren of the South* (Macon, Ga., 1983); and Louis A. Sigaud, *Belle Boyd: Confederate Spy* (Richmond, Va., 1944). Much information in all sources listed comes from Belle Boyd, *Belle Boyd in Camp and Prison*, 2 vols. (London, 1865).

21 Sigaud, *Belle Boyd*, 39; William R. Buck, ed., *Sad Earth, Sweet Heaven: The Diary of Lucy Rebecca Buck* (Birmingham, Ala., 1973), 1–18; and Entry of Kate Sperry, Oct. 26, 1861, in Thomas Felix Hickerson, *Echoes of Happy Valley: Letters and Diaries in the South Civil War History* (Chapel Hill, N.C., 1962), 88–95.

22 David Golightly Harris Farm Journals, 1855–70, 6 vols., Feb. 24, 1863, microfilmed copy of original, Southern Historical Collection, University of North Carolina, Chapel Hill (hereafter cited as Harris Farm Journals); and Philip N. Racine, ed., *Piedmont Farmer: The Journals of David Golightly Harris, 1855–1870* (Knoxville, Tenn., 1990), 277–8.

Inadequate soldiers' pay led to attempts to reconcile a growing conflict between a man's duty to fight for his country and his duty to support his family. Complaints poured into the Confederate secretary of war's office as conditions worsened, and soldiers failed to be discharged on expiration of their original enlistments. Citizens of Carroll County, Georgia, petitioned the secretary of war in 1863 because of the hardships of the family of the shoemaker, David Bryant, after he and two sons volunteered, leaving "a sickly and weakly wife and nine children at home a sickly daughter and the next oldest a cripple. So there is no one to make them a support – and owing to the very small pittance paid to him as a private soldier & the very high price of every necessity of life his family is reduced to want." Mrs. Lydia Bolton of North Carolina requested the discharge of her husband because: "i am a pore woman and i work as hard as eney slav in North Carolina." It was "impossible to cloth[e] and feed" her family when "tha only giv me thre dolars a month and fore in famely and corn too dollars per bushel … we will hav to go neked or starv and i beg you to hear the crye of the pore." After her husband had been a Confederate soldier for a year, Mrs. I. W. McLaughlin requested that her husband be detailed to some better-paying position. Otherwise, they would have to leave the Confederacy for help in the North since people in the Confederacy "pay no attention to soldiers wives and children." She believed many people would not hesitate to "put me out doors if I did not pay my rent by the month which is seven dollars now how can I liv on his army pay." Her two children were sick "without means to make them comfortable."[23]

Many officers also found it difficult to provide for their families, as one lieutenant did who was transferred to Virginia from his home in Louisiana. His wife, Mrs. Virginia King, requested that her husband be transferred nearer home because "$90.00 would suffice … did I receive it regularly, but as it is quite otherwise, and he so far away that there is both trouble and uncertainty in transmitting it to me."[24]

Worse off than women with husbands were widows. In this study, 266 out of 850 letters to the Confederate secretary of war on private hardships from the absence of men came from widows (see Table 20.2). Many widowed

<hr>

23 Petition of Citizens of Carroll County, Georgia, to secretary of war for David Bryant, Oct., 1863, LR, no. B800-1863, roll 84, 112-14; Lydia Bolton to secretary of war, Nov. 12, 1862, LR, no. B103-1865 (1862 case), roll 146, 667; and Mrs. I. W. McLaughlin to secretary of war, Aug. 12, 1862, LR, no. M1063-1862, roll 62, 98–101. For a similar case, see John Moore to secretary of war, May 23, 1863, LR, no. M441-1863, roll 103, 447–8, with War Department notation stating that his case was "worthy," but there were "too many like it to allow them all to be granted." Such letters were rarely answered.

24 Mrs. Virginia M. King to secretary of war, Oct. 29, 1861, LR, no. 7828–1861, roll 61, 1019–23. For another example of slow payment to officers, see George W. Peddy to Kate Peddy, Oct. 23, 1862, Cuttino, ed., *Saddle Bag and Spinning Wheel*, 123–4.

Table 20.2. *Letters to the Confederate Secretary of War Pertaining to Hardships of Widows from the Absence of Men*

War Year	1861	1862	1863	1864	1865	1861–65
All Widows (% of *N*)	24.1	35.2	39.2	20.7	27.5	31.3
(No. of Cases)	(32)	(127)	(65)	(31)	(11)	(266)
N = All letters about hardship from the absence of men	133	361	166	150	40	850

mothers asked for release of a son. Widows, like many other Confederate citizens, were slow to ask for help because of a stigma against charity. Two war widows finally sought relief from the Confederate government after their husbands had been dead two years or longer and the circumstances of their families had become desperate. In November 1864, Mrs. S. D. Beazley, whose husband "dide in 1862 in the war of the South a Soldier," described her own and other soldiers' families "who cannot get bread to eat half of our time yet thare is plenty around us. … Corn is selling [a] hundred dollars a barrel wheat 30 dollars [a] bushel and do you know how in this life we are to live do for the lands sake try to releave our suffring if you can send our husbin[s] and sons on call … it is a nuf to brake the hart of a Mother to heair her little children ask for bread and she has nothing to giv them. … " According to Mrs. Col. Charles C. Lee in February 1865, who had struggled to "feed and cloth[e]" her "little ones," people "were amassing the largest prices for common necessities." Her husband fell three years ago "leaving his widow & little children to the mercy of the government he nobly defended to the last." It should at least "make some provisions for the widow and permit her to buy at Government price such things as wood and clothing." The Confederate government set forth Order no. 69 to grant her request, but the action came in the last days of the Confederacy after many widows and soldiers' families had long suffered deprivation of basic necessities.[25]

Families had to cope with hardships from the intervention of government in their lives. Many people complained of abusive treatment and damages from Confederate troops who camped on their property and Confederate impressing agents who took slaves, animals, or crops. Complaints to the Confederate secretary of war described ruined crops, slaughtered livestock, fencing that was carried off and burned, stripped grass fields, and insufficient government payment for the loss. People resented Confederate officials as "upstarts puffed up with a little brief authority" who forcefully seized stock

25 Mrs. S. D. Beazley to secretary of war, Nov. 2, 1864, LR, no. B677-1864, roll 122, 31–4; and Mrs. Col. Charles C. Lee to President Davis, referred to secretary of war, Feb. 12, 1865, LR, no. L50-1865, roll 149, 420–2.

and work animals from plantations and farms.[26] Taxes-in-kind and property taxes were burdensome to everyone – most of all to the wives of yeomen farmers and small slaveholders. When he came home on furlough, Harris noted in November 1864: "My wife, children, and negroes have done well in my absence & have made enough to live upon if they are permitted to use it." With high taxes and high prices, his family's burden was "about as much as we can well stand."[27]

Families experiencing the most difficulty were those dependent on one man. The absence of men was a severe trial for wives of yeomen farmers or craftsmen without slaves, especially elderly widowed mothers, women in bad health, families of young children, families in invaded areas or those dislocated by war, women in isolated areas, or women without strong ties to kin or community. Women in those families had to shoulder alone duties requiring a man's strength such as plowing, planting, repairing fences or farm implements – duties far beyond the household chores expected of them in peacetime. Mrs. Elizabeth Leeson described in July 1863 her desperate need to have her husband out of service: "He might do his children some good & thare is no use in keeping a man thare to kill him & leave widows & poore little orphen children to suffer while the rich has aplenty to work for them ... my poor children have no home nor no Father."[28]

The shortage of skilled men in the community also complicated women's management of homes and farms. Letters to public officials attest that the depletion of craftsmen and physicians made life difficult. Women were unprepared to assume skills that required special training, mechanical know-how,

---

26   J. M. Botts et al., to secretary of war, June 13, 1863, June 26, 1863, and July 2, 1863, LR, nos. B491-1863, B710-1863, and B543-1863, all on roll 83, 2–11, 867–77, and 196–98; and W. M. Byrd to secretary of war, Mar. 22, 1864, LR, no. B324-1864, roll 120, 280–4.

27   Harris Farm Journals, entry for Nov. 8, 1864; and Racine, *Piedmont Farmer*, 348–9.

28   Anne Firor Scott, *The Southern Lady: From Pedestal to Politics, 1830–1930* (Chicago, 1970), 82; and Paul D. Escott, *After Secession: Jefferson Davis and the Failure of Confederate Nationalism* (Baton Rouge, La., 1978), 107–8; Elizabeth Leeson to secretary of war, July 22, 1863, LR, roll 100, 664–6. See also Paul D. Escott, "Poverty and Government Aid for the Poor in Confederate North Carolina," *North Carolina Historical Review* 6 (Oct. 1984): 462–80; Paul D. Escott, "The Cry of the Sufferers:" The Problem of Welfare in the Confederacy," *Civil War History* 23 (Sept. 1977): 228–40; and Paul D. Escott and Jeffery J. Crow, "The Social Order and Violent Disorder: An Analysis of North Carolina in the Revolution and Civil War," *Journal of Southern History* 52 (Aug. 1986): 373–402. On backwoods women who refused to become victims, see Victoria Bynum, "'War Within a War': Women's Participation in the Revolt of the North Carolina Piedmont, 1863–1865, "*Frontiers*, no. 3 (1987): 43–9; and Victoria E. Bynum, "Unruly Women: The Relationship Between Status and Behavior Among Free Women of the North Carolina Piedmont, 1840–1865," Ph.D. diss., University of California, San Diego, 1987. On the hardships of poor women during the absence of their husbands, see George C. Rable, *Civil Wars: Women and the Crisis of Southern Nationalism* (Urbana, Ill., 1989); and for poor women's ideology, Drew Gilpin Faust, "The Altars of Sacrifice: Or How Confederate Women Lost the Civil War," a paper presented in San Diego, California, to the Research Seminar of the Focused Research Program in Southern History on June 23, 1989.

or physical strength. Ann Summerlin explained the hardships of women from the absence of such men to the secretary of war in March 1865: "please do send Mr. Lemon Atkinson home for the accommodation of this vicinity we have no one to make our shoes, to mend our ploughs, & to fix our hoes or axes, an[d] our wells are broke down, we cant do this work it is too laborous for we poor females." Martha J. Bates and other citizens petitioned the governor of Mississippi in June 1862 for the discharge of the blacksmith, James Alexander, to repair farming utensils for soldiers' wives and children, a service especially needed when all of the men were away. One miller in Virginia in a petition noted that many families were dependent on his mill for their daily bread, that he reserved some grain to send to the "destitute women & children free of charge because their *men* were in the army." People sought to exempt men from service whose skills were essential to the families of soldiers.[29]

Some women did try to carry on their husbands' businesses in their absence, but letters to the secretary of war show their difficulties managing their shops and their dependence on male labor, white and black. Mrs. Virginia J. Melton of Virginia requested that her husband be discharged after the slave blacksmith had attempted to escape. Susan Austin, a widow in Virginia, sought the discharge of her son to manage the blacksmith shop and the hired slave. It was difficult for her to manage the shop along with a farm, fourteen slaves, and household containing a lunatic brother and epileptic son. Mrs. Ann G. Matley of Virginia requested a furlough for her husband to repair the wheel of the grist mill that she was managing in his absence along with a household of nine children all under thirteen years of age and a crippled elderly mother. Of the urgency to have her husband home long enough to make a new water wheel, she wrote that the stoppage of the mill was disastrous for her family as it was "their chief dependence for bread. ... " Soldiers' wives needed to have a nearby mill because "they often had no other way of carrying" their wheat to the mill other than "on their sides or shoulders."[30]

Out of a sample of 2,085 letters of hardship to the secretary of war between 1861 and 1865, 27 percent of all complaints pertained to the difficulties of communities from the absence of such skilled men as blacksmiths, tanners, millers, and carpenters (see Table 20.3). Also included in the sample are

---

29 Ann Summerlin to secretary of war, Mar. 9, 1865, LR, no. A41-1865, roll 146, 171–2; petition of Mrs. Martha J. Bates and others to governor of Mississippi, referred to secretary of war, June 3, 1862, LR, no. B584-1862, roll 33, 450–2; and petition for detail of S. A. Campbell to secretary of war, Oct. 1862, LR, no. C81-1865, roll 147, 297–300.

30 Virginia J. Melton to secretary of war, Apr. 16, 1862, LR, no. M362-1862, roll 60, 72–4; Susan Austin to secretary of war, received Oct. 24, 1862, LR, no. A39-1865, roll 146, 161–63; petition of Ann G. Matley to secretary of war, Feb. 20, 1865, LR, no. M89-1865, roll 149, 989–91.

Table 20.3. *Hardships from Absence of Skilled Men in Service*

War Year	No. of Absence-of-Skilled-Men Letters	Percentage	All Hardship Letters
1861	31	13.4	232
1862	293	36.6	800
1863	143	29.2	490
1864	85	19.3	440
1865	11	8.9	123
1861–65	563	27.0	2,085

physicians and teachers. The highest percentage of such letters occurred in 1862 with the rush to volunteer to avoid conscription before laws granting exemptions were defined. After exemptions were defined, numerous notations on the War Department letters attest that men who were already in service were not able to be exempt except in cases of physical disability. Only late in the war were some men detailed from the military for those services.

Letters to public officials such as the secretary of war do not tell of the resourcefulness of Confederate women in devising makeshifts and substitutes for scarce necessities. Women did not take over male positions requiring mechanical know-how and strength, but necessity compelled them to find ways to carry on their homes and provide for their families in the absence of their men. Parthenia Hague, a governess in Alabama, noted in her memoirs the ingenious devices that two yeomen farmer women contrived for cultivating wheat in the absence of the men in their families. One woman converted a barrel so that she "flailed as much as a bushel or two at one time," and pounded the wheat on the ground so that the "wind acted as a great fan" to separate the good grain from the chaff. Another neighbor, a soldier's wife, with the help of her five small children, beat wheat free of the chaff in a smokehouse pork salting trough with "little wooden mauls she had roughly shaped." Women experimented to find substitutes for coffee, ink, medicines, leather, and many other basic items. Castoffs were recycled, and women recorded with pride the makeshifts that they devised. Slaves and white women of all classes learned to spin, weave, knit, and crochet. Ladies experimented with berries and other plants for dyes for homespun cloth. Old fabric was made over into new garments, as Cornelia McDonald indicated:

I had ripped up a cotton mattress and had it carded and spun, had dyed one half brown with walnut hulls, and left the other white. Out of this a very neat check was made which clothed Kenneth and the three little boys, while Nelly was dressed in some red Turkish cotton which had been used in former times for bed curtains, with aprons and white frocks of muslin that had also served as window and bed curtains.

Substitutes for shoe leather included wood, old carpets, canvas, and knitted materials.[31] Women devised makeshift items for the needs of their own families.

Although the absence of men most severely affected women in nonslave-holding families, it also created problems for many women in slaveholding families. The formidable adjustment from cotton to food production was made largely under women's management. Hague described a transition in southern Alabama from cotton to wheat, rye, rice, oats, corn, peas, and pumpkins. The changeover required the most adjustments for large slave-holders. Before the war, large slaveholders had devoted a greater percentage of their resources to cotton production for the world market than yeomen farmers with few or no slaves. Since they lacked a large-scale source of labor, most yeomen farmers raised stock and food crops.[32] For example, John Cotton of Alabama did not mention cotton in his correspondence to his wife. He emphasized wheat. The 1860 census listed the products of his farm as wheat, rye, corn, oats, peas, sweet potatoes, and livestock.[33] The management of the farm did not require a change of crops for Mariah Cotton.

Nevertheless, a labor force of slaves placed women in planter families at an advantage over nonslaveholding families. In November 1862, while her husband was at war, Catherine Edmondston, as with a number of mistresses, expressed confidence in her slaves: "Here have I been for three days and nights, the only white soul on a plantation of eighty odd negroes and not another white soul within five miles of me and that a man of near seventy surrounded with 300 or more slaves as safe as tho'an army with banners were encamped around without even a fear for myself."[34] Not everyone felt so secure, and others who did changed their minds later.

As the war continued, many women encountered difficulties supervising slave labor. Even the mistresses who had earlier praised the conduct of their slaves observed that slaves resisted and ran off when the Yankees were near. References to trouble occurred much earlier in the private writings of mistresses who lived in areas that were subject to invasion. Of the Mississippi

31 Parthenia Antoinette Hague, *A Blockaded Family: Life in Southern Alabama During the Civil War and Reconstruction* (Boston, 1888), 22–5; Cornelia McDonald, *A Diary with Reminiscences of the War and Refugee Life in the Shenandoah Valley* (Nashville, Tenn., 1935), 225; and Mary Elizabeth Massey, *Ersatz in the Confederacy* (Columbia, S.C., 1952), 80–4.

32 James Roark, *Masters Without Slaves: Southern Planters in the Civil War and Reconstruction* (New York, 1977), 77; Hague, *A Blockaded Family*, 16–30; Steven Hahn, *The Roots of Southern Populism: Yeomen Farmers and the Transformation of the Georgia Upcountry, 1850–1890* (New York, 1983), 46–7; Gavin Wright, *The Political Economy of the Cotton South: Households Markets, and Wealth in the Nineteenth Century* (New York, 1978), 55–9.

33 In the 1860 Census, John Cotton owned 65 acres of improved land and 285 acres of unimproved land. Cotton, *Yours Till Death*, vii–viii, 1.

34 Entry, Nov. 24, 1862, Crabtree and Patton, eds., *Journal of a Secesh Lady*, 303–7.

Valley area, Kate Stone wrote in June 1862 that there was "much excitement as the Yankees took the Negroes off the places below Omega, and the Negroes went willingly because the Yankees offered them their freedom." Her neighbors' servants would "not pretend to work and were impudent."[35]

Many slaveholding women were afraid to be alone with their slaves. Although the women of slaveholders were less likely to complain of hardships than women of nonslaveholders, many of them did write letters to public officials describing physical hardships from the absence of men, trouble with slaves, or both of these when their men first went away to war, whether Yankees were nearby or not. Although slaveholders' letters to government leaders also linked problems with slaves to invasion, there were more far-ranging implications. Unlike the private diaries and correspondence that linked slave unrest with the proximity of Yankees, letters to public officials early in the war emphasized problems caused by the initial loss of male authority, when inexperienced mistresses first faced the problem of managing slaves themselves or had to find new managers. Many mistresses felt insecure when they were surrounded by many slaves and few white men. They lacked the forcefulness necessary to manage slaves.

In large slaveholding families, it was more likely that a man remained on the premises – an overseer, a male kinsman, or neighbor who was too old for or exempt from military service under the Exemption or Substitution Acts. Under the Exemption Acts, one white man could be exempt from the military for each twenty slaves. The qualifying slaveholding families with twenty or more slaves also had the strongest bonds in a community, so that women of those families could at least turn to a man for advice and help when they needed it. Most likely to experience problems managing slaves and raising provisions were small slaveholding mistresses whose men were ineligible for the Exemption Act, and who could not afford to hire overseers or substitutes.

J. Oscar Howell of Louisiana wrote to President Davis as early as December 1861 of his wife's problems managing fifteen slaves with a black driver. Two slaves had revolted against the driver. His wife who was "soon to be confined" had become alarmed and gone to her mother's home "leaving the negroes to themselves." What few neighbors Howell had opposed his military service for fear that his place would become a "general rendez-vous for all the negroes in the county to carry on their rascality." Many poor white squatters lived in the area, and he feared that they would "prey upon his stock." Mrs. Mary Bishop of Georgia wrote President Davis in May 1862 to request that her husband be granted permission to stay home since her sons were not old

---

35   Entry, June 30, 1862, Anderson, *Brokenburn: Kate Stone*, 126–7.

enough to help supervise the slaves, who were "rather unmanageable." She knew of no one on whom she "might call for assistance in times of need or distress." She did not feel safe alone with only her "little helpless children." Mrs. W. E. Johnson of Virginia wrote in January 1862 that she and her four small children were insecure, for she had no male relative to assist her, and her farm was near a "large population of free negroes who have already commenced their depredations. ..." Her slaves would "not work if they know their [sic] is no one to attend to them."[36]

Widowed mothers were vulnerable to hardships in the absence of adult and older teenaged sons to manage slaves and plantation business. Their letters reflected the problems that plantation life posed for elderly women. Mrs. Savannah Mills of Virginia asked the secretary of war in May 1862, to let her oldest son come home and get a substitute because of her dependence on him for raising her seven other children and managing her plantation of fifty slaves "who were so unruly and unmanageable that...I shall be ruined since my son left me. ... " Another sixteen-year-old son had "no authority with the Negroes." In November 1862, she wrote again that she was "alone with a large family to provide for no father brother or ruler." Her slaves were "so unmanageable" that she was "almost afraid to be in my house at night." Mrs. J. M. McKie of Mississippi requested the discharge of her sixteen-year-old son in July 1862, after her overseer was conscripted for military duty. According to her letter: "I have tried my utmost and have failed, my negroes are unmanageable, my farm going to rock. ... "[37]

Private writings, as well as the correspondence to the secretary of war, justify the uneasiness many women expressed about managing their slaves and their fears of being alone with them before Yankee invaders or the Emancipation Proclamation offered slaves freedom. For example, Mary Chesnut noted the murder of her husband's elderly cousin, Betsey Witherspoon, in her diary on September 21, 1861, and in several later entries. According to Chesnut, "She was smothered – arms & legs bruised & face scratched. William, a man of hers, & several others suspected of her own negroes, people she has pampered & spoiled and done everything for." Later Mrs. Chesnut added that she had "never thought of being afraid of negroes," but the thought of "those black hands strangling and smothering Mrs. Witherspoon's gray head

36   J. Oscar Howell to President Davis, Dec. 22, 1861, referred to secretary of war, LR, no. 9193–1861, roll 20, 1689–92; Mary Bishop to President Davis, May 4, 1862, referred to secretary of war, LR, no. B482-1862, roll 33, 165–7; and Mrs. W. E. Johnson to secretary of war, Jan. 28, 1862, LR, no. 10358-1862, roll 24, 1585–8.
37   Mrs. Savannah D. Mills to secretary of war, May 2, 1862, LR, no. M447-1862, roll 60, 342–5, and Nov. 12, 1862, no. M1584-1862, roll 63, 970–5; and Mrs. J. M. McKie to secretary of war, July 27, 1862, LR, no. M1051-1862, roll 62, 64–6.

under the counterpane haunted" her. On October 20, 1861, as an aftermath of the murder, James Chesnut wrote to the secretary of war for his kins-woman, Mrs. William Evans, to request a furlough for her husband because "She has a number of little children, her health undermined...by recent events & personal calamities. ... The negroes of the Mother of Mrs. Evans, & one of his own in the house, have lately murdered the old lady."[38] Suffici-ent references to similar incidents and antebellum references to rumors of slave uprisings justified women's fears of being alone among their slaves.

Rebecca Barr described to her husband in February 1863 the care that mistresses had to take to meet obligations that slaves expected: "I was to blame. I weighed off one weeks allowance for two and only gave them three lbs. for two weeks, so you see they had a cause to complain. ... I looked on the books where you had it written and found my mistake and gave them more meat immediately." She, like other mistresses, had to provide accus-tomed provisions and privileges for slaves despite wartime shortages and high prices to assure their cooperation.[39]

The women best able to carry on in the absence of their men were first, women with teenaged sons and other children old enough to help, and second, women from established families in an area. Long-time settlers were more likely to have accumulated the wealth to be slaveholders or to be pros-perous townsmen or yeomen. More established settlers, whether slaveholders or not, were more likely to have exempt male family members or neighbors to turn to for help. Women in those families had nearby female relatives and friends to provide emotional support. Women sought to head their own nuclear families as independently as possible, but those who managed best had assistance as they gradually developed self-reliance.

For example, Kate Peddy could turn to her father, a lawyer and substantial planter, for assistance. In his earliest correspondence, her husband sent instructions for paying his debts, and he expressed his expectations that she would seek the advice and assistance from her father in major financial trans-actions. Later letters show Kate's increasing independence from her father as she developed confidence. In February 1862, George Peddy instructed Kate to "pay to Dave Grimes the amt. of the cash account if it is not over fifty dollars. If it is, just pay him that amt. & no more. If he has got mad about it,

38 Entry, Sept. 21, 1861; Woodward and Muhlenfeld, *The Private Mary Chesnut*, 162; with other ref-erences to the event on 159 (before cause of death was understood), 173, 177, 190; entries Sept. 21, 1861; Oct. 7, 1861; Oct. 18, 1861; and Oct. 25, 1861; Woodward, *Mary Chesnut's Civil War*, 198–9, 209–12, 217–18, 224–5; and Letter, Hon. James Chesnut to secretary of war for Mrs. William Evans, Oct. 20, 1861, LR, no. 7002–1861, roll 13, 637–9. Mrs. Chesnut wrote of how Mrs. Witherspoon's death had made her uneasy about her own slaves in her revision of her diary after the Civil War.
39 Rebecca Barr to James M. Barr, Feb. 22, 1863, McDaniel, *Confederate War Correspondence*, 52.

do not pay him one cent until I get home. I want your Pa to buy me Dr. Watkins' case of Trephineing instruments if he can get them for ten or twelve dollars. ... I am offered $90.00 just for my case of amputating & trephineing instruments." In April 1862, he mentioned the tension surrounding his dependence on his father-in-law: "I have no doubt that he would be better and more comfortably situated if I had you in a house of my own & not trouble him so much with my business. ..." In January 1863, he suggested: "You can hire y'r Negro out about Atlanta for $125 dollars per year, & her clothing & shoes will be furnished, but I had rather you would hire her for less about home. She would not be so liable to take the prevalent diseases. Do as you think best. ...I leave all my business at home with you & you have so far managed it excelently." Shortly afterward, he praised his wife's hiring out her slave for more than he would have. His letter in November 1863 mentioned her discontent from living with her parents: "Honey, you spoke in yours as if you would like to be at a home of your own. Then you could prepare some thing that you like to eat.... If you want to, you can rent Mrs. Boon's house. ... " Mrs. Peddy so competently managed the finances that before the end of the war, they had paid off all debts. Their correspondence mentioned shortages, high prices, concern over debts, and emotional turmoil from separation, but no physical suffering from the want of necessities. Invasion did not threaten western Georgia until late in the war, and Kate had been able to look to her family for assistance as she gained competence.[40]

Cotton's wife, Mariah, with the help of a hired slave and assistance from her father, father-in-law, other kin, and neighbors, became a resourceful manager who raised a surplus. Mariah could call on her kin for assistance, but she made the key decisions herself. John worried at the end of each year about whether or not she would be able to hire the slave for another year because the one laborer was crucial to her ability to carry on in his absence. He described his fears: "I am afraid you hant got nobody to make a crop for you if you dont get somebody to make a crop for you I dont no what you will do." When Mariah had a surplus of money, John suggested that she lend it, buy land, or buy slaves, all of which she disregarded. Although she was reluctant to act on her own and her husband did not agree with all her decisions, he supported her choices, as he made clear in a letter after she had

---

40 George W. Peddy to Kate Peddy: Feb. 6, 1862; Apr. 1, 1862; Jan. 6, 1863; Jan. 9, 1863; and Nov. 2, 1863; Cuttino, *Saddle Bag and Spinning Wheel*, 53–5, 79–81, 144–6, 184–5. In earlier transactions in letters to his wife on Mar. 22, 1862, and Mar. 29, 1862, Dr. Peddy mentioned consultation with Kate's father concerning transactions such as renting a house for Kate and the purchase of a horse, 72–4, 78–9. References to Dr. Peddy's indebtedness can be found in letters on Dec. 31, 1862, and Feb. 14, 1863, 140–2, 150–1. On Apr. 21, 1863, he was optimistically planning for the future with all debts paid, 163–5.

marketed the crops, "I was sorry you sold your corn for I think if you had kept it till spring you could get two dollars as easy as one but I dont blame you for selling it for I no you done the best you could if you do the best you can I will bee satisfied." He expressed relief that she had become a resource-ful manager in 1863, "there is one thing that gives me great consolation you have plenty to live upon and from what I lern there is lots of soldiers wives that has not much to eat. ..."[41]

Most married women preferred to live in their own nuclear family units with access to assistance from larger kinship and neighborhood groups. Although many absent husbands preferred their wives to live with other kinsmen, the tensions from crowded living quarters and interference with their nuclear-family group led most women to prefer homes of their own. Much tension occurred when a woman with children lacked a household of her own and was dependent on others for a place to live.

Whether she stayed with her own or her husband's family, Fanny Pender was discontent because her own parents and her parents-in-law interfered when she disciplined her children. Gen. William Dorsey Pender assured her that he had written to his parents and told them that "They must not spoil Turner. I told Papa that he must not give him things to eat that you did not want him to have. ... I told them they must not interfere in your whipping affairs either." When she was staying with her own parents, Mrs. Pender's dissatisfaction can be ascertained from her husband's letter as well as the drawbacks that prevented her from setting up her own household:

The children are too young to receive much damage by the interference of others with your discipline, and to rent a house and furnish it now, would take a great deal of money. ... You shall do as you wish and I will be satisfied. ... I fully agree with you that it would be well not to live on your father and am desirous of bearing the burden of your support.

In April 1863, she still was dissatisfied living with her father. Pender admitted that in her place, he "could not stand it," and he would not blame her if she left.[42]

Many proud men were uncomfortable as their women devised ways to supplement their family incomes as wartime shortages and soaring prices complicated their efforts to make ends meet. On the whole, soldiers' wives sought economic independence whether they had other male relatives to

---

41 John Cotton to Mariah Cotton, Dec. 26, 1862; Apr. 1, 1863; and Dec. 9, 1862; Cotton, *Yours Till Death*, 40–1, 56–7, 59–60.
42 Gen. William Dorsey Pender to his wife, Fanny Pender: Oct. 4, 1861; Oct. 21, 1861; and Apr. 26, 1863; William W. Hassler, ed., *The General to His Lady: The Civil War Letters of William Dorsey Pender to Fanny Pender* (Chapel Hill, N.C., 1962–65), 74–6, 183–7, 230–3.

look to for advice or not. One decision that many women made independently of their men was to work either inside or outside their homes for an income. Women worked from economic necessity to provide for the needs of their families. They also worked from patriotism and a sense of duty when wartime requirements and shortages opened new positions to women. When women did decide to work, men from the genteel classes were uncomfortable. Because of notions of honor, many men felt that working wives represented to others their failure to provide for their families.

Women extended domestic duties to the public, especially spinning, weaving, sewing, knitting, food preparation, and other household duties. Working with women's organizations, they made clothing for soldiers. It was not such a radical departure to make cloth and clothing in their homes for cash or barter. Married women were compelled to earn money on their own because the income of Confederate soldiers was inadequate, especially when soldiers could go for months without drawing their pay. Dr. Peddy wrote to his wife: "I have drawn no money sence I came back from home. The Government owes me now $1400.00. … If I cannot get any opportunity to send it to you, you will have to borrow it and give my note payable in confederate issue."[43] Mrs. Peddy, like many other women, worked at home within the accepted roles to make ends meet. She became increasingly autonomous. She sought to support herself and her daughter, to help pay off her husband's debts, and to rent a home of her own. Dr. Peddy objected: "Honey, I did not get you to work; I got you to worship and love. … So, darling, quit the weaving." Over her husband's protests, she continued to spin and weave in her home for an income, and she did not stop when she became pregnant. She chose to work out of her determination to be as independent as possible. Dr. Peddy feared his wife's working for an income was an indication of his failure to provide for his family. It was important to him that he support his family because he had risen from the yeomanry by working his way through medical training and by marrying into a much wealthier family. He was anxious to establish a respectable place. Of his discomfiture over his wife earning an income, he wrote: "I did you an injury in not letting you alone for someone who could have treated you better than I could, both as regards personal comfort and genuine unalloyed pleasure. My wants in youth were many, my extravigance was great; now, alas, I see to[o] late my folly. Instead of my reaping the bitter rewards of my indescretion, it has fallen with a crash on those who are dearer to me than my own life."[44]

43   George W. Peddy to Kate Peddy, Jan. 31, 1863, Cuttino, *Saddle Bag and Spinning Wheel*, 149–50.
44   George W. Peddy to Kate Peddy, Jan. 31, 1863; Nov. 2, 1863; ibid., 149–50, 184–8.

The men of the plain folk were less concerned with appearances. Since producing goods at home for either extra cash or barter had been common long before the war, the home manufacture of cloth was merely an extension of what yeomen women had been doing all along. Women of the yeomanry were more familiar with spinning and weaving than were women of slaveholding classes or their slaves. They often taught wealthier women and their slaves to spin and weave. Wealthy families and regiments of soldiers paid poorer women to make cloth for them, as did the small slaveholders, David Harris and his wife, Emily. In June 1862, David recorded in his journal that Emily had just finished "the first piece she has woven for many years." By October 1862, his family had a good lot of homemade cloth, though there was a severe shortage of yarn and cotton cards. In December 1862, when her husband was away at war, Emily wrote that their slave, Ann, was "trying to weave, and a poor weave it is." By April 1863, the Harrises were purchasing yarn from a factory and paying yeomen women to make it into homespun. In May 1863, David "paid Mrs. Miller $5.00 for making a bolt of cloth."[45] Spinning and weaving made it possible for some women to earn marginal amounts of extra income to help their families. Mrs. Cotton made extra money by weaving. Her husband did not object to her working. He was more concerned about her health: "you said you rote it one nite after weaveing 7 yards of cloth I dont want you to kill your self at work. Just because you can you had better work as you can stand it."[46]

It was even more problematic for men when their wives, mothers, daughters, and sisters chose to work for wages outside the home. No matter how temporary her position was, a husband felt that a wage-earning wife called attention to contradictions between a man's duty to support his family and his duty to fight for his country. Among slaveholding and educated classes, it was difficult for a man to admit that his family might have a genuine need that was beyond his ability to supply. A wife's income called into question a husband's leadership of his family. In a society based so much on honor and the good opinion of others, men worried about how their wives' wages reflected upon their manhood.

Yankee schoolmarms and male teachers left their positions when the war began. A shortage of teachers and the closure of many schools seriously disrupted the educational system. However, unlike the gaps in other skills and professions caused by the shortage of men, educated women could fill the teaching vacancies. Many younger women had supported themselves by

45 Harris Farm Journals, entries for June 19, 1862; Oct. 4, 1862; Dec. 5, 1862; Apr. 11, 1863; May 16, 1863; May 19, 1863; and May 22, 1863; Racine, *Piedmont Farmer*, 251, 270, 287, 291–3.
46 John W. Cotton to Mariah Cotton, June 23, 1863, 75–6, Cotton, *Yours Till Death*, 75–6.

teaching in antebellum times, though it was harder for older women to accept social changes. On the eve of the war in January 1861, Mrs. Eliza Roberts of Marietta, Georgia, described her daughter's governess job as "another trial to bear," when "through the kindness of Dr. Stewart, Mary Sophia was offered a place to teach four little girls in his brother's family. … Sophia seemed anxious to try and do something for herself, and I consented to let her go, although it cost me bitter pangs and tears to have my poor child go so far from home [to Alabama] to teach."[47] Sarah Morgan was not enthusiastic about teaching. In July 1862, she wrote in her diary that she wondered what she would do if her homeless family was left penniless: "I'll work for my living. How, I wonder? I will teach…I would rather die than teach. … Teaching before dependence, death before teaching. My soul revolts from the drudgery."[48] Whether women looked upon teaching as a welcome challenge or an unpleasant necessity, the Civil War speeded up a trend that began before the war. Many women who had not previously worked became teachers either from a sense of duty or from a need to lessen economic hardship.

Married women and mothers with children also became teachers. Citizens of Union Springs, Alabama, petitioned President Davis in May 1863 to discharge M. Butterfield because his wife had tried for eighteen months and had been unable to fill his place as teacher and principal of a school because her health was failing, and the support of his family depended on the school's successful operation.[49] General Pender was pleased with his wife's self-reliance, but he could not see a need for her to earn an income. Fanny taught music despite her husband's fear of family criticism. He protested: "I do not want any of your relations to say that I brought you to do teaching. We can live without it yet." After her husband's death in July 1863, Mrs. Pender refused outside help, never married again, and supported herself and her three sons by running a school and working as a postmistress.[50]

Sergeant Fay, a teacher himself, expressed his uneasiness when his wife decided to teach at a boys' school: "I think you would undertake a very large job if you should undertake the male school…, not that I doubt your capabilities of teaching any boys around Minden, but there are a great many considerations connected with it. … Where would you go when *you wanted to go out*? How would you keep your school house cleaned out, or in fact manage

47 Mrs. Eliza Roberts to Rev. C. C. Jones Sr., Jan. 26, 1861, in Robert Manson Myers, ed., *The Children of Pride: A True Story of Georgia and the Civil War* (New Haven, Conn., 1972), 646–8.

48 Entry, July 5, 1862, Dawson, *A Confederate Girl's Diary*, 104–5.

49 Petition of Citizens of Union Springs, Alabama, for M. Butterfield to President Davis, May 15, 1863, referred to secretary of war, LR, no. B464-1863, roll 82, 976–9. A note from the War Department shows that the request was not granted.

50 William D. Pender to Fanny Pender, June 18, 1861; Nov. 18, 1861; and afterword; Hassler, *The General to His Lady*, 36–7, 94–5, 259–62.

the bad boys? ... But, is it necessary for my own loved wife to descend to the unthankful occupation of teaching? ... I admire your resolution to do something and indeed regard you, my dearest, as a helpmeet indeed...." He worried about the welfare of their only surviving son when his wife worked: "Now that you are in school do not neglect Thornwell and leave him entirely to Laura's [the slave's] care. You had better take him to school with you if he will not be too much trouble. ... Laura may steal him off some time and he may get hurt. He is our only pet lamb and we cannot be too careful of him." Sarah Fay, like many other educated Southern women, made the decision to work independently of her husband.[51]

The shortage of trained medical personnel and the tremendous wartime requirements created an opportunity for many women to extend to sick and wounded soldiers their prewar role as nurses in their families. Early in the war, nursing was considered inappropriate for refined, modest ladies who were not supposed to nurse strange men, and certainly not crude soldiers from all walks of life.[52] According to Kate Cumming, "it was not considered respectable for ladies to be in hospitals." For a precedent, she looked to Florence Nightingale: "It was strange that what aristocratic women of England did was a disgrace for southern women." She felt a sense of purpose filling a critical need for nurses because "if soldiers fought in the battles, the least women could do was bind up the wounds, for it had been in all ages a special duty of women."[53] During her first day at a Richmond hospital, Phoebe Yates Pember confronted objections to women nurses from the male hospital staff when she overheard a surgeon inform a friend in "ill-concealed disgust that, 'one of them had come.'"[54] Despite male prejudice and lack of formal training, many women became capable hospital managers and nurses. Of her widowed mother's duties nursing soldiers, Constance Cary Harrison wrote: "Sleeping on a soldier's bunk, rising at dawn laboring till midnight, my mother faced death and suffering with the stout spirit that was a rock of refuge to all around her." Women nurses showed strength and courage, as Mrs. Pember did when she stayed when most of Richmond fled ahead of Yankee invaders. She explained that, "my duty prompted me to remain with my sick on the ground that no general ever deserts his troops."[55] The entry of women into

51 Edwin Fay to Sarah Fay, Jan. 24, 1863; Apr. 20, 1863; Wiley and Fay, *This Infernal War*, 213–20, 251–5. See also introduction, 3–21.
52 Massey, *Bonnet Brigades*, 44–5.
53 Kate Cumming, *The Journal of a Confederate Nurse, 1862–1865*, ed. Richard Harwell (Baton Rouge, La., 1959; reprint: Savannah, Ga., 1975), 54–5.
54 Phoebe Yates Pember, *A Southern Woman's Story Life in Confederate Richmond*, ed. Bell Irvin Wiley (New York, 1959), 26.
55 Mrs. Burton Harrison, *Recollections Grave and Gay* (New York, 1911), 49–55, 77–83, 184–5; Pember, *A Southern Woman's Story*, 128.

medicine did not extend to the position of physician. Nursing became acceptable because it was an extension to strangers of a family duty.[56]

Ironically, although the Confederate government sought to perpetuate the patriarchy, it became a leading source of a new public role for women when it hired women to work in Civil Service office jobs. Gen. Albert G. Blanchard suggested to the secretary of war in August 1862 that too many men were avoiding service as postmasters when the duties could be performed by a woman just as well as a man.[57] However, the urgent financial need and low pay of the women employed in Confederate Civil Service clerk positions prevented major changes in women's status. Because there were no women managers, all women worked under male supervisors. That made their jobs extensions of the subordinate role that some women had at home keeping records for their husbands.

Necessity compelled many educated women to seek government employment. Malvina Black Gist, a young South Carolina war widow, signed Confederate bills in the Treasury Note Department.[58] Judith McGuire, a minister's wife, worked as a clerk in the Commissary Department at $125.00 per month in 1863 and 1864 because she felt compelled to earn an income when her elderly husband's Confederate Civil Service salary was only slightly above their living expenses in Richmond. The McGuires were refugees from Alexandria, which fell under Federal control at the beginning of the war. She worked in an office with thirty-five other ladies. Many of them were refugees, and a large number of them were wearing mourning for relatives and other victims of the war.[59]

Many ladies in financial need wrote to the secretary of war, president of the Confederacy, or other Confederate department heads to ask for clerkships. Often the ladies had fled to Richmond from conquered areas. Many of them were unable to support themselves, as Louisa C. Boulevare appealed to the secretary of war: "I am living in Richmond with two orphan nieces under my charge, with no other kindred near, and finding my limited means, very inadequate to my support, in these most exorbitant and trying times, find it necessary to appeal to you, for a situation, as clerk in your Department. ... " Mrs. E. J. Fisher, a refugee from New Orleans to Richmond,

56 Massey, *Bonnet Brigades*, 62–3.
57 Gen. Albert G. Blanchard to secretary of war, Aug. 6, 1862, LR, no. B960-1862, roll 34, 820–1.
58 Introduction; Diary Entries of Malvina Black Gist, Feb. 13, 1865; Feb. 14, 1865; Feb. 15, 1865; and Mar. 1, 1865; Jones, *Heroines of Dixie*, 356–60, 376–83.
59 Entries for Mar. 5, 1863; Nov. 11, 1863; Nov. 13, 1863; Dec. 12, 1863; and Jan. 3, 1864; in Judith White (Brockenbrough), McGuire, *Diary of a Southern Refugee During the War* (New York, 1867; reprint: New York, 1972), 195–8, 243–5, 247, 250–1; and Willie T. Weathers, "Judith W. McGuire: A Lady of Virginia," *Virginia Magazine of History and Biography* 82 (Jan. 1974): 100–13.

also sought employment in a Confederate government office in March 1865. She had lost almost everything to the Yankee invaders. General Butler had imprisoned her husband, her sons were all in Confederate service, and one of her sons had been killed. Mrs. C.V. Baxley, a widow, asked President Davis for employment in January 1864 after Yankees had imprisoned her son. J. B. Jones, a clerk in the War Department, noted in his diary in September 1864 a lack of clerkships for the most needy: "There is a project on the topic of introducing lady clerks into this bureau – all of them otherwise able to subsist themselves – while the poor refugees, who have suffered most, are denied places."[60] A shortage of men to fill government positions and the economic needs of so many women led the Confederate Civil Service to become a major employer of women.

Women also worked in both private and government-controlled factories such as textile mills and munitions plants. Many private companies filled government contracts. Women labored in low-paying positions that were subordinate to male authority. Women did not work in higher-paying positions that required skill and mechanical know-how. Those positions were dependent on exempted and detailed men. Women's jobs did not threaten the positions of male machinists or male supervisors either before or during the war. Textile factories sought the exemption of white male operatives because managers considered their skills essential to the operation of the factory and to the continuation of women's employment. In 1863, William Bradley of the Manchester Cotton and Woolens Factory in Georgia requested the exemption of fourteen white male factory operatives from any military service other than local defense because their positions were essential to the continued operation of the plant. If they were called into active service, their absence would throw 100 women and girls and 110 slaves out of work. Major E. B. Bentley petitioned in August 1864 for the discharge of six male operatives to continue making tent cloth in Richmond for the Confederate government. The loss of those men would cause approximately 100 women, girls, and boys to be cut off from support.[61]

Some factory jobs for indigent women could be risky. In his diary, J. B. Jones recorded in 1863 the tragic deaths of several women who were working

60 Louisa C. Boulevare to secretary of war, Nov. 16, 1864, LR, no. B733-1864, roll 122, 275–81; E. J. Fisher to President Davis, Mar. 28, 1865, referred to secretary of war, LR, no. F37-1865, roll 148, 199–202; C. V. Baxley to President Davis, Jan. 7, 18, 1864, referred to secretary of war, LR RG109, M437, no. B379-1864, roll 120, 451–8; entry, Sept. 1, 1864, John B. Jones, *A Rebel War Clerk's Diary*, ed. Earl S. Miers (New York, 1958), 415–16; see also John B. Jones of War Department to secretary of war, Feb. 1, 1865, LR, no. J7-1865, roll 149, 20–1.

61 William Bradley, Supervisor of Manchester Cotton and Woolens Factory, Manchester, Georgia, to secretary of war, Dec. 16, 1863; and Major E. B. Bentley, Confederate Tent Factory in Richmond, Virginia, to secretary of war, received Aug. 22, 1864, LR, no. B530-1864, roll 121, 259–60.

in a government laboratory when "an explosion took place, killing instantly five or six persons, and wounding fatally, some thirty others. Most of them were little indigent girls!"[62]

Women's work provided for their families in the absence of male support, but it rarely interfered with male authority. Women were only managers in situations where a woman's home role was most directly extended to the public, such as in teaching, serving as hospital matrons, or running boarding houses. They were paid less than men, and many jobs that women held were dependent on the employment of males in skilled or managerial positions. Men and women alike looked upon women's work as a temporary expedient of war, although the long-range effects of the widespread war disabilities and deaths would result in an impoverished labor force of war widows and orphans. The Civil War did open up some new opportunities for women, but not in leading positions.

Many women welcomed the chance to utilize their talents, among them young widows and spinsters of well-to-do families who had previously been tied to codes that discouraged ladies from working outside their homes. Mrs. Pember expressed in a letter to her sister the sense of purpose that her position as a hospital matron gave her in comparison to the dissatisfaction she had felt as a dependent widow in her father's house:

> I thank God every night for the courage He gave me to leave those who never cared for me and I believe disliked me for the gifts he had given me. I bring comfort, strength and I believe happiness to many sick beds daily and lie down at night with a happy consciousness of time well and unselfishly spent.[63]

Economic necessity and patriotism led many women to seek employment, although they did not think of their roles as more than emergency expedients to deal with the absence of men.

Many women derived confidence, self-esteem, and a sense of purpose from participation in the war efforts. Absent men were more content when their wives were able to carry on without them, whether they agreed with their wives' choices or not. A yeoman farmer's wife expressed her satisfaction in a letter to Parthenia Hague in which she described how she managed the support of her family after Yankees captured her husband and oldest son, and the $11 support that she received from each one was cut off:

> We had a hard time; myself and two oldest daughters making a living for ten in the family. ... We spun and wove cloth to sell by day and we took in sewing, which was done by night. We knit a great deal, and worked so hard . . . we never went to bed

62 Entry, Mar. 13, 1863, J. B. Jones, *Rebel War Clerk's Diary*, 175.
63 Phoebe Yates Pember to her sister, Jan. 30, 1863, Pember, *Southern Woman's Story*, 151–2.

hungry. ... There is one thing I am proud of, and that is, the advantage we took of our resources and our own independence.[64]

It was impossible for many other poor women to feel self-esteem in the absence of their men. The ideal of honor did not help destitute women to provide for themselves and their children. Many women questioned old ethical standards when their families suffered starvation while many slave-holders and merchants were exempt from military service and seemed to be profiting from the poor families of the soldiers who were fighting. From the point of view of many poor women, the well-to-do had failed to uphold their obligations.

Many women of the plain folk wrote letters to public officials requesting the discharge of their men from service or other relief when the situation of their families became desperate. Invaders caused many families to become refugees in unfamiliar areas. Although the number of destitute women increased as the war progressed, the letters to public officials on hardships owing to the absence of male breadwinners were most numerous at the beginning of the war as poor women who had never been without a man faced an uncertain future with no one to help them along. Many of the women who could not carry on without a man were physically unable to perform the labor required for them to subsist because they suffered from old age or ill health. Children were too small to assist others. They did not feel familiar enough with the people in their neighborhood to ask for assistance, they lacked emotional support, and they did not believe that they could get along on their own.

Numerous women, often barely literate, wrote to elected officials of their need for their husbands, sons, brothers, or other male family members. Mrs. Elizabeth Huxtept expressed her despair to the secretary of war in February 1862: "I am entirely without friends all alone with three little children and has been down with the dropsey for near ten months and scarcely able to go about sense my Husban been in Survise. ... " There was "no one to guit mee wood or to tote mee water I am bound to suffer." Mrs. Martha J. Bell of Virginia described similar "distresses" in April 1862, and two later letters to the secretary of war: "I am left alone with no one to keep me from suffering & two little children not one able to keep the other out of the fire also I have bin sick in bed for more than a year & not able to do anything and is still declining, and the neighbors is so thinly settled & all the men gone to war about here; I don't know where to look to." Of her need for the discharge of her son, Mrs. June McVeigh wrote to President Davis: "I am a Widdow upward of seventy years of age a cripple for life my home and property distroyed and

---

64 Letter, n.d., quoted in Hague, *A Blockaded Family*, 108–9.

dispoiled by the inhuman enemy and left entirely without resources of any kind and no one in the world to look to for support... but my son (or the cole charities of the public) with the rigours of winter stairing me in the face."[65]

How much good did it do for destitute women to request relief from government officials? They requested furloughs, discharges, or exemptions for their men, not charity. Most letters do not have answers, but the existing responses indicate that after the passage of the Conscription Acts in the Spring of 1862, it was difficult for a common soldier to be discharged from the military except for his own physical disability, no matter how destitute his family. The only exception was for a man wealthy enough to hire a substitute. Mrs. Bettie Bayliss of Virginia wrote several letters to President Davis and the secretary of war. Her children were small, she was poor, she was unhealthy, she had no servants, and she lived in an unfamiliar area. She felt she had nowhere else to turn. Early in 1862, before the passage of the Conscription Acts when she was near the birth of her fourth child, she and her husband, Silas, were successful in getting him discharged from the Virginia militia. But he did not remain at home long before the Second Conscription Act in Fall 1862 extended the draft to men between thirty-five and forty-five years of age. She did not believe that she could get along without her husband. On October 24, 1862, she expressed her fears:

I will be left alone with no one but my little children the oldest not large enough to keep the others out of danger. My health is very bad. ... I am living in a strange neighborhood away from my friends and have no one to look up to do anything for me not even to cut me a stick of wood or cook my children a mouthful to eat when I am sick... my husband is a sole dependence for a support... we have nothing to live on but what he labors for. ...

In March 1863, she described her despair to President Davis after her husband had been conscripted. His pay as a soldier would not permit them to get things that were "necessary to keep body and soul together," and they were "very poor and it was as much as" they "could do to make out to live" when her husband was at home. On April 20, 1863, she again appealed for her husband's discharge when one of her children was ill:

Oh, Sir ... if you have any pity or compassion for the poor little helpless children one of my children is now very ill and I am unable to procure things which are very necessary for the comfort of that sick child.

---

65 Elizabeth Huxtept to secretary of war, Feb. 1, 1862, LR, no. 10346-1862, roll 24, 1554–5; Martha J. Bell to secretary of war, Apr. 1, 1862, Apr. 7, 1862, and July 7, 1862, LR, nos. B234-1862, B243-1862, and B730-1862, roll 31, 794–5, 823-4, and roll 34, 80–3; and June McVeigh to President Davis, received Nov. 18, 1862, referred to secretary of war, LR, no. M1535-1862, roll 63, 751–3.

People "would take the last cent out of the purse of a poor woman" whose husband was in service. Bayliss's appeals were in vain, but she was not totally without kin, for her husband's sister in a letter, signed M. Bayliss, also of Virginia, wrote to the secretary of war in November 1864 to request the discharge of her own husband because of her hardships supporting fifteen children and managing a farm. She wrote that not only her husband, but his brothers, Silas and Thomas, were both in service and could not assist her. There were no more letters from Bayliss. Her efforts to get her husband discharged had been unsuccessful, and she did the best she could in poverty, as did countless other poor women.[66]

In September 1864, Robert Garlick Hill Kean, head of the Confederate Bureau of War, described the inability of the War Department to approve the numerous appeals from desperate women: "The conscription is now being pressed mercilessly. It is agonizing to see and hear the cases daily brought into the War Office, appeal after appeal and all disallowed. Women come there and weep, wring their hands, scold, entreat, beg, and almost drive me mad. The iron is gone deep into the heart of society."[67]

Before the Civil War, welfare had been a local problem. It carried a social stigma that made people reluctant to seek aid beyond discharge of their men unless they were destitute.[68] People turned to the Confederacy because they believed that a soldier and his family should receive relief from the leaders of the cause for which they were sacrificing. Common soldiers could not be discharged for family hardships while many planters and merchants were exempt from military service and charging high prices for essential items. It appeared to hard-pressed soldiers and their families that many wealthy people were profiting from the war and not sharing equally in the sacrifices. Soldiers and their families were concerned with honor and doing their duty, but honor also meant consideration from noncombatants and protection against profiteers. When the government was unable to help them, many women redefined honor and influenced their men to do so.

Refusing to be passive victims, some women resorted to bread riots by the Spring of 1863. Poor women in cities faced a severe problem because food

---

66 Letters of Bayliss family to the Confederate secretary of war, LR: Silas Bayliss to secretary of war enclosing a letter from Bettie Bayliss to Hon. R. M. Hunter, received Mar., 1862, no. B186-1862, roll 31, 635–41; Bettie Bayliss to secretary of war, Oct. 24, 1862, no. B1301-1862, roll 35, 1050–5; Bettie Bayliss to secretary of war, Dec. 12, 1862, no. B99-1865, roll 146, 657–9; Bettie Bayliss to President Davis, Mar. 7, 1863, referred to secretary of war, no. B2971863, roll 82, 264–71; Bettie Bayliss to secretary of war, Apr. 20, 1863, no. B314-1863, roll 82, 332–4; and M. Bayliss to secretary of war, Nov., 1864, no. B49-1865, roll 146, 350–3.
67 Entry, Sept. 4, 1864, in Edward Younger, ed., *Inside the Confederate Government: The Diary of Robert Garlick Hill Kean* (New York, 1957), 173–4.
68 Escott, "Poverty and Governmental Aid," 462–80.

was scarce, and their families suffered most of all from the high prices. Riots occurred not just in Richmond but in cities throughout the Confederacy both before and after the Richmond Bread Riot on April 2, 1863: Atlanta, Macon, Columbus, and Augusta, Georgia; Salisbury and High Point, North Carolina; and Mobile, Alabama. The riots appeared radical to many contemporary observers, but the women who participated had no intentions beyond the survival of their families. Rioters expressed similar grievances as authors of letters to government officials. A participant in the Richmond riot told a gentlewoman, Agnes, of the rioters' intentions: "We celebrate our right to live. We are starving. As soon as enough of us get together we are going to the bakers and each of us will take a loaf of bread. This is enough for the government to give us after it has taken all our men."[69]

Many rioters wanted only to be able to purchase food at reasonable prices, and they resorted to rioting before seeking the dole. The Bread Riots were not spontaneous aimless violence. They were planned and carried out against merchants with a reputation for extortion, profiteering, and charging the highest prices. The riots only affected a few stores. The participants who have been identified were often illiterate, though not necessarily poor. A study of the merchants who suffered losses to the mob shows that some of those who had been in business in 1860 had improved their positions during the war. Also, a number of them were of military age, had not volunteered, and had escaped conscription. To women who were suffering from high food prices in the absence of their men, the merchants represented a conflict that had become a "rich man's war and a poor man's [and woman's] fight."[70]

Women's riots called attention to the failure of both the Confederate government and the men fighting to live up to the reciprocity built into the code of honor. Soldiers were unable to provide for or protect their families when they were away at war, and the Confederate government, too, failed to live up to the expectations of soldiers and their families. The riots demonstrated the failure to uphold major obligations upon which Confederate leadership was based. Government officials did not fully comprehend the extent of hardships that many soldiers' families endured, or when they did, they did not understand the limited goals of the rioters. Many sympathetic observers

---

69 Quoted from letter of Agnes, Apr. 4, 1863, Jones, *Ladies of Richmond*, 154–6; also quoted from Mrs. Roger A. Pryor, *Reminiscences of Peace and War* (New York, 1904), 251–9.

70 Michael B. Chesson, "Harlots or Heroines? A New Look at the Richmond Bread Riot (April 1, 1863)," *Virginia Magazine of History and Biography* 92 (April 1984): 131–74. Other articles on the Richmond Bread Riots are William J. Kimball, "The Bread Riot in Richmond, 1863," *Civil War History* 7 (1961): 149–54; and Douglas O. Tice, "'Bread or Blood!': The Richmond Bread Riot," *Civil War Times Illustrated* 12 (1974): 12–91. See also Emory M. Thomas, *The Confederate Nation: 1861–1865* (New York, 1979), 202–5. See also Bynum, "War Within a War," 43–9.

described the essential nature of the goods that the rioters took from the stores. According to a Georgia soldier, W. H. Winn, who was in Richmond during the riots, the articles that "the women said to be soldiers' wives" took from the stores were scarce essentials: bacon, flour, candles, soap, brooms, beef, lard, shoes, boots, and fabric." Constance Cary Harrison observed that a "large number of women and children marched through Main and Cary Streets, attacking and sacking several stores kept by known speculators." Mrs. McGuire and J. B. Jones were sympathetic to the rioters and critical of the merchants.[71]

President Davis appeared at the scene of the Richmond Bread Riot, and the Confederate government issued rations of rice as a short-term solution, but little was accomplished to alleviate the widespread destitution of soldiers' families in Richmond or elsewhere. Many government officials saw riots as radical and did not see that the women sought only to care for their families. On April 4, 1863, S. S. Baxter reported that the "riot originated in the desire to plunder." He believed that many rioters were refugees "suffering great depreviations" who had fled Yankee conquest, but also government employ-ees who "were not suffering privations were active in it."[72]

Other men did not approve of women's violence. Before the Richmond riot, Thomas McCollum responded to his wife's letter describing a women's protest in Georgia: "You mention about the women turning out on the stores. I hope you will not have a hand in that business. But try and do the best you can. I hope you can get some sewing to help you along." G.W. Peddy also disapproved of riots and rioters. Over a year after the Richmond Bread Riot when he was at Adiersville, Georgia, he wrote to his wife Kate that the hardships of the ladies in that section had reduced them to a "female raid," to get through the hard times. He hoped that she would not "join such a class."[73]

A woman's turning to charity was an act of desperation for family survival when all else failed. Judith McGuire worked with a cooperative association of Richmond ladies in aiding wives, widows, and orphans of soldiers. She offered aid to a "wretchedly dressed" refugee with three children. She pro-mised the woman that "a soldier's widow shall not suffer from hunger in Richmond." The widow, Mrs. Brown, was seeking work over charity, but she accepted the help offered because of the pressing needs of her children. She could not supply her family's wants from odd jobs.[74]

71 W. H. Winn to his family, Apr. 2, 1863, Lane, *Dear Mother*, 223–4; Harrison, *Recollections Grave and Gay*, 137; entry, Apr. 2, 1863, McGuire, *Diary of a Southern Refugee*, 203; and entry, Apr. 2, 1863, J. B. Jones, *A Rebel War Clerk's Diary*, 183–5.
72 S. S. Baxter to secretary of war, Apr. 4, 1863, LR, no. B296-1863, roll 82, 260–3.
73 Thomas McCollum to Margaret McCollum, Dec. 28, 1862, Lane, *Dear Mother*, 207–8; and George W. Peddy to Kate Peddy, May 17, 1864, Cuttino, *Saddle Bag and Spinning Wheel*, 242.
74 Entry, Feb. 28, 1864, McGuire, *Diary of a Southern Refugee*, 252–5.

Many women offered what they could to suffering soldiers' families, while other women suffered so many deprivations that they had little to share. Many states provided assistance to soldiers' families, but it was not enough to alleviate widespread need in the face of soaring prices, scarcity of basic necessities, property destruction, homelessness, and the absence of so many essential men. Kate Stone learned when she was a refugee that it was not always the rich who were the most generous. The charity of the well-to-do toward the less fortunate varied from "extremes of generosity to extremes of meanness."[75]

Although many individuals and communities did offer small amounts of aid to soldiers' families and widows, there was much insensitivity. Stinginess disheartened women at home and the men fighting. Class divisions widened between the plain folk and the well-to-do. Many instances of lack of charity came to the attention of various public officials. Mrs. Virginia Berry of Virginia wrote to the secretary of war in April 1864 concerning the stinginess of an exempt neighbor man. It looked as though

the poor man who has been used to hard labour is obliged to serve his country while the rich man who has never handled a plough or hoe is left to humiliate & hoard up all he can get his hands on. … We poor soldiers' wives ought to have some provisions made for us or our families will starve.[76]

Ella Gertrude Clanton Thomas did not fully comprehend the destitution of some soldiers' families. Her response varied according to how direct her encounter with the woman was. In April 1862, her father offered to sell meal to soldiers' wives for $1.00 a bushel. Mrs. Thomas was outraged when a poor soldier's wife wrote to the newspaper in response to his offer that she wondered "how they were to get the meal." Also, "the mill was in the country, they had no horses and could not be expected to turn themselves into beasts of burden," and "it would not be cheap at 10 cts pr bushel unless delivered." To Mrs. Thomas, the woman was an "ungrateful wretch." She was more sympathetic when she directly encountered a victim. In July 1864, Mrs. Thomas offered a ride to a poor soldier's wife and her small son, both barefooted and carrying berries into town after moving out of the poor house the day before. After she bought the fruit and left the woman, she could only see "a bright smile of contentment," not the woman's continuing problems of survival.[77]

---

75 Mary Elizabeth Massey, *Refugee Life in the Confederacy* (Baton Rouge, La., 1964), 139–41; and Anderson, *Brokenburn: Kate Stone*, 361.

76 Mrs. Virginia Berry to secretary of war, Apr. 2, 1864, LR, no. B382-1864, roll 120, 469–72.

77 Journal of Ella Gertrude Clanton Thomas, 13 vols., Apr. 14, 1862 and July 12, 1864, typescript, Duke University, Perkins Library; Virginia Ingraham Burr, ed., *The Secret Eye: The Journal of Gertrude Clanton Thomas, 1848–1889* (Chapel Hill, N.C., 1990), 202–3, 227–8; see also Mary Elizabeth Massey, "The Making of a Feminist," *Journal of Southern History* 39 (Feb. 1973): 3–22.

Table 20.4. *Letters to Confederate Secretary of War Requesting Passes to Leave Confederacy over Civil War Period*

War Year	No. of Letters for Passes	Percentage of N All Letters	N = Total Hardship Letters
1861	16	6.9	232
1862	32	4.0	800
1863	53	10.8	490
1864	80	18.2	440
1865	20	16.3	123
1861–65	201	9.6	2,085

When they could not support their families in the Confederacy, many women sought passes to cross Union lines if they had relatives there. Requests for passes to leave the Confederacy increased in percentage of total complaints as the war progressed, and they reflected the growing hardships of Southern families (see Table 20.4). Requests at the beginning of the war came from people who wished to leave the South because it was not home to them, while later requests came from destitute families with Southern sympathies. Requests to leave the Confederacy showed the hopelessness of women who could not feed their families inside Confederate lines. Such refugees went either to the North or to conquered areas of the Confederacy, where basic necessities at least were available.

In October 1863, Ann I. Munroe and Eliza C. Perkins wrote to the secretary of war for permission to return to their homes in North Carolina, which they had left to avoid being under Yankee occupation. They sought to return "after striving in every honorable way to make a living, we now feel constrained by our necessaries to ask permission to return to our homes where we still have property, and where we believe we can subsist on much less means than is now required among strangers." In November 1863, Mrs. Mary J. Buck asked to leave the Confederacy after her husband's death. She believed that she could support herself and her children within Union lines where she had friends and family. The Confederate government granted her request as it did similar requests. In August 1864, Bridget Macauley of Richmond, Virginia, stated that the destitute condition of herself and her five children forced her to request a passport because she had no relatives in the Confederacy, but there were relatives who would assist her in Washington, D. C. She and her family were in "the most painful state of want and have no prospect of adequate relief while they remain in the Confederacy." Mrs. E. F. Kellum asked Major Carrington for a pass in March 1865, after her husband was wounded and taken prisoner. She wanted to go because "I am here without a protector or means of support except my own labor and what little I can make by my own needle barely supports myself and child. I am frequently in great want."[78]

Most difficult for soldiers was the knowledge that their families were in severe deprivation. It was not possible for many women to achieve autonomy. When letters of hardships at home reached men in the military, they caused discontent and sometimes rationalization of desertion, although desertion was considered the ultimate violation of honor early in the war. By 1864, the failure of the Confederacy to remedy the destitution of families meant the failure of leaders and well-to-do citizens to adhere to common soldiers' notions of reciprocity, and desertion became more justifiable. Common soldiers redefined honor. It was easier to rationalize desertion after the war had become a "rich man's war and a poor man's fight" than when it was a war for independence.[79]

From the letters that came to her hospital, Phoebe Yates Pember described the plight of the families of many common soldiers and the dilemma of many men:

For the first two years of the war, privations were lightly dwelt upon and courageously borne, but when want and suffering pressed heavily as times grew more stringent, there was a natural longing for the stronger heart and frame to bear part of the burden. Desertion is a crime that meets generally with as much contempt as cowardice and yet how hard for the husband... knowing that his wife and little ones were literally starving at home – not even at home for few homes were left.[80]

While visiting her husband at camp in North Georgia, Catherine Rowland described her sympathy for a soldier who was shot for desertion: "The poor man who was shot to-day deserted to go home to provide for his wife & five children who were in a destitute condition, & I cannot think his life ought to have been taken."[81]

78 Ann I. Munroe and Eliza C. Perkins to secretary of war, Oct. 13, 1863, LR, no. M754-1863, roll 104, 665–6; Mary J. Buck to secretary of war, Nov. 8, 1863, LR, no. B808-1863, roll 84, 155–6; and Bridget Macauley to secretary of war, Aug. 3, 1864, LR, no. M510-1864, roll 136, 793–4; Mrs. E. F. Kellum to Major Carrington, Mar. 28, 1865, referred to secretary of war, LR, no. K29-1865, roll 149, 214–15.
79 Richard Reid, "A Test Case of the 'Crying Evil': Desertion Among the North Carolina Troops During the Civil War," *North Carolina Historical Review* 58 (Summer 1981): 234–62; Stephen E. Ambrose, "Yeomen Discontent in the Confederacy," *Civil War History* 8 (1962): 259–68; Frank L. Owsley, "Defeatism in the Confederacy," *North Carolina Historical Review* 3 (1926): 446–56; and Georgia L. Tatum, *Disloyalty in the Confederacy* (Chapel Hill, N.C., 1934). See also Bynum, "War Within a War," 43–9.
80 Pember, *A Southern Woman's Story*, 132–3.
81 Catherine Whitehead Rowland diary, 1863–65, Mar. 15, 1864, typescript, Georgia Department of Archives and History, Atlanta.

According to General Battle, the presiding officer at Edward Cooper's court-martial, Mary Cooper unintentionally caused her husband to desert. Of the situation at home, she wrote during the winter of 1862–63:

I would not have you do anything wrong for the world; but before God, Edward, unless you come home we must die! Last night I was aroused by little Eddie's crying. I called and said "What's the matter, Eddie?" and he said, "Oh, mamma, I'm so hungry?" And Lucy, Edward, your darling Lucy, she never complains, but she is growing thinner and thinner every day.

Mary did not sanction desertion, but furloughs were difficult to get. When Edward went home without leave, she urged him to return. Edward was found guilty by the court but was pardoned by Gen. Robert E. Lee. He returned to die on the battlefield.[82]

Letters from slaveholding families caused some men to desert, as in an incident recorded in Mary Chesnut's diary in May 1864. According to Chesnut, Varina Davis influenced Jefferson Davis to grant a pardon to the husband of a shabbily dressed woman:

The army had to pass so near her. Poor little Susie had just died, and the boy was ailing. ... The negroes had all gone to the Yankees. There was nobody to cut wood, and it was so cold. ... I wrote ". ... if you want to see the baby alive, come. If they won't let you–come anyhow." ... He only intended to stay one day, but we coaxed, and then he stayed. ... He did not mean to be a coward nor to desert. So he went on the gunboats on the river, to serve there. And then some of his old officers saw him. ... "I would not let him alone, you see, I did it."[83]

It was better for a man's peace of mind for his wife to make decisions without him, even when he did not fully approve, than it was for her to complain of wartime hardships. Many women gained self-esteem from their temporary assumption of power, but it was impossible for others to gain autonomy because of the severity of their poverty and the inability of the Confederacy to offer remedies. Desertion was one result of a crisis in honor when neither the man nor the government for whom he was risking his life could support his family. It became a solution to a breakdown in reciprocity when a man's family was left with nowhere to look for relief in his absence. When he could not fight and support his family, the only reason to stay for many men was

---

82 Rev. J. L. Underwood, ed., *The Women of the Confederacy* (New York, 1906), quoting Gen. C. A. Battle, presiding officer at the court-martial, Confederate States vs. Edward Cooper, read the letter, 169–71, in "Two Specimen Cases of Desertion," *Southern Historical Society Papers* 8 (Jan. 1880): 28–31.
83 Entry, May 27, 1864, Woodward, *Mary Chesnut's Civil War*, 610–11.

protection of their families, but this too would become difficult to rationalize as greater portions of the Confederacy fell to the enemy and women had to face Yankees without male protection. For Confederate men, the male gender role itself seemed to have collapsed with their nation.[84] Hardships on the home front caused a total war in the sense that they broke down the wills of both soldiers and civilians to continue fighting.

84   Krug, "The Folks Back Home," 301–63.

21

German Patriotic Women's Work
in War and Peace Time, 1864–90

JEAN H. QUATAERT

In the early 1970s, a new generation of women's historians opened the discipline to searing attack. The critics rightly pointed out that the field's standard themes – among the most time-honored were wars and state building – had shaped the larger conceptual grid surrounding the historical narrative. Indeed, historical turning points, the basis of periodization as well as the very understanding of historical significance – all matched, more or less perfectly, major political events, wars, or revolutions. And, as traditionally defined, these topics failed to include anything about women's roles, experiences, and contributions. Not surprisingly, women's history tended early on to ally with social or labor history and made pathfinding steps across the disciplinary borders to adopt innovative theories and methods of inquiry. But time has a way of changing history, and recently women's historians have come full circle. What once was a declaration of war on the topic of war now emerges as a fruitful arena for meaningful dialogue.[1]

Gender inquiry has a lot that is new to say about war. And once military historians move beyond biographies of generals, battle tactics, and weapons – important as these themes may be on one level – and into society, they too must confront the gender implications of their subject. For war culture rests squarely on powerful assumptions about gender roles, and the disruption of war itself seems to crystallize the complex systems of gender embedded in state structures and social values. Certainly since the early nineteenth century and the anchoring of the western state on a new nationalist basis, masculine identity has been increasingly linked to the prescribed role of citizen-soldier. Indeed, the continuous tie between full-fledged citizenship and military

---

1 For examples of recent feminist thinking on the theme of women and war, see, among others, Jean Bethke Elshtain, *Women and War* (Oxford and New York, 1988); Jean Bethke Elshtain and Sheila Tobias, eds., *Women, Militarism and War: Essays in History, Politics and Social Theory* (Savage, Md., 1990); and Margaret Higonnet et al., eds., *Behind the Lines: Gender and the Two World Wars* (New Haven, Conn., and London, 1987).

449

participation has not been severed fully even with the end of the Cold War. The citizen-soldier, in turn, found its necessary counterpart in the mother-helpmate, a female nurturer whose civic identity is bound up with her fighting sons.[2] These ideological constructs work to encourage men and women to play appropriate roles for the war effort. Yet the actual war experience can turn this normative world on its head. For example, during World War I, soldiers' letters and fictional accounts reveal the desperate feelings of dependency and demasculinization of men in the trenches in striking contrast to their own descriptions of strength and control that presumably characterized the home front, women's domain. Similarly, growing numbers of working-class women, in this case German, became politically alienated from the state precisely because wartime dislocations prevented them from being adequate mothers and helpmates for their families. They increasingly entered the ranks of mobilized opposition that brought down the imperial German state in November 1918.[3] War clearly is a gendering activity, even if in unexpected ways.

The twentieth-century era of total wars has proven to be a subject of considerable interest to women's historians as well as those involved in military history. Both share a similar research agenda, even if the overlap has not been acknowledged explicitly. On the one hand, part of the effort of military historians is to define total war in its fullest meaning, which brings them inexorably to questions of civilian mobilization, political and familial transformation, changes in the nature and implementation of public policy, and other vital issues in which women are central actors.[4] On the other hand, women's historians involved in issues of war and peace recognize that total wars have mobilized women in increasingly central ways, for example, in defense work or military units. They look not only to these "real" changes in work, power, or authority that women experienced during the war years but raise a more complicated issue that addresses the definitional question of modern, totalizing war. What did women and men later make of the changes experienced by women? What cultural resources were used to give meaning to women's

2   The two works by Elshtain cited in note 1, *Women and War* and *Women, Militarism and War*, summarize particularly well the nature of the polarized imagery that makes up a large component of the ideological representation of war in the Western world.

3   Two articles in Higonnet's collection are of particular interest. See Elaine Showalter, "Rivers and Sassoon: The Inscription of Male Gender Anxieties," and Sandra M. Gilbert, "Soldier's Heart: Literary Men, Literary Women, and the Great War," both in Higonnet et al., eds., *Behind the Lines*, 61–9 and 197–226. For the German example, see Elisabeth Domansky, "World War I as Gender Conflict in Germany," paper presented at a conference on "The Kaiserreich in the 1990s: New Research, New Directions, New Agendas, at the University of Pennsylvania," Feb. 23–5, 1990.

4   The topic of total war was a central one at the conference "On the Road to Total War" sponsored by the German Historical Institute in April 1992, the proceedings of which comprise the chapters in this volume.

worlds under wartime conditions? To what extent did these cultural values and metaphors end up thwarting or furthering the potential for change?

This chapter also addresses key points around which the military and women's perspective intersect, but it moves the inquiry a half-century earlier, to the German Wars of Unification. These wars, too, involved an extensive tapping of human and material resources for the war effort and brought civilians into the struggle in ways that clearly foreshadowed the future. The chapter focuses on the short-and long-term implications of the mobilization of a group of patriotic German women for war work, a subject that is insufficiently explored in the historical literature to date. It represents, however, a preliminary investigation, at times more suggestive than definitive. Nonetheless, through a women's history perspective, it seeks a new understanding of how the Wars of Unification shaped imperial German society and politics.

Central Europe in the 1860s was in flux. It still was the old particularist world of the monarchical courts and aristocratic largess facing, however, the new economic power of the bourgeoisie as well as a growing politicization of the general populace. But it also was a period in which the version of nationalism later fostered by government circles was ill-defined. At the time, there were several conflicting definitions of the nation inherited from the Wars of Liberation against Napoléon I, the Restoration era, and the democratic forces of 1848. Furthermore, traditional parameters of philanthropy were being seriously strained in the decade, encouraging state elites and ordinary subjects to develop new policies and definitions of public and private activism. And there hardly was one conception of the family or even a shared understanding of motherhood. In fact, differing notions of motherhood structured vastly different political activities among middle- and upper-class German women.[5] By contrast, the war ideology seemed simple enough with

---

5   In a very useful book, Ann Taylor Allen points to the centrality of maternalist thinking in the emergence and evolution of German feminism. From the start, a powerful conception of the mother–child bond underlay reform feminists' political orientation; in this reading, these bonds supported an organic vision of a new society, in which maternal values of care and support were central to state purposes and, over time, the conception justified increasingly radical calls for feminist reform. However, Allen fails to acknowledge an alternative understanding of motherhood that also was present in German political culture—an older version tied in to royal authority as adult responsibility, which rested on a more hierarchical conception of social and familial organization. This "reading" of motherhood, I believe, underlay conservative women's conception of their political activities. Indeed, as the nineteenth century progressed, middle- and upper-class German women's political activities were shaped as much by cultural differences (alternative understandings of motherhood, differing conceptions of historical connections, different lessons drawn from the war decade, etc.) as by actual "class" membership. That is, over time in imperial Germany, patriotic women and reform feminists increasingly shared so-called "objective" class membership. Their distinct politics, therefore, are not simply a sociological issue. I am dealing in more detail with these themes in my larger study of women, war, and the state in Germany. For the importance of maternal thought in German political culture, see the very suggestive ideas of Allen, *Feminism and Motherhood in Germany, 1800–1914* (New Brunswick, N.J., 1991).

its gendered emblems and identities, comprising a polarized world assigning men and women distinct roles in the war zone as well as the home front. While the meaning of these roles later were open to varying interpretations, the memory of the war lived on long after the peace, justifying, among other activities, the ongoing political work of patriotic German women and helping to translate abstract values like "the nation" into more tangible and imagined popular sentiments.

I

The Franco-Prussian War, culminating a half-decade armed struggle for German national unity, exercised a strong fascination on contemporary Europeans for all the obvious reasons. To the English Charles Ryan, who rode with the Anglo-American ambulance that included veteran campaigners of the American Confederate Army, it was the "fiercest war of the century." James McCabe, succumbing to myth making, called the year 1870–71 the "most wonderful of the century equal in attractiveness to the most brilliant passages of the world's history. [It offered a] record of battles which have shaken Europe to its center... of patriotism, heroism, military skills and statesmanship never surpassed, and of the fall and rise of the mightiest Empires of modern times."[6] The minutest details of each military engagement were noted and battles themselves were memorialized in art, for the war was one of the first to be illustrated for the avid reading public.[7] In short, the war record was made to contain all the drama that Europeans expected of a good war story, but one that now involved civilians, a dramatic siege of Paris ("a wicked, useless act of vengeance which tarnishes the honour won by the German army") and ended, on the one hand, with German unification supported by the princes and the people ("who had heard of a parliament on campaign?" quipped a correspondent for the *Daily News*) and, on the other, with the apparent end of civilization in the unsanctioned violence surrounding the Paris Commune.[8]

Above all, the war permitted commentators to draw distinctions between the French and the Germans, which they did so with abandon. Most

---

6 Charles E. Ryan, *With an Ambulance during the Franco-German War: Personal Experiences and Adventures with Both Armies, 1870–1871* (London, 1896), 3, 19, 37; and James Dabney McCabe. *History of the War Between Germany and France* (Philadelphia, 1871), 4.

7 See, e.g., reports in *The War Correspondence of the Daily News, 1870*, vol. 1, edited with notes and comments forming a continuous narrative of the war between Germany and France (London, 1870–71); and Irving Montagu, *Wanderings of a War Artist* (London, 1889).

8 The first quote about the siege of Paris is in the *Daily News*, 1: 248; the second is found in vol. 2 of the same publication: *Correspondence Continued from the Recapture of Orleans by the Germans to the Peace* (London and New York, 1871), 37.

expressed these differences in standard military idiom. A professional army had triumphed over a people's army or, for those enamored by modern weaponry, 1871 was hailed as the victory of Krupp over the *meilleuse*. The French, most concluded, had committed two blunders: They underestimated their enemy and trusted to worn out tactics against modern improvements.[9] One would-be historian, citing words drawn from George Sand, called the outcome a victory of science over civilization. But science had a variety of meanings. For many in Germany, their so-called "scientific" superiority not only preserved their homeland against the French, who after all had marched on German lands earlier in the century, but safeguarded German family life and its women and children from the Turcos, those turbaned "half-wild" Africans in French employ, hallmarks of an emerging age of Empire.[10] In the newspaper correspondence and the war stories read avidly by a population that, in turn, was shaped by those very stories, messages of racism and sexual fears commingled with the lessons of tactics and strategies.

Commentators also were eminently aware that the war had advanced the move toward German unification in ways that supported the proclamation of Empire on January 18, 1871. The dispatches, war correspondence, and letters to the home front, all comment half-consciously on how the war helped to lay a material, almost structural, foundation for subsequent unity. For example, the requirement of the army for telegraph and telephone service became a larger project of establishing extensive communication networks throughout Germany.[11] Central depots were set up to coordinate production and delivery of war materiel from diverse localities, and many associations brought forth by the war also became unifying instruments in subsequent years. The Seven Weeks' War with Austria still had elicited the old particularist response: a decentralized mode of war work and care for invalids. From the perspective of the organizational life in Germany, the Franco-Prussian war represents a "turning point," promoting centralization and integration among the separate organizations, first in the states of the north and then with those

---

9   *Kriegs-Depeschen von 1870 und 1871: Nach den amtlichen Bekanntmachungen des Königlichen Polizei-Präsidiums in Berlin* (Strasbourg, n.d.). Also, *Daily News*, 1 : 334, 2 : 46. In addition, consult the judgments of Ryan, *With an Ambulance*, 78, and Maurice Irisson d'Hérisson, *Journal of a Staff Officer in Paris, 1870–1871* (London, 1885), 41.

10   The contrast between science and civilization is found in Ryan, *With an Ambulance*, 169. References to the North African soldiers are in Heinrich Adolf Köstlin, *Im Felde: Bilder und Erinnerungen aus dem Jahre 1870–71* (Friedberg, 1876), 14; and also the *Daily News*, 1 : 86. A racist subtext is also in the works of some Americans who participated in both the American Civil War and the Franco-Prussian War. In addition to Ryan, see also Mary Olnhausen, *Adventures of an Army Nurse in Two Wars: From the Diary and Correspondence of Mary Phinney Baroness von Olnhausen*, comp. J. P. Munroe (Boston, 1903), 138–73.

11   Otto Kuss, *Bei der Feldtelegraphie des Generals von Werder: Heitere Erinnerungen eines Kriegs-Veteranen* (Darmstadt, 1907); *Daily News*, 1 : 47–8, 2 : 166.

branch organizations in the south. It also reinforced growing pressures for meaningful legislative uniformity. Indeed, the Kaiser himself in March 1871 acknowledged the role of the war associations in setting the stage for greater integration. "German unity was carried out successfully first through the humanitarian labor of the [war organizations] at a time when the political unification of our Fatherland remained but an ambition."[12]

A similar process of centralization, coordination, and uniformity characterized the associations and clubs that organized women's war work. The wars elicited an unprecedented response by German women; a large range of women's clubs and associations mushroomed in towns and cities throughout the territory that became Germany, and women also "served" in France, following the invading troops from Sedan to Ravon L'Elappe to Paris. This record has been misrepresented, however, surprisingly at the outset by contemporary leaders of the German bourgeois women's movement, which had been constituted in 1865 during the war decade itself.[13] A truer rendering of women's war experiences permits an equally new reading of state elite's construction of German charity in the new imperial nation and of women's essential role in that side of state building.

The mid-century Wars of Unification mobilized a distinct and identifiable strata of German women for the war effort. Perhaps not surprisingly, aristocratic women were the most prominent, followed by the wives of state-elites like district presidents, members of the chancellery, or councilors at the regional and local levels. These two groups comprise what can be called a veritable female political "class" spearheading women's war work.[14] With the breakdown of corporate structures in the early nineteenth century, women

---

12 The kaiser's speech was reprinted in the *Neue-Preussische [Kreuz] Zeitung* (hereafter cited as *KZ*), no. 68, March 21, 1871. He was referring specifically to the Central Committee of the Association Caring for Soldiers Wounded in Battle, a prominent war organization. Reports from the *KZ* during the Franco-Prussian war demonstrate unmistakably the ongoing process of centralization and coordination of former local and separate associations. Among other possible references, see, specifically, *KZ*, Jan, 19, 1870; no. 43, Feb. 20, 1870; and supplement to no. 106, May 7, 1870. For references to the earlier models of decentralized charity, consult no. 134, July 12, 1870, and no. 166, July 20, 1870.

13 I develop this point in more detail later. For the bias of the early women's movement, see, specifically, Gotthold Kreyenberg, *Mädchenerziehung und Frauenleben im Aus- und Inlande: Mit einem Anhange: Deutsche Frauentätigkeit während des Krieges, 1870–1871* (Berlin, 1872).

14 I am using the notion of political class persuasively developed by Lynn Hunt in her innovative study of politics in the French Revolution. Lynn Hunt, *Politics, Culture and Class in the French Revolution* (Berkeley and Los Angeles, 1984). Hunt makes the case that the leading groups of revolutionaries were shaped by the rhetoric, symbols, and rituals of the revolution itself. In her analysis, language and political practice were more important than socioeconomic "class" membership in shaping the revolutionary vanguard. As noted earlier, in the German case, objective class membership cannot fully explain German upper- and middle-class women's subsequent political orientations. Therefore, a good case can be made that patriotic women were influenced as much by a range of cultural forces as by material structures.

royalty came to function as "protectresses" of new female organizations, providing them official status and legitimacy.[15] In the 1860s, for example, the Queen Dowager of Bavaria was the patron of the Bavarian Women's Association (*Baierische Frauen-Verein*), Queen Augusta of Prussia protected the extensive network of Patriotic Women's Associations (*Vaterländische Frauenvereine* or *VFV*) and the Dowager of Prussia, Elisabeth, oversaw the Central Berlin Relief Association caring for children and wives of soldiers (*Berliner Haupt-Unterstützungsverein*).[16] Aristocratic and state-elite women dominated the leadership of these clubs and were themselves active in wartime endeavors. They founded and ran hospitals from Berlin to Kaiserswerth, supervised much of the nursing operation in France, and administered ambulance services and war-front hospitals in enemy territory. Women's memoirs of war work in France confirm the presence of ladies of the high German aristocracy in France. Rosa Behrends-Wirth, for example, nurse-administrator of a mobile German medical team, identified a woman who arrived supervising a group of Silesian nursing sisters, as a member of the "high aristocracy."[17] Aristocratic women, in this war, got their feet wet.

Next in importance in terms of numbers were the religious sisters, Catholics and Protestants, who through their religious orders did many of the practical tasks of nursing at the front and helping minister to the ill and wounded back home. Equally distinct in terms of organizational affiliation and more peripheral to the war effort were the reform feminists, daughters and wives of the educated and business community, the groups that historians identify as the rank and file of the bourgeois women's movement. Granted, these distinctions are essentially political and partly arbitrary. Daughters and wives of Germany's educated and business leaders worked in and for and on occasion even played a leadership role in the associations dominated by the female political "class." But reform feminists had their own organizations which, in larger cities, essentially worked independently of the patriotic associations. Significantly, after the war, the distinct institutional groups continued to play very different roles in the new political world of imperial Germany.

---

15 Women royalty increasingly assumed the role of patron of women's organizations in the era after the Wars of Liberation. At the time, Queen Louise of Prussia (by then deceased), Queen Carolina in Bavaria, and the Granduchess Stephanie of Baden all sponsored, in name or in person, women's philanthropic associations. See Helene Lange and Gertrud Bäumer, *Handbuch der Frauenbewegung*, 2 vols. (Berlin, 1901), 19.

16 *KZ*, Jan. 2, 1870 and Kreyenberg, *Mädchenerziehung*, 295.

17 Rose Behrends-Wirth, *Frauenarbeit im Krieg: Selbsterlebtes aus den Jahren 1870–1871* (Berlin, 1892), 43, 87. The German high military command, according to the author, reluctantly permitted women of the "high aristocracy" to travel to the front, an indirect testimony to their participation.

Not surprisingly, the survival of war records preserves mainly the names and backgrounds of upper- and middle-class women. But another more anonymous group of working women participated in the war effort—in this case by manufacturing for pay needed war materiel. Women elites arranged for the making of jackets, shirts, socks, bandages, and pillows on a large scale throughout the territory, preferring to employ the wives of reserves and other soldiers at the front. For example, a Berlin women's auxiliary of the city's Relief Association, which supported a hospital in the Bavarian Palatinate, organized the production of linens and surgical bandages for its hospital, partly by employing women whose husbands were at the front. In other cases, money was solicited privately and after "careful investigation of the situation of each case," used to support soldiers' wives. At the front, hospital adminis- trators used local, that is French, seamstresses for their work force. In one case, Behrends-Wirth had twenty-one young girls making stuffed pillows on sewing machines, and the clinic "hummed like a factory." Not all the work was paid, however. The *Kreuz-Zeitung* of October 1870 reported with pride that in Memmel even the "poorest women" of the town were volunteering to sew woolen socks and underclothing for the town's regiment.[18]

On the most general level, the appeal to women to become involved in war work was most successfully launched on patriotic grounds, on the unam- biguous duty to the threatened fatherland. Listen to how women themselves expressed this sentiment.[19] A predominantly female executive committee of the Victoria Bazaar prepared an appeal to German and Prussian women in July 1870 at the start of the war that captures much of the emotional content and imagery used to galvanize civilian support. The Fatherland, it wrote, is in danger, although which specific lands were included in the notion re- mained unspecified. The historic enemy of Germany threatens once again to destroy "our districts, houses and property, our family and community, our happiness and honor." These words could not but resonate with an older generation who, a half-century earlier, had experienced firsthand the invasion by Napoléon I. The eighty-year-old mother of Mrs. Behrends, who otherwise might have been skeptical of her daughter joining a mobile hospital in enemy lands, never forgot the "horrors of the Napoléonic wars." In her view, one had to be "steadfast" in the defense of the country, which included, perhaps, the carving out of new public roles for women.[20] Continuing with its historical

---

18 See the following reports in *KZ*, Aug. 16, 1870, supplement to no. 3, Jan. 4, 1871, no. 240, Oct. 1870, and Sept. 19, 1871. The latter refers to an obituary of Caroline von Normann, a prominent leader in organizing women's war work, including the dispensing of sewing contracts for soldiers' wives. Also, Behrends-Wirth, *Frauenarbeit*, 65–6, and Kreyenberg, *Mädchenerziehung*, 294.
19 *KZ*, supplement to no. 165, July 19, 1870.
20 Behrends-Wirth, *Frauenarbeit*, 3.

analogy, the executive also connected the present day with the world of the wars against Napoléon I. "Today represents a return to the spirit of 1813 ... so once again father is separated from wife and child, son from father, mother and sister, and bridegroom from bride." Yet soldiers willingly go off to fight now as then because they know why they fight. Implied not only is the need to defend the fatherland but, specifically, the women and children left at home. And for the women at home, their task also is clearly defined. They must assure the fighting men that "love accompanies them, that millions of hands are ready to bind the wounds and dispense the last penny to bring bread to those in need." In this particular address, women were called on to help the sick and wounded as well as needy soldiers' families, for the sake of the war's heroes as much as for their families. A bipolar world of distinct gender roles is evoked, as another author put it succinctly, to mold men to "bravery" and women to "sacrifices."[21]

As might be expected, however, given the distinct organizational contexts, there were subtle differences in the political notions and concepts that motivated women to join the war effort. And these differences, later, would shape how women (and men) read these war experiences, the meanings they gave to the war years, and the conclusions drawn for future collective activity. Religious motivations are the most transparent and easily identifiable, and they were not confined to the sisterhood alone; in highly Christian Germany, middle- and upper-class lay women believed in charity, care, and succor as paramount Christian duties (as well as embodiments of womanhood). Indeed, many lay organizations during the war had close ties to the religious orders, a relationship that continued well into the twentieth century. In religious conceptions, nursing, which was the foremost war activity of sisters and nuns, was the quintessential vocation that perfectly expressed female virtues. It required "utmost precision in domestic tasks, faithfulness and circumspection in carrying out doctors' orders, devotion, willingness to sacrifice, patience in caring for the sick as well as self-control, courage and presence of mind during operations."[22] These attributes, self-evidently, were put at the service of the Fatherland in need during the war crisis.

As members of the court, the titled aristocracy, and government service, the female political class could not but respond to the nation threatened by its enemies. But more was involved. These privileged groups also acted out of older concepts of rule that gave women of the higher orders responsibility to care for the less fortunate, a noblesse oblige that still was powerful in

---

21 Kreyenberg, *Mädchenerziehung*. The book was dedicated to documenting women's sacrifices in light of men's bravery.
22 Lange, *Handbuch*, 2:13–14.

458 *Jean H. Quataert*

mid-century and authorized these women to organize philanthropic war work on new bases. These public responsibilities, indeed, rested on assumptions about the state as an institution caring for its needy. And women royalty could easily personify the caring nature of the state, supported by ranks of privileged women doing its philanthropic bidding. The widened public roles, in addition, were reinforced by equally prescriptive conceptions of mothers caring for the family's needy – its children, sick, and disabled. Rules of public behavior rested on assumptions of appropriate family behavior. In turn, women's motherly roles at home could be extended to the care of society's needy in general. And in the course of the war, as a united Germany was being formed, an additional political element joined this equation. A speaker at a nationalist festival in 1871 summed this up in the following way. "The pulse of the nation can be measured precisely in the care and love given by women to invalids since the Wars of Liberation. Through the sympathetic nurture of mothers, wives, and sisters in the innermost sanctuary of the family, a sense of national identity grows to its present heights."[23] In this conception, which does not necessarily follow, a logical step nonetheless is made from women's roles as nurturers of war's victims in the heart of the family to their promotion of nationalist consciousness as mothers. Significantly, these varying sentiments demonstrate the effort made to integrate women into a developing nationalist ideology.

Reform feminists, also, were motivated by patriotic duty. It was part of their understanding of female responsibilities, which they inherited from the past. They looked back in history, too, and drew inspiration from the Wars of Liberation, although their reading might stress more the thwarted democratic, constitutional ideals of the struggle against Napoléon I. Indeed, ironically, in the 1860s, politically active women in the patriotic and reform camp shared an "origin myth," which located women's initial political awakening and activity in war. In 1848, Louise Otto, a prominent liberal women's rights leader, expressed the relationship abstractly as follows: "when the times become forcefully loud, it cannot but be that women also raise their voices and respond accordingly."[24] When expressed with historical specificity, Otto was arguing that the Wars of Liberation had encouraged women's first systematic participation in the public arena. At the time, they founded charity and philanthropic associations for the care of war's casualties. Indeed, a number of such clubs continued operation in peacetime. The Frankfurt women's association, for example, traced its origin back to 1813 and had been involved in local charity for three-quarters of a century.

---

23 *KZ*, no. 153, July 5, 1871.
24 In Lange, *Handbuch*, 1:27.

Aristocratic and state elite women sought essentially to perpetuate this earlier philanthropic and charity work occasioned by war. Reform feminists drew more complex conclusions from the same historic record. They also acknowledged women's earlier patriotic involvement and held up a principle inherited from the liberal, nationalist movement of 1848 (an event, hardly surprising, absent in aristocratic reading of history). That prescript stressed women's "duty" to participate in the fate of the state. But the implications surrounding the notion of duty were multiple. Bourgeois feminists were quite aware that women's earlier patriotic involvement had not been solidified by concrete educational and occupational gains, and they expected to win meaningful reform after these specific wars. And, in addition, filling the gap in logic in the nationalist argument, these activists believed that to do their patriotic duty, women needed better education and a restructuring of the girls' curriculum, a position which, again, reinforced their expectations of significant feminist reform in the near future.[25]

Thus, German women embarked on war work with quite different notions and motivations. But to assume a lock-step trajectory is an error, for the war experience itself opened unanticipated avenues, with implications for the subsequent political development of Germany. By far, the mass of war work was spearheaded by members of the Patriotic Women's Associations founded, symbolically, on armistice day September 11, 1866, to remedy the lack of adequate nursing personnel for wounded soldiers, which the Seven Weeks' War had made painfully clear.[26] From the start, its bylaws stressed both war and peacetime operations. During war, the members were to provide care for stricken soldiers and support the institutions serving them; in peacetime, the women were to offer extraordinary help to the needy during crises like floods, fires, epidemics, or other disasters, as well as support the education and training of nurses. The Patriotic Women's Association never had the organizational field to itself, however. During the war, a range of other women's clubs assisted and supplemented its work. There was, for example, the Berlin group headed by the Baroness Wrangel and Countess Bismarck, with the pithy title of Central Relief Committee for Needy Families whose Breadwinners were Called to Arms, an 1866 ad-hoc club recalled to life in July 1870 with the declaration of war between France and the North German Confederation. Active, too, was the Women's Club of the Lazarus Hospital for the Care of Wounded and Sick Soldiers and the women of the Stuttgart

---

25 Margrit Twellmann, *Die deutsche Frauenbewegung im Spiegel repräsentativer Frauenzeitschriften: Ihre Anfänge und erste Entwicklung, 1843–1889*, vol. 2: *Quellen* (Meisenheim/Glan, 1972), 11; and Lange, *Handbuch*, 1: 35–6.
26 Twellmann, *Quellen*, 47–9.

Medical Association. The list is hardly exhaustive. There also were reform feminists' organizations affiliated with the German Women's Association (*Allgemeiner deutscher Frauenverein*), the umbrella body of the emerging bourgeois women's movement. Prominent here was Lina Morgenstern's creation of peoples' kitchens, in operation already at the start of the Prussian-Austrian war. In conception, these kitchens were designed to offer urban poor access to "good, nutritious and plentiful meals at fair prices." The whole economic undertaking of buying and producing food in bulk was run exclusively by women. During the wars, the kitchens fed the troops that came through Berlin. And there also was the Lette Association, dedicated to the improvement of women's and girls' education and employment opportunities. It, too, played a distinctive role during the war, pushing for improved training of nurses and supporting hospitals like the Königin-Auguste-Hospital in Berlin, where both female professionals and volunteers could acquire necessary training.[27] In subsequent years, the feminist Association based its ongoing struggle for women's professional advancement on their sterling performance during wartime.

Not alone, then, in promoting women's activities for the war effort, the *VFV* nonetheless was the most extensive, successful, and permanent organization of the genre. Its national leadership overwhelmingly was aristocratic and included two countesses (the president was Charlotte Countess von Itzenplitz). Four of six women on the executive committee had "von" in their surnames, and several of its male members were princes and barons. A similar leadership composition was found on the local level where the organization took roots in most medium-sized towns and cities of Germany. Several examples adequately capture the leadership mix. In Aachen, in the western part of Prussia, the local branch had been founded in 1867; its president was the Countess Johanna von Nellessen, the secretary was the wife of the district president Hasenclever, and in the executive committee, among others, was the wife of a member of the chancellery (*Kanzleirathin* Hermsen) and a Helene von Hoselt. The Cologne branch of the *VFV* had 310 members at the end of 1870 and was headed by a five-member female executive committee comprised of Johanna von Bernmuth, wife of the district president (*Regierungspräsident*), a Frau Karoline Neven, Frau Josephine von Niesewand, Fräulein Emilie Nourney, and the Baroness Amalie von Oppenheim. An account of its day-to-day activities confirms the extensive involvement of well-born women. "Hundreds of ladies of the very best (*besten*) and the better

27   For information on Lina Morgenstern's kitchens, see Kreyenberg, *Mädchenerziehung*, 279; Twellmann, *Quellen*, 181; Lange, *Handbuch*, 1 : 61–2. For the *Lette Verein*, see *KZ*, supplement to no. 29, April 17, 1870, and no. 222, Sept. 23, 1870.

(*besseren*) classes (*Stände*) worked daily from 8 A.M. to 8 P.M. cutting material which then was given over to poorer wives of reservists to make into soldiers' shirts and clothing." Reports from the local level also reveal the organizational separation between war work by the female political class on the one hand and reform feminists on the other. The example of Braunschweig captures vividly this division. The city's Patriotic Women's Association was founded in 1869 and had 195 members at the end of the war; it was headed by the wife of the State Minister, Auguste von Campe, and its secretary was the wife of the Court Preacher, Frau Elisabeth Thiele. During the war, it had been busy soliciting funds and, from its own revenues, had set up a hospital with seventy-four beds. The city's Women's Association also originated in 1869; it had 146 members at war's end and was headed by Frau Dorette Sack, and the secretary was Fräulein Marie Selenke. Its members had been busy gathering needed war materials and caring for the wounded in a hospital for reservists. The report pointedly noted, however, that the feminist club had functioned more as an educational institution, supporting a continuing school, which offered instruction in the use of the sewing machine, and organizing evening entertainment.[28]

Membership of the Patriotic Women's Associations recorded steady advances, which continued well beyond the war years. By October 1870, three months into the war, there were 359 branches with a total of 31,382 members, a gain of over 9,000 members since the outbreak of the war. Two years after the end of the war, its membership had increased slightly to 32,741. By 1880, there were 493 locals with a total membership of around 48,000, and one year later, through its amalgam with the Red Cross, it boasted 151,359 female members organized in 1,508 locals.[29] By then, the *VFV* had established an important niche in German political life, fulfilling a philanthropic role outlined by government officials as a result of wartime experiences and long-term needs occasioned by war's casualties.

During the war, the Patriotic Women's Associations, and their sister philanthropic societies, pursued an expanded and increasingly coordinated form of "private" charity, sanctioned by high government officials. At the national level – indeed Berlin became the national headquarters for most of these war associations – the women organized fund-raising campaigns, sponsored bazaars and lotteries to raise more money, and ensured that adequate supplies of war materiel (which was procured from their local branches throughout the German states) reached the depots in Germany and France in a timely

---

28 These details on Patriotic Women's Associations and parallel reform feminist groups are drawn from local reports reprinted in Kreyenberg, *Mädchenerziehung*, 313, 319, 344–5.
29 *KZ*, supplement to no. 251, Oct. 27, 1870, and Twellmann, *Quellen*, 48.

fashion. Indeed, success rested on the work at the local level, which essentially was geared to the needs of soldiers and their families but moved inexorably beyond to care for the area's poor in general. A few examples suffice to make the point. The local branch in the town of Stettin concentrated mainly on the world of soldiers and their families. There, *VFV* members solicited funds; supervised the manufacture of shirts, underclothing, socks, pillows, hand towels, and clothing for the sick; and prepared thousands of bandages, enough to supply three private hospitals. They arranged for seamstress commissions from local businessmen to be given to reservists' wives (for which 6,243 taler were paid); provided relief for pregnant women or sick family members of soldiers; paid the room and board of convalescents; offered general charity to soldiers who had fallen on hard times; gave Christmas presents to people in hospitals; and even set up a school to teach sewing and mending. The Weissenfels example, by contrast, demonstrates the more fluid line between support for soldiers' families and that of the area's needy in general. Association members were also involved in war work; indeed, they took over the feeding and procuring of medicine and equipment for the local hospital, which cared for 648 wounded. But the club also helped widows, sick people, the aged, unemployed, and so-called degenerates. It worked in tandem with a group promoting day care, aid for orphans, and relief for impoverished pregnant women, and it also set up a people's kitchen in which four executive committee ladies cooked roughly 200 portions daily. The official report of the association's activities concluded that "overall it stepped in when help [was] needed."[30]

Indeed, this wartime involvement in expanded charity placed the national leadership in a morally strong position to enter a debate about the state's future obligations to its disabled soldiers, veterans, war widows, and orphans. This debate, in the midst of war, is remarkable for the various positions that it elicited – positions that foreshadowed the whole spectrum of views that would reemerge over the next several decades as the German state slowly was transformed along more modern welfare lines. The discussion was prompted by publication of the Prussian government's official position toward its long-term obligations, which it made known in September after the Battle of Sedan convinced authorities that they would win the war and could begin to think about the peace. Crown Prince Frederick William, in whose name the policy was formulated, had wrestled with similar concerns in the 1864 and 1866 wars; he now called on all Germans to support the government's program, and he based his authority on his wartime role. Just as he had led an

30 Kreyenberg, *Mädchenerziehung*, 366–7, 370–1.

army in which the Badenese, Bavarians, and Württembergers fought next to the Prussians, so he felt empowered to appeal to the hearts of all Germans. As crystallized by William, the policy was straightforward: State help alone, even if it were relatively generous, was incapable of supporting the large numbers of projected invalids, orphans, widows, and their families. Public moneys provided only the bare necessity, measured on standardized norms, and could not be geared to individual cases. Thus, voluntary help (that is, private charity) was essential to the state's mission. "In the same way as the war has created a uniform and united German army in which the sons of all the social orders fought in brotherly expression of bravery, the care for the invalids and helpless whom the war leaves behind must become the common business of Germany, the north and south of our Fatherland taking a like share in it." And the Prince resurrected a National Invalid Foundation to co-ordinate the solicitation of funds and oversee the establishment and functioning of branch organizations.[31]

The response was mixed. To be sure, large segments of the leaders of wartime organizations, tied in closely with high government officials, supported William's position, but a surprising number of urban officials did not.[32] While most councilors in Nuremberg, for example, voted a 35,000 florin grant for the Crown Prince's Foundation, a number of magistrates opposed the policy on the basis of alternative assumptions about the state's proper role. The dissidents regarded it as a clear "duty of the state" to provide adequate support for invalids, going so far as to say that these people had a "right" to such support instead of being forced to rely on private charity. A legal councilor Marx (no relation, of course, to the famous namesake!) argued in no uncertain terms that if the state did not have the means to provide long-term support, it would have the right to levy a general tax (an *Invalidensteuer*), since each citizen enjoyed the protection of the army. While the argument remained confined to the military context, it evoked the language of the modern welfare state – a language of state responsibility, of support as a right underpinned by a general tax. In Braunschweig, urban magistrates also sought to establish new lines of responsibility. There, the local Citizen's Association (*Bürgerverein*) called on the Reichstag to pass a new law expanding public responsibility for the victims of war. Diplomatically, its members acknowledged the Crown Prince's call for private initiatives

31 *KZ*, no. 217, Sept. 17, 1870.
32 For example, the Central Committee of the German Relief Association in Dec. 1870 pledged money for invalids, widows, and orphans, and the Wilhelm Foundation reorganized its priorities to provide the same groups with a single monetary payment as a stopgap measure to cover the period of time until state support began. See, *KZ*, no. 285, Dec. 6, 1870, and no. 287, Dec. 8, 1870.

but read history in a way that made it impossible to accept that conclusion: Private charity had been sorely wanting since the Napoléonic Wars. Their solution was elegantly put. "We believe that the question of compensation for disability or long-term support for surviving families is not a question of humanity, of [heartfelt commitment of] private charity, or that of the municipality but is an affair of the [nation] state alone which must emanate from the state in the form of national, uniform legislation."[33] This association of professionals, businessmen, and artisanal groups shifted sole responsibility to the national public structures.

The debate was not confined to the issues of rights and responsibilities alone. It included the voicing of considerable fear and worry about public money eroding individual initiative and undercutting hard work. The Crown Prince himself had expressed concern that the distribution of money and ongoing financial support might discourage individual self-reliance. He wanted precautions taken that the money spent not "weaken instead of strengthen the power to earn which may still exist" and that it really prove "beneficial to the life of those assisted."[34] Included early on as well was the play of sexual politics. Indeed, the involvement of privileged women in war work itself already had evoked considerable dismay in aristocratic circles. These concerns are captured well in Count Paul Hatzfeldt's letters to his wife, which he wrote when he accompanied Bismarck in France during the war as representative of the Foreign Office. In no uncertain terms, he cautioned her against tending French prisoners of war in Berlin hospitals. He hoped she would cease that activity altogether, adding "you must have read in the papers how upset people are with the interest our ladies are giving French soldiers."[35] The sexual innuendo is unmistakable. Hatzfeldt expressed his concern over the loss of control of his wife's daily routine due to his absence – essentially a political issue – in sexual terms. Similarly, with publication of the new war veterans' and widows' pension law, numerous correspondents wrote fearfully about the public moneys earmarked for war widows. The money (representing a paltry fifty taler yearly) surely would discourage widows from remarrying, many said, resulting in a dramatic rise in illegitimacy and common-law relationships, although most quickly added only for women of the lower orders (among soldiers', not officers', widows). It was most pointedly asserted that the need to honor war's heroes with a morally correct policy took precedence over the claims of war widows. Since the widows lost their

---

33 For Nuremberg, see *KZ*, no. 232, Oct. 5, 1870, and the Braunschweig example is found in no. 241, Oct. 15, 1870.

34 The Crown Prince's appeal is reprinted in McCabe, *History of the War*, 345–6.

35 *Hatzfeldts Briefe: Briefe des Grafen Paul Hatzfeldt an seine Frau: Geschrieben vom Hauptquartier König Wilhelm, 1870–71* (Leipzig, 1907), 56.

pensions if they remarried, one enterprising letter writer proposed that a small amount of capital be given each widow upon remarriage to encourage the new conjugal union.[36]

But what about the women's voices in this debate? The documents are silent about their response to the veiled sexual charge of impropriety; presumably, Frau Hatzfeldt continued her rewarding work in the hospital. The spokeswomen of the female political class, however, were not silent; they had their own agenda. Their work throughout Germany had made them realize the inequalities of wealth in the new nation in the throes of capitalist industrialization. Traditional charitable approaches in which support reflected the level of local resources were inadequate; wealthy communities could offer more and poorer ones less. "Just as the sacrifices at the front are equaled among fighting soldiers, so those at home should expect justice and a fair division of money."[37] These women, however, did not join those magistrates and citizens' associations calling for expanded or exclusive state responsibility; they accepted the government's combined policy of public and private initiatives. But they spoke for greater coordination and expansion of the national philanthropic side to the enterprise. And they did so partly because of the sense of patriotism, which had involved them in war work in the first place. These philanthropic endeavors later were seen to uphold the social order. And their language hardly was "feudal" in the sense of representing a decentralized, particularistic, local solution. Their position was fully compatible with the new geographic realities of a united Germany undergoing uneven industrial advance. They spoke about justice and the fair distribution of resources coordinated by a well-administered center.

Indeed, in subsequent years, it was patriotic women's extensive network of charitable associations that helped realize the government's own understanding of its collective responsibilities for its populace: a shared commitment divided between public support and government-sanctioned private endeavors. The imperial German state never really gave up this dual face, although considerable change occurred in the nature of its public commitments. On the one hand, there was the trend toward health, disability, and old-age entitlements geared to paid labor – an evolution toward the "modern" welfare model. On the other hand was a functionally differentiated

---

36 For concerns about potential abuse by widows, see, specifically, *KZ*, supplement to no. 91, April 19, 1871, and supplement to no. 117, May 17, 1871. The pension law, whereby the government committed monies to support the casualties of war (wounded soldiers, veterans, war widows, and orphans) was aired in the *Kreuz-Zeitung*, April 18, 1871. The key provision of the law, as far as soldiers' families were concerned, geared payment to the soldier's rank, not to the size of his surviving family or their geographic location (not to individual family need).

37 *KZ*, supplement to no. 206, Sept. 4, 1870.

municipal support system for the needy in terms of health care, supervision of children and youths, unemployment provisions and housing policies – a move toward a more modern, updated poor relief system. And at the heart of overseeing municipal poor relief were the charitable organizations and voluntary labor of Germany's elite and middle-class women. These public and voluntary initiatives coexisted well into World War I, when wartime exigencies required new initiatives, policies, and institutions and once again pushed the German state in new directions.[38]

Indeed, patriotic women's organizations became the life blood of charity in the decades of the 1870s and 1880s, paving the way for growing municipal commitments to its needy inhabitants through the utilization of female voluntary labor. And, in the process, these patriotic women became involved in change that had a decisively, if not self-consciously, feminist character. This evolution of women's charitable and philanthropic activities in peace time can be captured easily by a few concrete examples drawn over several decades.

In the immediate postwar years, many local patriotic associations continued to operate along earlier organizational guidelines, essentially supplementing local poor law administration, which officially was in the hands of men – teachers, businessmen, master craftsmen – who worked on an honorary basis. At the time, most communities excluded women from involvement in the official poor law relief system, so the women's associations set their sights on the poor outside the workhouses who, anyway, had come to their attention during the war. They continued to solicit funds for relief in times of emergencies; sought work, food, fuel, and clothing for war widows specifically; and often joined forces with local churches, supporting hospitals with nursing sisters. In addition to these more traditional undertakings, a number of associtions as in Karlsruhe helped to train nurses as well as daycare attendants and supported the education of teachers in girls' sewing schools.[39] And they remained on alert in the event of renewed outbreak of war. As the times increasingly favored peace, however, the national Association officially shifted emphasis away from its nursing orientation and stressed its willingness to work with municipal officials in poor relief administration, a commitment

38 For example, in a survey taken in 1915, in forty-five large towns, there still were around 10,000 female volunteers and only 761 paid women in municipal welfare, supervising infants, children, and orphans, working in the housing and educational divisions, and staffing employment exchanges. See Ute Frevert, *Women in German History: From Bourgeois Emancipation to Sexual Liberation*, trans. Stuart McKinnon-Evans (Oxford, Hamburg, and New York, 1989), 104; see also Karin Hausen, "The German Nation's Obligations to the Heroes' Widows of World War I," in Higonnet et al., ed., *Behind the Lines*, 126–40.

39 Kreyenberg, *Mädchenerziehung*, reports from Bergen auf Rügen, 317; Bernburg, 318; Görlitz, 336; Graudenz, 337; Posen, 361; Quedlinburg, 362, among others.

paralleled by local officeholders' greater willingness to use women in official, although still unpaid, capacities. Ongoing urbanization and industrial change had taxed severely the older system of personal visitation by male volunteers.[40] Consequently, municipalities throughout Germany began to institute a series of changes, essentially centralizing local poor law administration under the direction of a few trained (male) professionals who used growing numbers of volunteers, above all patriotic women. The Frankfurt Congress of the *VFV* in 1880 facilitated the change by calling on its members "to make themselves available to provide additional and auxiliary services for the public care of the poor."[41] Its local clubs were to establish permanent ties with both state and municipal poor relief bureaus and work out agreeable procedures with the local officials.

Over the course of the next decade, then, municipalities extended their involvement into new areas that included overseeing youth, housing, and health. In short, the traditional local system of poor relief in Germany with its limited clientele and reliance on male volunteers had evolved into a broad-based set of communal social policies (*soziale Fürsorge*) that rested on women's extensive, unpaid participation.[42] Not surprisingly, the activities of the Patriotic Women's Associations had grown commensurably. A report in the late 1890s on the work of a Baden branch, still under the "protection" of Louise of Baden, demonstrates the organization's impressive transition from war work into a multifaceted range of peacetime relief activities. The report, however, says nothing about the impact of such work on the lives of the poorer clients.

The Baden club divided its competencies into four areas. First came efforts to promote women's work in general, which included the training of teachers of sewing, supporting girls' continuing education, and sponsoring an employment bureau for female clients. Philanthropic work played an unspoken role in shaping the local gendered capitalist labor market.[43] The second involved work with children, which meant sponsoring daycare as well as an institute to train its staff and overseeing the health and well-being of foster

40 Christoph Sachsse and Florian Tennstedt, *Geschichte der Armenfürsorge in Deutschland: Fürsorge und Wohlfahrtspflege, 1871–1929*, 3 vols. (Stuttgart, 1988), 2:25. Also, Florian Tennstedt, *Sozialgeschichte der Sozialpolitik in Deutschland: Vom 18. Jahrhundert bis zum Ersten Weltkrieg* (Göttingen, 1981).
41 Lange, *Handbuch*, 2:40.
42 Sachsse and Tennstedt, *Geschichte*, 9.
43 Interestingly enough, the two key laws structuring Germany's national poor relief system, the Law on Freedom of Movement (1867) and The Law of Settlement (1870), by facilitating labor migrations, contributed greatly to the creation of a capitalist labor market in Germany. Patriotic women's municipal work in public relief had a similar effect on the local level. See George Steinmetz, "The Myth and the Reality of an Autonomous State: Industrialists, Junkers, and Social Policy in Imperial Germany," paper presented at the conference on "The Kaiserreich," Univ. of Pennsylvania, Feb. 23–5, 1990.

children and boarders. The third division was its original commitment to the training of nurses, in this case to staff sixty hospitals and also provide aides for local clinics. The fourth was the branch working in public charity itself, aiding destitute, pregnant, and sick people, running an asylum for "fallen" girls and a home for clerks, providing services for wage-earning women, running schools to teach cooking and sewing, and administering an employment agency. Female members of this association, clearly, had become deeply entwined in the social, educational, and work world of the less fortunate in the local community. Their work was duplicated in many other localities throughout Germany. Indeed, the Patriotic Women's Association was the largest women's organization in imperial Germany. The official chroniclers of the bourgeois women's movement around the turn of the century acknowledged the predominance of the *VFV* in social work. No second "equally important and extensive women's" organization devoted to the goals of social welfare [exists] in Germany."[44]

Given its prominence, then, and the key role of patriotic women in the evolution of public charity, it is surprising that the record of *VFV* activities is inconsistent. The reasons partly are due to perspective and partly to chronology: On the one hand, the feminist perspective largely has written the story of women's political involvement in German public life; on the other hand, most accounts of women's activities in imperial Germany neglect the critical war years.[45] This omission is all the more serious in the case of German women's involvement in charity and philanthropy. From the start, bourgeois women's movement leaders differentiated reform feminists from members of the *VFV*. In their terms, the war decade, which had led to a multiplication of patriotic local clubs, actually thwarted for a time the development of the bourgeois women's movement. This conscious effort to draw clear distinctions apparently reflected very different readings of the war experience. Bourgeois women's movement leaders, as noted, used women's unmistakable display of competency during the war to push later for increasingly important feminist reform legislation in a variety of spheres. *VFV* women did not, although they consistently sought professional training for nurses and later on

---

44 These details are drawn from reports of the Karlsruhe branch association which, in 1899, had 717 members . In the state of Baden, generally there were 227 affiliate clubs of the *VFV*, comprising a total of 42,330 members. Lange, *Handbuch*, 2: 24–8 . The quote is the conclusion drawn from one of the most prominent women involved in welfare reform, Alice Salomon, in her article in Lange's collection, "Die Frau in der sozialen Hilfstätigkeit," 28.

45 This perspective effects the analysis of Roger Chickering who otherwise has written a very informative article on patriotic women's organizations. However, he does not relate these women's activities to the ongoing process of state building, as I seek to do here. Chickering, "'Casting their Gaze More Broadly': Women's Patriotic Activism in Imperial Germany," *Past and Present* 118 (Feb. 1988):156–85.

for aides and childcare providers and, in time, also promoted widened educational and employment opportunities for women. But patriotic women did not push for reforms favorable to women at the national level and, apparently, had a very different understanding of their own experiences from the war. They were not alone in this understanding, for the war itself had left an ambiguous legacy. Since women had been mobilized partly as mothers and nurturers who naturally cared for sick and ill people at home, no conclusions about the need to improve women's educational opportunities or training would follow necessarily from their exemplary services. Their work, after all, had been a matter of the heart. This was the judgment of Behrends-Wirth, who wrote in no uncertain terms that women's war work (including her own example as a highly efficient administrator) did not demonstrate hitherto unacknowledged competency, which should be extended to other spheres of life; it simply expressed mother love.[46]

The official handbooks of the bourgeois women's movement, to be sure, credited the *VFV* with playing an important role in public relief in the postwar period (that they could not gloss over). The authors also acknowledged that reform feminists had taken at least ten to fifteen years longer (than patriotic women) to become involved in charity, notwithstanding the appeals as early as 1868 of a few feminist leaders to admit women into official poor law administration. But when it came time to honor individuals who had played a crucial part in the war effort, their official history shunned mention of patriotic women.[47] Subsequent historians have had their own assumptions, which also masked part of the story. Studies by historians Ute Frevert or Christoph Sachsse and Florian Tennstedt, for example, argue that middle-class women (that is, organized bourgeois feminists) had been the movers of local charitable activities; indeed, in these authors' analyses, philanthropy perfectly expressed a bourgeois impulse toward reform. Thus, these historians, too, neglected patriotic women's experiences and activities.[48] In addition, failure to include debates and practices during the war years distorts the later narrative. As this chapter has demonstrated, in matters of policy, institutional coordination, and hands-on experience in organizing relief at the local level, the war itself had set the stage for subsequent developments. And a perspective that spans war and peacetime, as is offered here, also raises important

46 Behrends-Wirth, *Frauenarbeit*, 113. In discussing those best utilized for war, she drew an analogy to mothers who had a heart for the matter; the issue was not training but rather reflected natural sentiments – only those with a natural disposition to sacrifice should be drawn into the efforts to ameliorate the hard conditions of war. See also the detailed chapter by Alice Salomon, "Die Frau in der sozialen Hilfstätigkeit," in Lange, *Handbuch*, 2.
47 Kreyenberg, *Mädchenerziehung*, 398–409.
48 Frevert, *Women*, 104–6 and Sachsse and Tennstedt, *Armenfürsorge*, 15–16.

questions about causality at the heart of the analysis of the German welfare state. The question of cause always is complicated. The favored model of material changes from below (for example, disruptions of industrialization and urbanization mobilizing groups which then pressured state elites to redraw policies) captures part of but not the full story.[49] For it locates the cause for change in society alone and makes state policy reflective of social interests. But, as seen, wartime government officials had their own agenda for the future care of war's victims and shaped the broad outlines of German charity already in 1870–71. That mix of public and private initiatives, indeed, accommodated ongoing material changes partly because of the large-scale voluntary involvement of patriotic women.

II

If positions and policies set under wartime exigencies shaped the ongoing evolution of German charitable institutions, the wars themselves, and particularly the Franco-Prussian War, helped to define ingredients of German national identity through the ideological representations of war that characterized peacetime. Peacetime was not devoid of war; war lived on in German collective memory through a variety of mediums: in men's and women's war memoirs published at varying dates in the late nineteenth and early twentieth centuries; in the histories of the war that retold war's stories; in artistic monuments and statuary glorifying war and increasingly marking public space; and in commemorative festivities and rituals celebrating specific battles, victories, and peaces. The construction of a shared social memory becomes important in countries undergoing dislocating industrial and urban change; connection with a specific past fosters social cohesion and helps to structure new social relationships. Thus, Eric Hobsbawm has recognized that in the period 1870–1914, European nations embarked on an unprecedented venture to "invent traditions."[50] However, this common undertaking was doubly significant in Germany, for there collective traditions and rituals not only provided historical legitimacy for a new nation; they helped to forge a national identity—one that resonated among the new male citizens to be sure but also among females, who stood in a different relationship to the state. Defining the meanings of the Franco-Prussian War was central to the nationalist project, because the war was the first major political event that all new

49 This is the standard causal model adopted, e.g., by Sachsse and Tennstedt, *Armenfürsorge*, 17–18, 42–5. For new ways of thinking about the state, see, among others, Peter Evans, Dietrich Rueschemeyer, and Theda Skocpol, eds., *Bringing the State Back In* (Cambridge, 1985).

50 Eric Hobsbawm, "Mass-Producing Traditions: Europe, 1870–1914," in Eric Hobsbawm and Terence Ranger, eds., *The Invention of Tradition* (Cambridge, 1983), 263–307.

Germans had in common. And the symbolic uses of gender stood at the heart of its celebration.

This subject, clearly, is a fascinating theme in its own right. Only a few general observations are offered here. It appears that men's war memoirs tended to reflect a sense of the nation compatible with the evolving nationalist ideology promoted from above. In the literature, this version had three specific components. First, the war itself had unified a diverse people, setting the stage for a cohesive new political entity. The memoir of Otto Kuss, who laid telegraph lines during the war, captures this argument well. As he put it, his crew was a "mini" Germany, consisting of five Prussians from the traditional homeland, three Silesians, two from the new Rhenish territories, one each from Hanover, Holstein, Saxony, Braunschweig, and Hamburg, and three other inhabitants from elsewhere in the North German Confederation.[51] Similarly, the fighting armies themselves became representatives of a united Germany; their colors and uniforms—the true blue uniform of the Bavarians, the darker colors of the Württembergers, and spiked helmets of the Prussians—were made to symbolize diversity in the service of unswerving unity and common purpose.[52] Second, the war was seen to transcend class and all manner of social distinctions. It was a war that resonated among the populace, and "the people" cheering the troops on at railroad stations or greeting the kings were identified explicitly as workers as well as middle- and upper-class folk—in short, representative types of the entire social order. In Hatzfeldt's account, a group of workers in Essen enthusiastically met the train transporting Bismarck to the front and "[each] worker gave Bismarck [his] hand."[53] Hatzfeldt's letters were published in 1907, and his point was obvious and ideological: Germans of all socioeconomic backgrounds supported the Fatherland despite the divisive machinations of the godless and nationless social democrats. Third, what was at stake in victory was nothing less than German family life resting on German virtues of propriety, stability, and tranquillity, all implicitly safeguarded by German womanhood. Indeed, the salient point about these memoirs is the ideological division between men's and women's worlds in the accounts of war. In men's stories, women at the front are either missing, or they appear in highly stereotypical roles—as sacrificing mothers or solicitous nurses. Interestingly enough, women's memoirs of life at the front do not challenge the depiction of distinct worlds; rather, female authors fill in the missing details about women's work. They

51 Kuss, *Bei der Feldtelegraphie*, 24.
52 *Daily News*, 2:87.
53 *Hatzfeldts Briefe*, Mainz, Aug. 2, 1870.
54 This is true in the accounts of both Behrends-Wirth, *Frauenarbeit*, 22–3; and Olnhausen, *Adventures*, 32, 37–8, 61.

have their own stories to construct, including describing what surely were considerable sexual antagonisms toward female nurses by army doctors, recording their Herculean efforts to serve the troops despite all obstacles and touting their eventual success in winning over the skeptical male medical personnel.[54] But unintentional points are equally revealing. Note, for example, the simple statement by Charles Ryan about his daily routine at the front: "We breakfasted at 7:30 A.M., dined at noon, and supped at 6:30 P.M." Now contrast his words with those of Behrends-Wirth, who administered an equivalent hospital and writes about the unacknowledged support system behind men's activities. "Daily work was strictly organized and regimented," she states simply. "I awoke at 4:00 A.M., at 5 A.M. I was in the hospital checking the provisions, noting what was missing and seeing that everything was in order; at 6:00 A.M. the daily help arrived whom I needed for washing and cleaning; 7:00 A.M. all had to be ready in the dining hall ... for the doctors and their assistants arrived punctually."[55]

Memoirs, then, capture the bipolar universe of male warriors and female helpmates at the root of much of the inherited traditions of war making in the era of the citizen-army of the nation-state. And similar gendered understandings are found in the historical treatments of war, those "master narratives" that glorify the great men, events, and battles while simultaneously neglecting the average soldier's fate and most women. An absence of explicit mention of women does not mean a lack of gender usage; the latter often slips into the text. Those budding historians of war, writing at the time of the professionalization of the discipline, used gender imagery to make judgments, even as many – particularly, British and Americans – sought to be "objective, impartial, and unbiased" narrators. But what was disapproved of was feminized (in McCabe's account, the government of Napoléon III was "the council of old women at Paris" while Hérisson made the newly mobilized popular opinion "impressionable as a woman") just as what was praised was forceful, resolute, and masculine.[56] Indeed, the dominant theme in the inscribed literature – the genre of memoirs and narratives – is that "war is men's business not ladies'," a position ideologically charged and not reflective of the war experience.[57] Through its dominant voice – the masculine

---

55   Ryan, *With an Ambulance*, 166; Behrends-Wirth, *Frauenarbeit*, 54.
56   McCabe, *A History*, 231; and Hérisson, *Journal*, 33. The latter could not refrain from offering crass stereotypes about women as irrational. Speaking of the French response after the Battle of Sedan, Hérisson notes: "The women, as usual, made themselves remarkable by their enthusiastic, violent, and hysterical demonstrations," 59. See also, Daniel Colt Gilman, *The Victory of Germany as Seen in Connecticut: An Address to the German Residents of New Haven on the Festival of Peace, April 10, 1871* (New Haven, Conn., 1871).
57   This popular saying is from the movie "Gone with the Wind" as quoted by Higonnet et al., eds., *Behind the Lines*, 1.

voice – women are absent, although they nonetheless lurk in the background, caring for the troops and safeguarding all that is worth while back home. But collective memory also is created and nurtured in festivals, festivities, and rituals. Here, memory is incorporated in repeated or ritualized behavior, postures, and gestures, as well as dress.[58] The early festivities around the Wars of Unification reflected a similar bipolar world created, in this case, by the notable participation of patriotic women. That is, real women, who communicated meanings through their physical presence as well as symbolically, played a central role in the rituals celebrating war, glorifying and honoring the troops, and later, commemorating war during the long years of peace after 1871. It appears important, however, to distinguish between two separate political traditions in this ideological work. The first harked back to the older world of the patrimonial despotic court in Central Europe. After all, the particularist state was the court *writ large* and its military apparatuses dominated by the aristocracy. And royal women were closely associated with the military in a variety of highly stylized contexts. Newspaper accounts capture numerous moments in which women royalty lent support to the troops. In April 1870, for example, prior to the outbreak of war, the Queen Dowager of Bavaria had been embroidering colorful ribbons for an infantry regiment; these were later affixed on the flag at a specific ceremony. Also, when the Berlin populace rushed to the royal palace seeking news of the victory at Wörth, they demanded to see the Queen, who stepped out, bowed, and reassured the crowd. British war correspondents reported the following account. The Prince of Saxony-Weimar, son-in-law of the King of Württemberg, was making the rounds at a hospital for wounded soldiers. After hearing a particularly pitiful tale, he "dip[ped] into his pocket and gave the wounded a gold piece. 'Here my man, send that to the mother and let her know it comes from the Queen'."[59] For those within hearing range, this gesture evoked memories of mothers and reinforced bonds of loyalty to a caring monarchy through the Queen and, thus, to the King. And, when the troops were reviewed (after the 1866 war and again in 1871, for example), they paraded before the King, Queen, Queen Dowager, and numerous carriages of ladies of the court. The ceremony lasted several days and was geared to impress not only the army but the spectators who thronged along Unter den Linden.[60] For the fighting men, the large presence of women of the court signified the

58 An extremely interesting study analyzing different forms of social memory, which I found particularly useful for the following section, is Paul Connerton, *How Societies Remember* (Cambridge, 1989).
59 *KZ*, no. 95, April 24, 1870; McCabe, *A History*, 162, describes the response of the populace after the Battle of Wörth; *Daily News*, 2 :20–1.
60 H. M. Hozier, *The Seven Weeks' War: Its Antecedents and Its Incidents*, 3d ed. (London and New York, 1872), 455–66.

home front and what they had been fighting for; for the spectators, the very bipolar world of war meant that the women present could represent the home, hearth, and happiness – in short, stability and the promise of normalization. For the female spectators, perhaps, the appearance of so many other women helped to forge a common sense of achievement and reinforced a commitment to a regime that offered women few tangible channels of official participation.

A different political agenda was involved when the women participating in the rituals were representatives of female civil society of the new nation-state. This was a world in which public opinion increasingly counted (a factor already recognized in the war), and the government saw clearly that it needed to court the civilian population, including its women, for future wars. Thus, in 1871, the same victorious troops, royalty, and the ladies-in-court, in turn, were greeted by a Berlin magistrate and fifty-five young girls who spoke stylistically in rhyme and meter. And in later years, in the festivities honoring the troops, victory wreaths were handed out by young women typically dressed in white.[61] In many ways, white is the antithesis of war, which is blood, gore, and mud. These young women, after all, could be seen as representing peace, which also was being honored. Peace was glorified through the girls in white, who were depicted as humanitarian, clean, pure, and loving, denying the horrors of war – in essence, sanitizing war. But more was at stake. Their ongoing presence at the festivals represents a public recognition of the necessity to integrate women into the nation, which derived part of its legitimacy from its war-making prerogatives. Indeed, these roles in the commemorative festivities ultimately served to prepare the body-politic for future wars. In these arrangements, however, the young girls were not truly agents. Their presence, their dress, and their ritualized performances imparted information and metaphors by which some nationalists in German society were seeking to handle war and peace. In time, however, these girls could grow up to become patriotic agents, like our "female political class" who, in the new civic world of immediate postwar Germany, helped to organize similar commemorative festivities with charged political meanings. These members of the Patriotic Women's Associations sponsored, among others, "July 3," a festival celebrating Königgrätz, Prussia's victory over Austria (which made possible, of course, the small-German solution to nationhood).[62] This celebration brought veterans of Germany's wars together (going back to the Wars of

---

61   *KZ*, supplement to no. 152, July 3, 1870, and no. 153, July 5, 1870; no. 164, July 17, 1870; supplement to no. 143, June 23, 1871; and no. 153, July 5, 1871. See also Julius von Hartmann, *Erlebtes aus dem Kriege 1870–71* (Wiesbaden, 1885), 223; and Olnhausen, *Adventures*, 286.

62   *KZ*, supplement to no. 152, July 3, 1870, and no. 153, July 5, 1870, as well as no . 153, July 5, 1871.

Liberation) to eat, sing, and hear speeches. Keeping alive the memory of this victory served multiple political purposes in the new Germany. In the first place, thematically, it commemorated a key birth event of the imperial state. Equally to the point, it was orchestrated by women who, officially disenfranchised, nonetheless were able to demonstrate their commitment to the new nation-state by sponsoring these types of events. Second, it honored war veterans who, in the celebration, were hailed as war's heroes. Honored was not the individual man who had lost his eye, or leg, or arm; the whole ritual romanticized and depersonalized the soldier and deprived him of his context – death and dying on the battlefield – which disappeared. Indeed, these festivals abstracted and distilled out the meanings most appropriate for the creation of stories that worked to reproduce war. They, too, reinforced the state's war-making powers that underlay much of its legitimacy. Finally, these types of commemorative festivities reinforced the gender hierarchy; objects of esteem were males as were chosen speakers; and women were in the background, seeing to it that the events ran smoothly.

These representations of war rested on notions of difference that were partly grounded in assumptions about the two worlds of men and women in wartime. Two sets of values were juxtaposed and contrasted: war and peace, soldiers and mothers, battlefield and the home front, bravery and sacrifices, heroes and their nurses. Indeed, the war decade – one particular version of it – was essential to the nationalist cause, providing myths, stories, and images that infused the new political structure with life. Such beliefs increasingly exercised cognitive control among the nationalist bourgeoisie in imperial Germany, submerging the alternative traditions of a more democratic and liberal nationalism. The change is captured graphically in a talk by Louise Otto-Peters, the early women's rights leader who, as we have seen, lived the democratic nationalist ideals of 1848. Her writings had kept those liberal beliefs alive for reform feminists. In 1883, however, she gave an ode to "Germania" at a festival.[63] The framework of her talk was war's gender division of labor. To the extent, she said, that men rally to the defense of the German Reich, they should look to the monument of Hermann in the Teutoburg Forest and use it as their inspiration. (A monument to Hermann, defender of the Teutons against the Romans, was being built at the time.) In contrast, women look trustingly to Germania to which they also are dedicated to serve at home and in the family, in arts and science, as protectresses of morality and educators of German youth. In Otto-Peters's formulation, Germania had become the home front, served by its women as a duty and

---

63   In Twellmann, *Quellen*, 569.

a right. It is hardly surprising that in subsequent years a liberal monument in Frankfurt am Main, dedicated to the ideals of 1848, was transformed into a statue honoring the precursors of German unity in the years before unification.[64] It was shorn of its ties to the democratic nationalist tradition. A version of the past was being remembered, and memory largely conditions the hierarchy of power.

III

Historians long have recognized that major twentieth-century wars – from the two world wars to the colonial wars of liberation – were *total wars*, even if they disagree on the full definition of the phenomenon. In essence, these monumental conflicts blur the distinctions between soldiers and civilians as well as the war zone and the home front, involve massive state interventions, and mobilize labor, resources, and technology in ways that leave very few unaffected, indeed. This total involvement of society, in turn, has stimulated new inquiry into war's complex and multiple meanings for the men and women of the belligerent countries. Joining an older tradition of military history with a newer sensitivity to gender has opened up promising avenues of historical research.

But so-called *total wars* did not spring full-blown in Europe in, say, 1914, as reputedly Athena did long ago from the head of Zeus. From the perspective of women, an examination of Germany's mid-century Wars of Unification has offered some rewarding insights into the complex stages "on the road to total war." A few suggestive conclusions can be drawn. In the first place, war and peace are not as distinct as their ideological representations have maintained. As seen clearly in the German example, different versions of the wars lived on long after the peace to structure political life in a variety of ways in the ever-changing present. Second, and concretely, the war years fed into the making of a patriotic female group that played an indispensable role in war work. Fashioned by a variety of forces – Germany's earlier wars, evolving readings of mothers' roles, and ties to an older aristocratic heritage, among others – and in continuous evolution, these patriotic women derived their basic justification for their extensive public activities from the need to support the war effort. Indeed, the patriotism initially generated by the war and the hands-on experiences gained in caring for war's casualties continued to underpin these privileged women's growing public presence as volunteers in municipal charity and social services. And,

64 The example is found in Thomas Nipperdey, "Nationalidee und Nationaldenkmal in Deutschland im 19. Jahrhundert," *Historische Zeitschrift* 206 (1968): 563.

third, these same patriotic women helped to create a war culture, which served to keep the memory of war alive. Through commemorative festivities, they were tied into a process that gave new centrality to the place of war in German nationalism. If total war requires that war as a policy option becomes a democratic passion, then the patriotic norms that these women helped to bring into daily consciousness at the very birth of imperial Germany contributed to the realization of that commitment of warfare at a future date.

PART FIVE

The Reality of War

22

Tactics, Trenches, and Men in the Civil War

EARL J. HESS

The Civil War has long been perceived as a total war, or modern war – as a conflict which presaged a future filled with horrible new weapons, relentless strategies, and terrible loss of life. The characteristics of total warfare certainly manifested themselves on and off the battlefield. Those changes were much less pronounced off the battlefield, where the reality of warfare remained largely the same for Civil War soldiers as it had for the veterans of America's previous conflicts. On the battlefield, however, modern war making demanded new tactics that significantly changed the combat experience of Northern and Southern soldiers. Some men found it difficult to adjust and lost their faith in what they were fighting for, but most veterans of the Civil War retained their belief that war was a justifiable, albeit horrible, solution to political problems. Caught in the middle of a quickly changing military environment, Civil War soldiers were tested by the reality of combat more terribly than any previous American warriors.

Civil War soldiers benefited only slightly from new technology, communications, and transportation, for their society had not yet reached an accelerated phase in its modern development. America was only a partially industrialized nation in the 1860s. It stood poised on the threshold of world industrial leadership, but that would not occur until at least three decades after the war.

Off the battlefield, Civil War soldiers lived much like their predecessors in earlier wars. The processes of food preparation had not yet advanced enough to provide them with more convenient or healthy fare than their ancestors in the Revolution had eaten. Pork, saturated with salt, which was used as a preservative, and a hard bread made of flour and water (called *hardtack*) were staples of the soldier's diet. The universal method of preparation was to fry the meat in animal fat. The Federals experimented with processed foods, distributing condensed milk and desiccated vegetables to some troops. These foods were easier to transport, did not spoil, and could be prepared easily in the field by adding water. The soldiers universally hated the taste of these preparations, calling them "condemned" milk and "desecrated" vegetables. This type of food represented the cutting edge of modern military cuisine, but Civil War soldiers remained unimpressed.[1]

The state of medical knowledge was hardly more advanced than that of food preparation. The Civil War occurred before a fully developed germ theory had been accepted, before the practice of blood transfusion had been developed, before modern internal medicines had been conceived, and before an efficient administrative structure for the care of large numbers of men had been worked out. Diseases ranging from diarrhea to measles to typhoid ravaged the armies. For every soldier who died of combat-related causes, at least two died of disease. The modern weaponry of the Civil War created complex wounds. The primitive surgical techniques usually were painfully inadequate to deal with them, thus amputation became the common and all too comprehensive treatment for injuries of the limbs. Head wounds, stomach trauma, and infection of the trunk were usually inoperable: Luck and the will of the patient to survive determined whether the man would live or die. Only in the area of developing a more efficient administrative model for hospitals did the Civil War produce any large-scale improvement in military medical care. Generally, soldiers suffered horribly because they had the misfortune of fighting a war in a premodern medical world.[2]

Transportation and communication capabilities were much farther advanced than either food preparation or medicine. The United States had more railroad mileage than any other nation in the world, and rapid, cross-country communication via telegraph was a fact of national life. The railroad proved to be a particularly vital strategic weapon. Large numbers of men and supplies could be transported over long distances in short spans of time, helping to lessen the vast geographical spaces of the South. Steam-powered, shallow draft boats provided the same advantage on the South's river systems. But there were limitations. Railroad tracks often did not extend to areas that armies needed to occupy, and the river system was much less generous than the railroads in this way. Modern transportation facilities offered little help on the battlefield, except in rare cases; soldiers still had to maneuver to the battlefield and move around it by marching. Only the employment of the internal combustion engine, beginning in the early twentieth century, would help to change that fact of military life. Nearly every soldier rode on a train or boat at least once in their Civil War

---

1 Bell Irvin Wiley, *The Life of Billy Yank: The Common Solider of the Union* (Baton Rouge, La., 1983), 224–46.
2 Ibid., 124–52.

experience, but the overwhelmingly common mode of transit for all of them was walking.[3]

Most of the significant changes in the experience of soldiering during the Civil War were felt not in camp life but on the battlefield. A new weapon, the rifled musket, was used for the first time on a large scale in the Civil War. The rifling inside the barrel increased the range of this weapon to five hundred yards, compared to the range of a smoothbore musket, about one hundred yards. In addition, an improved projectile allowed a good soldier to fire the rifled musket three times per minute, compared to the pre–Civil War weapon, which was fired some three times slower. These improvements increased the size of the killing zone on Civil War battlefields and dramatically thickened the volume of lethal projectiles in that zone.[4]

Tactical formations remained unchanged. The battle line was standard, consisting of two ranks of men placed shoulder to shoulder. The line delivered fire on the defensive and moved forward into a hail of balls on the offensive. Either way, unless protected by the terrain, vegetation, or fortifications, the line offered a tightly packed target to the enemy. In the face of persistent, disciplined fire, men fell in droves. Little significant attention was paid to the need to alter these formations to reduce casualties and offer attacking forces a better chance of success. The volunteer army of the Civil War had no institutional means of self-examination; there were no military commissions charged with finding out why linear tactics were so wasteful and offering recommendations for new tactics. The regular army was too small and overwhelmed with other duties, such as providing professional engineers for the building of fortifications, to fulfill that all-important role.[5]

The result was a persistent tactical stalemate that characterized most Civil War engagements. The use of the rifled musket combined with linear tactical formations were only two reasons for this stalemate. Ironically, the rifled musket was not advanced enough to allow for improved tactics. The logical development would have been the creation of loose-order tactics – men positioned several yards from each other advancing or delivering fire individually or in small groups while taking cover as much as possible. These tactical formations became standard by the twentieth century but were possible only if the men were armed with either breech-loading rifles or weapons equipped with magazines. The rifled musket's improved rate of fire simply was not fast enough to give a single soldier the ability to deliver enough balls in a short

3   George Edgar Turner, *Victory Rode the Rails* (Indianapolis, Ind., 1953), 29–38.
4   Robert V. Bruce, *Lincoln and the Tools of War* (Indianapolis, Ind., 1956), 37–43
5   Herman Hattaway and Archer Jones, *How the North Won: A Military History of the Civil War* (Urbana, Ill., 1983), 11–19.

time to make loose-order tactics feasible. Such new weapons as the Spencer and Henry repeaters provided that increased firepower but were not widely distributed enough to foster a change in tactics.[6]

In addition to weapons, the huge size of Civil War armies contributed to the tactical stalemate. Total war demanded mass mobilization, and that led to field armies that could consist of as many as 120,000 men. The United States regular army, consisting of only 16,000 men before the war, had no officers who had commanded more than a brigade in battle. At least regular officers had a modicum of training for command; volunteer officers had to learn everything on the job. The lack of experience in handling large numbers of men on the battlefield contributed to the persistent failure of Civil War armies to win decisive victories. Assaults were far too often uncoordinated, and the defending force had little difficulty repelling them. Complicated tactical plans, which demanded precisely timed movements, usually fell apart. Northerners and Southerners alike paid a heavy price in blood, and endured an unnecessarily prolonged war, because of the traditional American policy of maintaining a small, poorly trained army in peacetime. This premodern policy was barely adequate to meet the demands of total war.[7]

Overall it is inaccurate to term the Civil War the first *modern war*. That conflict contained many modern features that pointed the way to massed conflict in the twentieth century, but it was essentially an old-fashioned war. The modern components of that war puzzled many participants. Few men had the foresight to deal with the new tactical situation or the intuition to develop quickly better methods of caring for the sick and injured. Civil War soldiers were the unwitting subjects of a vast, often cruel, experiment in modernization.

The grinding clash of traditional and modern methods of making war can best be seen in the realm of tactics. Contrary to the general perception of Civil War tactics as inflexible and unchanging, two major innovations took place. By 1864, the principal armies began to engage in continuous campaigning rather than the sporadic, brief contact that had characterized operations during the preceding three years. This led to the second innovation, the use of sophisticated earthen field fortifications, which intensified the physical and emotional suffering of the soldiers. The experience of combat altered in traumatic, significant ways, and soldiers found it much more difficult to retain traditionally positive attitudes toward war as a justifiable means of settling political issues. These new methods of fighting dramatically foreshadowed the future of warfare.

6 Jack Coggins, *Arms and Equipment of the Civil War* (Wilmington, N.C., 1990), 26–9.
7 Hattaway and Jones, *How the North Won*, 8–11.

Continuous campaigning was a new experience for American soldiers. During the first three years of the war, operations had centered on the pitched battle, a distinct engagement lasting from a few hours to a few days, each engagement separated by weeks if not months of preparation, maneuvering, and idleness. The Federal Army of the Cumberland and the Confederate Army of Tennessee, for example, spent six months recuperating from the horrible battle of Stone's River before resuming the series of campaigns along the railroad line that penetrated the southeastern portion of the Confederacy. Nearly all field armies entered winter camps rather than exhaust themselves by struggling over mud-engulfed roads. In Europe, where geographical distances were shorter and improved road systems offered armies a greater opportunity to achieve strategic gains in shorter time, seasonal campaigning did not unnecessarily prolong the conflicts attending German unification. But in America, with its dirt roads, huge areas, and massed armies, seasonal campaigning prolonged the fighting and loss of life. Ulysses S. Grant's promotion to command of all Federal armies in March 1864 changed this pattern. Grant intended to apply continuous pressure on the two major Confederate armies in Virginia and Georgia in order to wear down their strength and prevent them from taking the strategic offensive into territory already cleared of Rebel troops. The war would be more vigorously pursued, and the losses would be great for the immediate future, but the war would be shortened and fewer lives sacrificed in the long term.[8]

As a result, the campaigns of 1864–65 would be a new and terrible experience for the American soldier. The combination of new weapons, old tactical formations, and massed armies had already made the pitched battles of 1861–63 prohibitively costly. That would not change. Essentially, Grant's strategy would pack several battles the intensity of Gettysburg and Chickamauga into a compressed time span, each one linked by only a few hours or days of maneuvering into new positions while under the guns of an alert and desperate enemy. The war would shift into "overdrive," and the pressures placed on the common soldier would dramatically intensify.

Taking personal charge of the Army of the Potomac, Grant began the new campaign in the first week of May 1864. Robert E. Lee's Army of Northern Virginia struck the Federals in a densely wooded area known as the Wilderness, fifty miles north of the Confederate capital of Richmond, Virginia. The Wilderness was as bloody and indecisive as previous pitched battles had been, but Grant surprised his men by continuing the advance southward instead of retreating northward to recuperate. The Federals cheered as they

8 Ibid., 529–30.

realized they were marching toward, not from, the enemy. They knew the futility of engaging the Rebels in costly battles only to allow them a chance to recover by withdrawing to fight another day.[9]

Those men who cheered their commander on that pleasant day in spring had no idea what Grant's new strategy would mean to them by the hot and humid days of summer. In mid-May, Grant's and Lee's armies met in an even more intense battle at Spotsylvania Courthouse. For fourteen days, soldiers tore at each other in some of the most vicious combat any Americans had ever endured, climaxed by a massed assault on a bulge in the Confederate lines known as the Mule Shoe Salient on May 12. As at the Wilderness, the fighting at Spotsylvania was indecisive and costly. The salient was reduced but the Confederate line held.[10]

Several weeks of maneuvering preceded the next major clash, and it came to symbolize the waste of modern war more than any other battle. Confronted by well-entrenched enemy positions near Cold Harbor, Grant threw men into frontal assaults – 7,000 fell in only thirty minutes. Cold Harbor was an ominous precursor of World War I, with massed frontal attacks against determined men armed with modern weapons and protected by a sophisticated system of trenches. The casualty rate was roughly similar as well.[11]

The early stages of the Petersburg campaign, which began by mid-June, continued the bloody confrontation that had so far failed to break Lee's army. Offered a chance to capture this small town south of Richmond and force the Confederates to evacuate their capital, the Federals suffered a heartbreaking defeat. The troops were physically exhausted and emotionally drained. Subordinate commanders grew timid in the face of desperate Confederate resistance. By the time both armies settled down into a stalemate in the trenches outside Petersburg, Grant had lost 65,000 men in six weeks of fighting, a number equal to Lee's effective strength at the beginning of May. The Confederates had lost about 35,000. All that could be shown for the sacrifice, so far, was a tactical and strategic draw.[12]

The effect of this continuous campaigning on the men of both armies was dramatic. Previous pitched battles had been traumatic experiences, but the rank and file had always had an opportunity to recuperate during the interim periods between confrontations. Now they had no time to rest physically or to recover their spirits. Campaigning in the field was never easy; now it drove the men to the breaking point. Constant marching, digging

---

9 Bruce Catton, *A Stillness at Appomattox* (Garden City, N.Y., 1953), 92.
10 William D. Matter, *If It Takes All Summer: The Battle of Spotsylvania* (Chapel Hill, N.C., 1988), xiii.
11 Frances H. Kennedy, ed., *The Civil War Battlefield Guide* (Boston, 1990), 220.
12 James M. McPherson, *Battle Cry of Freedom: The Civil War Era* (New York, 1988), 742–3.

entrenchments, skirmishing, repelling or launching frontal assaults, hastily burying the dead, and beginning the cycle of combat all over again was the rule for nearly two months without cessation.

"We all look very much like a horse after a weeks hard driving on the shortest kind of rations," wrote Frank Johnson of the 45th Georgia Infantry in late May. More than rest was at stake for some soldiers. "Many a man has gone crazy since this campaign began from the terrible pressure on mind & body," reported Captain Oliver Wendell Holmes Jr. The relentless pressure at Spotsylvania pushed men to an extreme. At the Mule Shoe Salient, two Federal regiments moved up to relieve a third regiment late in the day's fighting.

They took their position along the crest, standing in mud halfway to their knees, with bodies all around them. From there, they fired at the top of the Confederate works until they were numb with fatigue. Some of them sank down into the bloody mud and fell asleep under fire. Their officers, who were just as tired as the men, moved among the prostrate forms, shaking them and shouting at them to resume their places on the firing line. In many cases the officers were exhorting dead men, but they were too numb with exhaustion to know it.[13]

While the armies grappled in Virginia, William Tecumseh Sherman launched his own continuous campaign against Joseph E. Johnston's Army of Tennessee in Georgia. Commanding an army group that outnumbered his opponent by nearly two to one, Sherman aimed to wear down the Confederates and capture the important industrial and transportation center of Atlanta. Sherman proceeded with more caution than Grant, relying on maneuver to pry the entrenched Confederates from one strong defensive position to another, but he did not hesitate to engage the enemy in several pitched battles. Beginning with the engagement at Resaca in mid-May, Sherman's Federals were in almost daily contact with Johnston's Confederates. Large and bloody battles followed at New Hope Church, Pickett's Mill, Dallas, and Kennesaw Mountain before the Confederates gave up northwestern Georgia. Additional conflicts at Peach Tree Creek, the Battle of July 22, Ezra Church, and Jonesboro took place before Atlanta fell on September 2, 1864. After four months of continuous campaigning and the loss of some 23,000 Union and 29,000 Confederate soldiers, the western armies knew the hardships of modern welfare as well as the eastern armies.[14]

---

13   Frank Johnson to Emmie, May 23, 1864, Civil War Letters – Pulliam Gift, Special Collections, University of Georgia; Mark DeWolfe Howe, ed., *Touched With Fire: Civil War Letters and Diary of Oliver Wendell Holmes, Jr., 1861–1864* (Cambridge, Mass., 1946), 149-50; Matter, *If It Takes All Summer*, 257.
14   McPherson, *Battle Cry of Freedom*, 750, 755.

The long campaign wore heavily on the men. Major Stephen Pierson of the 33rd New Jersey Infantry described the experience of his regiment at New Hope Church as the Federals pushed forward through the woods until they could push no more. "But soon through the green of the forest we caught a glimpse of fresh red earth; the strong earthworks were there. Over them we saw leap the skirmish line we had been forcing back, and, the next instant, the storm of shot, shell, shrapnel and minnie burst upon us." As Rebel artillery cut the limbs from the trees, the regiment entrenched with bayonets, hands, and shovels. They remained in this position for a week. The lines were so close to each other that burying the dead was impractical so bodies "lay there and festered" in the hot May sun. A few men cooked rations behind the lines for the rest and, under cover of darkness, brought food forward to those on duty. Companies remained on duty until the men had fired off the sixty rounds of ammunition that had been issued to them when they took their places in the trenches. Like nearly all of Sherman's and Johnston's men, the 33rd New Jersey performed this kind of duty for four months until Atlanta fell.[15]

Continuous campaigning tested Civil War soldiers as they had never been tested before. Physically and psychologically, they were pushed to the limits of their endurance. Yet there was no alternative. This new method of pressuring the enemy was the key to the North's military victory. Given the nature of the Confederacy, its vast geographical space, comparatively poor road system, and the determination of its people, the South could have endured indefinitely as long as Federal armies continued to pull their punches. The Rebels had to be ground down before peace and the Union could be restored.

The practice of continuous campaigning fostered another key feature of modern warfare, the extensive use of earthen field fortifications. Earthworks had been used widely from 1861 through 1863 but primarily to protect fixed assets such as towns, artillery emplacements, and river passages. The nature of pitched battles, which lasted only a few hours or a few days, discouraged the construction of even temporary earthworks in the field — soldiers usually had no time to dig them and lacked the incentive to rely on them if they knew the battle would end soon.

When armies remained in longer contact with each other, both the time and incentive appeared. Living, fighting, even marching within sight of the enemy placed a premium on protection. Soldiers learned to construct earth-

---

15 Stephen Pierson, "From Chattanooga to Atlanta in 1864, "*Proceedings of the New Jersey Historical Society* 16 (1931): 339–40.

works quickly, often doing so while under fire. Henry Dwight of the 20th Ohio Infantry explained this tactical development in an article published in 1864. "Wherever the army moves, either in gaining the enemy's work, or in taking up a new line of attack, the first duty after the halt is to create defensive fortifications. . . . It is now a principle with us to fight with movable breastworks, to save every man by giving him cover, from which he may resist the tremendous attacks in mass of the enemy."[16]

The citizen soldiers of the Civil War became instant experts on military engineering. In both Virginia and Georgia, men learned how to strengthen the basic trench with embellishments. Traverses, embankments accompanied by a trench, were built at an angle to the main trench to prevent the enemy from outflanking it and pouring a destructive fire into the position. In front of the main trench men built elaborate obstructions of tree branches, palisades of sharpened stakes, or even wire entanglements, anything to trip up an attacking enemy. Trench lines were constructed to take full advantage of the lay of the land, even incorporating rocky outcroppings into the trench's parapet for added strength. Often, as at Cold Harbor, elaborate systems of interconnected trenches formed a formidable defense in depth, forcing the enemy to deal not just with one trench line but several lines placed a few yards behind each other. Modern trench warfare, an eerie foreshadowing of World War I, became a fact of military life.[17]

Field fortifications hardened the life of the Civil War soldier. They restricted his already limited view of the enemy and the battlefield. Theodore Lyman, an aide on Gen. George G. Meade's staff, was struck by the fact that nothing showed above the enemy trenches "but the bayonets, and the battle-flags stuck on top of the work." Living in the trenches for any length of time was a trial of discomfort and danger. "We are lying here resting from the fatigues of the ditches," wrote a Rebel staff officer in mid-June, 1864. With the armies stalemated at Petersburg, the constant digging of earthworks turned the area into a dust bowl. "We are still without rain," reported the artillery chief of the Federal Fifth Corps, "and as there has been so much turning up of the dirt, the slightest wind renders the dust intolerable. It fills

---

16   Henry O. Dwight, "How We Fight at Atlanta," *Harper's New Monthly Magazine* 29 (1864): 664.
17   There is no substantial study of field fortifications in the Civil War or the use armies made of them. Two recent authors have briefly discussed this topic: Edward Hagerman, *The American Civil War and the Origins of Modern Warfare: Ideas, Organization, and Field Command* (Bloomington, Ind., 1988), index; Paddy Griffith, *Battle Tactics of the Civil War* (New Haven, Conn., 1989), 123–35. Most of my conception of the significance of field fortifications in the Civil War is derived from reading numerous published and unpublished personal accounts by soldiers and by my examination of trench remains on more than ninety battlefields.

our tents even here at headquarters, where there is but little passing close by, making everything very dirty."[18]

The use of fortifications fixed the lines in close proximity, intensifying the already fierce nature of Civil War combat. Early in the Petersburg campaign, enterprising Federals devised a plan to dig a mine under no-man's land, blow up a Confederate fort, and advance through the gap in the Rebel defenses. On July 30, 1864, the mine exploded, creating a crater thirty feet deep, sixty feet wide, and one hundred seventy feet long. The attacking divisions went in with inadequate preparation and the men were awestruck at the sight of the hole and its horrors. The attack was stalled. "Every organization melted away, as soon as it entered this hole in the ground, into a mass of human beings clinging by toes and heels to the almost perpendicular sides. If a man was shot on the crest he fell and rolled to the bottom of the pit." Men struggled for life within a few yards of enemy guns for many hours, while the crater became a hellhole. Major Charles Houghton of the Fourteenth New York Heavy Artillery described the scene. "The sun was pouring its fiercest heat down upon us and our suffering wounded. No air was stirring within the crater. It was a sickening sight: men were dead and dying all around us; blood was streaming down the sides of the crater to the bottom, where it gathered in pools for a time before being absorbed by the hard red clay." The Rebels held on.[19]

The worst example of how fortifications could turn a very small space into a hell of flying metal and desperate survival occurred on May 12 at Spotsylvania. The Mule Shoe Salient, a large bulge in Lee's lines, became the object of a powerful attack by the Federals. Rain fell, keeping the powder smoke low over the battlefield as the Unionists lodged themselves against the outer slope of the entrenchments while the Rebels clung to the inner slope. The two armies were separated only by an earthen parapet. "Like leeches we stuck to the work," wrote a Federal, "determined by our fire to keep the enemy from rising up." For twenty-three hours, the men fought savagely. "So continuous and heavy was our fire that the headlogs of the breastworks were cut and torn until they resembled hickory brooms." A tree twenty-two inches in diameter was cut down by rifle fire. "The dead and wounded were torn to pieces by the canister as it swept the ground. ... The mud was half-way to our knees, and by our constant movement the dead were almost buried at

---

18 Theodore Lyman, *Meade's Headquarters, 1863–1865: Letters of Colonel Theodore Lyman from the Wilderness to Appomattox*, ed. George R. Agassiz (Boston, 1922), 100–1; Francis Marion Coker to wife, June 17, 1864, Florence Hodgson Heidler Collection, Special Collections, University of Georgia; Charles S. Wainwright, *A Diary of Battle: The Personal Journals of Colonel Charles S. Wainwright, 1861–1865*, ed. Allan Nevins (New York, 1962), 434.

19 Robert Underwood Johnson and Clarence Clough Buel, eds., *Battles and Leaders of the Civil War* (New York, 1956), 4: 551, 562, 663–64.

our feet." Confederates who tried to surrender were shot down by their comrades. When the inconclusive fighting ended, the men were awestruck by the sight of the horribly mangled corpses. One man found the body of an acquaintance that had been so riddled there was no spot on it larger than four square inches which was untouched. Another man had to rely on the color of a beard and the torn pieces of a letter to identify a friend, for the body "no longer resembled a human being but appeared more like a sponge."[20]

In Georgia, the life of the soldier was little different. The constant round of marching, digging, fighting, and maneuvering was less intense and concentrated, but it was elongated in time. In all types of weather and often in sparsely populated areas, Federals and Confederates alike had their endurance tested like it had never been tried before. John W. Geary's division of the Twentieth Corps was in the thick of the action from Resaca to the outskirts of Atlanta. Geary's Yankees took up positions in the valley of Mud Creek, near Kennesaw Mountain, on June 16, 1864. According to Geary, the stream was aptly named.

After dark commenced a series of very severe rainstorms, which lasted, with occasional short intermissions, for several days and nights. Our skirmish pits were filled with water, and the occupants suffered much from cramps. All the troops bivouacked in fields of soft, low ground, and without adequate shelter, suffering much from these rains, which were accompanied by chilly winds. Muddy [sic] Creek and its small tributaries became swollen to the size and power of torrents, and the low ground adjoining, part of which were unavoidably occupied by my troops in line, were flooded with water.[21]

Life for the Confederates was equally exhausting and hazardous. After a month of continuous contact with Sherman's army, the Ninth Kentucky Infantry found its entrenched position within range of Federal skirmish fire. Private Johnny Green recalled how difficult it was to rest. "We could not even stretch our blankets as dog tents but had to just squat in the trenches or behind trees with out blankets wrapped around us & take the rain & catch what sleep we could in this squatting posture." The constant pressure of the Federal fire also prevented Green's comrades from properly recuperating. "We could not show our heads outside the trenches without having a minnie ball come whizzing at us, but the boys would lay around out side notwithstanding." Green saw one man, Tom Wimms, doing just that and told him to take cover. Wimms said, "'I am sleepy for I was out there on picket all last night & I am

20 Ibid., 172–3; Matter, *If It Takes All Summer*, 266–7.
21 *The War of the Rebellion: A Compilation of the Official Records of the Union and Confederate Armies*, ser. 1, vol. 38, pt. 2 (Washington, D.C., 1891), 131.

going to have a good stretched out sleep if they kill me for it." Ten minutes later, Wimms was dead.[22]

Although Sherman generally avoided frontal attacks against trenches, he duplicated the horror of the Mule Shoe Salient on a much smaller scale when he launched an assault on a heavily defended Confederate position at Kennesaw Mountain. The focal point of the worst fighting was an angle in the Rebel works, later named the Dead Angle. Some of the best troops in the Confederate army defended this spot against a massed attack on June 27, 1864. The weather was hot and humid. Confederate soldier Sam Watkins of the First Tennessee Infantry recalled "a solid line of blazing fire right from the muzzles of the Yankee guns being poured right into our very faces, singeing our hair and clothes, the hot blood of our dead and wounded spurting on us, the blinding smoke and stifling atmosphere filling our eyes and mouths, and the awful concussion causing the blood to gush out of our noses and ears. ..." The Federals were stopped, but only after hand-to-hand fighting across the parapet. Watkins looked around and "never saw so many broken down and exhausted men in my life. I was as sick as a horse, and as wet with blood and sweat as I could be, and many of our men were vomiting with excessive fatigue, over-exhaustion, and sunstroke; our tongues were parched and cracked for water, and our faces blackened with powder and smoke, and our dead and wounded were piled indiscriminately in the trenches."[23]

For all the horror, discomfort, and disease in the trenches, field fortifications made continuous campaigning possible. Only by digging in could the armies maintain close contact for long periods of time. In addition, living in the trenches itself had a debilitating effect on the Confederates, who were chronically short of men and supplies. During the latter stages of the Petersburg campaign, which lasted eleven months, Lee's army suffered a desertion rate as high as eight percent per month. Pinned to the cold, bare earth with inadequate food and outnumbered by their opponents, the Army of Northern Virginia suffered an attrition rate between battles that foreshadowed the slow hemorrhage that World War I armies commonly endured between offensives. Modern warfare had fostered a depressingly effective weapon.[24]

When the fighting ended, most soldiers realized that they had experienced something unprecedented not only in their individual lives but in the collective life of the nation. What they made of that experience was laden with meaning for the future of American culture, for wars never end when the

22 John Williams Green, *Johnny Green of the Orphan Brigade: The Journal of a Confederate Soldier*, ed. Albert D. Kirwan (Lexington, Ky., 1956), 134–5, 138.
23 Sam R. Watkins, "Co. Aytch" (New York, 1962) 158, 160.
24 James M. McPherson, *Ordeal by Fire: The Civil War and Reconstruction* (New York, 1982), 468.

fighting stops. They have to be refought, reimagined, and reinvented if need be, or they lose their meaning. How soldiers did this and what they concluded at the end of this process was very important in shaping the role of the Civil War in the American consciousness.

Most veterans continued to believe in the ideals that impelled them to fight, yet a small minority could not sustain that belief. These men, who foreshadowed the Lost Generation of half a century later, have become overly prominent in the historiography because they were superb writers and they represented a highly modern attitude toward war and its effects on the mind. Twentieth-century historians can hardly be faulted for taking to soldier-writers like Ambrose Bierce, for he wrote with a clarity, an irony, and a deep cynicism that came into vogue as a meaningful way to interpret modern war in the twentieth century. Bierce's view was echoed by other veterans, such as Abner Small, who saw nothing ennobling in their war experiences. For them, the conflict had wasted lives, replaced innocence with empty suffering, and ruined the future of its victims. "He resented it all," wrote Small of the common soldier, "and at times his resentment grew into a hatred for those who formed the whirlpool of war. ... He might have the courage of his convictions, yet behind his bravery there lay something that mystified and repelled him. He didn't know what it was, so inevitably he went to find out. I don't know that he ever got an answer. I didn't."[25]

The overwhelming majority of soldiers who wrote about the war did not share the sentiments of Bierce or Small. Many did not attempt to assess in any major way the impact of the war on the ideology or psychology of its participants, preferring to recount amusing incidents, exciting adventures, or glorious feats. They often acknowledged the horror of combat, but seldom dwelled on its significance. Most soldier-authors included an acknowledgment that the suffering was worth the sacrifice, even though it often was done in a perfunctory, even obligatory fashion.[26]

These men had an opportunity to bear testimony to war's waste, as Bierce and Small had done, but they refused to do so. A recent author has characterized this refusal as a sell-out; he believed it was a denial of the true nature of war and its effect on the minds of its participants. Society demanded that its collective sacrifice in the conflict be worth something, and the only way this could be accomplished was by ignoring the waste of war and inventing a cause

---

25 See Ambrose Bierce's "Bits of Autobiography" and his many fictional stories about the war in *The Collected Works of Ambrose Bierce* (New York, 1909), vols. 1 and 2; Abner Small, *The Road to Richmond* (Berkeley, Calif., 1939), 194–5.

26 See, e.g., Charles Mackenzie, "The Great American Civil War," *War Sketches and Incidents as Related by Companions of the Iowa Commandery* (Des Moines, I., 1893), 1:359–60, and Jacob C. Switzer, "Reminiscences of Jacob C. Switzer of the 22nd Iowa," in Mildred Throne, ed., *Iowa Journal of History* 56, no. 1 (Jan. 1958): 75–6.

or result that would justify the carnage. This is an overtly modern reading of soldier memoirs that gives little credit to the ideological sincerity of those men who risked their lives and survived America's greatest conflict. Rather than a denial of war's reality, the mass of soldier-authors presented a great, often muted, testimonial to the power of faith over reality. By continuing to assert that worthy ends had resulted from the war, they continued to meet the challenge that combat had offered to their motivations for engaging in war, and they continued to triumph over that challenge. They did not deny the reality of war but continued to assert their ability to deal with it.[27]

These veterans expressed their sentiments in a variety of literary styles, ranging from a romantic or sentimental voice borrowed from fiction to a remarkably direct, often stoic style. William Camm, a twenty-five-year-old English immigrant, first realized the horror of modern warfare at Shiloh. As the lieutenant colonel of the 14th Illinois Infantry, Camm confronted the worst reality of combat but had not time to ponder its meaning until the fighting ended on the evening of the first day. "Now, we had time to think. … Everything seemed very unpleasant but very real, and very far from exciting or romantic. We had been whipped; all our camp and stores were in the hands of the enemy, but Moore's lines came to me:

> Night closed around the conqueror's way,
> But lightnings show'd the distant hill,
> Where those who lost that dreadful day
> Stood few and faint but fearless still,
> The soldier's hope, the Patriot's zeal,
> Forever dimm'd, forever crost –
> O! who can say what hero's feel,
> When all but life and honour's lost?"

As he penned this entry in his journal that night of April 6, 1862, Camm found great comfort in countering his horror of combat with romantic poetry. Years later, after he had plenty of time to rethink his war experience, he still used the same method. Camm inserted another romantic, even jingoistic, bit of doggerel into his April 1862 entries:

> By the fields thy sons left gory,
> Make the past thy future story,
> On and on to greater glory,
> Hail, Illinois.[28]

27 Gerald F. Linderman, *Embattled Courage: The Experience of Combat in the American Civil War* (New York, 1987), 275–97.

28 William Camm, "Diary of Colonel William Camm, 1861 to 1865," *Journal of the Illinois State Historical Society* 18 (Jan. 1926): 853, 864.

Years after the war, Ira Seymour Dodd of the Twenty-sixth New Jersey Infantry wrote a series of articles about his war experiences. Adopting a clear, direct, and highly expressive style, sanitized of romantic or sentimental elements, Dodd did not hesitate to describe combat in its true light. He recalled battle scenes at Chancellorsville: the shower of gravel kicked up at his feet by a Confederate sharpshooter's bullet; the sound made by a volley of rifle fire ("Like the pattering roar of rain after thunder"); the voice inflections of retreating men as they told his regiment how the battle progressed ("they said it in a tone of tired reproach, as though you ought to know and had insulted them by asking"). Dodd remembered the sight of these soldiers. "Here a man holding up his hand, across which a bullet has ploughed a bloody track; there one with a ragged hole though his cheek; and then an officer leaning on two other men, both wounded, the ashy hue of death on his face and the blood streaming from his breast." Each one wore a "fixed expression, not of terror, but of stony despair." Dodd dwelled on the haunting idea that the youngest, most promising men of his society fell in battle. In fact, he intimately described such a man in an essay entitled "One Young Soldier." But, in another essay entitled "Sacrifices," Dodd movingly described the death of this ideal Northerner and resoundingly affirmed the value of his loss. For Dodd, the goals of the conflict were worth the human cost.[29]

Overall, the soldiers of the Civil War struggled to hold on to traditional attitudes toward war although they were faced with a new style of warfare. Continuous campaigning and trench warfare would so dominate tactics in World War I that twentieth-century soldiers would find it nearly impossible to view armed conflict as an acceptable solution to political problems. Civil War veterans had the luxury of refighting, in their old age, a "good" war.

Although their conflict was not fully like the war of the future, Civil War combatants sometimes described their experiences in images that were surprisingly modern. Living, working, and dying in trenches only a few yards from the enemy imposed an awful tyranny on the lives of men who were born to till the soil or turn a lathe rather than kill other Americans.

Young William Ketcham sensed this tyranny and expressed it in his memoirs. Barely seventeen years old when he joined the Thirteenth Indiana Infantry in 1864, Ketcham served for extended periods of time in the earthworks of the Army of the James near Petersburg, Virginia. The lines were so close to the enemy that a sudden rush could be made that might breach the Federal position. "As the result, every morning before the cold gray dawn

---

29   Ira Seymour Dodd, "The Song of the Rappahannock," *McClure's Magazine* 8 (1896–97): 314–20; Ira Seymour Dodd, *The Song of the Rappahannock: Sketches of the Civil War* (New York, 1898), 165–201, 208, 253.

began to think of breaking, we were invariably drawn in line at the works with everything ready to resist an attack and there stood until the broken day would give us full warning of any movement." Fifty years later, many soldiers would mechanically follow the same routine as they tried to survive the trenches of France.[30]

In the war's other major theater, Col. John Charles Black of the Thirty-seventh Illinois Infantry participated in one of the last infantry assaults of the conflict. A Federal army invested Mobile, Alabama, and began to dig its way across no-man's land toward the well-fortified but outnumbered Confederates. On the evening of April 9, 1865, the very day that Lee surrendered to Grant in Virginia, the Federals suddenly jumped out of their trenches and rushed toward the Rebel positions. "I was in front of the center of the Regt. and springing to the top of the parapet cast one glance around. For a mile on either side the earth seemed giving birth to men as they leaped up from the works, and cheering shouting raging swept on like in color force & effect to a blue ocean wave." The attack succeeded, but the kind of warfare that could elicit such a striking image in the mind of an Illinois colonel was the same kind of war making that would warp the consciousness of thousands of future soldiers as they repeatedly "went over the top" in futile attacks across no-man's land.[31]

The reality of warfare in the Civil War created a tension between faith and despair among soldiers, a tension that most of them were able to subdue. It would be the last time that the participants of a major, modern war would be able to do so.

---

30   William A. Ketcham, "Reminiscence," 22, Indiana Historical Society.
31   John Charles Black to Mary, April 12, 1865, Black papers, Illinois State Historical Library.

23

Daily Life at the Front and the Concept of Total War

THOMAS ROHKRÄMER

Until recently, German military history has largely ignored the daily lot of the common soldier. Whereas historians have generally concentrated on grand strategy, decision-making processes, and a few highly influential persons, the vast majority involved in the war effort have been subsumed under the label "unknown soldier" – not important enough to be studied in closer detail as individuals.[1] The argument that the hardship, brutality, and anxiety of daily life at the front is incomprehensible to the outsider, although ostensibly a sympathetic one, was usually no more than a pretext to avoid widely available sources: Most soldiers described the reality of war in letters; most veterans talked about this exceptional part of their lives and communicated their experiences and reflections; and many tried to come to terms with it by writing memoirs and novels. These documents teach a lot about the experience of war, its suffering and destructiveness, monotony and boredom, cruelty and pain, but also its comradeship, adventure, and excitement. Studying the anthropological dimension of wars reveals their inhumanity as well as the psychological dispositions that are necessary for wars to take place.[2]

To study the attitude, behavior and beliefs of soldiers of all ranks is of particular importance when talking about the concept of total war. Some

---

1   Wolfram Wette, "Militärgeschichte von unten," in Wette, ed., *Der Krieg des kleinen Mannes: Eine Militärgeschichte von unten* (Munich, 1992), 10–23.

2   My reconstruction of the war experience draws on autobiographical memoirs of common soldiers, which were published in magazines of veterans' organizations and as books. Some of them were written by members of the educated middle class, others by common people. As both social groups describe their war experience in very similar terms, I will not distinguish between them.

Obviously, it is problematic to reconstruct the reality of war by using sources that were mostly published many years later in order to keep up the nationalistic enthusiasm of the war period. But more intermediate sources have disadvantages, as well. Letters are not objective, because they are usually censored and often try to set the minds of friends and family at rest. Diaries tend to be very brief and matter-of-fact, as the war does not leave time for reflections.

Under these difficult conditions, it seems unavoidable to draw on all available sources and compare the results based on the different source material. From what one can say at this preliminary point, the similarities of the results are more striking than the differences.

features of total war can, of course, be studied using a purely systemic approach, one that focuses on macro-historical structures and processes. Modern transportation has made it possible to mobilize huge masses of people, concentrate them in one place, and supply them with food and weapons; modern means of communications have made it possible to deploy and direct them. As a result, technological developments have gained a central influence in modern warfare, and economic factors have become decisive. Weapons of mass destruction have made it impossible to distinguish between combatants and noncombatants. In modern wars, the whole of society, civil and military, is mobilized to support the war effort, and, likewise, the whole of society is threatened by the enemy's weapons. Traditional "restraints imposed by custom, law, and morality" on military means, such as the protection of noncombatants, tend to lose their meaning in the age of industrial and technological warfare.[3]

This systemic view highlights two elements of total war: the "militarization of the whole of society, politics and economy as a means of warfare,"[4] and the increasingly destructive potential of modern weapons, which has reached its peak in the age of atomic bombs.[5] From this perspective, one can perceive a gradual totalization of warfare, which corresponds with the process of industrialization.

But any definition of total war is incomplete without taking into account more subjective factors such as the intensity of the war effort, the population's preparedness for extreme sacrifices as well as extreme military measures, and a rigid binary way of thinking, which glorifies one's own nation and condemns the enemy or other. All the means of total war – total war effort, guerrilla warfare, mass destruction, and extermination – can only be justified by demonizing the enemy, the leaders as well as the common people. These attitudes and beliefs associated with total war, which only came into view with the growing interest in the war experience, do not seem to follow a clear developmental pattern. This not only questions our belief in a "road to total war," it also demands a new reflection on the term *total war* itself.

In this chapter, I first look at the daily life at the front during the Franco-Prussian War, concentrating on those aspects of the war experience that are

3 James Turner Johnson, *Just War Tradition and the Restraint of War: A Moral and Historical Inquiry* (Princeton, N.J., 1981), 229.
4 Michael Geyer, "Der zur Organisation erhobene Burgfrieden," in Klaus-Jürgen Müller et al., eds., *Militär und Militarismus in der Weimarer Republik* (Düsseldorf, 1978), 26.
5 Edward P. Thompson, "Notes on Exterminism, the Last Stage of Civilisation," in Thompson et al., eds., *Exterminism and Cold War* (London, 1982).

most closely related to the concept of total war.[6] This war provides a good example for the tendencies toward totalization inherent in modern wars, since it started as a limited war led by authoritarian governments but gained its own momentum and developed into a *guerre à outrance*. Next I show in what way the two apparently disparate aspects of total war, the collective will to fight without any restraints and the industrial means for total mobilization and destruction, are actually interrelated. This suggests a new understanding of the concept of total war.

Since universal conscription was introduced at the beginning of the 1860s, the German Wars of Unification for the first time mobilized a large percentage of the German population. Whereas the wars against Denmark and Austria did not meet with any national enthusiasm – the population remained unconvinced by the reasons for the war – the news about the war against France met with varied reactions. Draftees from traditional areas and occupations, such as farmers, regarded the war with little enthusiasm. They took part in the fighting only because they had to. Married men adopted a similar attitude, tending to worry more about their families than about the nation. In contrast, younger members of the middle classes and professional soldiers greeted the war with enthusiasm. In particular, students from grammar schools and universities, traditionally a very nationalistic group, often joined the army voluntarily. The wish to prove their manliness in a great national event was mixed with anti-French sentiments.[7] France was widely seen as the eternal troublemaker, and the war as a legitimate defense against outside aggression. This reached its peak when the troops were on their way to the front, and national enthusiasm inflamed the whole army. It was clear from the outset that the attitude toward the war against France was different than that toward the two previous wars against Denmark and Austria. Although there was very little explicit hatred and chauvinism, many common soldiers felt that it was high time to "teach France a lesson."

Although many soldiers had prejudices against France and the French, the war was limited until the battle of Sedan on September 2, 1870. In this period, there was very little personal bitterness, anger, or brutality. Although excesses did occur in the heat of the battle, the opponents in principal

6 For a wider discussion of the daily life at the front, and more detailed references to primary and secondary sources, see Thomas Rohrkrämer, *Der Militarismus der "kleinen Leute": Die Kriegervereine im Deutschen Kaiserreich, 1871–1914* (Munich, 1990).
7 "Wie in den Jahren der Knechtschaft und der Erhebung Preussens gegen das Joch des französischen Unterdrückers Napoléon I. wurden auch diesmal die Universitäten die Herde der glühensten Begeisterung und des freudigsten Opfermutes." Karl Mewes, *Leiden und Freuden eines kriegsfreiwilligen Hallenser Studenten vom Regiment Nr. 86 in den Kriegsjahren, 1870–71* (Magdeburg and Leipzig, 1898), 12.

recognized the validity of the traditional *ius in bello* as defined in the "just war" tradition. Of course, the common soldiers were not aware of the long tradition of attempts to distinguish between justified and unjustified reasons for a war and to limit the amount of violence and hatred against the opponent, which has its origin in medieval Christianity and the knightly codex. This idea found a new basis in the concept of "natural law" in the Renaissance, and was expressed in modern legal terms in the Hague LandWarfare Convention.[8] Nevertheless, the common soldier's belief in the immunity of noncombatants, their attempt to avoid unnecessary violence against the French soldiers, and their fair treatment of prisoners of war closely corresponded with the traditional *ius in bello*. Cruelty and aggression were to be found in intense moments of battle, and ruthlessness against civilians was to be expected in any war. But the common soldiers had a clear understanding of "right" and "wrong," which was in accordance with the "just war" tradition.[9]

For the German army, whose campaign was marked by exceptional success, there was very little temptation to intensify warfare and violate the traditional *ius in bello*. Most soldiers came to expect the quick victories that they had experienced in the two previous wars of unification and expected to be home by Christmas. Central food supplies were sufficient, and the army did not have to live off the land.

With the spectacular victory at Sedan (September 2, 1870), when the major part of the French regular army capitulated and Emperor Napoléon III was taken captive, a traditional limited war led by an authoritarian government, a *Kabinettskrieg* or cabinet war, would have ended and been followed by a moderate peace. But in the age of industry, "mass participation, citizenship and nationalist fervour,"[10] Germany wanted to weaken its opponent permanently and was not interested in a moderate peace, whereas France did not acknowledge defeat at this point. Instead, the new republican government mobilized a national guard, which grouped itself around the remnants of the regular army and urged the population to participate in the fighting as franc-tireurs.

After Sedan, part of the German army lay siege to the French capital, Paris, and to the town of Metz, into which the army of Marshall Bazaine had fled. Other troops, under their commanders Tann and Edwin von Manteuffel, pushed deep into the south of France as far as Orléans. They tried to establish

8 Johnson, *Just War*, 121–89; Carl Schmitt, *Theorie des Partisanen: Zwischenbemerkung zum Begriff des Politischen* (Berlin, 1963), 28.
9 Michael Fellman and Mark E. Neely Jr. use the terms *honor* and *Victorian* values to describe the same inhibitions among soldiers in the American Civil War. I prefer my terminology, because it calls attention to the striking correspondence between the just war tradition and the moral values of common soldiers.
10 Martin Shaw, *Dialectics of War: An Essay in the Social Theory of Total War and Peace* (London, 1988), 29.

control over all strategically important points in order to be able to attack newly emerging French troops while they were still weak. Apart from a few major battles, the Germans pursued the French troops in long and tiring marches, which were frequently interrupted by small military encounters.

The German sieges of French towns tried the patience of the German soldiers. The besiegers had to be continually alert, even though nothing much ever happened. The living conditions were dreadful. During the siege of Metz, the weather was bad, and the homemade wooden huts proved to be poor shelter. Once uniforms got wet, there was no chance of them ever drying out.

It is hardly possible to give a true picture of the hardship. The dear reader has certainly been wet to the skin before, maybe he even did not get out of his wet clothes for 24 hours, but then he was able to dry himself and put on dry things. But just imagine ten nights and ten days in this condition in constant cold rain without any protection, in fields, up to your ankles in water.[11]

Under these circumstances, it is not surprising that the health of the troops deteriorated; they suffered from colds, diarrhea, typhoid fever, and dysentery.

The soldiers hated outpost duty in particular. They had to stand alert in the open, under the constant strain of knowing that something might happen. Furthermore, French rifles had a longer range than the ones used by the Germans. Thus, until the Germans started to use weapons captured from the enemy, there was no possibility of returning fire and inflicting damage.

When the first starving civilians tried to leave town, a conflict arose for the soldiers on outpost duty. On the one hand, it was in the interests of the besieger to keep the population inside so that food reserves would be used up faster. On the other hand, this meant a violation of a just war's fundamental principle of conducting war only against the opponent's army, not against civilians. In the Middle Ages, noncombatants were usually allowed to leave town, but in modern times, besiegers often violated this custom, until it finally became an extreme but legitimate measure to keep the whole of the population inside the town.[12]

In most cases, the German soldiers allowed French civilians to pass through guard posts and scavenge for potatoes in the field. The soldiers often gave food to civilians who begged. It is true that some soldiers occasionally displayed their power by frightening and chasing away the civilians with warning shots, and in rare cases even aimed at them, but usually they left them in peace. It was only when the army command ordered that there was to be no

---

11 Günther Boschen, *Kriegserinnerungen eines Einundneunzigers, 1870–71* (Oldenbourg, 1897), 59.
12 Michael Walzer, *Just and Unjust Wars: A Moral Argument With Historical Illustrations* (London, 1977), 166.

contact with the inhabitants of the town, who were to be kept inside by whatever means, that all this changed. The soldiers accepted the military logic of the command, although they obeyed reluctantly and with a bad conscience.[13]

The same ambivalence and compassion is apparent in reports of the capitulation of the city. Although the soldiers rejoiced in their victory, most felt guilty when they saw the famished and emaciated civilians, and they handed out food to them. They did not criticize the course of action that the German command had taken but were horrified by its consequences.

The sieges in the Franco-Prussian War raised a new moral problem. Traditionally, the besieger bombarded fortifications in his attempt to gain a breach for an attack, but with the longer range of cannons, it became possible to bombard the town and thus strike at the defenders through the morale of the civilians. Both the French and the Germans showed little inhibition in bombing the opponent's towns, although this method of fighting, which became an accepted one in the twentieth century, clearly violated the just war's principle of noncombatant immunity.[14]

As to the question of bombing towns, the ranks had as few moral scruples as their leaders. In the case of Paris, the siege had gone on for about three months. The German troops had been mainly inactive, suffering from the tedious routine of daily drill and all around boredom. Worse, they had to endure the heavy cannons of the French, which continually threatened their lives, without any means of fighting back. Under these circumstances, it is not surprising that they greeted the bombardment of the city, which began on January 5, 1871, with universal rejoicing.

Now I will tell of the weeks, which stand out from the suffering we had experienced in winter, from all the hardship, which has taken such a lot of space in the narration (I am afraid probably too much space for the taste of the readers, but – as my comrades will agree – much shorter than in reality). Everybody involved will forever remember the three weeks of the bombardment of Paris. ... With us the first gunshot brought a great change. It raised our spirits by a hundred percent. From now on, it was no longer them only shooting at us, now it also went the other way. The German guns had a noble sound by which you could tell their tremendous effect.[15]

After Paris capitulated, it was agreed that the German troops should not occupy the capital but only celebrate their victory with a triumphant pro-

13 Karl Geyer, *Erlebnisse eines württembergischen Feldsoldaten im Kriege gegen Frankreich und im Lazarett zu Paris, 1870–71* (Munich, 1890), 96. See also Michael Howard, *The Franco-Prussian War: The German Invasion of France, 1870–1871* (London, 1962), 280.

14 Howard, *Franco-Prussian War*, 274.

15 Oskar Leibig, *Erlebnisse eines freiwilligen bayerischen Jägers im Feldzuge 1870–71* (Munich, 1905), 206, 208.

cession through the city. This very limited demonstration of victory not only failed to satisfy the emperor and the military commanders but also the ranks, who would have preferred a more clamorous way to demonstrate and celebrate their victory. They wanted to triumph over their enemies and did not consider the ill feelings that it might arouse.

While parts of the German troops were engaged in the sieges, others marched further south to continue the fight against the *guarde civile* (citizens' militia). In the early months of the war, many soldiers had looked forward to combat to prove their fighting strength and manliness, but by then, most of them showed clear signs of war-weariness. The prospect of finishing a war that had already been won did not fill them with enthusiasm. National euphoria had evaporated, and most soldiers felt that they had done their share. Why should they look forward to fighting again, when they had already proved their courage in the first combats?[16] As many reports from different wars clearly show, soldiers do not get used to the dangers of war. On the contrary, the longer they are in combat, the more they understand the dangers involved and the weaker their nerves become. "War must rely on the young, for only they have the two things fighting requires: physical stamina and innocence about their own mortality. ... Knowledge will come after a few months, and then they'll be used up and as soldiers virtually useless – scared, cynical, debilitated, unwilling."[17]

In addition, living conditions were dreadful. Winter was approaching and the temperature dropped, and shoes and uniforms were gradually wearing out. The soldiers had to replace pieces of their own uniforms with what clothes they could get from civilians. The troops must have been quite a picturesque sight, one unit wearing uniforms repaired with materials of all colors and French nightcaps over their helmets.[18]

Since the national guard and the franc-tireurs tried to avoid major battles with the superiorly equipped enemy, the second part of the war mainly consisted of endless marches through the rain and snow.

When we started to move our legs in the morning to continue the march, most of us probably thought: today I won't make it, this is the last day, the machine is going to stop. At noon one thought, just another hour, then all my strength is certainly gone. Afternoon approaches and the mechanical movement of the legs still continues. Evening arrives, and still the tired body drags along. ... Certainly, quite a few

16 Boschen, *Kriegserinnerungen*, 33; Otto Kopelke, *Kriegserlebnisse eines Veteranen von, 1870–71* (Berlin, 1902), 63. See also Hans Meier-Welcker, "Der Kampf mit der Republik," in Wolfgang von Groote and Ursula von Gersdorff, eds., *Entscheidung 1870: Der deutsch-französische Krieg* (Stuttgart, 1970), 128.
17 Paul Fussell, *Wartime: Understanding and Behaviour in the Second World War* (Oxford, 1989), 52.
18 Hermann Tiemann, *Vor fünfundzwanzig Jahren: Feldzugserinnerungen eines Kriegsfreiwilligen* (Braunschweig, 1895), 68–9.

strong men had to pay with their lives. It often happened that healthy and fit persons just collapsed while marching and were dead.[19]

Routine, obedience, and willpower kept the ranks marching on, and sometimes simply the fear of being left behind. When the train was unable to follow the troops and give exhausted soldiers a lift, soldiers were left at the side of the road, exposed to the danger, since they feared falling into the hands of the franc-tireurs and being killed.

The cold weather made it impossible to sleep outside. The soldiers therefore had to take up quarters in French homes, coming into close contact with the population for the first time. Many soldiers, for whom it was the first experience of staying in a foreign country, reacted aggressively to the problems of communication. Misunderstandings were often interpreted as passive resistance, which had to be overcome by violence. For the soldiers who were able to speak French, contact with the population was more relaxed. Although there were a few well-educated soldiers who expressed strong prejudices against the French, most of them lived in harmony with the population and praised their friendly and helpful manner. When soldiers stayed in the same quarters for a long period of time, the close contact could even overcome previous prejudices. At one point, an author recounts the story of a friendship that developed during the war and lasted for many years afterward.[20] Such strong ties were rare, of course. But outright hatred of the enemy in toto – a feature that is commonly associated with total war – was equally exceptional.

The centralized food supply of the German army had worked well during the summer, and looting had been strictly prohibited. But in winter, the system collapsed, and every unit had to organize its own food through requisitions.[21]

In general, we…were not as good-hearted as we used to be. At first, when the French complained that they hadn't enough food, we just took money out of our pockets and paid them, a method they understood and liked a lot. … But this stopped completely. Food was just requisitioned, if necessary by force. The French had to feed us, if we did not get any supplies from the army. Until then we were victorious.[22]

19 Ernst Esch, *Erlebnisse eines Einjährig-Freiwilligen des VII. (rheinisch-westfälischen) Corps im Feldzug 1870–71* (Munich, 1898), 102.

20 Heinrich Schmitthenner, *Erlebnisse eines freiwilligen badischen Grenadiers im Feldzuge 1870–71* (Karlsruhe, 1891), 26.

21 One author reckons that the central supply broke down after the siege of Metz. Ernst Stier, *Unter Prinz Friedrich Karl: Erlebnisse eines Musketiers vom X. Armeekorps im Feldzug, 1870–71* (Munich, 1883), 125ff.

22 Julius Hüggelmeyer, *Im Feldzuge 1870–71: Feldzugserinnerungen und Selbsterlebtes eines Einjährig-Freiwilligen des I. Hannoverschen Dragoner-Regiments Nr. 9* (Hanover and Leipzig, 1909), 160.

When the troops were quartered in houses that had been abandoned by their owners, they often devastated them by looting all the food supplies, by burning the furniture, and occasionally by outright vandalism. They cared little for lodgings that they planned to leave the following day. A lot of damage was also inflicted when different military units were stationed in the same village. Each soldier strove to meet his own needs for as long as supplies lasted, not caring about economical usage. When the French "host" supplied the soldiers with enough food "voluntarily," he was usually spared the rest of his possessions. Civilians did not have enough food in store to provide for the exceptional circumstances of a war. They therefore began to hide their provisions, while the Germans tried to find food through violence and cunning. Even if the soldiers took pity on the population, it did not solve the inevitable conflict caused by scarce food supplies.

Although I honestly tried to spare poor people, it was not always possible. Often I had to witness dreadful scenes, when families had to sacrifice their only or last cow. The receipts we handed out did not console at all. Crying women and children begged for mercy so that I felt like an avenging angel. But what could I do? Our good soldiers should not suffer deprivation.[23]

Some soldiers felt pity for the French population and refused to confiscate their last provisions. For many, however, it was much more convenient to assume that the French had enough provisions and were simply denying the soldiers access to them.

"The inhabitants do not have a single drop of wine, no piece of bread," one soldier tells the others. "Just wait, Froggy, then we will get twice the amount ourselves!" And without mercy the village was devastated. The more the soldiers got drunk, the wilder the witches' sabbath became. ... The havoc I saw was beyond description.[24]

In retrospect, many soldiers described the requisitions as a sporting competition in which French and Germans tried to outwit each other. When cunning did not help, threats and torture were used until hiding places were disclosed. Some soldiers even enjoyed their power over civilians and played cruel "jokes."

It cannot be denied that cruelty and unnecessary violence did occur. If a mob of soldiers forces an old woman under threat of instant death to drink oil from a jug after which she was ill for months, this is a cruelty for which one can hardly find an excuse.

23 Franz v. Wantoch-Rekowski, *Kriegstagebuch 1870–71 des jüngsten Offiziers im Königs-Grenadier-Regiment* (Munich, 1914), 523.
24 Karl Zeitz, *Kriegserinnerungen eines Kriegsfreiwilligen aus den Jahren 1870–71* (Altenburg, 1893), 119–20.

And if an old and honourable gentleman is forced with guns and sabers to drink the first sip of each bottle of wine he hands out to the mob, until he loses his balance and senses, this is a heartless procedure, which nobody can accept.[25]

Whereas the French population mainly suffered under the requisitions, the Germans' hatred focused on the groups of franc-tireurs, formed after the capitulation of the regular army out of men who wanted to join the fight without being identified as soldiers. Although their numbers remained small, they terrified the German soldiers with surprise assaults and ambushes, after which they would again go into hiding among the noncombatant population. They also killed a few wounded and lost soldiers. Some franc-tireurs probably took up weapons spontaneously to defend their country or to take revenge for damage inflicted by the German troops, but the new authorities also officially encouraged the population to start a partisan war. Léon Gambetta, one of the new military leaders, stated:

> We must set all our resources to work – and they are immense. We must shake the countryside from its torpor, guard against stupid panic, increase partisan warfare and, against an enemy so skilled in ambush and surprise, ourselves employ ruses, harass his flanks, surprise his rear – in short inaugurate a national war.[26]

And the prefect of Côte d'Or proclaimed guerrilla warfare by posting the following bill in his department:

> Your fatherland does not ask you to gather in large numbers and oppose the enemy openly; it only expects that each morning three or four resolute men will leave their village and go to where nature has prepared a place suitable for hiding and for firing on the Prussians without danger.[27]

Karl Marx, who never believed in the possibility of limiting a war, mocked the storm of indignation among the Germans by saying: "It is a real Prussian idea that a nation commits a crime when it continues to defend itself after its regular army has lost."[28]

The whole situation contains a certain irony when one remembers that Prussia tried to employ exactly the same means in its wars against Napoléon.[29] On a deeper level, however, partisan war raises an objective dilemma.

---

25 Karl Klein, *Fröschweiler Chronik: Kriegs- und Friedensbilder aus dem Jahre 1870* (Munich, 1896), 130–1. But the French author admits that such incidents were rare.

26 Quoted in Howard, *Franco-Prussian War*, 62.

27 Quoted in Geoffrey Best, *Humanity in Warfare: The Modern History of the International Law of Armed Conflicts* (London, 1980), 198.

28 Karl Marx, "Brief an Ludwig Kugelmann in Hannover," Dec. 13, 1870, in Karl Marx and Friedrich Engels, *Marx-Engels-Werke*, ed. Institut für Marxismus-Leninismus beim ZK der SED, 39 vols. (Berlin, 1956–1989), 33:163.

29 Gerhard Ritter, *Staatskunst und Kriegshandwerk: Das Problem des "Militärismus" in Deutschland*, 4 vols. (Munich, 1965), 1 : 100.

Although it is understandable that a patriot will defend his country by all means without regard for war conventions, one cannot expect soldiers to respect the immunity of the population if they are attacked "deviously, without warning and in disguise. ... Soldiers must feel safe among civilians if civilians are ever to be safe from soldiers."[30] The problem of distinguishing between combatants and noncombatants in a partisan war turns the entire population into potential enemies. Thus, measures against guerrillas tended to inflict harm on the population as a whole, mostly noncombatants.

A journalist from a neutral country, Edward Hamley, described the way in which the Germans conducted war as "horrible": The requisitions were "nothing but a system of organized plunder," their way of fighting the franc-tireurs was a "system of terrorism," which compelled the French, "through fear of instant and tremendous penalties, not only to refrain from acts of hostility, but to aid in protecting their oppressors by betraying the enterprises of their own country men."[31] But is this view a balanced one?

As far as official policy was concerned, the Germans soon adhered to the generally accepted war conventions.[32] It is true that in the beginning they viewed all irregular soldiers as criminals, but on August 31, they officially accepted as soldiers all troops that would be distinguished from civilians. Only franc-tireurs were still regarded as murderers and treated accordingly.[33] In reality, however, not only were there cases of overreaction, but there were also generals who, as a common practice, shot all captured soldiers lacking military identification.[34]

Whereas the troops usually accepted the French soldiers as equals, hardly any of them even tried to understand the motives of the franc-tireurs.[35] Most common soldiers regarded them as cut-throats and treated them harshly. The continual fear of hidden, unavoidable dangers wore the soldiers down and filled them with hatred and rage. That the danger of dying in an open battle was still much greater did not alter this violent reaction against the invisible enemy.

The soldier is not angry about the enemy in open battle. He knows that the opponent is just fulfilling his duty when he tries to wound or kill. But he gets enraged when people, who pretend to be peaceful citizens and expect security from the

---

30 Walzer, *Just and Unjust Wars*, 182.   31 *The Times* on Feb. 22, 1871.

32 Admittedly, they are not very satisfying in regard to partisan warfare.

33 Fernand Thiébaut, "Der Krieg in französischer Sicht," in Groote and Gersdorff, eds., *Entscheidung, 1870*, 165ff, 192–5; Howard, *Franco-Prussian War*, 251.

34 Best, *Humanity in Warfare*, 199; Howard, *Franco-Prussian War*, 208, 378–81; Thiébaut, *Krieg*, 195.

35 In only two memoirs was an understanding expressed that the distinction between a terrorist and a freedom fighter might depend on one's own point of view. *Parole: Deutsche Kriegerzeitung*, no. 43 (Oct. 21, 1892), 736; Edmund Pfleiderer, *Erinnerungen und Erfahrungen eines Feldgeistlichen aus dem Kriege des Jahres, 1870–71* (Stuttgart, 1874), 89.

soldiers, suddenly attack him. – This was not a war any more, it was dreadful murder, in particular for patrols. There was no way to protect oneself, one could just hope for good luck.[36]

After the first German soldiers were killed by franc-tireurs, their comrades lost all inhibitions. Thus, one author reports proudly that his unit killed a captured franc-tireur, and others freely tell about having taken cruel revenge. Another author details a troop's reaction to German soldiers being fired upon by a sniper hiding in a house.

…running up the stairs, stabbing the merchant who had fired the shot, dragging him down by his feet and throwing him into the street, while the neighbors watched with horror–all this happened within a few minutes. … While some demolished the house of the murderer (though his bullet did not hit anybody) according to the law of war, a huge soldier came running along, jumped in full rage on the corpse and shouted: "You bastard! I have to take my revenge as well! You pig!" … We had to act like this, just to protect our lives; if the situation were reversed the French would have probably burned the whole town.[37]

Apart from spontaneous acts of revenge, there were also military commanders who were responsible for unjustifiably strict procedures. They ordered the plunder and destruction of towns, which had allegedly supported or accepted franc-tireurs, and asked for high contributions when incidents with franc-tireurs had occurred. Some commanders took towns' notables as hostages and threatened to kill them in the event of partisan activities. In such tense situations, innocent people had to suffer: The Germans killed some peasants from Averton and burned the village of Souche in an attempt to force the inhabitants to turn the franc-tireurs over, or at least discourage them from further attacks.[38]

Although "throughout the autumn and winter of 1870 the terrorism of the franc-tireurs and the reprisals of the Germans spiraled down to new depths of savagery,"[39] the soldiers did not forget about their obligation to refrain from inflicting damage on noncombatants. Many war memoirs contain lengthy passages justifying harsh measures taken against franc-tireurs as unavoidable self-defense. In one incident, a soldier succeeded in restraining his comrades from lynching a civilian by pointing out that they could not be sure that he was a franc-tireur.

Judged objectively, the German troops often overreacted. They got carried away by their desire for revenge and certainly on occasion killed innocent

---

36 Schmitthenner, *Erlebnisse*, 62–3; Hüggelmeyer, *Im Feldzug*, 143.
37 S. Husser, *Erlebnisse eines badischen Trainsoldaten im Feldzuge, 1870–71* (Karlsruhe, 1895), 60–1.
38 Rohkramer, *Militärismus*, 111.
39 Howard, *Franco-Prussian War*, 380.

civilians. But most tried to treat the French population correctly, as long as this did not harm them and the German cause. In many cases, even contemporaries were unable to untangle the reports of war crimes and decide whether an act of self-defense or of cruelty had occurred.

> A consumptive was shot in his bed; but others believe, that he only pretended to be ill and hid, after he had committed the deed. An innkeeper and his wife were killed on the doorsteps; his two children were badly wounded. ... What had they done? Is it true that they shot at the soldiers, that they refused to give them food and drink? Go and ask the graves, they will be silent, and with the living there is neither voice nor answer.[40]

Although the franc-tireurs did not pose a real threat to the German troops, it is understandable that the German soldiers were primarily concerned with their own safety. Without playing down individual cases of excessive cruelty, one has to conclude that a national war necessarily includes violence of this kind. The soldiers are less responsible than the circumstances of war.[41]

Any definition of total war must necessarily include the polarization of people into either friend or enemy, the hatred of and aggression toward the opponent. On this point, most authors of war memoirs agree that it was not aggression that motivated them but patriotism and "manly" joy in fighting. There is some truth to this interpretation: Most enthusiastic soldiers saw the war as an opportunity to prove their courage and their eagerness to sacrifice their life for the common good. Group processes also played an important part in motivating soldiers to fight: comradeship, buddy relationships, eagerness to please the officers, the fear of disobeying. Nevertheless, aggression and the pleasure of dominating other people were important factors, too.

Many soldiers quite simply enjoyed the power they had over civilians. Often they were friendly and sociable, but since their superiors only intervened in extreme cases, they could also be rude and aggressive. Requisitions provided a good opportunity to experience the feeling of power. The soldiers searched the house, used force against the inhabitants, and took what they liked. If they were in a good mood, they tried to be fair, but they could also claim all food and sleeping facilities for themselves. Many soldiers particularly liked to "teach" French women, whom German soldiers often regarded as "Xanthippes," to be "good housewives." More generally, most Germans just liked the chance to be the master of the situation.

---

40 Klein, *Fröschweiler Chronik*, 122–3.
41 If one can talk of guilt, it applies more to military commanders and officers, who could formulate a policy without being personally threatened. In their case, their distrust in the effectiveness of war conventions in general might have been responsible for taking excessively harsh measures.

If we wanted to play billiards, while some French were playing, it was usually enough to put a cue on the table to make them stop and leave. If they did not get the hint, one of us would lean on the billiard table, not getting out of the way until the players were forced to end the game. Of course, it was a drastic measure, but the French had to realise that we were the bosses.[42]

The pleasure of exerting power over others is also part of civilian life, but only in war is it both legal and a matter of course to kill human beings. What has been a terrible crime suddenly becomes a collective enterprise. Most people seem to have no difficulty in temporarily putting aside the cultural norm "Thou shalt not kill."

Psychology and behavioral science agree that aggression is an essential element of human existence, necessary to maintain oneself vis-à-vis nature and vis-à-vis fellow human beings, who are often perceived as rivals. Unconsciously every human wishes to destroy all obstacles to his desires, wishes, needs, and interests. "Every day and every hour we destroy in our unconscious life all the people who get into our way, those who insult and harm us."[43]

Human beings are also social creatures and need a group for survival. Aggressive impulses are therefore controlled or at least constrained by cultural norms and by an instinctive inhibition against killing a member of the same species. Although this inhibition is weaker in human beings than in predatory animals, the war memoirs studied prove that it does indeed exist. Most soldiers had strong inhibitions to kill a completely helpless opponent. One veteran remembers a scene where a group of French soldiers unknowingly strolled toward a German post. The German soldiers could not bring themselves to shoot, because under those circumstances their adversaries appeared harmless and sociable. Instead, they alerted the French to their danger by throwing snowballs at them. On another occasion, a soldier happened to lie in the flank of the opponent's position. Well-protected himself, he found the French an easy target. But it was only when he saw that the soldiers were shooting at his comrades that he overcame his inhibitions and felt able to open fire.[44]

Such behavior is objectively absurd: Although soldiers normally use all means at their disposal to defeat the opponent, they threw those particularly favorable opportunities away. Why did they not seize the occasion? They

42 Karl Tanera, *Ernste und heitere Erinnerungen eines Ordonanzoffiziers im Jahre 1870–71* (Munich, 1887), 193.

43 Siegmund Freud, "Zeitgemässes über Krieg und Tod" (1915), in Freud, *Studienausgabe* (Frankfurt/Main, 1982), 9:57.

44 Zeitz, *Kriegserinnerungen*, 700–1; *Die Bayern im Kriege seit 1800: Taten und Kriegserlebnisse bayerischer Kämpfer* (Munich, 1911), 175.

were not able to do so, precisely because most people can kill only when an opponent is not acknowledged as an individual human being.

In the Franco-Prussian War – as in all modern wars – the soldiers rarely perceived the effects of their actions. The opponents were separated physically, and shot at each other without actually seeing whether the bullet had hit its target. The obligation that soldiers felt toward their buddies and their superiors was a more important motivation than aggression. Strong aggressions only surfaced in the course of the battle and the war when a soldier was wounded himself or saw comrades being wounded or killed.

With a heartrending cry of rage: "These rascals have shot my lieutenant!" The heroic man jumped out of his position. Burning with anger, blood in his eyes, he advanced all by himself, eager to attack the enemy.[45]

In circumstances like this, the opponent is not recognized as a human being but is viewed as a malicious and destructive enemy. Similarly, soldiers always described their first aggressive action as a reaction against an evil doing of the enemy. They were always fully convinced that their acts of aggression were legitimate forms of self-defense, to help comrades, or for revenge.

Although long-range weapons had gained in importance, hand-to-hand combat still took place in the Franco-Prussian War. After successful charges, the soldiers fought each other with bayonets, unless the opponent retreated or fled. In these situations, the mixture of fear and hatred stimulated brutal encounters. Many memoirs barely touch upon these kinds of situations, but others manifest a delight in killing.

Two steps ahead is my comrade, pushed into the trench, with a French soldier on his back. Now he lifts his hand for the deadly stroke. – At this moment the moon appears. I can see the delicate face of the French man, the cloak he is wearing over his shoulders, the glittering weapon. – The shot – The Frenchman falls into the trench.[46]

The deed is justified as helping a comrade, but the tone of satisfaction and the sensuous description of the opponent's face and of the killing (whereas his comrade is hardly mentioned) make it apparent that the author proudly and joyfully remembers the killing.

Although there was a lot of talk about *Erbfeindschaft* (traditional enmity) between France and Germany, the soldiers accepted each other as human beings and equals. But the French army also included colonial troops with soldiers from Africa and Arabia, the so-called *Turkos*, against whom many German soldiers had strong prejudices. They were regarded as bloodthirsty

45   *Parole*, no. 12 (Feb. 11, 1906), 111.
46   K. H. Lindenmann, "Kriegsberichte 'Vor vierzig Jahren,'" *Mittelbadischer Kurier* (1910–11), 57.

beasts, although the memoirs studied do not contain any evidence of particular cruelty on their part.

I look up and see a Turko standing nearby, pressed against a tree. ... With loathing I see his naked legs, covered with long hair, under the ripped uniform, with disgust the bald head, blown apart by a bullet in his brain. ... I was filled with horror by the sight of this typical negro face with its mean expression, full of wild wrath and malicious rage.[47]

When the opponent was perceived as subhuman, there was no inhibition against acting aggressively:

Partly hidden by a small bush, there is a Turko behind me. His eyes are bloodthirsty, his half-opened mouth exposes fang-like teeth. In his hands he holds the rifle, from which smoke is still rising. ... With two jumps I reach my mortal enemy. I am overcome by a boundless anger, as can only be caused by a murderous fight and the malicious behavior of the African. ... I push the handle of the gun into the side of the black guy.... "Pardon!" he cries and lifts his hands. ... I will save the bullet, they are rare. ... One stab! The bayonet goes right through the breast of the black guy, deep into the moss of the forest.[48]

The author justifies his own behavior by saying that the inhuman enemy had shot at him from behind. But nevertheless, it is a grave violation of any war convention to kill an opponent who pleads for mercy. The joy of killing also becomes apparent: His decision to stab his opponent instead of shooting him reveals that he wanted to experience physically the act of killing.

This text was not the report of a particularly cruel soldier, but an article printed in the journal of the Prussian ex-armymen's organizations, which included about 15 percent of the male population as members. In a short afterword, the editor even praised the author for this deed. From today's point of view, this racist and murderous attitude can be seen as a prelude to the colonial wars in Southwest and East Africa, which were directed against the whole population,[49] and to the attack on the Soviet Union in World War II, where all war conventions were suspended because Slavs and communists were regarded as subhuman.

Even without the added dimension of racism, anger and aggression could reach an intensity that made soldiers enjoy torturing an opponent to death.

One of the monsters among the villagers, who had intended to kill our poor wounded comrades, was caught. ... It was an old woman. She had stabbed the eyes of a

47   Adolf Fausel, *Ein Ritt ins Franzosenland: Bilder aus dem Kleinleben im Feld* (Leipzig, 1909), 28.
48   *Parole*, no. 33 (Aug. 12, 1898), 526–7.
49   For this less well-known war in East Africa, see Detlef Bald, "Afrikanischer Kampf gegen koloniale Herrschaft: Der Maji-Maji-Aufstand in Ostafrika," *Militärgeschichtliche Mitteilungen* 20, no. 1 (1976): 23–50.

wounded Prussian soldier, who came into her house for shelter and care. When our soldiers found out about this atrocity, their rage was limitless. The woman was pulled out of the house, tied to the wheel of a cannon and literally tortured to death with stabs and blows.[50]

As the war continued, the hatred against the enemy grew, and the inhibitions about the use of excessive violence were lowered. In this situation, aggressive behavior as well as killing became commonplace.

"Ordered to bring down the enemy's post." A huntsmanlike role of command, aiming at the noblest of game. Taking aim – estimating the distance – and shooting. "Great!" said the colonel, "Right into the head! Revenge for the noncommissioned officer we buried yesterday."[51]

One can notice clear distinctions between the soldiers. A few of them had few inhibitions about using force and violence against franc-tireurs, soldiers, and civilians, whereas others tried to behave correctly. But even soldiers who had strong moral scruples occasionally got carried away by their aggression.

Yesterday at noon a soldier was trying hard to kill me. The man was a bad shot: out of spite I got one of his comrades. I would have hardly imagined the cold-heartedness, with which you can put the rifle on a pole, aim and take a shot at a human being. I would have preferred to get the rascal, who tried to get me, but he was too sheltered.[52]

To summarize the evidence about violence in the wars of unification, one can say that aggression was certainly not one of the primary emotions motivating the soldiers to fight. Rather, they were motivated by a desire to prove their manhood and fulfill the expectations of their comrades, superiors, relatives, friends, and country.

When acts of aggression did surface, they were often brought about by the circumstances of the war itself. Even unjustified acts of violence usually occurred in situations where the soldiers felt threatened and thus behaved violently. Most aggression against franc-tireurs falls into that category. A modern war with mass participation necessarily leads to barbaric violence, the motivation of which is mainly "defensive aggression."

Occasionally, the memoirs bear testament to situations where soldiers did enjoy using violent means, torturing and killing people. But these situations were exceptional, and one should not regard them as an essential part of the behavior of soldiers. Only in a few cases was "offensive aggression" the motivator for actions.

---

50 Richard Martin, *Dr. Martins Kriegserinnerungen*, ed. F. Bücker (Wiesbaden, 1898), 159–60.
51 *Parole*, no. 18 (May 4, 1896), 289.
52 *Parole*, no. 53 (July 5, 1914), 526.

Thomas Rohkrämer

Although human beings are potentially aggressive, one can also find evidence of attempts to avoid unnecessary cruelty and injustice. Some soldiers tried to avoid hardship when requisitioning food, and tried to protect noncombatants. These examples indicate that some are able to control their aggressions by natural as well as moral inhibitions even in the extreme circumstances of war.

There is, however, one type of situation that is frequently characterized by excessive violence. When German soldiers came into contact with *Turkos*, they often acted extremely aggressively. They were partly motivated by irrational fears and partly by the lack of inhibitions against using violence. Evidently, the soldiers were capable of excluding the *Turkos* from the community of human beings – with terrible consequences.

In comparison to the factors already mentioned, ideology played a minor but nevertheless important role in the daily life at the front. Many authors of memoirs explicitly mentioned that they did not fight for honor and glory (although the descriptive parts of their writings often prove the opposite) but rather to defend their country against foreign aggression. Proving the legitimacy of national and personal motivations was a necessary prerequisite for glorifying the war and one's own part in it.

During the campaign, questions of ideology lost their importance. The soldiers were occupied with their own lives and their immediate social circle. It is true that there was a feeling of solidarity among all ranks of the army, and it was important for the common soldier to believe that his deeds were respected and honored, and that everybody – including kings and generals – was doing his duty and carrying his share of the war burden. But generally their immediate superiors and comrades were more important in motivating the common soldier to fight than all the kings, princes, and generals in the command headquarters.

The same applies to nationalistic feelings: It was mainly common experience of hardship, endurance, and fighting that fostered a powerful sense of group and national unity. At the beginning of the Franco-Prussian War, there were some tensions between the troops of the different German countries, probably caused in the main by the fact that some of them had fought against each other only four years earlier. But after the first battles in which the troops fought together and supported each other, the differences lost their divisive force.

On a more abstract level, too, ideology played only a marginal role. Patriotic speeches and religious ceremonies left as small an impression on the soldiers as the news about the founding of the German Empire and the proclamation of the Kaiser. The only political event that was greeted with real enthusiasm was the conclusion of the peace treaty.

The universal rejoicing that broke out when the fighting ended suggests that, in the long run, hardly any of the soldiers truly enjoyed the war. Whatever enthusiasm they might have felt at the beginning of the war waned after the victory at Sedan. The hardships of winter, in particular, destroyed any positive attitudes that they had held toward the war. Living in mortal danger, suffering great privation, and growing frustration regarding a war that dragged on much longer than expected, all dominated the soldier's thinking and feeling.[53] In spite of all this, the soldiers continued to fulfill their duty. The German army's successes, hopes for a speedy end to the war, and the unconditional obedience that became habitual prevented any major disintegration of the fighting morale. The attitudes and feelings of the common soldiers did not prolong the war, but neither did they do anything to shorten it.

In comparison to the limited wars against Denmark and Austria, the Franco-Prussian War gained its own momentum and developed into a *guerre à outrance*, which displayed many characteristics of a total war. The features of totality were less connected with its destructiveness and more with its elements of strategy, ideology, and emotional fervor. Since Germany did not accept a moderate peace and France could not accept defeat after Sedan, the French government started a national war by mobilizing the masses, building an irregular army, and initiating partisan warfare. In response, the Germans violated the immunity of noncombatants through the bombardment of cities, through requisitions, which probably brought some of the population close to despair, and through antipartisan tactical measures. All these elements, which for Europe marked a new level of intensity "on the road to total war," were a logical consequence of nationalistic sentiments and mass participation. When fighting against a nation whose citizens identify with the war aims, it is not enough to defeat the government and the regular army; it is also necessary to break the population's will to resist. If the French had concentrated more upon partisan warfare instead of trying to free Paris by mobilizing new troops, the war would probably have reached an even higher level of intensity and national hatred.

In other respects, however, the Franco-Prussian War does not correspond with the concept of total war. There was no national enthusiasm comparable with the onset of World War I, the combatants mostly tried to fight according to the conventions of war, and the opponent was generally not demonized.

53 Rohkrämer, *Militarismus*, 112–15, 132–6.

This moderation becomes particularly clear at the end of the war, which was concluded relatively quickly and without an unbridgeable gulf of hatred or ideological enmity. When it became apparent that even the extreme measure of mass mobilization had failed, the French were nearly as happy as the Germans about the peace settlement.

Another indication that the Franco-Prussian war did not provoke any lasting animosity in Germany is the fact that hardly any of the memoirs express hatred against France or the desire for a new war. Whereas military leaders such as Helmut von Moltke soon came to consider the possibility of waging a new war against France, and many members of the younger generation grew quite fond of this prospect, even nationalistically oriented veterans abhorred the idea of provoking a war. One of them wrote:

When I hear others saying light-heartedly: "There will be another war against France. That's why it would be better not to wait until France has regained its strength, but attack now while we still know that we are superior," then I think: "If you had seen how the dead were buried on November 1st and December 20th in Dijon, if you had seen the battle field of Chênebier and Frahier after the battle at Belfort, if you had just seen one person painfully die of his wounds, you would consider it sinful to say any such words."... When a war breaks out, we want to be prepared and fight until complete victory, without any considerations about the cost, but we do not want to start a war. We can never be certain whether a war which we regard as unavoidable, really has to take place. The nation which unnecessarily starts a war deserves to be beaten.[54]

Although the Franco-Prussian War displayed some elements of total war, the belief in the concept of just war (just cause for going to war and correct conduct in war) still prevailed among the majority of soldiers and set limits to its intensity and horrors.

As suggested previously, our understanding of the term *total war* consists of two distinct aspects: first, the unlimited destructiveness; and second, the intensity of the war effort. These two aspects do not necessarily occur at the same time and are even mutually exclusive in their absolute form, because the totality of destruction, which is reached with the nuclear strategy of MAD (mutually assured destruction), literally annihilates the anthropological factor. This suggests that the concept of total war is an ideal type, which can never occur in its pure form.[55]

---

54 Schmitthenner, *Erlebnisse*, 41.
55 The other possibility would be to say that total war is a war conducted without any limitations with different concrete expressions, e.g., nuclear warfare and guerilla warfare. But this would lead to an inflation of the term.

But these two aspects of total war are more closely connected than it seems at first sight. If we exclude the possibility of a technological "accident," nuclear destruction takes more than just pushing a button. A person or social group that is prepared to use this means against another group is under the obligation.

also to destroy these other people, that is, their victims and objects, on a moral level. They must declare every aspect of the opponent as inhumane and criminal, as absolutely unworthy. Otherwise they themselves are criminals and inhumane.[56]

The only conceivable moral justification for threatening to inflict ultimate destruction on others is to see them as the ultimate evil. Thus, exterminism includes both objective and subjective aspects: the technical means and the moral justification to use them.

With regard to the anthropological dimension of warfare, Michael Fellman's article in this book (Chapter 24) draws attention to the violence of the Thirty Years' War. His comparison with the American Civil War clearly shows that not only modern wars have the tendency to become increasingly violent and absolute, making all attempts to limit violence and enmity increasingly difficult. The far-reaching similarities of daily life at the front in different wars and armies are indeed striking and need to be studied further.

Important differences nevertheless remain. The intensity of the war effort and being prepared for extreme sacrifices as well as extreme military measures are not independent of time and space. A closer look at partisan warfare, which is the most important nontechnological factor in the breakdown of the customary limitations on violence in war, reveals that total people's war is dependent on a number of historical conditions:[57]

1. As partisans fight in small groups, they cannot – like common soldiers in a regular army – be forced to fight but must be convinced of the war aim. Also, they are dependent on the support of the population so that they are able to move "like fish in water." Thus, guerrilla warfare demands a strong ideology that prepares the whole population for an absolute war effort. The wide majority must identify with the fate of their country against a real enemy; otherwise, they will not tolerate great sacrifices. These strong nationalistic feelings, which are necessary to endure guerrilla warfare, are a phenomenon of modern history.[58]
2. Both the spread of a nationalistic ideology and the necessity to coordinate the war efforts of the extremely mobile partisan groups demand a nationwide communication system.

---

56 Schmitt, *Theorie des Partisanen*, 95.
57 This list does not pretend to be complete, but only serves to prove the point in this argument.
58 Wolf Kittler, *Die Geburt des Partisanen aus dem Geist der Poesie: Heinrich von Kleist und die Strategie der Befreiungskriege* (Freiburg, 1987), 218–324.

3. In most cases, partisans are dependent on an interested third party, whose engagement secures some limitations to antiguerrilla warfare. An international public, which gives weight to humanitarian considerations and stops the regular army from treating their irregular opponents as murderous criminals, tends to be a necessary prerequisite for the success of guerrilla warfare.[59]
4. The need for the guerrillas to be mobile and avoid major battles, however, shows that a country must not be too highly developed. The territory must contain uncontrolled areas into which the irregular troops can disappear.
5. In a fully developed modern society, human beings are too dependent on a functioning infrastructure to endure a sustained guerrilla war.
6. As history shows, guerrilla warfare is the warfare of the poor. People with some property tend to believe that they have more to lose than a war.[60]

These necessary conditions show that partisan warfare cannot develop in all wars or even in all modern wars. In its most extreme form, it is clearly related to a specific historical constellation: Total guerrilla warfare is the defense of a partially modernized country in a highly developed, modern world.[61]

The Franco-Prussian War manifested some features of a total war, and some politicians and military leaders demanded an even greater effort from the population. But this does not allow us to assume that had the war continued, it would have developed into total war. Despite the creation of a *theory* of guerrilla warfare after 1806, the Prussian military was unable to put it into practice; in similar fashion, the appeals of French politicians and military leaders could not have led to unlimited people's war. The citizens were too dependent on a functioning infrastructure and had more to lose than Alsace, Lorraine, and five billion francs. The fall of Paris was not only a political but also a societal symbol, because it showed the price that the population would have had to pay for the continuation of the war, namely, the relinquishing of civilized life. Faced with this prospect, capitulation must have appeared as the lesser of two evils.

---

59 Carl Schmitt, *Theorie des Partisanen*, 78; and Carl Schmitt, "Conversation with Joachim Schickel about the 'Theorie des Partisanen,'" May 22, 1969, television broadcast on the Third Program, Germany.
60 From Michael Geyer's contribution to the conference in Washington, D.C.; see also Schmitt, "Conversation with Joachim Schickel."
61 In the Thirty Years' War, e.g., violance never became part of an overall partisan strategy. The population was never mobilized to fight for a political goal but just defended their own existence, and the armies' violence against the population was not the expression of a warfare against civilians and noncivilians alike.

24

At the Nihilist Edge:
Reflections on Guerrilla Warfare
during the American Civil War

MICHAEL FELLMAN

As defined in our times, total war is a twentieth-century outcome of twentieth-century capacities for social mobilization, ideology, and technology applied to war-making ends. What look, in certain respects, like its predecessors, such as the American Civil War and the German Wars of Unification, prove on closer examination to be markers on an undulation in levels of wartime violence reaching far back into the history of warfare, rather than developmental stops on a simple linear and progressive development of modern war that culminated during the twentieth century.[1]

Many "premodern" wars reached horrific levels of destruction. Perhaps the most dramatic example of a much earlier war that reached a far greater level of violence than did those of the 1860s was the Thirty Years' War, which destroyed much of Germany during the period from 1618 to 1648.

The story in the reports is repeated a hundred times: the bands of mercenaries destroyed domestic utensils, tools and furniture, ruined stores and seeds, slaughtered or took away cattle and the domestic animals, inflicted cruel tortures on the inhabitants or killed them and set fire to the farm. ... This was expressly forbidden by all the rules. In addition, it also frequently happened that young plants and ripe corn were deliberately trampled down by the armed plunderers or military detachments on the march and not without the senseless killing of the village inhabitants either. It is likewise occasionally reported that the healthy and able-bodied inhabitants were driven away and sold ... for eternal labor, far worse than death.[2]

In this instance of war against all civilians, the purchasers were Turks, the enslaved inhabitants German peasants, the sellers Swedish invaders. During the Thirty Years' War, waves of foreign troops, Danes, French, Spanish, and especially Swedish, invaded the disorganized Holy Roman Empire. Linguistic

---

1 I wish to thank Robert H. Wiebe, John Gillingham, and Santa Aloi for their perceptive readings of earlier drafts of this chapter.

2 Johann Jakob Christoffel von Grimmelshausen, *Theatrum Europaen* 1 (Frankfurt/Main: Meridan, 1643), 1050, paraphrased in Herbert Langer, *The Thirty Years' War* (Poole, 1980), 105.

and ethnic hatreds multiplied religious conflicts between Catholics and Protestants; invading soldiers and local rulers alike also despised, exploited, and slaughtered the German peasantry peopling the countryside through which all the armies marched. "When the German peasants [of Brandenburg-Kulmbach] attempted to drive out the [Swedish] invaders, in November, 1631," Geoffrey Parker writes, "they were massacred: a chronicler who visited the site of the peasants last stand was appalled to find the vineyards and fields red with blood, with corpses scattered in bizarre positions over a three-mile radius."[3]

Horrendous as were these invasions of organized armies, even more profoundly destructive were the freebooting actions of marauding mercenaries, most often foreigners, who were demobilized each winter, without pay, but with their arms, the better to prey, in the name of foraging, on villagers and peasants. By the war's end, in Rhineland-Lauten, thirty-six of sixty-two towns were deserted, while the chief town of Kaiserslautern had dropped in population from 4,200 to 500. The peasants fared the worst – when not raped and murdered, they were, even more frequently, plundered and burned out of home and crops and left to wander or to camp unwelcome in towns where they faced malnutrition, which vastly increased rates of death by typhus, dysentery, and bubonic plague while lowering birth rates. In many places, the war was such as to inspire Thomas Hobbes. One village near Nuremberg was plundered eighteen times in two years. Peasants organized guerrilla forces of their own to counterslaughter the mercenaries when opportunities arose, but more often, the outgunned peasants died or fled. Desperation induced all inhumanities, cannibalism included.[4]

Coolly discussing death rates rather than terror, modern historians of the Thirty Years' War have fully debated the probable level of the decimation of the German population by violence and by epidemics. Conservative estimates are that "only" 3 or 4 million of the 20 million Germans alive in 1626 died or were killed during the war. Even by these cautious reckonings, between one-half and two-thirds of the people of Mecklenburg, Pomerania, and Württemberg perished.[5]

3 Geoffrey Parker, *The Thirty Years' War* (London, 1984), 127. For this passage, Parker cites Ernst L. Sticht, *Markgraf Christian von Brandenburg-Kulmbach und der dreissigjährige Krieg in Ostfranken, 1618–1635* (Kulmbach, 1965), 154.
4 Harry Kamen, "The Economic and Social Consequences of the Thirty Years' War," *Past and Present* 39 (April 1968): 44–62; Parker, *The Thirty Years' War*, 164.
5 Parker, *The Thirty Years' War*, 208–15. In addition to Parker's macro-military and political analysis, and Langer's cultural history, the best narrative of this war in English remains C. V. Wedgwood, *The Thirty Years' War* (London, 1938). The cold-bloodedness of much of the historiography of the Thirty Years' War is approximated perhaps only by that found in the discussion of the demographic catastrophe in the central valley of Mexico during the first 100 years after white contact and

As the Thirty Years' War demonstrates, if the central test of the level of destructiveness reached during war is the degree of erasure by soldiers of the discrimination between combatant and civilian, then nothing was new about the behavior of German or American troops in the wars of the 1860s. That is an understatement. Although there were episodes in the Civil War and the German Wars of Unification that paralleled those of the Thirty Years' War, neither approached the general level of human destruction of that earlier conflict. Indeed, one can discover episodes of massive military destruction of civilians in the military behavior of the first so-called Western civilizations. The slaughter or enslavement of enemy civilians, and the destruction of their home fields and home cities, was common wartime practice among the Greeks and Romans and their competitors.

Conflating the scale of war with the modernization of war is anachronistic not only in mismeasuring the ebb and flow of slaughter during the long history of armed conflict; it also distorts the contemporaneity of the ability to wage total war. Rather than growing directly from earlier wars, the twentieth-century meaning of total war owes more to the pen of General Erich Ludendorff, whose 1935 book, *Der Totale Krieg*, suggested a mass economic and social mobilization, such as was approached by Nazi Germany, but only in 1944, guided by Albert Speer.[6] Beyond Ludendorff-style total social and economic mobilization and newly available technological advances such as allowed massive strategic bombing in World War II, the systematic ideological dehumanization and thorough bureaucratization achieved by the Nazis in their slaughter of 6 million unarmed Jews, killed as a purely civilian category, form parts of the contemporary meaning of total war. In addition, the full contemporary meaning of total war is predicated on the omnipresent fear of the annihilation of the entire human race by nuclear war, for which the Americans provided the horrendous test cases at Hiroshima and Nagasaki. Roman swords, not to mention seventeenth-

---

conquest. The refusal to focus on the "micro-level" sufferings of ordinary people, while examining huge and hugely impersonal demographical "death rates," strikes me as monumentally insensitive. A second early modern conflict filled with dehumanization and slaughter of civilians was the epoch of the French civil wars of religion. See Denis Crouzet, *Les Guerres de Dieu! La Violence en Temps des Troubles de Religion: vers 1525 vers 1610*, 2 vols. (Paris, 1990). For a brief summary by Crouzet of his thesis, see his "Violence Catholique et Désir de Dieu," *Notre Histoire* (April 1992): 36–40. I am much obliged to Annette Becker for these references. It is one of Russell F. Weigley's themes in *The Age of Battles* (Bloomington, Ind., 1991) that eighteenth-century military leaders consciously attempted, not always with success, to pull back from the horrors of seventeenth-century warfare, which had gone much too far to suit their minds and stomachs.

6 For a good scholarly analysis of the twentieth-century linguistic creation of the term *total war*, argued in the context of the American Civil War depicted as less than a total war, see Mark E. Neely's stimulating essay, "Was the Civil War a Total War?" *Civil War History* 37 (1991): 5–28, reprinted in this volume.

century muskets, were sufficient to produce a level of slaughter of civilians not much improved upon prior to 1945, and nuclear weaponry has proven to be so globally threatening that it has thus far remained unusable, leaving killing to the old-fashioned weapon systems. Modernization theory will not go far in explaining thresholds of violence, either observed or crossed. Not technology, nor thorough organization, but cultural factors have always determined the level of slaughter and restraint from slaughter in war – "totality" linked to "modernization" are just historians' words, as the marauding mercenaries and peasants fighting in Germany well realized 350 years ago.

If chronological progressivism and modernization theory distort far more than they illuminate, how then can we understand this seemingly arbitrary record of greater and lesser intensities of warfare over the centuries? One crucial variable is what one might call the cast of the cultural net: the treatment accorded by warriors to those whom they consider to fall inside their culture as opposed to the treatment that they apply to those whom they consider to be cultural outsiders. Consciously or unconsciously, warriors of all nations apply their cultural standards while at war. In addition, their level of cultural inclusion and exclusion and of destructiveness is amplified by the form of combat in which they engage. Irregular warfare, where formal command structures are weak or absent, frequently has provided fertile grounds for the most devastating enactment of war against the people, restrained by the fewest cultural inhibitions.

During the American Civil War, the military theater most nearly approximating that of the marauders and peasants of the seventeenth century was in the hill country of the border states and the up-country South, where guerrilla war broke out spontaneously between local communities internally divided between Union and Confederate sympathies. In some areas, particularly in up-country North Carolina and East Tennessee, Unionists took to the bush to fight a guerrilla war against Confederate troops, while in other areas, particularly Kentucky and Missouri, young men of Confederate leanings banded together to fight Union authorities. Although I know most about Missouri, from which my primary evidence is drawn, most of the phenomena found there were replicated elsewhere in the warring border regions. If all war is the application of collective violence with implicit and explicit limitations, the guerrilla war was, owing to its fundamental disorganization, the locale with the fewest explicit limitations during the Civil War. The tendency toward indiscriminate slaughter of an enemy's civilians as well as of its soldiers, present in all wars (and perhaps in the human breast), and the infatuation with nihilism, both found their fullest, but by no means exclusive, play in the guerrilla aspects of the Civil War.[7]

Pro-Confederate guerrillas in Missouri formed not in regular units, with uniforms and flags waving, but in temporary small bands, in ordinary clothes, gathering in secret places, and then striking out with stealth and bursts of violence at the Union enemy or at whom they deemed to be the enemy's civilian supporters, thence dispersing to melt back into the civilian population. Union troops could not discern which among all those smooth-talking civilians actually were deadly guerrillas or guerrilla sympathizers, and badly frightened and furious over the loss of their comrades' lives, they therefore tended to strike out blindly at anyone who seemed threatening or untrustworthy to them. This shared dialectic of negation created a cycle of destruction, where justice came to mean vengeance, where one death was to be answered by ten retributive killings, and ten by a hundred. Over four years, perhaps 10,000 Missourians were killed this way and perhaps 300,000 (of 1.2 million) fled their homes for the relative safety of Union garrison towns, or for more distant and safer states, leaving behind burned homes and fields, slaughtered livestock, bands of wolves, and armed marauders of both political persuasions.

Both sides adopted a slash, burn, and kill policy. Pro-Confederate guerrillas operated on their own, far from Confederate military or civilian control. On the other side, although some legal controls remained in civilian hands, most Union authority in the ravaged countryside devolved into military hands – the Provost Marshal at the local outpost exercised such police authority as remained in rural areas often dominated by enemy guerrillas.

General Union policies varied wildly – war taxes and land confiscation, loyalty oaths, banishment or jailing of known (or more often suspected) civilian guerrilla supporters, all proved ineffective and were applied unevenly or abandoned outright. In the most dramatic incident of this long and formless conflict, after a guerrilla raid on Lawrence, Kansas, on August 21, 1863, in which at least 150 unarmed civilian men and boys were executed, the Union general in Kansas City issued a general order depopulating the four Missouri counties from which the raid had been staged. Approximately 20,000 civilians of all political persuasions were forced to vacate their homes and lands, all of which then were torched. These four burned-over counties were a sizable chunk not of a Confederate but of a *Union* state, and this undiscriminating official attack on all civilians, including Unionists, and on women

---

7 These generalizations, and the discussion of guerrilla war that follows are extrapolations from my book, *Inside War: The Guerrilla Conflict in Missouri During the American Civil War* (New York, 1989). The notes to that book also provide bibliographical and historiographical contexts.

and children as well as men, produced such an outcry all over the North that this extreme policy was quickly withdrawn, never to be repeated. This revocation demonstrated the cultural and political limits imposed by American public opinion, expressed through a free press, even in the midst of a civil war, against the potential application of draconian antiguerrilla policies to civilians and their property.[8]

All other Union antiguerrilla policies were less sweeping, but all suffered from the fundamental impossibility of distinguishing guerrillas from civilians, and enemy from friendly civilians. While in command in Missouri early in 1862, General Henry Halleck had issued a general order that captured guerrillas be shot summarily rather than being taken prisoners of war. After he went to Washington as general in chief, Halleck commissioned Francis W. Lieber, a German-American legal scholar, to draft what became General Order no. 100 – the application of martial law to guerrilla-infested regions. Guerrillas, Lieber wrote, were "not entitled to the privileges of prisoner of war, but shall be treated summarily as highway robbers or pirates." Likewise, civilians who guided guerrillas or gave them military information were "war traitors" whose punishment was to be death. On the other hand, Lieber's orders insisted that sheer military tyranny was wrong, that every commander "who possesses the power of arms against the unarmed" had for that very reason to be "strictly guided" not by "cruelty but by the principles of justice, honor, and humanity." The honorable commander thus would treat enemies with summary execution, and all others with justice.[9]

Of course, only the most Solomonic commander could have distinguished his enemies from innocent bystanders in the deep haze of guerrilla war. In the fury of action, it often proved impossible to determine which execution was just and which arbitrary, and, after the bloody deed had been done, mere suspicions were easily enough rationalized as having been real threats. Union commanders in the field, urged on by their men as well as by their own fear and anger, tended therefore to shoot when in doubt. In practice, neither side took many prisoners – the torch and immediate capital vengeance were the norm.

8   The best discussions of General Order no. 11 are Charles R. Mink, "General Orders no. 11: The Forced Evacuation of Civilians During the Civil War, "*Military Affairs* 34 (Dec. 1970): 132–6, and Ann Davis Niepman, "General Orders no. 11 and Border Warfare During the Civil War," *Missouri Historical Review* 67 (Jan. 1972): 185–210.

9   War Department, General Order no. 100, Washington, D.C., April 24, 1863, *The War of the Rebellion: A Compilation of the Official Records of the Union and the Confederate Army*, 130 vols. (Washington, D.C., 1880–1902), ser. 3, vol. 3, 148–64. This compilation is hereafter cited as *OR*. For Halleck's request to Lieber for an analysis of the legal context in which to consider guerrilla warfare, and Lieber's reply, see Lieber's essay, "Guerrilla Parties Considered with Reference to the Laws and Usages of War," *OR*, ser. 3, vol . 3, 301–9.

It was the brutal guerrilla slaying of one of his men that led General Samuel R. Curtis, a West Point man, to his no-prisoner stance. He wrote to St. Louis headquarters in May 1862, that "a set of assassins are prowling about Little Red River. One of our men bathing in that river was shot down and beaten to death with clubs. I have ordered such villains not to be taken as prisoners." Curtis was far from alone in his willingness to declare openly to headquarters such a no-prisoner policy. "We take no prisoners," Col. James Ford wrote to St. Louis in 1864. Such officers instructed their men to show no quarter. Private George Woltz wrote to his parents from southern Missouri in 1864, "there are strict orders against taking any more prisoners that is found in arms or as bushwhackers but to leave them on the ground we found them on." Nevertheless, guerrilla prisoners sometimes were taken because shooting disarmed enemies in cold blood was morally too much for some Union troops. Such hesitancy could annoy commanders such as Colonel Bazel F. Lazear, who responded to the capture of guerrilla chieftain Bradaway and several of his men, "I am sorry that they are prisoners on my hands, as they should have been shot on the spot." In such instances, a no-prisoners policy for guerrillas could be rendered somewhat more "legitimate" through a quick kangaroo court. For example, William C. Long wrote to his children from the field in 1862, "we captured a bushwacker yesterday. ... He has been tried by drum-head court-marshall [*sic*] and condemned to death. He will be executed in about one hour. His grave is now digging." A widely used formula allowing for an even quicker quasi-moral execution was expressed by Union Cavalry Captain Thomas Thomas, in his official report from the Ozarks in 1864 concerning the capture and fate of Jacob Rustin and John Inman, two "notorious bushwhackers. On the march to camp the prisoners attempted to make their escape by running, and both were instantly killed."[10] This common formulation provided safety against possible official recriminations as well as psychological defense for the executioners against the nakedness of committing outright murder.

Guerrillas reported to no one but littered the countryside with the corpses of their enemies whom they executed as they would be executed. Not merely did both camps of fighters kill one another; they frequently scalped and

---

10 Major General Samuel R. Curtis to Captain J. C. Kelton, Batesville, May 19, 1862, *OR* ser. 1, vol. 13, 392; Colonel James H. Ford to O. D. Greene, Independence, July 26, 1864, Two or More Name file 2635, record group 393, Records of U.S. Army Continental Commands, 1821–1920. Dept. of the Missouri, National Archives, Washington, D.C.; George Woltz to His Parents, Springfield, Aug. 11, 1862, Joint Collection, University of Missouri, Western Historical Manuscript Collections – Columbia, State Historical Society of Missouri Collections (hereafter cited as JC); Lieutenant Colonel Bazel F. Lazear to Captain Dyer, Jackson, February 14, 1863, *OR*, ser. 1, vol. 22, pt. 1, 224–5; William C. Long to His Children, Butler, Dec . 23, 1863, William C. Long papers, JC; Captain Thomas Thomas to Captain J. Lovell, Houston, Jan. 11, 1864, *OR*, ser. 1, vol. 34, pt. 2, 57.

otherwise mutilated the bodies of their murdered foes. Fighters took body parts – ears, noses, scalps, teeth, facial skin, fingers – to keep or give away as trophies. On September 14, 1864, Major Austin King's command killed five of the notorious Bill Anderson's men, "some of their bridles being decked with human scalps." Two months earlier, Archie Clement, by reputation the leading executioner in Anderson's gang, had attached a note to the remains of a Union soldier, which proclaimed proudly, "You come to hunt bushwhackers. Now you are skelpt. Clenyent skelpt you."[11]

Union troops doubtless reciprocated in kind, but as the victors purged the records, little direct evidence of their mutilations remains. Something of Union fury toward the enemy can be recaptured in the order that General Clinton B. Fisk gave to a Colonel of his command on April 16, 1864, "Try the bushwhacker by drumhead court-martial tonight, and let every soldier in Macon shoot him if he is guilty, as he doubtless is."[12] One bullet, or at most a firing squad, would have sufficed; Fisk prescribed collective, ritualized dismemberment. Killing the enemy was incomplete; one had to finish the dehumanization, literally deface the enemy, by rending his flesh, which somehow contained his evil soul. Drenched in the endless terrors of a guerrilla war, combatants sought release in the obliteration of the face of the Other. Some guerrilla warriors wished to push on toward a place of total destruction, some land where "we" in all our force are all and "they" are rendered into nothing at all. Each side could seek this end for their enemies, as each knew they had been targeted. This urgent, two-way, furious desire amounted to a mutual aesthetic of destruction, placing the fighters at the edge of the nihilist abyss, their repellent and attractive genocidal dreamland.[13]

---

11   Major Austin A. King to Brigadier General Clinton B. Fisk, Fayette, Sept. 14, 1864, *OR*, ser. 1, vol. 41, pt. 3, 194; *Missouri Statesman*, Aug. 5, 1864. Concerning scalping, the most sophisticated discussion is James Axtell, "The Unkindest Cut, or, Who Invented Scalping," in Axtell, *The European and the Indian: Essays in the Ethnohistory of North America* (New York, 1981), 16–35.

12   Brigadier General Clinton B. Fisk to Lieutenant Colonel Daniel M. Draper, Macon, Ga., April 18, 1864, *OR*, ser. 1, vol. 24, pt. 3, 216.

13   For a brilliant discussion of the aesthetic of destruction among men in war, see J. Glenn Gray, *The Warriors: Reflection on Men in Battle* (New York, 1959). For psychological analyses of soldiers who commit atrocities, see William Barry Gault, "Some Remarks on Slaughter," *American Journal of Psychiatry* 128, no. 4 (Oct. 1971): 450–4; William Goldsmith and Constantine Cretekos, "Unhappy Odysseys: Psychiatric Hospitalizations among Vietnam Returnees," *Archives of General Psychiatry* 30 (Jan. 1969): 78–83; Sarah A. Haley, "When the Patient Reports Atrocities: Specific Considerations of the Vietnam Veteran," *Archives of General Psychiatry* (Feb. 1974): 191–6; Joel Yager, "Personal Violence in Infantry Combat," *Archives of General Psychiatry* (Feb. 1975): 257–61. In general, my analysis of the psychological meanings of warfare owes a great deal to the work of Robert J. Lifton. Of his opus, see in particular *The Nazi Doctors: Medical Killing and the Psychology of Genocide* (New York, 1986); *Death in Life: Survivors of Hiroshima*, 2d ed. (New York, 1967; reprinted: New York, 1982); *Thought Reform and the Psychology of Totalism: A Study of Brainwashing in China*, 2d ed. (1961; Chapel Hill, N.C., 1989); *Explorations in Psychohistory: The Wellfleet Papers* (New York, 1974); and, with Eric Markusen, *The Genocidal Mentality: Nazi Holocaust and Nuclear Threat* (New York, 1990).

Surely the likes of Bill Anderson and Fisk were psychologically equipped to have replicated the full experience of central Germany centuries earlier. And yet, horrendous as was the guerrilla war in Missouri, it stopped short of the level of destruction and slaughter reached in that earlier conflict, in part because people on both sides had so much in common. In Missouri, there was no arrogant aristocracy that observed the poor as a less than human subspecies of peasants, who were subject to separate and unequal laws and social consideration. Then, too, the combatants, 90 percent of them, shared the Protestant faith. There were both northern and southern branches of the dominant Baptist and Methodist sects, but all shared a basic pool of religious practices and values. Ninety percent of Missourians were small landholders or aspiring tenant farmers. Only 10 percent of these held slaves, and then only small groups of slaves, unlike the huge gangs of slaves characteristic of slaveholding in the lower South. The issue of slavery divided the state, of course, although the Confederate party was far larger than its slaveholding leadership. Seventy-five percent of Missourians on both sides were "Butternuts," descendants of Anglo-Saxon migrants from the upper South. Racially, ethnically, linguistically, religiously, and economically, in terms both of livelihood and of aspirations, the vast majority of Missourians of both political persuasions were cut from the same cultural cloth.[14] Their brutal war was not a war of religion, nor a class war, nor a war of race or ethnicity. Although impossible to document conclusively, these absences of fundamental social fissures both lent special horror to what really was a brother's war, and served to limit the full-blown dehumanization necessary to something more nearly approaching a genocidal Armageddon.

In addition to sharing a pool of demographic, economic, and social characteristics, fighters on both sides shared fundamental cultural values. Although wildly distorted by the lying and violence that they inflicted upon one another during war, they also clung to at least vestiges of their peacetime values, perhaps to prove to themselves that they still retained their core personalities and their membership in what they thought to be the human family. These were Evangelical Christians, American republicans who shared the egalitarian belief that each individual ought to be free and freely respectful of the personhood of others. They also shared values of honor – that a man (or woman, though here the male fighters and hence masculinity are more to the point) ought to be forthright with others while defending the integrity of his person and his family through mutual fellow-dealing at best, and fair fighting at worst. Most especially, the honor of men was tested

14   Fellman, *Inside War*, 3–11.

by their protective attitude toward the weak, especially the elderly, women, and children, the necessary complements to themselves in the proper family, which was the indispensable core unit of their otherwise lightly institutionalized society, the central building block of their society. By extension, fighters on each side sought to preserve not only their own women, children, and families, but the abstract principles of loyalty and service to kinship, represented by their own families, yet equally embodied in other families like their own. Even when they maimed and killed one another, men did so in perverse testimony to these core values.[15]

The clearest demonstration of male service to the code of honor was the manner in which women understood the verbal and behavioral latitude that men afforded them, even while they slaughtered one another. Iowa Private Dan Smith wrote back home about his responses to the "rampant secesher" women of Boonville. "They said the Iowa boys conducted themselves more like gentlemen than any other troops that had been here. The women were the spunkiest I ever seen and when a squad of us would visit a house we would have to take a few broadsides but our orders were to do things as civil as possible but I felt several times like if I could see them strangled." Smith's reactions to the traitorous Boonville women were complex. He admired their sauciness (which he would never have taken off enemy men) and also the gentlemanly reflection he sometimes saw coming back from their eyes, but he also held a partially acknowledged homicidal fantasy toward them – one expressed, however, only in the passive voice. His peacetime sense of gender proprieties, and that of the Boonville ladies, was stretched but not broken under guerrilla war duress.[16]

Union Captain Edwin F. Noyes reported his much angrier and surlier reaction to a similar scenario early in the war. When he requested water for his thirsty troops, one Missouri woman had said that she would not give a drop to his "beer-swilling, nigger loving, cowardly dogs to save their lives." Noyes had replied to the woman "you are a woman: if you were a man, we would have an answer in our guns."[17] Unlike Private Smith, Captain Noyes was not even partly amused; neither, however, did he pull his trigger. His foul-mouthed enemy knew to what extent her gender lent her immunity, even during military action.

15 An ambitious book on many of these themes is Bertram Wyatt-Brown, *Southern Honor* (New York, 1982). See also Dickson D. Bruce Jr., *Violence and Culture in the Antebellum South* (Austin, Tex., 1979), and Edward Ayres, *Vengeance and Justice: Crime and Punishment in the 19th-Century American South* (New York, 1982).
16 Daniel R. Smith to His Parents, Jefferson City, Aug. 28, 1861, Daniel R. Smith papers, Illinois State Historical Library, Springfield.
17 Edwin F. Noyes to Mr. Stephenson, Camp Benton, Aug. 21, 1861, Nathaniel Wright Family papers, Library of Congress, Washington, D.C.

Confederate guerrillas observed the same limits of attitude and behavior toward women, and whereas there was a Union command structure to reinforce the forbearance of Union soldiers, the guerrillas had none – they restrained themselves in service to implicit cultural constraints not reinforced by external institutions. Sometimes even the most brutal of guerrillas in the middle of bloodbaths would stop to observe the cultural ban on directly harming women. To give one horrendous example, on the night of May 6, 1865, Mrs. Mary Hall was awakened by a group of guerrillas. They demanded she light a candle and then took it and set light to her children's clothes, shoving them under the bed where the three children were sleeping. "I caught the clothes they were burning and threw them in the fire place. One of them says God damn you let them; if you don't I will burn up the house. I answered they will burn just as well where they are and will give more light." They then went to the bed of her eighteen-year-old son and demanded his pistol. He said he had traded it for a watch and added, "its hanging by the glass though some of you have it – as I do not see it. One of the guerrillas then said god damn him. Shoot him. I thought they would shoot him and knocked up the pistol several times, injuring my shoulder by so doing," Hall reported. "They finally succeeded in shooting him the head killing him instantly. I was screaming and entreating them all the time to spare his life. After they had killed him one of they says shut your God damn mouth or I will blow a hole through you head. … All this time my niece, 16 years of age was lying in bed. One of the guerrillas stood by her bedside and as she made an effort to rise ordered her to lie still saying one woman was enough at a time. After they had killed my son and plundered the house one guerrilla ordered me out of the house and shut the door. The door had scarcely closed before I heard my niece scream and say Lord Aunt Mary run here to me. I started and as I reached the door my niece who had succeeded in effecting her escape from the men came rushing out. I says let the poor girl alone you have done enough. … I do not think they effected their designs on the girl."[18] Mary Hall could not protect her son from slaughter, but she could aid in preventing her niece's rape, mainly because the guerrillas were unwilling to complete a rape under even these circumstances. The assault went up to the edge of rape and murder of women. This was the most negative version of the observation of the code of protection of women.

Part of the perversity of armed chivalry was the God-like power it gave the warrior over the fate of women. In their moments of armed domination, guerrillas had the power to do what they alone willed, including murder; thus

18   Deposition of Mrs. Mary Hall, Franklin County, May 11, 1865, Letters Received file 2593, Record Group 393, National Archives.

withholding destruction could also give them an enormous sense of potency. During the Lawrence raid, two guerrillas had their pistols drawn on Henry Bissell, when his pretty sister Arabella, according to a later report by their mother Sophia, began "pleading ... with the leader to spare her only brother, running from him to the other and back again in agony. The leader relented and spoke to the man. He let go his hold, and Henry ran for corn. ... They tipped their hats and bid me good morning."[19] Such an incident no doubt heightened the self-image of the gentleman for these two guerrillas; it was a demonstration of their total power over Arabella, even more than over Henry, who in this situation would have had no effective means to plead for himself.

Many on the Union side attested to this guerrilla maintenance of the manly code. An Illinois journalist wrote during the worst summer of guerrilla violence around Independence: "In this country the old notion that men are the protectors of women has exploded, the tables are turned, men are now the weaker vessels, and women the protectors. A man dare not travel five miles from Kansas City, but with his wife he feels comparatively secure. Bushwhackers have not yet raised a hand against a woman, they sometimes burn a house over her head but are careful not to injure her person."[20] In fact, customary deference had been twisted into the power game between men who could proclaim that their slaughter of one another was done in service to their protection of women.

At least the occasional warrior was conscious of the weird mutation of the male code prescribing the proper treatment of women that he had adopted during the guerrilla war. Discussing his self-awareness during a typical search of a suspected guerrilla lair, inhabited only by women, Lieutenant Sardius Smith recorded one night in his diary, "We are getting quite hardened to this kind of thing and can go into a house with a pistol in my hand, with a smile on my face, speak politely to the ladies, ask where their men are in order that I may shoot them with as much grace as though I was making a call for friendship sake."[21]

However partial, however selective was its observance, the male code of honor continued to limit some aspects of masculine behavior during the guerrilla war, even while serving to license other outbreaks. What one sees in action are cultural inhibitions intertwined with cultural licenses, combining to create a nastily dynamic dialectic. Destructive impulses most often overrode peacetime reserve, especially when groups of young men attacked

---

19 Sophia L. Bissell to Her Cousin, Lawrence, September 8, 1863, Sophia L. Bissell letters, Chicago Historical Society.
20 Charles M. Chase to the editor of the Sycamore, Illinois *True Republican and Sentinel*, Independence, Mo., Aug. 12, 1863, reprinted in *The Kansas Historical Quarterly* 26 (1960): 124.
21 Entry for May 28, 1862, Sardius Smith diary, Illinois State Historical Library.

other groups of young men, but the code of honor, strangely reworked and sporadically reasserted, served to dampen somewhat the rush toward total destruction.

Vestiges of honor applied only to those whom the warriors considered to be within their cultural net. The exclusion of people as the Other, as anti-beings, eliminated almost all inhibitions for these same fighters. During the Civil War, as has been generally true in the history of the United States, those Others have been defined by race. In Europe, class and ethnocultural divisions, which had none of these nihilistic consequences during the American Civil War, had justified, as they still do, slaughters at least as apoc-alyptic as those that nineteenth-century Americans enacted on the racial Others.

The code of honor, this marginal reticence, applied in the American guerrilla war only to white women and white families. Indeed, there is evidence that German-American men, who were nearly all Unionists and recent immigrants, never were spared by Confederate guerrillas and were strung up or shot with special glee. Even if Germans were feared and loathed as aliens by Anglo-Saxon Missourians, however, there is evidence that German women were spared rape and murder. A common race, differ-ing ethnicity notwithstanding, placed Germans at least tentatively within the recognized racial community, marginally inside rather than outside American culture.[22]

Unlike German women, black and Indian women lived below the racial pale – the code of honor did not apply to them. Many black women were abused, beaten, and raped during the war as they had been during slavery times. Escaping slave women who attached themselves to Union armies found in their newfound freedom that Union soldiers took up much of the physical tyranny of their former owners. One explicit example of rape in the Missouri guerrilla war context comes from the testimony of Francis Kean at the court-martial of guerrilla James Johnson. Kean testified that Johnson and two other bushwhackers had seized her eighteen-year-old slave girl. "They rode on a piece and said to her, 'God damn we will punish you.' … Johnson then got off his horse and said now ride boys and she told me they all done with her what they wanted to – she said they violated her person." In March 1864, a slaveholder named Tapley of Pike County recaptured his escaping slave woman. As she refused to tell him where she had hidden her three children, she was, an unsigned letter to the *Chicago Tribune* later reported, "stripped and beaten on the bare back with a band saw until large blisters

22   Fellman, *Inside War*, 28, 39–40, 181, 206, 252.

formed, and the wretch sawed them open, under which treatment the poor woman died."[23]

The most horrendous example of the general violation of nonwhite women in Missouri was the Sand Creek, Colorado, massacre of a peaceful tribe of Cheyenne Indians on November 19, 1864. This extermination of about five hundred Indians, mainly women and children, took place west of Missouri, but socially similar Union volunteers carried it out. A sickened young officer, who came from New Mexico but was temporarily attached to the Colorado militia, later reported that in addition to the widespread shooting down of fleeing women and children, he saw widespread mutilation of them. "I also heard," James D. Cannon reported, "of numberless instances in which men had cut out the private parts of females and stretched them over…their hats while riding in the ranks."[24] The guerrilla war in Missouri, of whites against whites, never crossed those barriers.

Not merely in the guerrilla war or in Indian warfare did white soldiers treat other races by significantly lower standards than they treated enemies of their own race. As opposed to the no-prisoner policy among white fighters in Missouri, elsewhere regular armies on both sides were nearly always scrupulous about taking prisoners rather than shooting them summarily, treating others as they would wish to be treated. However, this military and cultural inhibition of slaughter did not apply to the treatment accorded by Confederate captors to black Union prisoners, particularly in the western theater. On April 12, 1864, screaming "No Quarter!" and "Kill the damn niggers, shoot them down!" Confederate troops under the command of the renowned General Nathan Bedford Forrest overran Fort Pillow, Tennessee and, following Forrest's orders to shoot them down like dogs, massacred over 100 blacks who had surrendered, burying some alive, setting fire to tents containing wounded blacks, shooting four little boys and two black women and throwing their bodies in the Mississippi River. That same month, other Confederates under General John S. Marmaduke, a well-bred Missourian,

---

23 Court-Martial of James Johnson, Jefferson City, May 18, 1863, case MM 1021, record group 153, Judge Advocate General – General Court Martial Records, National Archives; Mrs. J. R. Roberts to General James L. Long, Quincy, Illinois, April 7, 1864, Provost-Marshal file, Letters Received file 2786, record group 393, National Archives. On white treatment of blacks, particularly but not exclusively those in the Union army, see Joseph T. Glatthaar, *Forged in Battle: The Civil War Alliance of Black Soldiers and White Officers* (New York, 1990).

24 Report of First Lieutenant James D. Cannon, 1st Infantry, New Mexico Volunteers, Fort Lyon, Colorado Territory, Jan. 16, 1865, *OR*, ser. 1, vol. 41, pt. 1, 970–1; Joint Committee on the Conduct of the War, Massacre of the Cheyenne Indians, 28th Congress, 2d session (Washington, D.C., 1865); Report of the Secretary of War, 29th Congress, 2d session, Senate Executive Document 26 (Washington, D.C., 1867). Parts of these two official investigations are reprinted in John M. Carroll, ed., *The Sand Creek Massacre: A Documentary History* (New York, 1973). See also Stan Hoig, *The Sand Creek Massacre* (Norman, Okla., 1961).

executed a perhaps larger number of black prisoners at Poison Springs, Arkansas. Subsequently, black soldiers sometimes would murder Confederate prisoners, shouting "Remember Fort Pillow!"[25]

White Confederate and Union soldiers generally regarded decent treatment of prisoners of war, even those taken immediately after the killing of their squad mates, as a mark of manly honor, thus demonstrating their subscription to rules of a fair fight, which they did not extend to black soldiers. At those moments when the Civil War was also a race war, the different rules that applied lowered the threshold of legitimated violence. When the fight was between white Americans, soldiers generally were willing to limit their killing in combat, not because they lacked firepower or because of tactical shortcomings, and not just because their officers enforced restraint, but primarily because they continued to act at least in part within the restraints of their implicit, shared moral code.

If the guerrilla war theaters of the Civil War provided a brutal testing ground of the tension between approaching nihilism and preserving cultural and personal inhibitions, the psyche of Gen. William Tecumseh Sherman provided another key venue of inner conflicts, both acted out and constrained. Sherman was the representative man of the western war; he was lean, hard, mean, and relentless. He had been deeply affected by the guerrilla war that he had seen when he was posted in Missouri early in the conflict. He was bright, sometimes depressed, sometimes manic, endlessly and carelessly garrulous about his feelings as well as about his opinions, and he transformed himself into a fighting leader beloved to his men and hated as the devil incarnate in the South. During his incendiary march through Georgia and the Carolinas, he not only trailed destruction but all the while gleefully proclaimed his mission to destroy the very soul of the Confederacy. This self-declared grim reaper transformed himself into the implacable embodiment of the Union war against the South.

The argument over whether or not the Civil War was a total war often focuses on assessments of Sherman's intentions and activities.[26] The

25 Albert Castel, "The Fort Pillow Massacre: A Fresh Examination of the Evidence," *Civil War History* 4 (1958): 37–40; John Cimprich and Robert C. Mainford Jr., "Fort Pillow Revisited: New Evidence about an Old Controversy," *Civil War History* 28 (Dec. 1982): 293–306; James McPherson, *Battle Cry of Freedom* (New York, 1988), 748; Glatthaar, *Forged in Battle*, 155–9; and for Poison Springs, *OR*, ser. 1, vol. 39, pt. 1, 554–7. One can only approximate the exact number of blacks who surrendered and were then executed. There were 295 whites and 262 blacks garrisoned at Fort Pillow when Forrest's men attacked. One-hundred and twenty-seven whites were killed, and 168 taken prisoner. Of the blacks, only 58 were taken prisoner. Assuming, for the purposes of estimation, that approximately the same proportion of blacks as whites (36 percent) or 94 men) were killed in battle, 110 were killed after surrendering.

26 See, e.g., the debate between Neely's, "Was the Civil War a Total War?" (Chapter 2) and James McPherson's essay in this volume (Chapter 14).

Atlanta Campaign, the inexorable march through Georgia to the sea at Savannah and then up through the Carolinas, burning a broad swath through the countryside and the cities, without doubt were intended by Sherman to break the fighting spirit of the Southern rebels. Sherman succeeded. Lest any Confederate miss the point of his actions, Sherman also loudly advertised the meanings of his campaigns, which he clearly realized to be psychological even more than military events. On the eve of the march from Atlanta to the sea, Sherman wrote to Grant, "If we can march a well-appointed army right through [President Jefferson Davis's] territory," we will make "a demonstration to the world, foreign and domestic, that we have a power that Davis cannot resist. ... Thousands of people abroad and in the South will reason thus: If the North can march an army right through the South, it is proof positive that the North can prevail in this contest, leaving only open the question of its willingness to use that power ... I can make the march and make Georgia howl!"[27] The last part of this letter, because of its pungent phrasemaking, is the best remembered. Even more chilling than the authentic anger of the letter, however, is Sherman's cool calculation of the impact that a campaign of organized terror would have on the South.

Six weeks earlier, when he had been shelling Atlanta, which the Confederates had turned into an armed fortress with civilians living inside, Sherman traded invective with Confederate General John B. Hood, who condemned Sherman for his "studied and injurious cruelty," which was the worst ever in "the dark history of war." Rejecting Hood's charges as they applied to Atlanta in particular, Sherman accepted them in general. Sherman wrote to Hood:

You cannot qualify war in harsher terms than I will. War is cruelty, and you cannot refine it; and those who brought war into our country deserve all the curses and malediction a people can pour out. ... You might as well appeal against the thunderstorm as against these terrible hardships of war. They are inevitable, and the only way the people of Atlanta can hope once more to live in peace and quiet at home, is to stop the war, which can only be done by admitting that it began in error and is perpetuated in pride ... I want peace, and believe that it can only be reached through union and war, and I will conduct war with a view to perfect and early success. But then my dear sir, when peace does come, you may call on me for any thing. Then will I share with you the last cracker, and watch with you to shield your houses and families against danger from every quarter.[28]

---

27 OR. ser. 1, vol. 39, pt. 3, 660.
28 William Tecumseh Sherman, *Memoirs* (1875; reprint: New York, 1983), 2: 126–7.

Sherman's rhetorical purpose was clear – he was after not only the material but, even more significantly, the moral and emotional center of the Confederacy. He did not burn all of the South, which he could not have accomplished even if he had wished to do so. But he wanted to make an explicit demonstration that he could burn it piece by piece if this proved necessary, and he also wanted to show that he had the necessary destructive energy to accomplish whatever was required. Not only did Sherman write this message; he broadcast it to the people, South and North. A well-known hater of the press and a reactionary antidemocrat in many ways, Sherman also understood the necessity of reaching the hearts and minds of the people, which, owing to the newly available telegraph and high-speed, cheap newspaper technology, were available to him. Sherman seized hold of the new technology in an effort to subdue the rebellion. In propagandistic abilities, Sherman was indeed the first of the modern generals. And in his equally acute consciousness of the impact of terror on civilians, proclaimed as loudly as possible, Sherman was also a powerful psychological warrior of a kind that we usually associate with twentieth-century military leaders, although Sherman himself probably would have considered Napoléon to have been the great innovator in this realm, and Genghis Khan had been no slouch either. Writing a decade after the war, Sherman concluded about his intentions during the last year of his campaigning, "My aim then was, to whip the rebels, to humble their pride, to follow them to their inmost recesses, and make them fear and dread us."[29]

On the long march through the Confederate heartland, although he sponsored the burning of the Southern food supply, the theft and killing of draft animals, and the burning of barns, fields, and fences, Sherman also prohibited the rape of Southern women, the killing of civilians, and, on the whole, the burning of occupied rural houses and of towns. Unlike the combatants on both sides of the guerrilla war, Sherman never intended in actual practice, nor would he permit, a level of destructive war that would erase the line between civilian and military enemies. He intended to induce terror and to make psychological war, but unlike guerrillas, he did not even dream of genocide against Southern whites, whom he viewed as errant fellow-civilians to be defeated as efficiently as possible in war in order to welcome them back, chastised and redeemed, into the bosom of the Union family. In his attack on Southern hearts, Sherman stopped well short of total warfare. He certainly had the military means to make total war – overwhelming force and no viable opposing army – which allowed his torch-bearers to fan out over a broad

29 Sherman, *Memoirs*, 2:249.

swath of land, and he perhaps had sufficient personal anger and self-right-eousness to wage a total war if he had really wanted one, but he held himself and his men back because of the shared cultural value system, which would not permit the slaughter of white American civilians.

As was generally true in his culture, as the Sand Creek massacre of 1864 had demonstrated once again, Sherman too did not consider Indians to be part of the true American family – these were not errant kin, as were white Southerners, but alien savages. Toward Indians, he could at least countenance a war of extermination, the killing of all civilian men, women, and children. In mid-nineteenth-century America, paternalistic, protective, and even romantic images of Indians vied with the picture of nomadic heathens fit to be slaughtered. Sharing these ambiguities, Sherman rarely expressed com-pletely genocidal feelings toward Indians. However, especially writing in pri-vate to old Civil War comrades, when he was in charge of the war against the Plains Indians, which accompanied the building of the transcontinental rail-road after the Civil War, Sherman not only used a language approaching genocide, but he seemed to predict the death not merely of Indians but of the Indian culture and people in a manner in which he had never conceptualized Georgians and Carolinians even when he was in the midst of attacking them.

Exasperated by the guerrilla tactics of the childlike red devils, Sherman wrote from his St. Louis headquarters to Ulysses S. Grant, the Army com-mander in Washington in 1867, "In time we must take these wild Indians in hand and give them a devil of a trashing. They deserve it now, but they are so scattered and so mixed up that even if we were prepared, we would hardly know which way to strike." However exasperated he was, Sherman had only a tiny army to cover a huge area of the West, and thus only limited means to act out his urgent feelings (unlike his far stronger military situation in 1864–65 in the South). Even in a cooler mood, writing again to Grant in 1868, Sherman viewed Indians as a separate and inferior race to be "removed." Whether or not ultimate justice was on the side of the white race, History was, Sherman believed, and he also believed himself to be Destiny's Agent. "I have no doubt our people have committed grievous wrong to the Indians and I wish we could punish them but it is impracticable," Sherman wrote to Grant in 1868, in one of his more complex formulations of the "Indian problem." "Both races cannot use this country in common and one or the other must withdraw. We cannot withdraw without checking the natural progress of Civilization. The only course is for us to destroy the hostile, and to segregate the peaceful and maintain them." To this point in his analysis, Sherman saw himself as a compromising father, mediating between furious white settlers and hostile Indians, seeking to protect the good Indians while punishing only the bad. Sherman, however, went on. Although he would not commend or sponsor the slaughter of tame bands, as had been the case at Sand Creek, Sherman wrote to Grant, "I would not hesitate to approach the extermination of a camp . . . from which they send out their thieving and murderous parties to kill and steal." Selecting only the bad Indian women and children for death might well merge, Sherman considered, into a more wholesale slaughter. If Indians did not distinguish between white soldiers and white settlers, Sherman wrote to Grant, "We in our turn cannot discriminate among the Indians – all look alike and to get the rascals, we are forced to include all."[30]

If a touch of ambivalence remained here while he was at his calmest, if generally he did not seek to enact the exterminatist values he shared with almost all white settlers in the West, Sherman often could override his humane inhibitions when he considered the Indians that he was fighting on the Plains, in a manner impermissible to him when he had attacked white Southerners. Indeed, at his most furious, Sherman could lift his verbal censorship. On December 28, 1866, after Captain William J. Fetterman and eighty-one of his men were killed near Fort Phil Kearney, in what is now northern Wyoming, Sherman wrote to Grant, "We must act with vindictive earnestness against the Sioux, even to their extermination, men, women and children. Nothing else will reach the root of this case."[31]

30 Sherman to Grant, June 11, 1867, May 8, 1868, in John Y. Simon, ed., *The Papers of Ulysses S. Grant* (Carbondale, Ill., 1967), 18:174–5, 261. Also revealing is Sherman's later correspondence with General Philip H. Sheridan, when Grant became President, Sherman the army commander in Washington and Sheridan the Indian killer in charge in the West. Cf. The Sheridan papers, Library of Congress. Sherman's place for the Indian in his value structure, far from being original, was the standard one for nineteenth-century Americans, particularly those in the West. "Frontiersmen" were, after all, physically displacing Indians. Such had been the task of the Ohioans of Sherman's father's generation, and such was central to Sherman's purpose on the Great Plains from after the Civil War until his retirement in 1883. For a telling example of this process as it was carried out by civilian settlers in Illinois from approximately 1800 until 1850, see John Mack Faragher, *Sugar Creek: Life on the Illinois Prairie* (New Haven, Conn., 1986). New England's first settlers brought exterminationist sentiments with them, folk beliefs which only increased on contact. See Richard Slotkin, *Regeneration Through Violence: The Mythology of the American Frontier, 1600–1860* (Middletown, Conn., 1973).

31 Sherman to Grant, Dec. 28, 1866, quoted in Robert G. Athearn, *William Tecumseh Sherman and the Settlement of the West* (Norman, Okla., 1956), 110. Sherman had to operate within a political arena that included former abolitionists and other Christian activists, including his own wife and brother-in-law, who sought to prevent the killing of the Indians and to promote their salvation through conversion to Christianity and to farming. On all elements of this conflict, see the magisterial two volumes by Francis P. Prucha, *The Great Father* (Lincoln, Neb., 1984). Of course, one might argue from our own perspective that destroying Indian religion and economic forms amounted to genocide by softer means, but the narrower point here is that Sherman could not have gotten away with actual genocide, given American public opinion, which included what Sherman considered to be stupidly humanitarian "Indian lovers," whom, whatever his opinion, he could not entirely dismiss. This context can lead us both to underplay and to exaggerate the possible meanings of Sherman's widely shared if ferocious attitudes.

What had been unthinkable to the erstwhile father leading the honor-bound family, the incorporation of even errant children who were to be punished before they were redeemed, was quite thinkable toward others outside one's concept of shared peoplehood. Thresholds of violence varied in both varieties of warfare, of course. White warrior brother shot and mutilated white brother in Missouri, and this was not the case when two regular armies faced off in the larger Civil War. But in neither the guerrilla nor the regular war sector was sister, mother, wife, or daughter raped or murdered as a general rule. Not only guerrillas but regular soldiers too could rape and slaughter Indian women and children, and Confederates would shoot disarmed black soldiers, which they would not allow themselves to do to members of the white culture, even enemy ones. Sherman, who consciously fought with brutality against Georgia to make reunification and peace, warred against the Sioux to drive them off the land, and if necessary to exterminate them. On the great stage of the Civil War, even Sherman, the most articulate mass terrorist, held back at the gate of total war against civilians. Only toward the Indians did he reach toward this level of destructiveness of a whole people.

In the guerrilla war and in the war against the Indians, one can catch glimpses of what might be called the great chain of cultural antibeing. In the Anglo-American experience of this chain, one might start with the English treatment of the "barbarian," "heathen" Irish, who were to be treated as the English refrained from treating one another. English martial debasement and destruction of the Irish had a long lineage, dating back to at least the twelfth century, when, John Gillingham has argued, the developing rules of chivalric combat, including exchange of prisoners rather than their enslavement or slaughter, simply were not applied by the English to the Irish, who were not conceptualized as fellow humans with whom to bargain equally but as aboriginal savages to be killed when they were in the way.[32]

England's more direct moral predecessor to Sherman, one to whom he was compared frequently after the war, would be Oliver Cromwell, a morally upright and generally humane man, who told his officers when he assumed command in Ireland in 1649, "I have often had these thoughts within myself which perhaps may be carnal and foolish: I had rather be overrun by a Cavalierish interest than a Scotch interest, I had rather be overrun by a Scotch interest than an Irish interest, and I think that of all this is the most dangerous. ... If they shall be able to carry on their work they will make this the most miserable people in the earth, for all the world knows their barbarism."

32 John Gillingham, "The English Invasion of Ireland," in Brendan Bradshaw, Andrew Hadfield, and Willy Maley, eds., *Representing Ireland* (Cambridge, 1992), and "Conquering the Barbarians: War and Chivalry in Twelfth-Century Britain," *Haskins Society Journal* 4 (1993).

Cromwell proceeded to storm Drogheda, slaughtering its 2,800 inhabitants, and then Wexford, killing 1,500. Far from showing remorse for these massacres, after Drogheda he wrote "I am persuaded that this is a righteous judgment of God upon those barbarous wretches, who have imbrued their hands in so much innocent blood, and that it will tend to prevent the effusion of blood for the future; which are the satisfactory grounds of such actions, which otherwise cannot but work remorse and regret." After Wexford, Cromwell deepened rather than reversed his blooded certainty; he then wrote that he had been God's minister, doing justice to His enemies. "God, by an unexpected providence, in His righteous justice brought a just judgment upon them, causing them to become a prey to the soldiers who in their piracies had made preys of so many families, and with their bloods to answer the cruelties which they had exercised upon the lives of divers poor Protestants."[33]

The following year, Cromwell warred against the Scots, who were to him not Papist savages to be slaughtered but errant Protestants who were to be chastised and then welcomed back into the English family: They were "one's own," Cromwell proclaimed. And within England, Cromwell and the Royalists usually tried to limit collateral damage to civilians: Barbara Donagan has argued that for reasons both of "utility and professional honor," they shared "a kind of contractual etiquette of belligerence."[34]

It has been argued that what the English learned about the aboriginal Irish they then applied to the Indians of America.[35] When they reached for an analogy to analyze what was to their sensibilities barbaric behavior among the Indians, New England Puritans often alighted on the Irish parallel. Observing native funeral customs, including face painting with lead and

33 The passages on Ireland are quoted in Charles Firth, *Oliver Cromwell, and the Rule of the Puritans in England* (New York, 1900; reprinted: London, 1956), 252, 256. Such English attitudes toward the Irish have persisted in England, much as have American prejudices toward Indians and blacks. On nineteenth-century English slurs against the Irish, see two books by Lewis P. Curtis Jr., *Anglo-Saxons and Celts: A Study of Anti-Irish Prejudice in Victorian England* (Bridgeport, Conn., 1968); and *Apes and Angels: The Irishman in Victorian Culture* (Washington, D.C., 1971), a study based on cartoons in the popular press. One high victorian, the historian Edward A. Freeman, noted of the Anglo-American Others during his first visit to America, "This would be a grand land if only every last Irishman would kill a negro, and be hanged for it." Edward A. Freeman to F. H. Dickinson, New Haven, Dec. 4, 1881, in W. R. W. Stephens, ed., *The Life and Letters of Edward A. Freeman*, 2 vols. (London, 1895), 2: 242.
34 Barbara Donagan, "Codes and Conduct in the English Civil War," *Past and Present*, no. 117 (Feb. 1988): 78–9.
35 Winthrop D. Jordan, *White Over Black: American Attitudes Toward the Negro, 1550–1812* (Chapel Hill, N.C., 1968), 85–91. Jordan entitles this portion of his study, "The UnEnglish: Scots, Irish, and Indians." Also sensitive to white treatment of Indians as well as of blacks is George M. Fredrickson, *The Black Image in the White Mind: The Debate on Afro-American Character and Destiny, 1817–1914* (New York, 1971). Nicholas P. Canny makes the link between sixteenth-century English attitudes toward the Irish and later English-settler takes on the Indians of the new world in "The Ideology of English Colonization: From Ireland to America," *William and Mary Quarterly*, 3d ser., 30 (Oct. 1973): 575–98.

soot, William Wood noted that the ceremonies were accompanied with "Irish-like howlings." Roger Williams, that most benevolent of New Englanders, argued against the enslavement of Indians who had surrendered, lest they be encouraged to remain enemies "or turn wild Irish themselves."[36] Such a melding of cultural categories among seventeenth-century English settlers in America does lead us toward Sherman, whose attitude about the Indians so resembled those of Cromwell concerning the Irish – set, as both men were, in the context of cultures that would prescribe treating the aliens as Others, as they were at Sand Creek and Drogheda, Wexford and Fort Pillow.

In their guerrilla conflict, American warriors had approached the destruction of all possible enemies, civilian and soldier alike – the nihilist desire – but, because of their cultural values, however perversely reworked, they had held back from plunging all the way into the abyss. Their attitudes and behavior shifted significantly when they warred against enemies of other races. In this, they resembled seventeenth-century European soldiers and those of our century, who often war against others as they would not against those whom they consider as their own. Attention to levels of destructiveness of civilians during wars reveals a great deal about the meanings of human conflict obscured by modernization theory. Argument by linear development toward the *modern* or the *total* in war is a kind of teleological trap that obscures more than it reveals about warfare as a widespread and varied cultural institution. Instead of assuming that everything leads to now, by examining the throw of the cultural net, with differing levels of destruction applied to one's own than to the Others, one can begin to understand not a false and foreshortened progression but a long and jagged record, one that reflects concrete cultural circumstances, not abstract chronological imperatives.

---

36 Both quotations are from Alden T. Vaugham, *New England Frontier: Puritans and Indians* (Boston, 1965), 42–3, 208. Vaugham points out that Williams nevertheless requested an Indian captive for himself.

25

The Wars against Paris

ROBERT TOMBS

INTRODUCTION

Two wars were waged against Paris between September 1870 and May 1871, the first by the German army, the second by the French. The German attack was the siege of the largest fortress in the world, carried out by blockade and bombardment. The French attack was the suppression of an insurrection by the legal government. Their common target was regarded by many, and especially by its inhabitants, as unique: the center and symbol of modern civilization in some of its most admirable, but also in some of its most dangerous, forms. Both attacks were ultimately political, intending not merely to reduce a fortress but to chastise its inhabitants. The German purpose was to alter the will of the population by privation and intimidation. The French purpose, at first merely to disarm dissidents, became radicalized during the course of the civil war until it became, for some of those in authority, the elimination of sections of the Parisian population regarded as a social and political danger.

Paris was not a fortress like any other in France or Europe. The ramparts of other capital cities were relics of the past. Those of Paris, conceived in the early 1830s, were built only in 1840–41, when the Mehemet Ali crisis made another European war seem likely. The French calculated that modern war, on the pattern of the revolutionary wars, would have as its object the domination of the state and the nation, not merely the seizure of frontier territory.[1] Paris had become the essential target because of its unique political importance in postrevolutionary France, encapsulating the political life, and even the sovereignty, of the country.

In the days of our forbears, its occupation had little influence on the rest of France; Charles VII, Henri III, Henri IV did not cease to be kings by ceasing to reign over

---

1 Hence, the focus of recriminations over the frontier alterations of 1815 was that they made a march on Paris easier. See Gary P. Cox, "Facing the Germans: The Beginning of French Strategic Planning, 1815–1848," Ph.D. diss., University of Virginia, 1987.

Paris; [but] two recent examples have proved that this great capital ... [now] takes with her the destiny of all our provinces. ... Because of this importance of Paris we have to defend her.[2]

As 1814 and 1830 had shown, as Paris went, so went France.

Fortifying the city had a double significance. It defended the French State both against foreign invasion and – many argued – against popular insurrection. A ring of suburban forts could be new Bastilles in which governments could seek refuge, launch counterattacks, and imprison enemies. In the face of public outcry, the government compromised by building in addition a continuous rampart around the city, which could shelter its citizens from domestic tyrants as well as foreign invaders.[3] The fortification question aptly summed up the multiple significance of Paris: bulwark of France; seat of government; source of sovereignty; hotbed of revolution.

Not until 1870–71 would all these roles be simultaneously played out and fought over. Contemporaries were riveted by the spectacle, which gave dramatic proof of the horrors of modern war. They were correct in seeing the involvement of civilians in war both as a reversion to earlier religious or revolutionary forms of conflict, and as a sign of barbarities to come. This chapter looks in detail at the motives and beliefs animating the attacks on Paris. It argues that they help us to identify at an early stage key political and ideological developments, not fully understood by contemporaries, that were to contribute to the twentieth-century concept of total war.

THE GERMAN SIEGE, SEPTEMBER 1870–JANUARY 1871

The march on Paris of the German armies after their victory at Sedan followed the logic of the French strategists of the 1830s: control of Paris could alone give control of France. Yet this had not been the German's plan, and they were slow to appreciate their strategic predicament.[4] The consequence of Sedan, they thought, should have been French surrender. Indeed, the new Government of National Defense duly asked Bismarck what his peace terms would be. But Sedan had also meant a revolution in Paris and the seizure of political initiative by the city's population. Consequently, the terms that the government was free to accept were circumscribed by

---

2 General Lamarque in Chamber of Deputies, April 13, 1831, *Archives Parlementaires*, 2d ser., 68 (1831): 546. (Unless otherwise stated, translations are mine.)

3 Patricia O' Brien, "*L' embastillement de Paris*: The Fortification of Paris during the July Monarchy," *French Historical Studies* 9, no. 1 (1975): 63–82.

4 Moltke had thought only of marching to meet the French army for a decisive battle that would overthrow the dynasty and end the war. Helmut von Moltke, *Moltke's Military Correspondence, 1870–1871* (Oxford, 1923), 1:25, 34.

Parisian susceptibilities: the Foreign Minister Jules Favre, although "dying to make peace,"[5] had proclaimed that "we will not give up an inch of our territory or a stone of our fortresses." Hence, the war continued. Moltke sarcastically wrote, "*La France qui est 'plus forte que jamais'* is still boasting even in this situation. Her field army no longer exists, but she has *Mr. Rochefort, professeur de barricades and la poitrine des patriotes invincibles.*"[6]

From September 1870 until the armistice the following January, all efforts were focused on Paris: "Let us win in Paris," wrote the prefect at Lille, "the rest is a detail."[7] The military mobilization of the provinces was directed solely toward raising the siege, and that of the Germans toward maintaining it.[8] This was not because Paris was the center of the railway network or of industrial production, for these were cut off anyway from the rest of the country, whose military effort had to do without the capital's resources. It was rather because Paris was "the sacred city," "where the sovereign resides …the intellectual, moral and political centre of France."[9] "The sovereign" was the people of Paris, who had assumed the right to speak for France. The situation was quite different from the American Civil War, for example, when neither Richmond nor even Washington were of decisive importance.[10]

As winter dragged on and repeated military failure, occupation, requisitions, fines, and reprisals sapped the will to resist of a growing proportion of Frenchmen outside Paris, the war became increasingly a battle of wills between Germans and Parisians: "The Republican dictators in Paris do not dare to consult the country," noted Moltke on October 12.[11] The strength and danger of Paris lay not in the strength of its fortifications or the resources of its arsenals and factories, but in the minds and hearts of its people, and in particular the Republicans who, inspired by the great legend of 1792, were convinced that a *levée en masse* of patriotic citizens could roll back the German armies. Favre understood this perfectly:

The generals should remember that they are not merely the defenders of a citadel, they are also and above all the champions of a great city, which encloses a large

---

5   According to the Austrian ambassador, quoted by J. P. T. Bury, *Gambetta and the National Defence: A Republican Dictatorship in France* (London, 1936), 79.
6   Helmut von Moltke, *Moltkes Briefe*, ed. Willy B. Andreas (Leipzig, 1922), 2: 395–6 (Sept. 21, 1870). French passages, in the original.
7   Stéphane Audoin-Rouzeau, *1870: La France dans la guerre* (Paris, 1989), 178.
8   The best analysis of the campaign is Michael Howard, *The Franco-Prussian War: The German Invasion of France, 1870–1871* (London, 1960) .
9   Words of Louis Blanc and J. B. Millière in *Annales de l'Assemblée Nationale* (hereafter cited as *AAN*), (1871), 1:271, 277 (March 10).
10 During our discussions in Washington, Richard Current pointed out that the war did not end because Richmond fell, but rather Richmond fell because the war ended. Jay Luvaas noted that General Sherman regarded the possible loss of Washington with some equanimity.
11 *Moltkes Briefe*, 2: 400.

population, whose passions and political and social movements impose their own requirements. The city of Paris wants to be defended *à outrance*.[12]

For diplomats such as Bismarck and for soldiers such as Moltke, this was the world turned upside down. Public opinion, so Napoléon III told them after Sedan, had forced him into war, and now the war was essentially being directed by "journalists and the mob," in Bismarck's words, following no political or military logic.[13] Although disagreeing over means, the German leaders wanted to make the French people, especially the "invincible patriots" sheltering behind the ramparts of Paris, painfully aware of the impossibility of victory and the penalties of senseless resistance. This, to the Germans, had gone beyond legitimate patriotism and was sustained only by lying propaganda and what Moltke called "the lawyers' reign of terror."[14] Professional principle was outraged by what seemed the callous futility of the results:

It is lamentable and irresponsible to send an army like that into action. They have no idea what soldiering is … their artillery fires into the air, and hits practically nothing. They have no cavalry. Their weapons are appalling. In spite of [their] undeniable bravery, [they] can hardly put up any resistance.[15]

It was also alarming because there seemed no neat military and political conclusion to what was becoming in their eyes a regression to more barbarous ages: "The war takes on an ever more hateful character," wrote Moltke on October 27. "It is bad enough that armies must slaughter each other; one must not lead whole peoples against each other."[16] The response of Bismarck and Moltke was to order reprisals against the civilian population.[17] But these had the effect of further escalating the conflict.

Paris had to fall for resistance to end. As it was too strong to be stormed, the Parisians had to be forced to surrender. Moltke and most soldiers saw no alternative to starvation; Bismarck, supported by the German press, demanded a bombardment of the city which "in five or six days" would bring "the mob" to their senses.[18] There was a shared element of vindictiveness toward

12 Speech to council of war, Dec. 31, quoted in *Enquête sur les actes du gouvernement de la défense nationale* (hereafter cited as *EGDN*), in *AAN*, 21 (Paris, 1874), 314.
13 See Napoleon's and Bismarck's words after Sedan in Moritz Busch, *Bismarck: Some Secret Pages of His History* (London, 1898), 2 : 155, 164; corroborated by Bismarck's report to the king dated Sept. 2, 1870, *The Correspondence of William and Bismarck* (London, 1903), 1 : 126. Moltke agreed that "it is dreadful how the mob in power has wreaked havoc, and ridiculous too," in *Moltkes Briefe*, 2 : 400 (Oct . 12) .
14 *Moltkes Briefe*, 2 : 412 (Dec. 22). The French government was largely composed of lawyers.
15 A German officer quoted in François Roth, *La Guerre de 1870* (Paris, 1990), 296.
16 Moltkes Briefe, 2 : 404 .
17 Moltke had ordered the shooting of captured franc-tireurs as early as Aug. 22, 1870. *Military Correspondence*, 1:105 . Bismarck urged an intensification of the war in a memorandum to the king dated Dec. 14. *Die gesammelten Werke*, 15 vols. (Berlin, 1924–32), 6b : 634–5.
18 Busch, *Bismarck*, 2 : 333.

Paris, the "house of Satan," the city of jingoism, corruption, and revolution.[19]
The relatively moderate Crown Prince wrote in his diary:

May we then soon see an end of the resistance of this reputed metropolis of civilization, and finally break the chain that surrounds this so-called "holy city" – "the modern Babylon" were the better designation – and inflict on her the chastisement she
deserves [and] punish that section of the population whose wickedness was the guilty
cause of the war.[20]

The soldiers resisted Bismarck's desire to bombard Paris because it would
be costly and arduous, would strain transport resources, and would be unlikely to succeed. Moreover, they detested having strategic decisions made
by politicians and journalists:

If we give in ... we shall soon arrive at the same condition of affairs as the French
... and shall return to 1848. If we allow ourselves to be driven by the so-called "Voice
of the People" ... it will be an end to generalship.[21]

Their objections, however, gave way before Bismarck's unscrupulous pressure. For example, he spread the story that reluctance to bombard was owing
to the liberal scruples of the Crown Prince's English wife.[22] The king made
the final decision: Bombardment was necessary to frighten "the sovereign
Paris mob ... which has the final word" into surrender.[23]

On January 5, 1871, shelling of the city began. It continued with varying
intensity until January 26. Some 12,000 shells, according to a French estimate, fell inside the ramparts, causing about 400 casualties. The effect was
slight and, if anything, increased popular determination to resist. So small
was the danger that the shells – which, noted the composer Vincent d'Indy,
came whistling over in B flat – became a popular spectacle. Small boys set up
a trade in fragments, and shouted "Gare à la bombe!" to make respectable
bourgeois throw themselves flat in the mud.[24] There was another side to
the daytime bravado, however. The explosion of a shell every few minutes
during the night, "as regular as a steam piston," noted Edmond de Goncourt,
frayed nerves and led to a sizable migration to the Right Bank.[25]

19 War Minister von Roon, in Roth, *La Guerre*, 198.
20 *The War Diary of the Emperor Frederick III, 1870–1871*, ed. and trans. Alfred R. Allinson, (London,
    1927), 247 (Jan. 3). He clearly had in mind Victor Hugo's much-quoted declaration, "I shall enter
    once more within thy holy walls, O Paris, O my mother, and bear a link of thy chain."
21 *Journals of Field-Marshal Count von Blumenthal for 1866 and 1870–71*, ed. Albrecht von Blumenthal,
    trans. Maj. A. D. Gillespie-Addison (London, 1903), 229.
22 For details of the quarrel, see Stig Förster's essay (Chapter 6, this volume).
23 Quoted in Howard, *Franco-Prussian War*, 357 n. 1.
24 Vincent d' Indy, *Histoire du 105e bataillon de la Garde nationale de Paris en l'année 1870–1871* (Paris,
    1872), 101; Francisque Sarcey, *Le Siège de Paris* (Paris, 1871), chap. 10.
25 Edmond de Goncourt, *Paris Under Siège, 1870–1871: From the Goncourt Journal*, ed. and trans.
    George J. Becker (Ithaca, N.Y., and London, 1969), 192; Audoin-Rouzeau, *1870*, 275.

The intention behind the bombardment is clear from its execution. While most effort was always directed at the forts and ramparts, some guns were ordered to shell the city itself (see Figure 25.1). They fired as far as they could reach, mostly at night and without precise targets. Their range covered the whole of the Left Bank, which was sprayed with fire. The outraged French accused them of aiming at public monuments and hospitals, but the areas that suffered most intensely (the Champ de Mars district, Montparnasse, and the Latin Quarter) show not even such perverse consistency. Perhaps these hardest-hit zones were where the roughly directed fire of the various batteries intersected; and perhaps the gunlayers, when visibility permitted, aimed roughly at or between landmarks such as the domes of the Invalides, the Panthéon, the Salpetrière, and the Val de Grâce. The industrial district of Grenelle, within easy range of the batteries on the high ground south of the city, received no more than a random allotment of shots. The well-known Cail engineering factory there, the city's biggest armaments producer, was hit only seven times. The large Javel chemical works, close to the German batteries, was outside the main bombarded zones. But Montparnasse cemetery received 400 shells – more than anywhere else in the city.[26]

The bombardment drew restrained protest from diplomats still in Paris. They complained that the shelling had begun without a warning to permit noncombatants, especially foreign citizens, to seek shelter.[27] The Germans, in other words, had not made even a token gesture at distancing civilians from military operations – something that progressive writers on war and international law laid down as a basic principle of limited, civilized warfare. Yet, ironically, this very separation was also the aim of the Germans themselves. Each side accused the other of disregarding the conventions of civilized warfare. The Germans criticized the French for mobilizing civilians – franc-tireurs were a German nightmare. The French criticized the Germans for punishing civilians. Both had in mind the grim precedent of the revolutionary wars: The Germans had enlisted civilian volunteers in 1813, protested Favre; yes, answered Bismarck, "and the French shot them whenever they caught them."[28]

The bombardment of Paris was the most spectacular German reprisal against civilian involvement in the war, not directly as franc-tireurs, but as citizens demanding *la guerre à outrance*. Diplomatic protests missed the point. Civilians were not being caught up in siege operations owing to the

26 H. de Sarrepont, *Le Bombardement de Paris par les Prussiens en lanvier 1871* (Paris, 1872) gives most detail.
27 Text in United States Embassy, ed., *Franco-German War and Insurrection of the Commune: Correspondence of E. B. Washburne, Envoy Extraordinary and Minister Plenipotentiary of the United States to France* (Washington, D.C., 1878), 124.
28 Busch, *Bismarck*, 1:499.

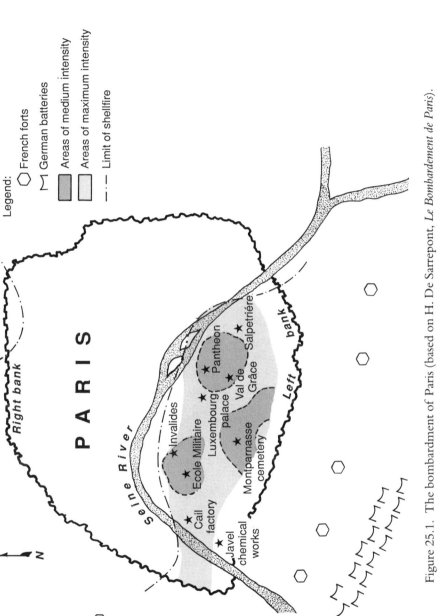

Legend:

⬡ French forts

⋏ German batteries

▨ Areas of medium intensity

▨ Areas of maximum intensity

–·– Limit of shellfire

N

P A R I S

Right bank

Seine River

Left bank

★ Invalides

★ Cail factory

★ Javel chemical works

★ Ecole Militaire

★ Luxembourg palace

★ Pantheon

★ Val de Grâce

★ Salpetriére

★ Montparnasse cemetery

Figure 25.1. The bombardment of Paris (based on H. De Sarrepont, *Le Bombardement de Paris*).

carelessness of the soldiers: They were the ultimate target of those operations, which had no other aim but to intimidate them into political surrender.

[In Paris] the Reds are instituting a reign of terror and are so eager for the continu-
ance of the war for their own selfish ends that even honourable peace-loving men,
as, for instance, Jules Favre, can make no headway against it."[29]

In other sieges, the Germans used civilian sufferings as a weapon to induce
surrender of the fortress, and this, French outrage notwithstanding, was a
recognized "usage of war."[30] But Paris, as Favre had said, was not just a
citadel, a bigger Belfort: It was a great city and the political heart of France.
Bismarck, in his reply to the diplomatic protest, came fairly close to formulating this point:

The determination, standing alone in modern history, to transform the capital of a
great country into a fortress...including nearly three millions of inhabitants, has created...a distressing state of things which is much to be regretted. The responsibility
falls exclusively upon those who have chosen to make of this capital a fortress and a
battlefield.[31]

Bismarck and other spokesmen were, however, disingenuous in pretend-
ing that the target was military and that civilians were suffering only what
would now be termed "collateral damage." Moltke claimed that fog and distance made gunnery inaccurate; Bismarck told Busch to suppress references
in press communiqués to shells falling in the Luxembourg gardens. The
Crown Prince was franker in his diary: "All that is in question is to punish
that section of the population whose wickedness was the guilty cause of the
war."[32]

The bombardment caused great interest but restrained reaction abroad.
The major newspapers followed Bismarck's line. For *The Times* (January 23),
while "the bombardment of a great and populous capital...in our time is
very deeply to be deplored,...Paris is a regular fortress." The London *Daily
News* (January 16) concluded more succinctly that "a fortress is a fortress."
The *New York Herald Tribune* regretted the "impending ruin" of the great city
but shrugged it off as an unfortunate consequence of modern war, in which
the Parisians would suffer the fate of the "people of Petersburg and
Vicksburg."[33] The German press tended to answer any criticism by pointing

29 Allinson, ed., *War Diary of Frederick III*, 140.
30 See, e.g., M. Bluntschli, *Le Droit international codifié*, 2d ed. (Paris, 1874), which incorporated the
    Instructions for the Government of Armies of the United States in the Field (May 1863), drawn up
    by the prominent liberal lawyer Francis Lieber, and widely considered to sum up enlightened mod-
    ern practice.
31 United States Embassy, ed., *Franco-German War*, 138.
32 Allinson, ed., *War Diary of Frederick III*, 247.
33 Jan. 1 and 2, 1871.

to French or British bombardments – of Delhi, Rome, Sebastopol – and repeating Bismarck's point that Paris was a fortress like any other.[34]

There are several probable reasons for this rather toneless response to a sensational event. News from inside Paris, dependent on balloon flights, was slow to emerge, so that vivid live reporting, even in leading papers, was up to two weeks late. Moreover, first reports in *The Times* and the slightly faster *Daily News* stressed how much less terrible the effects had been than expected: Far from causing a Great Fire of Paris, slaughtering the innocent and pulverizing art treasures, as had been feared, the shells were "very few, and have done slight mischief either to persons or property."[35] Harrowing details of civilian casualties, along with outspoken criticism, did not begin to appear in *The Times* until January 23, only two days before it announced the armistice negotiations that ended the bombardment.

Furthermore, most foreign press correspondents were in Versailles, briefed by the German authorities. They did not know where the shells were going, and they accepted the German version that the bombardment was aimed at the city's fortifications, with only overshooting shells landing on civilian targets. An emotive drawing in the *New York Harper's Weekly* (February 11), for example, showed a dead mother and baby in a shell-torn Paris apartment, but with the caption "A Stray Shot." Interestingly, the *New York Herald Tribune* suggested before the bombardment started that "the most desirable part of Paris to shell" would be the Faubourg Saint-Antoine, "the quartier where the rabble live ... those fierce fighting moblots [*Garde Mobile*] who tore down the Bastille years ago" (January 1), but editorialists never followed up this shrewd guess. The fact that shelling was deliberately aimed at civilians – against international law as then understood – never clearly emerged. Public protest was consequently muted: A demonstration in Trafalgar Square on January 23 attracted "some few hundreds"; by that time, the war was practically over.[36]

Although the bombardment was the most spectacular and controversial aspect of the German attack on Paris, it was the blockade that really counted. Food and fuel shortages greatly increased the death rate, especially among the very young and the old. Intestinal and respiratory diseases were the main killers. Nearly 42,000 more people died during the siege than in the corresponding months of 1869–70.[37]

Bismarck had refused to permit the city to be revictualled as part of a temporary armistice when this had been requested by Adolphe Thiers on

34   See, e.g., *The North German Correspondent* [Berlin], Jan. 1, 4, 6, 1871.
35   *The Times*, Jan. 21, 1871, 10; report dated Jan. 6.
36   *The Times*, Jan. 24, 1871, 9.
37   *EGDN*, xxi, 464–5. See also L. Vacher, *La mortalité à Paris en 1870* (Paris, 1871).

November 3, as this would have increased the city's capacity to resist and hence encouraged a continuation of the war. Moltke was reluctant even to permit the establishment of emergency food stocks close to Paris, arguing that this would encourage the Parisians to hold out until the last moment. Rather, they should be made to understand that famine would be the consequence of intransigence. News of hardship in the city did cause much press comment, but it was never suggested that the Germans were wrong to impose a blockade, or that this marked a new kind of warfare; indeed, criticism was often directed at French advocates of *la guerre à outrance* for causing useless suffering to their own noncombatants.[38] The imminent exhaustion of food stocks was what forced Paris to surrender at the end of January.

The surrender of Paris brought with it that of France. Bismarck had insisted on offering relatively moderate armistice terms for the city, making it possible for the Government of National Defense to maintain its authority and end the war for the whole country. For peace as for war, provisional national sovereignty was still exercised by Paris, and this justified the strategy of the siege. The German army had won crushing military victory by the previous September; but final political victory had required a major campaign against civilians, aimed at wresting control of the war from their hands. Some French generals were by the end desperately pursuing the same aim. In order to be able to seek an armistice, they had to persuade the Parisians that further resistance was useless and, hence, agreed under civilian pressure to a hopeless sortie on January 19, 1871: "These National Guard clowns are determined to get their heads blown off; we'll give them the opportunity."[39]

THE FRENCH SIEGE, APRIL–MAY 1871

I address several questions in this section. What were the links between the war and the insurrection, and between the war and the severity of the repression? Does this, the most extreme example of its time of an ideological war against civilians, constitute another symptom of a society in which the conditions for total war were developing?

The war created the conditions for the Paris Commune. Yet the connection is very different from that between war and revolution in the twentieth century, a consequence of the intolerable burden of war on State, economy, and society. The Paris insurrection was not a revolt against the burden of war. On the contrary, popular protests in Paris had been prowar, not antiwar, aimed at radicalizing and galvanizing the defense *à outrance*. The insurrection

38   See, e.g., *The Times*, Jan. 14, 1871; *Daily News*, Jan. 16, 1871.
39   Sarcey, *Siege*, 164.

reflects the different experiences and perceptions, and in some ways the lighter impact, of the war on Paris compared with the rest of the country, which had suffered or was threatened by occupation, requisitions, fines, and economic disruption, and which had provided conscripts as cannon fodder for an almost unbroken series of defeats. These experiences aggravated already deep divisions between the capital and the provinces, and also between Republicans and conservatives.

The Republican Government of National Defense, composed almost entirely of Parisian politicians, had come to power in the bloodless revolution of September 4, 1870, and faced with Bismarck's demands, undertook a Republican-nationalist crusade, with Léon Gambetta directing the military effort in the provinces.[40] The revolution seemed to have altered the nature of the war in the eyes of both French and Germans, who were ready to see in Gambetta a dictator in the Jacobin mold. This was a major reason, in conservative eyes, to press for peace: The "Jacobins" were prolonging a disastrous war to keep power and revolutionize the country.[41] Some thought that the Germans were deliberately using revolution as a weapon: The bombardment of Paris, for example, was feared by some to be intended to provoke a working-class revolt, and there would later be persistent accusations that the Germans had fomented and supported the Commune.[42]

In reality, the Republicans were concerned about preventing revolution and limiting upheaval, and they mobilized the country to only a limited extent by twentieth- or late-eighteenth-century standards.[43] Even in the extreme case of Paris, economic controls did not go beyond – or arguably did not even attain – the minimum necessary.[44] In the most basic aspect of mobilization, that of manpower, the government in Paris held back far more than did Gambetta in the provinces. He thrust barely trained and badly armed conscripts into the firing line; but masses of Parisian men, enrolled in the National Guard, were kept as far as possible out of major combat in the belief that their use would lead to futile slaughter. As Favre had said, Paris wished to be defended *à outrance*, but, in the eyes of its more ardent patriots, it had not been: Paris, they charged, had not been defeated by the Germans but rather betrayed by the provinces and the government, who had "abandoned the country that we wished to defend."[45]

40 Bury, *Gambetta*, is the best account.
41 For an anthology of such attitudes, see *EGDN*, xxi.
42 See, e.g., Sarcey, *Siège*, 167.
43 For example, significant aspects of the war effort were left to local or private initiative; and major guerrilla warfare was not seriously contemplated. Roth, *La Guerre*, 218, 224–5, 334, 366.
44 See Audoin-Rouzeau, *1870*, 273–4, and William Serman, *La Commune de Paris (1871)* (Paris, 1986), 143–8.
45 *La Commune*, March 21, 1871.

Consequently, after the armistice, Parisians elected to the new National Assembly a majority of left-wing nationalists committed, in principle, to continuing the war. But the rest of the country, reflecting its very different experiences, elected a large majority of propeace conservatives, most of them royalists. The political and economic implications of the armistice increased Parisian resentment and added to the crisis. These implications were (1) conservative political control and the possibility of a monarchist restoration; and (2) a precipitate return to economic normality, threatening thousands of Parisians with ruin and destitution by lifting the wartime moratorium on rents and commercial debts, and ending the subsistence payment to National Guards and their families.

Provincial opinion had little understanding of or sympathy with the Parisian plight, and it feared a further outbreak of revolution: "ten times in eighty years Paris has sent [France] governments ready made, by telegraph ... and she wants no more of it."[46] This resentment (and an answering contempt on the part of Parisians for provincials) had intensified during 1869–70, and further during the war, when the capital, as has been seen, exercised effective national sovereignty.[47] From this provincial conservative viewpoint, all Parisians were to some extent to blame for the recurrent turbulence, including the upper classes, who failed to keep revolutionary elements in check. No concessions should be made to Paris: on the contrary – and here there is a similarity with the Prussian view – Paris should be forced to realize that it could no longer overrule the wishes of the rest of France. As Thiers said, Paris must be governed "like Lyons, like Marseilles ... like the other towns of France ... there will be only one law, and no privilege." Its power and pride would be broken; "any attempted secession ... will be energetically repressed in France as it has been in America."[48] If damage was done in the process, the lesson would be all the more salutary.

That this political crisis could blow up into a full-scale civil war with revolutionary implications was owing to (1) the mobilization of the Parisian population in the increasingly politicized National Guard, expanded during the war to include all able-bodied men; and (2) the weakening of government authority at the armistice, causing in effect an interregnum. Bismarck's willingness to offer relatively moderate armistice terms had the unintended consequence of perpetuating the illusion of Parisian invincibility, and also of leaving the city in a state of near anarchy. Most of the regular army was

---

46 *AAN* (1871), 1: 276–7, speech of Belcastel (March 10).
47 Louis Girard, *Nouvelle Histoire de Paris: La Deuxième Republique et le Second Empire, 1848–1870* (Paris, 1981), 418.
48 Circular of April 12, 1871, Archives Historiques de Guerre (hereafter cited as AHG), series Lu, carton 95.

disarmed under the armistice terms, but the National Guard was left intact. Its escape from effective government control meant that by early March, the government and its agents – police, army, and loyalist National Guard–were no longer in control of the streets of the capital. The center of legal power had moved to Bordeaux (the meeting place of the new National Assembly), which increased the power vacuum in Paris. Even then, insurrection came only when the government made a reckless attempt on March 18 to begin disarming the National Guard and arresting dissident leaders. This proved to be impossible and led to the visible collapse of government authority, followed by the retreat of the government and its remaining armed forces to Versailles.

That various attempts at a negotiated settlement failed is due, in the last analysis, to the fact that two centers of political and military power had formed, and that in both the most intransigent elements believed that they could win. On the other hand, the revolt remained largely confined to Paris, with only minor outbreaks in the provinces, a further sign that the war and the armistice had produced a very different reaction inside and outside Paris, and demonstrating that the events in Paris were, in Marx's well-known words, "the rising of a town under exceptional circumstances." Yet the fact that Paris was quickly defeated shows that the war against Germany had not devastated French society, the State, or the army.

The French attack on Paris had in common with that of the Germans its ultimate target, the revolutionary section of the population – "the mob." The methods adopted were quite different. The accepted military means to coerce and punish the whole population – that is to say, blockade and bombardment – were not used. Although interrupting food supplies was discussed and eventually decided on, no serious attempt was made to organize a complete blockade; and although the army did for military reasons shell the western and southern suburbs and ramparts and their immediate vicinity, there was no indiscriminate bombardment of the city like that undertaken by the Germans. It would have been politically and morally difficult for the French government to follow in the footsteps of the Germans by bombarding and starving its own capital, especially as the Germans' cooperation would have been required. It would have placed the French even more than they already were at their mercy. It would have alienated supporters within the capital and moderate Republicans in the provinces. Moreover, many of the western parts of the city, closest to the siege batteries, were wealthy districts hostile to the Commune. Blockade or bombardment might have provoked, as earlier against the Germans, a desperate sortie against Versailles–a continual fear of the Versailles commanders. Finally, the effectiveness of such action was doubtful. As the first siege showed, no rapid result was likely. Besides, it was the government's public line, and probably genuine belief, that the Commune held power by force, and so measures to make the general population suffer were unlikely to force its surrender. Consequently, the only way to defeat it was to storm the city and engage its defenders in battle – the course that the Germans had prudently avoided.

What began as an attempt to neutralize the revolutionaries by disarming them, ended, after an increasingly bitter civil war of seven weeks, in the determination to eradicate revolution if necessary by killing *en masse* those regarded as especially blameworthy. The resulting massacre was the worst seen in Europe between the French and the Russian revolutions. Only in colonial contexts did western European governments ever feel similarly exposed to catastrophe and show comparable ruthlessness toward their opponents. The resemblance is more than simply coincidental; annihilation is a logical response to enemies who are seen as belonging to no state, and who cannot be attacked through their property (as by bombardment or devastation).[49]

Slaughter on this scale within France is unimaginable except in the context of the recent disastrous war. Defeat by Germany convinced many Frenchmen that the country was afflicted by a deep malaise, caused above all by revolutionary turbulence. Defeat followed by insurrection seemed to be threatening France with catastrophic breakdown: "The ancient world in its darkest hours affords us no spectacle of such a collapse."[50] Many commentators made lugubrious comparisons with eighteenth-century Poland, paralyzed by internal divisions and falling prey to foreign aggression. The shock of defeat encouraged a search for scapegoats: Both left and right denounced their political enemies for betraying national interest in the hour of greatest danger. This desire to shift the responsibility for the country's predicament onto other shoulders was strong in the army, whose commanders blamed their defeat on (among other things) indiscipline and disorder caused by left-wing agitation. The generals were also eager to prove their military capacities by defeating the rebellion: In their eyes, victory over the rebels was a revenge for defeat by the Germans. These widely held fears and recriminations encouraged and justified an extreme reaction to the insurrection, colored by the political and social analyses outlined in the following.

For many provincials in 1870–71, both soldiers and civilians, suspicion of both Paris and the Left dated at least from the Second Republic of 1848, which had imposed a heavy land-tax increase that aroused violent peasant

49   I owe this point to Michael Geyer.
50   *Le Soir*, March 19, 1871.

opposition. For much of rural France, the Republicans, especially those in Paris, were people who wanted to live at the expense of the peasantry – a view encouraged by the Parisians' demand that the wartime pay of the National Guard should be continued.[51] Versaillais propaganda played on this resentment, as in this message to the troops: "they steal public funds and … everyone's savings. … Their Republic is no more than an odious tyranny that would force the provinces to feed them in Paris without working."[52] Some of the slaughter in Paris doubtless stemmed from such attitudes: It was fairly indiscriminate killing by the army, most of whose rank and file were young peasant recruits, of anyone suspected of being a "Red."

Yet this traditional rural – urban resentment, even aggravated by the circumstances of 1871, is not the whole, or even the main, cause of the killing. Few provincial volunteers answered the National Assembly's call to join up to fight the insurrection: There was nothing like the flood of men who marched on Paris in June 1848 to put down the insurrection then.[53] The conscripts mustered to fight for the government did not, contrary to many accounts then and since, carry out a wholesale massacre: Thousands of Communards were allowed to surrender and some were even sent home.[54] The troops did not run amok, in the age-old manner of the *soldatesca* sacking a captured city. Their commanders feared that they could not be wholly relied on to fight, and there were numerous reports in the days immediately following the final battle that soldiers were fraternizing with Parisians, drinking with "people who could very well have fought them from behind the barricades."[55]

Neither the soldiers nor their commanders thought that they were fighting against all Parisians but rather against certain identifiable groups within the city. The official version of the struggle, reiterated in the Assembly and the press, was that the majority of Parisians involved in the insurrection were merely the victims or dupes of a ruthless minority of revolutionaries: "unfortunates led astray by criminals," in Thiers's words.[56] These "unfortunates" were said to serve the Commune only from fear or economic necessity. This analysis denied the Commune legitimacy, while heaping blame for the insurrection and its deeds on an active minority declared to be atypical of

51   Allain Corbin, *Village des Cannibales* (Paris, 1990), 31–46.
52   Ordre General no. 1, April 11, 1871, AHG, series Lu, carton 16.
53   For details, see Robert Tombs, "Paris and the rural hordes," *Historical Journal* 29, no. 4 (1986): 795–808 ; and for 1848, J. Vidalenc, "La province et les journées de juin," *Etudes d'Histoire Moderne et Contemporaine* (1948): 83–141.
54   See, e.g., statement of J. Quesnot (commander of 120th National Guard battalion), AHG, 6e Conseil de Guerre, dossier 229.
55   Prescriptions du rapport, May 31, 1871, AHG, series Lu, carton 16.
56   *Le Soir* (Versailles ed.), April 5, 1871.

Paris or France. These were clearly identified by Versaillais propaganda. The leaders were professional revolutionaries, ambitious fanatics motivated by frustrated ambition: "criminals who have usurped power," said the Foreign Minister Favre, "not to establish a political principle, but to satisfy the most debasing passions."[57] Such assertions depoliticized the conflict and denied any validity to the rebels' demands.

Many of the insurgents, it was endlessly affirmed, were foreign, and some were Prussian agents working for the destruction of France: "The movement is no longer essentially Parisian ... the adventurers of every country, dedicated makers of European revolution, have come together in Paris."[58] The stress on foreign participation in the Commune fulfilled several political and psychological functions. It redefined the Communards as being outside the nation. It shifted the odium for the rebellion outside France completely, making the French people and government the innocent victims of what was declared to be another foreign attack, less open but scarcely less dangerous than that led by Moltke. The most active insurgent units, reported an army intelligence unit, were "nearly always composed of foreigners," and the main reason why ordinary Parisians did not reject the Commune was "the terror inspired by these foreigners."[59] The Communards – whom some of the regular troops nicknamed "the Prussians of Paris" – were persistently accused of being the unconscious or conscious agents of the national enemy: "It is Germany who profits from the anarchy ... She waits, eyeing her prey."[60]

The most ardent rank-and-file supporters of the Commune were claimed to be the criminal underclass that flocked to the urban jungle of Paris: In the words of two army officers, the "*direct agents*" of the Commune were "all vagabonds, all people out of prison, all that is worst in Paris"; "ex-convicts, drunkards, pimps, déclassés, in short, all the vermin of the *faubourgs*."[61] These beliefs had a fairly long history. The concept of the *classes dangereuses* – an underclass of vicious poor always seeking opportunities for crime or revolution – had emerged in the 1840s, though it probably fed on legends of the Terror.[62] The insurrections of 1848 and 1851 evoked fanciful stories of crimes and atrocities; they were echoed in 1871. Similar notions inspired the law of May 31, 1850, disfranchising those without fixed abode, with police records,

---

57 Speech to Assembly, quoted in *Le Gaulois*, May 16, 1871.
58 *Le Gaulois*, April 20, 1871.
59 May 1, 1871, AHG, series Lu, carton 95.
60 *Le Soir* (Paris edition), March 27, 1871.
61 Captain Garcin to the *Enquête parlementaire sur l' insurrection du 18 mars, no. 740, Assemblée Nationale 1871,* [hereafter cited as EPI] 3 vols. (Versailles, 1872), 2:236; Gen. Alexandre Montaudon, *Souvenirs militaires,* 2 vols. (Paris, 1898–1900), 2:266.
62 Louis Chevalier, *Labouring Classes and Dangerous Classes in Paris during the First Half of the Nineteenth Century* (London, 1973).

or who paid no taxes.[63] The debate on the law was notorious for Thiers's speech stigmatizing the "vile mob that has … delivered over to every tyrant the liberty of every Republic," but which was quite distinct from "the people." Such stereotypes were commonplace: They are reflected in such widely read novels as Eugène Sue's *Les Mystères de Paris* (1842–43) and Victor Hugo's *Les Misérables* (1862). As recently as 1870, an unimpeachable republican, Charles Hugo, had used terms very similar to those of Thiers, with reference to the crowds who attended public executions: "scum of the chaingang and the brothel, the twilight world … denounced by thinkers in every age, which degraded Rome on circus days, and which dishonors Paris."[64]

Fears and fantasies about crime had recently been displayed in the emotional public response to the sensational "Pantin crime," judged in January 1870 in Paris. A nineteen-year-old psychopath, Troppmann, had murdered a family of seven, apparently for money. What alarmed the public was the incongruity of the horrifying crime and his pleasantly normal manner and appearance. People were used to the idea, inculcated by popular works of phrenology and "physiognomy," that criminal tendencies were reflected in physical appearance. In Troppmann, they were frighteningly undetectable. The press desperately scrutinized the shape of his head, his teeth, and above all his big bony hands for signs of his criminal nature: "That hand … is frightening."[65] His inborn tendencies had been aggravated, it was believed, by a "monomania" about money and social promotion, seen as the archetypal vice of Second Empire France. The idea for the crime had come from an obsessive reading of Sue's melodramatic *Le Juif Errant* (1845), in which the villain kills a family of eight for their money.[66]

Flaubert saw in the Troppmann case and the interest it aroused the first symptom of an "epileptic crisis" that culminated in the Commune.[67] We may see in it vivid evidence of an intense public awareness and fear of criminality; its association with what seemed pathological tendencies within modern urban society; the belief that thwarted social ambition, aggravated by inflammatory reading, could engender murder; and the rooted expectation that outward appearance betrayed psychological makeup. These attitudes colored conservative perceptions of the Commune. War and revolution, it seemed,

---

63 Paul Raphael, "La loi du 31 mai 1850," *Revue d'Histoire Moderne et Contemporaine* 13 (1909): 277–304; 4 (1910): 44–79, 297–331.

64 *Le Rappel*, Jan. 4, 1870, quoted by M. Perrot, "L'affaire Troppmann (1869)," *L'Histoire* 30 (1981): 36.

65 *La Gazette des Tribunaux*, Dec. 29, 1869. Phrenologists regarded the hands as the second most important guide, after the head, to behavioral propensities, as Alison Winter has kindly pointed out to me.

66 Ibid.; *Le Figaro*, Dec. 29 and 30, 1870; *Le Crime de Pantin: edition complète illustrée* (Paris, [1870]).

67 Letter to George Sand, April 29, 1871, quoted by Perrot, "Troppmann," 36.

had unleashed these dark forces against a suddenly vulnerable society. The head of the Sûreté, Claude, who had been in charge of the Troppmann case, was closely questioned by a parliamentary inquiry about criminal participation in the Commune, the numbers of criminals in Paris, and why seemingly law-abiding workers had joined what the parliamentarians saw as a gigantic criminal enterprise.[68] Versaillais propaganda stressed crude material motives among Commune leaders, with repeated stories of their frustrated ambition, greed, and corruption, and of their drunken orgies. The Communards were described and drawn as hideous and subhuman, echoing the criminological pseudosciences of phrenology and physiognomy.[69] To conservatives, they were reincarnations not only of the *Septembriseurs* of 1792 but also of Troppmann: "I used to think ... that criminals of Troppmann's type were very rare individuals, that it took fifty or sixty years to hatch one out in the lower depths of society"; but since the Commune, "I am convinced that when revolution occurs there are thousands in Paris."[70]

The army and the police tried to weed out the potential Troppmanns from the "harmless wretches" among the Communards that they captured. During the fighting, Sûreté agents checked Communard prisoners for known criminals and "thought they recognized many ex-convicts and dangerous people."[71] A staff officer, Captain Garcin, who became the specialist on Communard prisoners, stated that "we could recognize those led astray by poverty ... we showed them the greatest indulgence, we fed them and put them into a special category."[72] General de Cissey, one of the principal commanders, agreed that most prisoners were "quite inoffensive ... the mass of National Guards do not want to fight; there is only a hard core of fanatics recruited among the vagabonds and idle workers, and ready for anything"; some had "most ugly faces," which seemed to indicate "a long habit of evildoing."[73] Garcin put it more scientifically: "Their physiognomies were as revolting as could possibly be imagined."[74] Once the army was fighting inside Paris, in the last violent convulsions of the civil war, large numbers of men suspected as belonging to this imaginary "hard core" were shot. For many officers, it was an

---

68 *EPI*, 2 : 203–4
69 See, e.g, *Gustavé Doré: Versailles et Paris en 1871* (Paris, 1979), 93–103.
70 Abbé Lamazou, *La Palace Vendôme et la Roquete* (Paris, 1872), 260.
71 General de Cissey, report May 4, 1871, AHG, series Lu, carton 119.
72 *EPI*, 2 : 237.
73 Reports to Marshal de MacMahon, May 12, 1871, AHG, series Li, carton 123; and May 19, 1871, AHG, series Lu, carton 92.
74 *EPI*, 2 : 238.

opportunity to purge the country of all the scum that is spreading grief and ruin everywhere ... the government should not have the right of mercy ... a court martial must function at once, otherwise they will tell us that it is too late to execute the guilty, and we shall have to start all over again with the same men; ... military law should be applied in all its rigor [so] that in a few days this monstrous insurrection will have been settled with ... in such a way as to break with the revolutionaries for good.[75]

Paris became a battlefield, which gave the army a largely free hand under martial law to destroy the forces of revolution. Politicians were unable or unwilling to restrain it. As Thiers wrote to one of his ministers who was worried by the summary executions, "during the fighting we can do nothing, and it would be useless to get ourselves mixed up in it."[76] The slaughter was applauded in the press and by many prominent intellectuals, who with a few exceptions were virulently hostile to the Commune.[77]

The full rigor of military law[78] was indeed applied, with orders to shoot summarily prisoners taken "les armes à la main" who, if they were still fighting at this late stage of the conflict were assumed to be doing so by choice.[79] Those belonging to volunteer units, those above or below the age of compulsory military service, foreigners, officers, suspected criminals – all who could be taken for "picked agents let in by the Commune," in Garcin's words – risked summary shooting. So too did the dirty and the ugly, identifiable by amateur phrenologists as criminally inclined. Hands were inspected for gunpowder stains: Was this also an echo of the Troppmann case? A British journalist witnessed General de Galliffet's selection of prisoners to be shot: "It was not a good thing on that day to be noticeably taller, dirtier, cleaner, older or uglier than one's neighbors. One individual in particular struck me as probably owing his speedy release from the ills of this world to his having a broken nose."[80] Those who could not show that they had worked for their living during the insurrection were suspect, too.

Those who survived were dispatched to Versailles and then to other prisons to await more formal trial by regular courts martial. The criteria applied

---

75   Letter from Colonel Quinel to Colonel Leperche, May 17, 18 71, AHG, series Lv, carton 10 .
76   Letter, May 27, 1871, Archives Jules Ferry, Bibliothéque Municipale de Saint-Dié. For Thiers's role, see John P. T. Bury and Robert Tombs, *Thiers 1787–1877: A Political Life* (London, 1986), 207–9.
77   See Paul Lidsky, *Les écrivains contre la Commune* (Paris, 1970).
78   Not statutory law, but military usage (as for example defined in section 82 of the U.S. Instructions for the Government of Armies, which provided for the summary shooting of armed irregular bands). By a decree issued on Oct . 2, 1870, the government of national defense established drumhead courts martial with sweeping powers for the duration of the war.
79   For details of orders given, see Robert Tombs, *The War Against Paris 1871* (Cambridge, 1981), 174–5 .
80   *Daily News*, June 8, 1871, 6.

were much the same. Prisoners and witnesses were repeatedly questioned about criminal records. Elaborate efforts were made to track down those implicated in "pillage." Drinking habits were a theme of such probing and censorious questions by army officers – not a group noted for abstemiousness – that the records could almost be the minutes of an unusually severe temperance society. In short, the civil war was treated not as a political conflict but as a vast criminal saturnalia.[81] This was reflected in later conservative writing on the Commune, such as Maxime du Camp's *Les Convulsions de Paris* (Paris, 1878), and it provided a spur to the work of criminal anthropologists all over Europe for a generation.[82] In short, the repression, though extreme, was far from indiscriminate; it was targeted and rationalized.

It was also formalized and depersonalized. Orders were given and the military hierarchy respected. Courts martial following a semblance of regular procedure oversaw the process. The arrest of prisoners, their conveyance to recognized places of detention, their judgments, and their executions were separate stages of the process. Individual responsibility was diluted, for no one was clearly responsible for, carried out, or even witnessed the whole process. The slaughter bore the marks of a modern, organized society, desiring to control and conceal violence, to remove it from the realm of popular spectacle into that of social policy.[83] The random violence of ordinary soldiers[84] and the organized massacres of the generals were thus quite different phenomena. The death of the Communard leader Eugène Varlin exemplifies both the "archaic" and the "modern": When caught, he was paraded around the streets and beaten half to death by a mob; but he was removed by the military authorities to be summarily sentenced and officially shot.

Like that of the Germans, the French war against Paris achieved its object. Paris was reduced to, and even below, the legal level of "the other towns of France." It was purged of its "dangerous" elements in perhaps the first tentative application of characteristically "modern" mass violence against civilians. The Commune was thus the last Parisian revolution, the lurid "sunset" of a popular tradition.[85]

---

81 For details, see Robert Tombs, "Crime and the Security of the State: The 'Dangerous Classes' and Insurrection in Nineteenth-Century Paris," in V. A. C. Gatrell et al., eds., *Crime and the Law: The Social History of Crime in Western Europe since 1500* (London, 1980), 221–3.

82 Daniel Pick, *Faces of Degeneration: A European Disorder, c. 1848–c. 1918* (Cambridge, 1989), 140–3.

83 For thoughts on the control of popular violence, see Corbin, *Village*, 121–39; for an analysis of the infinitely more developed horrors of twentieth-century violence, which characterizes them as essentially modern, see Zygmunt Bauman, *Modernity and the Holocaust* (Cambridge, 1989).

84 Similar in some ways to that during the American Civil War analyzed by Michael Fellman in Chapter 24, this volume.

85 Jacques Rougerie, *Procès des Communards* (Paris, 1964), 241.

CONCLUSIONS

Bismarck was much impressed in September 1870 by General Sheridan's advice, based on his experience in the American Civil War, to cause "the inhabitants so much suffering that they must long for peace, and force their government to demand it. The people must be left with nothing but their eyes to weep with over the war."[86] There was more to this dictum than its poetic phrasing. It makes clear that military operations were deliberately aimed at making civilians suffer so as to bring about a political result – something that made sense only in at least partially democratic societies, but which was a logical and essential feature of wars waged between such societies, which we might term *citizens' wars*. As for Philip H. Sheridan, William Tecumseh Sherman, and Abraham Lincoln in their war, this political aim was reinforced by moral condemnation of the enemy, also necessary in citizens' wars. As with the slave-owning rebels of South Carolina, the Parisians deserved special chastisement both for what they were – the arrogant, untrustworthy inhabitants of the New Babylon – and for what they had done – their "wickedness" in starting and continuing an unjustifiable conflict. Theirs was "the woe due to those by whom the offense came," in Lincoln's words.[87]

There is a paradox here. The Germans were fighting a modern war, with that basic feature of total war, a politically motivated attack on civilians. Yet they did so (as when shooting franc-tireurs, burning villages, or taking hostages) in order to punish the involvement of civilians in war. The revolutionary *levée en masse* was their enemy, the cause as they saw it of the rising barbarity of the war, which distinguished it from those civilized, professional "cabinet wars" against Denmark or Austria, in which civilians remained as onlookers, and the State was autonomous and free.[88] The paradox is that in attempting to stamp out the *levée en masse* in the provinces, and using cannon fire to encourage lucid decision making in Paris, Bismarck and Moltke had extended the scope of warfare and seemed to have opened an era of wars between peoples. The bombardment of "journalists and the mob" in Paris was, as Leonhard von Blumenthal noted with disgust, a victory over rational generalship won by the "Voice of the People" in Berlin.

Yet the lessons of the war were ambiguous. It may be doubted whether the bombardment of Paris was seen as a model for future wars: The political role of Paris was unique, and after all, bombardment failed. The real level of

---

86 Busch, *Bismarck*, 1 : 171.
87 Quoted by James McPherson in Chapter 14, this volume. Charleston was singled out for bombardment with incendiary shells.
88 Although Moltke had already deplored the role of "lawyers, journalists and politicians" who decreed all-out resistance from safety in Copenhagen. *Moltkes Briefe*, 2 : 308 (April 23, 1864).

popular participation and of mobilization in this people's war was limited. The ineffectiveness of citizen-soldiers convinced professionals (including those fighting for the Commune) that "militias" were useless, and that efficient modern armies had to operate by militarizing society, rather than through civilianizing the military. Whereas Moltke expected future wars to be long, drawn-out peoples' wars, his successors, most notably Alfred von Schlieffen, calculated that professionalism (combined with severe repression of any popular resistance) could win the knockout blow that had eluded Moltke in 1870.

One conclusion would be that 1870–71 was a nail in the coffin of the progressive nineteenth-century illusion that modern wars were the business of states and their regular armies, and that their peoples were and should be bystanders. On both sides, amateurs had taken the initiative, foisting their patriotic enthusiasm on invariably dubious professionals. The "laws and usages of war" proved inadequate to regulate a people's war, because their "rigorous" execution meant violence against civilians on a scale that was morally unacceptable. What in 1870–71 were arguably legal reprisals would by the twentieth century be regarded as war crimes.[89] Moreover, where public opinion was able to influence policy, civilians became *ipso facto* parties in the conflict, whatever the theories of international lawyers: Hence, the Parisians, while scarcely allowed the role of soldiers, were forced to participate as targets. Yet this was a passing phase, and we should beware of too-ready comparisons with later European wars; groups of citizens were not again to exercise popular control over generals and diplomats as had the Parisians in 1870. Bismarck, Moltke, and Blumenthal need not have worried – citizens' war was not a vision of the future. It was not total war in embryo.[90]

The French war against Paris shared some elements with the German. Bismarck, Thiers, Moltke, and Cissey held similar views of "the vile mob" and the lawyers and journalists who led it. Bismarck regretted that German guns could not reach the working-class district of Belleville,[91] the real and symbolic center of revolutionary nationalism; and Belleville was where the Communards made their last stand. Moltke had mocked the journalist Rochefort, "professeur des barricades"; and Cissey referred with similar contempt to "Citizen Rochefort, cravenly fleeing from Paris at the moment

---

89 Bismarck had argued that it was legally permissible to impose collective punishments, such as destruction of property and taking of hostages, on the civilian inhabitants for any resistance activity. Memorandum of Dec. 14, 1870, *Gesammelte Werke*, 6b:634–5.

90 As was pointed out at the Washington conference, the nearest approach to total war, on the eastern front from 1941–45, was fought by the subjects of totalitarian states, and the sufferings and wishes of civilians were not a consideration for the rulers.

91 Busch, *Bismarck*, 1:333.

of danger."[92] But whereas for the Germans "the mob" was the dynamo of continuing French resistance, for French conservatives the patriotism of the revolutionaries was false, a cloak for ambition and treachery, and their destruction was the first step toward the regeneration of France and revenge.

Was the civil war of 1871 a symptom of embryonic *total war*? The war against Germany had profound domestic repercussions. It mobilized large numbers, including those habitually apolitical or moderate. It modified the usual structures of power (for example, by arming civilians and weakening the regular army). It suspended the usual political and legal safeguards (for example, through the imposition of martial law). It meant the subordination of society to the needs of the state, and hence the suppression of opposition. Gambetta took modest steps in this direction, but the real conflict came in Paris, always the focus of the war, and where the choice of war or peace was made.

For the French, the war of 1870 was the continuation of domestic politics by other means. Fighting the Germans was fighting the reactionaries; making peace with the Germans was forestalling the revolutionaries. This dimension was not unfamiliar to contemporaries, and certainly not to Bismarck: Political and social upheaval, whether as a deliberate auxiliary to conflicts between States or as an accidental byproduct, had been seen in the previous two decades in Russia, the Habsburg monarchy, and the United States. Yet, unlike the revolutionary wars of the 1790s or of the world wars of the twentieth century, or indeed the Italian war of 1859 or the American Civil War, the interstate conflict in 1870–71 was kept formally separate from the domestic conflict. That is to say, Bismarck was set against imposing any political or social change on France. Here, German aims fell far short of total war, and this is surely a reason why the majority of Frenchmen were fairly soon ready to accept peace. It also meant, however, that the domestic struggles in France were not resolved by the ending of the war: German victory did not impose a regime but, on the contrary, left a near vacuum in power and two rival authorities in Paris and Versailles. Hence, as in Germany and Russia after the World War I, wartime domestic struggles spilled over into the postwar period and culminated in civil war. Lenin and Trotsky, students of the history of the Commune, had drawn the conclusion that the revolution must stop at nothing to defend itself against the danger of another *semaine sanglante*: This time, the boot was to be on the other foot.

The war against Germany raised the stakes in France's domestic conflict. Each faction saw the others as taking the country toward catastrophe.

92   May 20, 1871, AHG, series Li, carton 123.

Opponents, by causing dissension, seemed to be objective allies of the enemy; the distinction between domestic opponents and foreign enemies disappeared; and domestic opponents provided an obvious scapegoat for defeat – in 1871, each faction had its own "stab-in-the-back" theory. In France, where domestic conflicts were already bitter and had historic links with war and defeat (the Jacobin dictatorship and the Terror had stemmed from Revolutionary Wars, the Restoration and White Terror from the defeats of 1814 and 1815), it was especially likely that foreign and domestic conflicts would merge. It is along these lines that one would try to account for the difference in scale between the "peacetime" violence of June 1848, which cost some 1,500 lives,[93] and that of May 1871, when at least 12,000 insurgents were slaughtered.

The two "wars against Paris" fascinated and shocked contemporaries because Paris, seen as the center of modern European civilization, had been confronted with the barbarities of war, revolution, and massacre. Contemporaries regarded modern civilization and barbarity as opposites; we can see them as complementary. Had the war of 1870 not been a modern war, one waged by "journalists," "lawyers," and "the mob," as well as by professional soldiers and diplomats, there would have been no sense in trying to win it by bombarding civilians. Had the Commune not aroused characteristically modern fears of social and national catastrophe, it would not have been treated with such characteristically modern, impersonal, and amoral ruthlessness. The level of violence used against Parisians was not new; the motives of those using it were.

What fundamentally the German and the French wars against Paris had in common was their enemy: a population considered to constitute the most virulent revolutionary strain in modern urban society. What the wars of the next century would have in common with both was the willingness to use ever harsher forms of blockade and bombardment against an ever larger part of the enemy population, and a willingness to act ruthlessly against any part of one's own population seen as posing a threat to a united war effort, and even, in some cases, to seize on the disruption of normality caused by war as an opportunity to destroy real or imaginary domestic enemies.

---

93   The estimate of Charles Tilly and L. M. Lees, "The People of June 1848," in Roger Price, ed., *Revolution and Reaction: 1848 and the Second French Republic* (London, 1975), 186.

26

"Our Prison System, Supposing We Had Any":
The Confederate and Union Prison Systems

REID MITCHELL

Pvt. Henry G. Adams served in the Fifty-sixth Georgia Volunteer Infantry. He enlisted in May 1862, which suggests that he was a reluctant volunteer who wished to avoid the draft. He was twenty-eight years old when he was captured at the battle of Champion Hill, Mississippi, in May 1863. The Union army sent him first to Camp Morton, Indiana. From there, he went to Fort Delaware, arriving in June. He was exchanged on the Fourth of July – the same day that Vicksburg fell. The exchange did him little good; the Confederate army immediately placed him in a hospital in Richmond, where he was diagnosed as having "Phtyisis Pulmonatis." Still, he was thought to be well enough to travel – on August 2, he was given a forty-five-day furlough, presumably to go home and recuperate. He did reach home – according to Adams family stories, he walked – where he died of pneumonia on September 13, 1863. He left behind a widow, three sons, and one daughter. He was my great-great-grandfather.

During the Civil War, approximately 195,000 Union soldiers and 215,000 Confederates spent some time in enemy hands. Over 56,000 soldiers died in captivity – roughly 30,000 Union soldiers and 26,000 Confederates. The systems for keeping prisoners developed by the Union and the Confederacy were subject to much controversy during the war. Their failures, particularly their failures to maintain the health of the inmates, were the source of grief, bitterness, and recriminations. Supporters of both the Union and the Confederacy pointed to the wounds inflicted by the other side, while denying those inflicted by their own. Men of good will on both sides covered up the truth, and the debate lasted far longer than did the Confederacy itself. The issue of prisoners aroused as much passion as any other aspect of the Civil War, and more than most.[1]

---

1   James M. McPherson, *Ordeal by Fire: The Civil War and Reconstruction* (New York, 1982), 451.

Yet the passion suddenly ceased. Prisons are now one of the least studied subjects relating to the Civil War. Indeed, it is hard to think of any other subject so significant to the war that remains so in need of investigation; for example, we still do not have a reliable institutional history of the prison systems. The last monograph that discussed the issue of Civil War prisons as a whole, William Hesseltine's brilliant *Civil War Prisons*, appeared in 1930.

Perhaps more significant than the place of the prison systems in Civil War historiography is their place in the national imagination. Compared to the way people felt about, remembered, and debated the Union and Confederate prisons in 1860 or in 1880, the issue has more or less been forgotten. True, at the site of the Andersonville prison, there is now a memorial maintained by the National Park Service. It is a moving site. Fittingly, it has been transformed from a place of Union remembrance to one devoted to the sufferings of all prisoners of war at all times – although its otherwise thorough exhibits still require one on Confederate prisoners of war in Union hands.

I said the change of public memory at Andersonville is fitting, but I am not certain that that is so. It is not always fitting to universalize the sufferings of individual people at specific places and times – indeed, sometimes it is almost sacrilegious. The emphasis on universal suffering at Andersonville reveals one of the principal reasons why Civil War prisons are now forgotten: the desire for reconciliation between the North and the South. For some reason, the fact that several million men put on uniforms and proceeded to slaughter one another is not viewed as obstructing reconciliation; sometimes commemorations are so celebratory that the war seems a matter of national self-congratulation. Nobody finds much to celebrate in the prison system. Furthermore, the accusations and counteraccusations made at the time did obstruct sectional reconciliation: The frequently waved bloody shirt often came from the body of a prisoner at Andersonville. Yet the price paid for reconciliation and self-congratulation was, as usual, a little less access to historical reality. It was easier to forget the prison systems than to justify them.

Hesseltine's *Civil War Prisons* was anything but celebratory. Hesseltine condemned both the Union and Confederate systems, although he tended to accept some of the Confederate line of defense. Confederate prisons were nightmarish. The nightmare occurred because the Confederacy lacked the resources to maintain the system. That was unavoidable. Union prisons, Hesseltine argued, were also nightmarish. That, however, had been avoidable. The Union had the resources that the Confederacy lacked. The Union, acting out of wartime hysteria, diminished the rations and supplies in their prisons to match what were thought to be Confederate conditions, and thus increased the deaths – not to the level of POW deaths in the Confederacy but to a level higher than it should have been. Both sides were guilty.[2] Nonetheless, things could have been worse. We might start our examination of Civil War prisons by considering the ways in which Americans of 1861–65 resisted the impulse toward total war. One way that war becomes total is when people act on the logical conclusions of the ideology that drove them to war; such logic too often points toward extermination. During the Civil War, if either side had acted on the logical conclusions of their ideology, the treatment of prisoners would have been far more barbaric; if logic had been followed – rather than common sense – mass executions would have resulted. By law and logic, each could view prisoners of war as criminals. This was particularly true for the Union in the early portion of the war, and Confederates in the second half. In 1861, the crime committed by Confederates was treason; after January 1, 1863, the crime committed by Federals, at least white officers in the United States Colored Troops, was insurrection. Both crimes were punishable by death. Of course, if either side had chosen to conduct large-scale executions, the other side would have retaliated with executions of their own.

Confederate Gen. Braxton Bragg summarized the Union problem well for his opponent Union Gen. W. S. Rosecrans. "Our soldiers are either traitors to be hung or prisoners of war to be treated as such."[3] Before the Union recognized the Confederacy's belligerent status, the army, the navy, and the administration had to determine what to do with such rebels as they captured. Confederate soldiers were traitors; worse than that, they were "traitors taken in arms," as Secretary of War Simon Cameron put it. In July 1861, when Gen. George B. McClellan agreed to treat captured Confederates as prisoners of war, he warned them that "it was not in my power to relieve them from any liability incurred by taking arms against the United States." And in December 1861, Gen. Henry Halleck explained to McClellan that exchanging prisoners was a sound policy as exchange was "a mere military convention."

---

2 William B. Hesseltine, *Civil War Prisons: A Study in War Psychology* (Columbus, Oh., 1930). See also William B. Hesseltine, "Civil War Prisons – Introduction," *Civil War History* 8, no. 2 (1962): 117–20. Hesseltine's attitudes toward the prisons and toward the Civil War came in part as a reaction to World War I: He was against war, period. He was also opposed to militarism, conscription, and American entry into World War II. Specifically, Hesseltine interpreted the propaganda use of the treatment of prisoners in the Civil War in light of the uses made of German treatment of Belgians in World War I. "In each case, the stories fed the fires of hate and inspired war-crazed peoples with savage impulses." Richard N. Current, "Introduction," and William B. Hesseltine, "Propaganda Literature of Confederate Prisons," in William B. Hesseltine, ed., *Sections and Politics* (Madison, Wis., 1968).

3 U.S. War Department, ed., *The War of the Rebellion: A Compilation of the Official Records of the Union and Confederate Armies* [hereafter cited as OR], 70 vols. (Washington, D.C., 1880–1901), ser. 2, 5:102–3.

"A prisoner exchanged under the laws of war is not thereby exempted from trial and punishment as a traitor. Treason is a state or civil offense punishable by the civil courts."[4]

While this legal distinction was crucial to justify treating traitors as prisoners of war, what mattered more, both at the time and in the long run, was the practical decision that Confederate soldiers were to be so handled. The fact that the Confederacy had in its possession a number of Union prisoners who wanted to be exchanged was not coincidental. The men who established Union policy toward prisoners also had to deal with prisoners other than captured Confederate soldiers. There were blockade runners, Northern dissidents, Southern secessionists, bushwhackers, and spies. These generally were thought undeserving of exchange. But should they be treated as traitors?

Since Confederates understood individual states to be sovereign, they too occasionally discussed using the charge of treason against prisoners of wars. Southern Unionists in the Federal army could be viewed as traitors to their states. Thus, in July 1862, Governor John Letcher requested that Virginians in the Union army be turned over to the commonwealth for trial; in September 1862, seven German immigrants, who had lived in Louisiana but joined the Union army, were tried and executed for "desertion and treason." (The Confederates were not entirely alone in this practice; the state of Kentucky indicted Confederate Gen. Simon B. Buckner for treason.)[5]

The great test case for the treatment of any Confederate prisoners as traitors operating outside the conventions of war dealt not with Confederate soldiers but with Confederate privateers. In autumn 1861, the federal government prosecuted the crew of the captured ship *Jeff Davis* as pirates. In the trial of the privateers, the defense pleaded that the captured pirate William Smith had committed his acts under duress, because the state of Georgia obliged men to serve in the Confederate army or navy. As Judge Robert C. Grier observed, "Every one knows there has been great violence used down there, men compelled to enlist, & c." The defense used the Union understanding of secession as a conspiracy based on fraud and force against the Southern people to justify Smith's acts of rebellion. Judge Grier asked, "If there is a great insurrection on this theory may not every fellow say, 'I had to go with them; there was so much violence and excitement I was forced to act with them,' and thus may not the whole hundred or hundred thousand escape?" One of the defense attorneys responded, "that is the only way you can deal with

4   *OR*, ser. 2, 3:9, 49, 150–1.
5   *OR*, ser. 2, 3: 280; 4: 708–10, 829, 849–50.

communities." Judge Grier had already suggested that the defense "might more justifiably plead the total insanity of the people of the South."[6]

The court rejected "this theory," and the jury found William Smith guilty. It took threats of retaliation on the part of the Confederate government to prevent the execution of William Smith and the other crew members of the *Jeff Davis*. In practice, however, the United States allowed far more than a whole hundred or hundred thousand rebels to escape. Ideologically, the Confederate soldiers were rebels; practically, the Union chose to treat them as legitimate belligerents.

Confederates, of course, denied the right of the Union to wage war against secession. But it was when the Union threatened the Confederate institution of slavery that the Confederate ideology of slavery and race began to influence the treatment of prisoners. While Confederates viewed white captives as prisoners of war, they refused to grant the same rights to black prisoners or the white officers who led them.

In June 1862, W. H. C. Whiting wrote the Secretary of War to ask, "Am I authorized by law of Virginia or Confederate States of America to hang or shoot by drum-head court martial marauding parties of the enemy captured kidnapping slaves." The answer was *no*. Governor Letcher, who had requested that Virginia-born Union soldiers be tried by the state for treason, also demanded that Union officers who had been "stimulating slaves to resist the laws of the Commonwealth and encouraging them to abscond from their lawful owners," be delivered to the state so they could be tried for insurrection. In August, Robert E. Lee complained to the Union army that certain of their generals were recruiting Southern blacks; using Jefferson Davis's words, he said "Major General Hunter has armed slaves for the murder of their masters, and has thus done all in his power to inaugurate a servile war, which is worse than that of the savage, inasmuch as it superadds other horrors to the indiscriminate slaughter of all ages, sexes, and conditions." For these "crimes and outrages," the Confederate War Department declared Generals David Hunter and John W. Phelps "outlaws." When he heard of the Emancipation Proclamation, G. T. Beauregard advocated raising "the black flag" for "abolition prisoners." "Let the execution be with the garrote."[7]

As the War Department orders indicate, the sentiments expressed toward abolitionists were not merely personal: they were the foundation of considered Confederate policy. In his January 1863 message to Congress, Davis announced that, in view of the Emancipation Proclamation, "all commis-

6   *OR*, ser. 2, 3: "Trial of William Smith for Piracy," 58–121.
7   *OR*, ser. 2, 4: 328-9, 776, 829, 835, 857, 916.

sioned officers of the United States that may hereafter be captured by our forces in any of the States embraced in the proclamation may be dealt with in accordance of the laws of those States providing for the punishment of criminals engaged in servile insurrection." The customary state penalty for such a crime was death. Davis intended to spare Union soldiers, however: "The enlisted soldiers I shall continue to treat as unwilling instruments in the commission of these crimes."[8]

A few months later, Congress backed off some. It passed resolutions saying that captured officers should be handled by the Confederate government, not the state governments. While the Congress justified retaliation, it limited its scope to white officers actually commanding black soldiers. "All negroes and mulattoes" who were captured either as Union soldiers or giving aid to Union soldiers, however, were to be turned over to the state authorities.[9] From an ideological standpoint, all the Union army could be viewed as fomenting insurrection, but Congress decided to narrow that charge so it applied only to whites commanding blacks. Davis had been willing to go further, but not as far as regarding the rank and file as insurrectionists. And both Congress and Davis insisted that the matter was one best handled by the court system, giving Union officers and men some sort of state or military trial.

Other Confederates, high and low, went further than that. The killing of black prisoners at Fort Pillow and the Crater is well known. But some Confederates tried to make the immediate execution of black soldiers official policy. Gen. Kirby Smith, commander of the department of the Trans-Mississippi, ordered that no quarter be given black troops, so the problem of turning black prisoners of war over to state governments could be avoided.[10]

Unionists rejected as crazy this logic that turned black soldiers into runaway slaves. Even Confederates had trouble with bits of it. For example, what should be done with black prisoners who had never been enslaved and who were not Southern born? The immediate instinct of Southern whites was to treat such men the same as slaves, not as prisoners of war. But legally, such thinking was dubious. Such prisoners could not be regarded as reclaimed property. When Beauregard captured several Massachusetts blacks near Charleston, he had to write to the War Department for instructions: "Shall they be turned over to State authorities with the other negroes?" The governor of South Carolina claimed them not as slaves but as men guilty of violating the state code against inciting insurrection. In this case, they were turned over to the State of South Carolina, as the congressional resolutions on retal-

---

8   *OR*, ser. 2, 5:807–8.
9   *OR*, ser. 2, 5:940–1.
10   *OR*, ser. 2, 6:21–2.

iation had not distinguished between free blacks and slaves. But then the governor of South Carolina, who was eager to try and execute Southern free blacks, became uncertain as to what he should do with Northern free blacks. James Seddon, the Confederate Secretary of War, resolved the practical issue, if not the legal one, by deciding that Northern blacks should neither be executed nor treated as prisoners of war, but be put to "hard labor."[11]

But free blacks remained an anomaly. Some black prisoners were sent to Andersonville.[12] Looking for some concession to make so that exchange would be resumed, in June 1864, general and politician Howell Cobb advocated exchanging free blacks. In October, Lee wrote to Ulysses S. Grant denying that free blacks had been held to hard labor and saying they were considered "proper subjects of exchange." And on February 8, 1865, in the last weeks of the war, the Confederate Congress finally amended the 1863 resolution on retaliation to recognize blacks as soldiers and to repeal the sections proclaiming the commanders of black troops leaders of servile insurrection. The Confederate decision to enlist black soldiers had made this shift in policy necessary.[13]

Despite the proclamations of Davis and the Confederate Congress, and despite the racist violence directed toward black soldiers, the Confederacy never implemented its policy of executing black troops or white officers. That such men were treated worse than other prisoners was undeniable; that they were treated as other than prisoners of war was a fact. But while such officers and men were sometimes murdered by their captors, they were not brought to trial and executed as insurrectionists. When the South Carolina trial of black prisoners finally occurred, the provost-marshall's court in Charleston infuriated the governor by declining jurisdiction.[14]

So neither the Union nor the Confederacy pushed their ideologies to their logical conclusions – a mass war accompanied by a series of trials and executions. Nonetheless, the possibility of extermination remained. The number of men who died in Civil War prisons – some 30,000 Union prisoners and some 26,000 Confederate prisoners – was high. The conditions under which they suffered, particularly Union prisoners, were miserable. And the rage that their suffering and their deaths inspired in turn created yet more suffering and more dying.

At the start of the war, few people in the North or South seemed to realize that a prison system would be needed. Part of the education in modern

11   *OR*, ser. 2, 6: 125, 134, 139–40, 145, 159, 193–4.
12   *OR*, ser 2, 7: 198.   13   *OR*, ser. 2, 7: 203–4, 1010–12; 8: 197.
14   *OR*, ser. 2, 7: 673. For fuller discussion of the treatment actually received by black prisoners, see Ira Berlin, Joseph P. Reidy, and Leslie S. Rowland, eds., *Freedom: A Documentary History of Emancipation, 1861–1867*, ser. 2: *The Black Military Experience* (Cambridge, Mass., 1982), 567–70.

warfare that the Civil War represented was the lesson that not all prisoners were paroled and exchanged. Both sides believed that that was the way that gentlemen fought wars. Each side disillusioned the other. Furthermore, the notion of a short war, popular on both sides, implied few military prisoners. In July 1861, the farsighted Montgomery C. Meigs, the quartermaster general, pointed out to then U.S. Secretary of War Cameron that the war would create prisoners, military and civilian, and that provisions must be made for them. He advocated appointing a commissary of prisoners to manage a prison system and to handle the exchange of prisoners; he also recommended renting an island in Lake Erie to use as a prison. Colonel William Hoffman was appointed commissary.[15]

The early prison system was no system. After a victory or any battle in which large numbers of prisoners were taken, Union and Confederate generals would have to telegram their war departments to ask where to send the prisoners – or ship the prisoners off hoping somebody somewhere down the line would know what to do with them. The war departments, meanwhile, would telegram the governors of various states, asking how many prisoners they could accept. For example, after the capture of Island No. 10, Union General Halleck telegraphed the governor of Illinois. "General Pope has taken over 2,000 prisoners of war today and expects to take more. How many can you accommodate at Springfield and Chicago?" He instructed the governors of Indiana and Wisconsin that they would also receive prisoners. His final orders to Pope on what to do with the prisoners reveals how complicated and improvised the prison system was in April 1862. "Send sick to this city [St. Louis]; general and field officers, prisoners of war, to Fort Warren Boston Harbor; other officers to Columbus, Ohio. Send 1,500 prisoners to Chicago, 1,000 to Springfield and the remainder to Madison and Milwaukee via Prairie du Chien, Wis."[16]

Despite the best efforts of men like Meigs, both sides clearly were improvising. It took until April 1862 for the Union army to issue its revised orders on prisoners of war. In March 1862, Halleck had to remind the commander at Columbus, Ohio, that "Prisoners of war should not be permitted to leave their barracks nor permitted to carry their side arms without special orders"; in June 1862, it was reported that captured Union officers were permitted to walk around Charlottesville, Virginia, gathering information about supplies.[17] The policy both North and South was to view prisons as holding

15   *OR*, ser. 2, 3: 8, 32, 48–9.
16   *OR*, ser. 2, 3: 433–5; for similar telegrams to Southern governors from the Confederate secretary of war, see 3: 730–4.
17   *OR*, ser. 2, 3: 355, 417–18, 899.

pens, where men would be stored until they were exchanged. As long as authorities believed that the exchange cartel would eliminate large numbers of prisoners, they saw no reason to build prisons sufficient for the numbers they would eventually receive.

The cartel for exchanging prisoners was signed in July 1862. It formalized a practice that had been going on almost since the war began. Prisoners had been paroled and exchanged by agreements between Union and Confederate authorities. The rank and file were generally paroled and exchanged en masse. Officers were exchanged more or less one-on-one. When it came to exchanging officers, the initial "system" was based on political favors and sentimental wire pulling. Fathers, wives, brothers, and friends tried to use their influence with generals and politicians to arrange for the exchange of their sons, husbands, kinsmen, and companions. Specific exchanges – that of rebel Major Y for Yankee Major Z – occupied much of the time of authorities in the early part of the war; frequently, prisoners were paroled on the condition that they arrange an exchange when they got home.

The cartel was designed to regularize these informal practices. "Prisoners to be exchanged man for man and officer for officer" – and in case there were not enough officers of the same rank, it explained how many lower-grade officers should be bundled up to equal an officer of higher rank. Citizens could only be exchanged for other citizens; the imprisonment of civilians was one issue that negotiations never resolved. Significantly, the cartel included privateers as military personnel. The cartel (1) arranged for prisoners to be paroled until exchanged; (2) designated where prisoners of war should be delivered – the James River in Virginia and Vicksburg, Mississippi; and (3) decided how the paperwork should be filed. Most important to the POWs themselves, the cartel stipulated that "all prisoners, of whatever arm of service, are to be exchanged or paroled in ten days from the time of their capture, if it be practicable to transfer them to their own lines in that time; if not, as soon thereafter as practicable."[18]

In theory, the cartel solved the prisoner of war issue. There would be no prison system, because prisoners would be held for only short periods of time. In fact, the cartel was always about to break down, usually because of Confederate prickliness. Whether or not Bertram Wyatt-Brown is correct in his understanding of Southern honor, Confederate authorities insisted on respect being shown their new nation.[19] Any slight which suggested that their government was illegitimate infuriated them. More important, they needed

18   *OR*, ser. 2, 4: 265–8.
19   Bertram Wyatt-Brown, *Southern Honor: Ethics and Behavior in the Old South*, (New York, 1982).

to establish the Confederacy as an independent country in the eyes of the world. Refusing to exchange prisoners was one more means to coerce the Union; and they played the card too often. Thus, Confederate authorities would stop exchanging officers to obtain the treatment of Confederate privateers and guerrillas as prisoners of war, or to retaliate for incidents such as Benjamin Butler's hanging of William Mumford in New Orleans in spring 1862. In effect, like many nationalistic movements, they held prisoners as hostages.

The cartel required good faith and trust. Trust had been in notoriously short supply during the sectional crisis, and while both sides believed that they showed good faith, each was inclined, probably unknowingly, to favor its own needs – all the time doubting the good faith of the other side and claiming that the enemy had distorted the cartel in its favor. The cartel provided no clear guidelines for certain kinds of prisoners. One class of prisoners taken during the war who nonetheless were not regarded as prisoners of war were civilians – Union men down south, secessionists and their sympathizers up north, and Confederate die-hards in territory occupied by the Federal army. Inevitably, a war over the nature of the political process itself created such political prisoners. But neither side readily recognized the right of the other to imprison such dissenters. Then there was the question of soldiers who had committed crimes against their captors – crimes that their side was always reluctant to concede. Finally, neither side was happy when the other side claimed that their bushwhackers were entitled to prisoner of war status, and each side claimed such status for their own guerrillas.

So the cartel was doomed to failure. Union officers involved in the arrangements – E. A. Hitchcock, Hoffman, and Sullivan A. Meredith – concluded that the Confederate agent of exchange, Robert Ould, was a liar who invented paroles and exchanges whenever necessary to put soldiers back in the army. On October 21, 1863, Hoffman wrote Meredith that "Mr. Ould is so utterly reckless of integrity and fairness and so full of finesse in his declarations and in the foundations which he claims for them, that I do not see how it is possible to continue longer with your efforts to carry out the cartel with him, or any engagements he may enter into." When Ould protested against the accusation that he had declared paroled prisoners exchanged illegally so they could participate in the battle of Chickamauga, Meredith answered him with insulting mockery. "Of course, a Government in as prosperous a condition as the Confederacy, with men in superabundance to put into the field, would not declare men exchanged for their purpose, nor would a high toned, honorable gentleman, who has reserved for himself the right to declare exchanges, use that right with the idea of putting men in the field. Yet it is well known that many officers and men captured at Vicksburg were in the battle of Chickamauga." In particular, Ould enraged them by announcing that the prisoners taken by Grant at Vicksburg and Banks at Port Hudson were exchanged. Probably Hitchcock, Hoffman, and Meredith would have been surprised, but not impressed, to learn that in October 1863, Ould scrupulously informed the secretary of war that "in making recent declarations of exchange he has exhausted very nearly all the paroles in his possession" and therefore could exchange no more paroled prisoners at the present time. Ould believed he continued to act in good faith. But he had long decided that the Yankees did not. He believed that they were dilatory in delivering Confederate prisoners in the flesh who had been exchanged on paper. He also thought that they showed lawyerly nitpicking that violated the spirit of the cartel. If they pointed to his handling of paroles from Vicksburg and Port Hudson, he objected to their disregarding paroles issued by Lee at Gettysburg and Richard Taylor in the Red River Campaign. The Union army was quick to declare paroles invalid and return former prisoners to the field. In fact, at one time, Ould had to tell Confederate commanders to cease issuing battlefield paroles. The fact that by November 1863 Ould hated and was hated by the Union officials with whom he dealt did nothing to strengthen the cartel.[20]

But personal dislike and ill-trust were not the sole reason that the cartel proved inoperable. While the cartel might have broken down in any event, the Confederate ideology of race and slavery ensured that it did. The Confederacy refused to accept black soldiers as prisoners of war. Instead of exchanging black prisoners of war, they treated them as criminals and slaves. The Union insisted that Confederate policy must change or the cartel must cease. In July 1863, Abraham Lincoln announced, "The Government of the United States will give the same protection to all its soldiers; and if the enemy shall sell or enslave any one because of his color, the offense shall be punished by retaliation upon the enemy's prisoners in our possession." Edwin M. Stanton, the secretary of war, wrote General Butler that November that "It is known that the rebels will exchange man for man and officer for officer, except officers in command of black troops. These they absolutely refuse to exchange. This is the point on which the whole matter hinges." His conclusion: "Exchanging man for man and officer for officer, with the exception the rebels make, is a substantial abandonment of the colored troops and

---

20 *OR*, ser. 2, 6:41–7, 95–7, 105, 151–2, 209, 306–8, 313–16, 320, 336–47, 364, 369–71, 387, 400, 403 4, 419, 426, 441–2, 444–5, 452–5, 457–8, 471–2, 504–7, 523–4, 537, 549–50, 552–4. At the time that Grant and Banks paroled their prisoners at Vicksburg and Port Hudson, federal authorities worried the paroles were improper. *OR*, ser. 2, 6 92–3, 147–8.

their officers to their fate, and would be a shameful dishonor to the Government bound to protect them."[21]

Once the combatants abandoned the system of parole and exchange, each had to rely on a system of prisons. The Union at least had a system; the Confederacy had just started creating one. It was as late as October 1863, after he realized the cartel had broken down, that Lee wrote the secretary of war to suggest that "we should commence at once to make thorough and effective arrangements to keep our prisoners of war during the period of hostilities between the two Governments." Modern war uses mass armies – a corollary of this truism is that mass armies tend to produce mass prisoners of war. Maintaining a large prison system was yet another strain of war that the Union was able to absorb and that the Confederacy failed to stand. As with the Union army, the Union prison system grew stronger as the war progressed. As with the Confederate army, the Confederate prison system disintegrated under the strain of this new warfare. Yet while the burden of their prison system certainly hurt the Confederacy by using time, resources, energy, and talent that they would have preferred to spend elsewhere, the principal sufferers from the Confederate failure were the Union prisoners themselves.[22]

Most notoriously, they suffered at Andersonville – a shelterless stockade built over a marsh in Georgia occupied by prisoners before the building was even done. In April 1864, the commander of the post – not the prison – reported that the "foul, fetid malaria and effluvia coming from the prison" had spread disease through the prisoners, through the guards, and into the countryside. Surgeons learned that gangrene was so prevalent at Andersonville that guards standing on their perches at the fence and never entering the stockade could develop gangrene in scratches and sores on their feet and ankles. In May, General Cobb recommended that no more prisoners be sent there as the prison was already too crowded; he predicted a "terrible increase" in death if the crowding got worse. There was nowhere else prepared for Union prisoners, however, so they still came as the hot summer wore on. By June, the prison, intended to hold 10,000 men, held over 26,000; by August, the figure was over 30,000. General Winder called for the immediate establishment of some other prison to relieve Andersonville. Henry Wirz, commander of the prison itself, began complaining that the bread issued was made from unbolted meal and was increasing diarrhea and dysentery – the two diseases that killed more men than any other cause during the war. Later on, the prisoners went for periods with no rations at all. In June, James E. Anderson, a Confederate private stationed at Andersonville, was so

21   *OR*, ser. 2, 6:163, 225–6, 528.
22   *OR*, ser. 2, 6 438–9.

appalled that he wrote to President Davis to tell him of "things revolting to humanity" that he witnessed. A Confederate inspection officer called Andersonville "a hell on earth." In August, Colonel Robert H. Chilton pronounced Andersonville "a reproach to us as a nation."[23]

Chilton was right. Many of the deaths at Andersonville were avoidable. Even if rations, both of food and of clothing, could not have been improved, shelter could and should have been provided, and there is little excuse for the camp's sanitary arrangements – or lack of them. Other prisons should have been built, and Andersonville should have been built larger, more comfortable, and in another spot entirely. Yet the failures of Andersonville had more to do with bureaucratic incompetence than with a deliberate conspiracy to murder Yankees.

One of the more grotesque exercises of Lost Cause defensiveness was the effort to turn Wirz into a hero. Doubting the justice of his execution is possible without admiring the man, yet some Southerners–specifically, the Georgia United Daughters of the Confederacy–tried to place Wirz in the Confederate pantheon. Since there was nothing heroic in his administration of the camp, they looked elsewhere. Wirz's defense attorney claimed that Wirz could have avoided execution by perjuring himself and implicating Davis. Wirz refused. This testimony was all that justified the erection of a memorial to Wirz in the town of Andersonville, a memorial that stands to this day.

Andersonville, it must be remembered, was the most famous but arguably not the worst of the Confederate camps. There were other camps that winter of 1864–65. With few exceptions, such as the ones in Richmond, the other camps also suffered from disorganization, haste, and lack of supplies. Two major Confederate prisons were located at Salisbury, N.C., and Florence, S.C. The Salisbury prison lacked adequate water, wood, even a place to build latrines: "The stench is insupportable both to the prisoners and the people in the vicinity." The "ration issued daily" at Florence "amounts almost to starvation." Men were trying to live on one pound of meal and one-half pound of peas daily. The prisoners died at the rate of six a day, primarily from diarrhea. The Confederate commissary-general replied, "Unless more money is furnished the bureau it will be impossible to continue to issue the present ration to prisoners of war, much less increase it." In November 1864, Chilton said, ordering an inspection of all Confederate prisons, "The shocking conditions of those poor wretches at Andersonville and other points, as heretofore report, is calculated to bring reproach upon our Government." Besides the dictates of humanity, the specter of Union retaliation frightened

23   OR, ser. 2, 7:63–4, 119–20, 135–9, 167–9, 207, 386–7, 403, 426–7, 493, 499, 521–2, 541–53, 759; 8:588–632.

Chilton. "They have already taken advantage of the reports respecting our prison system, supposing we had any, to inflict sad cruelties upon those captured from us."[24]

By 1865, a consensus emerged among the Confederate officials most directly involved with Union prisoners: Send them home. General Winder said in a panic, "I am at a loss to know where to send prisoners from Florence. In one direction the enemy are in the way. In the other the question of supplies presents an insuperable barrier. I again urge paroling the prisoners and sending them home." Bradley Johnson, commanding at Salisbury, begged for tents to shelter the prisoners, who were living in holes dug in the ground. "They are a terrible burden. It would be better to send them home at once upon parole." There was no longer a Confederate prison system, just anxious, guilty men sending desperate messages to one another and transporting sick, starving prisoners from place to hopeless place.[25]

After the war was over and Wirz was sentenced to death, the judge advocate-general of the U.S. Army, Joseph Holt, pronounced that by looking at the cemeteries filled from Confederate prisons, "we can best understand the inner and real life of the rebellion." For many Northerners, Andersonville summarized the Confederate cause. Propaganda stories about prison atrocities may seem to be nonideological. Surely portraying the enemy as a brute was a natural portion of making any war, almost a reflex action. While this is true, there also was an ideological dimension to the pictures drawn of the enemy's prisons. In particular, the descriptions of Southern prisons fit well with the Republican Party's understanding of the rest of Southern society. During the years of the antislavery struggle, abolitionists had portrayed the South as a land of unmitigated brutality. Slavery was cruelty unmatched, which permitted men to unleash all their worst instincts. In this depiction, the domination enjoyed by Southern white people led them to incidents of physical violence and mental cruelty. As anyone would know from *Uncle Tom's Cabin*, masters beat their slaves, fed them poorly, clothed them in rags, and tyrannized over them generally. With the exception of sexual abuse, these same crimes seemed to characterize Confederate treatment of Union prisoners. It was not much of a jump from Simon Legree to Wirz. Prewar portrayals of slavery were in perfect accord with wartime portrayals of prisons. Indeed, what other kind of behavior would one expect from slave masters turned prison keepers? The U.S. Sanitary Commission, which argued that the ill-treatment of Union prisoners was the product of a con-

24   *OR*, ser. 2, 7:1129–30, 1162, 1219–21; 8 :137–8, 160.
25   *OR*, ser. 2, 7:1304; 8 96–7, 211–12, 245–55.

spiracy, explained Southern brutality by saying "A too positive denial of humanity to another race, and a too positive contempt for a poorer class of their own race, have fostered those perverted principles, which would undermine a government filled with a more generous idea, and excite a hatred toward the people who would uphold it."[26]

Yet Confederates, too, pointed to their enemy's prisons as proof of their iniquity. They were not without evidence. Consider the prevalence of smallpox within Union prisons. In April 1863, smallpox spread throughout the Union prison system. Prisoners carrying the disease left Camp Douglas in Chicago and brought it to Baltimore and then to City Point, Virginia; it was feared that other prisoners spread it from Alton to St. Louis. The camp officials sent prisoners away without proper inspections; at Camp Douglas, they blamed this on a rebel surgeon failing to do his duty. Orders were given to minimize the spread of the disease. Yet Colonel Hoffman confessed that "if the transfer of troops or prisoners of war can only be made from camps or places free of this disease a moment's reflection will show how much expense and how much embarrassment to the service must grow out of such a rule." In June and July, smallpox still prevailed in the camps at Alton and St. Louis. In August, the commander at Alton prison had to admit that he had not yet succeeded in "isolating the cases of smallpox from this prison." In September, the commander at Alton said it was now free from smallpox – yet in October the commander at Johnson's Island claimed prisoners from Alton brought smallpox to his camp. At the same time, the commander at Point Lookout was complaining that the prisoners he received from Fort Delaware were likewise infected. In November, the surgeon at Fort Delaware acknowledged he had "126 cases of smallpox" in the hospital. "The deaths had averaged about $2\frac{1}{2}$ per diem, but it may be observed that this mortality is not owing to the character of the disease, but to the existence of other exhausting affections, such as chronic diarrhea, &c., prior to its onset."[27]

The 1863 smallpox epidemic suggests no malice on the part of the prison-keepers, just an incompetence bred from unfamiliarity with their jobs. The newly created system could not yet handle an outbreak of smallpox coincident with the need to move prisoners around the system. Yet, it was easy to take this incompetence and make it sinister. In March 1865, the Confederate

26   *OR*, ser. 2, 8:731; *Narrative of Privations and Sufferings of United States Officers and Soldiers while Prisoners of War in the Hands of the Rebel Authorities: Being the Report of a Commission of Inquiry Appointed by the United States Sanitary Commission* (Philadelphia, 1864), 97. For further discussion, see William B. Hesseltine, "Propaganda Literature of Confederate Prisons," *Sections and Politics* (Madison, Wis., 1968); Reid Mitchell, *Civil War Soldiers* (New York, 1988), 44–55.

27   *OR*, ser. 2, 5:449–52, 461–2, 495–7, 693; 6: 61, 70, 104–5, 179, 191, 265; 6:391, 422, 477.

joint committee on prisoners of war accused the Union army of deliberately infecting prisoners with smallpox. "It was equivalent to murdering many of them by the torture of a contagious disease."[28]

Manifestly, the Union prison system was imperfect. Yet within this system, variations were extreme. Except for a few days early in the war, prisoners at Fort Warren underwent very few hardships; remarkably, only twelve prisoners died there. Johnson's Island, a prison camp primarily for officers, had 221 deaths among approximately 12,000 prisoners. At Rock Island Prison, 1,960 of the 12,409 prisoners died in captivity – approximately one quarter of them in a smallpox epidemic that broke out when the prison first opened. The Yankee hellhole was Elmira, where the death rate was 24 percent – 2,963 deaths from 12,123 prisoners.[29]

If the high death toll in Confederate prisons – roughly 15.5 percent of all Union prisoners – was caused by incompetence and deteriorating supplies, what about the somewhat lower – roughly 12 percent – death toll in Union prisons? The figures alone suggest that conditions were poor; a reading of the official correspondence of the Union army will show that they were often chaotic. Conditions varied not only from prison to prison but also from month to month. Henry G. Adams spent his brief time at Fort Delaware during a period that the water there made people ill. A few days after Adams was exchanged, Ould wrote to his Union counterpart, "You yourself see the living wrecks that come from Fort Delaware – men who went into the cruel keep hale and robust, men inured to almost every form of hardship and proof against everything except the regimen of that horrible prison." Was it Adams's bad luck simply to pass through Fort Delaware at the wrong time?[30]

Or was Union policy the key to the Confederate death toll? In 1864, the Union instituted a policy of retaliation. Was Hesseltine's concentration on this aspect of the Union prison system justified by its centrality, or was *Civil War Prisons*'s focus determined primarily by his ethical concerns? Was it retaliation that made the Union prison system what it was?

In November 1863, Stanton ordered that Confederate prisoners of war would henceforth be treated the same as Union POWs were in Richmond. The army officers associated with the cartel and the prison system reacted variously. General Hitchcock immediately protested that such ill treatment

---

28 *OR*, ser. 2, 3:348.
29 Minor H. McLain, "The Military Prison at Fort Warren," *Civil War History* 8, no. 2 (1962):136–51; Edward T. Downer, "Johnson's Island," *Civil War History* 8, no. 2 (1962):202–17; T. R. Walker, "Rock Island Prison Barracks," *Civil War History* 8, no. 2 (1962):152–63; James I. Robertson Jr., "The Scourge of Elmira," *Civil War History* 8, no. 2 (1962):184–201. *OR*, ser. 2, 6:938–40, 948–9, 1000; 7:15.
30 *OR*, ser. 2, 6: 80, 104, 113.

would result in revolt in the prison camps: "Human nature would not endure such treatment under an ordinary system of guards, and the prisoners ought either to be put under lock and key (as in penitentiaries) or on islands under the control of fortified batteries." General Halleck advised Stanton that retaliation, while "fully justified under the laws and usages of war," would be "revolting to our sense of humanity." Butler supported the idea of retaliation, although practically he looked for ways to avoid the need for it. In May, Stanton urged the Joint Committee on the Conduct of the War to visit Annapolis and see returning Union prisoners. "There appears to have been a deliberate system of savage and barbarous treatment and starvation, the result of which will be that few, if any, of the prisoners that have been in their hands during the past winter will ever again be in a condition to render any service or even to enjoy life." Colonel Hoffman's reaction to the sight was to counsel Stanton to start retaliation "by subjecting the officers we now hold as prisoners of war to a similar treatment." Presumably, he meant starving them to death. In May 1864, Hoffman officially proposed a smaller ration for prisoners, Halleck reduced it even further, and Stanton approved the retaliatory measure.[31]

The notion of retaliation for Confederate treatment had never been far from the surface of Union consideration of prisoners of war. In fact, the Confederacy itself had introduced the idea of retaliation into the Union–Confederate dialogue on prisons. Hesseltine saw war hysteria as key to Union retaliation. A "people's war" – as the war for the Union was so often proclaimed – might also be expected to be particularly rough on prisoners of war. A democratic government should be responsive to the passions and demands of the people; and the people, with so many more members of their families in the new mass armies, will be passionate. But retaliation also seemed, to those who ordered it if not to those who implemented it, the only way to force the Confederacy to treat Union prisoners well, whether they were white or black. The fact that retaliation had little demonstrable impact on the condition of Union prisoners of war failed to discourage its practitioners – indeed, it may have provided them with a sense of grim satisfaction that they were avenging their fellow soldiers.

Was retaliation primarily responsible for the deaths of Confederate prisoners in the North? Official retaliation, which was limited primarily to short rations, probably killed some men. Unofficial retaliation – brutalities not ordered by Washington – killed some more. But neglect, incompetence, and haste were responsible for many deaths as well – the same culprits found south

31   *OR*, ser. 2, 6: 485–6, 523–4, 956–8; 7: 31–2, 110–14.

of the Mason-Dixon Line. Consider the following facts. Camp Douglas had
sewerage problems that resulted in disease. The prison at St. Louis was over-
crowded, and sickness was rampant. The barracks at Camp Butler were
insufficiently heated. At Johnson's Island, the prisoners – "the coldest set
I ever saw" – lacked overcoats. Camp Morton was "a disgrace to the name of
military prison." And in September 1863, over 300 prisoners – 317 soldiers
and fourteen civilians – died out of about 7,000 prisoners. All of this occurred before retaliation was ordered against Confederate prisoners. Many
of the poor conditions in Union prisons developed early in their existence,
before officers had learned their jobs and problems had been identified and
eliminated. It is true that death rates went up during the winter of 1864–65,
but it is hard to establish whether this was owing to the general policy of
retaliation, the increased number of prisoners owing to the breakdown of the
cartel, the weakened condition of captured Confederates, particularly those
from Hood's army, the severity of winter, or poor health conditions at specific
prisons such as Point Lookout and Elmira.[32]

Colonel A. J. Johnson, commandant at Rock Island, resented charges
that prisoners were being deliberately mistreated or that they were being mistreated at all. But his apologia, written to a local newspaper, reveals much
about the man. Perhaps it reveals much about the attitude of other wardens
as well. First, Johnson denied any individual responsibility for conditions at
Rock Island. "The treatment of them here and all issues are made strictly in
accordance with orders from the War Department." Then he admitted how
he would treat his prisoners if he had "discretionary power." Instead of in a
camp with well-heated barracks, "I would place them in a pen with no shelter but the heavens, as our poor men were at Andersonville." Instead of plentiful rations, "I would give them, as near as possible, the same quantity and
quality of provisions that the fiendish rebels give our men." Instead of new
clothing, "I would let them wear their rags, as our poor men do in the hands
of the rebel authorities are obliged to do." To sum up, Johnson frankly
admitted, "had I the power, strict retaliation would be practiced by me."[33]

This was an understandable emotion. Did it color his behavior as commandant at Rock Island? Johnson denied that his desire to retaliate against
his captives made any difference in the way he treated them. But the rage
that Johnson expressed at having to treat prisoners humanely when he would
prefer that they suffer was hardly a good sign. I suspect it was a rage shared
by other wardens, North and South. And if it did not lead them into sys-

---

32   *OR*, ser. 2, 4: 106–8, 110, 739; 5: 48–50, 250–51, 492; 6: 353, 359, 368, 424–6.
33   Walker, "Rock Island Prison Barracks," 161; *OR*, ser. 2, 8: 17.

tematically murdering their prisoners, as was charged during and after the war, it led to a drying up of sympathies at a time when an anonymous web of bureaucratic misconception and mismanagement was sufficient to make prison deadly. If men like Johnson did not propose to kill their prisoners, they still were not highly motivated to protect them.[34]

Consider Elmira, where according to historian James I. Robertson, the death rate was higher than Andersonville. There the prisoners received little clothing. They had insufficient shelter–men slept in tents in the dead of winter. The swampy areas, particularly a stagnant pond, that gave rise to disease remained undrained until midway in the prison's existence. The prison-keepers, wishing to retaliate for the sufferings of their soldiers in the South, refused to let the prisoners buy vegetables and rarely issued them themselves. The prisoners lived on bread and water. The result was scurvy and weakened resistance to disease in general. In October 1864, after many prisoners moved from Elmira died on the road, Hoffman concluded that "both the commanding officer and the medical officers" at Elmira "neglected the ordinary promptings of humanity in the performance of their duties toward sick men"; he recommended that they all be transferred.[35]

The impression conveyed by Civil War prisoners' memoirs is as often one of incompetence as one of cruelty. The prison-keepers had no training for their post, and many of them showed little aptitude. Commanding hostile but helpless men, they alternately wheedled and bullied them; far from the battle front, they paid back their enemies with cruelties, both petty and large; frustrated with their unadmirable task, they took out their frustrations on their prisoners. At other times, they acted pathetically in their desire to gain the respect of the prisoners; some even wished to be liked. Bernhard Domschcke hated Confederate Captain W. Kent Tabb, whom he described as "half-barbarian, half fool." He accused him of theft and physical cruelty. Yet he admitted that Tabb sometimes "seemed to suffer remorse at his brutality." One day Tabb asked a prisoner, Gen. Alexander Shaler, the former commandant of Johnson's Island Military Prison, "whether that assignment had caused him regrets." Shaler told him, "No. I always obeyed the laws of humanity and justice."[36]

34 One of the most thoughtful condemnations of Civil War prisons is Frederic Trautmann's introduction to his translation of a German-language POW memoir, Bernhard Domschcke, *Twenty Months in Captivity: Memoirs of a Union Officer in Confederate Prisons* (Rutherford, Madison, and Teaneck, N. J., 1987).

35 Robertson, "The Scourge of Elmira," 184–201. *OR*, ser. 2,7: 603–15, 677, 878, 892–4, 996–7, 1003–4, 1025.

36 Domschcke, *Twenty Months in Captivity*, 86.

One problem remains. What does this story of two highly interactive systems tell us about the American "road to total war?" It is a little embarrassing for me to attempt to answer this question, as I am on record arguing that the old adage that the Civil War was the first modern war may have reached the end of its interpretative value. Yet the experience of creating and operating the prison system was clearly a step in the evolution of U.S. Army institutions suited for modern war. The Union, once again, proved more modern than the Confederacy and succeeded in establishing a prison bureaucracy that looked something like a modern corporation. For its time, it was well organized and efficient. From the perspective of a more bureaucratic time, it seems a little sloppy and inefficient. Yet no army successfully carries a complete, humane, and efficient system for dealing with prisoners of war with it onto the field – as the recent controversy over the treatment of POWs by Eisenhower's army in 1945 suggests.[37]

The relationship of Civil War prisons to the evolution of total war is a historical problem; the concept of total war itself is problematic. Where do we look for our model of total war? Should we look toward the Great War or to World War II? If the first provides a model of total war, then we might conclude that, just as modern wars are crueler to noncombatants, they are kinder to combatants, at least when the combatants have been captured. The professionalization of war, at least, has been somewhat kind to prisoners of war. In the system that the Union set up – at least on paper – one finds evidence of the desire to treat prisoners humanely, and in the Confederacy, the ill-treatment of prisoners – when the prisoners were white – aroused condemnation, if ineffectual condemnation. If World War II provides our model of total war, the picture becomes much grimmer – and more in line with the actualities of both Union and Confederate prisons. John Keegan has pointed to "some unconscious recognition that it was to be in a camp – concentration camp, extermination camp, labor camp, prisoner of war camp; the differentiation blurs easily – to have been the enemy's chattel not his opponent, that was really dangerous in World War II, and that to have been a fighting soldier was to have lived in relative safety." If World War II is our model, we might decide that modern wars, at least when they are wars of ideology and race, are detestably cruel to prisoners, whether civilian or military. Insofar as ideology motivated the Union and Confederate war efforts, this too seems to be true; and when racism made itself felt, the immediate result was all too often Confederate atrocity. But to confuse Elmira or even Andersonville with Treblinka or the Bataan Death March, as the product of

---

37   Reid Mitchell, "The First Modern War, R.I.P.," *Reviews in American History* 17 (1989): 552–8.

a conscious design for cruelty, trivializes the horrors that the twentieth century concocted – although perhaps no more than the occasional confusion between Sherman's march to the sea and Hiroshima. Getting at evidence for the prison system is easy enough; weighing that evidence is no more difficult than the usual task of historical evaluation; but fitting this into a picture of total war is complicated by the fact that the historian's image of total war will be a matter of personal choice – or, even more likely, the image of total war will be something thrust on the historian by history.[38]

One final example. In December 1959, Saul Levitt's "The Andersonville Trial" opened in New York. This successful play explored the question of the treatment of prisoners and the nature of obedience to military authority. It left out such concerns of 1865 as whether or not Wirz conspired with Davis to focus primarily on one question: "When was a soldier justified in disobeying orders?" "The Andersonville Trial" was as much about the Nuremberg trials as it was about the Andersonville prison. And, in case anyone should miss the point, the "arrogant, defiant, fatalistic, contemptuous" Wirz spoke with a "slight Germanic accent."[39]

---

38 John Keegan, *The Face of Battle: A Study of Agincourt, Waterloo, and the Somme* (New York, 1977), 283.

39 Saul Levitt, *The Andersonville Trial* (New York, 1960).

27

French Prisoners of War in Germany, 1870–71

MANFRED BOTZENHART

Prisoners of war are among the forgotten victims of history. Historical scholarship has so far shown little interest in them, although studies of the situation and treatment of prisoners of war could be a very interesting subject for international, interdisciplinary research projects. For the era of the German Wars of Unification, this subject has yet to be studied on either the French or the German side. After becoming aware of this general research gap while doing work on the Napoléonic era, I have begun over the last few years to search German archives for materials on the history of prisoners of war. In what follows, I present some initial, preliminary results of my research. Owing to the loss of the Prussian collections, results are based primarily on materials from the Bavarian War Archives in Munich and the Main State Archives in Stuttgart. However, these materials need to be supplemented and verified through additional research, particularly in French archives.[1]

During the Franco-Prussian War of 1870–71, the problem arose – for the first time in European history – of supplying housing and provisions for large masses of prisoners. Prior to that time, this was not an issue in Europe primarily because it was customary to exchange prisoners at frequent intervals in the middle of field campaigns on the basis of cartel agreements. To my knowledge, the first international treaty that provided for the protection and humane treatment of soldiers during their imprisonment was the Friendship and Trade Treaty between Prussia and the United States of 1785.

The French Revolution brought with it a significant turning point in the treatment of prisoners of war when the National Convention renounced the previous system of exchange agreements and issued a decree in May 1793 stating that prisoners could henceforth only be exchanged on a "man for man" basis. Apparently, a scale of tariffs establishing wide variations in the

1 This essay was translated from German by Sally E. Robertson of Arlington, Virginia. A revised and expanded version of this essay has already appeared in German in the April 1995 issue of *Francia* (21, no. 3), the journal of the German Historical Institute in Paris.

value of enlisted men and officers was inconsistent with the Convention's ideas on equality and human dignity. During the great French Revolution and the Napoléonic era, there were no longer any generally recognized rules for the treatment of prisoners of war.

During the Franco-Prussian War, the number of French prisoners of war brought to Germany, especially after the capitulation of Sedan, Metz, and other fortresses, rose to around 12,000 officers and 372,000 enlisted men by the end of the war.[2] The prisoners were transported by train wherever possible. They were distributed among the different German states in proportion to the population of each state and were housed in approximately 200 fortresses or camps with an average of 10,000 prisoners per facility. Treatment of the prisoners in all parts of Germany followed a "Regulation regarding the treatment, care, etc. of prisoners of war after their arrival in the prisoner of war facilities," which the Prussian Ministry of War had issued on July 30, 1870.[3] According to this regulation, the housing and provisions for lower-ranking officers, noncommissioned officers, and enlisted men were based "generally on the existing principles for housing Prussian troops in wartime."[4] They were to be separated as much as possible from the civilian population and were to be kept busy with work on fortress construction and at military maneuver grounds and military workshops. They were required to work five hours a day as compensation for their housing and provisions, but they were given the opportunity to work longer hours for private employers and thus earn additional income.

Higher-ranking officers from the rank of major were allowed to rent private quarters for themselves and their orderlies as long as they gave their word of honor that they would not attempt to escape and would not make contact with the local populace or with France. They were allowed to move about freely in the town of their imprisonment and to enjoy social contacts of all kinds.

The sources that I have found to date contain no indication of special treatment of captured franc-tireurs. However, only members of the regular French army identifiable by military insignia had the right to be treated as prisoners of war. All others who bore arms against German troops were court-martialed and sentenced to not less than ten years of hard labor.[5]

Given the unexpectedly high number of prisoners of war, it was not a

---

2   See the "Nachweisung der Kriegsgefangenen-Depots in Deutschland am 19. Februar 1871 und des Gesamt-Bestandes der Kriegsgefangenen überhaupt": Württembergisches Hauptstaatsarchiv (hereafter cited as WürttHStA) Stuttgart, Militärarchiv M 271 c, Nr. 4792.

3   Ibid., Nr. 4764.   4   Ibid., 1.

5   Cf. the decree countersigned by Otto von Bismarck and Albrecht Count von Roon on Aug.

simple matter to carry out the regulation governing their treatment. The assumption that the prisoners could be accommodated in fortresses or empty barracks was quickly shown to be an illusion. It therefore became increasingly necessary to prepare magazines, stables, riding grounds, and other publicly owned buildings, such as underused monasteries, to house prisoners. Moreover, the Germans were soon forced to build new barracks within the fortresses and even to set up entirely new barracks camps. At least at the start, it was not always possible to fulfill the requirement that each prisoner have a wooden bed frame with a straw mattress and two sheets. In addition to meals, the prisoners initially received the same pay as German soldiers and later a higher "prisoner's pay" from the French government, the disbursement of which was made possible by the mediation of the British government.

The Bavarian files give the impression that the responsible military authorities were sincerely trying to make the lot of the prisoners as bearable as possible. Nevertheless, there were some shortcomings and some cases of appalling conditions. During an inspection of prisoner of war (POW) camps by Bavarian physicians at the end of January or the beginning of February 1871, the following were the most frequent deficiencies found:[6] overcrowding of the camps, inadequate heating, poor cleaning and disinfecting of latrines, muddy hallways during rainy or snowy weather, inadequate clothing such as coats and boots, inadequate supply of warm blankets and straw mattresses. Surprisingly, there is no mention of vermin such as fleas or lice, at least in this case. Their presence was probably taken for granted and therefore not specifically mentioned.

There were supposedly no complaints about the provisions, with the exception of occasional demands by the prisoners for red wine and more white bread. In some camps, there was a general prohibition against alcohol; for others, excessive drinking and gambling was reported. In all camps, care was taken to ensure that the prisoners exercised out-of-doors for at least an hour and a half each day.

27, 1870, in the Bayerisches Hauptstaatsarchiv (hereafter cited as BayerHStA), Kriegsarchiv B 938, Fasz. 2:

Prisoners who have borne arms against German troops may be treated as prisoners of war only if they: 1, are assigned, by means of an order directed to them personally by the French government, to a military corps organized by the French government; 2, are consistently identified as a fighting member of the French army by means of standard military insignia permanently attached to their clothing and clearly visible with the naked eye at firing distance. Prisoners who have borne weapons but are not supported by the foregoing conditions, shall not be regarded as prisoners of war but shall instead be court-martialed and, if they have not committed any act punishable with a harsher sentence, shall be sentenced to ten years hard labor and shall be sent to Germany to serve this sentence.

    Further research is necessary to determine how many such courts martial took place and what verdicts were issued.

6   BayerHStA, B 939, Fasz. 6.

It was inevitable that all sorts of communicable diseases would spread throughout the camps. The prisoners were already in extremely poor health upon their arrival. During the occupation, there had been hunger and epidemics in the fortresses from which they came. Some of the prisoners were wounded or physically and mentally exhausted from the strain of battle, and the stress of the transport to Germany had put an additional burden on them. Many prisoners arrived in Germany "almost without shoes, with frozen toes, torn trousers, shoddy coats or jackets teeming with vermin,"[7] and many died within the first days from injuries or exhaustion. At times during the first weeks, as many as 14 percent of the prisoners were sick, with the percentage dropping later to 5 percent or lower. The diseases mentioned most frequently were typhus, smallpox, dysentery, diarrhea, pneumonia, and bronchitis. Nevertheless, the physicians managed to keep the mortality rate relatively low, as compared with the wars of the Napoléonic era. By the end of June 1871, of the 39,339 prisoners who had been sent to POW camps in Bavaria, 1,508, or 3.8 percent, had died.[8] In the camps located in the member states of the North German Confederation, by mid-February 1871, 7,230, or 2.5 percent, of 285,124 prisoners had died.[9] The prisoners who remained healthy probably suffered most from cold, dampness, homesickness, and boredom.

It is impossible to decide, based on the sources that have come to light so far, whether the Bavarian inspectors, despite all the criticism, glossed over the conditions in the camps. One should also interpret with a certain amount of caution the fact that the almoner of the French army, after visiting thirteen prison camps in northern Germany, is said to have made quite a positive report on the conditions in the camps and military hospitals.[10] The fact that only relatively few escape attempts were made may support the conclusion that, despite all the adversity, the conditions were to some extent tolerable.

It appears to have been possible only in exceptional cases to obey the July 1870 regulation that the prisoners be kept busy doing meaningful work repairing fortresses, restoring wasteland, or engaging in river and dike construction. For only six out of fifty-six camps in Prussia are there reports of this kind of prisoner labor for the end of 1870, and barely 3 percent of the prisoners were working for private employers by the end of 1870.[11]

---

7   Ibid., Report on the inspection of the Lechfeld camp on Feb. 3, 1871.
8   Ibid., B 940, Fasz. 8. Final report of Dec. 19, 1872.
9   Compare the "Nachweisung der Kriegsgefangenen-Depots."
10 According to an article in the *Militärwochenblatt* 56, 1871, Nr. 101, 779ff. The author refers to a published report of the almoner, Count v. Damas, to his "spiritual lord bishop" on Jan. 5, 1871.
11 Hauptstaatsarchiv Hannover, Hann. 122a, XXXIV Nr. 6650, Table, dated Berlin, Dec. 31, 1870.

Whereas the labor of all prisoners of war was a significant prerequisite for maintaining German agricultural and industrial production during World War I, there was no prison labor to speak of in 1870–71.

A number of clubs and organizations attempted to ease the prisoners' disheartening situation. As early as September 1870, the commander at Ingolstadt reported that the prisoners were receiving "not insignificant monies from all sides,"[12] and he mentioned in this context banks and aid societies from Geneva, Basel, Zurich, Stuttgart, Munich, Frankfurt am Main, and Cologne. In November, the International Agency for Aid to Wounded Soldiers (Agence internationale de secours aux militaires blessés) appealed to all German governments under the auspices of the Red Cross to allow them to deliver to the prisoners not just letters and money, as had previously been allowed, but also "warm articles of clothing of all kinds, red wine, etc."[13] After initial hesitation, this was permitted. Another of these organizations was the International Aid Society for Prisoners of War (Societé internationale de secours pour les prisonniers de guerre), founded in Brussels in December 1870.

Once such centralized information offices for transmitting lists of prisoners had begun operations, postal service between the prisoners and their homeland functioned so well that the post offices in the camps were soon completely overloaded. For example, the commander at Ingolstadt complained in January 1871 that over 600 letters a day were received for the approximately 8,000 prisoners, plus hundreds of postal money transfers and a considerable number of packages with clothing of all sorts, the contents of which had to be inspected.[14]

The relationship between the prisoners and the population seems to have been essentially free of tension. At one point, the commander of the Lechfeld camp even speaks of a decidedly friendly attitude of the population toward the prisoners, which created a very favorable environment for escape attempts.[15] The files rarely speak of conflicts between the locals and the prisoners. There were minor property offenses and barroom brawls, and the guards occasionally had to step in when French officers loudly demanded wine after curfew or came into conflict in bordellos with members of the Bavarian army.

The relatively extensive free movement of the prisoners, the access to money and civilian clothing, and the often inadequate guarding of the camps

12 BayerHStA, B 938, Fasz. 1, Sept. 19, 1870.
13 Ibid., Fasz. 2, Nov. 17, 1870.
14 Ibid., B 939, Fasz. 4, Jan. 21, 1871.
15 Ibid., B 940, Fasz. 7, May 11, 1871.

offered favorable conditions for escape attempts, which moreover were punished only with disciplinary measures. Nevertheless, prisoner escapes did not become a serious problem. For example, only seventeen prisoners escaped by mid-April 1871 from the Lechfeld camp, which had an average occupation of 5,000 prisoners, despite the fact that it was surrounded only by a loose chain of guards, was poorly lit, and was often shrouded in fog during the long winter nights – all ideal conditions for escape.[16]

The living conditions of the higher-ranking officers who had been captured were as pleasant as they could possibly have been under the circumstances. They usually lived with their orderlies in hotels or private quarters and associated with the officers of the garrison and the prominent citizens of the town. Officers could apply, with good hope of success, to be transferred to certain locations, perhaps in order to live with friends or relatives or, in one case, to study art in Munich. To be sure, the treatment of the captured officers appears to have been particularly generous in Bavaria, whereas the government of Württemberg pointed out that being a prisoner of war was not "a time for amusement."[17]

As the capitulation of Paris neared in mid-January 1871, an urgent search began throughout Germany for adequate winter accommodations for the expected 250,000 or so new prisoners. There was certainly great relief when it was established in the armistice of January 28 that the troops trapped in Paris would be required to surrender their weapons but would otherwise be allowed to remain in the city.

The repatriation of prisoners began immediately after the signing of the preliminary peace treaty in accordance with the provisions of a special convention of March 11, 1871. The severe shortage of train cars, however, led to serious transport difficulties, and repatriation was interrupted in April. When it appeared questionable for a time whether the French government would be able to prevail over the uprising of the Paris Commune, Bismarck ordered that the prisoners be held back as pawns to be used "to force acknowledgment and implementation of the peace treaty under any circumstances."[18] By the end of June, however, the repatriation at least of the prisoners from Bavaria had been completed, and in spring 1872, the first memorials were erected to the French soldiers who had died in Bavarian military hospitals.

The Franco-Prussian War of 1870–71 made the European public aware to an unprecedented degree of the problem of prisoners of war. The activity of international organizations for the relief of prisoners of war, which began at

16   Ibid.
17   WürttHStA, M 271 c, Nr. 4764, Draft of a reply to a Bavarian inquiry of Aug. 18, 1870.
18   Berlin, April 10, 1871: Ibid., Nr. 4864, copy.

that time, developed into efforts toward permanent agreements on the treatment of prisoners of war. In June 1872, the International Society to Improve the Lot of Prisoners of War (Societé internationale pour l'amélioration du sort des prisonniers de guerre) was founded in Paris. Its goal was to bring about a treaty on the treatment of prisoners of war corresponding to the Geneva Convention of 1864 on the special protection and care of the wounded. On the initiative of Czar Alexander II, a congress on issues of international law in wartime was held in Brussels in July–August 1874 and attended by delegates from the European powers and the United States, but it took more than thirty years for these efforts to result in the Land Warfare Convention, signed at The Hague in 1907.

I would like to conclude this chapter by tendering the thesis that the prisoners of the war of 1870–71 in Germany were treated respectably, presumably better than prisoners in any other European war before or since. Their unexpectedly large numbers caused the responsible military authorities many difficulties and aggravating problems, which they attempted in good faith to solve. Sympathy rather than hatred for a "sworn enemy" characterized the attitude of the population toward the prisoners. In dealing with information on the French prisoners in Germany, I am unable to discover any evidence of a people's war or of a development in the direction of total war. It is impossible to say whether the prisoners would have been treated differently had the war lasted longer or had the French troops advanced into Germany.

PART SIX

The Legacy

28

The Influence of the German Wars of Unification on the United States

JAY LUVAAS

On June 15, 1866, Field Marshal Helmuth von Moltke, chief of the Prussian General Staff, ordered three armies – about 278,000 men – to commence operations against Austria. For more than a century, the two powers had been rivals for supremacy in the German states, and with the appointment of Otto von Bismarck as minister-president of Prussia in 1862, it soon became evident that Germany could be united under Prussian leadership only if Austria were excluded. The two had been allies in the brief and successful war against Denmark in 1864, but Prussian demands for supremacy in northern Germany made war inevitable. "It was a struggle long foreseen and amply prepared for," Moltke admitted, "recognized as a necessity by the cabinet... for an ideal end – the establishment of power."[1]

Prussia's success owed itself to several factors, including good prewar planning by the General Staff in creating a superior military machine that could be mobilized quickly, the maximum utilization of railroads and the electric telegraph in both mobilization and operations, and a superior infantry weapon, the needle-gun, which could be loaded faster than the Austrian muzzle-loader and in a prone position. Moving through narrow mountain passes into Bohemia in three widely separated columns, the Prussians closed in against the Austrian position at Königgrätz on July 3 to win "the greatest battle of encirclement" in modern history.[2] At a cost of about 10,000 men, they had soundly trounced a respected army of equal size and inflicted losses of some 44,000 casualties, nearly half of them prisoners.

The military world was stunned. Soldiers everywhere began to probe for the secrets and implications of this new military power. As the American *Army and Navy Journal* put it, "The grand strategic victory won by Prussia's

---

1   Gordon A. Craig, *The Battle of Königgrätz: Prussia's Victory over Austria, 1866* (Philadelphia, 1964), 1.
2   Walter Goerlitz, *History of the German General Staff, 1657–1945* (New York, 1953), 87.

maneuvering in Saxony – itself equivalent to a campaign – has been crowned and consummated by a tactical triumph" at Königgrätz.³

Four years later, the new confederation of North German states, led by Prussia, invaded France. In August 1870, three German armies, nearly half a million men, poured across the French frontier, won a series of battles at Weissenburg, Worth, Spicheren, Borny, Mars-la-Tour, and Gravelotte, and then bottled up half of the French army at Metz. The other half was soon enveloped and defeated at Sedan. With losses substantially less than the Confederates had suffered at Gettysburg, the French commander surrendered an army of 83,000 men and 449 guns to the German Third Army, which then moved on to the outskirts of Paris to commence siege operations. New French armies raised in the provinces by a provisional government failed to break the German grip on Paris, and after a few unsuccessful sorties and attempts to raise the siege, the city was surrendered in late January 1871.

In retrospect, the Franco-Prussian war stands as a major watershed in modern history. It ended one empire and established another, for on January 18, 1871 – less than five months after Emperor Napoléon III had surrendered at Sedan – Wilhelm I was proclaimed emperor of a united Germany. The war signified also a shift in the military and political center of gravity from Paris to Berlin as professional soldiers everywhere scrutinized the latest wrinkle in German military doctrine, practice, and literature. The German General Staff and system of compulsory military service found imitators in every major army in Europe except in Britain, and in 1881, the U.S. Army replaced the French *kepi* (cap) with the German *Pickelhaube*, or spiked helmet, as standard military headdress.⁴

For the next half-century, these battles and campaigns would be refought in military books throughout the western world. Earlier wars and even the American Civil War often were discounted on the ground that tactics before the universal introduction of the breechloader were no longer relevant. The German campaigns came to be generally regarded as the fount of all military knowledge; if soldiers could not always agree on specifics, few outside of the United States argued that any other war offered so many instructive lessons for the future.

I

Perhaps because they were oceans apart from any external military threat, American soldiers did not rush to the corner as quickly as military men else-

---

3   *Army and Navy Journal* 3 (1866) : 764.
4   Herbert Knotel Jr., *Uniforms of the World: A Comendium of Army, Navy, and Air Force Uniforms, 1700–1939*, trans. Ronald G. Ball (New York, 1980), 438.

where to watch the Prussians march by. In 1866, the *Army and Navy Journal*, a weekly professional journal devoted "to the impartial discussion of military questions," had been forced to rely mainly upon accounts of English war correspondents for "graphic" pictures from the theater of war.[5] In a subsequent editorial on the Prussian Staff School, the *Journal* proclaimed: "This method of securing competent and trained staff officers … is so sensible and appropriate to the needs of our army, that its adoption – or the adoption of one substantially like it – should be urged by all who desire [to] see the efficiency of our Army increased."[6]

The *Journal* provided better coverage of the campaigns of 1870–71. From articles written by the Special Correspondent of the *New York Tribune*, details from German official reports, and translations from German and French newspapers and military journals, it was possible for American officers to get a good picture of what was happening.

A few high-ranking American soldiers visited Europe during the war. Gen. J. G. Barnard, who had been in charge of the Washington defenses until 1864, and Gen. H. G. Wright, whose corps had defended Washington when it was threatened by a Confederate raid in July of that year, were sent to Europe in 1870 "for the purpose of studying the present condition of military engineering abroad." "With every opportunity for observation," however, they discovered "that there was but little … to learn from the study of European examples."[7] Indeed, according to the *Army and Navy Journal*, the judgment of all American officers who visited the German or French armies was "that we suffer nothing by the comparison."

No American officer who has followed the daily story of this war will believe that Spicheren Hill would have been taken, even by the determined von Steinmetz, had our veterans held its crest, or that an American army of 120,000 men would have been pushed back from the woods and hills west of Metz, as Bazaine was in the middle of August.[8]

The ranking American officer to visit the theater of war was Lt. Gen. Philip Henry Sheridan, then commanding the Division of the Missouri. William Tecumseh Sherman, now general in chief, supported his desire to see something of the war, and Sheridan, convinced from what he had learned of the French army in Mexico a few years earlier that "indications pointed to the

5　Donald Nevius Bigelow, *William Conant Church and the Army and Navy Journal* (New York, 1952), 97.
6　*Army and Navy Journal* 4 (1866): 28.
7　Peter D. Skirbunt, "Prologue to Reform: The 'Germanization' of the United States Army, 1865–1898," Ph.D. diss., Ohio State University, 1983, 57; "Foreign Armies and Ours," *Army and Navy Journal* 8 (1870): 261.
8　Ibid.

defeat of the French," decided to accompany the Germans on the assumption that more could be learned by observing a successful army. He obtained permission to accompany Prussian royal headquarters in the field, where he was privy to campaign plans and enjoyed candid conversations with the king, the chancellor, the minister of war, the chief of staff, and subordinate commanders. He witnessed the battle of Gravelotte as Moltke explained the positions of the different corps and the nature and object of their movements.[9] Later he rode over the battlefield with Bismarck and "was astonished to observe how little harm had been done the defenses by the German artillery," even the famous Krupp guns.[10] At Sedan, he was surprised by the "ridiculously small number" of French dead that had been killed by artillery – "not much more than one dead man for each Krupp gun on that part of the line."[11] And at Versailles, he encountered Gen. Ambrose P. Burnside, who was in Europe on a business trip and had seen a little bit of the war from the French side, and Col. (formerly Maj. Gen.) William B. Hazen, the official observer from the United States accompanying the German armies.

Sheridan's memoirs are anecdotal rather than analytical, but there is no mistaking his admiration for German military organization and leadership. It was Moltke's "marvelous mind" that had perfected the military system by which 800,000 men were mobilized and maneuvered "with unparalleled celerity and...certainty of combination." While finding much of interest and instruction in the methods of subsisting, equipping, and maneuvering large armies in the field, Sheridan concluded that "nowadays war is pretty much the same everywhere, and this one offered no marked exception to my previous experiences." He credited the initial German successes to the "strikingly prompt mobilization of their armies," and their later victories largely to "French blunders and stupendous errors." He witnessed one "unfortunate" German cavalry charge at Gravelotte, which led him to conclude that had they massed their cavalry as Union commanders had done in the final campaign of the Civil War and maneuvered against the French line of communications, it would have contributed more to the final victory. The Prussian infantry on the other hand impressed him. The regiments perhaps were too large for a colonel to command "unless he has the staff of a general," but this objection was counterbalanced by the territorial system of recruiting, "the foundations of the German system."[12]

Sheridan was well aware that marching, camping, and subsisting in France was a different proposition from the conditions that had existed in the Civil

---

9   *Personal Memoirs of P. H. Sheridan*, 2 vols. (New York, 1888), 2:359.
10   Ibid., 383–4.   11   Ibid., 412.   12   Ibid., 446–50.

War. "Under the same circumstances our troops... would have done as well, marched as admirably, made combinations as quickly and accurately, and fought with as much success." He wondered, however, how the Prussians would have fared on the bottomless roads and in the swamps and quicksand of Northern Virginia or in following Sherman to the sea. Nor could he detect any new military principles in strategy or in the operations of the Prussian armies from the battle of Gravelotte to the siege of Paris, "the movements of the different armies and corps being... governed by the same general laws that have so long obtained – simplicity of combination and maneuver, and the concentration of a numerically superior force at the vital point."[13]

What *did* impress Sheridan was the Prussian General Staff, particularly its mobilization plans and ability to place well-trained armies in the field. The American army, he contended, should pay close attention to the role of the staff as a planning agency. He was less inspired by the way in which the Prussians had supplied their units in combat. In this phase of warfare, he confided to Sherman, "their staff systems are not as good as ours," and he doubted that the Prussian model would be acceptable to the American public because "it gave enormous potential power to the professional soldier and the central government."[14]

General Burnside apparently wrote nothing of his impressions, but Hazen published a detailed record of his personal observations of German military life and service in 1870–71. Described by one of his staff officers in the Civil War as "a born fighter" and "educated soldier" whose "missionary efforts were directed chiefly against the spiritual darkness of his superiors in rank," Hazen had visited the French camp of instruction at Chalons in 1867, and in August 1870, by direction of the President, he was sent to visit the theater of war.[16]

Hazen reached Sedan three weeks after the battle. Scars of the fighting remained, but he was struck by the relatively small number of graves in evidence. In contrast to the Civil War soldiers, who tried to move near the enemy before halting and fighting in fixed positions where "heavy losses occurred in small spaces," Prussian soldiers were inclined to keep advancing "until the enemy runs away or they themselves turn back."[17] He was impressed with their

13 Ibid., 451.
14 Richard Allen Andrews, "Years of Frustration: William Tecumseh Sherman, the Army, and Reform, 1869–83," Ph.D. diss., University of Illinois, 1968, 83 .
15 Ambrose Bierce, *Ambrose Bierce's Civil War*, ed. William McCann (Washington, D.C., 1956), 40–1. If Burnside left any notes of his impression of the siege of Paris, there is no indication in his most recent biography, where his experience was summarized in half a paragraph. See William Marvel, *Burnside* (Chapel Hill, N.C., 1991), 420.
16 Bvt. Maj. Gen. W. B. Hazen, *The School and the Army in Germany and France, with a Diary of Siege Life at Versailles* (New York, 1872), iii–iv, 9–11, 36.
17 Ibid., 24.

success at concealment and noted that the French, "like ourselves in the late war," often preceded an attack by a long cannonade, thereby advertising their intentions. "Such use of artillery impressed him as one of the absurdities of modern warfare."[18] Hazen agreed with Sheridan that French cavalry should have been used to attack the enemy's line of communications – "if free in France, under a Wilson or an Upton, and divided into five or six detachments," the 30,000 cavalry penned up in Paris would cut the enemy line of communication, check and harass all their advancing columns, and in many ways make themselves felt. In the future, he predicted, as a consequence of the use of long-range and close-shooting small-arms, this would be the main use of cavalry."[19]

Nor was Hazen impressed with the weaponry that he saw. "The French *mitrailleuse* had failed to live up to expectations. The Germans hold it in great contempt, and it will hardly become a permanent military arm." The Gatling gun seemed to have many advantages over the mitrailleuse. The famed German needle-gun was "capable of about the same rapidity of firing as our own breechloader," but according to Hazen, it did not stand service well: "Such an arm at Shiloh during the rainy, dirty ninth and tenth of April, 1862, would have proved our ruin." The French chassepot was a superior infantry arm, but Sheridan regarded neither weapon comparable to half a dozen firearms used in the United States. In the hands of troops "imperfectly disciplined," he doubted whether either could be kept in serviceable condition.[20] "The new strength of the defense" made possible by recent improvements in firearms led Hazen to conclude:

It may be safely said that a single line in two ranks, composed of thoroughly good troops, with the new style of breech-loading arms, and protected by some slight work, can defy any sort of attack ... provided it be made in front, and over ground affording no cover. ... It is scarcely possible to hope for success in attacking an entrenched position in future, defended by firm men armed with the new breech-loaders.[21]

As for artillery, Hazen claimed that the Civil War Parrott and Rodman rifled pieces were more accurate than the German Krupp guns, even though the latter excelled in "lighter and easy maneuver and safe and rapid firing." He was not particularly impressed by the captured French guns. "We have much to learn about artillery," he concluded, particularly in the application of the breech-loading mechanism to steel guns for field purposes and rifling for heavy guns.[22]

18   Ibid., 59.   19   Ibid., 61.   20   Ibid., 71–2, 86–7.
21   Ibid., 99, 165.   22   Ibid., 123–4.

Hazen did not limit his observations to weapons and tactics. He was interested in every phase of the Prussian army – "its organization, composition, system of supply, drill, discipline, conduct in battle, and methods of living on the march, in the field, and in cantonment." Bored with the siege of Paris, he went to Berlin to acquire more information.[23] He commented on the Press, the commissariat, the mobilization process, and the field administration of the invading army in France that contained more than half a million men – over half the population of New York City at the time.[24] Comparing the Civil War experience with what he had learned abroad, Hazen was struck by the fact that "in our war ... no sooner was a regiment formed than it began to waste away from every imaginable cause."

We had no system of recruiting, but preferred to have new regiments formed, in hope that the desire of gaining commissions would promote volunteering. As soon as our regiments arrived at their posts, details began to be made for all the uses of administration. Then came that greatest of all enemies of "fighting-strength reports." ... Its greed for men knew no limits. We even detailed men from the infantry regiments to serve with batteries. ... A regiment would be left at the end of six months with a full complement of officers, a thousand men on its rolls, and about three hundred in the ranks, and these the miserable remainder after subtracting its best components. ... The wonder is, how we ever accomplished anything.

The Prussians on the other hand seemed to have anticipated everything. No details were made from the regiment. Hazen praised the German school system, which provided the best talent to the army, whereas in the United States, a newly commissioned officer felt free to drop his books and slip backward in his professional studies.[25]

Hazen summarized the special characteristics that made the Prussian army preeminent. First, the absence of exemptions and substitutes, which "secured for the army the best men." Second, "a thorough knowledge of duty." Third, a general educational system that produced superior soldiers and officers. Fourth, an effective system for keeping the ranks full. Fifth, superior training and careful selection for merit alone of the higher staff. He also mentioned a decentralized administration, impartial justice, adequate rewards for enterprise and industry, "a strict but not harsh discipline" throughout all grades, and, finally, "a rigid economy in all things."[26]

The Prussian staff and administration were "models of efficiency." In size, the United States army in 1872 was 30,000 – nearly as large as the wartime strength of a Prussian corps, yet the United States army register showed 542 "staff" officers where a typical Prussian corps had but fourteen! To compound

23   Ibid., 128.   24   Ibid., 173.   25   Ibid., 177–80.
26   Ibid., 185.

the error, U.S. staff departments had become "substantially independent bodies," whereas in Prussia, the General Staff provided "connected links of a great chain of military administration."[27]

Hazen's most interesting comments concern military education. He was impressed by the fact that German military schools made service universal and respectable and enabled the army to secure "the best possible officers." Each year, about one-third of the officers needed came from the military schools – the Cadet Schools for boys, the War Schools for engineers, and the Engineer and Artillery school and the higher War Academy for officers of all arms with several years' service. The rest were provided by "a superior civil education" that made it possible for young men to join the army for one year as unpaid volunteers and then transfer as officers to the reserves for the remaining six years of obligatory service.

The most remarkable feature of the system is the attention paid to forming and disciplining the mind, and encouraging habits of reflection. The regulations repeatedly assert that the object of education is not acquisition of positive knowledge, but to develop the intellectual faculties, and cultivate powers of thought and reasoning. The education is eminently practical, and frequent visits are made to manufactories and other places where actual work is carried on. At least one foreign language must be spoken by a Prussian officer.[28]

II

While claiming that the U.S. Military Academy graduated "better technical soldiers than any army in the world," Hazen contended that it produced predominantly engineers and that the most talented graduates were usually placed in the "least military" branches of the service – the engineers, the Quartermaster's Department, and the Ordnance Department.[29] Moreover, in peacetime, the regular army had become "exclusive and separated from the sympathies of the people," while officers of the administrative departments, separated officially from the line, "became also entirely divided from it in heart and sympathy." Moreover, their "peculiar relations" to the government and civil life usually enabled them to succeed whenever their interests ran counter to the welfare of the service.[30]

Hazen recalled that during the Civil War the adjutant general had created all possible obstacles to regular officers serving with volunteer units, which often meant that West Point graduates who took volunteer commands "were looked upon with distrust by many … while our honest efforts to secure discipline were viewed as absurd martinetisms."[31]

27 Ibid., 226–9.   28 Ibid., 265.   29 Ibid., 230–1, 291.
30 Ibid., 233.   31 Ibid., 291–2.

III

"We actually appoint men at the mere wish of influential persons, without any evidence of... qualification," whereas the Prussian system made it "nearly impossible" for an unworthy or inefficient candidate to get a commission.[32] These thoughts were echoed by Sherman when he visited Europe later in 1872. Asked by a correspondent in Geneva whether he had seen much of the Prussian army, he responded:

> You may be sure I did not fail to do that. It is unquestionably the finest army in the world... a perfect machine of war. The men who have recreated it have made every separate force, aptitude, and impulse that can contribute to military success the subject of the most rigorously scientific study. ... By hard thinking and close observation of the mental as well as the bodily habits of men, the Prussians have established a system exactly adapted to their national traditions, temperament, and moral and political organization.

In a different society, "an imitation of the Prussian scheme in its details instead of in its spirit would... be a mistake." What particularly impressed Sherman was the ability of the Prussian to recognize the individuality of the soldier. "You may talk contemptuously of the Prussian drilling, but their idea seems to be to drill men to do so without drill." Drill had become a kind of synonym "for the aggregate union of the most thorough individuality with the most thorough subordination for its highest end and aim."[33]

Later, Sherman was asked whether Moltke had in fact likened the Civil War armies to "an armed mob." "I have seen Moltke in person," he snapped. "I did not ask him the question because I did not presume that he was such an ass as to say that." What he may have said was that the Civil War armies, organized and composed as they were and operating over terrain vastly different from Europe, "form no guide or rule in European warfare."[34] Convinced that the Union army was "as good an army as the Prussians ever had," Sherman was not about to imitate slavishly a foreign system in detail simply because it had won. "The condition of our country, the smallness of our army, the jealousy of civilians and mistrust of our authorities," he explained, "make our situation so different from anything abroad that I do not see that we can do any good by comparison with the military experience of others."[35] Doubtless, Sherman agreed with sentiments expressed in the *Army and Navy Journal* the previous year, where the author of an article on "Prussian Staff Organization" had questioned "whether such thoroughness

32 Ibid., 238, 240.
33 *Army and Navy Journal* 9 (1872): 782.
34 Ibid., 10 (1873): 634.
35 Sherman to Sheridan, Sept. 26, 1872, in Andrews, "Years of Frustration," 87.

... is possible to any but the patient German race," while another officer concluded his analysis of German cavalry in France by asserting that European examples "have but little to teach us ... except in respect to thoroughness of training and preparation." These may have been lessons that the American army most needed, but they also were the lessons that American soldiers would be "least likely to learn."[36]

One other high-ranking Civil War commander analyzed the German military system. In 1874, Gen. George B. McClellan, then traveling in Europe, published his detailed thoughts on army organization. Writing for the general reader, McClellan explained what was meant by organization – "the entire system" of recruiting, leadership, military education, discipline, armaments, and supply of armed forces. Organization depended on the character, institutions, and topographical and political relations of a nation, and since no two armies of great nations can ever be organized precisely the same, he claimed that it would be a mistake to copy "blindly" the organization of any other army – including the Prussian army.[37]

But obviously he believed that this was the army most worthy of study.[38] McClellan preferred the Prussian company of 250 men to the U.S. company of 100 because it required proportionally fewer officers and most readily permitted a rapid expansion on the eve of war.[39] He acknowledged that "the relative value and the sphere of action of the cavalry have decidedly diminished" since the general introduction of breechloaders and rifled field-guns.[40] He admired the Prussian administrative branches no less than the combat arms, and he regarded the General Staff Corps as the best in the world. "In our own last war infinite difficulty, not only in the organization, but also in the subsequent handling of the armies, arose from our lack of such a body of men."[41] The War Academy at Berlin was "undoubtedly the best institution of the kind in the world," and the entire Prussian system was designed to produce a moral force throughout the army that would "impel and enable every man to do his best" – an important factor now that greatly improved weapons demanded "a higher order of intelligence and better discipline and instruction."[42]

These weapons would change the traditional balance among the arms, with a large increase in the relative strength of artillery. Infantry would be

36   "Prussian Staff Organization," *Army and Navy Journal* 8 (1871):540.
37   Gen. George B. McClellan, "Army Organization [pt. l]," *Harper's New Monthly Magazine* 47 (1874):670.
38   Ibid., 671.
39   Ibid., 674.
40   Ibid., 678.
41   McClellan, "Army Organization [pt . 2]," *Harper's New Monthly Magazine* 49 (1874):104.
42   Ibid., 408.

organized much like the Prussian company columns, 250 men to each company and every four companies led by a battalion commander. Cavalry would find its most useful action in small bodies.[43] No nation, McClellan asserted, can ever be perfectly assured of perpetual peace. The United States must make up its mind to maintain a military academy and a standing army that not only would meet the ordinary demands of peace but would also provide the nucleus capable for rapid expansion in time of war.[44]

Three years later, McClellan wrote again on behalf of army reform, urging specifically that the regular army be increased to the point where it could bear the brunt of the initial fighting in a future war, act as a solid nucleus around which volunteers could form, and at the same time furnish the necessary staff officers and instructors needed for the expanding army. He urged the adoption of the Prussian infantry organization of three battalions of four companies for each regiment and a general staff corps of officers picked and especially trained for the highest field duties.[45]

Unfortunately, the post–Civil War army was hardly in a position to assimilate the lessons of any foreign war. Over a million volunteers and militia who had served were quickly mustered out, and the regular army, which had been neglected during the war, was left far below strength, scattered in hundreds of tiny forts and posts throughout the vast west, and for a time was also distributed as an "army of occupation" in the military districts of the South. Recruitment lagged, promotions were slow, and the ranks were no longer filled with enthusiastic volunteers. Responding to the charge in a New York newspaper in 1877 that "the Regular Army is composed of bummers, loafers, and foreign paupers," a recent historian has commented that this was only partially true. "There were other undesirables as well – criminals, brutes, perverts, and drunkards, to name a few."[46] The soldier serious about his profession found little opportunity for intellectual development. "We are four," a typical company officer wrote in jest but with strong feelings, "forty miles from a railroad, a one-company post, a tri-weekly mail subject to the vicissitudes of imperfect horseflesh... we languish for excitement." Having read all books in the post library, "we are now all competent to command armies!"[47]

Indeed, Sherman, the commanding general, did not in fact command the army. The War Department staff remained beyond his control, and as general

---

43   Ibid., 409.
44   Ibid., 411.
45   Gen. George B. McClellan, "The Regular Army of the United States, " *Harper's New Monthly Magazine* 55 (1877): 779–81.
46   Robert M. Utley, *Frontier Regulars: The United States Army and the Indian, 1866–91* (New York, 1973).
47   Quoted in *Army and Navy Journal* 10 (1872): 122–3.

in chief responsible for the conduct of military operations, he constantly struggled with the administrative departments that maintained, armed, and fed the army. As he himself described it, each head of a bureau was in daily consultation with the Secretary of War, leaving Sherman to command "without an adjutant, quartermaster, commissary, or any staff except his own aides, often reading in the newspapers of military events and orders before he could be consulted or informed."[48]

Occasionally, Sherman tried to get away from the problem by visiting Europe in 1872 and later by moving army headquarters to St. Louis. Yet his hopes for reorganizing the War Department remained unfulfilled. In the concluding chapter of his memoirs in which he analyzed the "lessons learned" from the Civil War, Sherman noted that the French Marshal MacMahon, who had been defeated at Wörth (August 6, 1870) and again at Sedan (September 2, 1870), had blamed his "misfortunes" upon a similar two-headed system. This French report, Sherman declared, "is well worth the study of our army."[49]

One of the most promising officers in the postwar army was Gen. Emory Upton, an outstanding tactician who had successfully commanded each of the three combat arms during the Civil War. In January 1866, Upton wrote from his post in Colorado requesting that a Board of General Officers be convened to consider his new system of infantry tactics based upon Civil War experience. The Board unanimously recommended the adoption of his tactical manual as the standard manual for the U.S. Army, pointing to its practical application for all the arms, the ease with which the principles could be acquired by new troops, the simplicity of the maneuvers, and the fact that it provided for a superior system of skirmishing and "for a single-rank formation especially adapted to the use of breechloaders."[50] Grant, still general-in-chief, recommended the new manual for immediate adoption as the standard tactical manual for the army, noting that this was no mere translation, "but a purely American work." It was also, according to one authority, "the greatest single advance in exercises and maneuvers since the regulations of Steuben," which had been improved from time to time by added details borrowed from the French.[51] Upton later assimilated his manual with the tactical manuals for cavalry and artillery, thus creating a uniform system of tactics for the three arms. Perhaps with the Prussian needle-gun in mind, he asserted:

---

48 William Tecumseh Sherman, *Memoirs of Gen. W. T. Sherman* (New York, 1891), 2: 442. See also Oliver Lyman Spaulding, *The United States Army in War and Peace* (New York, 1937), 395–6.
49 Ibid., 403–4.
50 Peter S. Michie, *The Life and Letters of Emory Upton* (New York, 1885), 197.
51 Ibid., 201–4.

The introduction of the breech-loader has changed none of the principles of grand tactics; and, while it has given a great impetus to the employment of skirmishers, which is to be encouraged, experience will prove that the safety of an army cannot be entrusted to men in open order with whom it is difficult to communicate; but that, to insure victory, a line or lines of battle must ever be at hand to support or receive the attack.[52]

Upton's tactics won broad support throughout the army, and one officer declared in 1886 that they "were so sound in principle, and the formations they authorize are so elastic, that they seem to possess the germs of every change that could be desired."[53] It was only in his last days that Upton, like McClellan, specifically advocated the German system of organization and urged that the ten-company regiment that had fought the Civil War be replaced by one comprising two battalions of four companies each, with the two remaining companies to constitute the regimental depot.[54] Not until 1898, however, was infantry finally organized along the lines Upton had suggested, reflecting not only the German wars but a shift to the more modern practice of treating the battalion as the tactical subdivision while the regiment exercised administrative control.[55]

In June 1875, Sherman sent Upton on an extensive tour of the Far East and Europe. His mission was to report upon the organization, tactics, discipline, camps of instruction, and the maneuvers of the major foreign armies. In Germany, he was to pay special attention to officer education in strategy, operations, applied tactics, "and the higher duties in the art of war."[56]

One issue of intense concern to Upton was the expandable army. Whereas the Prussians in 1870 had put their army on a war footing in eight days and a week later had 400,000 soldiers in France, it had taken the Union nearly one year to raise an army of comparable size, and it was far from cost effective. Accepting the fact that the United States could not maintain a great army in peace, Upton could see no reason why the army could not at least provide a scheme for officering a large force in case of war.[57] Some of his recommendations, particularly those calling for an expandable army and interchangeable service between staff and line, eventually found their way into a bill that a joint congressional committee under the chairmanship of Senator Burnside

52 Emory Upton, *Infantry Tactics Double and Single Rank Adapted to American Topography and Improved Firearms* (New York, 1874), viii.

53 Bvt. Maj . J. B. Babcock, "Fighting Drill, "*Journal of the Military Service Institution of the United States* (hereafter cited as *JMSIUS*) 19 (1886):168.

54 Emory Upton, *Armies of Asia and Europe; Embracing Official Reports on the Armies of Japan, China, India, Persia, Italy, Russia, Austria, Germany, France, and England* (New York, 1878), 337, 340; Michie, *Life and Letters of Emory Upton*, 471–3.

55 John K. Mahon and Roman Danysh, *Army Lineage Series: Infantry Part I: Regular Army* (Washington, D.C., 1972), 34–8

56 Michie, *Life and Letters of Emory Upton*, 299–300.   57 Ibid., 387.

proposed for adoption in 1878, but the debate was purely along partisan lines, and the bill was defeated. The army was still mentally preoccupied with chasing Indians, and as Sherman admitted a few years later, it remained "in reasonably good condition, considering the fact that peace and politics are always more damaging than war."[58]

Nor had Sherman any desire to imitate the Prussian system simply because it had been successful. As he explained to Sheridan soon after the latter's return from Germany, "the condition of our country, the smallness of our Army, the jealousy of civilians and mistrust of our authorities make our situation so different from anything abroad that I do not see that we can do any good by comparison with the military experience of others."[59] Sherman demonstrated a more active interest in military education than any of his predecessors. Modern war, he contended, required greater intelligence than ever on the part of all soldiers and officers, "thus necessitating more study and preparation" than before – a situation further complicated by the normal dispersal of the Army throughout frontier posts. He encouraged the proprietor of *The Army and Navy Journal* to devote space in his weekly to serve as a forum for debates over new weapons, tactics, and organization; he fostered the growth of the army school system by creating the School of Application for Infantry and Cavalry at Fort Leavenworth in 1881; and he constantly encouraged officers to be more professional in the study of military science. If lawyers and doctors needed a good professional education, he argued, "how much more necessary with us who hold in our hands the lives of so many people."[60]

We occupy the most enviable position. ... We have no foreign enemies. We can at leisure study their systems, adopt what suits our purposes, and reject the surplus. Our wars are spasmodic and short, whilst the resulting periods of peace are long, affording ample time for study and preparation for the "next war."[61]

As the School of Application evolved into what eventually became the Staff College, students were increasingly exposed to ideas from foreign armies, "particularly the German." Instructors studied the wars of 1866 and 1870, translated German tactical literature, and diligently applied the German applicatory method of tactical instruction. Instead of remaining passive listeners, students became actively involved in analyzing "the endless diversity of the conditions of modern battle," even to the point of becoming exposed to the stresses of command.[62] To bridge the gap between theory and practice,

58   Charles W. Abshire, "American Military Policy, 1865–79," Ph.D. diss., Duke University, 1952, 129.
59   Sherman to Sheridan, Sept. 26, 1872, as quoted in Skirbunt, "Prologue to Reform," 67.
60   Ibid., 241, 249.
61   Sherman, "The Militia," *JMSIUS* 6 (1885): 2–13.
62   Timothy K. Nenninger, *The Leavenworth Schools and the Old Army: Education, Professionalization, and the Officer Corps of the United States Army, 1881–1918* (Westport, Conn., 1978) .

they worked out tactical schemes based upon real or probable military situations in the United States, applying theory and their own ideas to concrete cases. Because most German tactical studies were often too ambitious for the typical American officer and the problems he would likely encounter, the process was simplified so that he could make his applications on familiar ground with the aid of a good map. The student was also given a basic tool for organizing thought and communication, the now-familiar five-paragraph field order, as he worked out his tactical schemes. The original idea, of course, came from the Germans, who according to Capt. Eben Swift, the foremost military educator of the day, "have utterly dispelled the fallacy that 'war alone teaches war.' Under a careful system of peacetime training, they have been able to develop safe leaders for great armies in the field."[63]

The *Kriegsspiel* (war game) was essential to the applicatory method. Manifestly, this elaborate game also came from the Germans, who had devoted half a century to developing map maneuvers that would educate officers by developing specific tactical problems and possibilities.[64] This required "that a great mass of facts be analyzed, sifted, tabulated and arranged in such a way that a man of limited experience can find from the tables in a minute the probable results of any series of circumstances."[65] Complete with maps and scales, military pieces denoting combat and support units, timetables for marches and maneuvers, transportation statistics, tables of casualties expected from modern weapons, and seemingly endless data, *Kriegsspiel* even included formulas for computing the results of a charge, the losses and consequence of a pursuit, or the effect of fatigue, all for the purpose of enabling the player to make the necessary calculations for determining the "possibility, effect, consequence, and result" of his projected "operations."[66] An official version of *Kriegsspiel*, which included several applications of "purely American features" not included in any of the European War Games, was issued by the War Department in 1880.[67]

One early pioneer in military education was Capt. Arthur L. Wagner, who graduated from the Military Academy in 1875, participated in several campaigns against the Indians, and later served as professor of military science and tactics at two Southern state institutions. In 1884, Wagner published a prize-winning essay on "The Military Necessities of the United States."

63 Capt. Eben Swift, "The Lyceum at Fort Agawam," *JMSIUS* 20 (1887): 236, 239, 276–7. Swift was responsible for introducing the applicatory system at Leavenworth and developing the five-paragraph field order. Nenninger, *The Leavenworth School*, 45–6.

64 Skirbunt, "Prologue to Reform," 100.

65 Swift, "The Lyceum at Fort Agawam," 258.

66 Capt. W. R. Livermore, *The American Kriegsspiel* (Boston, 1879), 6.

67 Lt . Charles A. L. Totten, *Strategos: A Series of American Games of War Based upon Military Principles* (New York, 1880), l: xi.

Two years later, still only a first lieutenant, he was assigned to Leavenworth as assistant instructor in tactics and military art. In 1889, he published his first book, *The Campaign of Königgrätz*, which was the outgrowth of lectures on the German army and a trip to Europe to study German military schools.[68]

This was not a work of original or extensive research. Based upon four or five basic sources (including the Prussian *Official History*), Wagner's objective was not so much to produce a definitive history as to compare some of the military features of the Civil War with corresponding characteristics in the Seven Weeks' War. Too often, he contended, European soldiers had dismissed the "lessons" of the Civil War simply because they regarded American generals and soldiers as inferior to European regulars, and Wagner feared that this prejudice was shared also by "a small class" among American professional soldiers who admired recent European military operations not so much "because they were excellent" but "because they were European!"[69]

Wagner admired the Prussian army, especially the machinery for rapid mobilization that had placed nearly half a million men on a war footing in two weeks and provided for a steady stream of trained soldiers as replacements. As individuals, too, the Prussians had been superior to the Austrians because, as Hazen had also pointed out, their school system made every soldier "an educated man." Moreover, the Prussian army was the first ever to take the field armed *entirely* with breech-loading rifles, although Wagner noted that the needle-gun "would seem but a sorry weapon at the present day."[70]

He admired the thorough military preparation of Prussia and Moltke's strategical preparations to eliminate any threat from the rear. His strategy was "perfect." "The Prussian objective was the Austrian army, wherever it might be."[71] Wagner was not impressed with Prussian tactics, however, noting that in the first engagement some 33,000 Austrians had defeated 35,000 Prussians, despite the fact that the latter, armed with breechloaders, had managed to inflict the greater number of casualties.[72] Had the Austrians learned the lessons taught at Atlanta, Franklin, and Petersburg and utilized field entrenchments, they "could certainly" have held the mountain passes separating the two Prussian armies long enough to concentrate against the

---

68 Information on Wagner is found in Major Eben Swift, "An American Pioneer in the Cause of Military Education," *JMSIUS* 44 (1909):68–72; Timothy K. Nenninger, "Arthur Lockwood Wagner," in Roger J. Spiller, ed., *Dictionary of American Military Biography* (Westport, Conn., 1984), 3:1146–9.
69 Arthur L. Wagner, *The Campaign of Königgrätz, a Study of the Austro-Prussian Conflict in Light of the American Civil War* (Westport, Conn., 1972), 4.
70 Ibid., 11–12.
71 Ibid., 19–21.
72 Ibid., 34.

main enemy force.[73] As it was, however, the Prussians managed to maintain the initiative and force the Austrians into a purely defensive mode.[74]

As for the battle, the greatest conflict of modern times involving nearly half a million men, Wagner observed that in only three Civil War battles – Fredericksburg, Chattanooga, and Cold Harbor – did the victors exceed, in proportion to the numbers engaged, the losses of the defeated Austrians at Königgrätz. "A bit of reflection upon these facts might convince certain European critics that the failure of victorious American armies to pursue their opponents vigorously was owing to other causes than inefficient organization or a lack of military skill." Had Lee commanded his own army at Königgrätz, even if defeated "the next day would have found him on the left bank of the Elbe, under the shelter of hasty entrenchments, presenting a bold front to the Prussians." And had the Austrians profited from the American experience to cover their position with field entrenchments, they "should have been able to repulse the combined Prussian armies."[75]

Manifestly, the Prussians had won because of greater numbers and superior tactics and not because of their superior rate of fire.

> The needle gun was of inestimable value to the Prussians, but it was by no means the principle cause of their triumph. The great cause of the success of Prussia was, without doubt, the thorough military preparation which allowed her to take the field while her adversaries were unprepared, and to begin operations the minute war was declared. This, combined with the able strategy of von Moltke, enabled the Prussians to seize the initiative, to throw the Austrians everywhere upon the defensive, and to strike them with superior numbers at every move. ...[76]

Wagner criticized both armies for failing to make good use of cavalry. Commanders were unwilling to let mounted units get out of sight. Had the Austrians studied the far-flung raids of Civil War leaders like Forrest, Grierson, or Sheridan, they might have learned a valuable lesson, and he could well imagine the effect upon the Prussians during their advance to the Danube had such cavalry commanders been available to operate against railroads supplying their armies. He also faulted the cavalry of both armies for failure to provide their columns with a strategic veil to cover their operations.[77]

As for the artillery, Wagner contended that the full offensive value of this arm was not yet understood. The Austrian artillery was superior, "but in every case it was used defensively," and the gunners originated no new tactical features and therefore taught no lessons that could not have been learned equally well from Civil War battles.[78]

---

73 Ibid., 42–4.   74 Ibid., 78.   75 Ibid., 72.   76 Ibid., 83.
77 Ibid., 88–90.   78 Ibid., 94–7.

Wagner concluded that the art of war had reached a higher development in America by 1865 than it would attain in Europe the following year. Despite the superior organization and thorough preparation of the Prussians, despite even the genius of Moltke and the energy of his subordinates, the prime failure of the Austrians was their failure to study the Civil War. Had they done so and had they gleaned the right lessons, their infantry, taking advantage of entrenchments, might have held off the Prussians. Then their commander, using interior lines, could have thrown superior numbers against one or another of the Prussian army, and the correct employment of cavalry should have enabled the Austrians to sever enemy communications and thus gain time to seize the initiative. At the very least, Wagner concluded, the war would have been a matter of months rather than weeks and the Prussian victory would have been far less impressive.[79]

Another young proponent of army professionalism to study German operations was Lieutenant John Bigelow of the 10th cavalry. Concerned about military education and influenced by Wagner, Bigelow likewise questioned the assumption that the more recent German wars had eclipsed the lessons of the Civil War. The son of Lincoln's former minister to France and the brother of a prominent traveler, journalist, and author, Bigelow had been a student in Germany.[80] In 1880, some three years after graduating from the Military Academy, he delivered a remarkable lecture on the battle of Mars-la-Tour before the newly organized U.S. Military Service Institute. This was followed two years later by a series of lectures on Gravelotte, all of which were published in *Ordnance Notes* the following year, accompanied by twenty-nine elaborately detailed maps depicting individual cavalry squadrons, infantry companies, and artillery batteries. Convinced that the United States Army must never be unprepared to wage effective combat, as the French had been in 1870, Bigelow admired Germany's military planning and performance, and he considered the study of German military thought a logical way to augment the limited experience of the Indian wars.

In contrast to Wagner's *Königgrätz*, Bigelow's elaborate study of these two battles was based on solid research, much of it among German sources provided by his father, and his detailed maps would have delighted even the most meticulous German staff officer. His judgments were impartial and based not on what Civil War soldiers might have done in similar situations but on the circumstances and perceptions of the moment. Nor did Bigelow commit the error, so common in tactical studies of that period, of inferring motives from

79 Ibid., 99–100.
80 Howard K. Hansen Jr., "The Remarkable John Bigelow Jr.: An Examination of Professionalism in the United States Army, 1877–91," M.A. thesis, Old Dominion University, 1986, 32–3.

the outcome of a particular decision. Bigelow was struck by the "intense aggressiveness" of the Germans, especially when compared with the French, who historically had been noted for this quality. The cause of this "uncommon intensity" in the thoughts and actions of the Germans, he decided, was not the ordinary German nature nor even "the rules and principles of modern warfare." It came instead from "the moral conditions of a German's thought and action as a soldier," from a pervasive unique spirit of emulation that animated the entire army from corps to the individual soldier. Instead of concentrating merely on tactical forms, Bigelow maintained that it would be profitable to examine the cause of this emulation – the ways in which the German soldier was recruited and organized and the customs and opinions of German society and educational institution.[81]

He cautioned against looking at a battle strictly from the tactical level.

There are those who are ready to assert that the victory at Mars-la-Tour belonged to the French. They cannot get around the fact that the Germans achieved an important strategic success, but they claim for the French what is called a *tactical* victory. Those who … support this claim have lost sight … of the broad meaning of the word "tactics," and use it as a synonym with fighting. … They need to be reminded that "tactics" means, broadly, *the execution of strategy* – to see that, in one sense at least, a tactical victory cannot be logically predicated of a strategic defeat.

If indeed the Germans were "defeated," which conventional wisdom often asserted, then Bigelow could only hope that the United States Army, whenever it found itself at war, might experience "many such defeats."[82]

His lectures on Gravelotte, delivered in three weekly sessions, were more of the same – a blow-by-blow, hour-by-hour description followed by detailed analysis. Even his comments on the advantages and disadvantages of the French position could have been enlightening to a professional soldier seeking to learn from the experience of others.[83]

We do not know how these lectures, so detailed and technical, were received, but those in the audience who had already been exposed to the applicatory method should at least have enhanced their understanding about the use of terrain by a force on the defensive. Bigelow ended his remarks with a similarly detailed list of what today would be called "lessons learned": To him, they were "conclusions of professional concern."[84] For an army scattered throughout the west and increasingly limited in practical experience to campaigns against the Indians, he offered a practical way for the professional soldier to learn from the German wars.

81 Lt. John Bigelow Jr., "Mars-la-Tour and Gravelotte," *Ordnance Notes*, no. 390 (1884):21–3.
82 Ibid., 24.
83 Ibid., 39.
84 Ibid., 64–5.

Although Wagner and Bigelow had viewed the German campaigns from opposite ends of the telescope, their future development ran along parallel lines. Both turned next to military treatises on more general topics. Wagner produced substantial treaties on *The Service of Security and Information* (1893) and *Organization and Tactics* (1895) that replaced European works on the subjects and stressed the Civil War experience.[85] His published lecture on strategy likewise reflects a belief that American officers could learn as much about the subject from the Civil War campaigns as from analyzing Moltke's operations against Austria and France.[86] Instead of the usual maxims and principles borrowed from abroad, Wagner posited his own rule of strategy. "Remember," he cautioned,

> your object is to ... defeat the enemy, and endeavor to take the most direct means to accomplish this end. Look carefully to the supply of your army; protect your flanks and guard your communications; aim, if possible, at the flanks and communications of your adversary; remember that the enemy has as much cause to worry about you as you have to feel anxiety about him, having made your plan, stick to it unless compelled to change. Plan carefully and deliberately; then move quickly and strike hard.[87]

As might be expected, Bigelow wrote on the subject in graphic detail. In 1894, he produced *The Principles of Strategy Illustrated Mainly from American Campaigns*, a substantial treatise intended to furnish instruction for American officers. The Swiss theorist Henri de Jomini (1779–1869), who had exerted a powerful influence on most Civil War commanders, would have been delighted with his description of "the strategic chessboard" – and of almost eighty titles listed in his bibliography – only 10 percent were by German authors.[88] This book was followed some fifteen years later by *The Campaign of Chancellorsville: A Strategic and Tactical Study*, a comprehensive analysis that remains, despite the later flood of Civil War literature, far and away the best book on the subject.

By the turn of the century, both Wagner and Bigelow had come fully to appreciate the unique value of the Civil War in educating American officers. A large percentage of the after-action reports for each Union and Confederate battery, regiment, brigade, division, corps, and army were now available in print, and from the official correspondence of the commanders, it was possible to gain access to the thinking process and the assumptions of those who

85 Carol Reardon, *Soldiers and Scholars: The U.S. Army and the Uses of Military History, 1865–1920* (Lawrence, Kan, 1990), 102–7.
86 Col. Arthur L. Wagner, *Strategy* (Kansas City, Mo., 1904), 30.
87 Ibid., 54–5.
88 John Bigelow, *The Principles of Strategy Illustrated Mainly from American Campaigns*, 2d ed. (New York, 1968), 11–13.

had planned campaigns, directed operations, and fought the battles. There was no comparable source for the German wars, and because memoirs often were self-serving and official history tended to present campaigns in the best possible light – frequently serving primarily to illustrate doctrine – the *Official Records* became the ideal source for the applicatory method.

"One of the most important qualifications of a commander," Bigelow asserted, "is the ability to sift the truth from conflicting rumors and reports, and deduce therefrom the dispositions, movements, and intentions of the enemy." Thanks to the availability of the *Official Records*, authors could now make available the information to enable a military reader to do this. It was then up to the reader "to test or perfect himself" by occasionally pausing

> to put his own construction on bits of information about the enemy, and consider what he would have done in the position of a particular commander. As a rule, he should not criticize without amending. Purely analytical criticism is easy but comparatively unprofitable. Criticism should be positive rather than negative, synthetical rather than analytical. Where a plan or a movement seems faulty, a correct one should be substituted for it.[89]

Another officer who had an impact upon the development of U.S. army officers at this time was Capt. Matthew Forney Steele, who had charged up San Juan Hill and later campaigned in the Philippines before being assigned to Leavenworth in 1903 as an instructor. Even in his lecture on "the campaign of Königgrätz," Steele raised the question, "How long would it have taken Moltke to reach Vienna if Joseph E. Johnston had commanded the army opposed to him and it had been composed of Americans?" Prussian success, he asserted, was primarily the result of superior preparation for war – a system of army organization, training, recruitment, mobilization, and a plan of campaign worked out long before hostilities by the Great General Staff (*Grosser Generalstab*) that had enabled the Prussian army to seize the initiative. Steele was "astonished," however, to see how poorly the cavalry had performed in the campaign of 1866, and he was convinced that both armies might have learned how to entrench, make better use of the field telegraph, and move troops around at night had they studied the Civil War.[90]

With generous support from his superiors, both at Leavenworth and in Washington, Steele later published his lectures on the American campaigns in a two-volume textbook that provided soldiers with the historical informa-

89 John Bigelow Jr., *The Campaign of Chancellorsville: A Strategic and Tactical Study* (New Haven, Conn., 1910), xii.

90 Department of Military Art, Infantry, and Cavalry School. Course in Strategy, 1905–06. Extracts from Lecture no. 26, "The Campaign of Königgrätz." Matthew Forney Steele papers, U.S. Army Military History Institute, Carlisle Barracks, Pa.

tion needed to support their military studies.[91] Such studies, he insisted, must take into account American military policy, institutions, and traditions, "bad as they may be from a military point of view." If it was desirable for soldiers to be familiar with the organization of German forces, to understand the way they were recruited and mobilized, and to learn how the German fighting machine is handled, it was more important still for American officers to know how to handle such forces "as our own national conditions must produce."[92]

This is not to say that American soldiers turned their backs completely on the German wars. Any book or article devoted to the evolution of tactics devoted appropriate attention to the wars of 1866 and 1871, but increasingly the pace of technology – particularly in the improvement of field artillery – outdated any tactical lessons from the German wars.

What can we conclude about the nature and extent of the German influence on the U.S. Army? Clearly, most American soldiers did not mistake form for substance. From the first, they stressed the superiority of the German military organization, as McClellan had defined the term. "Such combinations, such preparation, such work!" declared one former Civil War cavalry general.

The profession of arms has always been one of great labor for those at the head of armies, and one of partial indolence for subalterns and the rank and file. Now, this is all changed. Study, application, intelligence and labor must be the rule throughout.[93]

Sherman's initial reactions to the wars of 1866 and 1870 had stressed the spirit of German military education and the thoroughness of German planning. His influence – and the reforms that Upton had proposed – set the agenda for military study and debate for the rest of the century and, according to the foremost authority on the subject, "were for the most part eventually accepted." These included (1) the three-battalion system for infantry regiments – which Sherman in his memoirs had advocated as one of the "military lessons" of the Civil War – (2) an army school system for enlisted men and officers receiving commissions and to "further train officers in the finer points of their profession," (3) a mobilization scheme similar to the German system, with regimental depots and universal obligations, (4) the establishment of a General Staff Corps, and (5) an American equivalent to the *Kriegsakademie* (war college).[94] After the administrative and organizational

---

91 Reardon, *Soldiers and Scholars*, 123.
92 Capt. Matthew F. Steele, "The Conduct of War," JMSIUS 42 (1908):25.
93 Bvt. Maj. Gen. Wesley Merritt, "Important Improvements in the Art of War in the Last Twenty Years and the Probably Effect on Future Military Operations," *JMSIUS* 4 (1883):185, 187.
94 Skirbunt, "Prologue to Reform," 173–8.

defects exposed during the war with Spain in 1898, Congress finally voted in 1903 to establish a General Staff Corps. The way had been paved by Gen. John M. Schofield, commanding general from 1888 to 1895. Schofield, who had served under Sherman in the Atlanta campaign and whose aide-de-camp had been Upton's traveling companion on his world tour to investigate the armies of Asia and Europe in 1875–76, initially "created a means to accomplish the function of the Great General Staff of determining and guiding the operational readiness of army units."[95]

Several years later, Brig. Gen. William Ludlow submitted a manuscript of nearly 200 pages describing the organization of the German army, its system of recruiting and training, the supply of officers, military administration, the General Staff, military schools and colleges, and military education and training.[96] When Secretary of War Elihu Root established the War College in 1903, he confessed that he had been significantly influenced by a book that had recently appeared in England on the German General Staff. "I created a General Staff," he confided to the author, "but not quite on the Prussian system."[97] That would have been incompatible with American institutions. Nevertheless, Root initially viewed the Army War College as "a great adjunct to the General Staff," particularly in the area of planning.[98] Indeed, so prevalent were German practices and military texts at Leavenworth in the first decade of this century that one lecturer could comment: "Our Field Service regulations unmistakably show the impress of German thought. Moltke teaches us our strategy, Griepenkerl writes our orders, while Von der Goltz tells us how they should be executed."[99]

But this is misleading, and one should not assume that the American "art of war" was ever in fact "made in Germany." By this time, German tactics and formations had little influence in the United States army. Even though the *Pickelhaube* had been officially introduced in 1881, what concerned most American soldiers from Sherman to Root was the thinking process that went on under the spiked helmet. And this they consistently tried to adapt to American military institutions.

95 Col. Harry P. Ball, *Of Responsible Command: A History of the U.S. Army War College* (Carlisle Barracks, Pa., 1983), 36.

96 William Ludlow, "Principles and Practical Methods in Organization, Training, Administration of German and Other Armies," typescript dated Feb. 16, 1901, U.S. Military History Institute.

97 Capt. T. A. Bingham, "The Prussian Great General Staff and What it Contains that is Practical from an American Standpoint," *JMSIUS* 13 (1880): 675–6. Henry Spenser Wilkinson, *Thirty-Five Years, 1874–1909* (London, 1933), 260–1.

98 Ball, *Of Responsible Command*, 79.

99 Nenninger, *The Leavenworth Schools*, 87.

29

From Civil War to World Power: Perceptions and Realities, 1865–1914

RICHARD N. CURRENT

Between 1865 and 1914, the United States rose to recognition as one of the world's great powers. This would seem, at first glance, to be a legacy of the Civil War, one that Americans perceived and appreciated at the time. But was it really a result of that war, and did contemporary Americans perceive it as such? A review of the evidence will suggest a negative answer to both questions. The truth seems to be that people had to live down the Civil War before the country could become a great power and they could accept and applaud its new status.

To qualify as a great power, the United States needed to develop the following: (1) a party system that would tend to unite rather than to divide the country; (2) a sense of psychological as well as political reunion; (3) a strong, assertive presidency; (4) an aggressive and expansive foreign policy; (5) a large military and naval capability; and (6) a highly industrialized and productive economy. By 1914, the United States had obtained or was on the verge of obtaining each of those half-dozen elements of national greatness. Not one of the items, however, could be traced back directly and continuously to the events of 1861–65, as even a brief look at each of them will show.

POLITICAL REUNION

With apologies to Carl von Clausewitz, it might be said that politics is warfare carried on by other means, and American politics for many years could certainly be considered a continuation of the Civil War. The war, which followed a sectionalization of political parties, led to an increase rather than a decrease in sectionalism. It intensified the anti-Yankee bitterness of Southerners and made them less willing than before secession to acknowledge Northerners as fellow citizens.

"I here declare my unmitigated hatred to Yankee rule – to all political, social and business connections with the Yankee and to the Yankee race." So wrote the Virginian Edmund Ruffin in the hour of final defeat. "Would that I could impress these sentiments, in their full force, on every living Southerner and bequeath them to every one yet to be born! May such sentiments be held universally in the outraged and down-trodden South, though in silence and stillness, until the now far-distant day shall arrive for just retribution for Yankee usurpation, oppression and atrocious outrages, and for deliverance and vengeance for the now ruined, subjugated, and enslaved Southern States!" Having written those words, Ruffin put the muzzle of a shotgun in his mouth and pushed the trigger with a forked stick.[1]

Ruffin had been a fanatical secessionist. The Georgian Howell Cobb, by contrast, had resisted extremes of sectionalism while serving as a prewar congressman, governor, and secretary of the treasury. After the war, Confederate General Cobb advised Union General James H. Wilson: "The prejudices and passions which have been aroused in this contest, crimsoned in the blood of loved ones from every portion of the land, will yield only to the mellowing influence of time, and the younger participants in the struggle will scarcely live to see the last shadow pass away." The abolition of slavery, Cobb went on, was "calculated to excite the most serious apprehensions" and would be "unfortunate" for both blacks and whites. The task of statesmanship now was to find a "substitute" for slavery. "I take it for granted," Cobb concluded, "that the future relations between the negroes and their former owners ... will be under the control and direction of the State Governments."[2]

As long as President Andrew Johnson had his way, the Southern states did keep control of race relations, and each of the states enacted its "black code" to limit the freedom of blacks and thus provide a substitute for slavery. To assure real freedom to the former slaves, the Republicans in 1867 launched their program of congressional Reconstruction, which gave black men political rights. This further embittered the majority of white Southerners.

A temporary dissenter from the majority was the Mississippi planter James L. Alcorn, who had been the state's largest slaveholder next to Jefferson Davis's brother Joseph but had been unenthusiastic about secession. In January 1869, shortly before Ulysses S. Grant's inauguration as president, Alcorn wrote to Grant's friend Elihu B. Washburne, an Illinois congressman: "Is there a man in Congress so stupid as to believe that there is a Democrat in the South who regards Gen. Grant with other than the most intense hatred? Who considers the American government other than a stupendous tyranny?

1   Avery Craven, *Edmund Ruffin, Southerner: A Study in Secession* (New York, 1932), 259.
2   Cobb to Wilson, June 14, 1865, Andrew Johnson papers, Library of Congress.

Who would not hail with joy the overthrow of that government by France, England, or any other power, as a Christian would hail the coming of the Messiah?"[3]

Rebelliousness on the part of Southern whites persisted as long as Southern blacks continued to vote and hold office. The issues of the Civil War now reemerged in a somewhat altered form—state rights instead of secession, "white supremacy" instead of slavery. The Democratic party, North as well as South, took up what had been the Confederate side. Democrats vilified the Republican state governments in the South, grossly exaggerating their extravagance and corruption and falsely characterizing them as instruments of "Negro rule." After the Democrats got control of the national House of Representatives, the federal government quit trying to enforce the political rights of Southern blacks, and Reconstruction came to an end in 1877.

Republicans, with considerable justification, had been denouncing the Democratic Party as the party of treason, and they continued to do so even after the Reconstruction issues were dead. Not all the Democrats were traitors, Republicans said, but all the traitors were Democrats. Republicans urged ex-soldiers in the North to vote as they shot, thus appealing to the hundreds of thousands who belonged to the Union veterans' organization, the Grand Army of the Republic (G.A.R.), which functioned as a virtual auxiliary of the Republican Party.

Democrats accused Republicans of "waving the bloody shirt"—that is, reviving wartime hatreds for political effect—although in the South, the Democrats were doing likewise as they continually rearoused devotion to the Lost Cause and its heroes. In the South, Confederate war service became practically a requirement for election to state or local office, and Union war service was equally essential in the North. Republican candidates were almost always former officers, almost never common soldiers. A Wisconsin member of the Grand Army of the Republic claimed in 1872 that the veteran vote had "elected 274 Generals and Colonels to the State Legislature and not one private."[4]

In every presidential election except one between the end of the war and the end of the century, the Republicans ran a former officer of the Union army. Only Grant had been a professional soldier; all the rest of those elected had served as volunteers – Rutherford B. Hayes, James A. Garfield, Benjamin Harrison, and William McKinley. The Democrats could not very well take

3 Alcorn to Washburne, January 1, 1869, Washburne papers, Library of Congress.
4 Madison, Wis., Soldiers' Record, April 30, 1872, quoted in Mary R. Dearing, *Veterans in Politics: The Story of the G.A.R.* (Baton Rouge, La., 1952), 195.

advantage of the politics of patriotism in the same way. A Confederate veteran on their ticket would turn away voters in the North, and a Union veteran could not be expected to attract very many in the South. Still, the Democrats tried their luck with Winfield Scott Hancock in 1880. Hancock, a West Point graduate, still held a generalship in the regular army. Against the "citizen soldier" Garfield, he had no chance.

The election of 1884 was the only one in which the Republicans risked a candidate with no war record – James G. Blaine. They tried to make up for Blaine's defect by picking John A. Logan as his running mate. Logan had been not only a general of volunteers but also a commander in chief of the Grand Army of the Republic. Even so, the ticket did not attract enough of the soldier vote to carry the election. Grover Cleveland, who, like Blaine, had escaped war service, became the first Democrat to be elected president in almost thirty years.

Some observers thought that Cleveland's election marked an end to sectional politics. Once Cleveland had begun his presidency, however, Gen. William Tecumseh Sherman accused him of appointing "open Rebels" to office, and Cleveland did indeed appoint ex-Confederates to positions as high as his cabinet. G.A.R. leaders raised the question whether the fruits of Northern victory were now to be sacrificed. Republicans waved the bloody shirt with renewed vigor. Before the end of Cleveland's first term, the British observer James Bryce could nevertheless declare that from 1850 to 1876, "questions, first of the extension of slavery, then of its extinction, then of the reconstruction of the Union, had divided the nation," but now the "controversies raised by the war" had been settled.[5]

During the 1890s, farmers of the South and West came together to resist the "money power" of the Northeast, and the new Populist alignment tended to offset the old sectionalism of South against North. A Populist writer quoted Abraham Lincoln (apocryphally) as having predicted that the money power would "endeavor to prolong its reign by working upon the prejudices of the people." Sure enough, "it had kept aflame the sectional bitterness engendered by the War."[6] To emphasize the spirit of reunion, the Populist party in 1892 nominated a former Union general for president and a former Confederate general for vice-president.

The Spanish-American War, drawing support from both parties and both sections, contributed further to political reunion. Former Union soldiers, as represented by the G.A.R., endorsed the war. Along with them, former

---

5 James Bryce, *The American Commonwealth*, 2 vols . (London and New York, 1889), 2:179–80.
6 Milford W. Howard, *The American Plutocracy* (New York, 1895), quoted in Norman Pollard, ed., *The Populist Mind* (Indianapolis, Ind., and New York, 1967), 239–40.

Confederates enlisted in it. Two ex-Confederate generals, Fitzhugh Lee and Joseph Wheeler, now served as generals in the U.S. Army. Veterans of the blue and the gray no longer refought the old war with their accustomed bitterness, and their influence for good or ill declined as they gradually died off.

Politics became still less divisive as, around the turn of the century, the Southern states completed the disfranchisement of blacks by means of laws and constitutional amendments. As Bryce had said, "thoughtful observers in the South" expected that "for many years to come the negroes, naturally a good-natured and easy-going race," would be "content with the position of an inferior caste, doing the hard work, and especially the field work, of the country."[7] Few Northerners objected to this substitute for slavery. The war aim of reunion had finally been achieved – at the expense of the war aim of emancipation.

PSYCHOLOGICAL REUNION

It took more than political reunion to bring about the psychological reunion of Northerners and Southerners. It also required the reeducation of Northerners. They had to learn to look back on the Civil War in more or less the same way that Southerners did.

In this reeducation, the public schools naturally played an important part. History texts and teachers gave a great deal of attention to the war but concentrated almost exclusively on campaigns and battles, recounting them in what seemed to students like boring detail. "What a farce the teaching of American history was," an Indiana schoolboy of the 1880s later recalled; "for tomorrow take four pages, and we sat down and learned those pages over and over until we could answer how many men were shot in such and such a battle, and how many miles they marched and whether Antietam came before Gettysburg – what a waste of time."[8] Such teaching was not likely to raise a generation of Civil War enthusiasts and Yankee partisans.

Neither were the textbooks themselves likely to do so. At first, some of those used in Northern schools displayed a strong Yankee bias, portraying Confederates as the veriest traitors. But the larger publishers, aiming at the Southern as well as the Northern market, made their books quite impartial from an early date.

The publisher A. S. Barnes and Company – with offices in New York, Chicago, and New Orleans – announced the following objective in its 1871

---

7   Bryce, *American Commonwealth*, 2:708.
8   Mark Sullivan, *Our Times: The United States, 1900–1925,* vol. 2: *America Finding Herself* (New York, 1927) 58.

edition: "To write a National history by carefully avoiding all sectional or partisan views." Indeed, the book hardly expressed any views at all. It made only a passing mention of the Emancipation Proclamation and the Thirteenth Amendment, while recounting the campaigns and battles at length. It gave equal billing to Union and Confederate heroes in the illustrations as well as the narrative. In the book, Lincoln and Davis faced each other in pictures of the same size on opposing pages, and Union generals appeared in poses no more flattering than those of Stonewall Jackson and Robert E. Lee.[9]

Northerners seemed to accept, without complaint, that kind of bland and boring treatment of the war until the mid-1880s, when some of the Union veterans began to object to it. A Wisconsin veteran found his teenage son and daughter "lamentably ignorant" of the war's causes and the Union's aims. He discovered why when he looked at the history books that the Wisconsin schools were using. "In making text-books for the whole country, publishers have eliminated everything that might offend the Southern people." Apparently, in Wisconsin and other Northern states, young people born since the war were being brought up to feel guilty about it, while in the South they were being taught to take pride in the Lost Cause and to revere its heroes.[10]

The Grand Army of the Republic finally undertook to correct the teaching of history in the schools. At the G.A.R. national encampment in 1888, the commander in chief presented a report from the Wisconsin branch, which had appointed a committee to examine textbooks. Those used in the North, the committee found, made such concessions to the South that pupils could not tell "which was right and which was wrong." The committee concluded: "It is time that a broad, comprehensive, constitutional, Union-loving patriotism should be taught in our common schools." This the G.A.R. advocated throughout the 1890s, without a great deal of success.

The G.A.R. succeeded better in its attempt during the 1890s to instill patriotism through flag worship. Local posts donated flags to schools and encouraged the schools to fly the flags. The G.A.R. instructed its own members to stand whenever "The Star-Spangled Banner" was played, and school authorities soon required students to follow the veterans' example. In 1899, the G.A.R. adopted the "pledge of allegiance" to the flag and began to persuade schools to adopt it.[11]

The veterans' agitation for patriotism was not a direct outgrowth of the Civil War, nor did it do much to overcome the war's legacy of sectional

9   *A Brief History of the United States for Schools* (New York, Chicago, and New Orleans, La., c. 1871), v. and passim.
10 Richard N. Current, *Those Terrible Carpetbaggers* (New York, 1988), 404–5.
11 Dearing, *Veterans in Politics*, 402–4, 471–5.

divisiveness. Not until twenty years after that war did the G.A.R. even start its educational program, and not until after the Spanish-American War and a new wave of patriotism did the G.A.R. make much headway with the program. The more the G.A.R. appealed to Northerners, the more it alienated Southerners, especially with its demand for pro-Union schoolbooks.

Unlike the G.A.R., Grant and other former officers, Confederate as well as Union, usually emphasized national harmony rather than sectional animosity when they recalled the war. Reminiscences of many of them were published in the 1880s in a series of magazine articles and then in four volumes under the title *Battles and Leaders of the Civil War*, which stressed the "skill and valor of both sides." Although Sherman had (unintentionally) stirred up Southern resentment with his too-candid *Memoirs* (1875), Grant said nothing to antagonize his late foes in his *Memoirs* (1885). Southern military memoirists were too busy quarreling with one another to spend much time denouncing Federals, even if they had been inclined to do so. The ex-Confederates tried to shift the blame for losing the Lost Cause – Davis pointing the finger at various opponents; P. G. T. Beauregard and Joseph E. Johnston at Davis; John B. Hood at Johnston. Hood and Johnston were friendly enough with Sherman but could not contain their hatred for each other.[12]

Historians also contributed to the growing spirit of reunion. During the late nineteenth and the early twentieth century, the leading authorities – James Ford Rhodes, Frederick Jackson Turner, Edward Channing, John Bach McMaster, Woodrow Wilson – took a nationalist rather than a sectionalist stance. Instead of assigning guilt for the war, they attributed it to impersonal causes. They expressed satisfaction at its consequences, the most significant of which they unanimously held was the preservation of the Union and the destruction of slavery. None of them mentioned the nation's rise to world power as one of the legacies.[13]

By 1911, a half-century after its start, the war had become the subject of nearly 7,000 works of nonfiction, according to the Librarian of Congress. Many of these books sold well and were widely read. Nevertheless, when Francis Trevelyan Miller was preparing his ten-volume *Photographic History of the Civil War* (1911), he noted: "military writers have informed me that they cannot understand why the American people have been so little interested in this remarkable war." (Perhaps these military writers had their own treatises

12 Clarence C. Buel and Robert U. Johnson, eds., *Battles and Leaders of the Civil War*, 4 vols. (New York, 1887); William T. Sherman, *Memoirs of General William T. Sherman*, 2 vols. (New York, 1875); Ulysses S. Grant, *Personal Memoirs of U. S. Grant*, 2 vols. (New York, 1885–86); John A. Garraty, *The New Commonwealth, 1877–1890* (New York, 1968), 287–8; John B. Hood, *Advance and Retreat*, ed. Richard N. Current (Bloomington, Ind., 1959), v.
13 Thomas J. Pressly, *Americans Interpret Their Civil War* (Princeton, N. J., 1954), 187–90.

in mind.) Miller came to the conclusion that the "lack of popular interest" was because the United States was "not a military nation." He dedicated his compilation "to the men in blue and gray whose valor and devotion have become the priceless heritage of a united nation."[14]

Americans were being psychologically reunited through fictional as well as historical writing. "Not only is the epoch of the war the favorite field of American fiction to-day," the novelist Albion W. Tourgée noted in 1888, "but the Confederate soldier is the popular hero. Our literature has become not only Southern in type, but distinctly Confederate in sympathy." Stories by Southern writers were driving "from the Northern mind the unfriendly [wartime] picture of the South," as Paul H. Buck has written. The South now appeared as a land of "noble lives ... heroic sacrifices ... magnolias ... romance." In the writings of the North Carolinian Thomas Dixon Jr., the South also began to appear as the bastion of white civilization against a threat of black barbarism. Dixon's 1902 book *The Leopard's Spots: A Romance of the White Man's Burden – 1805–1900* sold more than a million copies. Two of his novels formed the basis of the racist movie *The Birth of a Nation* (1915), which in turn inspired the revival of the Ku Klux Klan.[15] The Columbia University historian William A. Dunning agreed with Dixon on at least one essential point – that it had been a serious error to give blacks the right to vote and hold office. Of course, the suffrage had been necessary for assuring freedom to the freed and thus clinching the war aim of emancipation. By the time of World War I, most Northerners were ready to abandon that aim.[16] Psychological reunion was achieved; it had been made possible by the intellectual Southernization of the North.

PRESIDENTIAL AUTHORITY

To behave like a great power, the United States needed a strong executive, one who, at least in matters of peace and war, would be free from the constraints of the people or their representatives in Congress, so as to be able to act quickly and decisively. Recent presidents have claimed that kind of author-

14 Francis T. Miller, *The Photographic History of the Civil War*, 10 vols. (New York, 1911), 9:15–16.
15 Current, *Those Terrible Carpetbaggers*, 405; Paul H. Buck, *The Road to Reunion, 1865–1900* (Boston, 1937), 234-5; Raymond A. Cook, *Fire from the Flint: The Amazing Careers of Thomas Dixon* (Winston-Salem, N.C., 1968), 161–83. "Contrary to general opinion, the fiction of the Civil War is not predominately southern," Robert A. Lively argues in *Fiction Fights the Civil War* (Chapel Hill, N.C., 1957), 22–3, but he bases his conclusion on a count of titles and does not attempt a comparison of sales.
16 Five Southerners and five Northerners, including Dunning, wrote essays that were published in the *Atlantic Monthly* in 1901 and republished in Richard N. Current, ed., *Reconstruction in Retrospect: Views from the Turn of the Century* (Baton Rouge, La., 1969), esp. 159. See also Buck, *Road to Reunion*, 283–97.

ity. They, together with journalists and political scientists who cater to them, trace the authority back to the Civil War example of Abraham Lincoln.

Harry S. Truman, for one, thought the Korean War justified his seizure of steel mills in the same way that the Civil War justified Lincoln's seizure of railroad and telegraph lines between Washington and Annapolis. At a press conference, Truman was asked: "Are there any limitations at all on a President's actions during an emergency?" He replied, in effect, that there were none. "Mr. Lincoln," he explained, "exercised the powers of the President to meet the emergencies with which he was faced."[17]

Actually, the Civil War was followed by a decline in the powers of the president and an increase in those of Congress. The impeachment of Andrew Johnson, though falling short of conviction, contributed to this result. Grant and his successors in the White House assumed that it was the business of Congress to make the laws and of the president to carry them out. In his book *Congressional Government* (1885), Wilson acknowledged the dominant position of the legislative branch; he proposed a closer connection between the legislative and the executive branches, the British parliamentary system being his preferred model.[18]

But the British observer Bryce did not seem to think a reform of that kind was necessary. In *The American Commonwealth* (1889), Bryce wrote:

The domestic authority of the President is in time of peace very small.... In war time, however, and especially in a civil war, it expands with portentous speed. Both as commander-in-chief of the army and navy, and as charged with the "faithful execution of the laws," the President is likely to be led to assume all the powers which the emergency requires. How much he can legally do without the aid of statues is disputed, for the acts of President Lincoln during the earlier part of the War of Secession, including his proclamation suspending the writ of *Habeas Corpus*, were subsequently legalized by Congress; but it is at least clear that Congress can make him, as it did make Lincoln, almost a dictator. And how much the war power may include appears in this, that by virtue of it and without any previous legislative sanction, President Lincoln issued his emancipation proclamations of 1862 and 1863, declaring all slaves in the insurgent States to be thereafter free, although these States were deemed to be in point of law still members of the Union.[19]

As Bryce here indicated, experts in the 1880s disagreed in regard to the president's constitutional ability to act without the approval of Congress even in a time of overwhelming emergency such as the Civil War. Bryce might also

---

17 News conference, April 24, 1952, in *Public Papers of the Presidents of the United States: Harry S. Truman* (Washington, D.C., 1961–66), 8 : 295–6.
18 See the excerpts from Wilson's *Congressional Government* in E. David Cronon, ed., *The Political Thought of Woodrow Wilson* (Indianapolis, Ind., and New York, 1965), 61–78.
19 Bryce, *American Commonwealth*, 1 : 50–1.

have indicated—if he had known—that Lincoln himself harbored serious doubts as to the efficacy of his "war power" and the enduring constitutionality of his emancipation proclamation once the war should be over.

As late as 1897, Wilson believed that Lincoln's case was highly exceptional and was no model for later presidents. According to Wilson, "Lincoln made the presidency the government while the war lasted ... but ... his time was a time of fearful crisis, when men studied power, not law. No one of these men [Washington, Jackson, Lincoln] seems the normal President, or affords example of the usual course of administration."[20]

Wilson noticed a change, however, after the Spanish-American War and the diplomatic exploits of Theodore Roosevelt. "Foreign questions became leading questions," Wilson wrote in 1908, "... and in them the President was of necessity leader. Our new place in the affairs of the world has ... kept him at the front of our government, where our own thoughts and the attention of men everywhere are centered upon him." That is to say, the Spanish-American War, not the Civil War, had prepared the way for the president to become the "leader" in foreign affairs.[21]

In 1913, the year Wilson took office, ex-President Roosevelt said his own principle had been the same as Jackson's and Lincoln's, namely, that the executive was "bound to serve the people affirmatively in cases where the Constitution does not explicitly forbid." But, he went on, James Buchanan and William Taft had taken the "narrowly legalistic view that the President ... can do nothing ... unless the Constitution explicitly commands the action." Taft was amused at Roosevelt's calling him a "Buchanan President" and himself a "Lincoln President." Later Taft wrote that Roosevelt's notion of an "undefined residuum of power" in the executive was an "unsafe doctrine" and that Lincoln had provided no precedent for it. Lincoln had "always pointed out the [constitutional] source of the authority which in his opinion justified his acts" and "never claimed that whatever authority in government was not expressly denied to him he could exercise."[22]

In trying to maintain neutrality from 1914 to 1917, Wilson was much too cautious to suit the bellicose Roosevelt. "Whoever is too proud to fight ... whoever demands peace without victory ... is false to the teachings and lives

---

20 Woodrow Wilson, "Mr. Cleveland as President," *Atlantic Monthly* (March 1897), reprinted in Wilson, *College and State: Educational, Literary and Political Papers* (1875–1913), ed. Ray Stannard Baker and William E. Dodd (New York, 1925), 1: 286–7.

21 Woodrow Wilson, *Constitutional Government in the United States* (New York, 1908; reprinted: New York, 1917), 57–9.

22 Theodore Roosevelt, "The Presidency: Making an Old Party Progressive, " *Outlook* 105 (Nov. 22, 1913): 637–8, 640, 642; William H. Taft, *Our Chief Magistrate and His Powers* (New York, 1916), 143–8.

of Washington and Lincoln," Roosevelt declaimed. "Whoever seeks office … on the ground that 'he kept us out of war' … is treacherous to the principles of Washington and Lincoln; *they* did not 'keep us out of war.' "[23]

But Lincoln's legacy was complex and confusing. As a congressman during the War with Mexico, he had condemned James K. Polk for exceeding the constitutional powers of the president. In 1918, after the United States had entered World War I, Roosevelt denounced Wilson as a would-be wartime dictator and quoted against him Lincoln's criticisms of Polk! Roosevelt said: "The President is merely the most important of a large number of public servants." This did not sound like the "Lincoln President" who could exercise any and all powers that the Constitution did not deny him in so many words.[24]

By the time of World War I, not one of Lincoln's successors had found an unequivocal precedent for the uninhibited executive in Lincoln's conduct of the Civil War.

EXPANSIONISM

If the Civil War had been the determining influence, the United States would not have joined the hunt for overseas possessions in the 1890s, nor would it have leaned toward Great Britain and France when the European powers formed their alliances in preparation for the war of 1914. Instead, the United States would have steered clear of imperialism, and if it had aligned itself with any of the European powers, the most likely choice (after Russia) would have been Germany.

"They [the Americans] have a well-grounded aversion, strengthened by their experience of the difficulty of ruling the South after 1865, to the incorporation or control of any community not anxious to be one with them and thoroughly in harmony with their own body." So it seemed to Bryce in 1888. "Although they would rejoice over so great an extension of their territory and resources [as Canada], they are well satisfied with the present size and progress of their own country."[25]

In *The United States as a World Power* (1908), Harvard Professor Archibald Cary Coolidge agreed that after the Civil War "public opinion occupied itself but little with foreign affairs; for the nation was engaged in recovering from

---

23 Theodore Roosevelt, "Washington and Lincoln: The Great Examples," in his *The Foes of Our Household* (New York, 1917), reprinted in *The Works of Theodore Roosevelt* (New York, 1923-26), 21:56.

24 Theodore Roosevelt, "Lincoln and Free Speech," *Kansas City Star*, April 6 and May 7, 1918, reprinted in *Works of Theodore Roosevelt*, 21:327–8.

25 Bryce, *American Commonwealth*, 2 :398.

the effects of the struggle," and "territorial expansion did not appeal either to statesmen or to the people, the general feeling on the subject being very different from what it had been just before 1860." True, the United States acquired Alaska in 1867, "but the new territory was on the same continent," and with the anticipated annexation of Canada, "Alaska would be united to the rest of the republic." After the Alaska purchase, "the feeling in America for over a generation remained hostile to further expansion."

For thirty years, expansionists made no headway in their efforts to acquire Santo Domingo, the Danish West Indies, Samoa, Hawaii, or Cuba; and they did not even think of the Philippines. If the war with Spain had occurred during the Cuban insurrection of 1868–78, the American people would not have been ready for overseas colonies or protectorates. At that time, they were still preoccupied with issues growing out of the Civil War. "In 1898 the country … was prepared to meet the situation with a spirit quite unlike that which would have animated it twenty years earlier," as Coolidge said.[26]

Even in the 1890s, Americans retained much of their anti-expansionist feeling, and, to cultivate it, opponents of imperialism appealed to memories of the Civil War. "Only a very few of the public men of the time [1861–65] still delighted in 'manifest destiny' dreams," Carl Schurz reminded the people in his 1893 argument against President Harrison's proposal to annex the Hawaiian Islands. According to the well-known Presbyterian divine Henry Van Dyke, the issue in 1898 was the same as in 1860: "Could the Republic continue to exist 'half slave, half free'?" *The Arena* magazine said in 1900: "Strange things are happening in America when an Administration representing the party of Lincoln – the party that freed the blacks – stands squarely against liberty in the Philippines."

When Emilio Aguinaldo led the Filipinos in revolt against American rule, the imperialist Theodore Roosevelt also found a lesson in the Civil War. "The men in our own country who, in the name of peace, have been encouraging Aguinaldo and his people to shoot down our soldiers in the Philippines might profit not a little if they would look back to the days of the bloody draft riots … when the mob killed men and women in the streets and burned orphan children in the asylums as a protest against the war." The enemy at that time, the Confederacy, "was helped by the self-styled advocates of peace." So, in Roosevelt's opinion, the anti-imperialists of 1899–1901 were no better than the Copperheads and draft resisters of the 1860s.

While anti-imperialists appealed to the idealism of that earlier period, expansionists made the most of racist feelings that had recently been

---

26   Archibald C . Coolidge, *The United States as a World Power* (New York, 1908), 37–8, 172–3.

intensified. The "little brown brother" in the Philippines, like the black brother in the Southern states, seemed to need the firm hand of the master race. Alfred T. Mahan, whom Roosevelt characterized as "a Christian gentleman," confided to the imperialist senator from Massachusetts, Henry Cabot Lodge: "I try to respect, but cannot, the men who utter the shibboleth of self-government, and cloud therewith their own intelligence, by applying it to a people in the childhood stage of race development."[27]

By this time, the British government was encouraging Americans, in the words of Rudyard Kipling, to "take up the white man's burden," and Mahan and Roosevelt looked upon Great Britain as a foreign-policy model for the United States. The Anglo-American rapprochement was by no means a product of the Civil War. England had been the historic enemy, the only one whose armies had ever invaded the country, and they had done it twice. By recognizing the Confederacy as a belligerent, and by permitting it to obtain British-built warships, the British government antagonized the North while giving insufficient aid to satisfy the South. The Civil War led to a worsening of Anglo-American relations.

Afterward, the British deliberately cultivated American friendship. In the 1872 Treaty of Washington, they agreed to a settlement of the *Alabama* claims and other U.S. grievances arising from the Civil War. They, conspicuously alone among the Europeans, were friendly during the Spanish-American War. Later, they made other concessions, to win the ultimate reward of U.S. assistance in World War I.

During the Civil War, the French, to an even greater degree than the British, offended Northerners while failing to please Southerners. The French flouted the Monroe Doctrine when they intervened in Mexico, and in the postwar decades, the Monroe Doctrine became increasingly a sacred tenet of Americans, both North and South. This is one reason why most Americans favored the Prussians during the Franco-Prussian War, but there is also another reason. German immigrants vastly outnumbered French immigrants in the United States. As Coolidge said of the German-Americans in 1908, "In the Civil War they played a creditable part, and they have shown

---

27   Schurz, "Manifest Destiny, "*Harpers' Magazine* 87 (Oct . 1893): 737–46; Van Dyke, Thanksgiving sermon, Nov. 24, 1898, in *The Independent* 50 (Dec. 1, 1898): 1579–85; Frank Parsons, "The Preservation of the Republic: The Great Issue of 1900," *The Arena* 23 (June 1900): 561–5; Roosevelt, "Expansion and Peace," *The Independent* 51 (Dec. 21, 1899): 3401–5; Mahan to Lodge, Feb. 7, 1899, manuscript in the Massachusetts Historical Society; all reprinted in Richard E. Welch, ed., *Imperialists vs. Anti-Imperialists: The Debate over Expansionism in the 1890s* (Itasca, Ill., 1972), 45–6, 72–3, 84, 105, 116.

themselves ready to support their adopted country on all occasions, even – if necessary – against their native one."[28] Certainly, the Civil War had nothing to do with the ultimate estrangement from Germany and reconciliation with France.

MILITARISM AND NAVALISM

The Civil War left the United States with no strong military establishment and no tradition of militarism – even though, by the war's end, this country had become as mighty a military and naval power as any in the world. Congress had "provided for the assembling of a host that grew in magnitude until it surpassed in numbers the largest military force ever put in the field by a European power."[29] The navy had grown strong enough that it could have defended the American coast against any European foe. But the navy soon dwindled to a mere skeleton of its wartime self, and only the regular army remained in 1866, after more than a million volunteers had been mustered out of the service. Congress then authorized an increase in the size of the regular army, but three years later reduced its strength to a maximum of 25,000 officers and men, a limit that was to continue in effect until the Spanish-American War.

As far as the national defense was concerned, the lesson that most Americans drew from the Civil War was that a small professional army, to serve as the cadre for an expanded volunteer force, would suffice. "The two services [regular and volunteer] were rapidly and most happily combined, and demonstrated by their joint powers the strength of the country for defense, and, if need be, for offense," Blaine stated in 1884. "Without maintaining a large military establishment, which besides its expense entails multiform evils, it was shown that the Republic possesses in the strong arms and patriotic hearts of its sons an unfailing source of military power."[30]

As late as 1897, less than a year before the outbreak of the Spanish-American War, the secretary of war himself, Russell A. Alger, expressed a view similar to Blaine's. Alger, a former commander in chief of the Grand Army of the Republic, was addressing its members at a banquet. He assured his fellow veterans that the U.S. Army, "as far as it went," was "the best under God's footstool." He said an English friend had recently asked him what the

---

28 Coolidge, *United States as a World Power*, 196–7.
29 James G. Blaine, *Twenty Years of Congress: From Lincoln to Garfield*, 2 vols. (Norwich, Conn., 1884), 2: 672. On the postwar demobilization, see Walter Millis, *Arms and Men: A Study in American Military History* (New York, 1956), 132–3 and T. Harry Williams, *The History of American Wars: From 1745–1918* (New York, 1981), 303.
30 Blaine, *Twenty Years of Congress*, 2: 33.

United States would do if a strong power should attack. "I answered that in thirty days we could put five millions of fighting men in the field, and back them up with a wall of fire in the person of the veteran." The G.A.R. members roared their applause.[31]

While the veteran volunteers continued to be honored, the professional soldiers of the postwar army gained little respect. They added to their unpopularity when they served as strikebreakers during the depressions of the 1870s and 1890s. In the 1870s, federal and state troops together seemed inadequate to the task. Concerned citizens then began the revitalization of the National Guard as a military reserve for war and as a strikebreaking force in times of peace.

Except in the National Guard, the army, and the military academies, there was little opportunity for military training. The Morrill Act of 1862 provided that colleges benefiting from federal land grants should teach military tactics as well as agriculture and mechanical arts, but the law did not specify whether military tactics was to be compulsory or optional. After the war, the A and M colleges did little with the subject. They could seldom find qualified instructors until 1893, when Congress authorized the army to detail officers for educational duty. From time to time, congressmen meanwhile introduced resolutions to discontinue the military academy at West Point.

During the Franco-Prussian War, some Americans were so well impressed by the efficiency of the Prussian army that they lauded the Prussian system of compulsory military training for all able-bodied young men. But other Americans denounced the militarism of both Prussia and France. Massachusetts Senator Charles Sumner declared that Prussia was a military despotism and that compulsory service was a form of "bondage."[32] There was, at that time, no serious movement for the adoption of the Prussian system in the United States.

But there later developed a serious movement for the introduction of some kind of military training in the public schools. In the 1890s, the G.A.R. advocated it, and ex-President Harrison endorsed it. The New York legislature passed a bill requiring it, despite the opposition of prominent citizens who said the measure would "encourage in America the growth of the spirit of militarism" that had "done so much to hamper the civilization and prosperity of Europe."[33] Although the governor vetoed the bill, some schools in New York and in other states soon were drilling their students.

31 Graham A. Cosmas, *An Army for Empire: The United States Army in the Spanish-American War* (Columbia, Mo., 1971), 5–6.
32 Arthur A. Ekirch Jr., *The Civilian and the Military* (New York, 1956), 120–1.
33 Dearing, *Veterans in Politics*, 479–80.

The great majority of Americans continued to rely on untrained volunteers to fight future wars, the assumption being that the Civil War had shown they could safely do so. But some army and navy officers drew a very different lesson from that war and from subsequent events. Armies and navies of European powers were developing new technologies and techniques, and the armed forces of the United States, once so powerful, were lagging far behind.

The navy began a slight buildup in 1883, when Congress appropriated money for three small cruisers with auxiliary sails. These vessels were intended for coastal defense and commerce raiding, as ships of the Civil War had been. There was, as yet, no thought of far-flung naval engagements. As President Chester A. Arthur explained in his annual message, "It is no part of our policy to create and maintain a Navy able to cope with that of the other great powers of the world."[34]

Mahan changed the concept of the navy's role with his writings on seapower, which began to appear in the 1890s. While Mahan did not neglect coastal defense, he conceived of operations a long way from American shores. To some extent, he derived his ideas from his Civil War experience and study – he had written a history of the Gulf Coast blockade – but he adapted his ideas to the world scene as it had evolved since the Civil War. Mahan's doctrines had little influence on American policy until the U.S.S. *Maine* exploded and sank in Havana harbor on February 15, 1898. Not the Civil War but the Spanish-American War gave a great impetus to the Big Navy movement.

What Mahan did for the navy, Emory Upton had tried to do for the army. Upton's *Military Policy of the United States from 1775* came out in 1904, twenty-three years after his suicide. A West Point graduate and a Civil War veteran, Upton argued that the United States had never really had a military policy but had repeated the same mistake in one conflict after another and had won only with luck and with a horrific waste of time, money, and lives. "History," he wrote, "records our triumph in the Revolution, in the War of 1812, in the Florida War, in the Mexican War, and in the Great Rebellion, and as nearly all of these wars were largely begun by militia and volunteers, the conviction has been produced that with us a regular army is not a necessity." He insisted that, on the contrary, the country needed a sizable, well-trained, well-equipped professional force. "Twenty thousand regular troops at Bull Run would have routed the insurgents, settled the question of military resistance, and relieved us from the pain and suspense of four years of war."[35]

34   Millis, *Arms and Men*, 147–9.
35   Ibid., 139–40; Emory Upton, *The Military Policy of the United States from 1775* (Washington, D.C., 1904), vii–xv [introduction, dated 1880], excerpted in Walter Millis, ed., *American Military Thought* (Indianapolis, Ind., and New York, 1900), 180, 192.

Leonard Wood took up the cause that Upton had advocated. Colonel of the Rough Riders in Cuba, commanding general in the Philippines, and then chief of staff from 1910 to 1914, Wood led the "preparedness" campaign that preceded the entry of the United States into World War I. He wanted this country to adopt a military system such as that of Germany or France, including peacetime conscription and universal military training. "Manhood suffrage," he said, "means manhood obligation for service in peace or war."[36]

Wood, like Upton, used the Civil War as a negative example to support the preparedness argument; the progress of militarism and navalism through 1914 was not a result of the war. It was, instead, a response to more recent events and, in particular, to the military and naval developments on the part of the European powers.

INDUSTRIALIZATION

"The output of American iron and steel – that measure of modern power – was, in 1870, far below the tonnage of England or France; within twenty years the United States had outstripped them and was pouring from its forges more than one-third of the world's total annual supply." So wrote Charles and Mary Beard in 1927. Moreover, "twenty-five years after the death of Lincoln, America had become, in the quantity and value of her products, the first manufacturing nation in the world."

Undoubtedly, the country had industrialized at a rapid rate between the Civil War and the end of the nineteenth century. The question is how much the war had to do with the industrialization that followed it.

The Beards thought that the war, which they termed "The Second American Revolution," was a prime cause of economic development. "Through financing the federal government and furnishing supplies to its armies, northern leaders in banking and industry reaped profits far greater than they had ever yet gathered during four years of peace." Thus, they "accumulated huge masses of capital" to invest in postwar enterprises. Other wartime policies, according to the Beards, also helped – tariff protection, the national banking system, grants of public land to railroads and other corporations, the provision of cheap labor through the immigration act of 1864, and the absence of hampering regulations of business.[37]

But in 1918, the economic historian Victor S. Clark held that the Civil War "of itself changed no existing economic tendency in America"; "the war did

36 Leonard Wood, *Our Military History* (Chicago, 1916), reprinted in Millis, *American Military Thought*, 273–4.
37 Charles A. and Mary R. Beard, *The Rise of American Civilization*, 2 vols. (New York, 1927), 2: 106, 166, 176.

not create new manufacturers," nor did it "create new forms of domestic industry." As for the tariff, it was "a post-bellum influence so far as it had permanent effect upon the growth of our manufactures." Later, in 1961, Thomas C. Cochran went even further. Undertaking to refute the Beards, Cochran raised and answered in the affirmative the question: "Did the Civil War *retard* industrialization?"[38]

Disagreeing as they do, historians since World War I have left the subject rather moot, and writers before 1914 did not even raise the issue. In 1884, Blaine boasted of the country's economic progress between 1861 and 1881, but he did not attribute it to the war, although he did say that if the Union had lost, "the progress of civilization on the American Continent" might have been "checked for generations." Wilson, in *Division and Reunion, 1829–1889* (1893), concluded that in the "twenty-four years since the close of the war between the States ... these twenty-four years of steam and electricity had done more than any previous century to transform the nation." He was refer-ring to the years 1865–89, not 1861–65, and to "steam and electricity," not to the consequences of the war. When in 1906 James Ford Rhodes completed the last of his seven volumes, he exclaimed: "What a change between 1850 and 1877! A political and social revolution had been accomplished." He did not mention an economic or industrial revolution as occurring during those years, nor did he do so when he referred to "Legacies of the War and Reconstruction" after 1877.[39]

The Civil War left a legacy that, from 1805 to 1914, discouraged more than it encouraged the rise of the United States as a world power. It left the American people with a divided psyche and divisive politics. It yielded no clear and compelling model for the "imperial presidency," despite the exam-ple of Lincoln's use of a presidential "war power." It made the nation less expansionist than before the war. It reinforced the longstanding tradition of opposing the maintenance of a large standing army, while it gave no perma-nence to the sizable wartime navy. And it gave no clear and certain stimulus to the industrialization of the country.

In short, the war exerted a negative rather than a positive effect on the growth of those necessary elements of world power: political and psycho-

---

38   Victor S. Clark, "Manufacturing Development during the Civil War," (1918), reprinted in Ralph Andreano, ed., *The Economic Impact of the American Civil War* (Cambridge, Mass., 1962), 41–3; Thomas C. Cochran, "Did the Civil War Retard Industrialization?" *Mississippi Valley Historical Review* 48 (Sept. 1961): 197–210.

39   Blaine, *Twenty Years of Congress*, 2:672; Woodrow Wilson, *Division and Reunion, 1829–1889* (New York and London, 1893), 298–9; James Ford Rhodes, *History of the United States from the Compromise of 1850 to the Final Restoration of Home Rule at the South in 1877*, 7 vols. (New York, 1892–1906), 7:291.

logical unity, presidential authority, expansionism, militarism and navalism, and industrialization. Moreover, contemporary Americans did not perceive the war as a cause of such developments.

There is, of course, one sense in which the war — resulting as it did in the defeat of the secessionists — facilitated the emergence of a world power. That power could hardly have arisen when and as it did if the continent had remained permanently divided between the United States of America and the Confederate States of America. But even the temporary division — and the struggle to overcome it — delayed the debut of the United States as a leading actor on the world's stage.

30

The Myth of Gambetta and the "People's War" in Germany and France, 1871–1914

GERD KRUMEICH

This chapter explores the question of whether and in what way French warfare after the defeat at Sedan was regarded as a step on the way to total war.[1] The point is not so much to determine whether the people's war (*Volkskrieg*) organized by the French leader Léon Gambetta between September 1870 and January 1871 objectively represents a new type of war but, rather, to ask the question of whether and in what way the *année terrible* (terrible year) and the people's war represented a milestone in German and French memory and military theory between 1871 and 1914. In what way was Gambetta's warfare considered exemplary; how was it adopted in later war theory? Did his contemporaries already consider it a step toward the "war of the future?" The following reflections are a first step onto previously neglected research terrain. There is a dearth of research on the Gambetta myth in the Third Republic, which is somewhat astonishing considering the obvious significance of this politician in French history. Likewise, little is known of how French military history and theory were received in Wilhelmine Germany.[2]

Military science began to explore the people's war of Gambetta's armies soon after the end of the Franco-Prussian War of 1870–71. Interestingly, this reflection began much sooner in Germany than in France. Colmar von der Goltz, certainly the most prolific representative of the "official" school of military history in Imperial Germany, published a study in 1877 on *Léon Gambetta und seine Armeen* (Léon Gambetta and his armies). The study was based on essays by the same author in the *Preussische Jahrbücher* (Prussian yearbooks) of 1874–75. The very same year, it was translated into French and

---

1 This chapter was translated from German by Sally E. Robertson of Arlington, Virginia.
2 To the best of my knowledge, there is only a short study by J. P. T. Bury, "Le gambettisme depuis Gambetta," in *Mélanges offerts à Gr. Jacquemyns* (Brussels, 1968), 99–114. Gerd Krumeich, "Le déclin de la France dans la pensée politique et militaire allemande avant la Première Guerre mondiale," in Jean Claude Allain, ed., *La Moyenne Puissance au XXe Siècle* (Paris, 1989), 101–15. There is nothing comparable to Claude Digeon, *La crise allemande de la pensée française, 1870–1914* (Paris, 1959), or Henry Contamine, *La Revanche, 1871–1914* (Paris, 1957).

served as a continual scientific reference in the domestic French discussion of the subsequent years. Above all, Gambetta's followers and comrades-in-arms consulted von der Goltz's study in order to repulse attacks against Gambetta's style of warfare.[3] Von der Goltz was actually of the opinion that Gambetta's organization of the people's war was in no way illusory or incompetent. Gambetta, he wrote, "succeeded, through sheer will, in rousing an unarmed land which was wearied even by resistance to a fight that occupied the German army for months and revealed to us forces which we would be underestimating to this day were it not for that experience."[4] This hymn of praise also contains early propaganda for a continuous German arms buildup, a form of military "worst-case" thinking which is found throughout the German Gambetta myth: a mixture of collective memory of the *levée en masse* (mass conscription) of 1792 – and Napoléon's *Grande Armée* – as proof of the collective energy, and perhaps the unpredictability and, therefore, danger which, for example, so greatly influenced Bismarck's image of France.[5] In his painstakingly detailed study of the military events of 1870, von der Goltz states that Gambetta wanted to "transform the entire people into an army"[6] and within six weeks had created "a field army of 180,000 men furnished with all the necessities."[7] He set himself up in the role of a "dictator," which would have been "quite impossible ... in Germany."[8] Gambetta's intentions, according to von der Goltz, were both grand and somewhat grandiose. The *nation armée* (nation at arms) that he enlisted was a technical masterpiece but a political absurdity. It could be effective only in the "stubborn defense of the homeland" and was unsuitable for rapid and decisive offensive action, which was necessary for political reasons. "Once he had activated such significant masses of troops at enormous sacrifice, in order to dazzle the country, the country demanded in turn that something be done with the large armies, that rewards be reaped from the sacrifices they had made."[9] Without explicitly citing Carl von Clausewitz here, von der Goltz's argumentation is certainly in line with Clausewitz's ingenious "formula" (Aron) of war as the continuation of politics by other means. In addition, he follows the same political pedagogy, namely, warning against carelessly unleashing the passions of the people. Von der Goltz makes the interesting judgment that, compared to the

3   Charles de Freycinet, *Souvenirs, 1848–1878*, 2d ed. (Paris, 1912), 188–9; Jean Jaurès, *L'Armée nouvelle*, 2d ed. (Paris, 1915), 110, 148.
4   Colmar von der Goltz, *Léon Gambetta und seine Armeen* (Berlin, 1877), 1.
5   L. A. Puntila, *Bismarcks Frankreichpolitik* (Göttingen, Zurich, and Frankfurt, 1971); Allan Mitchell, *Bismarck and the French Nation* (New York, 1971).
6   Von der Goltz, *Léon Gambetta*, 7.
7   Ibid., 9.
8   Ibid., 25.
9   Ibid., 30.

people's war of the Germans against Napoléon in 1813, Gambetta's *levée en masse* was only a flash in the pan, consisting of "artificially fanned flames,"[10] because the "national defense" was simply staged as propaganda, with much pomp, and carried out on a technical level, not built on an actual enthusiasm of the entire population for the national cause. Gambetta takes on an increasingly Napoléonic quality. "The dictator yearned to solidify his reputation with military successes,"[11] which is why he demanded sacrifices from the country that the country was not in a position to make. This is not an analysis of what Gambetta actually did but rather an opinion brought before the German people in line with the usual German stereotypes regarding Bonapartism and the "French national character." This picture had the intended effect, probably precisely because of its stereotypical character, all the more so because von der Goltz not only made ideological arguments but also showed with remarkable objectivity how hard the traditionally oriented French generals worked against Gambetta's plans. Nevertheless, von der Goltz believed that the defeats of the first Army of the Loire can be ascribed primarily to the "willfulness of the dictator." He was too morally indecisive to be a dictator who could actually unite all of the forces. Unlike Bonaparte, he left the work half done, robbing the generals of their independence and decision-making powers, but without putting anything in their place as an emanation of the *volonté générale* (general will) to focus the energies of the people.[12] The innovation that Gambetta employed was "completely reprehensible," according to von der Goltz, because it repeatedly goaded the people into new battles by means of unbridled propaganda, regardless of the actual military situation. For example, when the Army of the Loire was crushed and Orléans was evacuated on December 3–4, 1870, Gambetta cynically portrayed the situation by saying that the morale of the troops was excellent, that they were in safe positions, and that they had plenty of materials, but that General d'Aurelle de Paladines had nevertheless decided to retreat without consulting the government. This is the intentional fabrication of a legend with consequences that cannot be exaggerated in terms of the irrationality of the conduct of the war. It is here that von der Goltz closes the loop of his argumentation. The objective of his ground-breaking study of Gambetta and his armies was to awaken German authorities to the new possibilities opened up for the wars of the future by Gambetta's mobilization of national energies, the new people's war. However, the aim of his critique was not actually to include propaganda and public energies in Germany's own strategic plan. In the end, Gambetta's people's war was a failure. His mass mobilization remained eclectic and clearly inferior to the order and discipline of the

10   Ibid., 31.   11   Ibid., 38.   12   Ibid., 83.

recruited Prussian army. Although the German war theoretician was unsettled by this new force in the conduct of war, the Gambetta experience is more a warning to him than an impetus for change. We shall see that the French reception of the events of 1870 was similarly ambivalent and that there, too, the new people's war was considered more a dangerous disruption of order than a productive innovation in the theory and practice of war. This had already been recognized by Clausewitz, whose brilliant analysis of absolute war had always stood as a warning against being pulled into that whirlpool.

As one would expect, Gen. Field Marshal Helmuth Count von Moltke also repeatedly addressed Gambetta's conduct of war in his *Geschichte des deutsch-französischen Krieges* (History of the German-French war), and we may assume that Moltke adopted material from von der Goltz. Moltke's extremely sober, even pedantic, portrayal attempts to show that the unexpectedly stubborn resistance of Gambetta's armies prolonged the war unnecessarily. In the long run, these armed mobs were technically and tactically inferior, but their desperate resistance, fanned by unquestioned patriotism as well as extravagant and irresponsible propaganda, led to very stubborn street-to-street and house-to-house fighting.[13] This guerrilla warfare contrary to all established military expertise[14] forced the Germans into numerous battles that were actually superfluous. It was for this reason, Moltke argued, that the war claimed such a disproportionately high number of victims.[15] The following sentences summarize Moltke's overall interpretation of Gambetta's people's war:

> With a rare energy and unshakable perseverance, Gambetta was able to arm the country's entire population, but not to devise a unified plan to guide the troops he had brought into being. Without giving them time to organize themselves into combat-ready groups, he ruthlessly sent them poorly equipped into disjointed operations against an enemy whose solid front need must shatter their bravery and devotion. He prolonged the fight, with all its victims on both sides, without turning fate in France's favor.[16]

These disparaging remarks on Gambetta's people's war only appear to contradict the effects of the war experience of 1870 on Moltke's subsequent strategic thought as researched by the historian Stig Förster.[17] What Moltke

---

13 Helmuth von Moltke, *Geschichte des deutsch-französischen Krieges von 1870–71* (Berlin, 1891), reprinted in Helmuth von Moltke, *Gesammelte Schriften und Denkwürdigkeiten des General-Feldmarschalls Grafen Helmuth von Moltke*, 8 vols. (Berlin, 1891–93), 3:155–6.

14 Ibid., 168, 234, 273, 298.

15 Ibid., 413.

16 Ibid., 113–114.

17 Stig Förster, "Optionen der Kriegsführung im Zeitalter des 'Volkskrieges' – Zu Helmuth von Moltkes militärisch-politischen Überlegungen nach den Erfahrungen der Einigungskriege," in Detlef Bald, ed., *Militärische Verantwortung in Staat und Gesellschaft* (Munich, 1986), 83–107; Stig Förster, ed., *Moltke: Vom Kabinettskrieg zum Volkskrieg* (Bonn and Berlin, 1992).

understood and what surfaces again and again in von der Goltz's writings is the fact that the experience of Gambetta's people's army, despite all its momentary shortcomings, was regarded as a significant new factor in the theory and conduct of war. The very emphasis on the unreadiness and inadequacy of Gambetta's army immediately raised the question of what the consequences of a possible well-prepared and well-organized future *nation armée* would be. If Gambetta's more or less enthusiastic mob, with entirely inadequate weapons, had been able periodically to stop the Prussian army in its tracks, what would have been the consequences of a really well-organized *nation armée*?[18] Förster has summarized the lessons that Moltke drew from the experience of 1870: preventive war in order to avert total war. Bismarck was presumably also greatly impressed by the experiences and perspectives of the people's war. This negative fascination appears to me to be elucidated by his severe and certainly disproportionate reaction – viewed by the French as a deliberate annoyance – not to the French troop buildup in general but to the cadre law first drafted in 1875.[19] From the French perspective, the cadre laws served only to provide a sufficient number of officers for the conscripted army being formed. For the Germans following the experience of 1870, however, this painted a picture of what they most feared: a Gambetta-type army, but this time with efficient military order. Moltke expressed this quite clearly in the April 24, 1877, session of the Reichstag:

It appears that our neighbors believe that victory in a future war lies with the masses, with overwhelming numbers, and that is certainly a matter which weighs heavily. … The French are quite definitely superior to us in the respect that, with all their numerous formations for war, they already have their cadres in peacetime.[20]

The fact that the German army paid less and less attention to the French army in the years prior to 1914, to the point of the grandiose underestimation contained in the Schlieffen Plan, has to do with the pseudo-Darwinist view of France as a "dying people," which gained prevalence beginning in the 1890s; the new German militaristic mentality interpreted French demographic problems as a simple sign of decadence. Gen. Erich von Falkenhayn's "annihilation" strategy in planning the attack on Verdun is a direct extension

---

18 This is also the conclusion that Fritz Hoenig reaches repeatedly in his comprehensive *Der Volkskrieg an der Loire im Herbst 1870* (Berlin, 1894), 1:5, 7, 17, 23, 27. In addition to his massive criticism of Gambetta's despotism and poor understanding of strategy, Hoenig strongly criticizes German underestimation of the mass mobilization by Gambetta, which led to avoidable defeats – before Orleans. For this, Hoenig probably drew upon himself the fury of the military "establishment."

19 For bibliography on the war-in-sight crisis of 1875, cf. Raymond Poidevin and Jacques Bariéty, *Les relations franco-allemandes, 1815–1975* (Paris, 1977), 142–3.

20 Quoted from von Moltke, *Gesammelte Schriften*, 7:123.

of the ideas of General von Bülow and Friedrich von Holstein,[21] which shattered against the reality of the well-organized *nation armée* of 1914. Gen. Alfred Count von Schlieffen, who had always warned in vain against under-estimating the French army, has nothing left to say about the Gambetta experience in his somewhat prophetic 1911 essay on the "Krieg der Gegen-wart" (Contemporary warfare).[22] For him, there remained only the logistical problem of how to appropriately equip the army of millions and set them in motion, the problem of the fortifications considered nearly impregnable (Antwerpen!) and the "bitter...fight between the engineers and the artil-lery."[23] The "moral" dimension of the *nation armée*, the tactical relevance of the conviction that one could call upon all citizens to defend their threatened homeland, no longer played the same role in this fetishist organizational thinking that Moltke apparently still attributed to it. The distance covered between 1871 and 1914 by the German assessment of Gambetta and the peo-ple's war is illustrated by one final look at von der Goltz's *Das Volk in Waffen* (The nation at arms) from 1883, which, along with Friedrich von Bernhardi's *Deutschland und der nächste Krieg* (Germany and the next war),[24] is certainly the most significant work of military theory from Wilhelmine Germany.[25] Gambetta figures only in the epilogue, namely, with regard to the problem of what role the "growing national consciousness" plays in the ability of a nation to resist during an invasion. In this regard, von der Goltz cites Gambetta's defense before the commission of inquiry of the national assembly in 1872 – that France had had sufficient resources to rid herself of the invaders in the long run, and that he would have succeeded in completely mobilizing the people, had the government not capitulated prematurely. Certainly, von der Goltz argues, it is conceivable "that it may be necessary, in order to emerge victorious with weapons against the will of a stubborn people led by a great man, to completely flood the enemy's territory and exert pressure on the pop-ulation for years on end." But von der Goltz considers this perspective of total war unrealistic since he believes that the classes responsible for upholding civilization in the beleaguered land would do their utmost to prevent such a war, which could annihilate all productive resources. In order to generate this perspective, it is important for the military leader "to prepare himself in any case for the idea that one might have to go to the extreme in order to

---

21 Gerd Krumeich, "Le déclin de la France dans la pensée politique et militaire allemande avant la Première Guerre mondiale," in Allain, ed., *La Moyenne Puissance au XXe siécle*, 101–15.
22 Alfred von Schlieffen, *Gesammelte Schriften*, 2 vols. (Berlin, 1913), 1:11–22.
23 Ibid., 19.
24 Friedrich von Bernhardi, *Deutschland und der nächste Krieg* (Stuttgart and Berlin, 1912).
25 The 14th edition from 1890 was used.

achieve the objectives of the war."[26] In other words, this implied the threat of annihilation in order to produce a limited war, although this threat of escalation was expressly motivated by the problems that Gambetta's army had created for the Germans in 1870. The war of the future, according to the strategic summary of von der Goltz, must (and can!) be kept short by force, because Gambetta's people's war of 1870 showed how a war can be prolonged when one fails to end it with a decisive battle "annihilating" the enemy's main armies.[27]

When one sets out to study the French reception of Gambetta's people's war, one first encounters an astonishing fact: There is still no coherent portrayal of the Gambetta myth, despite the fact that there is probably no French city without at least a rue Gambetta. It is also amazing, from the German perspective, that French historians apparently have a somewhat reserved approach to the phenomenon of Gambetta's people's war. The *armées révolutionnaires* of 1792 are only rarely mentioned as a possible precursor. The attitude toward Gambetta's armies is usually a mixture of skepticism and defensiveness. As he so often does, Gaston Bonheur in his *L'Album de famille de Marianne* (The Marianne family album) finds precisely the right words when he says that, in the French memory, Gambetta is the man in the balloon, tirelessly trying to excite the population about the republic. In addition, he is "the Lazare Carnot of a strange epic created from defeat. … It is not Year II. France has developed a paunch. She has already kissed Alsace-Lorraine goodbye. She votes to the right – for amputation"[28] – a charming and appropriate formulation, reminiscent of Adolphe Thiers's famous accusation whereby he called Gambetta a "furious fool" who agitated the people into resistance against all political reason and governing skill.[29] The catalogue of "Cent ans de République" (The republic at one hundred), the large exhibition in Paris in 1978, is similarly skeptical. Of course, Gambetta's balloon flight and personal courage are addressed, but there is a sense of extreme mistrust of his improvised people's war. The three armies that Gambetta successively deployed are depicted as having been smashed all too quickly because they were in fact improvised and were led by too few competent generals. In addition to this were Gambetta's well-known strategic mistakes, namely, "too exclusive a preoccupation with lifting the blockade of Paris."[30] Even the well-known military historian

26   Von der Goltz, *Das Volk in Waffen*, 426–30.
27   Jehuda Wallach, *Das Dogma der Vernichtungsschlacht*, 52–99. However, Wallach overlooks the degree to which Schlieffen's idea of the "decisive battle" of "annihilation" is borne by his concern regarding a prolonged war.
28   Gaston Bonheur, *La République nous appelle: L'Album de famille de Marianne* (Paris, 1965), 250.
29   Freycinet, *Souvenirs, 1848–1878*, 181–2.
30   *Cent ans de République* (Paris, 1978), 19.

Henry Contamine, for all his acknowledgment of Gambetta's courage, sees the reason for the defeat in the hasty organization of the people's armies. Not enough value was placed on their cooperation with the troops of the regular army, Contamine argues.[31] The handbook by Michel Winock and Jean-Pierre Azéma is similarly skeptical, pointing out above all that, unlike 1792 and the revolutionary uprising of the people in arms against the international aristocratic reaction, the dividing line in 1870 between the *république populaire* and the *république bourgeoise* was so clear that no *union sacrée* was possible. This is the most profound reason for Gambetta's failure, the handbook says. In 1870, the ruling classes in France wanted peace at any price because they were afraid of the democratic republic that would have been a necessary consequence of the people's war.[32] The historian William Serman, in his recent book on the Paris Commune, raises the sensitive issue of the French National Guard's inadequacy for any kind of offensive operation, although such operations were necessary to relieve Paris. Serman describes – for the first time – how unwilling the population of Paris in its entirety was to join in Gambetta's plan. Gambetta's conviction that he, like a latter-day Danton, could enlist a whole army of citizen soldiers was cruelly disappointed when it turned out that, of the 30,000 National Guard troops prepared to defend Paris, a full 7,000 followed General Trochu's call to undertake a sortie from Paris along with the regular army.[33] Military expert Maurice Faivre describes a similar "nonchalance" in his new overview of the history and future of the *nation armée*:

However, Gambetta's inflamed rhetoric fell far short of arousing the enthusiasm and inciting the resistance of all Frenchmen. Only the regions to the east and north were undergoing the ordeals of occupation. The inadequacy of replenishments gave rise to nonchalance and lack of discipline on the part of the troops, over which their fearful commanders had little control. … And, above all, there was not enough time to structure the divisions and train them for a type of combat with which they were unfamiliar.[34]

The overall impression gleaned from the most important historical writings is that, to a considerable extent, most historians would agree with the analysis of the events given by Jacques Bainville in the 1920s in his royalist *Histoire de la III. République* (History of the third republic): "With the passage of time, these events have taken on a heroic character. At the time, one saw, first and foremost, the incoherence and unease, and the absurdity of combating a disciplined enemy while disorder and confusion reigned in France."[35]

31   Henry Contamine, *La Revanche* (Paris, 1957), 26.
32   Michel Winock and Jean-Pierre Azéma, *La IIIème République* (Paris, 1971), 48–51.
33   William Serman, *La Commune* (Paris, 1989), 121.
34   Maurice Faivre, *Les nations armées: De la guerre des peuples à la guerre des ètoiles* (Paris, 1990), 28.
35   Jacques Bainville, *La IIIème Republique* (Paris, 1936), 23.

After this cursory overview of the historical literature, let us turn to the protagonist himself. In the situation of August 1870, Gambetta as head of the opposition had repeatedly urged that all citizens be called to arms.[36] In the late fall and winter of 1870–71, he made this as much a reality as possible for the "Government of National Defense." In contrast, Gambetta appears to have had no interest after 1871 in reinforcing the myth of the unlimited people's war. As early as his great justification speech before the investigative committee of the national assembly on September 7, 1871, what mattered to him was to portray the predicament in which he had found himself. He had had to rule in a rather dictatorial manner from Tours to ward off the threatened secession of parts of the French provinces. His intention had been "to restore order."[37] In addition, he argued, he had not recklessly armed the revolutionary mob, as many conservatives accused him of doing; he armed only "men of good heart and goodwill." He had therefore also not balked at integrating patriotic royalists into the cadre of the army.[38] The improvised armies, he continued, had "done battle as well as inexperienced troops could" in the absence of a regular army, which was almost entirely in the hands of the enemy. He was a man of order, he said, who turned away regiment volunteers, such as those from the "League of the Midi," if they pursued separatist, revolutionary tendencies.[39] Moreover, his warfare had often enough consisted of palliative measures only: "We had to resign ourselves to waging war with the weapons we possessed."[40] It was quite apparent that Gambetta, at least in the situation following the defeat of 1871, was not at all interested in portraying his people's war of 1870 in too positive a light. Nor is there any trace of an attempt to draw a parallel to the legendary energy of the *armées révolutionnaires* of 1792.

This impression is confirmed by Gambetta's behavior during the 1870s. It is well known that his main mission was to stabilize the republican institutions throughout the country against the threat of monarchist restoration. His politics, mocked by the radical left as "opportunistic," cannot be explored here in detail. However, it is interesting that, in the important military policy debates of the 1870s, Gambetta was by no means an advocate of a radical *nation armée* concept, which of course permits conclusions regarding the ephemeral character of his people's army of 1870.

36   Joseph Reinach, ed., *Léon Gambetta, Discours et plaidoyers politiques* (Paris, 1881), 1:311, 315, 346, 384, 388.
37   Ibid, 2: 95.
38   Ibid., 96.
39   Ibid., 114 –15.
40   Ibid., 133.

As far as the military issue is concerned, during the entire nineteenth century, one of the theorems of republican radicalism (and later socialism) was that all citizens must fundamentally be equal with regard to military service, that exemptions should be completely eliminated if at all possible. The result of this egalitarian thinking, which harked back to the principles of 1789, was of course as short a period of service as possible. The ideal was the *armée citoyenne* (citizens' army), where the barracks was simply a transition site for short-term weapons training in order to give all citizens the actual opportunity to take up arms in defense of the fatherland in the hour of danger.

Remarkably, this egalitarian defensive principle was expressed in particularly drastic form in Gambetta's *Programme de Belleville* (Belleville program) of 1869: "abolition of standing armies – ruinous to the finances and interests of the nation, a source of hatred between peoples and internal defiance."[41] However, when the debate over the *nation armée* flared up again in 1872 during the conflict over a new military service law, Gambetta was by no means among the supporters of a radical egalitarian solution. With peculiar restraint, he strongly insisted on the necessity of having a small, active, manageable army with a sufficiently large "cadre," or officers' corps. In the discussion of the cadre law of 1877, Gambetta also represented the viewpoint that one must keep a soldier in uniform for at least three years in order to train him adequately[42]. He even went so far in the debate as to oppose the reduction in the length of service from five years to three years, therewith falling in line with the military policy of his main domestic policy rival, Adolphe Thiers.[43] Gambetta's new "opportunism" became the bête noire of the republican left in the late 1870s and 1880s partly because of its military implications, although the details of this have yet to be investigated adequately.

It would not be correct to lump these concepts of military policy together with those of the conservatives; the difference between Thiers and Gambetta, even in their military views, remained considerable.[44] Nevertheless, it is important in our context to note as the net effect that Gambetta was certainly no longer a protagonist of the "people in arms" after the experiences of 1870. He was interested in creating an army with a strong enough "cadre" to remain truly maneuverable and with soldiers who received rather extensive military training. This thinking appears to me to be a direct reac-

41 Cited from Jean-Thomas Nordmann, ed., *La France radicale* (Paris, 1977), 33.
42 According to Richard D. Challener, *The French Theory of the Nation in Arms* (New York, 1955), 33, 56.
43 Even the German ambassador in Paris, Hohenlohe, was impressed by this shift. See Prince Chlodwig zu Hohenlohe-Schillingsfürst, *Denkwürdigkeiten* (Berlin, 1914), 2: 192.
44 Thiers's views have been best investigated by: Allan Mitchell, "Thiers, Mac Mahon, and the Conseil Supérieur de la guerre," *French Historical Studies* 6 (1969): 233–52.

tion to the defectiveness of the improvised *nation armée* in the fall of 1870, far from any positive mythology of the *levée en masse*. It was more important to Gambetta to republicanize the officers' cadre than it was to organize a people's army. He designed a whole system of grades and observations in which both the officers' behavior in battle against Germany and their political choices played a role. He apparently wanted to work in advance to prevent another situation such as Bazaine's capitulation at Metz.[45]

Another interesting indication that those responsible for the mobilization in the fall of 1870 were later critical of enlisting the people in a total war is found in the memoirs of Charles de Freycinet, the actual technical organizer of the Gambetta armies in 1870. Freycinet sincerely stated what was lacking in the people's war of 1870 and why it ultimately failed. First, he says, the mobilized soldiers did not have adequate technical training, whereas the Prussians had superbly trained recruits. Second, and at least as serious, the Gambetta armies were completely undisciplined. Military discipline must be decisively improved in the future, he added, not in the form of blind obedience, but as the *discipline raisonnée* of mature citizens:

Modern armies, particularly in France, should be based on moral concepts which their elders never knew. … Whereas contempt for authority and rebellion obsess the spirit of young recruits, they also affect both national defense and internal security at the same time.[46]

These quotations and explanations should make it apparent how difficult it was for Gambetta and Freycinet following the defeat with the armies that they had created, and how heavily the memory of the catastrophe of 1870 weighed upon them. Far from creating a positive myth of the people's army, they returned afterward to liberal-conservative army models. They were not interested in perfecting the armies of 1870, drawing military lessons from the actual people's war, which could have raised it to a more organized level, but rather in returning to a disciplined, well-trained, and always controllable barracks army which, contrary to the ideas of the left, was seen as the "real" army by both the liberals and the conservatives. We shall see that the "Gambettists" of the time just before the beginning of World War I cited precisely this Gambetta experience in their bitter debate with the leftist-republican supporters of the *nation armée* and wanted to place the defense of France primarily on the shoulders of a relatively small but powerful *armée de caserne*.

Thus, if the protagonists of the people's war of 1870 subsequently put a clear distance between themselves and that war, this throws some light on the

---

45 François Bédarida, "L'Armée et la République: Les opinions politiques des officiers français en 1876–1878," *Révue historique* 232 (1964): 119–64.

46 Freycinet, *Souvenirs. 1848–1878*, 254–5.

otherwise astonishing fact that the memory of the people's war of 1870 played a subordinate role in the Gambetta myth during the Third Republic. One gets the impression that the French tried just as hard to forget Gambetta's people's war as the Germans, from Moltke to Schlieffen, tried to hold it up as a warning. This attitude is particularly clear in the reaction of the press and parliament when the great tribune died suddenly on December 31, 1882, at the age of forty-three. On the left, the conflict with the opportunism of "Gambettism" in domestic politics prevailed. The radical republican faction in parliament was not even willing to participate in a joint meeting of all republican factions of the chamber to honor Gambetta. Gambetta's dedication to national defense was hardly evoked at all in the midst of these conflicts. For the left in the 1880s, Gambetta was synonymous with opportunism and clientele politics, in short, with betrayal of the Republic. And the radical newspaper, *Le Radical*, made no mention of the people's war of 1870 in articles on Gambetta's death.[47] The reaction of the moderate press amid the flood of obituaries was also restrained, settling for very metaphorical and casual mentions of Gambetta as a *grand patriote*.[48] The official eulogies conveyed a similar image, uniformly describing Gambetta as the organizer of national defense, as the *âme de la résistance* (spirit of the resistance) who had saved France's honor. Only the historian and Senator Henri Martin spoke explicitly in this context of the improvised armies of 1870. "With poorly trained soldiers and inadequate weapons," he recalled, "Gambetta succeeded in keeping the strongest military power in Europe in check for four months ... and he could even have won the war had not Bazaine's betrayal prevented it."[49] This speech was by far the most positive, however; elsewhere, the order of the day was skepticism and intentional omission of Gambetta's army and the failed people's war. Even *Le Drapeau*, the newspaper of the formerly Gambettist *Ligue des Patriotes* (League of patriots), asked in an obituary whether Gambetta had really done all he could to win the war: "He certainly did the impossible, but did he always do the possible?"[50]

This rather negative image of the failed people's war of 1870, evoked with restraint or sometimes even as a warning, did not change appreciably over time. When a *monument de la reconnaissance nationale* (monument of national recognition) was erected to Gambetta in Nice in 1909, the French premier Georges Clemenceau was the principal speaker. This was particularly notable since, throughout the 1870 and 1880s, Clemenceau had been the main oppo-

47   *Le Radical*, Jan. 3, 6, and 7, 1883.
48   See, e.g., *Le Temps*, Jan. 8, 1883.
49   All speeches from *Le Temps*, Jan. 8, 1883.
50   *Le Drapeau*, Jan. 6, 1883.

nent of Gambetta and "opportunism" in matters of domestic policy.[51] Clemenceau emphasized Gambetta's major contributions: "He was the soldier of the fatherland and freedom, organizer of the national defense and the principal founder of the Republic." This praise was merely stereotypical and businesslike, however. The remarks of Senator Rouvier, also president of the General Council of the Maritime Alps Department, on the same occasion were more emphatic and explicit. When the French armies had already been defeated or imprisoned, he said, there arose in Gambetta the man whose powerful patriotism restored the nation: "At his command, new legions arose, armies formed, national defense was organized, the struggle was prolonged to the astonishment of the entire world. Alas, it was too late to preserve the integrity of our frontiers, but this supreme effort at least salvaged our honor."[52]

This quite positive treatment of the people's war of 1870 was made more specific at the same celebration by the moderate republicans' military expert in Parliament, Raiberti. A nation that thinks patriotically and is determined to defend itself, he said, is undefeatable when and only when it understands how to convert this patriotic energy into a long-term military organization. The really essential point, he continued, is to provide sufficient "cadres," that is, a well-trained, numerically strong officers' corps. In addition, he added, the military power of a nation in war is naturally a direct function of the moral power that the nation has accumulated in peacetime.[53] Patriotism, as the result of social order and discipline, had always been an ideal of the moderates, and Gambetta had consistently shared this political theory, so it was appropriate that his legacy be evoked in this context. The "lessons from the people's war" were still quite clear to the most prominent French politicians nearly forty years after the war. War can be waged successfully only with a well-structured conscripted army enthused with patriotism and filled with a sense of internal social order. One sees how much average public opinion and politics had actually moved past the people's war of 1870, a rather negative event from which one can only learn what to avoid in the future.

How much this was the case is shown by a look at what is today probably the best known work of military theory from the time just prior to World War I, namely, Jean Jaurès's *L'Armée nouvelle* (The new army) of 1911. In this basic text of republican socialist military theory, Jaurès attempts to prove that only a militia system of "the people in arms" under the auspices of

---

51 The most important texts on this controversy are in Pierre Barral, ed., *Les fondateurs de la Troisième République* (Paris, 1968), 116–32.
52 Cited from *Le Temps*, April 26, 1909, 1.
53 Ibid.

modern war involving the entire population could guarantee France protection from aggression. However, even in this text, which attempts to bring the socialist concept of the *nation armée* into a symbiosis with republican military tradition since the *levée en masse* of 1792, the experience of the people's war of 1870 plays a relatively minimal role. Gambetta embodied patriotic determination. His armies unsettled even the well-organized invader, but they were too improvised and the idea of the *nation armée* was too new; "they were an inexperienced, disorganized people" whose republican convictions were still relatively unstable, which is why the "irresistible national movement" that Gambetta sought was unable to develop.

Into the chilly night, which the flaming rhetoric of Gambetta and Blanqui could not ... warm up, distraught and gloomy crowds rushed, suddenly opposed to an army doubly confident in its organization, confident of victory, and confident in its pride.[54]

There is a world of difference between Gambetta's armies, these *armées d'improvisation et de catastrophe*, and a real people's army. It is therefore important, Jaurès argued, to begin in peacetime to gather the energies of the people and organize them militarily; only then will France be invulnerable.[55]

The experience of 1870 was also not a relevant memory in the great armaments controversy of 1913–14, which, like the Dreyfus affair, split France into two antagonistic political camps. The question here was whether, in the event of a German attack, France's defense could be better guaranteed by the *nation armée* of trained reservists or by the standing army. The generals assumed that a war would be decided in the first great battles and that, therefore, the emphasis in armaments must be on the barracks army. The moderate politicians, Raymond Poincaré, Etienne, and Aristide Briand, among others, did their utmost to push this innovation through Parliament against the opposition of the republican left, which held fast to the traditional concept of the purely defensive *nation armée* of all citizens subject to the draft.[56] In this context, the memory of Gambetta and the war of 1870 played a certain role. This was evident in the *cérémonie des jardies*, a commemorative ceremony held annually in the house where Gambetta died. This ceremony was entirely in the grip of the military discussion in April 1913. A week earlier, the German imperial chancellor, Theobald von Bethmann-Hollweg, had defended the massive German armament project before the Reichstag. Minister of War Etienne, a personal friend of Gambetta's and a prominent colonial and military politician, did not miss his opportunity to justify his plea for an extensive arms

54 Jean Jaures, *L'Armée nouvelle* (Paris, 1915), 148.
55 Ibid., 149.
56 Gerd Krumeich, *Aufrüstung und Innenpolitik in Frankreich vor dem Ersten Weltkrieg* (Wiesbaden, 1980).

buildup using the example of Gambetta. Etienne pointed out expressly how much Gambetta had always concerned himself with the army, and how hard he tried in defense legislation after 1870 to turn the regular army into a truly powerful instrument. Joseph Reinach, military expert of the moderate republicans and also a friend of Gambetta's, likewise insisted on the fact that Gambetta had always wanted an active army capable of securing the boundaries of France with an "iron cover" against any invasion. If in 1870 Gambetta had had more than just untrained, albeit heroic, soldiers available, Reinach concluded, then France certainly would not have lost the war.

Bearing this cursory overview of the Gambetta myth between 1871 and 1914 in mind, it is possible to conclude that Gambetta's people's war was ever-present in the French and German memory, although in completely different ways. For the French, it was a heroic episode but not one particularly worthy of imitation. For the Germans, in contrast, it served to prepare them for the war that, with reference to the *furia francese* (furious French), they believed they would have to wage in order to prevent a new and more dangerous people's war.

31

War Memorials: A Legacy of Total War?

ANNETTE BECKER

In French, one says "monuments to the dead."[1] In English, one rather says "war memorials." This semantic distinction has guided my reflections on the memorials that were built in France after the Franco-Prussian War and in the United States after the Civil War. The French language emphasizes death, whereas the English language chooses to recall the war that not only produced deaths but also disrupted the lives of those who survived. The meaning of the English is therefore broader, implying that such monuments evoke both memories of the war and memories of the war dead. Beyond the mere words used to designate them, a study of monuments in these two countries shows that the construction of memory is itself complicated, multifaceted, and often difficult to comprehend.

The monumentalizing of memory begun during these two nineteenth-century wars was ineluctably linked to the battlefield and to those who had fallen. The honor immediately bestowed upon the dead was funerary, and the battlefield became their cemetery. The first monuments were built in order to help the survivors cope with the loss of their fallen comrades, that is, they were built to commemorate the dead. By not forgetting them, their friends were also exhorted to continue the fight. The funeral monument was thus transformed into a monument to battle, and it assumed a political meaning that it continues to have. After these wars had ended – and sometimes decades later, as in the case of the war of 1870–71, for which commemorative monuments in France were still being built in the summer of 1914 – the monuments, glorifying their political mission, in the etymological sense of the word, moved to the heart of the cities. In prominent public spaces, they proclaimed a message that enabled populations to accept and support the new political order that had resulted from the war. In dedicating

1 The introduction to this text as well as all of my reflection on war memorials owe much to the Australian historian Ken Inglis. I would like to thank him here. All my thanks to Elisabeth Rottenberg for her translation.

these monuments, significant speeches were made that insisted upon their allegorical content, a content that might otherwise have escaped a public poorly educated in the scholarly analyses of works of art.

In the material that follows, I present the results of my research, divided into two sections: first, memorials to cope with death; and second, memorials to cope with the new, postwar political order. In each section, I discuss individual monuments in the chronological order in which they were erected.

MONUMENTS TO COPE WITH DEATH

The mortality rates during these two wars speak for themselves: During the Franco-Prussian War, 300,000 French and German soldiers died within a period of six months; during the Civil War, 620,000 American soldiers died – more than the number killed in all subsequent American wars, including both world wars and Vietnam. One would also need to add the civilian casualties in the South, which have seldom been taken into account, to evaluate properly the losses inflicted upon American society by this war. The enormity of these numbers was further aggravated by the severity of the battlefield injuries, resulting from a lack of adequate medical supplies and the havoc wrought by various diseases. In total, 415,000 Americans fell victim to disease, which accounted for two out of three deaths. For every 1,000 French men mobilized in 1870, 37 fell in combat, and 140 fell victim to epidemics. (As a means of comparison, in the French army during World War I, the proportion was reversed: For every 1,000 men mobilized, 135 were killed at the front, and 20 died of disease.)[2]

Military Cemeteries and Obelisks

The tremendous slaughter brought on by these two wars explains in part why early on in these conflicts people arrived at the idea of creating funerary structures. Americans had, for the first time in their history, organized gravesites for the war dead of the conflict with Mexico, 1847–48. They did the same in 1862. The Department of State decreed that all graves of Union soldiers would be marked and registered by the federal government. One of the first Union cemeteries was created on the grounds of Robert E. Lee's plantation in Arlington, Virginia, as an act of reprisal.[3]

2 André Corvisier, "La mort du soldat depuis la fin du Moyen-Age" in *Les hommes, la guerre et la mort* (Paris, 1985), 367–94.
3 After the war, Lee's family received compensation for having been instrumental in the creation of the Arlington National Cemetery. This information comes from G. Kurt Piehler, *Remembering War the American Way* (Washington, D.C., 1995). I am indebted to Kurt Piehler, who sent me his book manuscript and without whose generosity this text would lack an essential comparative element.

Article 16 of the Treaty of Frankfurt, which formally ended the hostilities of the Franco-Prussian War, stipulates that, "the French and German governments here engage reciprocally to respect and maintain the graves of soldiers buried in their respective territories."

If military cemeteries were systematically organized for the first time following these two wars, it was not owing to historical chance. They followed the logic of a novel way of conceiving of death, and especially of death in battle. The death of young men was seen as tragic, all the more so in the American case since the fight was a civil war. People reconciled themselves to the deaths of soldiers – far from their families and far from the cemeteries in the communities to which they belonged – both through mourning and suffering and through collective commemoration organized by official or private veterans' associations. War monuments thus became guardians of the collective memory of mourning, and that of the cause for which young men had given their lives.

The architecture of battlefield monuments everywhere is consequently very similar – the somber obelisks that one finds in cemeteries and on individual graves since the eighteenth century. The neoclassicist aesthetic of the architecture of commemoration is especially well suited to collective death. In France, as in the United States, one finds these obelisks dispersed, far from the villages, in cemeteries where the dead have been assembled: new cemeteries created during the fight, or old, communal cemeteries where space had been reserved. In a different war space, such as German and French gravesites, German and French obelisks abut one another. Only the inscriptions in the two languages differentiate the dead. There are even some monuments where the soldiers of both countries are memorialized together. Would the same death allow for the same commemoration, because the suffering was the same for the survivors? On the present territory of the Czech Republic where the Battle of Sadowa was fought, near the town of Hradec-Kralove, the same kind of obelisks commemorate the defeated Austrian (that is, Czech) soldiers. Moreover, obelisks are seen as sacred everywhere, surrounded as they are by railings, gratings, box trees, or the archetypal cemetery trees – conifers.

Space for the war dead is thus marked by the monument, which is larger and taller than the other grave markers in the cemetery, and by the fact that the space itself is reserved and cannot be transgressed. The dead are many, and they died for a single cause. Their death is not "natural," it is exceptional. The memory is therefore organized around the exceptional: These dead were not repatriated, for a mark must be left on the foreign soil where they fought. They were not repatriated because the cause was just, and their memory must continue to assert this notion. By building nearly 200 monuments to their dead along the border between France and Germany, the Germans created a demarcation line of blood and honor. In creating the giant field of memory in Gravelotte, near Metz, they demonstrated that these territories were indeed German. Death, the memorials tell us, created the nation just as the nation justified these deaths. In France, around Mars-la-Tour, the French acted in much the same way. The novels of Maurice Barrès, from the *Déracinés* (1897) to *Colette Baudoche* (1909), proceed from this same love for the dead – a reflection of love for the nation. To create or recreate, through the worship of the dead; this is the goal that the Souvenir Français, an organization founded in 1887 by Xavier Niessen from Alsace, set for itself. Its motto was clear: "To us, memory; To them, immortality."

The two minutes that the *Gettysburg Address* lasted on November 19, 1863, were of such historical importance, I would suggest, because Lincoln spoke of death and the resurrection that would follow it.

We have come to dedicate a portion of that field as a final resting place for those who here gave their lives that the Nation might live. It is altogether fitting and proper that we should do this. But, in a larger sense, we can not dedicate – we can not conse-crate – we can not allow – this ground. The brave men, living and dead, who strug-gled here, have consecrated it, far above our power to add or detract. ... It is rather for us to be here dedicated to the great task remaining before us. ... That we here highly resolve that these dead shall not have died in vain, that this Nation, under God, shall have a new birth of freedom.... .

We return later to the purely political aspects of these monumental and verbal proclamations. It is enough, for the moment, to add that the Confed-erate soldiers who died in the Battle of Gettysburg were thrown into a mass grave a little further off. The American nation, which Lincoln defined as incorporating the living and the dead, did not yet include them.

Collective Death, Individual Death

The mass grave was not, however, exceptional in times of war. But it took the shape of a revalorized mass grave, otherwise known as the *ossuary*. In this, we touch upon a new aspect of the worship of the military dead in the middle of the nineteenth century. Until that time, the only deaths in battle that had been commemorated at all were the deaths of generals. Only generals had marked graves, while soldiers were forgotten or placed in mass, unmarked graves. Time quickly accomplished its task. Where are the hundreds of thou-sands of war dead from the French Revolution and the French imperial wars? One can visit the battlefields, Valmy, Austerlitz, or Waterloo, and one can see monuments commemorating the victories of the generals. But the soldiers have been obliterated, and with them the memory of their cause. To bury the dead is to recognize the individuality of the fighters and to recognize that their role was as important as the role of their generals. Underlying this practice is the democratization of war and death. In France, the evolution toward individual recognition of all of the men who died for the nation was slow. It was only in 1918 that the universal practice of inscribing all of the names, in alphabetical order, onto the list of merit of the Republic became a reality. Typically, the monuments of the war of 1870–71 only have the names of the regiments that were engaged in the fight. This includes thanking even those who did not die in battle for their participation.[4]

Although French regiments were organized by region – the mobile guard of the Loire or the Gironde, for example – the commemoration of battlefields united them by virtue of having sacrificed to a common cause. The same phenomenon occurred in Germany, where monuments to specific regiments evoke their Bavarian or Saxon origins and yet collectively commemorated the fallen soldiers. In the United States, each state built in succession a monument to Gettysburg and Vicksburg. Losing little time, the states of the Union were the first to build monuments on battlefields that had recently become memorials. But the war dead of the nation as a whole – regiment by regiment, state by state – were only slowly, sometimes grudgingly honored. For example, Texas built its memorial to Gettysburg only in 1964.[5]

From all over France, from the entire German Empire, from all over the United States – from the North, then the South – soldiers came and died as their nations took to arms. Monuments to these wars did not overlook military hierarchy, however, and the phenomenon of the hero-general. On German monuments, names engraved, if any, are always those of officers. The generals of all of the armies, victorious or not, have the right to a statue, usually featuring them on horseback. In fact, they adopt the pose of the victor no matter what the outcome of the combat. From Floing (Sedan) to Gettysburg, although the place of death and the place of commemoration are one and the same and proclaim equality before death, only ordinary soldiers lie beneath simple crosses. In these vast spaces devoted to battle deaths, generals inevitably have their own gravesite, their own monument apart from the rest (at Floing, for example, compare the monument to the "Africans" and Gen. Jean-Auguste Margueritte's grave). In the United States, heroes

---

4 Paradoxically, this recalls a tradition that was completely lost in France after World War I. In countries in which the army was entirely made up of volunteers, on the other hand, Australia for example, there are two separate lists – one containing the names of the dead, and another the names of all those who enlisted.

5 James A. Mayo, *War Memorials as Political Landscape, the American Landscape and Beyond* (New York, 1988), 174.

Figure 31.1. Provins, France: Winged figure embracing fallen soldier.

of the Civil War were commemorated by holidays – their achievement trans-
forms the calendar, the very passage of time.

This new way of conceiving of death in war carries with it new ways
of relating to life after the war. Two kinds of war memorials reflect this
phenomenon: statues of soldiers and ossuaries (see Figure 31.1). In France,

it was the *moblot*; in the United States, it was "Johnny Reb" and "Billy Yank." The familiarity of the nicknames given to soldiers showed how close the people felt to the soldiers who gave their lives for the common ideal. The Napoléon's *grognards* also had a familiar nickname, one of affection. But as individual soldiers, they cannot be found immortalized in stone or in bronze, either in cemeteries or in public squares. Along with their physical bodies, somewhere between the Rhine and Moscow, the memory of their sacrifice was also lost.

The statues of soldiers multiplied after the wars of the middle of the nineteenth century and rekindled among their own people the memory of the men who were born there, and who are regarded with familial, local, and political affection. They have brave, even swaggering poses, because one knows how brave they were, even though they are now dead, and even though they lost the war. Their uniforms are depicted in detail, as are their weapons. Standing on their pedestal, they are destined to fight an exemplary battle to which they have given their lives for all eternity. War has become sanitized in these monuments and can thus appear glorified. No mud, no lice, no blood. These warriors are fresh and clean like the toy soldiers of children. Soldiers of light opera who play the role that was theirs over and over again, without end, the heroic defense of the cause for which they volunteered to fight? There are no deserters to be found on these monuments, no rioters against conscription, no reluctance to take up arms against a common enemy.

These monuments are graves, however, empty graves. And the cenotaphs remind us that they are constructed on top of bodies. They are posthumous lists of merit (tableau d'honneur). The first of the class, the generals, have the right to their own particular monuments. All of the others are commemorated by this same monument. There are no dunces, no one is excluded: The very fact of having fought in the war (war memorial) is glorified. The very fact of having died in the war (monument to the dead) is exalted. And, as one cannot always glorify nor exalt death – whatever its cause may be, it is always intolerable – the monuments choose to deny death and to pretend that the soldiers are still alive. The bronze is their resurrection.

Ossuaries

Death takes a very particular form in the commemorative form known as the *ossuary*. The idea behind its construction follows a perfect logic: The remains of a large number of soldiers could not be identified, and common graves were therefore created where they could be buried. Together in battle, they were put to rest collectively, and the gravemarker, surrounded by a railing, testifies to their heroism and to the respect that survivors had for them. In Arlington National Cemetery, for example, a confederate ossuary was created not far from Lee's mansion. In France, the ossuaries are marked by the symbol of the Souvenir Français, which is the tricolored flag and a sword, both in wrought iron, and by the words "Military Grave, Law of April 4, 1873," for which the state, with a precision faithful to the execution of the republican law, was responsible. The giant obelisks signify simultaneously grave, death, and important grave, valiant death. Often constructed on mounds, these ossuaries dominate the battlefields where those who became merely bodies distinguished themselves. Or sometimes they dominate communal cemeteries where the other dead rest beneath the usual stelae.

These invisible remains were glorified beyond a simple inscription and a monument. In Bazeilles (Sedan), an enormous neo-Gothic building was constructed, topped by a pinnacle embellished with four sculpted and empty coffins. Below it, in underground chambers, there are skulls, tibias, humeri, walking boots, which have been piled up on both sides of an alley – all of them perfectly assembled. Until 1914, German bones were on the left and French bones on the right. The ossuary is 300 meters from the "House of the Last Cartouche," and the paintings that are exhibited within this museum/monument prove how difficult it must have been for the promoters of memories of death to identify the remains of each side. In 1914, German occupation authorities found these trophies to be too demoralizing for their men and decided to bury them. Today, the bones on the right, the French bones, are piously preserved in their original state, whereas the German bones are protected from visitors by a concrete shell. Those who are reminded by these piles of bones of the abject mass graves of World War II will have a hard time placing themselves back in the nineteenth century in an attempt to understand the historical provenance of such a project. This commemoration, however macabre it might have seemed at the time, tried to realize a physical demonstration of death in battle, of heroic death: These remains became relics; the soldiers were canonized by the cause and thus served as an example. Their spirit, exalted by speech, was not enough. One had to be able to see, and even to touch. The fact that the ossuary in Bazeilles is surmounted by medieval decorations proves my point: The valorous soldiers have become saints. Accordingly, their bodies do not decompose. This ossuary demonstrates in exalted fashion the faith of its promoters: religious faith in resurrection of the ideal – whatever it might have been – that animated the fighters.

Faith in the Resurrection of Soldier and Nation

From the *Gettysburg Address*, we have seen that an important part of commemoration and the construction of monuments lies in the faith in resurrection. When comparing texts of French and American sermons, the similarity in theological explanations of war and its conclusion are striking.[6] During the period of the inauguration of numerous war memorials, in the 1880s, French Catholic priests never missed an opportunity to repeat that the Franco-Prussian War and the French defeat were sent by God to punish a people that had become too frivolous. This kind of talk, however, was equally consistent with the strongly American Puritan tradition of the seventeenth century. President Lincoln himself echoes the tradition at various points.

It is the duty of nations as well as that of men to own their dependence upon the overruling power of God and to confess their sins and transgression in humble sorrow, yet with assured hope that genuine repentance will lead to mercy and pardon, and to recognize the sublime truth, announced in holy scripture, and proven by all history, that those nations only are blessed whose God is the Lord. We have been the recipient of the choicest bounties of Heaven. … But we have forgotten God. … It behooves us, then to humble ourselves before the offended power, to confess the national sins and to pray for clemency and forgiveness.[7]

Americans in both the North and South were convinced that they were the new chosen people, the eschatological role of which was to save the world, beginning with themselves (Redeemer Nation). If the Civil War belonged to the schemata of salvation because it was just, it reminded one, nevertheless, that one could not take the future for granted. According to the expression of Sacvan Bercovitch, war was a "dramatization of the national myth."[8] The Lincoln Memorial in Washington, erected in 1911, with its reproduction of the entire Gettysburg text, was an important milestone in the making of the civil religion of the American Republic. It belonged to the "Gesta Dei per Americanos," an expression that I use to parallel an old formulation reused during and following the Franco-German conflict, namely, that of "Gesta Dei per Francos."

There is at least one significant difference to be found in the two discourses. In the United States, the myth had its greatest effect among the upper classes of society. Born of evangelical Protestantism, this myth became the civil religion of the Republic by bringing together the God of the Jews and

---

6 This is true also for Germany, as is well shown by Hartmut Lehmann in "The Germans as a Chosen People: Old Testament Themes in German Nationalism," *German Studies Review* 14 (1991): 261–73.
7 Fast Day Proclamation, March 30, 1863.
8 Sacvan Bercovitch, *The American Jeremiad* (Madison, Wis., 1978), 174.

the Catholics with the God of the Protestants, without, however losing its Protestant foundation. In France, in contrast, the Catholics, far from belonging to the controlling circles of the state, were the ones who in the nineteenth century set about their search for a means of saving France. They were of the opinion, as were Lincoln and his compatriots, that in the war dead lay the answer.

Sin makes the people unhappy. ... Has there ever been seen a series of disasters so visibly portentous of the mark of divine justice? We must have been very guilty to have been punished so harshly. ... Public prayer, solemn, social, is salutary. ... Prayer for the dead is the most salutary. ... For these are not ordinary dead, but hostages of our ransom. ... They have been chosen by the justice of God to expiate our sins. ... France for whom they have suffered so much, France "fallen in her soul" must rise. ... [9]

Commemorative churches were constructed in Loigny and Mars-la-Tour. Later called "The Battle," the church in Loigny was built as an ossuary for 1,200 French who died here. At this site, the relics of saints assumed a function in religious politics, one that helped to push for the beatification of General de Sonis, who fought among the papal Zouvaves, the bearers of the flag of the sacred heart. The frontier village of Mars-la-Tour laid claim not to the political-religious heritage of Paray-le-Monial – a sacred site next to Lourdes and a frequently visited place of pilgrimage – but to that of Joan of Arc with regard to the contest over Lorraine. On the altar, a baroque imitation resounding with the spirit of the post-Tridentine Catholic Reformation, is inscribed the dedication of the church: "To the French soldiers who died for their country, 1870-71." In the chapel dedicated to the worship of the dead, plaques evoke the names of those whose remains rest in the adjacent ossuary. The name of Yves de Julienne d'Arc catches one's eye: "Following Joan, my sister, who knew how to fight and die for France, so too will I, when the occasion arises, devote myself to my country. The words of 1868 so bravely kept." In Mars-la-Tour as in Loigny, one appealed to the dolorous tone of the Christian message. At the gravesite, the pietà shows Christ and his mother at the time of death and suffering. The time of the *stabat mater* or the grieving mother standing before her son on the cross. These monuments tell of the death of soldiers, the death of France, and the death of Christ, and they show how they are all linked. In the 1890s, could the French not find a reason to be hopeful?

The example of the United States of America where the republican idea and the Christian idea are in agreement is there to attest that the thing is not impossi-

---

9   Abbé Chevalier, *Discours au service funèbre pour les victimes de la guerre* (Tours, Nov. 26, 1888).

ble. … The tricolor flag must be put in the churches … the soul of our heroes, in heaven, will applaud both our intelligence and our piety.[10]

Chronologically speaking, the war was being left behind. One could leave behind the suffering caused by the soldiers' deaths and move toward its possible political value. Commemorations and monuments allowed one to live with a new political order, born of the war.

The Grand Army of the Republic, an organization of Union veterans, was founded in 1866. Its head in 1868 was John A. Logan, senator from Ohio and ex-Union general, who declared that the dead were a "barricade between our country and foes."[11] On August 23, 1914, during a funeral service for the soldiers who had fallen on the field of honor, a Frenchman put forward his own conclusions regarding the years of commemoration: "It has been a perpetual mobilization of our dead for forty years to remind the living of their duty and to exhort them to stand ready."[12]

COMING TO TERMS WITH A NEW POLITICAL ORDER

Monuments more sophisticated than the funerary obelisks were generally placed in city centers, far from the battlefields and from the cemeteries. This conscious choice seems to move from death to life, from the outskirts to the center. These monuments were constructed later, not in the urgency of the loss of dear ones and suffering, but in strength, the strength of the memory of the loss; thus, they express the political impulses of the times. To follow the course of the commemoration of the Civil War properly, one needs to study the political battles of Reconstruction in the United States and the parallel course of the Third Republic in France. From the assassination of Lincoln to the republican campaigns, from the creation of the Grand Army of the Republic to the formation of the Ku Klux Klan, from the proclamation of the Third Republic to the Boulangist crisis and the Dreyfus affair, there are many crucial events that one must examine in order to understand fully the period of commemoration.

Neither the Spanish-American War in 1898 nor the colonial ventures of the French at the turn of the century produced a new wave of commemoration. Only a few anecdotes remind us today of these conflicts. This is evidence that monuments worthy of being called monuments were not built

10 Abbé Georges Fremont, *Les causes de nos malheurs en 1870 et leurs remèdes: Discours en la cathédrale de Poitiers pour l'inauguration du monument élevé en l'honneur des soldats poitevins victimes de la guerre franco-allemande* (Nov. 17, 1895).
11 Piehler, "Remembering War the American Way, 1783 to the Present," 70.
12 Abbé Julien, Le Havre, Aug. 23, 1914.

when a conflict resulted in too few deaths, deaths that could hardly represent the nation as a whole.

Historians are claiming that one cannot understand France during World War I without first returning to the Franco-Prussian War.[13] What is true for France can easily be said of the United States with respect to the Civil War and Reconstruction. Until the twentieth century, wars and their commemoration formed the basis of nationalism, whose duality historian Raoul Girardet describes best:

> On the one hand, the proud certainties of an officially sanctioned nationalism, which has become the essential element in the new republican legitimacy. ... On the other hand, ... the obsession with decadence, the haunting menace, a nationalism of dissatisfaction, of tension and demand. Yet how can one fail to remark that this duality is not unique to the French example?[14]

Girardet is thinking of Europe, of Germany, of Italy. Little prevents us from extending his thought to the United States; the commemorative monuments encourage us in this direction.

We will study these monuments in two groups: those that "writhe" in the pain of defeat and call for revenge; and those that glorify the Republic, the reconciled Union, and the new political legitimacies. Might these be seen as only the positive monuments to heroes? Yet all heroes of monuments are positive. It is here that the analytic frame risks being undone by the complexity of the monuments. In total, they rarely belong to either of the nationalisms described previously. As for those excluded and marginalized by commemoration – African-Americans, women, the Communards – they will be viewed as a separate group.

From Defeat to Revenge

The American South and France were vanquished in 1865 and 1871, respectively. Some historians argue with great conviction, however, that the military victory of the North masked a defeat, namely, the inability to avoid civil war in the first place. Lincoln's assassination added mourning to mourning, forbidding one from celebrating a victory so spoiled. If the first monuments were commemorative graves to dead soldiers, the reality of this political defeat was cloaked by the neutrality of their form and the lack of inscription; one could no longer hide behind death when it came time to sculpt later

---

13 Stéphane Audoin-Rouzeau, *1870: La France dans la guerre* (Paris, 1989); and François Roth, *La guerre de 70* (Paris, 1990).

14 Raoul Girardet, *Le nationalisme français* (Paris, 1983), 275–6.

homages. The financiers of the monuments demanded that reality be revised. We have already seen how the dead were made to live again; we will now see how it was that the vanquished became victors.

For this to occur, the focus had to be on heroism. Men had shown themselves to be paragons of military and civic virtues. They knew how to die; they glorified battles, even hopeless ones. Every year, people assembled and held speeches that recalled the bravery of the dead, and thus also that of the veterans, in front of monuments to the Confederates. These monuments were most often neutral stelae located in Southern cemeteries. To commemorate them as one would good soldiers was to silence the defeat; this was a way to show that their fight had been just and that their communities mourned them as honored dead. The sacrifice thus preserved its full meaning. If God permitted the South to be defeated, it was because it was part of a larger plan of salvation for the United States. The defeat, thus explained, became a victory.[15] The Confederate memorial in Arlington National Cemetery, built by the United Daughters of the Confederacy and dedicated in 1914, is a perfect example of this phenomenon: Men, women, and children gave their strength and their love to the struggle; Southern society in its entirety was represented (see Figure 31.2).

In France, the memorial to the chasseurs of Africa of Floing commemorates the cavalrymen killed during this particular offensive at the Battle of Sedan on September 1, 1870 (see Figure 31.3). The inscriptions and the sculpture outdo each other in spirit and gallantry. Beneath the enormous "In Honor of the French Cavalry," there is written twice, engraved below the sculpture by Emile Guillaume and in imitation of an original manuscript the words of Galliffet: "As long as you wish, my general, as long as one remains."[16] The monument is signed, "The Brave Men," the name given it at the dedication in 1910. This phrase was rumored to have come from the Prussian king who, as he watched the hopeless charges of the cavalrymen, referred to them as "die tapferen Leute!" Their heroism was recognized by the enemy, according to the tradition of chivalry, and saluted by the French Republic itself, as a giant Marianne standing at attention dominates the ossuary. However, she is veiled and evokes mourning more than does the tricolor flag. Beneath the monument rest the remains of 2,000 "brave" French

---

15 Gaines M. Foster, "Coming to Terms with Defeat: Post-Vietnam America and the Post-Civil War South," *Virginia Quarterly Review*, no. 66 (1990): 17–35.

16 A general who followed a career very typical of the military from the Empire to the Republic, from the repression of the Commune to the colonial wars. It is also very revealing that the sentence should not be signed by his name. The simple chasseurs of Africa were all commemorated for their act of heroism, which has only been emphasized by the general. Only the General Margueritte, fatally wounded in the battle, had the right to a separate grave beside the monument.

Figure 31.2. Arlington, Virginia: Confederate memorial.

and German soldiers. There is thus an attempt to show that national mourning was compensated for by patriotic heroism. This is the meaning of the monuments where, above the words "Gloria Victis," is stated "soldiers fight, are wounded, expire … and never give up." In sanitizing the war in this way, defeat is also sanitized. The Latin inscription on the Confederate memorial

Figure 31.3. Floing/Sedan: African "Honneur de la cavalerie française."

in Arlington reads: "The victorious pleased the gods but the defeated pleased Cato." Again, the classical mind represents the moral mind, which Cato epitomizes.

Nevertheless, early in the twentieth century, some in France began to think that these commemorations had gone on long enough.

Have we yet cried enough about this damned defeat, and by an incomprehensible aberration, have we glorified it enough? Not a single city without a Gloria Victis ... What will we be able to give to the winners if we give glory to these ones? What do we want? That France be the house of the living or the house of the dead.[17]

The French leader Léon Gambetta answered both of these questions at the dedication of the monument to the mobile guardsmen of the Lot, his native *département*, because France of the living is inseparable from France of the dead. It is very clear in this speech-program of commemoration.

A large nation must honor its dead, and I will freely say that those who should be honored, above all, are those who died in disaster and in defeat, those who died without hope but having nonetheless done their duty until the end, because they felt that there was nothing left to give France but their blood and their lives ... .

On monuments, defeat is made heroic because it is identified with the love for one's country, because it is attributed not to the weakness of the fighters but to the greater number of the enemy, or to their traitorous methods. The soldier of the monument of Sedan expired in the arms of the angel of victory, and he bears the crown of the hero *Impavidus numero Victus*.[18]

According to the monuments, not only were the Germans more numerous, but they also used barbaric methods of which the French were the victims. In Laon and Châlons-sur-Marne, monuments were built to the teachers who were shot. The choice of the teacher was not a neutral one. The republic commemorated its "black hussars." The monument to the three teachers at Laon, dedicated in 1899, shows them in heroic poses; admiring children bring them crowns. Far from defeat, far from the war. There were only heroes, and their story was told by the sculptor: The French Republic, cultivated and civilized, was a victim. The teachers of 1899 could teach their students "the horror of barbaric and iniquitous acts that render the inevitable evils of war more terrible still."[19]

Much like the war memorials, these teachers participate in the inculcation of hatred and a desire for revenge. The allegories of France sending their children to fight (monument of Lyon or Angoulême), their raised fist to the east, to the lost provinces: "We shall not forget" and "You must remember." The memory evoked by the inscriptions and the sculptures waxes

---

17 Louis Bertrand, *Le sens de l'ennemi* (Paris, 1917), 39 (Texte du 13 mars 1913).

18 Reinhart Koselleck notes that one can compare French monuments after 1871 with German monuments after 1918 and their "Im Felde Unbesiegt" (unvanquished in the field of honor); in "Les monuments aux morts, contribution à l'étude d'une marque visuelle des temps modernes," *Iconographie et Histoire des mentalités* (Paris, 1979), 113–23.

19 G. Texier, *Le monument des fusillés de Châlons-sur-Marne* (Jan. 22, 1891).

pedagogical. One reads upon them about a heroic past and an unjust defeat, both of which prepare for tomorrow's revenge.

> If the past saddens our hearts, the present gives us hope. ... The growth of national sentiment is evident everywhere. ... Crowds, on given days, gather to celebrate painful anniversaries before the ossuaries and on the road to the cross of the nation.[20]

The national monument of Mars-la-Tour exemplifies such pronouncements. The terrible battles of the summer of 1870 were commemorated on August 16 in that part of Lorraine that had remained French.[21] An allegory of France, the monument's eyes turned toward the frontier, carries in its arms a wounded soldier. He has not dropped his rifle – just the opposite. Romulus and Remus, the twin founders of Rome, with their faithful she-wolf by their side, hand him a symbolic sword. When this monument was built in 1875, it was decided that a new France would be created, the citizens of which would not blush at comparisons with the Roman Republic.

Monuments also became a source of political education, communicating knowledge on how to fight, how to suffer, and how to hate.

> You will bring your children before this work of art as you would on a pilgrimage where you will teach them to pay their respects with reverence. ... Then you will retell the history to them. It is thus that one elevates the soul; this is how one prepares courage for the ultimate hour when honor speaks and France calls to her children.[22]

The higher the monument, the bigger and more warlike are the soldiers represented on it, and the more defeat and the underlying fear of decadence are forgotten. Even victory often needs to be comforted by the grandiose, indeed, the grandiloquent. In portraying the bloody conflict, the enormous buildings or the columns built in Pittsburgh, Cleveland, and Indianapolis cultivate the aestheticism of the Roman Empire. These shrines reaffirm the mission assigned to the North for the United States and then to the United States for the world.

In Brooklyn, the Soldiers and Sailors Memorial Arch seeks to combine a Roman triumphal arch and the Arc de Triomphe in Paris. Lincoln and Grant sit squarely in this structure; thus, the political and military aspects of the war, united in the victory of the North, symbolize its strength. All of the sculptural

---

20   Texier, *Le monument des fusillés.*
21   Annette Maas, "Kriegerdenkmäler und Gedenkfeiern in Metz," in Rainer Hudemann, ed., *Développement urbain dans la région frontalière France, Allemagne, Luxembourg (XIXème et XXème siècles)* (Saarbrücken, 1991), 89–118.
22   From a speech given by General Thiery at the inauguration of the monument built in Marseilles to the memory of the children of the Bouches du Rhône, who died for their country in 1870–71, March 26, 1894.

Figure 31.4. Sadowa: Prussian monument.

details are borrowed from Roman art: eagles, lances, and helmets. As for the
winged victory at the pinnacle, it cannot help but recall Victoria and the
Quadriga atop the Brandenburg Gate in Berlin (compare Figure 31.4).[23] In

23 Significantly enough, in Berlin it is a "victory goddess" transformed from a "goddess of peace." The
    influence of antic art is also visible on the Prussian memorial built at Sadowa, which is topped by a
    Greek soldier's helmet.

these immense monuments, the North declares that it has won the war and shows that it is capable of embellishing its cities with works of art in which political and aesthetic value mesh. Proud and wealthy, it can permit itself such an urban luxury. The battles were not fought upon its territory, and thus it can build without having to rebuild.

Memory, however, must reconstruct itself. The veterans are not the last to participate in this reconstruction, which is also a reconstitution. Just as the Grand Army of the Republic resembled a secret society in some ways, the Ku Klux Klan, founded at the same time in the South, combined a hatred for the ex-slaves with the mystique of commemoration. The white robes were thought to represent the ghosts of fallen Confederate soldiers.[24]

In both the South and the North, the custom quickly developed of commemorating the war dead on a special day, called Decoration or Memorial Day. Moreover, beginning in 1865 in the South, women decorated the graves of Confederate soldiers, and commemorative services were held. Until 1889, the overwhelming bitterness of the South prevented it from participating in the Memorial Day established by the victor. On both sides, however, spring was the chosen season for such commemorations. The season of the rebirth of nature and the resurrection of Christ was also the season in which the memory of the dead led to the "resurrection" of the nation.

In France, the war dead were remembered on the anniversary of important battles, but usually in September, which was not only the month of the Battle of Sedan but also that of the collapse of the empire and of the proclamation of the Third Republic. Most monuments were dedicated at this time, as they were around (the) Memorial Day(s) in the United States. Therefore, it is not surprising to read of two triumphant republics when one looks at the monuments.

Two Nations: The Third Republic and the United States of America

I have been shown in the files of the War Department a statement ... that you are the mother of five sons who have died gloriously on the field of battle. ... I cannot refrain from tendering you the consolation that may be found in the thanks of the Republic they died to save. I pray that our Heavenly Father may assuage the anguish of your bereavement and leave you only the cherished memory of the loved and lost, and the solemn pride that must be yours to have laid so costly a sacrifice upon the altar of freedom.[25]

Based on a number of Lincoln texts, historian James M. McPherson notes that before 1861 the United States was considered in the plural: " 'The United

---

24 Piehler, "Remembering War the American Way, 1783 to the Present," 77.
25 President Lincoln to Mrs. Bixby, Nov. 21, 1864.

States are a republic,' one said. The war marked the transition toward the singular. The Union also became the Nation."[26] In the *Gettysburg Address*, the importance of which has already been remarked upon, Lincoln never said the Union but rather the Nation, and this he did five times, including in the now famous phrase: "That this nation, under God, shall have a new birth of Freedom – and that government of the people, by the people, for the people, shall not perish from the earth."

At the inauguration for his second term on March 4, 1865, the program of reconciliation that concluded his speech was first and foremost a call for commemoration:

With malice toward none, with Charity for all, with firmness in the right, as God gives us to see the right, let us strive on to finish the work we are in: to bind up the nation's wounds, to care for him who shall have borne the battle, and for his widow, and his orphan – to do all which may achieve and cherish a just and lasting peace, among ourselves and with all nations.

It is only after 1889 and the creation of the United Confederate Veterans that the South erected the majority of its monuments that lie outside cemeteries. In public spaces, the statues, often mass produced to the great displeasure of "serious" contemporary artists, portray an infantryman at parade rest. Nothing differentiates him from representations of his ex-enemy now compatriot from the North other than the later date of the monument's construction. Seventy-five percent of all Civil War monuments represent soldiers. In 1889, Memorial Day became a national holiday, and flowers were put on the graves of the Blue and the Grey. Was the war finally over?

The reconciled nation as described by Lincoln was the nation that knew how to commemorate the dead, all of its dead. The irony of his assassination a few weeks later made him a symbol of the dead of the Civil War. In a short time, statues of the assassinated president were built all over the country, from San Francisco to New York. The wave of "statue mania" surrounding Lincoln's death brought with it, however, a return to the past, a return to the American Revolution. When commemorating the founders of the new republic, was it not also fitting to raise memorials to Washington and to Jefferson, both Founding Fathers who were, in fact, sons of the South?

This same impulse toward retrospective commemoration took hold in France in the 1880s. In 1880, with the Third Republic well established,

---

26   James M. McPherson, *La Guerre de Sécession* [*Battle cry of freedom*] (Paris, 1991), 943.

July 14 became a national holiday, and it commemorated all of the battles from 1792 to 1814, "as if the occurrence of their respective hundredth anniversaries had coordinated its call with those of republican patriotism."[27] Furthermore, the victories of the "nation at arms" were far more satisfying to remember for a regime that could share pride in the government of national defense but not in the outcome of the war. However, the Third Republic never forgot those who died in 1870–71, for they too were its "founding fathers," as Gambetta reminded the crowd in Cahors during his speech at the dedication of the monument to the guardsmen of the Lot:

A people that wishes to remain free and independent has a duty to place before the eyes of the younger generations examples and memories that fortify the soul, that form character. ... All of the civilizations that were important in history ... possessed above all the love of sacrifice and military abnegation. But today more than ever we should applaud ourselves . . . for attending such ceremonies, for in our country the army has become identified with the nation.

"The army has become identified with the nation," as he put it, was what Gambetta hoped to realize in 1881. The war memorials built between 1880 and 1914 went even further. They identified the three colors with the nation, the three colors with the Republic; Marianne with the nation and with the Republic. Allegories in Phrygian cap and moblots bore the same banner. Even when a particular city (such was the case for the most famous monument, the Defense of Paris, designed by Ernest Barrias), glory, reputation, or victory replaced Marianne, the republican flag was omnipresent. It was the ultimate symbol of national legitimacy: "Standard bearer, my friend/you hold France in your hand."[28]

The reconciled United States, a universally accepted republic – this was what was conveyed by the large majority of commemorative monuments built in the last years of the nineteenth century. The same monuments were to be found everywhere, American soldiers at rest and mobile guards carrying the red, white, and blue flag. Behind the unified vision presented by these monuments, one may discover that which is left out of such monumental commemoration. In the United States, as in France, entire segments of the population have been voluntarily forgotten or marginalized in the commemorative monuments.

---

27 Maurice Agulhon, *Marianne au pouvoir, l'imagerie et la symbolique républicaines de 1880 à 1914* (Paris, 1989), 131.
28 Paul Déroulède "Au porte-drapeau du 14 juillet 1881," quoted by Raoul Girardet, "Les trois couleurs, ni blanc, ni rouge," in Pierre Nora, ed., *Les Lieux de mémoire, I-La République* (Paris, 1984), 5–36.

Unity Does Not Mean Pluralism

The principal cause of the Civil War was the desire on the part of the Southern states to maintain slavery. The most famous of Lincoln's words – "'A house divided against itself cannot stand.' I believe this government cannot endure, permanently, half slave and half free" – declared the conflict to be inevitable because the United States had its mission to survive whole. *The Emancipation Proclamation* (1861), the Thirteenth Amendment (1865) that abolished slavery, and the participation of soldiers who had been slaves should all have been commemorated. Yet they were not.[29] Lincoln's commemoration was altogether exemplary of this voluntary forgetting. In 1876, a small monument donated by African-Americans was inaugurated in a Washington, D.C., park. A standing Lincoln is portrayed, granting freedom to a slave who is kneeling. The statue also includes President Grant and Frederick Douglass, who reminds us that, above all, the war was a fight against slavery and that the victory of the North brought citizenship to blacks.[30] The Lincoln Memorial on the Mall completely disregards his role in the abolition of slavery. There is nothing surprising here: Reconstruction ended in segregation. The veterans' organizations of North and South minimized the role of slavery in the Civil War, and they emphasized instead the constitutional aspects of the fight. Such was the price of white reconciliation. The Veterans' associations were the groups most responsible for the construction of these monuments.

Southern and Northern women also had a substantial and fundamental role in the commemoration of the war dead. In positions of leadership of diverse associations and committees, they took charge of the moral support of their husbands and their brothers, such as The United Daughters of the Confederacy, for example, or the women of Columbus (Mississippi), who in 1867 put flowers on the graves of the Blue and Grey. The poem of Francis Miles Finch, written in memory of their action, became the symbol of reconciliation beyond the grave.

> … Under the sod and the dew
> Waiting for judgment day;
> Love and tears for the Blue
> Tears and love for the Grey.

Women, however, were not commemorated for the role played in the fight. Nurses or canteen women had no right to military honors. They were,

---

29   Or hardly. There is a black fighter to be found on the reliefs of the Brooklyn monument, but he is lost among other soldiers. The Boston monument honoring the African-American fighters is to my knowledge the only one.

30   Piehler, "Remembering War the American Way, 1783 to the Present," 68–9.

however, present in overwhelming numbers on monuments in the form of allegory: victory, glory, recognition, peace—they give funerary crowns or crowns of glory, receive soldiers in their arms. Although the figure of Columbia rarely appears in the United States, we have seen how Marianne was often chosen to represent France. According to the allegory of the feminine, weeping women are symbols of pain and not the "white widows" of monuments that followed World War I.

The historiography of the Commune has long overshadowed the historical field concerning 1871, leaving only the smallest part for the war. It would be equally wrong, however, to lean too much the other way and to forget the Communards altogether. The difficult commemoration of the Commune seems to me, in fact, to be a perfect example of what the monuments that we have studied prove—that the vanquished were not commemorated; they were transformed into victors. Historian Madeleine Rebérioux has shown that it was difficult to overcome the contradiction between love for the revolution and for the Republic.[31] The Communards were republicans defeated by the Republic. They had no place in official commemoration, all the more so as they claimed the red flag as their own at the moment when the tricolor flag was victorious.

At the Père Lachaise cemetery in Paris, the wall of the *Fédérés* stands on the opposite side from the monument-ossuary of the defense of Paris: Its four soldiers and their flag are those that the French nation commemorated. And it was done in a cemetery because their collective grave had become a memory.

This is the first time in our history that this ceremony has been held ... on this West Front of the Capitol. ... At the end of this open mall are those shrines to the giants on whose shoulders we stand ... George Washington ... Thomas Jefferson. ... And then, the Lincoln Memorial. Whoever would understand in his heart the meaning of America will find it in the life of Abraham Lincoln. Beyond those monuments to heroism is the Potomac River ... and Arlington National Cemetery, with its row upon row of simple white markers. ... They add up to only a tiny fraction of the price that has been paid for our freedom ...

In his inaugural address on January 20, 1981, Ronald Reagan, the fortieth president of the United States, described the heroes of American history, both great and small, and insisted on the privileged place of Abraham Lincoln. This rhetorical gesture was a brilliant political maneuver. It proved that in order to give meaning to the consequences of earlier wars, one had to know how they had been commemorated.

31 Madeleine Reberioux, "Le mur des Fédérés, Rouge, 'sang crache,' " in Pierre Nora, ed., *Les Lieux de mémoire*, 619–50.

President Reagan's speech continued by evoking the name of Martin Treptow, a soldier who died in World War I. Reagan made of him the incarnation of the American hero. In their youth, the French Martin Treptows had attended ceremonies in celebration of the monuments of 1871 and had followed the classes of their teachers whose message extended that of the sculptures and the speeches. Might the total engagement that took place in World War I be attributable to a national cohesion born in and out of the memory of the Franco-Prussian War? In this chapter, I have tried to show that, among the nineteenth-century roots of total war, the role played by commemoration was crucial. And commemoration, by essence, is total, like death.

Conclusions

32

The American Civil War and the German Wars of Unification: Some Parting Shots

ROGER CHICKERING

The story is probably apocryphal that Helmuth von Moltke, the chief of the Prussian general staff, once characterized the American Civil War as an affair of "two armed mobs chasing each other around the country, from which nothing could be learned."[1] Such sentiments were nonetheless rife among Prussia's military leaders in the early 1860s; and the performance of the armies that these soldiers thereupon led against Denmark, Austria, and France only encouraged their belief that the wars waged almost simultaneously on both sides of the Atlantic were not comparable phenomena. The present volume of essays leaves no doubt that the Prussian soldiers were mistaken and that historians can compare the German Wars of Unification and the American Civil War with insight and profit. Employing the idea of total war to frame this comparison has thrown light on both the differences and similarities in the conflicts. It has also, however, raised difficulties of its own.

As Carl N. Degler's essay (Chapter 3) makes clear, the simultaneity of these conflicts was not fortuitous. The wars on both sides of the Atlantic were instances of momentous civil strife, facets of the great mid-century political convulsions that Robert Binkley has characterized, in a wonderful but long-neglected book, as the "crisis of the federated polity."[2] The wars sealed the consolidation of new forms of rule, which were more unitary and centralized than the German Confederation (*Bund*) had provided in central Europe or the antebellum constitution, at least as construed by Southern observers, had foreseen in the United States. The tensions that undermined these looser federations reflected in both cases painful adjustments that accompanied the transition to industrial capitalism.

---

1 The story was first reported in J. F. C. Fuller, *War and Western Civilization, 1832–1932* (London, 1932), 99. See also Jay Luvaas, *The Military Legacy of the Civil War: The European Inheritance* (Chicago, 1959), 126.
2 Robert C. Binkley, *Realism and Nationalism, 1852–1871* (New York, 1935).

The simultaneity of the conflicts also registered in the military realm. These wars saw the mobilization of armies in the hundreds of thousands of men, whose deployment and supply depended on the capacities of new industrial economies. The mid-century conflicts featured the use of railroads and telegraphy to move soldiers, horses, supplies, and equipment to the battlefield, where mass-produced weapons shaped the character of combat.

These similarities notwithstanding, the contrasts between the German and American wars were so fundamental that they make plausible the bemusement of the Prussian soldiers who could not relate the Civil War to their own experience. The campaigns against Denmark, Bohemia, and France proceeded with a dispatch, order, and decisiveness that resembled more the cabinet wars of the eighteenth century than the contemporary war in America. The most protracted of these German campaigns, the one in France in 1870–71, lasted little more than six months and resulted in the loss of some 30,000 German lives, although the French lost far more.[3] The figures were imposing, but they paled in the light of statistics from America. In the Civil War, in geographical expanses that dwarfed the European theater of operations, some three million men saw action on both sides during the course of a conflict that exceeded four years; and over 600,000 of these men were killed.[4]

The statistical discrepancies reflected fundamental differences in the combatant forces. As Earl J. Hess has observed (Chapter 22), the composition and organization of the Union and Confederate armies frustrated the quest for a conclusive encounter such as Königgrätz or Sedan. To call them "armed mobs" stretches the point, but as Herman M. Hattaway (Chapter 8) has noted, these amorphous bodies, the bulk of which comprised ill-trained volunteers or recruits, remained in flux throughout the war. Their institutional structures were inchoate; much of their leadership was unsuited to manage or direct large-scale combat or to adjust to the tactical and strategic challenges of industrial warfare. Although the prolonged experience of combat welded these armies into seasoned fighting forces, their closest counterparts in the European theater were the volunteer armies raised by the French republican government; and the unhappy fate of these hastily mobilized bodies in the field only underscored the difference between them and the superbly organized and trained, professionally led Prussian conscript forces.

3 Michael Howard, *The Franco-Prussian War: The German Invasion of France, 1870–1871* (New York, 1961), 453; Alistair Horne, *The Fall of Paris: The Siege and the Commune, 1870–71* (Garden City, N.Y., 1967), 268. See also Stéphane Audoin-Rouzeau, *1870: La France dans la guerre* (Paris, 1989).

4 James McPherson, *Battle Cry of Freedom: The Civil War Era* (New York, 1988), 306–7n.

The vital advantages that these conscript armies enjoyed over all their antagonists, whether the volunteer armies of republican France or the professional armies of Austria or imperial France, accounted for the most striking distinction between the German Wars of Unification and the American Civil War. Because the military action was so much more abbreviated, the German campaigns did not require the extended mobilization of civilian economies, nor did they challenge systematically the distinction between the civilian and military spheres. German and Austrian civilians were largely spared the deprivations and burdens that mobilization and invasion visited on civilians during the American Civil War – particularly, as Donna Rebecca D. Krug's essay (Chapter 20) emphasizes, on the women of the Confederacy. If civilians in Paris and elsewhere in France were not similarly spared in 1870 – 71, their involvement was, as the essays of William Serman (Chapter 13) and Robert Tombs (Chapter 25) indicate, neither as extended nor as systematic as the participation of American civilians in their civil war.

The contrasts in the course, extent, and character of the campaigns have colored the historiography of the wars, and this fact has significantly complicated the problem of historical comparison. More precisely, the contrasts in the conflicts have been distilled in distinct historiographical traditions, which have long been governed by different concerns and methodological preferences. The German Wars of Unification have by no means suffered from the neglect of historians, but the precision of operations, the rapidity of resolution, and the sense of fulfillment that attached to the outcome of these campaigns assigned them a place in German historiography that was much less problematic than the place accorded to the Civil War in American historiography. Beyond minor miscalculations by the soldiers, there was little to criticize; and the losing side had few advocates in Germany, particularly among the men who wrote the history of the campaigns. In the aftermath of unification, a substantial corpus of historical scholarship appeared on the German wars, much of it officially or semi-officially commissioned. This literature examined the military operations in meticulous detail, as well as ancillary facets of the campaigns, such as supply, medical support, and railroads. Other studies, of which the multivolume work of Heinrich von Sybel set a standard, focused on the political and diplomatic background of the wars, particularly on the calculations of Bismarck.[5] If the accents in this

---

5 Heinrich von Sybel, *Die Begründung des deutschen Reiches durch Wilhelm I.*, 7 vols. (Munich, 1890–95). See also Georg Iggers, *The German Conception of History: The National Tradition of Historical Thought from Herder to the Present* (Middletown, Conn., 1983), esp. 90–123.

literature reflected the centrality that statecraft had already attained in German historiography, they also set an agenda that has to this day emphasized the military, political, and diplomatic dimensions of the Wars of Unification.[6]

The fact that the historiography of the American Civil War is much larger and broader is due to a number of circumstances. The Civil War was a more traumatic national experience, and the moral valences of this conflict were never as unambiguous in its aftermath. An enormous body of scholarship, much of it from authors who remained sympathetic to the Confederate cause, was nurtured in the ambiguities of heroic defiance defeated and the singular mix of moralism, ineptitude, and ruthlessness with which the stronger side prevailed. In the *Official Records* of both American armies, writers of all persuasions found a historical resource that addressed the experience of battle on levels absent from the German operational histories.[7] The study of war at these levels was, in addition, more cordial to American historiography than to German, as was the analysis of the social, economic, and cultural impact of the war, which was in all events far more massive and pervasive than in the German case.

The historiographical contrasts are evident throughout the present volume. The essays of Reid Mitchell (Chapter 26) and Manfred Botzenhart (Chapter 27) on the treatment of prisoners of war exemplify the problem: The essays on the American conflict paint a broader and richer picture. Scholars of the German wars, such as Ulrich Wengenroth (Chapter 11), Jean H. Quataert (Chapter 21), and Thomas Rohkrämer (Chapter 23), have labored at a disadvantage, for to pose the kinds of questions that have long engaged historians of the Civil War, they have had to undertake pioneering work. Their essays suggest the benefits that will accrue if others follow their lead into areas that provide routine occupation for scholars of the Civil War – such as the everyday experience of war for soldiers and civilians, the economic impact of war making, the ramifications of war for women and children, or the management of opinion in the press, schoolroom, and parish.

If only because scholars have traditionally asked different questions about them, the effort to span these conflicts with the concept of total war seems anomalous. But the massive disparities in the character of the wars also frustrate the effort. This conclusion seems particularly true of the Danish and Austrian wars, which have been neglected in this volume. But none of the

---

6 See Eberhard Kolb, *Der Weg aus dem Krieg: Bismarcks Politik im Krieg und die Friedensanbahnung, 1870–71* (Munich, 1990)

7 See the remarks of Jay Luvaas in Chapter 28, this volume, and in his *Military Legacy of the Civil War*.

German wars has been characterized in the terms that James M. McPherson (Chapter 14) has used to describe the American Civil War – the "overwhelming involvement of the whole population, the shocking loss of life, the wholesale devastation and radical social and political transformation that it wrought." On the other hand, invoking the idea of total war has invited more detailed examination of the disparities between the wars. The remarks of Richard E. Beringer (Chapter 4) and Hans L. Trefousse (Chapter 5) on the differences in nationalist ideologies on the two sides of the Atlantic are less convincing than the observations of Joseph T. Glatthaar (Chapter 9) on the profound implications of the Union's assault on slavery. The essays by Serman and Tombs confirm that the Germans never aspired to such far-reaching changes in the political or social structures of their antagonists; despite its eventual consequences, the German decision to annex Alsace-Lorraine represented no radical departure from common practices of European statecraft. The work of Manfred Messerschmidt (Chapter 12) and Wengenroth suggests that Germany escaped the kind of economic mobilization that Stanley L. Engerman and J. Matthew Gallman (Chapter 10) have analyzed in the Union, to say nothing of the Confederacy. Nor was German opinion evidently subjected to the kind of mobilization that Jörg Nagler (Chapter 16) and Phillip S. Paludan (Chapter 17) have described in America.

If the concept of total war seems to have little analytical relevance to the German Wars of Unification, it has defined a major debate in the historiography of the Civil War. This debate provides an important subtext in this volume. The poles in it are staked out in the essays by McPherson and Edward Hagerman (Chapter 7), on the one hand, and by Mark E. Neeley Jr.'s (Chapter 2), on the other.[8] The issue is whether or not the Civil War represented the first instance of the all-embracing, modern industrial warfare that is associated with the world wars of the twentieth century. The proponents of both sides have adduced an impressive body of evidence to support their cases, but given the absence of a shared definition of *total war*, weighting the combination of "modern" and "traditional" elements in the American Civil War has produced more frustration than consensus. Neeley and Hagerman appear at times to be writing about two different wars.

The debate has underscored the problematic features of total war and provoked some much-needed thinking about this concept, whose usage has

---

8 Neeley's essay in this volume, which was earlier published with the same title in *Civil War History* 37 (1991): 5–28, has provoked the controversy. The original statement of the other position is John B. Walters, "General William T. Sherman and Total War," *Journal of Southern History* 14 (1948): 447–80.

been as wide as it has been unreflecting.[9] At the very least, the essays in this volume have demonstrated the untenability of the easy correlation between total war and modernization, which has been one of the former concept's staple components. The work of Engerman and Gallman reveals that mobilization of the wartime economy was more extensive and fundamental in the Confederacy than in the more "modernized" Union. Michael Fellman's intriguing observations (Chapter 24) about guerrilla war in the west invites a similar conclusion. Nowhere was combat more brutal, nor the distinctions between soldiers and civilians more fluid, than in this "backward" theater of operations. Here, if anywhere, the "totalization" of the Civil War gestated, for as Hagerman points out, Sherman, Sheridan, and Grant – the soldiers most responsible for the Union's transportation of war to the civilians of the Confederacy – all saw action here against irregular forces early in the war.

It lies beyond the scope of this essay to venture a critical examination of the concept of total war. But if the concept is to have any heuristic value, it surely lies in directing attention to the limits on military violence and to the way these limits have historically broken down. From this perspective, the wars on both sides of the Atlantic do offer several instructive points of comparison. These lie at what might be called the "liminal features" of the conflicts. The first and most striking was the widening of warfare beyond the battlefield, the effort to encompass systematically the civilians without whose materials and moral support the conflict could not continue. In the depredations visited on Southern civilians by the armies of Sherman and Sheridan, the American Civil War offered the quintessential images of the breakdown of these "spatial" limits on warfare, but the mobilization of civilian economies for war implied a similar process. It documented the direct involvement of civilians in warfare and provided the warrant for extending the violence in their direction. Although the Franco-Prussian war concluded before it brought comparable mobilization to either the French or German economies, it, too, witnessed a systematic effort to carry the war to the civilian sector. The presence of Philip Sheridan at Prussian headquarters during the bombardment of Paris was more than a curious irony; it symbolized an essential common facet of the conflicts.

---

9 See, e.g., Ian F. W. Beckett, "Total War," in Clive Emsley et al., eds., *War, Peace, and Social Change in Twentieth-Century Europe* (Milton Keynes and Philadelphia, 1989); Martin Shaw, *Dialectics of War: An Essay in the Social Theory of Total War and Peace* (London, 1988); Thomas Powers and Ruthven Tremain, *Total War: What It Is, How it Got That Way* (New York, 1988); and Roger Chickering, "Total War: The Use and Abuse of a Concept," in Stig Förster et al., eds., *Anticipating Total War? The United States and Germany, 1871–1914,* the forthcoming successor to this book.

A second, though intrinsically related, category of limits that eroded during these wars might be called cultural or conceptual. These pertained to what Fellman has called the "level of cultural inclusion," or the expanding definition of "the other" that was required to justify extending the war to civilians. Irregular warfare – a mode in which the distinctions between soldier and civilian, friend and enemy, were by definition problematic – offered the most chilling illustrations of this process and its consequences. The savagery toward civilians that Fellman describes in the partisan warfare of Missouri had its analogue in the brutality to which the Germans resorted in their bewildered reprisals against the franc-tireurs.

A final category has to do with the temporal limits of warfare, or the problem of bringing war to an end once popular sentiments were mobilized in its prosecution. The wars in Europe and America did not end easily. The peace of Prague, which brought the Austro-Prussian war to its conclusion in August 1866, foretold the obstacles that emotions could present to compromise. The emotions in this case were principally those of the Prussian king, who insisted on a harsher settlement than Bismarck thought wise, but the Prussian minister president's calculations in the negotiations also frustrated in significant respects the demands of German nationalists. The annexation of Alsace-Lorraine accommodated these demands in the next war; it also conjured up unanticipated problems for the German leadership, as it heightened the French "nation's investment in the war," to use the terms of Stéphane Audoin-Rouzeau (Chapter 19), and prolonged the conflict well beyond the point where professional military wisdom prescribed that it end. The reasons for the prolongation of the American Civil War were numerous and complex, but they comprehended the same dynamics. The essays of Beringer, Trefousse, Nagler, and Paludan all leave little doubt that the mobilization of opinion on both sides ensured that the conflict end only in the destruction or capitulation of one of them.

The concept of total war invites comments about two additional problems raised in the Civil War and the German Wars of Unification. The first has to do with the face of battle. Despite the manifold differences in their conduct and outcome, these wars alike portended the dynamics of combat for the next half-century. The introduction of the rifled musket as the standard infantry weapon worked to the immense disadvantage of offensive operations. That the growing power of troops in defensive emplacements was encouraging tactical paralysis was evident in the initial clashes of the American war, as well as on the outworks of Düppel in 1864 and at Sadowa in 1866, where Prussian infantrymen armed with needle-guns held off a furious Austrian attack long enough for the Second Prussian army to complete the envelopment of the Austrian position.[10] Nor did the mobility of German operations in the war with France indicate a departure from this pattern, as a close analysis of early battles at Wissembourg, Mars-la-Tour, or St. Privat revealed.[11] The Germans' success was due instead to the virtuosity of their mobilization and strategic coordination, to the superiority of their artillery, and, as Serman has nicely shown (Chapter 13), to the fact that their opponents' operations were, from the moment mobilization began, consummately bungled.

Subsequent American students of the Wars of Unification were, as Jay Luvaas (Chapter 28) reports, undeceived by the spectacular nature of the German success in the field. The analysis of these observers reflect perhaps a certain defensiveness about the performance of American armies in the Civil War, but it also presents a sober appreciation of the common tactical dynamics that operated in the European and American wars. As a small number of later commentators recognized, the development of breech-loading, small-caliber, and rapid-fire infantry weapons only fortified these patterns; so did advances in artillery technology.[12] A case can thus be made that in their battlefield dynamics at least, the mid-century wars anticipated the next European war, when the apotheosis of defensive warfare led to a strategic stalemate so paralyzing that the resolution of the conflict could come only with the collapse of the home front.

But if the totality of World War I is to be the telos toward which the mid-century wars point, several contributors to this volume have issued a salutary caution. One scenario, foretold in the earlier conflicts, did not materialize. *Volkskrieg, guerre à outrance,* or "peoples' war" did not lead straightaway to total war. Variously hailed or deplored by contemporaries as a revolutionary new form of warfare – and regularly cited by military historians as a harbinger of total war – the mobilization of civilians for combat outside the traditional framework of military organization was an act of desperation, whether it took the form of partisan warfare in the American west or the *levée en masse* proclaimed by the new government of republican France. However, to most professional soldiers on all sides of these conflicts, it represented a repugnant spectacle, the descent into the kind of chaos and barbarism epitomized in the Paris Commune; and it bore no resemblance to the ordered violence of warfare properly understood. Stig Förster (Chapter 6) has shown that the specter of *Volkskrieg* plagued Moltke at the time that he first

10 Gordon Craig, *Königgrätz: Prussia's Victory over Austria* (New York, 1964).
11 Howard, *Franco-Prussian War.*
12 Roger Chickering, *Imperial Germany and a World without War: The Peace Movement and German Society, 1892–1914* (Princeton, N.J., 1975), 97–9, 387–92.

confronted it in France and for the rest of his career. Moltke was hardly alone. His disagreement with Bismarck, as Förster has shown, was not over the reprehensibility of peoples' war, but how best to bring it to an end. The reluctance of the Prussian war minister to employ *Landwehr* troops in France late in the war reflected similar apprehensions. Paradoxically, Generals Sherman and Sheridan, the soldiers who most brought war to the people during the American Civil War, themselves shared these apprehensions; and their depredations on Southern soil were calculated at least in part to discourage the kind of popular participation that the French tried shortly later to organize. Neeley's observations are especially apt in this connection, for he has emphasized the discipline and order that Sherman imposed on his troops even as they marched.

The idea of the *Volkskrieg* survived the mid-century wars not as a model but a bogey. Gerd Krumeich (Chapter 30) has pointed out that distaste for Gambetta's adventurism was rife in France itself, principally because the kind of military organization associated with his name had proved ineffective in the test of combat. In the aftermath of the war, the politicians and soldiers who rebuilt the French army accordingly looked elsewhere for their model, and they, like many others, found it in the Prussian conscript army, whose mid-century successes demonstrated that it was best designed to exploit popular energies without sacrificing discipline or professional direction. This principle of military organization represented, as Wilhelm Deist (Chapter 15) has put it, the "German path to total war." But it was the path trod by all. The legacy of the mid-century wars was everywhere, including the United States, a growing emphasis on the disciplined management of military force and the resources required to sustain it. The military history of the era that culminated in 1914 was devoted to this undertaking, which, as Annette Becker has vividly shown (Chapter 31), was so comprehensive that not even the war dead were exempt. Preparing for the next war extended to managing the memory of the last one. But that is another chapter.

Index